A Guide to Critical Reviews

Part IV: The Screenplay
from *The Jazz Singer* to *Dr. Strangelove*

by
James M. Salem

Volume 1

The Scarecrow Press, Inc.
Metuchen, N.J.   1971

ISBN 0-8108-0367-4
Library of Congress Catalog Card Number: 66-13733

TO JON

A GUIDE TO CRITICAL REVIEWS

Part I: American Drama from O'Neill to Albee

Part II: The Musical from Rodgers-and-Hart to Lerner-
           and-Loewe

Part III: British and Continental Drama from Ibsen to
           Pinter

Part IV: The Screenplay from The Jazz Singer to
           Dr. Strangelove

FOREWORD

The purpose of Part IV of A Guide to Critical Reviews is to provide a bibliography of critical reviews of feature length motion pictures released from October, 1927 through 1963. Approximately 12,000 American and foreign screenplays are included in this bibliography. Cross references are liberally provided to assist the reader in tracking down titles and to indicate films released under more than one title.

The reviews cited in this volume are those which appeared in American or Canadian periodicals and in the New York Times. With the exception of some now defunct movie periodicals, most of the reviews should be available in college and public libraries. No attempt has been made to include critical articles from the scholarly journals.

My primary source for film titles was Richard B. Dimmitt's excellent two-volume bibliography, A Title Guide to the Talkies (Scarecrow Press, 1965). Not only does Mr. Dimmitt provide a comprehensive list of film titles; he also includes copyright and release dates, and information on the producer and producing studio, screenplay author, and author and title of original works adapted to the screen. All films in this volume (except those introduced by an asterisk, which are my own additions) can be found in A Title Guide to the Talkies.

I should like to acknowledge a debt of gratitude to the cooperative Reference Division staff of the University of Alabama Library, and to Roy Underwood, Kay Holman, Judy Pritchard, and Ruth Rosborough. I am also indebted to my wife, Donna, and to Tim.

University, Alabama   James M. Salem
May 1970

TABLE OF CONTENTS

Screenplays

Aaron Slick from Pumkin Crick (1952)
  Commonweal 56:117, May 9, 1952
  New York Times p. 18, Apr. 19, 1952
  Time 59:100, Apr. 28, 1952

*A Nous La Liberte
  Nation 134:659-60, Jun. 8, 1932
  New Republic 71:74-5, Jun. 1, 1932; 71:130, Jun. 15, 1932
  New York Times VIII, p. 5, Jan. 10, 1932; VIII, p. 6,
    Feb. 14, 1932; p. 25, May 18, 1932; VIII, p. 3,
    May 29, 1932; VIII, p. 5, Feb. 10, 1935
  Saturday Review 37:31-2, Oct. 16, 1954; 39:50, May 19,
    1956

Abandon Ship (1957)
  America 97:179, May 4, 1957
  Commonweal 66:127, May 3, 1957
  Library Journal 82:1309, May 15, 1957
  National Parent-Teacher 51:36, Jun. , 1957
  New York Times p. 35, Apr. 18, 1957; II, p. 1,
    Apr. 21, 1957
  New Yorker 33:68, Apr. 27, 1957
  Newsweek 49:124, Apr. 22, 1957

Abandoned Woman (1949)
  Commonweal 51:160, Nov. 11, 1949
  New York Times p. 35, Oct. 27, 1949
  Newsweek 34:88, Oct. 24, 1949
  Rotarian 76:40, Jan. , 1950

Abbott and Costello Go to Mars (1953)
  National Parent-Teacher 47:36, May, 1953

Abbott and Costello in Hollywood (1945)
  New York Times p. 26, Nov. 23, 1945

Abbott and Costello in the Foreign Legion (1950)
  New York Times p. 14, Aug. 14, 1950

Abbott and Costello Meet Captain Kidd (1952)
  Christian Century 70:31, Jan. 7, 1953
  National Parent-Teacher 47:37, Jan., 1953

Abbott and Costello Meet Dr. Jekyll and Mr. Hyde (1953)
  National Parent-Teacher 48:37, Sep., 1953

Abbott and Costello Meet Frankenstein (1949)
  Commonweal 48:402, Aug. 6, 1948
  New York Times p. 17, Jul. 24, 1948

Abbott and Costello Meet the Invisible Man (1951)
  New York Times p. 18, Apr. 13, 1951

Abbott and Costello Meet the Keystone Kops (1954)
  National Parent-Teacher 49:38, Feb., 1955

Abbott and Costello Meet the Killer: Boris Karloff (1948)
  New York Times p. 18, Sep. 19, 1949

Abbott and Costello Meet the Mummy (1955)
  American Magazine 159:15, May, 1955
  National Parent-Teacher 49:38, Jun., 1955

Abdul the Damned (1936)
  New York Times p. 16, May 11, 1936

*Abdullah the Great
  Life 36:89-90, Mar. 22, 1954
  National Parent-Teacher 50:38, Mar., 1956

Abe Lincoln in Illinois (1940)
  Commonweal 31:367, Feb. 16, 1940
  Life 8:74-9, Feb. 12, 1940
  Nation 150:372, Mar. 16, 1940
  New Republic 102:308, Mar. 4, 1940
  New York Times p. 19, Feb. 23, 1940; IX, p. 4,
    Feb. 25, 1940; X, p. 5, Mar. 3, 1940; IX, p. 3,
    Jun. 9, 1940
  New Yorker 16:67, Feb. 24, 1940
  Newsweek 15:32-3, Jan. 29, 1940
  Photoplay 54:68, Apr., 1940
  Saturday Review 21:19, Mar. 9, 1940
  Scholastic 35:30-1, Dec. 11, 1939
  Time 35:60, Feb. 5, 1940

Abie's Irish Rose (1928)
  Motion Picture Classic 26:28-9+, Feb., 1928

Abie's Irish Rose (1928) (Continued)
New York Times IX, p. 6, Apr. 15, 1928; p. 26, Apr.
20, 1928; IX, p. 5, April 29, 1928; p. 7, Jul. 23,
1929
Outlook 149:65, May 9, 1928

Abie's Irish Rose (1946)
Commonweal 45:353, Jan. 17, 1947
New York Times II, p. 5, Dec. 22, 1946; p. 19, Dec.
23, 1946
Newsweek 29:69, Jan. 6, 1947
Scholastic 49:33, Dec. 2, 1946
Time 48:66, Dec. 30, 1946

Abilene Town (1946)
Commonweal 43:309, Jan. 4, 1946
New York Times p. 16, Mar. 4, 1946
New Yorker 22:89, Mar. 16, 1946
Time 47:99, Jan. 28, 1946

Abominable Snowman (1957)
Library Journal 82:2918, Nov. 15, 1957
National Parent-Teacher 52:34, Dec. , 1957

About Face (1952)
Catholic World 175:144, May, 1952
Christian Century 69:887, Jul. 30, 1952
New York Times p. 15, May 24, 1952
New Yorker 28:81, May 31, 1952
Newsweek 39:84+, Jun. 2, 1952
Time 59:94, Jun. 2, 1952

About Mrs. Leslie (1954)
America 91:426, Jul. 24, 1954
Catholic World 179:223, Jun. , 1954
Commonweal 60:388, Jul. 23, 1954
Farm Journal 78:92, Jul, 1954
Library Journal 79:1168, Jun. 15, 1954
National Parent-Teacher 48:38, May, 1954
New York Times p. 16, Jun. 28, 1954; II, p. 11, Jul.
11, 1954; II, p. 5, Nov. 15, 1953
New Yorker 30:60, Jul. 10, 1954
Newsweek 43:86, Jun. 21, 1954
Saturday Review 37:33, Jul. 3, 1954
Time 64:76, Jul. 5, 1954

Above and Beyond (1952)
Christian Century 70:175, Feb. 11, 1953

Above and Beyond (1952) (Continued)
Commonweal 57:499, Feb. 20, 1953
Good Housekeeping 136:16-17, Mar, 1953
Look 17:84-5, Feb. 10, 1953
McCalls 80:8, Feb., 1953
Nation 175:595, Dec. 20, 1952
National Parent-Teacher 47:37, Feb, 1953
New York Times p. 10, Jan. 31, 1953
New Yorker 28:56+, Feb. 7, 1953
Newsweek 41:77, Feb. 2, 1953
Saturday Review 36:27, Jan. 24, 1953
Scholastic 61:30, Jan. 14, 1953
Time 61:70, Jan. 5, 1953

Above Suspicion (1943)
Commonweal 38:514, Sep. 10, 1943
New York Times p. 10, Aug. 6, 1943
Newsweek 22:92, Aug. 16, 1943
Time 42:94, Aug. 23, 1943

Above Us the Waves (1955)
Commonweal 66:156, May 10, 1957
Library Journal 82:71, Jan. 1, 1957
National Parent-Teacher 51:37, Feb., 1957
New York Times p. 35, Apr. 18, 1957
Newsweek 49:110, Feb. 18, 1957

Abraham Lincoln (1930)
Commonweal 12:498, Sep. 17, 1930
Life (NY) 96:17, Sep. 12, 1930
Literature Digest 106:15-16, Sep. 20, 1930
National Magazine 59:144, Dec., 1930
New Republic 64:101-2, Sep. 10, 1930
New York Times p. 24, Aug. 26, 1930; VIII, p. 5., Aug.
    13, 1930
Nation 131:305, Sep. 17, 1930
Outlook 156:72, Sep. 10, 1930
Theatre Magazine 52:47, Nov., 1930
Vogue 76:126, Oct. 13, 1930

Absent-Minded Professor (1961)
America 105:25-6, Apr. 1, 1961
New York Times p. 25, Mar. 17, 1961
New Yorker 37:125, Apr. 1, 1961
Time 77:66, Mar. 10, 1961

Absolute Quiet (1936)
New York Times p. 11, May 2, 1936

Absolute Quiet (1936) (Continued)
   Time 27:28, May 4, 1936

Abused Confidence (1938)
   New York Times p. 29, Dec. 1, 1938

Accent on Youth (1935)
   Literature Digest 120:28, Aug. 17, 1935
   New York Times p. 10, Aug. 12, 1935
   Stage 12:2, Sep., 1935
   Time 26:42, Jul. 29, 1935

Accidents Will Happen (1939)
   Commonweal 28:49, May 6, 1938
   New York Times p. 19, Apr. 25, 1938

Accused (1937)
   Canadian Magazine 86:40, Dec., 1936
   New York Times p. 35, Dec. 17, 1936
   Time 28:19, Dec. 28, 1936

Accused (1949)
   Commonweal 49:377, Jan. 21, 1949
   Good Housekeeping 128:100, Jan., 1949
   New Republic 120:31, Jan. 31, 1949
   New York Times p. 26, Jan. 13, 1949
   New Yorker 24:71, Jan. 22, 1949
   Newsweek 33:73, Jan. 17, 1949
   Photoplay 34:16, Jan., 1949
   Rotarian 74:38, Mar., 1949
   Time 53:82+, Jan. 24, 1949
   Woman's Home Companion 76:10-11, Feb., 1949

Accusing Finger (1936)
   New York Times p. 35, Nov. 17, 1936

Ace in the Hole (1950) (see Big Carnival)
   Commonweal 54:334, Jul. 13, 1951
   Nation 173:37, Jul. 14, 1951
   New Republic 125:22, Jul. 16, 1951
   New York Times p. 8, Jun. 30, 1951; II, p. 1, Jul. 1,
      1951
   New Yorker 27:38, Jul. 7, 1951
   Newsweek 38:78, Jul. 2, 1951
   Saturday Review 34:24, Jul. 7, 1951
   Time 58:84, Jul. 9, 1951

Ace of Aces (1933)
New York Times p. 10, Nov. 11, 1933

Across the Bridge (1958)
America 98:228, Nov. 16, 1957
Catholic World 186:145, Nov., 1957
Commonweal 67:131, Nov. 1, 1957
Library Journal 82:2781, Nov. 1, 1957
Life 43:67-8, Oct. 21, 1957
Nation 185:396, Nov. 23, 1957
New York Times p. 24, Oct. 30, 1957
New Yorker 33:109, Nov. 9, 1957
Newsweek 50:112, Nov. 4, 1957
Senior Scholastic 71:25, Nov. 8, 1957

Across the Pacific (1942)
Commonweal 36:448, Aug. 28, 1942
New York Times p. 9, Sep. 5, 1942; p. 15, Oct. 19,
    1942
Newsweek 20:80, Sep. 7, 1942
Theatre Arts 26:693, Nov., 1942
Time 40:42, Aug. 17, 1942

Across the Wide Missouri (1951)
Catholic World 174:145, Nov., 1951
Christian Century 68:1359, Nov. 21, 1951
Library Journal 76:1818, Nov. 1, 1951
New York Times p. 35, Nov. 7, 1951
Newsweek 38:102, Nov. 19, 1951
Saturday Review 34:30, Oct. 27, 1951
Time 58:110+, Nov. 19, 1951

Across the World With Mr. and Mrs. Martin Johnson (1930)
Life (NY) 95:18, Feb. 21, 1930
New York Times VIII, p. 5, Jan. 12, 1930; p. 28, Jan.
    21, 1930; VIII, p. 5, Jan. 26, 1930

Across to Singapore (1928)
Life (NY) 91:26, May 17, 1928
New York Times p. 18, Apr. 30, 1928
Outlook 149:145, May 23, 1928

Act of Love (1953)
Catholic World 178:384, Feb., 1954
Commonweal 59:554, Mar. 5, 1954
Farm Journal 78:94, Mar., 1954
Library Journal 79:314, Feb. 15, 1954

14

Act of Love (1953) (Continued)
  National Parent-Teacher 48:38, Apr., 1954
  New York Times p. 20, Feb. 12, 1954; II, p. 1, Feb.
    21, 1954
  New Yorker 30:103, Feb. 20, 1943
  Newsweek 43:61, Jan. 4, 1954
  Saturday Review 37:29, Feb. 13, 1954
  Time 63:64, Jan. 4, 1954

Act of Mercy (1962)
  New York Times II, p. 9, Jan. 7, 1962

An Act of Murder (1948) (see Live Today for Tomorrow)

Act of Violence (1948)
  Canadian Forum 29:183, Nov., 1949
  Commonweal 49:424, Feb. 4, 1949
  Good Housekeeping 128:211, Mar., 1949
  New Republic 120:31, Jan. 31, 1949
  New York Times p. 16, Jan. 24, 1949
  New Yorker 24:76, Feb. 5, 1949
  Newsweek 33:75, Jan. 31, 1949
  Photoplay 34:21, Mar., 1949
  Rotarian 74:34, May, 1949
  Time 53:68, Jan. 31, 1949

Act One (1963)
  America 110:54-5, Jan. 11, 1964
  New Republic 150:26, Jan. 18, 1964
  New York Times p. 17, Dec. 27, 1963
  Time 82:57, Dec. 27, 1963

Action for Slander (1938)
  Canadian Magazine 89:29, Feb., 1938

Action in Arabia (1944)
  New York Times p. 18, Feb. 19, 1944

Action in the North Atlantic (1943)
  Commonweal 38:203, Jun. 11, 1943
  Life 14:90-3, May 31, 1943
  New Republic 108:794, Jun. 14, 1943
  New York Times p. 10, May 22, 1943; II, p. 3, May 30,
    1943
  New Yorker 19:38, May 29, 1943
  Newsweek 21:94, Jun. 7, 1943
  Photoplay 23:22, Aug., 1943

Action in the North Atlantic (1943) (Continued)
 Theatre Arts 27:552, Sep., 1943
 Time 41:92+, Jun. 7, 1943

Action of the Tiger (1957)
 National Parent-Teacher 52:33, Oct., 1957
 New York Times p. 41, Nov. 14, 1957

Actors and Sin (1952)
 Commonweal 56:245, Jun. 13, 1952
 Library Journal 77:1185, Jul., 1952
 Life 32:121-2+, Jun. 23, 1952
 National Parent-Teacher 47:38, Sep., 1952
 New York Times p. 11, May 30, 1952; II, p. 1, Jun. 15, 1952
 New Yorker 28:124, Jun. 7, 1952
 Newsweek 39:89, Jun. 9, 1952
 Saturday Review 35:28, Jun. 7, 1952
 Theatre Arts 36:42+, Apr., 1952
 Time 59:96+, Jun. 23, 1952

Actress (1928)
 Life (NY) 92:26, Jul. 26, 1928
 New York Times p. 25, Jul. 9, 1928; VII, p. 3, Jul. 15, 1928

Actress (1953)
 America 90:159, Nov. 7, 1953
 Catholic World 177:463, Sep., 1953
 Commonweal 59:92, Oct. 30, 1953
 Farm Journal 77:161, Nov., 1953
 Library Journal 78:1840, Oct. 15, 1953
 Life 35:107, Nov. 9, 1953
 National Parent-Teacher 48:38, Oct., 1953
 Nation 177:434, Nov. 21, 1953
 New York Times p. 34, Oct. 13, 1953; II, p. 1, Oct. 25, 1953
 New Yorker 29:129, Oct. 24, 1953
 Newsweek 42:101, Sep. 28, 1953
 Saturday Review 36:43, Oct. 3, 1953
 Scholastic 63:35, Nov. 4, 1953
 Time 62:112+, Oct. 19, 1953

Ada (1961)
 New York Times p. 15, Aug. 26, 1961
 Time 78:89, Sep. 8, 1961

Adam and Evalyn (1950)
 Christian Century 67:1311, Nov. 1, 1950
 New Republic 122:23, May 29, 1950
 New York Times p. 33, May 12, 1950
 New Yorker 26:105, May 20, 1950
 Rotarian 77:37, Dec., 1950
 Time 55:90, May 29, 1950

Adam Had Four Sons (1941)
 Commonweal 33:623, Apr. 11, 1941
 New York Times p. 26, Mar. 28, 1941; IX, p. 5, Mar.
  30, 1941
 Time 37:93, Mar. 17, 1941

Adam's Rib (1949)
 Commonweal 51:319, Dec. 23, 1949
 Cosmopolitan 127:15+, Dec., 1949
 New Republic 122:23, Jan. 9, 1950
 New York Times p. 33, Dec. 26, 1949; II, p. 1, Jan. 15,
  1950
 New Yorker 25:48, Jan. 7, 1950
 Newsweek 34:56-7, Dec. 26, 1949
 Rotarian 76:38, Feb., 1950
 Time 54:84, Nov. 28, 1949

Address Unknown (1944)
 Canadian Forum 25:42, May, 1945
 New York Times p. 20, Apr. 17, 1944
 Newsweek 23:93, May 1, 1944

Admirable Crichton (1958)
 America 98:522, Feb. 1, 1958
 Catholic World 186:382, Feb., 1958
 Commonweal 67:458, Jan. 31, 1958
 Library Journal 82:1994, Sep. 1, 1957
 National Parent-Teacher 52:32, Sep., 1957
 New York Times p. 45, Dec. 17, 1957
 Newsweek 50:119, Dec. 16, 1957
 Saturday Review 41:24, Jan. 18, 1958
 Time 71:74, Jan 6, 1958

*Admiral Nakhimov
 Commonweal 49:232, Dec. 10, 1948
 New Republic 119:29, Dec. 13, 1948
 New York Times p. 27, Nov. 25, 1948
 Theatre Arts 32:39, Summer, 1948

17

Admiral Was a Lady (1950)
New York Times p. 23, Oct. 13, 1950

The Adopted Father (1933) (see The Working Man)

Adorable (1933)
 Canadian Magazine 80:35-6, Aug., 1933
 New York Times p. 20, May 19, 1933; IX, p. 3, May 29, 1933
 Newsweek 1:31, May 27, 1933

Adorable Creatures (1956)
 Commonweal 63:483, Feb. 10, 1956
 New York Times p. 36, Jan. 11, 1956; II, p. 1, Jan. 15, 1956
 New Yorker 31:111, Jan. 21, 1956
 Newsweek 47:100+, Jan. 23, 1956

Adoration (1928)
 New York Times p. 20, Jan. 14, 1929

Adulteress (1957)
 Commonweal 67:513, Feb. 14, 1958
 New York Times p. 42, Jan. 14, 1958; II, p. 1, Jan. 19, 1958
 Newsweek 51:94, Jan. 27, 1958
 Time 71:92, Jan. 13, 1958

Adventure (1945)
 Commonweal 43:430, Feb. 8, 1946
 Cosmopolitan 120:55+, Jan., 1946
 New York Times p. 23, Feb. 8, 1946; II, p. 1, Feb. 10, 1946
 New Yorker 22:87, Feb. 16, 1946
 Newsweek 27:98, Feb. 18, 1946
 Photoplay 28:24, Mar., 1946
 Scholastic 48:33, Mar. 18, 1946
 Theatre Arts 30:159, Mar., 1946
 Time 47:94, Feb. 11, 1946
 Woman's Home Companion 73:11, Mar., 1946

Adventure Girl (1934)
 New York Times p. 14, Aug. 9, 1934

Adventure in Baltimore (1949)
 Commonweal 50:121, May 13, 1949
 New Republic 120:30, May 9, 1949

18

Adventure in Baltimore (1949) (Continued)
New York Times p. 27, Apr. 29, 1949; II, p. 1, May 1,
1949
Newsweek 33:90, May 9, 1949
Rotarian 75:36, Jul., 1949
Time 53:102, Apr. 18, 1949
Woman's Home Companion 76:10-11, Jun., 1949

Adventure in Diamonds (1940)
New York Times IX, p. 4, Jan. 14, 1940; p. 27, Apr.
4, 1940
Photoplay 54:68, Apr., 1940

Adventure in Manhattan (1936)
Canadian Magazine 86:38, Nov., 1936
New York Times p. 27, Oct. 23, 1936
Stage 14:12, Dec., 1936
Time 28:71, Oct. 26, 1936

Adventure in Sahara (1938)
New York Times p. 19, Dec. 19, 1938

Adventure in Washington (1941)
New York Times p. 27, May 20, 1941; IX, p. 4, May 25,
1941; p. 11, Aug. 1, 1941

Adventure Island (1947)
New York Times p. 29, Oct. 20, 1947

Adventure's End (1937)
New York Times p. 23, Dec. 20, 1937

Adventures of a Young Man (1962)
America 107:552, Jul. 28, 1962
New Republic 147:28-9, Jul. 16, 1962
New York Times II, p. 5, Jul. 22, 1962; p. 17, Jul. 26,
1962; II, p. 1, Aug. 5, 1962
New Yorker 38:46, Aug. 11, 1962
Newsweek 60:76, Jul. 30, 1962
Saturday Review 45:22, Jul. 21, 1962
Time 80:69, Jul. 27, 1962

Adventures of Casanova (1948)
New York Times p. 18, Mar. 27, 1948
New Yorker 24:72, Mar. 27, 1948

Adventures of Chico (1938)
Nation 146:310, Mar. 12, 1938

Adventures of Chico (1938) (Continued)
New Republic 94:195, Mar. 23, 1938
New York Times p. 9, Feb. 26, 1938; XI, p. 5, Mar.
20, 1938
Scholastic 32:12, Apr. 23, 1938
Time 31:47, Mar. 7, 1938

Adventures of Don Juan (1949)
Good Housekeeping 128:110, Feb., 1949
New York Times p. 10, Dec. 25, 1948
Newsweek 33:76, Jan. 10, 1949
Rotarian 74:38, Mar., 1949
Time 53:58+, Jan. 3, 1949
Woman's Home Companion 76:10-11, Feb., 1949

Adventures of Hajji Baba (1954)
America 92:83, Oct. 16, 1954
Library Journal 79:2095, Nov. 1, 1954
Life 37:51+, Sep. 27, 1954
National Parent-Teacher 49:39, Dec., 1954
New York Times p. 8, Oct. 9, 1954
Newsweek 44:101, Nov. 8, 1954
Time 64:98+, Nov. 1, 1954

Adventures of Huckleberry Finn (1939) (see also Huckleberry
Finn)
New Republic 98:336, Apr. 26, 1939
New York Times p. 21, Mar. 3, 1939
Newsweek 13:24, Feb. 27, 1939
Saint Nicholas 66:39, Mar., 1939
Scholastic 34:30, Feb. 4, 1939

Adventures of Huckleberry Finn (1960)
America 103:522, Aug. 6, 1960
Good Housekeeping 150:30, May, 1960
McCalls 87:6, Jul., 1960
New York Times p. 17, Aug. 4, 1960
Newsweek 55:105, Jun. 13, 1960
Time 75:67, Jun. 13, 1960

Adventures of Ichabod and Mr. Toad (1948)
Commonweal 51:70, Oct. 28, 1949
Cosmopolitan 127:13+, Oct., 1949
Life 27:65-7, Nov. 21, 1949
New Republic 121:23, Oct. 24, 1949
New York Times p. 18, Oct. 10, 1949; II, p. 1, Oct. 16,
1949

Adventures of Ichabod and Mr. Toad (1948) (Continued)
Newsweek 34:90, Oct. 10, 1949
Parents Magazine 24:15+, Sep., 1949
Rotarian 76:40, Jan., 1950
Time 54:104+, Oct. 17, 1949

Adventures of Marco Polo (1938)
Canadian Magazine 89:28-9, Feb., 1938
Commonweal 27:581, Mar. 18, 1938
Commonweal 27:728, Apr. 22, 1938
New York Times p. 17, Apr. 8, 1938
Newsweek 11:34-5, Jan. 3, 1938
Newsweek 11:20, Mar. 7, 1938
Scholastic 32:35, Apr. 2, 1938
Stage 15:66-8, Dec., 1937; 15:39, Mar., 1938
Time 31:37, Mar. 7, 1938

Adventures of Mark Twain (1944)
Christian Science Monitor p. 8-9, Apr. 15, 1944
Commonweal 40:63, May 5, 1944
Life 16:89-99, May 8, 1944
Musician 49:150, Aug., 1944
New York Times p. 25, May 4, 1944; II, p. 3, May 7, 1944
Newsweek 23:98-9, May 8, 1944
Photoplay 25:19, Jul., 1944
Scholastic 44:18-19, Apr. 17, 1944
Time 43:56+, May 8, 1944

Adventures of Martin Eden (1942)
New York Times p. 19, Mar. 16, 1942

Adventures of Maya (1929)
Nature Magazine 14:28, Jul., 1929
New York Times p. 27, Apr. 23, 1929; IX, p. 7, Apr. 28, 1929

Adventures of Robin Hood (1938)
Collier's 102:17+, Aug. 6, 1938
Commonweal 28:133, May 27, 1938
Nation 146:653-4, Jun. 4, 1938
New Republic 95:131, Jun. 8, 1938
New York Times p. 17, May 13, 1938; XI, p. 3, May 22, 1938
Newsweek 11:22-3, May 9, 1938
Life 4:60-62, May 23, 1938
Photoplay 52:39-41, Mar., 1938; 52:23, Jul., 1938

Adventures of Robin Hood (1938) (Continued)
Saint Nicholas 65:37+, Feb., 1938
Scholastic 32:30-3, May 14, 1938
Time 31:57, May 16, 1938

Adventures of Robinson Crusoe (1954)
Catholic World 179:220, Jun., 1954
Commonweal 60:413, Jul. 30, 1954
Farm Journal 78:92, Jul., 1954
Library Journal 79:1048, Jun. 1, 1954
Life 37:59-60+, Aug. 23, 1954
National Parent-Teacher 48:38, Jun., 1954
Natural History 63:426, Nov., 1954
New York Times p. 10, Aug. 6, 1954; II, p. 1, Aug. 15, 1954
New York Times Magazine p. 30, May 30, 1954
New Yorker 30:58, Aug. 14, 1954
Newsweek 43:106, Apr. 19, 1954
Reporter 11:46, Sep. 23, 1954
Saturday Review 37:27, Jul. 17, 1954
Scholastic 64:37, May 5, 1954
Time 63:102+, May 24, 1954

Adventures of Sadie (1955)
New York Times p. 35, May 18, 1955
New Yorker 31:78, May 28, 1955

Adventures of Sherlock Holmes (1939)
New Republic 100:190, Sep. 20, 1939
New York Times p. 20, Sep. 2, 1939

Adventures of Tartu (1943)
Collier's 112:4, Oct. 30, 1943
Commonweal 38:634, Oct. 15, 1943
Good Housekeeping 117:2, Nov., 1943
Nation 157:360, Sep. 25, 1943
New Republic 109:573, Oct. 25, 1943
New York Times p. 26, Sep. 24, 1943
New Yorker 19:56, Sep. 25, 1943
Newsweek 22:78, Oct. 11, 1943
Time 42:94, Sep. 20, 1943
Woman's Home Companion 70:2, Nov., 1943

Adventures of Tom Sawyer (1938)
Life 4:44-7, Mar. 7, 1938
New Republic 94:102, Mar. 2, 1938
New York Times p. 23, Feb. 18, 1938

Adventure of Tom Sawyer (1938) (Continued)
Newsweek 11:31, Feb. 28, 1938
St. Nicholas 65:37, Feb., 1938
Scholastic 32:30-1, Feb. 19, 1938
Time 31:63, Feb. 28, 1938

Adventures of a Young Man (1962)
America 107:552, Jul. 28, 1962
New Republic 147:28-9, Jul. 16, 1962
New York Times II, p. 9, Oct. 8, 1962
New Yorker 38:46, Aug. 11, 1962
Newsweek 60:76, Jul. 30, 1962
Saturday Review 45:22, Jul. 21, 1962
Time 80:69, Jul. 27, 1962

Adventuress (1947)
Commonweal 45:594, Mar. 28, 1947
Cosmopolitan 122:120, May, 1947
Life 22:60+, Apr. 7, 1947
Nation 164:339, Mar. 22, 1947
New Republic 116:42, Apr. 28, 1947
New York Times p. 19, Apr. 4, 1947; II, p. 1, Apr. 27, 1947
New Yorker 23:98, Apr. 12, 1947
Newsweek 29:94+, Apr. 14, 1947
Scholastic 50:45, Apr. 14, 1947
Time 49:98+, Mar. 24, 1947

Advice to the Lovelorn (1933)
Nation 137:745, Dec. 27, 1933
New Outlook 163:43, Jan., 1934
New York Times p. 28, Dec. 14, 1933; IX, p. 5, Dec. 24, 1933
Newsweek 2:31, Dec. 23, 1933

Advise and Consent (1962)
America 107:449, Jun. 30, 1962
Catholic World 195:379-80, Sep., 1962
Commonweal 76:280, Jun. 8, 1962
Esquire 58:127, Jul., 1962
Life 53:73-5+, Jul. 6, 1962
National Review 12:492+, Jul. 3, 1962
New Republic 146:28+, Jun. 4, 1962
New York Times p. 31, Jun. 7, 1962; II, p. 1, Jun. 17, 1962; II, p. 5, Jul. 1, 1962
New York Times Magazine p. 70+, May 13, 1962
New Yorker 38:116, Jun. 9, 1962

Advise and Consent (1962) (Continued)
Newsweek 59:99-100, Jun. 11, 1962
Saturday Review 45:23, Jun. 2, 1962
Time 79:13, Mar. 30, 1962; 79:66, Jun. 8, 1962

Aerial Gunner (1943)
New York Times p. 10, Jun. 26, 1943

Affair Blum (1948)
Christian Century 66:1527, Dec. 21, 1949
Commonweal 51:159, Nov. 11, 1949
New Republic 121:23, Oct. 24, 1949
New York Times p. 35, Oct. 18, 1949; II, p. 1, Oct. 23, 1949
New Yorker 25:115, Oct. 22, 1949
Newsweek 34:67-8, Oct. 31, 1949
Rotarian 76:38, Feb., 1950

Affair in Trinidad (1952)
Commonweal 56:462, Aug. 15, 1952
National Parent-Teacher 47:38, Sep., 1952
New York Times p. 14, Jul. 31, 1952
Newsweek 40:86, Aug. 11, 1952
Time 60:76, Aug. 4, 1952

Affair Lafont (1939)
New York Times p. 15, Oct. 9, 1939

Affair to Remember (1957)
America 97:451, Jul. 27, 1957
Catholic World 185:465, Sep., 1957
Commonweal 66:472, Aug. 9, 1957
Life 43:79-80+, Aug. 12, 1957
National Parent-Teacher 52:32, Sep., 1957
New York Times p. 8, Jul. 20, 1957; II, p. 1, Jul. 28, 1957
New Yorker 33:48, Aug. 3, 1957
Newsweek 50:100, Jul. 15, 1957
Saturday Review 40:27, Jul. 20, 1957; 40:24, Aug. 10, 1957
Time 70:76, Aug. 5, 1957

Affair with a Stranger (1953)
Commonweal 58:395, Jul. 24, 1953
National Parent-Teacher 48:38, Sep., 1953
New York Times p. 8, Jul. 11, 1953

*L'Affaire
   Commonweal 53:198, Dec. 1, 1950
   New Republic 123:23, Dec. 4, 1950
   New York Times p. 23, Nov. 13, 1950

Affairs of a Gentleman (1934)
   New York Times p. 16, Jun. 23, 1934

The Affairs of Annabel (1938)
   New York Times p. 29, Oct. 13, 1938

Affairs of Cellini (1934)
   New Republic 79:268, Jul. 18, 1934
   New York Times p. 22, Sep. 6, 1934; X, p. 3, Sep. 16, 1934
   Time 24:37, Aug. 20, 1934
   Vanity Fair 42:45, Jul., 1934

Affairs of Dobie Gillis (1953)
   National Parent-Teacher 48:36, Nov., 1953

Affairs of Jimmy Valentine (1942)
   Commonweal 36:16, Apr. 24, 1942

Affairs of Julie (1958)
   New York Times p. 53, Dec. 10, 1958

Affairs of Maupassant (1938)
   New York Times p. 20, Feb. 12, 1938; X, p. 4, Feb. 13, 1938

Affairs of Messalina (1953)
   National Parent-Teacher 49:38, Jan., 1955

Affairs of Susan (1945)
   Commonweal 41:649, Apr. 13, 1945
   Nation 160:371, Mar. 31, 1945
   New York Times p. 18, Mar. 2, 1945
   Newsweek 25:78, Apr. 2, 1945
   Photoplay 27:20, Jun., 1945
   Time 45:92, Apr. 2, 1945
   Woman's Home Companion 72:10, Jun., 1945

Affectionately Yours (1941)
   Commonweal 34:161, Jun. 6, 1941
   New York Times p. 18, May 24, 1941

Afraid to Talk (1932)
New York Times p. 19, Dec. 19, 1932; IX, p. 5, Dec.
    25, 1932

Africa Adventure (1954)
    Farm Journal 78:73, Nov., 1954
    National Parent-Teacher 49:38, Oct., 1954
    New York Times p. 23, Sep. 29, 1954
    Natural History 63:378, Oct., 1954
    Scholastic 65:29, Oct. 27, 1954

Africa Screams (1948)
    New York Times p. 34, May 5, 1949
    Rotarian 75:42, Aug., 1949

Africa Speaks (1930)
    Life (NY) 96:18, Oct. 10, 1930
    New York Times p. 15, Sep. 20, 1930; VIII, p. 3, Sep.
    28, 1930

African Lion (1955)
    Catholic World 181:59, Oct., 1955
    Commonweal 62:613, Sep. 23, 1955
    Nation 181:290, Oct. 1, 1955
    National Parent-Teacher 50:38, Nov., 1955
    Natural History 64:442, Oct., 1955
    New York Times VI, p. 78, Aug. 28, 1955; p. 39, Sep.
        15, 1955; II, p. 1, Sep. 25, 1955
    New Yorker 31:112, Sep. 24, 1955
    Newsweek 46:119, Sep. 19, 1955
    Saturday Review 38:34, Sep. 17, 1955
    Time 66:96+, Sep. 26, 1955

The African Queen (1951)
    Catholic World 174:457-8, Mar., 1952
    Christian Century 69:351, Mar. 19, 1952
    Commonweal 55:566, Mar. 14, 1952
    Library Journal 77:426, Mar. 1, 1952
    New Republic 126:21, Mar. 10, 1952
    New York Times p. 24, Feb. 21, 1952; II, p. 1, Feb. 24,
        1952
    New York Times Magazine p. 20-1, Feb. 10, 1952
    New Yorker 28:85, Feb. 23, 1952
    Newsweek 39:88, Mar. 3, 1952
    Saturday Review 35:29, Feb. 23, 1952
    Scholastic 60:24, Mar. 12, 1952
    Theatre Arts 36:48-9+, Feb., 1952; 36:45+, Mar., 1952
    Time 59:68, Feb. 25, 1952

After Mein Kampf (1940)
 New York Times p. 11, Sep. 14, 1940

After Office Hours (1935)
 New York Times p. 19, Mar. 9, 1935
 Time 25:16, Mar. 4, 1935

After the Ball (1933)
 New York Times p. 18, Mar. 20, 1933

After the Thin Man (1936)
 Canadian Magazine 87:23, Mar., 1937
 Nation 144:81, Jan. 16, 1937
 New York Times p. 19, Dec. 25, 1936
 Newsweek 9:24, Jan. 2, 1937
 Stage 14:63-4, Jan., 1937
 Time 29:21-2, Jan. 4, 1937

After the Verdict (1930)
 New York Times p. 21, Jan. 18, 1930

After Tomorrow (1932)
 New York Times p. 13, Mar. 7, 1932; VIII, p. 4, Mar.
    13, 1932

After Tonight (1933)
 New York Times p. 23, Nov. 3, 1933; IX, p. 4, Nov. 12,
    1933

Against All Flags (1952)
 Christian Century 70:207, Feb. 18, 1953
 Look 17:66-7, Jan. 13, 1953
 National Parent-Teacher 47:36, Dec., 1952
 New York Times p. 34, Dec. 25, 1952
 Newsweek 41:76, Jan. 12, 1953
 Time 60:67, Dec. 22, 1952

Against the Wind (1949)
 New Republic 121:27, Jul. 11, 1949
 New York Times p. 18, Jun. 27, 1949
 Newsweek 34:69, Jul. 11, 1949

*L'Age D'Or
 Nation 136:382-4, Apr. 5, 1933
 Vanity Fair 40:50-51, May, 1933

Age for Love (1931)
 New York Times p. 27, Nov. 13, 1931

Age of Consent (1932)
New York Times p. 16, Sep. 3, 1932

Age of Indiscretion (1935)
New York Times p. 21, May 18, 1935

Age of Infidelity (1958)
Commonweal 68:567, Sep. 5, 1958
New York Times p. 23, Aug. 19, 1958
New Yorker 34:67, Aug. 30, 1958
Saturday Review 41:28, Sep. 6, 1958

Age of Innocence (1934)
New York Times p. 27, Oct. 19, 1934

Aggie Appleby, Maker of Men (1933)
New York Times p. 14, Oct. 20, 1933; IX, p. 3, Oct.
29, 1933

Agitator (1945)
New York Times p. 12, Aug. 19, 1949
New Yorker 25:38, Aug. 27, 1949

Ah Wilderness! (1935)
Canadian Magazine 85:38, Feb., 1936
Literature Digest 120:22, Dec. 28, 1935
New Republic 85:198, Dec. 25, 1935
New York Times IX, p. 3, Sep. 1, 1935; p. 30, Dec. 25,
1935
Newsweek 6:38, Dec. 14, 1935
Scholastic 27:28+, Jan. 18, 1936
Time 26:44, Dec. 9, 1935

A-Haunting We Will Go (1942)
New York Times p. 18, Aug. 3, 1942

Aida (1954)
America 92:306, Dec. 11, 1954
Catholic World 180:66, Oct., 1954
Commonweal 61:290, Dec. 10, 1954
Harper 210:87, Jan., 1955
National Parent-Teacher 49:37, Sep., 1954
New York Times p. 17, Nov. 12, 1954; II, p. 1, Nov. 14,
1954
New York Times Magazine p. 26, Sep. 26, 1954
Newsweek 44:112, Nov. 15, 1954
Saturday Review 37:39-40, Nov. 6, 1954
Time 64:75, Nov. 29, 1954

Ain't Misbehavin' (1955)
New York Times p. 13, Jul. 2, 1955
Saturday Review 38:26, Jul. 30, 1955

Air Cadet (1951)
Christian Century 68:623, May 16, 1951
New York Times p. 32, May 11, 1951
Newsweek 37:100, Mar. 26, 1951

The Air Circus (1928)
Life (NY) 92:21, Sep. 21, 1928
New York Times p. 14, Sep. 3, 1928; IX, p. 5, Sep. 9,
   1928

Air Force (1943)
Collier's 111:36-7+, Jan. 16, 1943
Commonweal 37:423, Feb. 12, 1943
Life 14:61-2+, Feb. 8, 1943
Nation 156:283, Feb. 20, 1943
New Republic 108:254-5, Feb. 22, 1943
New York Times p. 29, Feb. 4, 1943; II, p. 3, Feb. 7,
   1943
New Yorker 18:52, Feb. 6, 1943
Newsweek 21:84, Feb. 8, 1943
Photoplay 22:16, Mar., 1943
Scholastic 42:28, Mar. 29, 1943
Theatre Arts 27:118, Feb., 1943; 27:551, Sep., 1943
Time 41:85, Feb. 8, 1943

Air Hawks (1935)
New York Times p. 26, Jun. 4, 1935

Air Hostess (1933)
New York Times p. 9, Jan. 23, 1933

Air Hostess (1949)
Rotarian 76:40, Jan., 1950

Air Mail (1932)
New Outlook 161:47, Dec., 1932
New York Times p. 20, Nov. 7, 1932

Air Raid Wardens (1943)
New York Times p. 15, Apr. 5, 1943

Al Capone (1959)
America 101:256-7, Apr. 25, 1959
Commonweal 69:651, Mar. 20, 1959

Al Capone (1959) (Continued)
　New Republic 140:20, Apr. 20, 1959
　New York Times p. 27, Mar. 26, 1959
　New Yorker 35:97, Apr. 18, 1959
　Newsweek 53:99, Mar. 30, 1959
　Saturday Review 42:27, Mar. 28, 1959
　Time 73:96+, May 18, 1959

Al Jennings of Oklahoma (1951)
　New York Times p. 34, May 18, 1951

Alakazam the Great (1961)
　Time 78:60, Jul 28, 1961

Alamo (1960)
　America 104:230+, Nov. 12, 1960
　Commonweal 73:124+, Oct. 28, 1960
　Good Housekeeping 151:28, Oct., 1960
　Life 49:120-3, Sep. 19, 1960
　McCalls 88:8, Jan., 1961
　New York Times p. 48, Oct. 27, 1960
　New Yorker 36:187, Nov. 5, 1960
　Newsweek 56:90, Oct. 31, 1960
　Redbook 116:11, Jan., 1961
　Senior Scholastic 77:38, Nov. 30, 1960
　Time 76:76, Nov. 7, 1960

Alaskan Seas (1953)
　National Parent-Teacher 48:39, Mar., 1954
　New York Times p. 13, Mar. 6, 1954
　Time 63:114, Mar. 22, 1954

Albert Schweitzer (1957)
　Christian Century 74:425, Apr. 3, 1957
　Commonweal 65:466, Feb. 1, 1957
　Library Journal 82:183, Jan. 15, 1957
　Nation 184:126, Feb. 9, 1957
　National Parent-Teacher 51:37, Feb., 1957
　New York Times p. 20, Jan. 21, 1957; II, p. 1, Jan. 27,
　　1957
　Newsweek 49:94, Jan. 28, 1957
　Saturday Review 40:25-6, Jan. 5, 1957
　Scholastic 69:24, Jan. 11, 1957
　Time 69:94, Feb. 11, 1957

Albuquerque (1948)
　New York Times p. 17, Mar. 1, 1948

Alcatraz Island (1937)
New York Times p. 22, Oct. 14, 1937

Alexander Hamilton (1931)
Commonweal 14:525, Sep. 30, 1931
Life (NY) 98:18, Oct. 9, 1931
Literature Digest 111:20-1, Oct. 3, 1931
New York Times p. 21, Sep. 17, 1931; VIII, p. 6, Sep.
20, 1931; VIII, p. 5, Sep. 27, 1931
Outlook 159:87, Sep. 16, 1931

Alexander Nevsky (1939)
Life 6:48-9, Apr. 10, 1939
Nation 148:413-14, Apr. 8, 1939
North American Review 247 no. 2:381-2, Jun., 1939
New Republic 98:279, Apr. 12, 1939; 98:222-3, Mar. 29,
1939
New York Times p. 27, Mar. 23, 1939; X, p. 5, Mar.
26, 1939
Time 33:40-1, Apr. 3, 1939

Alexander the Great (1955)
American Magazine 161:9, Apr., 1956
America 95:72, Apr. 14, 1956
Catholic World 183:146, May, 1956
Commonweal 64:96, Apr. 15, 1956
Library Journal 81:898, Apr. 15, 1956
Life 39:79-83+, Nov. 14, 1955
National Parent-Teacher 50:36, Jun., 1956
Nation 182:350, Apr. 21, 1956
New York Times p. 23, Mar. 29, 1956; II, p. 1, Apr. 1,
1956
New Yorker 32:110+, Apr. 7, 1956
Saturday Review 39:28, Mar. 31, 1956
Time 67:104+, Apr. 16, 1956

Alexander's Ragtime Band (1938)
Commonweal 28:411, Aug. 12, 1938
New York Times p. 7, Aug. 6, 1938
Newsweek 12:19, Aug. 1, 1938
Time 32:35, Aug. 15, 1938

Algiers (1938)
Canadian Magazine 90:58, Sep., 1938
Commonweal 28:370, Jul. 29, 1938
New Republic 95:363, Aug. 3, 1938
New York Times p. 13, Jul 15, 1938; IX, p. 3, Jul. 17,
1938

Algiers (1938) (Continued)
Newsweek 12:27, Jul. 11, 1938
Time 32:22, Jul. 25, 1938

Ali Baba and the Forty Thieves (1943)
New York Times p. 17, Mar. 16, 1944
Newsweek 23:76+, Jan. 24, 1944

Ali Baba Goes to Town (1937)
New York Times p. 14, Oct. 23, 1937; X, p. 5, Oct. 31,
   1937
Newsweek 10:29, Nov. 1, 1937
Scholastic 31:36, Nov. 13, 1937
Time 30:44, Nov. 1, 1937

Alias Bulldog Drummond (1935)
Literary Digest 120:28, Aug. 17, 1935
New York Times p. 26, Sep. 10, 1935

Alias French Gertie (1930)
New York Times p. 24, Apr. 14, 1930; VIII, p. 5, Apr.
   20, 1930

Alias Jesse James (1959)
New York Times p. 31, May 18, 1959
Time 73:98, Apr. 13, 1959

Alias Jimmy Valentine (1929)
New York Times X, p. 3, Nov. 11, 1928; p. 28, Nov. 16,
   1928

Alias Mary Dow (1935)
New York Times p. 16, Jun. 29, 1935

Alias Nick Beal (1949)
Canadian Forum 29:88, Jul., 1949
New Republic 120:30, Mar. 21, 1949
New York Times p. 35, Mar. 10, 1949
New Yorker 25:83, Mar. 19, 1949
Newsweek 33:82, Mar. 14, 1949
Rotarian 75:38, Oct., 1949
Time 53:105, Mar. 14, 1949
Woman's Home Companion 76:11, Apr., 1949

Alias the Deacon (1940)
New York Times p. 27, Mar. 14, 1940
Photoplay 54:60, Jul., 1940

Alias the Doctor (1932)
New York Times p. 22, Mar. 3, 1932; VIII, p. 4, Mar.
13, 1932

Alibi (1929)
Life (NY) 93:35, May 3, 1929
New York Times p. 29, Apr. 9, 1929; X, p. 7, Apr. 14,
1929; IX, p. 5, May 10, 1929

Alibi Ike (1935)
New York Times p. 22, Jul. 17, 1935; IX, p. 3, Jul. 21,
1935
Time 25:51, Jun. 24, 1935

Alice Adams (1935)
Commonweal 22:427, Aug. 30, 1935
Literary Digest 120:26, Aug. 24, 1935
New Republic 84:104, Sep. 4, 1935
New York Times p. 11, Aug. 16, 1935; IX, p. 3, Aug.
18, 1935
Time 26:26, Aug. 26, 1935

Alice in Wonderland (1933)
Literary Digest 111:20, Dec. 19, 1931; 117:31, Jan. 6, 1934
Nation 138:84, Jan. 17, 1934
New York Times X, p. 3, Sep. 17, 1933; IX, p. 4, Oct. 1,
1933; IX, p. 6, Dec. 17, 1933; p. 19, Dec. 23, 1933;
X, p. 5, Jan. 7, 1934; IX, p. 3, Sep. 15, 1935
Newsweek 2:30, Dec. 30, 1933
Vanity Fair 41:46, Feb., 1934

Alice in Wonderland (Disney) (1951)
Christian Century 68:999, Aug. 29, 1951; 68:1143, Oct.
5, 1951
Commonweal 54:430, Aug. 10, 1951
Library Journal 76:1239, Aug., 1951
Life 30:85-7+, Jun. 18, 1951
New Republic 125:21, Aug. 13, 1951
New York Times II, p. 5, Jun. 17, 1951; p. 24, Jul. 24,
1951; p. 12, Jul. 30, 1951
New Yorker 27:83-5, Aug. 6, 1951
Newsweek 38:83-5, Aug. 6, 1951
Saturday Review 34:30-2, Aug. 11, 1951
Time 58:69, Aug. 6, 1951

Alice in Wonderland (1951)
New York Times p. 15, Jul. 27, 1951; II, p. 1, Jul. 29,
1951

Alice in Wonderland (1951) (Continued)
New York Times Magazine p. 24-5, Mar. 20, 1949
Parents Magazine 24:73, Mar., 1949

Alimony Madness (1933)
New York Times p. 18, May 5, 1933

All About Eve (1950)
Christian Century 67:1439, Nov. 29, 1950
Commonweal 53:62-3, Oct. 27, 1950
Good Housekeeping 131:16, Dec., 1950
Harper 202:103-4, Jan., 1951
Life 29:79-80, Oct. 30, 1950
Nation 171:397, Oct. 28, 1950
New American Mercury 72:95-6, Jan., 1951
New Republic 123:21, Nov. 6, 1950
New York Times p. 13, Oct. 14, 1950; II, p. 1, Oct. 22,
    1950; II, p. 4, May 28, 1950
New Yorker 26:128, Oct. 21, 1950
Newsweek 36:94, Oct. 16, 1950
Rotarian 78:38, Jan., 1951
Saturday Review 33:31, Oct. 21, 1950
Scholastic 57:19, Nov. 29, 1950
Theatre Arts 34:8-9, Dec., 1950
Time 56:96+, Oct. 16, 1950

The All American (1932)
New York Times p. 18, Oct. 22, 1932

All-American (1953)
Commonweal 59:39, Oct. 16, 1953
National Parent-Teacher 48:35, Nov., 1953
Newsweek 42:114, Oct. 26, 1953
Scholastic 63:41, Nov. 11, 1953
Time 62:108, Oct. 5, 1953

All Ashore (1953)
National Parent-Teacher 47:27, Mar., 1953
Theatre Arts 37:89, Mar., 1953
Time 61:104, Mar. 9, 1953

All at Sea (1957)
America 98:522, Feb. 1, 1958
New York Times p. 18, Dec. 23, 1957
New Yorker 33:70, Jan. 4, 1958
Newsweek 51:69, Jan. 6, 1958
Saturday Review 41:24, Jan. 18, 1958
Time 71:92, Jan. 13, 1958

All By Myself (1943)
New York Times p. 20, Jul. 16, 1943

All Fall Down (1962)
America 107:210+, 1962
Commonweal 76:112+, Apr. 27, 1962
Esquire 58:28+, Oct., 1962
New Republic 146:37-8, Apr. 23, 1962
New York Times p. 41, Apr. 12, 1962; II, p. 1, Apr.
    22, 1962
New Yorker 38:170, Apr. 21, 1962
Newsweek 59:96-7, Apr. 23, 1962
Saturday Review 45:28, May 5, 1962
Time 79:100, Apr. 13, 1962

All Hands on Deck (1961)
New York Times p. 10, Apr. 1, 1961
Newsweek 57:108, Apr. 17, 1961
Time 77:72, Apr. 14, 1961

All I Desire (1953)
Commonweal 58:466, Aug. 14, 1953
McCalls 80:12, Jun., 1953
National Parent-Teacher 48:38, Sep., 1953
New York Times p. 10, Aug. 29, 1953
Theatre Arts 37:87, Jul., 1953

All in a Night's Work (1961)
America 105:227-8, Apr. 29, 1961
Commonweal 74:103, Apr. 21, 1961
McCalls 88:211, Apr., 1961
New York Times p. 28, Mar. 23, 1961
New Yorker 37:138, Mar. 25, 1961
Time 77:60, Apr. 7, 1961

All Mine to Give (1957)
Library Journal 83:71, Jan. 1, 1958
National Parent-Teacher 52:38, Jan., 1958
New York Times p. 32, Aug. 4, 1959
Senior Scholastic 72:42, Feb. 14, 1958

All My Sons (1948)
New Republic 118:33, Mar. 22, 1948
New York Times p. 17, Mar. 29, 1948; II, p. 1, Apr.
    18, 1948
New Yorker 24:58, Apr. 3, 1948
Newsweek 31:89, Apr. 12, 1948

All My Sons (1948) (Continued)
Photoplay 32:22, May, 1948
Time 51:100+, Apr. 12, 1948

All of Me (1934)
New York Times p. 19, Feb. 5, 1934; IX, p. 4, Feb. 11, 1934

All Over the Town (1948)
Commonweal 50:202, Jun. 3, 1949
New Republic 120:28, Jun. 6, 1949
New York Times p. 34, May 26, 1949
Newsweek 33:80, Jun. 6, 1949
Time 53:101, Jun. 13, 1949

All Quiet On the Western Front (1930)
Life (NY) 95:18, May 23, 1930
Literary Digest 105:19-20, May 17, 1930; 106:17, Aug. 30, 1930
New Republic 123:23, Jul. 31, 1950
New York Times p. 29, Apr. 30, 1930; XI, p. 5, May 4, 1930; p. 15, Oct. 9, 1939
New Yorker 26:38, Aug. 5, 1950
Outlook 155:72, May 14, 1930
Saturday Review 39:50, May 19, 1956
Theatre Arts 25:620, Sep., 1941
Theatre Magazine 52:44+, Jul., 1930
Time 34:49, Oct. 2, 1939
Nation 130:688, Jun. 11, 1930; 131:7-8, Jul. 2, 1930; 132:430, Apr. 15, 1931

All That Heaven Allows (1955)
America 94:647, Mar. 10, 1956
Catholic World 182:306, Jan., 1956
Commonweal 63:459, Feb. 3, 1956
Library Journal 81:74, Jan. 1, 1956
National Parent-Teacher 50:38, Dec., 1955
New York Times p. 35, Feb. 29, 1956; II, Mar. 4, 1956
Saturday Review 38:39, Dec. 3, 1955
Time 67:104, Mar. 26, 1956

All That Money Can Buy (1941)
Commonweal 35:51, Oct. 31, 1941
Life 11:87-90+, Oct. 27, 1941
New York Times p. 27, Oct. 17, 1941; IX, p. 5, Oct. 19, 1941
New Yorker 17:89, Oct. 18, 1941

All That Money Can Buy (1941) (Continued)
Newsweek 18:75, Oct. 20, 1941
Scholastic 39:32, Oct. 13, 1941
Time 38:98+, Oct. 20, 1941

All the Brothers Were Valiant (1953)
America 90:327, Dec. 19, 1953
Commonweal 59:165, Nov. 20, 1953
Library Journal 78:2098, Dec. 1, 1953
National Parent-Teacher 48:39, Dec., 1953
New York Times p. 19, Dec. 29, 1953
Newsweek 43:88+, Jan. 18, 1954
Saturday Review 36:37, Nov. 7, 1953
Time 63:103, Jan. 18, 1954

All the Fine Young Cannibals (1960)
America 103:623, Sep. 10, 1960
Commonweal 72:470, Sep. 9, 1960
McCalls 88:162+, Oct., 1960
New York Times p. 33, Sep. 23, 1960
Time 76:80, Sep. 12, 1960

All the King's Horses (1935)
New York Times p. 19, Mar. 9, 1935
Vanity Fair 44:47, Apr., 1935

All the King's Men (1950)
Christian Century 67:31, Jan. 4, 1950
Commonweal 51:181, Nov. 18, 1949
Library Journal 75:180, Feb. 1, 1950
Life 27:111-12+, Nov. 28, 1949
New Republic 121:21, Nov. 21, 1949
New York Times II, p. 4, Feb. 27, 1949; p. 37, Nov. 9,
    1949; II, p. 1, Nov. 13, 1949; II, p. 5, Nov. 20, 1949
New Yorker 25:101, Nov. 12, 1949
Newsweek 34:91-3, Nov. 21, 1949
Rotarian 76:36, Mar., 1950
Saturday Review 38:30, Jan. 8, 1955
Scholastic 55:22, Dec. 14, 1949
Time 54:102+, Dec. 5, 1949

All the Way Home (1963)
America 109:613, Nov. 9, 1963
Commonweal 79:257, Nov. 22, 1963
New Republic 149:48-9, Nov. 9, 1963
New York Times p. 46, Oct. 30, 1963
New York Times Magazine p. 130-131, Nov. 11, 1962

All the Way Home (1963) (Continued)
New Yorker 39:210, Nov. 9, 1963
Senior Scholastic 83:24, Nov. 1, 1963
Time 82:109, Nov. 1, 1963

All the Young Men (1959)
America 103:622-3, Sep. 10, 1960
Commonweal 73:17, Sep. 30, 1960
New York Times p. 8, Aug. 27, 1960
New Yorker 36:78+, Sep. 10, 1960
Newsweek 56:72, Sep. 5, 1960
Saturday Review 43:32, Aug. 20, 1960
Time 76:45, Aug. 29, 1960

All This, and Heaven Too (1940)
Life 9:35-6, Jul. 1, 1940
New York Times X, p. 5, Mar. 17, 1940; X, p. 5, May
    5, 1940; p. 10, Jul. 5, 1940
Newsweek 15:48+, Jun. 24, 1940
Photoplay 54:36-7+, Jul., 1940; 54:61, Aug., 1940
Time 35:89, Jun. 24, 1940

All Through the Night (1942)
New York Times p. 13, Jan. 24, 1942

All Women Have Secrets (1939)
Photoplay 54:58, Jan., 1940

Allegheny Uprising (1939)
New York Times p. 27, Nov. 10, 1939
Photoplay 54:59, Jan., 1940
Theatre Arts 23:802, Nov., 1939

Alligator Named Daisy (1957)
Catholic World 186:220, Dec., 1957
National Parent-Teacher 52:33, Dec., 1957
New York Times p. 23, Oct. 7, 1957
Newsweek 50:106, Oct. 7, 1957

Allotment Wives (1945)
New York Times p. 39, Nov. 22, 1945

Almost Angels (1962)
New York Times p. 34, Nov. 1, 1962

Almost Married (1942)
New York Times p. 23, Jun. 5, 1942

Along the Great Divide (1951)
  Commonweal 54:190, Jun. 1, 1951
  New York Times p. 38, May 17, 1951
  Time 57:108+, Jun. 11, 1951

Aloma of the South Seas (1941)
  Commonweal 34:496, Sep. 12, 1941
  New York Times p. 23, Aug. 28, 1941
  New Yorker 17:49, Aug. 30, 1941
  Newsweek 18:49, Sep. 1, 1941
  Scribner's Commentator 11:106-7, Nov., 1941

Along Came Jones (1945)
  Commonweal 42:192, Jun. 8, 1945
  New Republic 113:161, Aug. 6, 1945
  New York Times p. 18, Jul. 19, 1945
  New Yorker 21:51, Jul. 28, 1945
  Newsweek 26:84, Jul. 30, 1945
  Time 46:85, Jul. 9, 1945

Along Came Sally (1934)
  New York Times p. 20, Jun. 16, 1934
  Newsweek 3:36, Jun. 23, 1934

Always A Bride (1940)
  New York Times p. 43, Nov. 21, 1940

Always A Bride (1953)
  America 91:259, May 29, 1954
  National Parent-Teacher 48:39, Mar., 1954
  New York Times p. 19, May 28, 1954
  Saturday Review 37:28, Mar. 13, 1954
  Time 63:92+, Mar. 29, 1954

Always Goodbye (1931)
  Life (NY) 97:20, Jun. 12, 1931
  New York Times p. 13, May 23, 1931; VIII, p. 5, May
    31, 1931

Always Goodbye (1938)
  Life (NY) 97:20, Jun. 12, 1931
  New York Times p. 7, Jun. 25, 1938
  Time 32:18, Jul. 4, 1938

Always In My Heart (1942)
  New York Times p. 19, Mar. 14, 1942
  Time 39:74-5, Mar. 30, 1942

Always in Trouble (1938)
New York Times p. 27, Nov. 3, 1938

Always Leave Them Laughing (1949)
Commonweal 51:269, Dec. 9, 1949
New York Times p. 48, Nov. 24, 1949
New Yorker 25:74+, Dec. 3, 1949
Newsweek 34:87, Dec. 12, 1949
Time 54:102, Dec. 5, 1949

Always Together (1947)
New York Times II, p. 9, Dec. 7, 1947; p. 46, Dec. 11, 1947

Amateur Daddy (1932)
New York Times p. 11, Apr. 23, 1932

Amateur Gentleman (1936)
Canadian Magazine 85:59, Apr., 1936
New York Times p. 19, Apr. 27, 1936
Stage 13:8, Feb., 1936
Time 27:32, Apr. 13, 1936

The Amazing Colossal Man (1957)
New York Times p. 19, Oct. 26, 1957

Amazing Dr. Clitterhouse (1938)
Commonweal 28:390, Aug. 5, 1938
New Republic 96:18, Aug. 10, 1938
New York Times p. 14, Jul. 21, 1938
Newsweek 12:26, Jul. 4, 1938
Time 32:20, Jul. 18, 1938

Amazing Mr. Beecham (1949)
Christian Century 67:719, Jun. 7, 1950
Library Journal 75:410, Mar. 1, 1950
New York Times p. 33, Dec. 26, 1949
New Yorker 25:48+, Jan. 7, 1950
Rotarian 77:43, Aug., 1950

The Amazing Mr. Williams (1939)
New York Times p. 15, Jan. 19, 1940
Photoplay 54:6, Feb., 1940

Amazing Mrs. Holliday (1943)
Commonweal 37:471, Feb. 26, 1943
New York Times p. 20, Feb. 22, 1942; II, p. 3, Feb. 28, 1942

40

Amazing Mrs. Holliday (1943) (Continued)
Newsweek 21:70+, Mar. 1, 1943

The Amazing Monsieur Fabre (1952)
Christian Century 70:431, Apr. 8, 1953
Commonweal 57:38, Oct. 17, 1952
Library Journal 77:1605, Oct. 1, 1952
National Parent-Teacher 47:36, Nov., 1952
Natural History 61:424, Nov., 1952
New York Times p. 21, Sep. 9, 1952
Newsweek 40:112+, Sep. 22, 1952
Saturday Review 35:24, Aug. 30, 1952; 39:51, May 19,
    1956
Theatre Arts 36:96, Oct., 1952

The Amazing Transparent Man (1960)
New York Times p. 24, Mar. 30, 1961

Amazon Quest (1949)
New York Times p. 9, May 14, 1949

The Amazon Trader (1956)
New York Times p. 17, Nov. 17, 1956

Ambassador Bill (1931)
Life (NY) 98:56, Dec., 1931
New York Times p. 15, Nov. 14, 1931; VIII, p. 5, Nov.
    22, 1931

Ambassador's Daughter (1956)
America 95:576, Sep. 15, 1956
Catholic World 183:306, Jul., 1956; 184:66, Oct., 1956
Commonweal 64:611, Sep. 21, 1956
Good Housekeeping 143:142, Aug., 1956
New York Times p. 19, Aug. 30, 1956; p. 16, Sep. 8,
    1956
New Yorker 32:69, Sep. 8, 1956
Newsweek 48:90, Aug. 27, 1956
Saturday Review 39:29, Aug. 18, 1956
Time 68:104, Sep. 17, 1956

Ambush (1938)
New York Times p. 17, Feb. 9, 1939
Newsweek 13:24, Jan. 30, 1939

Ambush (1949)
Christian Century 67:191, Feb. 8, 1950

41

Ambush (1949) (Continued)
Library Journal 75:332, Feb. 15, 1950
New York Times p. 35, Jan. 19, 1950
New Yorker 25:75, Jan. 28, 1950
Rotarian 76:38, Apr., 1950

Ambush at Tomahawk Gap (1953)
National Parent-Teacher 47:37, May, 1953

America, America (1963)
America 110:173, Feb. 1, 1964
Commonweal 79:484, Jan. 24, 1964
Esquire 61:22+, Mar., 1964
Life 56:113-14, Mar. 6, 1964
National Review 16:413-15, May 19, 1964
New Republic 150:20-2, Jan. 4, 1964
New York Times II, p. 9, Dec. 15, 1963; p. 44, Dec.
    16, 1963; II & X, p. 3, Dec. 22, 1963
Newsweek 62:74, Dec. 23, 1963
Saturday Review 46:29+, Dec. 28, 1963
Senior Scholastic 84:28, Feb. 7, 1964
Time 83:78, Jan. 3, 1964
Vogue 143:64, Feb. 1, 1964

American Empire (1942)
Commonweal 37:328, Jan. 15, 1943
New York Times p. 25, Jan. 14, 1943

American Guerrilla in the Philippines (1950)
Christian Century 67:1471, Dec. 6, 1950
Commonweal 53:173, Nov. 24, 1950
Library Journal 75:2163, Dec. 15, 1950
New Republic 123:29, Dec. 11, 1950
New York Times p. 37, Nov. 8, 1950; II, p. 1, Nov. 12,
    1950
New Yorker 26:177, Nov. 18, 1950
Newsweek 36:103, Nov. 20, 1950
Rotarian 78:38, Jan., 1951
Time 56:98+, Nov. 27, 1950

American in Paris (1951)
Christian Century 68:1423, Dec. 5, 1951
Commonweal 55:39, Oct. 19, 1951
Life 20:150-2, Apr. 23, 1951
New Republic 125:21, Oct. 22, 1951
New York Times p. 24, Oct. 5, 1951; II, p. 1, Oct. 14,
    1951

American in Paris (1951) (Continued)
New Yorker 27:73, Oct. 6, 1951
Newsweek 38:100, Oct. 8, 1951
Saturday Review 34:28, Nov. 3, 1951
Scholastic 59:26, Nov. 14, 1951
Time 58:108, Oct. 8, 1951

American Madness (1932)
Commonweal 16:392, Aug. 17, 1932
Nation 135:199, Aug. 31, 1932
New York Times p. 14, Aug. 6, 1932; IX, p. 3, Aug. 14, 1932

American Romance (1944)
Commonweal 41:104, Nov. 10, 1944
Life 17:75-7, Oct. 2, 1944
New York Times p. 19, Nov. 24, 1944
Newsweek 24:112, Nov. 13, 1944
Photoplay 25:21, Oct., 1944
Scholastic 45:27-9, Oct. 23, 1944
Theatre Arts 28:669, Nov., 1944
Time 44:94, Oct. 16, 1944

American Tragedy (1931)
Life (NY) 98:18, Aug. 21, 1931
Literary Digest 110:18-19, Sep. 5, 1931
Nation 133:237, Sep. 2, 1931
New Republic 68:21-2, Aug. 19, 1931
Outlook 158:502, Aug. 19, 1931

Americano (1954)
National Parent-Teacher 49:38, Mar., 1955
New York Times p. 35, Jan. 20, 1955; II, p. 1, Jan. 30, 1955

*Americans All
Scholastic 38:27, Feb. 24, 1941; 38:41, Mar. 10, 1941
Time 44:96, Aug. 21, 1944

Among the Living (1941)
New York Times p. 25, Dec. 25, 1941

Ana-Ta-Han (see Devil's Pitchfork)

Anastasia (1956)
America 96:378-9, Dec. 29, 1956
Catholic World 184:381, Feb., 1957

Anastasia (1956) (Continued)
Commonweal 65:383, Jan. 11, 1957
Coronet 41:10, Dec., 1956
Library Journal 82:71, Jan. 1, 1957
Life 41:75-6+, Nov. 26, 1957
National Parent-Teacher 51:37, Feb., 1957
New Republic 136:22, Feb. 4, 1957
New York Times II, p. 5, Aug. 30, 1956; VI, p. 25,
    Sep. 9, 1956; p. 35, Dec. 14, 1956
New York Times Magazine p. 25, Sep. 9, 1956
New Yorker 32:65, Dec. 22, 1956
Newsweek 48:118, Dec. 10, 1956
Saturday Review 39:30, Dec. 8, 1956
Time 68:100, Dec. 17, 1956

Anatomy of a Murder (1959)
America 101:539, Jul. 18, 1959
Life 47:66-8, Jul. 27, 1959
Look 23:48+, Jun. 23, 1959
Nation 189:39-40, Jul. 18, 1959
New Republic 141:22, Jul. 13, 1959
New York Times p. 10, Jul. 3, 1959; II, p. 1, Jul. 12,
    1959
New Yorker 35:55, Jul. 11, 1959
Newsweek 54:88, Jul. 13, 1959
Saturday Review 42:24-5, Jul. 11, 1959
Time 74:68, Jul. 13, 1959

Anatomy of Love (1959)
New York Times p. 4, Sep. 29, 1959
Newsweek 54:118, Sep. 28, 1959
Time 74:112, Oct. 12, 1959

Anchors Aweigh (1945)
Commonweal 42:382, Aug. 3, 1945
Life 19:61-2, Aug. 13, 1945
New Republic 113:256, Aug. 27, 1945
New York Times p. 15, Jul. 20, 1945
New Yorker 21:51, Jul. 28, 1945
Newsweek 26:84, Jul. 30, 1945
Photoplay 27:2-3, Sep., 1945
Theatre Arts 29:587, Oct., 1945
Time 46:96+, Jul. 30, 1945
Woman's Home Companion 72:10, May, 1945

And Baby Makes Three (1949)
Christian Century 66:1559, Dec. 28, 1949

And Baby Makes Three (1949) (Continued)
New York Times p. 17, Dec. 23, 1949
Rotarian 76:38, Feb., 1950
Time 55:76, Jan. 23, 1950

And God Created Woman (1957)
Time 70:120+, Nov. 11, 1957

And Now Tomorrow (1944)
Commonweal 41:125, Nov. 17, 1944
Nation 159:725, Dec. 9, 1944
New York Times p. 38, Nov. 23, 1944
Newsweek 24:105, Dec. 4, 1944
Photoplay 26:21, Dec., 1944
Time 44:92+, Dec. 11, 1944

And One Was Beautiful (1940)
New York Times p. 32, Apr. 11, 1940

And Quiet Flows the Don (1960)
Commonweal 72:328, Jun. 24, 1960
New York Times p. 45, May 25, 1960
Newsweek 55:105, Jun. 13, 1960

And So They Were Married (1936)
New York Times p. 29, May 14, 1936
Time 27:48+, May 25, 1936

And Sudden Death (1936)
New York Times p. 18, Jul. 18, 1936
Time 27:40, Jun. 29, 1936

And the Angels Sing (1944)
Commonweal 40:231, Jun. 23, 1944
Nation 158:634, May 27, 1944
New Republic 111:133, Jul. 31, 1944
New York Times p. 14, Jul. 13, 1944
New Yorker 20:38, Jul. 22, 1944
Newsweek 23:90, Jun. 5, 1944
Time 43:93, May 29, 1944

And Then There Were None (1945)
Canadian Forum 25:265, Feb., 1946
Commonweal 43:94-5, Nov. 9
Life 19:89-90+, Oct. 29, 1945
Nation 161:441, Oct. 27, 1945
New York Times p. 20, Nov. 1, 1945
New Yorker 21:61, Nov. 10, 1945

45

And Then There Were None (1945) (Continued)
Newsweek 26:104+, Oct. 29, 1945
Scholastic 47:29, Oct. 15, 1945
Time 46:54, Oct. 15, 1945

Androcles and the Lion (1952)
Catholic World 176:303, Jan., 1953
Christian Century 70:399, Apr. 1, 1953
Commonweal 57:425, Jan. 30, 1953
Library Journal 77:2170, Dec. 15, 1952
National Parent-Teacher 47:37, Jan., 1953
New Republic 128:22-3, Jun. 15, 1953
New York Times p. 23, Jan. 15, 1953; II, p. 1, Jan. 18,
   1953
New Yorker 28:54, Jan. 31, 1953
Newsweek 41:89-9, Jan. 19, 1953
Saturday Review 35:27, Dec. 20, 1952
Theatre Arts 36:66-9, Dec., 1952
Time 61:94, Jan. 12, 1953

Andy Hardy Comes Home (1958)
Senior Scholastic 73:38, Sep. 19, 1958
Time 72:82, Aug. 18, 1958

Andy Hardy Gets Spring Fever (1939)
Commonweal 30:340, Jul. 28, 1939
New York Times p. 23, Jul. 19, 1939; IX, p. 3, Jul. 23,
   1939
Time 34:43, Jul. 24, 1939

Andy Hardy Meets Debutante (1940)
Commonweal 32:292, Jul. 26, 1940
New York Times p. 12, Aug. 2, 1940
Photoplay 54:61, Jul., 1940
Time 36:79, Jul. 22, 1940

Andy Hardy's Blonde Trouble (1944)
New York Times p. 17, May 5, 1944
Time 43:94, May 22, 1944

Andy Hardy's Double Life (1943)
New York Times p. 23, Feb. 12, 1943; II, p. 3, Feb. 21,
   1943

Andy Hardy's Private Secretary (1941)
New York Times p. 17, Mar. 7, 1941
Scribner's Commentator 10:108, May, 1941

Angel (1937)
Life 3:118-9, Oct. 11, 1937
Literary Digest 124 (Digest 1):34, Oct. 30, 1937
New York Times p. 29, Nov. 4, 1937
Newsweek 10:22, Nov. 8, 1937
Time 30:48, Nov. 8, 1937

Angel and Sinner (1947)
Commonweal 45:520, Mar. 7, 1947
New York Times p. 16, Feb. 24, 1947
New Yorker 23:82, Mar. 8, 1947

Angel and the Badman (1947)
Commonweal 45:540, Mar. 14, 1947
Nation 164:339, Mar. 22, 1947
New York Times p. 28, Mar. 23, 1947
Time 49:108+, Feb. 24, 1947

Angel Baby (1961)
McCalls 88:181, Mar., 1961
New York Times p. 43, Oct. 5, 1961
Newsweek 57:100, May 29, 1961
Saturday Review 44:36, Jun. 3, 1961
Time 77:61, May 26, 1961

Angel Face (1952)
America 89:118, Apr. 25, 1953
Commonweal 58:99, May 1, 1953
Library Journal 78:50, Jan. 1, 1953
McCalls 80:8, Apr., 1953
Nation 176:314, Apr. 11, 1953
National Parent-Teacher 47:37, Feb., 1953
New York Times p. 11, Apr. 25, 1953
Newsweek 41:95, May 4, 1953
Time 61:104, Feb. 23, 1953

Angel From Texas (1940)
New York Times p. 26, May 10, 1940

Angel on My Shoulder (1946)
New York Times p. 27, Oct. 21, 1946
New Yorker 22:114, Oct. 19, 1946
Newsweek 28:92, Nov. 4, 1946
Scholastic 49:37, Nov. 4, 1946
Time 48:104, Oct., 1946

Angel Who Pawned Her Harp (1956)
National Parent-Teacher 50:38, May, 1956

Angel Who Pawned Her Harp (1956) (Continued)
New York Times p. 35, Feb. 29, 1956
Newsweek 47:91, Mar. 5, 1956

*Angel With the Trumpet
Commonweal 55:350, Jan. 11, 1952
New York Times p. 21, Dec. 21, 1951
Newsweek 39:82, Jan. 14, 1952

Angel Wore Red (1960)
America 104:26+, Oct. 1, 1960
Commonweal 73:17, Sep. 30, 1960
Newsweek 56:102, Sep. 12, 1960
Time 76:80, Sep. 12, 1960

Angela (1954)
National Parent-Teacher 50:39, Sep., 1955
New York Times p. 9, Jun. 4, 1955

Angelina (1948)
Commonweal 48:654, Apr. 23, 1948
New Republic 118:20, Apr. 5, 1948
New York Times p. 27, Apr. 6, 1948
New Yorker 24:59, Apr. 3, 1948
Newsweek 31:94, Apr. 19, 1948

Angelo (1951)
Christian Century 68:1239, Oct. 24, 1951
Commonweal 53:495, Feb. 23, 1951
New York Times p. 19, Mar. 26, 1951
New Yorker 27:107, Apr. 7, 1951
Newsweek 37:81, Feb. 26, 1951

Angel's Holiday (1937)
New York Times p. 20, May 29, 1937

Angels in the Outfield (1951)
Catholic World 174:65, Oct., 1951
Christian Century 68:1207, Oct. 17, 1951
Commonweal 55:64, Oct. 26, 1951
New York Times p. 32, Oct. 18, 1951
New Yorker 27:82, Oct. 27, 1951
Newsweek 38:91, Sep. 17, 1951
Saturday Review 34:30, Sep. 22, 1951
Time 58:102, Oct. 1, 1951

Angels One Five (1953)
New York Times p. 28, Apr. 30, 1954

Angels Over Broadway (1940)
Commonweal 33:182, Dec. 6, 1940
New Republic 103:789, Dec. 9, 1940
New York Times p. 23, Nov. 18, 1940; IX, p. 5, Nov.
24, 1940
Newsweek 16:60, Oct. 21, 1940
Time 36:78, Nov. 4, 1940

Angels Wash Their Faces (1939)
New York Times p. 16, Sep. 4, 1939

Angels With Dirty Faces (1938)
Commonweal 29:133, Nov. 25, 1938
New York Times p. 18, Nov. 26, 1938; IX, p. 5, Nov.
27, 1938
Newsweek 12:28-9, Nov. 7, 1938
Photoplay 53:44, Jan., 1939
Stage 16:57, Dec., 1938
Time 32:28+, Dec. 5, 1938

Angry Hills (1959)
Library Journal 84:2054, Jun. 15, 1959
New York Times p. 31, Jul. 16, 1959

Angry Island (1960)
Commonweal 71:676, Mar. 18, 1960
New York Times p. 31, Feb. 29, 1960

The Angry Red Planet (1959)
New York Times p. 41, May 5, 1960

Angry Silence (1960)
America 104:549-50, Jan. 21, 1961
Commonweal 73:365, Dec. 30, 1960
McCalls 88:167, Feb., 1961
Nation 192:19-20, Jan. 7, 1961
New Republic 143:21-2, Dec. 26, 1960
New York Times p. 25, Dec. 13, 1960; II, p. 3, Dec. 18,
1960
New Yorker 36:51, Dec. 24, 1960
Newsweek 56:56, Dec. 26, 1960
Saturday Review 43:30, Dec. 17, 1960
Time 77:50, Jan. 2, 1961

Animal Crackers (1930)
Life (NY) 96:20, Sep. 26, 1930
Nation 131:355, Oct. 1, 1930

Animal Crackers (1930) (Continued)
New York Times XI, p. 6, May 4, 1930; p. 20, Aug. 29, 1930; IX, p. 5, Sep. 7, 1930

Animal Farm (1954)
America 92:408, Jan. 15, 1955
Catholic World 180:140, Nov., 1954
Commentary 19:156-61, Feb., 1955
Commonweal 61:478, Feb. 4, 1955
Library Journal 79:2095, Nov. 1, 1954
Nation 180:85, Jan. 22, 1955
National Parent-Teacher 49:38, Nov., 1954
New Republic 132:22-3, Jan. 17, 1955
New York Times VI, p. 70-1, Oct. 3, 1954; p. 14, Dec. 30, 1954; II, p. 1, Jan. 16, 1955
New York Times Magazine p. 70-1, Oct. 3, 1954
New Yorker 30:78, Jan. 8, 1955
Newsweek 45:86, Jan. 17, 1955
Saturday Review 37:27-8, Dec. 18, 1954
Scholastic 65:30, Jan. 12, 1955
Time 65:74, Jan. 17, 1955

Animal Kingdom (1932)
New York Times p. 14, Dec. 30, 1932
Time 21:37, Jan. 9, 1933
Vanity Fair 39:48+, Feb., 1933

Animal World (1956)
National Parent-Teacher 50:38, Apr., 1956
Natural History 65:333, Jun., 1956
New York Times p. 21, May 31, 1956; II, p. 1, Jun. 3, 1956

Ann Carver's Profession (1933)
New Outlook 162:43, Jul., 1933
New York Times p. 20, Jun. 9, 1933; X, p. 3, Jun. 18, 1933

Ann Vickers (1933)
New York Times p. 24, Sep. 29, 1933; X, p. 3, Oct. 8, 1933
Newsweek 2:30, Oct. 7, 1933

Anna (1953)
Christian Century 70:367, Mar. 25, 1953
Commonweal 57:551, Mar. 6, 1953
National Parent-Teacher 47:37, Jan., 1953

Anna (1953) (Continued)
New York Times p. 20, Feb. 19, 1953; II, p. 1, Mar. 8,
1953
Newsweek 41:90, Mar. 2, 1953
Theatre Arts 37:86+, Mar., 1953
Time 61:90, Mar. 2, 1953

Anna and the King of Siam (1946)
Commonweal 44:285, Jul. 5, 1946
Cosmopolitan 121:68+, Aug., 1946
Forum 106:175-6, Aug., 1956
Hollywood Quarterly 2:95-6, Oct., 1946
Life 20:81-4, Jun. 24, 1946
Nation 163:25, Jul. 6, 1946
New York Times p. 20, Jun. 21, 1946; II, p. 1, Jun. 30,
1946
New Yorker 22:43, Jul. 6, 1946
Newsweek 27:94, Jun. 24, 1946
Photoplay 29:4, Aug., 1946; 30:43, Feb., 1947
Theatre Arts 30:442, Aug., 1946
Time 47:98, Jun. 24, 1946

Anna Christie (1930)
Commonweal 11:590-1, Mar. 26, 1930
Life (NY) 95:20, Mar. 21, 1930
New York Times p. 22, Mar. 15, 1930; IX, p. 5, Mar.
23, 1930; p. 25, Jan. 6, 1931
Outlook 154:355, Feb. 26, 1930

Anna Karenina (1935)
Canadian Magazine 84:41, Nov., 1935
Literary Digest 120:29, Aug., 1931; 120:21, Sep. 21, 1935
Nation 141:391, Oct. 2, 1935
New York Times p. 16, Aug. 31, 1935; IX, p. 3, Sep.
8, 1935
Newsweek 6:26, Aug. 21, 1935
Time 26:46, Sep. 9, 1935
Vanity Fair 45:46-7, Oct., 1935

Anna Karenina (1948)
Canadian Forum 28:112, Aug., 1948
Commonweal 48:80, May 7, 1948
Life 24:101-4, Apr. 26, 1948
New Republic 118:31, May 10, 1948
New York Times p. 32, Apr. 28, 1948
New Yorker 24:92, May 8, 1948
Newsweek 31:72, Feb. 2, 1948; 31:81, May 10, 1948

Anna Karenina (1948) (Continued)
Scholastic 52:35, May 10, 1948
Time 51:90, May 3, 1948
Photoplay 33:26, Jul., 1948
Woman's Home Companion 75:10-11, Jul., 1948

Anna Lucasta (1949)
America 100:531, Jan. 31, 1959
Catholic World 188:416, Feb., 1959
Commonweal 50:490, Aug. 26, 1949; 69:497, Feb. 6, 1959
New Republic 121:22, Aug. 22, 1949
New York Times p. 13, Aug. 12, 1949; p. 27, Jan. 15,
    1959; II, p. 1, Jan. 18, 1959
New Yorker 25:49, Aug. 20, 1949; 34:111-12, Jan. 24,
    1959
Newsweek 34:70-1, Aug. 22, 1949; 52:95, Dec. 8, 1958
Saturday Review 42:66, Jan. 10, 1959
Theatre Arts 33:96, Oct., 1949
Time 54:78+, Aug. 15, 1949; 73:91, Jan. 26, 1959

Annabel Takes A Tour (1938)
New York Times p. 15, Dec. 29, 1938

Annabelle's Affairs (1931)
New York Times VIII, p. 4, Jun. 14, 1931; p. 20, Jun.
    29, 1931; VIII, p. 3, Jul. 5, 1931

Annapolis Farewell (1935)
New York Times p. 18, Aug. 24, 1935
Time 26:38, Sep. 2, 1935

Annapolis Salute (1937)
New York Times p. 18, Oct. 2, 1937

The Annapolis Story (1955)
New York Times p. 8, Apr. 9, 1955

Annapurna (1953)
America 90:346, Dec. 26, 1953
Commonweal 59:306, Dec. 25, 1953
Library Journal 79:56, Jan. 1, 1954
Life 35:34-6, Dec. 21, 1953
National Parent-Teacher 48:39, Feb., 1954
Natural History 63:94, Feb., 1954
New York Times p. 45, Dec. 14, 1953; II, p. 3, Dec.
    20, 1953
New Yorker 29:91-2, Dec. 12, 1953
Newsweek 42:90, Dec. 21, 1953

Annapurna (1953) (Continued)
Saturday Review 37:32, Jan. 9, 1954; 39:51, May 19, 1956
Time 62:90+, Dec. 21, 1953

Anna's Sin (1961)
Commonweal 74:47-8, Apr. 7, 1961

Anne of Green Gables (1934)
New York Times p. 21, Dec. 22, 1934
Vanity Fair 43:46, Jan., 1935

Anne of the Indies (1951)
Christian Century 68:1521, Dec. 26, 1951
New York Times p. 36, Oct. 25, 1951

Anne of Windy Poplars (1940)
New York Times p. 13, Aug. 23, 1940

Annette in Paradise (1936)
New York Times p. 11, Mar. 7, 1936

Annie Get Your Gun (1950)
Christian Century 67:879, Jul. 19, 1950
Commonweal 52:198, Jun. 2, 1950
Good Housekeeping 130:327, Apr., 1950
Library Journal 75:786, May 1, 1950
Life 28:174-5, Apr. 17, 1950
New Republic 122:22, May 29, 1950
New York Times p. 37, May 18, 1950; II, p. 1, May 21,
    1950; II, p. 1, Jun. 4, 1950; II, p. 5, May 29, 1949
New Yorker 26:105, May 20, 1950
Newsweek 35:86, Jun. 5, 1950
Rotarian 77:38, Sep., 1950
Time 55:66, Apr. 24, 1950

Annie Oakley (1936)
Literary Digest 121:23, Jan. 4, 1936
New York Times p. 10, Dec. 24, 1935
Scholastic 27:12, Dec. 7, 1935
Time 26:50, Nov. 25, 1935

Another Dawn (1937)
Commonweal 26:132, May 28, 1937
New York Times XI, p. 4, Jun. 13, 1937
Time 30:20, Jul. 5, 1937

Another Language (1933)
Nation 137:250, 326, Aug. 30, Sep. 20, 1933

Another Language (1933) (Continued)
New Outlook 162:44, Sep., 1933
New York Times p. 9, Aug. 5, 1933; IX, p. 3, Aug. 13,
1933
Newsweek 2:30, Aug. 12, 1933
Photoplay 44:12, Aug. 14, 1933
Time 22:22, Aug. 14, 1933
Vanity Fair 41:40, Oct., 1933

Another Man's Poison (1952)
Christian Century 69:231, Feb. 20, 1952
New York Times p. 14, Jan. 7, 1952
Newsweek 39:91, Jan. 21, 1952

Another Part of the Forest (1948)
Commonweal 48:185-6, Jun. 4, 1948
Life 24:63-4+, May 31, 1948
New Republic 118:29, Jun. 7, 1948
New York Times p. 30, May 19, 1948; II, p. 1, May 23,
1948
New Yorker 24:66, May 29, 1948
Newsweek 31:72, May 31, 1948
Photoplay 33:23, Jul., 1948
Time 51:86, May 31, 1948

Another Sky (1960)
New York Times p. 40, Oct. 25, 1960

Another Thin Man (1939)
New York Times p. 29, Nov. 24, 1939; IX, p. 5, Nov.
26, 1939
Newsweek 14:33-4, Nov. 27, 1939
Photoplay 53:20+, Dec., 1939; 54:59+, Jan., 1940
Time 34:78, Dec. 11, 1939

Another Time, Another Place (1960)
America 99:242, May 17, 1958
Library Journal 83:1528, May 15, 1958
New York Times p. 10, May 3, 1958
New Yorker 34:141, May 10, 1958
Newsweek 51:112, May 5, 1958
Time 71:96+, May 12, 1958

Anthony Adverse (1936)
Canadian Magazine 86:34-5, Aug., 1936
Commonweal 24:387, Aug. 14, 1936
Literary Digest 121:22, Jun. 13, 1936

54

Anthony Adverse (1936) (Continued)
Motion Picture 51:34-5+, Apr., 1936
New Republic 87:381-2, Aug. 5, 1936
New York Times p. 16, Aug. 27, 1936; X, p. 3, Sep. 13,
1936
Newsweek 8:24-5, Aug. 29, 1936
Scholastic 29:17, Sep. 19, 1936
Stage 13:44-5, Apr., 1936; 13:32-3, Jul., 1936
Time 28:43, Aug. 17, 1936

*Antigone
Esquire 59:32+, Feb., 1963
New Republic 147:28, Sep. 17, 1962
New York Times p. 30, Sep. 19, 1962
Saturday Review 45:22, Sep. 22, 1962

Antoine and Antoinette (1948)
New York Times p. 29, Apr. 26, 1948
New Yorker 24:59, Apr. 24, 1948

Any Number Can Play (1949)
Commonweal 50:319, Jul. 8, 1949
Good Housekeeping 129:169, Sep., 1949
New York Times p. 14, Jul. 1, 1949; II, p. 1, Jul. 10,
1949
New Yorker 25:38, Jul. 9, 1949
Newsweek 34:68, Jul. 11, 1949
Photoplay 36:22, Sep., 1949
Rotarian 75:42, Aug., 1949
Time 54:78, Jul. 25, 1949
Woman's Home Companion 76:10-11, Sep., 1949

Any Number Can Win (1963)
Commonweal 79:195, Nov. 8, 1963
New York Times p. 47, Oct. 9, 1963
New Yorker 39:146+, Oct. 19, 1963
Newsweek 62:110, Oct. 7, 1963

Anybody's War (1930)
New York Times p. 22, Jul. 11, 1930; VIII, p. 3, Jul.
20, 1930
Theatre Magazine 52:47-8, Aug.-Sep., 1930

Anybody's Woman (1930)
Life (NY) 96:18, Aug. 29, 1930
New York Times p. 8, Aug. 16, 1930; VIII, p. 5, Aug.
24, 1930
Theatre Magazine 52:48, Oct., 1930

Anything Can Happen (1952)
  Catholic World 175:63, Apr., 1952
  Christian Century 69:761, Jun. 25, 1952
  Commonweal 56:69, Apr. 25, 1952
  Holiday 11:105, May, 1952
  Library Journal 77:586, Apr. 1, 1952
  New York Times p. 21, Apr. 4, 1952
  New Yorker 28:119, Apr. 12, 1952
  Newsweek 39:95, Apr. 14, 1952
  Scholastic 60:23, Apr. 23, 1952
  Theatre Arts 36:104, May, 1952
  Time 59:106+, Apr. 14, 1952

Anything Goes (1936 and 1956)
  America 94:704, Mar. 24, 1956
  Catholic World 182:464, Mar., 1956
  Coronet 38:41-8, Aug., 1955
  Look 20:109-11, Apr. 3, 1956
  Motion Picture 51:29, Feb., 1936
  National Parent-Teacher 50:38, Apr., 1956
  New York Times p. 23, Feb. 6, 1936; p. 38, Mar. 22, 1956
  New Yorker 32:91, Mar. 31, 1956
  Newsweek 47:100, Mar. 26, 1956
  Time 27:57, Feb. 3, 1936; 67:110, Apr. 2, 1956

Apache (1954)
  Commonweal 60:413, Jul. 30, 1954
  Farm Journal 78:92, Jul., 1954
  National Parent-Teacher 48:38, Jun., 1954
  New York Times p. 7, Jul. 10, 1954
  Time 64:84, Aug. 9, 1954

Apache Ambush (1955)
  National Parent-Teacher 50:38, Nov., 1955

Apache Drums (1951)
  New York Times p. 22, May 7, 1951

Apache Rose (1947)
  New York Times II, p. 3, Jul. 27, 1947

Apache War Smoke (1952)
  National Parent-Teacher 47:37, Dec., 1952

Apache Warrior (1957)
  National Parent-Teacher 52:32, Sep. 1957

Apaches of Paris (1929)
New York Times p. 35, Dec. 11, 1928

*Aparajito
America 101:286, May 2, 1959
Catholic World 189:55, Apr., 1959
Commonweal 69:544, Feb. 20, 1959
Horizon 3:115, Jan., 1961
Library Journal 84:734, Mar. 1, 1959
Nation 188:484, May 23, 1959
New York Times p. 30, Apr. 29, 1959; II, p. 1, May 3, 1959
New Yorker 35:159, May 9, 1959
Newsweek 53:102, Feb. 23, 1959
Saturday Review 42:37, Feb. 14, 1959
Time 73:101, Feb. 16, 1959

Apartment (1960)
America 103:403, Jun. 25, 1960
Commonweal 72:351, Jul. 8, 1960
New Republic 142:20, Jun. 27, 1960
New York Times p. 37, Jun. 16, 1960; II, p. 1, Jun. 26, 1960
New Yorker 36:70, Jun. 25, 1960
Newsweek 55:110, Jun. 20, 1960
Saturday Review 43:24, Jun. 11, 1960
Time 75:47, Jun. 6, 1960

Apartment for Peggy (1948)
Commonweal 49:41, Oct. 22, 1948
Good Housekeeping 127:260, Nov., 1948
National Education Association Journal 37:608, Dec., 1948
Life 26:46, Mar. 14, 1949
New Republic 119:31, Nov. 15, 1948
New York Times p. 9, Oct. 16, 1948; II, p. 1, Oct. 24, 1948
Newsweek 32:108, Oct. 18, 1948
Photoplay 34:23, Dec., 1948
Rotarian 74:11, Jan., 1949
Scholastic 53:37, Sep. 29, 1948; 53:22T, Nov. 3, 1948
Time 52:106, Oct. 25, 1948

The Ape (1940)
New York Times p. 28, Nov. 28, 1940

Appassionata (1946)
Theatre Arts 31:42, Jan., 1947
Time 48:102+, Dec. 9, 1946

Applause (1929)
    Arts 16:240-41, Dec., 1929
    Life (NY) 94:24, Nov. 1, 1929
    Nation 129:503, Oct. 30, 1929
    New York Times IX, p. 5, Sep. 22, 1929; p. 24, Oct. 8,
        1929; IX, p. 6, Oct. 13, 1929
    Outlook 153:315, Oct. 23, 1929

Appointment for Love (1941)
    Commonweal 35:125, Nov. 21, 1941
    New York Times p. 27, Nov. 7, 1941; IX, p. 5, Nov. 9,
        1941
    Newsweek 18:57, Nov. 3, 1941
    Time 38:95, Nov. 10, 1941

Appointment in Berlin (1943)
    New York Times II, p. 3, Mar. 21, 1943; p. 8, Jul. 17,
        1943

Appointment in Honduras (1953)
    New York Times p. 41, Nov. 19, 1953
    New Yorker 29:131, Nov. 28, 1953
    Time 62:98+, Nov. 30, 1953

Appointment in Tokyo (1945)
    Commonweal 43:238-9, Dec. 14, 1945
    New Yorker 21:88, Dec. 8, 1945
    Theatre Arts 30:50, Jan., 1946

Appointment with a Shadow (1958)
    New York Times p. 24, Jan. 8, 1959

Appointment with Crime (1950)
    New York Times p. 19, Feb. 19, 1951

Appointment with Danger (1951)
    Christian Century 68:777, Jun. 27, 1951
    Commonweal 54:190, Jun. 1, 1951
    Nation 172:498, May 26, 1951
    New York Times p. 38, May 10, 1951
    Saturday Review 34:27, Jun. 9, 1951
    Time 57:102+, May 28, 1951

April in Paris (1952)
    Catholic World 176:301, Jan., 1953
    Christian Century 70:119, Jan. 28, 1953
    Commonweal 57:334, Jan. 2, 1953

April in Paris (1952) (Continued)
National Parent-Teacher 47:37, Feb., 1953
New York Times p. 34, Dec. 25, 1952; II, p. 5, Feb. 8,
    1953; II, p. 5, Feb. 15, 1953
Newsweek 41:61, Jan. 5, 1953

April Love (1957)
America 98:300, Nov. 30, 1957
Library Journal 82:3199, Dec. 15, 1957
National Parent-Teacher 52:38, Jan., 1958
New York Times p. 57, Nov. 28, 1957
Newsweek 50:97, Dec. 2, 1957
Senior Scholastic 71:32, Dec. 13, 1957

*April 1, 2000
National Parent-Teacher 48:38, Apr., 1954
New York Times p. 27, Feb. 17, 1954
New Yorker 30:106, Feb. 27, 1954

April Romance (1936)
New York Times p. 17, Jan. 27, 1937

April Showers (1948)
New York Times p. 10, Mar. 27, 1948
New Yorker 24:104, Apr. 10, 1948
Newsweek 31:85, Apr. 5, 1948

Arabian Nights (1942)
Commonweal 37:328, Jan. 15, 1943
Life 13:69-70, Sep. 28, 1942
New York Times p. 15, Dec. 26, 1942
Newsweek 21:60, Jan. 4, 1943
Time 41:88, Jan. 11, 1943

Arch of Triumph (1948)
Commonweal 48:80, May 7, 1948
Cosmopolitan 123:46+, Nov., 1947
Life 23:163-4, Nov. 17, 1947; 24:65-6+, May 3, 1948
New Republic 118:31, May 3, 1948
New York Times p. 33, Apr. 21, 1948; II, p. 1, Apr. 25,
    1948
New Yorker 24:59, Apr. 24, 1948
Newsweek 31:91, Apr. 26, 1948
Time 51:100+, May 10, 1948
Woman's Home Companion 75:11, Jul., 1948

Arctic Fury (1949)
Christian Century 67:63, Jan. 11, 1950

Arctic Fury (1949) (Continued)
New York Times II, p. 3, Jul. 17, 1949
Rotarian 76:36, Mar., 1950

Arctic Manhunt (1948)
New York Times p. 12, Aug. 19, 1949

Are Husbands Necessary? (1942)
Commonweal 36:328, Jul. 24, 1942
New York Times p. 17, Jul. 9, 1942
Time 40:46, Jul. 27, 1942

Are These Our Children? (1931)
New York Times p. 15, Nov. 14, 1931; VIII, p. 5, Nov.
22, 1931
Outlook 159:406, Nov. 25, 1931

Are These Our Parents? (1944)
New York Times p. 16, Aug. 23, 1944
New Yorker 20:50, Sep. 2, 1944

Are We Civilized (1934)
New York Times p. 28, Jun. 14, 1934; p. 19, Nov. 18,
1935
Newsweek 3:36, Jun. 25, 1934

Are You With It (1948)
Commonweal 48:675, Apr. 30, 1948
New York Times p. 31, Apr. 15, 1948
Newsweek 31:95, Apr. 26, 1948

Arena (1953)
America 89:366, Jul. 4, 1953
National Parent-Teacher 48:37, Sep., 1953
New York Times p. 201, Jul. 23, 1953; II, p. 1, Jul. 26,
1953

Aren't We All? (1932)
New York Times p. 19, Jul. 1, 1932; IX, p. 3, Jul. 10,
1932

Aren't We Wonderful? (1959)
Nation 189:408, Nov. 28, 1959
New York Times p. 27, Oct. 16, 1959
New Yorker 35:186, Oct. 24, 1959
Saturday Review 42:36, Sep. 26, 1959

Argentine Nights (1940)
New York Times p. 25, Oct. 11, 1940
Scribner's Commentator 9:197, Dec., 1940

Argyle Case (1929)
New York Times p. 13, Aug. 31, 1929; IX, p. 4, Sep. 8,
1929

Ariane (1934)
Nation 138:342, Mar. 21, 1934
New York Times p. 23, Mar. 7, 1934; X, p. 5, Mar. 11,
1934

Arise My Love (1940)
Commonweal 33:81, Nov. 8, 1940
New York Times p. 33, Oct. 17, 1940
Photoplay 54:69, Oct., 1940
Scribner's Commentator 9:106-7, Dec., 1940
Time 36:84, Oct. 28, 1940

Arizona (1940)
Commonweal 33:256, Dec. 27, 1940
Etude 58:519+, Aug., 1940
Life 9:81-4, Nov. 18, 1940
New Republic 103:756, Dec. 2, 1940
New York Times XI, p. 4, Jan. 19, 1941; p. 23, Feb. 7,
1941; IX, p. 5, Feb. 9, 1941
New Yorker 17:76, Feb. 15, 1941
Newsweek 16:64, Dec. 9, 1940
Photoplay 18:14, Feb., 1941
Scribner's Commentator 9:105-6, Apr., 1941
Stage 1:32, Nov., 1940
Time 36:92, Dec. 16, 1940

The Arizona Kid (1930)
New York Times p. 21, May 17, 1930; IX, p. 5, May 25,
1930

Arizona to Broadway (1933)
New York Times X, p. 3, Jul. 9, 1933; p. 14, Jul. 22,
1933

The Arizonian (1935)
New York Times p. 16, Jul. 27, 1935

Arkansas Traveler (1938)
Commonweal 29:105, Nov. 18, 1938

Arkansas Traveler (1938) (Continued)
New York Times p. 29, Nov. 17, 1938; IX, p. 5, Nov. 20, 1938
Time 32:26, Oct. 31, 1938

Armored Car (1937)
New York Times p. 15, Jul. 26, 1937

Armored Car Robbery (1950)
Newsweek 36:68, Jul. 24, 1950

Armored Command (1961)
New York Times p. 14, Oct. 7, 1961; p. 13, Jul. 4, 1962

Army Girl (1938)
New York Times p. 11, Aug. 12, 1938; X, p. 6, Aug. 14, 1938

Army Surgeon (1942)
New York Times p. 35, Nov. 5, 1942
New Yorker 18:77, Nov. 7, 1942

The Arnelo Affair (1947)
New York Times p. 8, Sep. 13, 1947

Around the World (1943)
New York Times p. 39, Nov. 25, 1943

Around the World in Eighty Days (1956)
America 96:140, Nov. 3, 1956
Atlantic 200:89-90, Sep., 1947
Catholic World 184:301, Jan., 1957
Christian Century 75:1239, Oct. 29, 1958
Commonweal 65:151-2, Nov. 9, 1956
Good Housekeeping 143:68, Nov., 1956
Holiday 20:77+, Oct., 1956
Library Journal 81:2676, Nov. 15, 1956
Life 41:81-5, Oct. 22, 1956
Look 20:144+, Dec. 11, 1956
Nation 183:417, Nov. 10, 1956; 183:470, Dec. 1, 1956
National Parent-Teacher 51:38, Dec., 1956
New York Times p. 37, Oct. 18, 1956; II, p. 1, Oct. 21, 1956
New Yorker 32:158, Oct. 27, 1956
Newsweek 48:98, Oct. 29, 1956; 48:114-15, Nov. 5, 1956
Reporter 16:36, Jan. 24, 1957
Saturday Review 39:28, Nov. 3, 1956; 42:41-4, Mar. 14, 1959

Around the World in Eighty Days (1956) (Continued)
Scholastic 69:53, Dec. 6, 1956
Theatre Arts 40:18-19+, Oct., 1956
Time 68:72+, Oct. 29, 1956
Travel 106:54-5, Sep., 1956

Around the World in 80 Minutes (1931)
New York Times p. 28, Nov. 20, 1931; VIII, p. 5, Nov. 29, 1931
Outlook 159:439, Dec. 2, 1931

Around the World Via Graf Zeppelin (1929)
New York Times p. 28, Nov. 4, 1929

Arrest Bulldog Drummond (1938)
New York Times p. 23, Jan. 12, 1939; IX, p. 5, Jan. 15, 1939

Arrow in the Dust (1954)
National Parent-Teacher 49:37, Sep., 1954
New York Times p. 13, May 1, 1954

Arrowhead (1953)
America 89:611, Sep. 19, 1953
National Parent-Teacher 48:38, Sep., 1953
New York Times p. 38, Sep. 16, 1953
Newsweek 42:104, Sep. 14, 1953

Arrowsmith (1931)
Hygeia 10:224-5, Mar., 1932
Nation 133:706+, Dec. 23, 1931
New York Times p. 36, Dec. 8, 1931; VIII, p. 6, Dec. 13, 1931
Outlook 159:503, 515, Dec., 16-23, 1932

Arsenal (1929)
Nation 129:640, Nov. 27, 1929
New York Times III, p. 3, Mar. 31, 1929; p. 20, Nov. 11, 1929; IX, p. 6, Nov. 17, 1929

Arsene Lupin (1932)
New York Times p. 21, Feb. 27, 1932; VIII, p. 4, Feb. 28, 1932; VIII, p. 4, Mar. 6, 1932

Arsene Lupin Returns (1938)
New York Times p. 21, Mar. 9, 1938

Arsenic and Old Lace (1945)
Commonweal 40:548, Sep. 22, 1944
Cosmopolitan 117:85, Oct. , 1944
New York Times p. 17, Sep. 2, 1944
Newsweek 24:110, Sep. 11, 1944
Photoplay 25:21, Nov. , 1944
Scholastic 45:30, Sep. 18, 1944
Theatre Arts 28:596, Oct. , 1944
Time 44:95+, Sep. 11, 1944
Woman's Home Companion 71:10-11, Sep. , 1944

Arson Racket Squad (1938)
New York Times p. 18, Jun. 18, 1938

Artists and Models (1937)
New York Times p. 19, Aug. 5, 1937; X, p. 3, Aug. 8,
1937
Time 30:36, Aug. 16, 1937

Artists and Models (1955)
National Parent-Teacher 50:38, Jan. , 1956
New York Times p. 20, Dec. 22, 1955
Time 67:86+, Jan. 9, 1956

Artists and Models Abroad (1938)
Commonweal 29:330, Jan. 13, 1939
New York Times p. 25, Dec. 22, 1938; IX, p. 7, Dec.
25, 1938
Photoplay 53:44, Jan. , 1939

*Arturo Toscanini
Etude 62:512, Sep. , 1944
Theatre Arts 28:727, Dec. , 1944

Arturo's Island (1962)
New Republic 148:29, Jan. 19, 1963
New York Times p. 5, Dec. 22, 1962
New Yorker 38:68, Jan. 5, 1963
Newsweek 61:58, Jan. 7, 1963
Time 81:87, Jan. 18, 1963

As Good As Married (1937)
New York Times p. 19, May 22, 1937

As Husbands Go
New York Times p. 20, Jan. 26, 1934; IX, p. 5, Feb. 4, 1934

As Long As You're Near Me (1956)
Catholic World 182:462, Mar. , 1956

64

As the Earth Turns (1934)
  American Review 3:155-7, May, 1934
  New Outlook 163:42, May, 1934
  New York Times p. 27, Apr. 12, 1934; IX, p. 3, Apr. 22, 1934
  Newsweek 3:35, Apr. 21, 1934

As the Sea Rages (1960)
  New York Times p. 41, May 18, 1961

As You Desire Me (1932)
  Commonweal 16:188, Jun. 15, 1932
  Nation 134:708, Jun. 22, 1932
  New York Times p. 23, Jun. 3, 1932; X, p. 3, Jun. 12, 1932

As You Like It (1937)
  Canadian Magazine 86:36, Nov., 1936
  Nation 143:613-14, Nov. 21, 1936
  New York Times p. 29, Nov. 6, 1936
  Stage 14:12, Dec., 1936
  Time 28:45, Nov. 9, 1936

As Young As You Feel (1951)
  Christian Century 68:831, Jul. 11, 1951
  Library Journal 76:972, Jun. 1, 1951
  New York Times p. 10, Aug. 3, 1951
  Newsweek 38:84, Jul. 23, 1951

Ashes and Diamonds (1961)
  Commonweal 71:45-6, Oct. 9, 1959; 74:230, May 26, 1961
  Nation 193:38+, Jul. 15, 1961
  New Republic 144:21-2, Jun. 12, 1961
  New York Times p. 8, May 30, 1961; II, p. 1, Jun. 4, 1961
  Newsweek 57:95, Jun. 12, 1961
  Saturday Review 44:37, Jun. 10, 1961
  Time 77:88, May 19, 1961

Ask Any Girl (1959)
  America 101:418, Jun. 6, 1959
  Commonweal 70:258, Jun. 5, 1959
  Library Journal 84:1801, Jun. 1, 1959
  New York Times p. 32, May 22, 1959
  New Yorker 35:90, May 30, 1959
  Newsweek 53:95, Jun. 1, 1959
  Saturday Review 42:24, May 23, 1959
  Time 73:60, Jun. 1, 1959

Asphalt Jungle (1950)
Christian Century 67:831, Jul. 5, 1950
Commonweal 52:249, Jun. 16, 1950
Good Housekeeping 131:17+, Jul., 1950
Library Journal 75:1201, Jul., 1950
Nation 171:65, Jul. 15, 1950; 171:397, Oct. 28, 1950
New Republic 122:23, Jun. 26, 1950
New York Times p. 29, Jun. 9, 1950; II, p. 1, Jun. 18, 1950
New Yorker 26:54, Jun. 17, 1950
Newsweek 35:88, Jun. 12, 1950
Saturday Review 33:34, Jun. 24, 1950
Time 55:92, Jun. 19, 1950

Assassin (1952)
America 89:175, May 9, 1953
Library Journal 78:897, May 15, 1953
New York Times p. 17, Apr. 18, 1953
New Yorker 29:113, Apr. 25, 1953
Newsweek 41:94, May 4, 1953

Assignment Children (1955)
New York Times p. 3, Feb. 10, 1955; p. 26, Mar. 27, 1955

Assignment in Brittany (1943)
Commonweal 38:75, May 7, 1943
New York Times p. 31, Apr. 22, 1943
New Yorker 19:38, Apr. 24, 1943
Newsweek 21:86, May 3, 1943
Photoplay 23:16, Jun., 1943

Assignment Paris (1952)
Catholic World 176:63, Oct., 1952
Library Journal 77:1801, Oct. 15, 1952
National Parent-Teacher 47:37, Oct., 1952
New York Times p. 12, Oct. 25, 1952
Newsweek 40:114, Oct. 27, 1952
Theatre Arts 36:73+, Oct., 1952
Time 60:124, Nov. 10, 1952

Astonished Heart (1950)
Christian Century 67:879, Jul. 19, 1950
Commonweal 51:537, Feb. 24, 1950
Library Journal 75:503, Mar. 15, 1950
New Republic 122:22, Feb. 27, 1950
New York Times p. 23, Feb. 15, 1959

Astonished Heart (1950) (Continued)
New Yorker 25:83, Feb. 18, 1950
Newsweek 35:80, Feb. 27, 1950
Rotarian 77:38, Sep., 1950
Time 55:100+, Feb. 27, 1950

At Dawn We Die (1943)
New York Times p. 19, May 8, 1943

At Gunpoint (1955)
National Parent-Teacher 50:38, Feb., 1956
New York Times p. 24, Feb. 4, 1956
Newsweek 47:106+, Feb. 20, 1956

At Sword's Point (1952)
New York Times p. 37, Apr. 10, 1952

At the Circus (1939)
Life 7:57, Dec. 4, 1939
New York Times p. 17, Nov. 17, 1939
Photoplay 53:64, Nov., 1939
Time 34:81, Dec. 4, 1939

At War With the Army (1951)
Christian Century 68:222, Feb. 14, 1951
Commonweal 53:544, Mar. 9, 1951
New York Times p. 21, Jan. 25, 1951; II, p. 1, Jan. 28,
    1951
Newsweek 37:80, Feb. 5, 1951
Time 57:104, Jan. 29, 1951

Athena (1954)
America 92:346, Dec. 25, 1954
Catholic World 180:303, Jan., 1955
Commonweal 61:224, Nov. 26, 1954
National Parent-Teacher 49:38, Jan., 1955
Newsweek 44:108, Nov. 22, 1954
Saturday Review 37:28, Nov. 27, 1954
Time 64:102, Nov. 22, 1954

Atlantic (1930)
New York Times X, p. 8, Dec. 8, 1929; VIII, p. 6, Jan.
    26, 1930; p. 21, Oct. 6, 1930; VIII, p. 5, Oct. 12,
    1930
Outlook 156:272, Oct. 15, 1930

Atlantic City (1944)
New York Times II, p. 4, Aug. 14, 1944

Atlantic Convoy (1942)
New York Times p. 18, Jul. 6, 1942

Atlantic Flight (1937)
New York Times XI, p. 5, Sep. 26, 1937; p. 24, Nov. 1,
1937

Atlantis, the Lost Continent (1961)
New York Times II, p. 5, Jul. 24, 1960; p. 12, May 27,
1961
Time 77:42, Jun. 2, 1961

Atomic City (1952)
Christian Century 69:863, Jul. 23, 1952
New York Times p. 21, May 2, 1952; II, p. 1, May 11,
1952
New Yorker 28:86, May 10, 1952
Newsweek 39:104, May 12, 1952
Theatre Arts 36:88, Jul., 1952
Time 59:103, May 12, 1952

Atomic Kid (1954)
National Parent-Teacher 49:38, Feb., 1955

*Attack
Commonweal 40:302, Jul. 14, 1944
Nation 158:743, Jun. 23, 1944
New Republic 111:16, Jul. 3, 1944
Newsweek 23:98, Jun. 26, 1944
Time 43:54, Jun. 12, 1944
Theatre Arts 28:496, Sep., 1944

Attack (1956)
America 95:632, Sep. 29, 1956
Catholic World 184:65, Oct., 1956
Commonweal 65:16, Oct. 5, 1956
Library Journal 81:2315, Oct. 15, 1956
National Parent-Teacher 51:37, Oct., 1956
Nation 183:294, Oct. 6, 1956
New York Times p. 29, Sep. 20, 1956
New Yorker 32:88, Sep. 29, 1956
Newsweek 48:116, Sep. 17, 1956
Saturday Review 39:25-6, Sep. 1, 1956
Time 68:116, Sep. 10, 1956

Attila (1958)
New York Times p. 19, May 19, 1958

Attorney for the Defense (1932)
New York Times p. 18, May 28, 1932; X, p. 3, Jun. 5, 1932

August Weekend (1936)
New York Times p. 21, Jan. 30, 1937

Auntie Mame (1959)
America 100:381, Dec. 20, 1958
Catholic World 188:416, Feb., 1959
Commonweal 69:340, Dec. 26, 1958
Library Journal 84:70, Jan. 1, 1959
New Republic 140:20-1, Jan. 19, 1959
New York Times p. 39, Dec. 5, 1958; II, p. 1, Dec. 7, 1958
Newsweek 52:112+, Dec. 15, 1958
Saturday Review 41:21, Dec. 27, 1958
Time 72:72, Dec. 22, 1958

Autumn Crocus (1934)
New York Times p. 26, Oct. 25, 1934

Autumn Leaves (1956)
America 95:432, Aug. 4, 1956
Catholic World 183:221-2, Jun. 1956
Commonweal 64:420, Jul. 27, 1956
National Parent-Teacher 51:39, Sep., 1956
New York Times p. 21, Aug. 2, 1956; II, p. 1, Aug. 5, 1956
New Yorker 32:58, Aug. 11, 1956
Newsweek 48:73, Jul. 2, 1956
Saturday Review 39:25, May 12, 1956
Time 68:80, Aug. 20, 1956

Avalanche (1946)
New York Times p. 11, Jul. 6, 1946

Ave Maria (1936)
Commonweal 26:580, Oct. 15, 1937
New York Times p. 18, Oct. 2, 1937

The Avenger (1933)
New York Times p. 28, Oct. 3, 1933

Avengers (1942)
Commonweal 37:208, Dec. 11, 1942
New York Times p. 18, Nov. 25, 1942
Scholastic 41:33, Jan. 18, 1943

The Avengers (1950)
New York Times II, p. 4, Jun. 26, 1949

L'Avventura (1961)
America 105:411, Jun. 3, 1961
Christian Century 78:1031, Aug. 30, 1961
Commonweal 74:79, Apr. 14, 1961
Esquire 55:21-2, Apr., 1961; 57:65-6, May, 1962
Horizon 4:110-12, Sep., 1961
Nation 192:329-30, Apr. 15, 1961
New Republic 144:26, Apr. 10, 1961
New York Times p. 30, Apr. 5, 1961; II, p. 1, Apr. 9, 1961
New Yorker 37:144-5, Apr. 22, 1961
Newsweek 57:107, Apr. 17, 1961
Saturday Review 44:41, Apr. 8, 1961
Time 77:60, Apr. 7, 1961
Yale Review 54:41-50, Oct., 1964

The Aviator (1929)
New York Times p. 21, Jan. 11, 1930

The Awakening (1928)
Life (NY) 93:29, Jan. 25, 1929
New York Times VIII, p. 6, Dec. 23, 1928; p. 9, Dec. 31, 1928
Outlook 151:141, Jan. 23, 1929

Awakening (1958)
America 98:706, Mar. 15, 1958
Catholic World 186:379, Feb., 1958
Commonweal 67:384, Jan. 10, 1958
New York Times p. 24, Mar. 3, 1958
New Yorker 34:113, Mar. 8, 1958

Away All Boats (1956)
Catholic World 183:306, Jul., 1956
Commonweal 64:419, Jul. 27, 1956
Coronet 40:8, Aug., 1956
Library Journal 81:1782, Aug., 1956
National Parent-Teacher 51:37, Oct., 1956
New York Times p. 14, Aug. 17, 1956
Newsweek 48:88, Aug. 20, 1956
Saturday Review 39:18, Jul. 7, 1956
Time 68:74, Aug. 27, 1956

Awful Truth (1937)
Commonweal 27:48, Nov. 5, 1937

70

Awful Truth (1937) (Continued)
New Republic 93:102, Dec. 1, 1937
New York Times p. 19, Nov. 5, 1937; XI, p. 5, Nov. 14, 1937
Scholastic 31:36, Dec. 18, 1937
Stage 15:87, Dec., 1937; 15:26, May, 1938
Time 30:45, Nov. 1, 1937

B. F.'s Daughter (1948)
New Republic 118:21, Apr. 12, 1948
New York Times p. 35, Mar. 25, 1948
New Yorker 24:59, Apr. 3, 1948
Newsweek 31:88, Apr. 12, 1948
Photoplay 32:23, May, 1948
Time 51:99, Apr. 26, 1948

Babbitt (1934)
New York Times p. 24, Dec. 17, 1934

Babe Ruth Story (1948)
Good Housekeeping 127:110, Oct., 1948
New Republic 119:28, Aug. 9, 1948
New York Times II, p. 1, Aug. 1, 1948
New Yorker 24:63, Aug. 7, 1948
Newsweek 32:68, Aug. 9, 1948
Time 52:94, Aug. 16, 1948
Woman's Home Companion 75:11, Aug. 16, 1948

Babes in Arms (1939)
Commonweal 31:14, Oct. 27, 1939
Life 7:37-8+, Nov. 6, 1939
New York Times p. 27, Oct. 20, 1939; IX, p. 5, Oct. 29, 1939
Newsweek 14:43, Oct. 16, 1939
Photoplay 53:65, Nov., 1939
Saint Nicholas 66:41, Oct., 1939
Scholastic 35:30+, Oct. 30, 1939

Babes in Bagdad (1952)
National Parent-Teacher 47:37, Jan., 1953
Newsweek 40:72, Dec. 22, 1952
Time 61:94+, Jan. 26, 1953

Babes in Toyland (1934)
New York Times p. 28, Dec. 13, 1934
Time 24:30, Dec. 10, 1934

Babes in Toyland (1962)
America 106:424-5, Dec. 23, 1961
Commonweal 75:341, Dec. 22, 1961
Dance Magazine 36:22-3, Jan., 1962
Life 51:55-6+, Dec. 8, 1961
New York Times p. 49, Dec. 15, 1961; II, p. 3, Dec. 17, 1961
Newsweek 58:98, Dec. 18, 1961
Time 78:85, Dec. 15, 1961

Babes on Broadway (1941)
Commonweal 35:296, Jan. 9, 1942
New York Times p. 37, Jan. 1, 1942; IX, p. 5, Jan. 4, 1942
Newsweek 19:54, Jan. 5, 1942
Scholastic 39:32, Jan. 5, 1942
Time 39:32, Jan. 19, 1942

Babette Goes to War (1960)
Commonweal 71:699, Mar. 25, 1960
McCalls 87:6, May, 1960
New York Times p. 46, Jun. 8, 1960
Saturday Review 43:27, May 7, 1960

Baboona (1935)
New York Times X, p. 4, Jan. 20, 1935; p. 21, Jan. 23, 1935

Baby and the Battleship (1956)
National Parent-Teacher 52:33, Dec., 1957
New York Times p. 37, Oct. 1, 1957
New Yorker 33:109, Oct. 12, 1957
Senior Scholastic 71:33, Oct. 25, 1957

Baby Doll (1956)
America 96:367, Dec. 29, 1956
Catholic World 184:302, Jan., 1957; 185:62, Apr., 1957
Christian Century 74:110-12, Jan. 23, 1957
Commonweal 65:335, Dec. 28, 1956; 67:202-4, Nov. 22, 1957
Cosmopolitan 142:23, Jan., 1957
Holiday 21:93+, Feb., 1957
Library Journal 18:2838, Dec. 1, 1956
Life 40:111-12+, Jun. 11, 1956; 42:60-5, Jan. 7, 1957
Look 20:95+, Dec. 25, 1956
National Parent-Teacher 51:36, Jan., 1947
Nation 183:567, Dec. 29, 1956

Baby Doll (1956) (Continued)
New Republic 136:21, Jan. 21, 1957
New York Times II, p. 5, Feb. 26, 1956; VI, p. 47,
    Apr. 22, 1956; p. 40, Dec. 19, 1956; II, p. 1, Jan.
    6, 1957
New Yorker 32:59, Dec. 29, 1956
Newsweek 48:106, Dec. 17, 1956
Reporter 16:36, Jan. 24, 1957
Saturday Review 39:22-4, Dec. 29, 1956
Time 68:61, Dec. 24, 1956; 69:100, Jan. 14, 1957

Baby Face (1933)
New York Times p. 16, Jun. 24, 1933

Baby Face Nelson (1957)
New York Times p. 35, Dec. 12, 1957
Newsweek 50:125, Nov. 25, 1957

Baby Take A Bow (1934)
New York Times p. 18, Jun. 30, 1934; IX, p. 3, Jul. 8,
    1934; p. 26, Sep. 13, 1934

Bachelor and the Bobby-Soxer (1947)
Canadian Forum 27:255, Feb., 1948
Commonweal 46:358, Jul. 25, 1947
Cosmopolitan 123:54+, Aug., 1947
Life 22:2, May 19, 1947; 23:82, Jul. 7, 1947
New Republic 117:38, Aug. 18, 1947
New York Times p. 12, Jul. 25, 1947
New Yorker 23:47, Aug. 2, 1947
Newsweek 30:88, Aug. 11, 1947
Time 50:95, Aug. 11, 1947
Woman's Home Companion 74:10-11, Sep., 1947

Bachelor Apartment (1931)
New York Times p. 13, May 16, 1931; VIII, p. 5, May
    24, 1931

Bachelor Father (1931)
New York Times p. 23, Feb. 2, 1931; VIII, p. 5, Feb. 8,
    1931

Bachelor Flat (1962)
New York Times p. 14, Jan. 13, 1962

Bachelor in Paradise (1961)
America 106:375, Dec. 9, 1961
New York Times p. 41, Nov. 17, 1961

Bachelor in Paradise (1961) (Continued)
New Yorker 37:235-6, Dec. 9, 1961
Newsweek 58:107, Nov. 13, 1961
Time 78:98, Dec. 8, 1961

Bachelor Mother (1939)
Commonweal 30:300, Jul. 14, 1939
Life 7:27-9, Jul. 3, 1939
Nation 149:155, Aug. 5, 1939
New Republic 99:307, Jul. 19, 1939
New York Times X, p. 5, Mar. 26, 1939; p. 17, Jun.
    30, 1939; XI, p. 3, Jul. 9, 1939
Newsweek 14:32, Jul. 10, 1939
Photoplay 53:63, Sep., 1939
Time 34:27, Jul. 10, 1939

Bachelor Party (1957)
America 97:152, Apr. 27, 1957
Catholic World 185:221, Jun., 1957
Commonweal 66:35-6, Apr. 12, 1957
Coronet 41:10, Apr., 1957
Library Journal 82:974, Apr. 1, 1957
Life 42:79-80, Apr. 29, 1957
Nation 184:379, Apr. 27, 1957
National Parent-Teacher 51:36, Jun., 1957
New Republic 136:29, May 27, 1957
New York Times p. 37, Apr. 10, 1957; II, p. 1, Apr.
    14, 1957
New Yorker 33:135, Apr. 20, 1957
Newsweek 49:124-5, Apr. 22, 1957
Saturday Review 40:25, Apr. 27, 1957
Time 69:116+, Apr. 15, 1957

Bachelor's Affairs (1930)
New York Times p. 18, Jun. 25, 1932; IX, p. 3, Jul. 3,
    1932

Bachelor's Daughters (1946)
New York Times p. 23, Oct. 7, 1946
New Yorker 22:115, Oct. 19, 1946
Newsweek 28:104, Oct. 21, 1946
Time 48:99, Oct. 21, 1946

Back Door to Heaven (1939)
Commonweal 30:49, May 5, 1939
New York Times p. 21, Apr. 20, 1939
Newsweek 13:33, Apr. 24, 1939
Time 33:69, May 1, 1939

Back From Eternity (1956)
Commonweal 64:634, Sep. 28, 1956
Library Journal 81:2174, Oct. 1, 1956
New York Times p. 20, Sep. 8, 1956
New Yorker 32:76+, Sep. 15, 1956
Newsweek 48:116+, Sep. 17, 1956
Saturday Review 39:22, Sep. 29, 1956
Scholastic 69:21, Oct. 18, 1956
Time 68:94, Sep. 24, 1956

Back From the Dead (1957)
National Parent-Teacher 52:37, Nov., 1957

Back in Circulation (1937)
Fortune 16:111, Dec., 1937
New York Times p. 17, Oct. 4, 1937; XI, p. 5, Oct. 10, 1937

Back Pay (1929)
New York Times p. 19, May 31, 1930

Back Street (1931)
Canadian Forum 13:78-9, Nov., 1932
New York Times p. 9, Aug. 29, 1932; IX, p. 3, Sep. 4, 1932

Back Street (1941)
Commonweal 33:424, Feb. 14, 1941
New York Times p. 25, Feb. 12, 1941; IX, p. 5, Feb. 16, 1941
New Yorker 16:63, Feb. 8, 1941
Newsweek 17:65-6, Feb. 17, 1941
Scribner's Commentator 9:105, Apr., 1941
Time 37:96, Feb. 24, 1941

*Back Street
America 105:839-40, Sep. 30, 1961
Commonweal 75:176, Nov. 10, 1961
New York Times p. 27, Oct. 13, 1961; II, p. 1, Oct. 15, 1961
Saturday Review 44:35, Oct. 21, 1961
Time 78:75, Nov. 3, 1961

*Back Streets of Paris
New York Times p. 9, Oct. 16, 1948
New Yorker 24:115, Oct. 16, 1948
Newsweek 32:81, Nov. 1, 1948
Time 52:106, Nov. 15, 1948

Back to Bataan (1945)
Commonweal 42:309, Jul. 13, 1945
New York Times p. 26, Sep. 13, 1945
New Yorker 21:36, Sep. 1, 1945
Newsweek 26:85, Jul. 23, 1945
Time 46:86, Jul. 9, 1945

Back to God's Country (1953)
National Parent-Teacher 48:36, Nov., 1953

Back to the Wall (1959)
Commonweal 70:522, Sep. 18, 1959
New Republic 141:21, Dec. 7, 1959
New York Times p. 43, Sep. 8, 1959
New Yorker 35:91, Sep. 19, 1959
Newsweek 54:118, Sep. 14, 1959
Saturday Review 42:27, Sep. 19, 1959
Time 74:107, Sep. 21, 1959

Background to Danger (1943)
Commonweal 38:323-4, Jul. 16, 1943
Nation 174:19, Jan. 5, 1952
New York Times p. 11, Jul. 3, 1943
Time 42:96, Jul. 19, 1943

Backlash (1946)
New York Times p. 10, May 24, 1947

Backlash (1956)
Commonweal 64:49, Apr. 13, 1956
Library Journal 81:821, Apr. 1, 1956
National Parent-Teacher 50:39, Apr., 1956
New York Times p. 11, Apr. 21, 1956

Bad and the Beautiful (1953)
Catholic World 176:302, Jan., 1953
Christian Century 70:303, Mar. 11, 1953
Commonweal 57:450, Feb. 6, 1953
Look 17:80-1, Jan. 27, 1953
National Parent-Teacher 47:37, Jan., 1953
New York Times p. 19, Jul. 16, 1953; II, p. 1, Jan. 25, 1953
New Yorker 28:89, Jan. 17, 1953
Newsweek 41:100-1, Jan. 26, 1953
Saturday Review 36:54, Jan. 3, 1953
Theatre Arts 37:80, Feb., 1953
Time 61:94, Jan. 12, 1953

Bad Bascomb (1946)
New York Times p. 13, May 23, 1946
Time 47:101, Jun. 17, 1946

Bad Boy (1936)
New York Times p. 16, Oct. 28, 1935

Bad Boy (1949)
New Republic 120:28, Apr. 11, 1949
New York Times p. 35, Mar. 23, 1949
Rotarian 75:36, Jul., 1949

Bad Company (1931)
Life (NY) 98:21, Nov. 27, 1931
New York Times p. 16, Nov. 7, 1931

Bad Day at Black Rock (1954)
America 92:518, Feb. 12, 1955
Catholic World 180:382, Feb., 1955
Colliers 135:6, Mar. 18, 1955
Commonweal 61:407, Jan. 14, 1955
Farm Journal 79:149, Feb., 1955
Library Journal 80:63, Jan. 1, 1955
Nation 180:165, Feb. 19, 1955
National Parent-Teacher 49:38, Mar., 1955
New York Times p. 22, Feb. 22, 1955; II, p. 1, Feb. 6,
    1955
New Yorker 30:92, Feb. 12, 1955
Newsweek 45:94, Feb. 21, 1955
Saturday Review 38:26, Jan. 29, 1955
Time 65:74, Jan. 17, 1955

Bad for Each Other (1953)
Library Journal 78:2208, Dec. 15, 1953
National Parent-Teacher 48:39, Jan., 1954
New York Times p. 9, Dec. 24, 1953
Time 63:98, Feb. 15, 1954

Bad Girl (1931)
Life (NY) 96:18-19, Oct. 24, 1930
National Magazine 59:453, Oct.-Nov., 1931
New York Times VIII, p. 3, Aug. 9, 1931; p. 18, Aug.
    15, 1931; VIII, p. 5, Aug. 23, 1931
Outlook 159:21, Sep. 2, 1931
Vanity Fair 35:46, Dec., 1930

Bad Guy (1937)
New York Times p. 25, Aug. 26, 1937

Bad Guy (1937) (Continued)
Time 30:62, Sep. 6, 1937

Bad Lands (1939)
New York Times p. 15, Aug. 9, 1939; IX, p. 3, Aug. 13, 1939

Bad Man (1930)
Child Life 20:165, Apr., 1941
New York Times p. 25, Apr. 4, 1941
Scribner's Commentator 10:108, Jun., 1941
Time 37:85, Apr. 28, 1941

Bad Man of Brimstone (1937)
New York Times p. 17, Feb. 4, 1938

Bad Men of Missouri (1941)
New York Times p. 18, Aug. 16, 1941

Bad Men of the Hills (1942)
New York Times VIII, p. 3, Apr. 26, 1942

Bad Men of Tombstone (1948)
New York Times p. 10, Mar. 5, 1949

Bad One (1930)
Life (NY) 95:17, Jul. 11, 1930
New York Times p. 28, Jun. 13, 1930; VIII, p. 3, Jun. 22, 1930
Outlook 155:311, Jun. 25, 1930

Bad Seed (1956)
America 95:604, Sep. 22, 1956
Catholic World 183:464-5, Sep., 1956
Commonweal 64:633, Sep. 28, 1956
Library Journal 81:1890, Sep. 1, 1956
Life 41:141-2, Sep. 17, 1956
Nation 183:333-4, Oct. 20, 1956
National Parent-Teacher 51:39, 1956
New York Times VI, p. 22, Jul. 15, 1956; II, p. 7, Sep. 9, 1956; p. 39, Sep. 13, 1956; II, p. 1, Sep. 23, 1956
New Yorker 32:159, Sep. 22, 1956
Newsweek 48:118, Sep. 17, 1956
Saturday Review 39:31, Sep. 22, 1956
Time 68:100+, Sep. 17, 1956

Bad Sister (1931)
Life (NY) 97:22, Apr. 17, 1931

Bad Sister (1931) (Continued)
New York Times p. 25, Mar. 30, 1931

Bad Sister (1948)
Commonweal 48:356, Jul. 23, 1948
New York Times p. 27, Jun. 11, 1948
New Yorker 24:68, Jun. 19, 1948
Newsweek 31:93, Jun. 21, 1948

Bad Sleep Well (1963)
Commonweal 77:157, Feb. 8, 1963
New Republic 148:26+, Jan. 26, 1963
New York Times p. 5, Jan. 23, 1963; p. 5, Feb. 6, 1963
New Yorker 38:122, Jan. 26, 1963
Newsweek 61:78, Feb. 4, 1963
Saturday Review 46:24, Jan. 19, 1963
Time 81:42, Jan. 25, 1963

Badlanders (1958)
Catholic World 188:63, Oct., 1958
New York Times p. 33, Sep. 4, 1958

Badlands of Dakota (1941)
Commonweal 34:548, Sep. 26, 1941
New York Times p. 27, Sep. 9, 1941

Badman (1941)
New York Times p. 25, Apr. 4, 1941
Time 37:85, Apr. 28, 1941

Badman's Territory (1946)
Commonweal 44:360, Jul. 26, 1946
New York Times p. 27, May 31, 1946
Woman's Home Companion 73:53, Apr., 1946

Bagdad (1949)
New York Times p. 11, Dec. 24, 1949
Newsweek 35:53, Jan. 2, 1950

Bahama Passage (1941)
Commonweal 35:438, Feb. 20, 1942
Musician 47:58, Apr., 1942
New York Times p. 23, Feb. 19, 1942
Time 39:82, Mar. 9, 1942

Bail Out at 43,000 (1957)
National Parent-Teacher 52:32, Sep., 1957
New York Times p. 13, Jun. 8, 1957

Bait (1954)
Commonweal 59:600, Mar. 19, 1954
National Parent-Teacher 48:39, Mar., 1954
New York Times p. 21, Feb. 24, 1954

*Baker's Wife
Canadian Forum 26:63+, Jun., 1946
Commonweal 31:436, Mar. 8, 1940
New Republic 102:474, Apr. 8, 1940
New York Times p. 17, Feb. 27, 1940; X, p. 5, Mar. 3, 1940
New Yorker 16:55, Mar. 2, 1940
Theatre Arts 24:321, May, 1940

Balalaika (1939)
Commonweal 31:227, Dec. 29, 1939
New York Times p. 33, Dec. 15, 1939; IX, p. 7, Dec. 17, 1939
Photoplay 54:59, Jan., 1940
Time 35:29, Jan. 1, 1940

Balcony (1963)
Christian Century 80:960-1, Jul. 31, 1963
Commonweal 78:74, Apr. 12, 1963
Nation 196:430-1, May 18, 1963
New Republic 148:34, Mar. 23, 1963
New York Times p. 7, Mar. 22, 1963
New Yorker 39:143-4, Mar. 30, 1963
Newsweek 61:81, Apr. 1, 1963
Saturday Review 46:34, Mar. 30, 1963
Time 81:92+, Mar. 29, 1963

Ball of Fire (1941)
Commonweal 35:369, Jan. 30, 1942
Life 11:89-92, Dec. 15, 1941
Nation 154:101, Jan. 24, 1942
New York Times p. 25, Jan. 16, 1942; IX, p. 5, Jan. 25, 1942
Newsweek 19:58, Jan. 19, 1942
Photoplay 20:24, Feb., 1942
Theatre Arts 26:132, Feb., 1942
Time 39:70, Jan. 12, 1942

Ballad of A Soldier (1960)
Commonweal 73:414, Jan. 13, 1961
Nation 192:420, May 13, 1961
New Republic 144:26, Jan. 9, 1961

Ballad of A Soldier (1960) (Continued)
New York Times p. 22, Dec. 27, 1960; II, p. 1, Jan. 1,
    1961
New Yorker 36:63, Jan. 7, 1961
Newsweek 57:80, Jan. 9, 1961
Saturday Review 43:42, Dec. 24, 1960
Time 77:47, Jan. 13, 1961

Ballad of Cossack Golota (1938)
New York Times p. 19, Feb. 28, 1938

Ballerina (1938)
    Commonweal 29:161, Dec. 2, 1938
    Current History 49:46, Jan., 1939
    Nation 147:574, Nov. 26, 1938
    New Republic 97:46, Nov. 16, 1938
    New York Times p. 27, Nov. 15, 1938; IX, p. 5, Nov.
        20, 1938
    Scholastic 33:29, Dec. 17, 1938
    Stage 16:57, Nov., 1938

Ballet of Romeo and Juliet (1956)
    Catholic World 183:145, May, 1956
    Commonweal 64:75, Apr. 20, 1956
    Dance Magazine 30:30-31, Apr., 1956
    Etude 74:17+, May, 1956
    Musical America 76:32, May, 1956
    Nation 182:418-20, May 12, 1956
    National Parent-Teacher 50:37, Jun., 1956
    New York Times p. 31, Apr. 3, 1956; II, p. 1, Apr. 8,
        1956
    New Yorker 32:78, Apr. 14, 1956
    Theatre Arts 40:85, Apr., 1956
    Time 67:54+, Apr. 9, 1956

Baltic Deputy (1937)
    Nation 145:274, Sep. 11, 1937
    New Republic 92:216, Sep. 29, 1937
    New York Times p. 8, Sep. 4, 1937; XI, p. 3, Sep. 12,
        1937
    Time 30:32, Sep. 13, 1937

Bambi (1942)
    Commonweal 36:374, Aug. 7, 1942
    Etude 60:588, Sep., 1942
    Good Housekeeping 115:4, Sep. 8, 1942; 115:8, Oct. 4,
        1942

81

Bambi (1942) (Continued)
Nature Magazine 35:350-52, Aug.-Sep., 1942; 35:441, Oct.,
1942
New Republic 106:893, Jun. 29, 1942
New York Times p. 13, Aug. 14, 1942
New York Times Magazine p. 16-17, Jul. 12, 1942
New Yorker 18:53, Aug. 15, 1942
Newsweek 20:70, Aug. 17, 1942
Time 40:78, Aug. 24, 1942

Bamboo Blonde (1946)
Newsweek 28:92, Aug. 5, 1946

Bamboo Prison (1955)
National Parent-Teacher 49:39, Dec., 1954

The Band Wagon (1953)
New York Times p. 10, Jul. 10, 1953; II, p. 1, Jul. 19,
1953

Band of Angels (1957)
Commentary 24:354-7, Oct., 1957
Commonweal 66:425, Jul. 26, 1957
Library Journal 82:1874, Aug., 1957
National Parent-Teacher 52:32, Sep., 1957
New York Times p. 21, Jul. 11, 1957
New Yorker 33:61, Jul. 20, 1957
Newsweek 50:86, Jul. 29, 1957
Time 70:76, Aug. 5, 1957

Bandido (1955)
National Parent-Teacher 51:39, Nov., 1956
Newsweek 48:114-15, Oct. 22, 1956

Bandit (1949)
Commonweal 50:201, Jun. 3, 1949
New Republic 120:28, Jun. 6, 1949
New York Times p. 26, Jun. 7, 1949
New Yorker 25:85, Jun. 11, 1949
Newsweek 33:87, Jun. 20, 1949

Bandit of Sherwood Forest (1946)
Commonweal 43:600, Mar. 29, 1946
Modern Music 23 no. 1, [Jan.], 1946
New York Times p. 8, Mar. 23, 1946; II, p. 1, Apr. 7,
1946
Newsweek 27:89, Apr. 8, 1946
Scholastic 48:27, Mar. 4, 1946

Bandits of Corsica (1954)
  Library Journal 78:724, Apr. 15, 1953
  National Parent-Teacher 47:37, Jun., 1953
  Time 61:110, Apr. 13, 1953

Bandits of the West (1953)
  National Parent-Teacher 48:38, Oct., 1953

Bandwagon (1953)
  America 89:405, Jul. 18, 1953
  Catholic World 177:384, Aug., 1953
  Colliers 132:44, Jul. 25, 1953
  Commonweal 58:423, Jul. 31, 1953
  Dance Magazine 27:68-9, Sep., 1953
  Farm Journal 77:118, Sep., 1953
  Holiday 15:17, Jan., 1954
  Life 35:79+, Aug. 10, 1953
  McCalls 86:6, Sep., 1953
  National Parent-Teacher 48:38, Sep., 1953
  New York Times p. 10, Jul. 10, 1953; II, p. 1, Jul. 19,
    1953
  New Yorker 29:63, Jul. 18, 1953
  Newsweek 42:48-50, Jul. 6, 1953
  Saturday Review 36:28, Jul. 25, 1953
  Scholastic 63:37, Sep. 16, 1953
  Time 62:94, Jul. 13, 1953

Banjo on My Knee (1936)
  New York Times p. 15, Dec. 12, 1936
  Time 28:23, Dec. 21, 1936

Bank Dick (1940)
  New Republic 103:900, Dec. 30, 1940
  New York Times p. 29, Dec. 13, 1940
  New Yorker 25:77, Jun. 25, 1949
  Time 36:35, Dec. 30, 1940

Bannerline (1951)
  Library Journal 76:1999, Dec. 1, 1951
  Time 58:84, Oct. 29, 1951

Bar Sinister (1955)
  Library Journal 80:2080, Oct. 1, 1955
  National Parent-Teacher 50:38, Nov., 1955
  Newsweek 46:110, Sep. 12, 1955

Bar-20 Rides Again (1935)
  Time 26:41, Dec. 16, 1935

Barabbas (1962)
America 107:863, Oct. 6, 1962
Christian Century 79:1294+, Oct. 24, 1962
Commonweal 77:176-7, Nov. 9, 1962
McCalls 90:8, Nov., 1962
New Republic 147:47, Oct. 20, 1962
New York Times p. 49, Oct. 11, 1962
New Yorker 38:216, Oct. 20, 1962
Newsweek 60:105+, Oct. 15, 1962
Redbook 120:16, Dec., 1962
Saturday Review 45:34, Oct. 20, 1962
Time 80:98+, Oct. 5, 1952

The Barbarian (1933)
New Outlook 161:48, Jun., 1933
New York Times p. 16, May 13, 1933

Barbarian and the Geisha (1958)
America 100:89, Oct. 18, 1958
Catholic World 188:241, Dec., 1958
Commonweal 69:73, Oct. 17, 1958
Library Journal 83:2825, Oct. 15, 1958
Look 22:108, Nov. 25, 1958
New Republic 139:21-2, Nov. 3, 1958
New York Times p. 25, Oct. 3, 1958; p. 32, Sep. 25,
    1958
New Yorker 34:94, Oct. 11, 1958
Newsweek 52:90-1, Oct. 6, 1958
Saturday Review 41:29, Oct. 11, 1958
Time 72:90, Oct. 6, 1958

Barbary Coast (1935)
Canadian Magazine 84:42, Oct., 1935; 84:43, Dec., 1935
New York Times X, p. 5, Sep. 29, 1935; p. 21, Oct. 14,
    1935; X, p. 5, Oct. 20, 1935
Newsweek 6:25, Oct. 19, 1935
Scholastic 27:28, Nov. 2, 1935
Time 26:45, Oct. 21, 1935
Vanity Fair 45:48, Nov., 1935

Barbary Coast Gent (1944)
New York Times p. 18, Sep. 29, 1944

Barbary Pirate (1949)
New York Times p. 29, Oct. 28, 1949

*Barber of Seville
Commonweal 46:118, May 16, 1947

*Barber of Seville (Continued)
   Musical Courier 135:20, May 15, 1947
   Nation 164:551, May 10, 1947
   New York Times p. 35, May 6, 1947; p. 21, Jul. 21,
   1949
   Newsweek 29:88, May 5, 1947
   Time 49:104, May 12, 1947

Barefoot Battalion (1954)
   Catholic World 178:382, Feb., 1954
   Commonweal 60:249, Jun. 11, 1954
   National Parent-Teacher 51:37, Oct., 1956
   New York Times p. 13, May 29, 1954
   Saturday Review 37:33, Feb. 20, 1954

Barefoot Contessa (1954)
   America 92:139, Oct. 30, 1954
   Catholic World 180:138, Nov., 1954
   Commonweal 61:15, Oct. 8, 1954
   Coronet 37:6, Nov., 1954
   Farm Journal 78:73, Nov., 1954
   National Parent-Teacher 49:39, Nov., 1954
   New York Times p. 37, Sep. 30, 1954; II, p. 1, Oct. 3,
   1954
   New Yorker 30:173, Oct. 9, 1954
   Newsweek 44:86-7, Oct. 4, 1954
   Saturday Review 37:31, Oct. 16, 1954; 37:8, Oct. 23,
   1954
   Time 64:102+, Oct. 18, 1954

Barefoot Mailman (1951)
   Commonweal 55:374, Jan. 18, 1952
   Library Journal 76:1948, Nov. 15, 1951
   Time 58:104+, Dec. 17, 1951

The Bargain (1931)
   Catholic World 183:62, Apr., 1956
   Life (NY) 98:18, Sep. 25, 1931
   New York Times p. 7, Sep. 5, 1931

The Barge Keeper's Daughter (1945)
   New York Times p. 23, Sep. 6, 1945

The Barker (1928)
   New York Times p. 35, Dec. 6, 1928; IX, p. 7, Dec. 16,
   1928

Barkleys of Broadway (1949)
  Commonweal 50:121, May 13, 1949
  Good Housekeeping 128:303, Apr., 1949
  Life 26:113+, May 16, 1949
  New Republic 120:23, May 16, 1949
  New York Times p. 34, May 5, 1949; II, p. 1, May 8,
    1949
  New Yorker 25:106, May 14, 1949
  Newsweek 33:83, May 2, 1949
  Photoplay 36:20, Jul., 1949
  Rotarian 75:42, Aug., 1949
  Theatre Arts 33:7, Jun., 1949
  Time 53:96, Apr. 25, 1949
  Woman's Home Companion 76:10-11, Jun., 1949

Barnacle Bill (1941)
  New York Times p. 12, Jul. 25, 1941

Baron of Arizona (1950)
  New York Times p. 29, Jun. 23, 1950

Baroness and the Butler (1938)
  New York Times p. 19, Feb. 19, 1938

Barrets of Wimpole Street (1934)
  America 96:492, Jan. 26, 1957
  Canadian Forum 15:109, Dec., 1934
  Canadian Magazine 82:38, Dec., 1934
  Catholic World 184:467, Mar., 1957
  Christian Century 52:295-7, Mar. 6, 1935
  Commonweal 65:466, Feb. 1, 1957
  Library Journal 82:349, Feb. 1, 1957
  Literary Digest 118:26, Oct. 13, 1934
  Nation 139:419-20, Oct. 10, 1934
  National Parent-Teacher 51:38, Mar., 1957
  New York Times p. 12, Sep. 29, 1934; p. 15, Jan. 18,
    1957; II, p. 1, Jan. 27, 1957
  New Yorker 32:95, Jan. 26, 1957
  Newsweek 4:28, Sep. 29, 1934; 49:90, Feb. 4, 1957
  Photoplay 48:65, Dec., 1935
  Pictorial Review 36:64, Dec., 1934
  Saturday Review 40:25, Jan. 26, 1957
  Scholastic 25:29, Nov. 17, 1934
  Time 69:82, Jan. 21, 1957
  Vanity Fair 43:49, Oct., 1934

Barricade (1939)
  New York Times p. 18, Dec. 9, 1939

86

Barricade (1950)
  Commonweal 52:46, Apr. 21, 1950
  New York Times p. 8, Mar. 25, 1950
  Time 55:94, Apr. 10, 1950

Barrier (1937)
  Commonweal 27:160, Dec. 3, 1937
  New York Times p. 21, Nov. 27, 1937

The Bat (1957)
  New York Times p. 51, Dec. 17, 1959

The Bat Whispers (1931)
  Life (NY) 97:20, Feb. 6, 1931
  New York Times p. 27, Jan. 16, 1931; VIII, p. 5, Jan.
    25, 1931

Bataan (1943)
  Commonweal 38:202, Jun. 11, 1943
  Good Housekeeping 117:2, Jul., 1943
  Nation 157:82, Jul. 17, 1943
  New Republic 198:829, Jun. 21, 1943
  New York Times p. 17, Jun. 4, 1943
  New Yorker 19:48, Jun. 5, 1943
  Newsweek 21:88, Jun. 14, 1943
  Photoplay 23:22, Aug., 1943
  Time 41:94, Jun. 7, 1943
  Woman's Home Companion 70:2, Jul., 1943

Bataillon Du Ciel (see They Are Not Angels)

Bathing Beauty (1944)
  Commonweal 40:353, Jul. 28, 1944
  Life 16:77-82, Apr. 17, 1944
  Nation 159:24, Jul. 1, 1944
  New Republic 111:133, Jul. 31, 1944
  New York Times p. 20, Jun. 28, 1944; II, p. 3, Jul. 2,
    1944
  Newsweek 24:81, Jul. 3, 1944
  Time 44:88, Jul. 3, 1944

Battle (1934)
  Nation 139:722, Dec. 19, 1934
  New York Times X, p. 5, Dec. 2, 1934; p. 23, Nov. 23,
    1934
  Time 24:44-5, Dec. 3, 1934

Battle at Apache Pass (1952)
New York Times p. 16, May 10, 1952

Battle at Bloody Beach (1961)
New York Times p. 18, Aug. 17, 1961; II, p. 1, Sep. 10,
1961

Battle Circus (1953)
America 89:87, Apr. 18, 1953
Christian Century 70:495, Apr. 22, 1953
Commonweal 58:53, Apr. 17, 1953
National Parent-Teacher 47:39, Apr., 1953
New York Times p. 27, May 28, 1953
Newsweek 41:101, Jun. 8, 1953
Saturday Review 36:36, Mar. 7, 1953
Time 61:108+, Mar. 16, 1953

Battle Cry (1954)
America 92:547, Feb. 19, 1955
Catholic World 180:464, Mar., 1955
Commonweal 61:551, Feb. 25, 1955
Farm Journal 79:89, Apr., 1955
National Parent-Teacher 49:38, Mar., 1955
New York Times p. 18, Feb. 3, 1955; II, p. 1, Feb. 6,
1955
New Yorker 30:93, Feb. 12, 1955
Newsweek 45:91, Feb. 14, 1955
Saturday Review 38:25, Feb. 19, 1955
Time 65:102, Feb. 14, 1955
Woman's Home Companion 82:14-15, Apr., 1955

*Battle for Music
New York Times p. 13, Oct. 15, 1945
Newsweek 26:104, Oct. 29, 1945
Theatre Arts 29:710, Dec., 1945

*Battle for the Marianas
Commonweal 40:614, Oct. 13, 1944
Nation 159:389, Sep. 30, 1944
New Yorker 20:54, Sep. 23, 1944
Time 44:92+, Oct. 2, 1944

Battle Hell (1957)
America 97:660, Sep. 21, 1957
New York Times p. 23, Aug. 22, 1957
Saturday Review 40:30, Sep. 14, 1957
Time 70:60, Sep. 2, 1957

Battle Hymn (1957)
  America 96:686, Mar. 16, 1957
  Catholic World 184:382, Feb., 1957
  Commonweal 65:591, Mar. 8, 1957
  Library Journal 82:349, Feb. 1, 1957
  National Parent-Teacher 51:38, Mar., 1957
  New York Times p. 14, Feb. 16, 1957; II, p. 1, Feb. 24,
    1957
  New Yorker 33:75, Feb. 23, 1957
  Newsweek 49:119, Feb. 25, 1957
  Saturday Review 40:28, Feb. 16, 1957
  Time 69:98, Mar. 11, 1957

Battle in Outer Space (1960)
  New York Times p. 10, Jul. 9, 1960

Battle of Broadway (1938)
  Commonweal 28:49, May 6, 1938
  New York Times p. 19, Apr. 25, 1938

Battle of Gallipoli (1931)
  New York Times p. 16, Dec. 7, 1931
  Outlook 159:503, Dec. 16, 1931

*Battle of Midway
  New York Times p. 19, Sep. 15, 1942; IV, p. 2, Sep.
    20, 1942; VIII, p. 3, Sep. 20, 1942
  Newsweek 20:80, Sep. 21, 1942
  Time 40:82, Sep. 28, 1942

Battle of Rogue River (1954)
  National Parent-Teacher 48:38, Apr., 1954

Battle of Russia (1943)
  Commonweal 39:72-3, Nov. 5, 1943
  Newsweek 22:98, Nov. 22, 1943
  Time 42:92, Nov. 29, 1943

Battle of the Rails (1950)
  New Republic 122:23, Jan. 9, 1950
  New York Times p. 27, Dec. 27, 1949

Battle of the River Plate (1956)
  New York Times p. 43, Oct. 30, 1956; II, p. 7, Nov. 18,
    1956

Battle of the Sexes (1928)
  Life (NY) 92:28, Nov. 2, 1928

Battle of the Sexes (1928) (Continued)
New York Times IX, p. 5, May 6, 1928; X, p. 6, Oct.
14, 1928; p. 16, Oct. 15, 1928; XI, p. 7, Oct. 21,
1928
Outlook 150:1121, Nov. 7, 1928

Battle of the Sexes (1960)
Commonweal 72:229, May 27, 1960
Nation 190:392, Apr. 30, 1960
New York Times p. 40, Apr. 19, 1960; II, p. 1, May 1,
1960
New Yorker 36:168-9, Apr. 30, 1960
Newsweek 55:89, May 2, 1960
Time 75:34, May 2, 1960

Battle Stations (1956)
National Parent-Teacher 50:39, Apr., 1956
Newsweek 47:91, Mar. 5, 1956

Battle Taxi (1955)
Farm Journal 79:103, Mar., 1955
National Parent-Teacher 49:38, Mar., 1955

Battleground (1949)
Christian Century 67:287, Mar. 1, 1950
Commonweal 51:213, Nov. 25, 1949
Good Housekeeping 129:218, Nov., 1949
Life 27:91-3, Nov. 21, 1949
New Republic 121:38, Nov. 28, 1949
New York Times II, p. 5, May 15, 1949; II, p. 5, Oct.
23, 1949; p. 8, Nov. 12, 1949; II, p. 1, Nov. 13, 1949
New Yorker 25:110, Nov. 19, 1949
Newsweek 34:88, Nov. 14, 1949
Parents Magazine 24:21, Nov., 1949
Photoplay 36:44-5, Dec., 1949
Rotarian 76:38, Apr., 1950
Scholastic 55:29, Nov. 2, 1949
Theatre Arts 33:2, Nov., 1949
Time 54:102+, Nov. 14, 1949
Woman's Home Companion 76:10-11, Nov., 1949

Bayou (1957)
National Parent-Teacher 52:37, Nov., 1957

Be Careful How You Wish (see Incredible Mr. Limpet)

Be Mine Tonight (1932)
New York Times p. 22, Apr. 14, 1933; X, p. 3, Apr. 23,
1933

Be Yourself (1930)
New York Times p. 20, Mar. 7, 1930

Beach Party (1963)
New York Times p. 40, Sep. 26, 1963
Time 82:74, Aug. 16, 1963

Beachcomber (1954)
America 92:463, Jan. 29, 1955
Library Journal 79:2315, Dec. 1, 1954
Nation 179:470, Nov. 27, 1954
National Parent-Teacher 49:38, Feb., 1955
Natural History 63:473, Dec., 1954
New York Times p. 27, Jan. 17, 1953; II, p. 1, Jan. 23,
   1953
Newsweek 44:83, Dec. 20, 1954
Time 65:75, Jan. 24, 1955

Beachcomber (1939)
Commonweal 29:302, Jan. 6, 1939
Life 5:34-7, Dec. 5, 1938
Nation 148:44, Jan. 7, 1939
New Republic 97:231, Dec. 28, 1938
New York Times IX, p. 7, Dec. 25, 1938; p. 29, Dec. 26,
   1939
Newsweek 12:23, Dec. 26, 1938
Photoplay 53:52, Mar., 1939
Time 33:17, Jan. 2, 1939

Beachhead (1954)
Library Journal 79:314, Feb. 15, 1954
National Parent-Teacher 48:38, Apr., 1954
New York Times p. 8, Apr. 17, 1954
Newsweek 43:80, Mar. 1, 1954
Time 63:104, Apr. 19, 1954

Beast From 20, 000 Fathoms (1953)
America 89:384, Jul. 11, 1953
Catholic World 177:305, Jul., 1953
National Parent-Teacher 48:39, Sep., 1953
New York Times p. 23, Jun. 25, 1953
New Yorker 29:48, Jul. 4, 1953
Saturday Review 36:33, Jun. 20, 1953
Time 61:88, Jun. 22, 1953

Beast of Hollow Mountain (1956)
National Parent-Teacher 51:37, Oct., 1956
New York Times II, p. 5, Jun. 26, 1955

Beast of the City (1932)
    Nation 134:380, Mar. 30, 1932
    New York Times p. 13, Mar. 14, 1932

Beast With Five Fingers (1947)
    New York Times p. 28, Dec. 26, 1946
    Time 49:100, Jan. 13, 1947

Beasts of Berlin (1939)
    New York Times p. 15, Nov. 20, 1939; IX, p. 5, Nov. 26,
        1939
    Newsweek 14:37-8, Dec. 4, 1939
    Time 34:82, Dec. 4, 1939

The Beat Generation (1959)
    New York Times p. 47, Oct. 22, 1959

Beat the Devil (1954)
    Catholic World 179:63-4, Apr., 1954
    Commonweal 59:600, Mar. 19, 1954
    Coronet 35:6, Apr., 1954
    Farm Journal 78:137, May, 1954
    Library Journal 79:444, Mar. 1, 1954
    Look 17:128-9+, Sep. 22, 1953
    National Parent-Teacher 48:38, Apr., 1954
    New York Times p. 11, Mar. 13, 1954
    New York Times Magazine p. 32-3, Sep. 27, 1953
    New Yorker 30:118, Mar. 20, 1954
    Newsweek 43:82, Mar. 8, 1954
    Saturday Review 37:28, Mar. 13, 1954
    Scholastic 64:27, Mar. 10, 1954
    Time 63:94+, Mar. 8, 1954

Beau Bandit (1930)
    New York Times p. 9, Jun. 14, 1930

Beau Brummel (1954)
    America 92:138, Oct. 30, 1954
    Farm Journal 78:141, Dec., 1954
    Library Journal 79:2095, Nov. 1, 1954
    Life 37:115-16, Oct. 18, 1954
    National Parent-Teacher 49:39, Dec., 1954
    New York Times p. 31, Oct. 21, 1954; II, p. 1, Oct. 24,
        1954
    New Yorker 30:126, Oct. 30, 1954
    Newsweek 44:102, Oct. 25, 1954
    Saturday Review 37:33, Oct. 23, 1954
    Time 64:102, Oct. 18, 1954

Beau Geste (1939)
  Commonweal 30:380, Aug. 11, 1939
  New Republic 100:20, Aug. 9, 1939
  New York Times p. 15, Aug. 3, 1939; IX, p. 3, Aug. 6,
    1939
  Newsweek 14:40-1, Aug. 7, 1939
  Photoplay 53:64, Oct., 1939
  Saint Nicholas 66:39, Sep., 1939
  Time 34:33, Aug. 14, 1939

Beau Ideal (1931)
  New York Times p. 25, Jan. 19, 1931; VIII, p. 5, Jan.
    25, 1931

Beau James (1957)
  America 97:392, Jul. 6, 1957
  Commonweal 66:377, Jul. 12, 1957
  Library Journal 82:1665, Jun. 15, 1957
  National Parent-Teacher 51:37, Jun., 1957
  New York Times p. 21, Jun. 27, 1957
  New Yorker 33:58, Jul. 6, 1957
  Newsweek 50:77, Jul. 1, 1957
  Time 70:80, Jul. 1, 1957

Beau Sabreur (1928)
  Life (NY) 91:24, Feb. 9, 1928
  New York Times p. 18, Jan. 23, 1928; VIII, p. 7, Jan.
    29, 1928
  Outlook 148:228, Feb. 8, 1928

Beauties of the Night (1954)
  Commonweal 59:651, Apr. 2, 1954
  Life 36:97-8, Mar. 29, 1954
  National Parent-Teacher 48:39, Jun., 1954
  New York Times p. 23, Mar. 23, 1954
  New Yorker 30:61, Mar. 27, 1954
  Newsweek 43:86, Mar. 29, 1954
  Saturday Review 38:63, Jan. 1, 1955; 37:41, Apr. 3, 1954
  Time 63:102+, Apr. 5, 1954

Beautiful Blonde From Bashful Bend (1949)
  New Republic 120:21, Jun. 13, 1949
  New York Times p. 11, May 28, 1949; II, p. 1, Jun. 5
    1949
  New Yorker 25:85, Jun. 11, 1949
  Newsweek 33:80, Jun. 6, 1949
  Rotarian 75:37, Sep., 1949
  Time 53:94+, Jun. 6, 1949

Beautiful But Dangerous (1958)
Commonweal 67:617, Mar. 14, 1958
National Parent-Teacher 51:38, Feb., 1957
New York Times p. 24, Feb. 6, 1958
Time 71:64, Feb. 17, 1958

Beauty and the Beast (1948)
Commonweal 47:227, Dec. 12, 1947
Life 23:61, Dec. 29, 1947
New Republic 117:35, Dec. 29, 1947
New York Times II, p. 7, Jan. 19, 1947; II, p. 1, Dec.
    21, 1947; p. 12, Dec. 24, 1947
New Yorker 23:56, Dec. 20, 1947
Newsweek 30:68, Dec. 29, 1947
Rotarian 74:11, Jan., 1949
Theatre Arts 32:20-6, 34, Jan., 1948
Time 50:62, Dec. 29, 1947

Beauty and the Boss (1932)
New York Times p. 13, Apr. 2, 1932; VIII, p. 4, Apr.
    10, 1932

Beauty and the Devil (1952)
New York Times p. 15, Aug. 26, 1952; II, p. 1, Sep. 14,
    1952
Newsweek 40:96, Sep. 8, 1952
Saturday Review 35:34, Sep. 13, 1952
Theatre Arts 35:34-5+, Jul., 1951; 36:93, Nov., 1952
Time 60:109, Sep. 15, 1952

Beauty for Sale (1933)
New York Times p. 9, Sep. 16, 1933

Beauty for the Asking (1939)
New York Times p. 19, Feb. 10, 1939

Beauty on Parade (1950)
New York Times p. 17, Aug. 18, 1950

Because of Him (1946)
Commonweal 43:458, Feb. 15, 1946
New York Times p. 26, Jan. 25, 1946
Newsweek 27:93, Feb. 11, 1946
Photoplay 28:26, Apr., 1946
Scholastic 48:37, Feb. 4, 1946
Time 47:90+, Feb. 4, 1946

Because of You (1952)
Commonweal 57:284, Dec. 19, 1952
McCalls 80:8, Nov., 1952
National Parent-Teacher 47:36, Dec., 1952
New York Times p. 47, Dec. 4, 1952
Newsweek 40:102, Dec. 15, 1952

Because You're Mine (1952)
Christian Century 69:1335, Nov. 12, 1952
National Parent-Teacher 47:36, Oct., 1952
New York Times p. 18, Sep. 26, 1952; II, p. 5, Nov. 16, 1952
New Yorker 28:74, Oct. 4, 1952
Newsweek 40:100, Oct. 13, 1952
Time 60:108+, Oct. 13, 1952

Becket (1963)
America 110:379-80, Mar. 21, 1964
Christian Century 81:1112-13, Sep. 9, 1964
Commonweal 79:722, Mar. 13, 1964
Life 56:81-2, Mar. 13, 1964
Mademoiselle 58:42, Apr., 1964
New Republic 150:26-7, Mar. 14, 1964
New York Times II, p. 5, Jun. 30, 1963; p. 40, Mar. 12, 1964; II, p. 7, Mar. 15, 1964
New Yorker 40:155, Mar. 14, 1964
Newsweek 63:95, Mar. 23, 1964
Saturday Review 47:24-5, Mar. 7, 1964
Senior Scholastic 84:32, Mar. 6, 1964; 84:5T, Apr. 10, 1964
Time 83:94-5, Mar. 20, 1964

Becky Sharp (1935)
Catholic World 141:727-8, Sep., 1935
Commonweal 22:243, Jun. 28, 1935; 22:316, Jul. 26, 1935
Literary Digest 119:26, Jun. 8, 1935
Motion Picture 49:37, Apr., 1935
Movie Classic 9:18, Sep., 1935
Nation 141:28, Jul. 3, 1935
New Republic 83:194, Jun. 26, 1935
New York Times p. 27, Jun. 14, 1935
Newsweek 5:22-3, Jun. 22, 1935
Photoplay 48:24-5+, Aug., 1935
Scholastic 26:28, May 11, 1935
Stage 12:36-40, Jul., 1935
Vanity Fair 44:44, Aug., 1935

Bed (1955)
Nation 180:590, Jun. 25, 1955
New York Times p. 26, Jun. 8, 1955; II, p. 1, Jun. 12, 1955
New Yorker 31:51, Jul. 2, 1955
Newsweek 46:77, Jul. 4, 1955

Bed of Roses (1933)
New Outlook 162:45, Aug., 1933
New York Times p. 20, Jun. 30, 1933
Newsweek 1:32, Jul. 8, 1933

Bedelia (1947)
Commonweal 45:469, Feb. 21, 1947
Cosmopolitan 121:183, Dec., 1946
Holiday 2:144, Mar., 1947
New Republic 116:39, Feb. 24, 1947
New York Times p. 10, Feb. 8, 1947
New Yorker 22:87, Feb. 15, 1947
Newsweek 29:92, Feb. 10, 1947
Time 49:97, Jan. 27, 1947

Bedevilled (1954)
America 93:194, May 14, 1955
Catholic World 181:220, Jun., 1955
Commonweal 62:150, May 13, 1955
National Parent-Teacher 49:38, Jun., 1955
New York Times p. 23, Apr. 23, 1955
Saturday Review 38:26, Apr. 23, 1955
Time 65:98, May 2, 1955

Bedlam (1946)
Life 20:117-18+, Feb. 25, 1946
Nation 162:354, Mar. 23, 1946
New York Times p. 16, Apr. 20, 1946
Time 47:97, May 27, 1946

Bedside (1934)
New York Times p. 23, Mar. 7, 1934

Bedtime for Bonzo (1951)
New York Times p. 31, Apr. 6, 1951
Newsweek 37:87, Mar. 12, 1951
Scholastic 58:19, Feb. 28, 1951

Bedtime Story (1933)
Motion Picture 43:40-41+, Jun., 1933

Bedtime Story (1933) (Continued)
New York Times p. 20, Apr. 20, 1933; IX, p. 3, Apr.
30, 1933
Vanity Fair 40:38, Jun., 1933

Beethoven Concerto (1937)
New York Times p. 29, Mar. 24, 1937; XI, p. 3, Mar.
28, 1937
Scholastic 30:28, Apr. 24, 1937

Before Dawn (1933)
New York Times p. 26, Oct. 17, 1933; IX, p. 3, Oct. 22,
1933

*Before Him All Rome Trembled
Commonweal 45:520, Mar. 7, 1947
Nation 164:340, Mar. 22, 1947
New York Times p. 16, Feb. 22, 1947; II, p. 5, Feb. 23,
1947
New Yorker 23:82+, Mar. 8, 1947
Newsweek 29:89, Mar. 10, 1947
Time 49:97, Mar. 10, 1947

Before I Hang (1940)
New York Times p. 13, Oct. 3, 1940

Before Midnight (1934)
New York Times p. 24, Jan. 10, 1934

Beg, Borrow or Steal (1937)
New York Times p. 33, Dec. 10, 1937

Beggars in Ermine (1934)
New York Times p. 25, Apr. 25, 1934

Beggars of Life (1928)
New York Times p. 25, Sep. 24, 1928; IX, p. 7, Sep.
30, 1928

Beggar's Opera (1954)
America 89:561, Sep. 5, 1953
Catholic World 177:465, Sep., 1953
Commonweal 58:561, Sep. 11, 1953
Farm Journal 77:118, Sep., 1953
Life 35:97-100, Sep. 14, 1953
Musical America 73:9, Aug., 1953
Nation 177:218, Sep. 12, 1953

97

Beggar's Opera (1954) (Continued)
National Parent-Teacher 48:36, Nov., 1953
New Republic 128:20, Jul. 20, 1953
New York Times p. 18, Aug. 25, 1953; II, p. 1, Aug.
30, 1953
New York Times Magazine p. 28, Aug. 16, 1953
New Yorker 29:59, Aug. 29, 1953
Newsweek 42:87, Sep. 7, 1953
Saturday Review 36:28-9, Aug. 15, 1953
Time 62:81, Aug. 31, 1953

Beginning of the End (1957)
New York Times p. 16, Jul. 4, 1957

Beginning or the End (1947)
Commonweal 45:519-20, Mar. 7, 1947
Good Housekeeping 124:13, Mar., 1947
Holiday 2:176, May, 1947
Life 22:75-8+, Mar. 17, 1947
Nation 164:259, Mar. 1, 1947
New Republic 116:41-2, Mar. 10, 1947
New York Times II, p. 1, Jun. 16, 1946; II, p. 5, Dec.
16, 1946; p. 15, Feb. 21, 1947; II, p. 1, Feb. 23,
1947; II, p. 1, Mar. 9, 1947
New Yorker 23:78, Feb. 22, 1947
Newsweek 29:81, Mar. 3, 1947
Scholastic 50:30, Mar. 31, 1947
Science Illustrated 1:42-3, Oct., 1946
Time 49:106+, Feb. 24, 1947
United Nations World 1:64, Apr., 1947

Behave Yourself! (1951)
Life 31:119, Dec. 10, 1951
Nation 174:66, Jan. 19, 1952
New York Times p. 35, Nov. 8, 1951
Newsweek 38:103, Nov. 19, 1951
Saturday Review 34:28, Nov. 3, 1951
Time 58:120+, Nov. 5, 1951

Behind Green Lights (1946)
New York Times p. 10, Feb. 16, 1946

Behind Office Doors (1930)
New York Times p. 5, Mar. 21, 1931

Behind Prison Gates (1939)
New York Times p. 9, Aug. 21, 1939

Behind That Curtain (1929)
New York Times p. 31, Jul. 1, 1929; VIII, p. 3, Jul. 7,
1929

Behind the Evidence (1935)
New York Times p. 13, Jan. 26, 1935

Behind the German Lines (1929)
New York Times p. 30, Dec. 3, 1928; X, p. 7, Dec. 9,
1928

Behind the Great Wall (1959)
New York Times p. 27, Oct. 17, 1959; II, p. 9, Dec. 6,
1959; p. 51, Dec. 10, 1959; II, p. 3, Dec. 13, 1959
New Yorker 35:125, Dec. 19, 1959
Reporter 22:38-9, Jan. 7, 1960
Saturday Review 43:27, Jan. 30, 1960
Time 74:57, Dec. 21, 1959

Behind the Green Lights (1935)
New York Times p. 14, Apr. 22, 1935

Behind the Headlines (1937)
New York Times p. 27, Jun. 1, 1936
Time 29:55, May 24, 1937

Behind the High Wall (1956)
National Parent-Teacher 51:39, Sep., 1956

Behind the Mask (1932)
New York Times p. 13, May 2, 1932; VIII, p. 3, May 8,
1932

Behind the Mike (1937)
New York Times p. 12, Jan. 29, 1938

Behind the News (1940)
New York Times p. 25, Jan. 16, 1941

Behind the Rising Sun (1943)
Commonweal 38:491-2, Sep. 3, 1943
New York Times p. 26, Oct. 14, 1943
New Yorker 19:44, Oct. 16, 1943; 19:63-4, Nov. 20, 1943
Newsweek 22:86+, Aug. 23, 1943
Photoplay 23:115, Oct., 1943
Time 42:94, Aug. 9, 1943

Behold A Pale Horse (1963)
   America 111:240, Sep. 5, 1964
   Catholic World 200:67-8, Oct., 1964
   Commonweal 80:579, Aug. 29, 1964
   Life 57:12, Aug. 21, 1964
   New York Times II, p. 5, Jul. 7, 1963; p. 16, Aug. 14,
      1964
   New Yorker 40:78, Aug. 29, 1964
   Newsweek 64:79, Aug. 24, 1964
   Saturday Review 47:24, Aug. 8, 1964
   Senior Scholastic 85:28+, Sep. 30, 1964; 85:10T, Oct. 7,
      1964
   Time 84:70, Aug. 28, 1964

Behold My Wife (1935)
   New York Times p. 19, Feb. 18, 1935

Bell'Antonio (1962)
   Commonweal 76:65, Apr. 13, 1962
   New York Times p. 43, Apr. 3, 1962
   New Yorker 38:148, Apr. 7, 1962
   Newsweek 59:109, Apr. 9, 1962
   Time 79:100, Apr. 13, 1962

Bell, Book and Candle (1958)
   America 100:437, Jan. 10, 1959
   Catholic World 188:328, Jan., 1959
   Commonweal 69:340, Dec. 26, 1958
   Good Housekeeping 148:24, Jan., 1959
   Library Journal 83:3418, Dec. 1, 1958
   Life 45:66-7+, Nov. 24, 1958
   New York Times p. 2, Dec. 27, 1958
   Newsweek 52:94-5, Dec. 8, 1958
   Saturday Review 41:36, Dec. 6, 1958
   Time 72:50, Dec. 29, 1958

Bell for Adano (1945)
   Commonweal 42:358, Jul. 27, 1945
   New York Times p. 8, Jul. 6, 1945; II, p. 1, Jul. 15,
      1945
   New York Times Magazine p. 17, May 20, 1945
   New Yorker 21:35, Jul. 14, 1945
   Newsweek 26:101, Jul. 16, 1945
   Theatre Arts 29:582-3, Oct., 1945
   Time 46:86, Jul. 2, 1945

Bella Donna (1935)
   New York Times p. 16, Feb. 26, 1935

The Bellamy Trial (1928)
New York Times p. 30, Jan. 24, 1929; IX, p. 7, Jan. 27, 1929

Bellboy (1960)
New York Times p. 17, Jul. 21, 1960
Time 76:58, Aug. 1, 1960

La Belle Americaine (1961)
Commonweal 75:415, Jan. 12, 1962
New Republic 146:22, Jan. 1, 1962
New York Times p. 42, Dec. 18, 1961
New Yorker 37:45, Dec. 30, 1961
Time 79:59, Jan. 5, 1962

Belle Le Grand (1951)
New York Times p. 34, May 18, 1951

Belle of New York (1952)
Christian Century 69:543, Apr. 30, 1952
New York Times p. 25, Mar. 6, 1952
Newsweek 39:103, Mar. 10, 1952
Saturday Review 35:30, Mar. 22, 1952
Time 59:100, Mar. 31, 1952

Belle of the Nineties (1934)
Literary Digest 118:32, Oct. 6, 1934
Nation 139:420, Oct. 10, 1934
New Republic 80:310, Oct. 24, 1934
New York Times p. 12, Sep. 22, 1934; X, p. 4, Sep. 23, 1934
Newsweek 4:28, Sep. 29, 1934
Time 24:34, Sep. 24, 1934
Vanity Fair 43:49, Oct., 1934

Belle of the Yukon (1944)
New York Times p. 18, Mar. 30, 1945; II, p. 1, Apr. 1, 1945
Time 45:92, Jan. 15, 1945

Belle Sommers (1962)
New York Times p. 23, May 31, 1962

Belle Starr (1941)
New York Times p. 20, Nov. 1, 1941
Newsweek 18:55-6, Sep. 29, 1941

101

Belle Starr's Daughter (1948)
New York Times p. 19, Jan. 10, 1949

Belles and Ballets (1960)
New York Times p. 46, Nov. 15, 1960

Belles of St. Trinian's (1954)
Library Journal 80:436, Feb. 15, 1955
Nation 180:38, Jan. 8, 1955
National Parent-Teacher 49:39, Mar., 1955
New York Times p. 13, Dec. 23, 1954
Newsweek 45:88, Jan. 17, 1955
Time 65:69, Feb. 7, 1955

Belles on Their Toes (1952)
Christian Century 69:791, Jul. 2, 1952
Commonweal 56:141, May 16, 1952
Library Journal 77:785, May 1, 1952
New York Times p. 17, May 3, 1952
Time 59:106, May 5, 1952

*Bellissima
Commonweal 58:152, May 15, 1953
National Parent-Teacher 47:39, Apr., 1953
New York Times p. 26, May 18, 1953; II, p. 1, May 31, 1953
New Yorker 29:73, May 23, 1953
Saturday Review 36:29, Mar. 21, 1953
Theatre Arts 37:88, Aug., 1953
Time 61:100+, May 25, 1953

Bells Are Ringing (1960)
America 103:463-4, Jul. 16, 1960
Commonweal 72:351, Jul. 8, 1960
New Republic 142:20, Jun. 27, 1960
New York Times p. 31, Jun. 24, 1960
New Yorker 36:55, Jul. 9, 1960
Newsweek 55:92, Jun. 27, 1960
Saturday Review 43:24, Jul. 9, 1960
Time 75:67, Jun. 20, 1960

Bells of St. Mary's (1945)
Commonweal 43:288, Dec. 28, 1945
Cosmopolitan 119:96, Nov., 1945
Harper's Bazzar 79:65, Jun., 1945
Nation 162:24, Jan. 5, 1946
New York Times p. 26, Dec. 7, 1945; II, p. 3, Dec. 16, 1945

Bells of St. Mary's (1945) (Continued)
New Yorker 21:87, Dec. 8, 1945
Newsweek 26:118-9, Dec. 17, 1945
Photoplay 28:22, Feb., 1946
Scholastic 47:36, Dec. 10, 1945
Theatre Arts 30:48-50, Jan., 1946
Time 46:94+, Dec. 10, 1945
Woman's Home Companion 73:8, Jan., 1946

Beloved (1934)
New York Times p. 9, Jan. 27, 1934
Newsweek 3:38, Feb. 3, 1934

The Beloved Bachelor (1931)
Life (NY) 98:19, Nov. 6, 1931
New York Times p. 20, Oct. 17, 1931

Beloved Brat (1938)
New York Times p. 38, Mar. 30, 1938; p. 13, May 2,
1938

Beloved Enemy (1936)
Canadian Magazine 87:25, Mar., 1937
Commonweal 25:333, Jan. 15, 1937
Life 1:48-9, Dec. 21, 1936
New York Times p. 15, Dec. 26, 1936
Newsweek 9:23, Jan. 2, 1937
Scholastic 29:24, Jan. 16, 1937
Time 29:21, Jan. 4, 1937

Beloved Infidel (1960)
New York Times II, p. 5, Aug. 2, 1959; p. 46, Nov. 18,
1959
Newsweek 54:65, Nov. 30, 1959
Saturday Review 42:33, Dec. 5, 1959
Time 74:87, Dec. 7, 1959

The Beloved Vagabond (1937)
New York Times p. 12, Feb. 8, 1937

Below the Sahara (1953)
Commonweal 58:348, Jul. 10, 1953
National Parent-Teacher 48:37, Sep., 1953
Natural History 62:284, Jun., 1953
New York Times p. 20, Sep. 2, 1953
New Yorker 29:62+, Sep. 12, 1953
Time 61:86+, Jun. 22, 1953

Ben Hur (1931)
New York Times p. 28, Dec. 4, 1931

Ben-Hur (1960)
America 102:333-4, Dec. 5, 1959
Christian Century 77:51-2, Jan. 13, 1960
Commonweal 71:320-1, Dec. 11, 1959
Cosmopolitan 147:26-9, Dec., 1959
McCalls 87:6+, Feb., 1960
New Republic 141:27, Dec. 28, 1959
New York Times p. 50, Nov. 19, 1959; II, p. 1, Nov. 22, 1959
New Yorker 35:153-4, Dec. 5, 1959
Newsweek 54:65, Nov. 30, 1959
Saturday Review 42:32, Dec. 5, 1959
Senior Scholastic 75:33, Jan. 13, 1960
Time 74:55, Nov. 30, 1959

Bend of the River (1952)
Catholic World 175:63, Apr., 1952
Christian Century 69:383, Mar. 26, 1952
Commonweal 56:15, Apr. 11, 1952
Library Journal 77:586, Apr. 1, 1952
New York Times p. 37, Apr. 10, 1952
New Yorker 28:93, Apr. 19, 1952
Newsweek 39:102, Feb. 25, 1952
Time 59:104, Mar. 24, 1952

Beneath the Twelve-Mile Reef (1953)
America 90:347, Dec. 26, 1953
Catholic World 178:381-2, Feb., 1954
Commonweal 59:331, Jan. 1, 1954
National Parent-Teacher 48:39, Feb., 1954
Natural History 63:95, Feb., 1954
New York Times p. 52, Dec. 17, 1953; II, p. 3, Dec. 20, 1953
New Yorker 29:54, Dec. 26, 1953
Newsweek 42:68-9, Dec. 28, 1953
Saturday Review 37:58, Jan. 2, 1954
Scholastic 64:30, Feb. 17, 1954
Time 62:56, Dec. 28, 1953

Bengal Brigade (1954)
America 92:222, Nov. 20, 1954
Farm Journal 78:141, Dec., 1954
Library Journal 79:1755, Oct. 1, 1954
National Parent-Teacher 49:39, Oct., 1954

Bengal Brigade (1954) (Continued)
New York Times p. 13, Nov. 13, 1954
Time 64:116, Dec. 6, 1954

Bengal Tiger (1936)
New York Times p. 22, Jul. 30, 1936
Time 28:26, Aug. 10, 1936

Bengazi (1955)
New York Times p. 13, Oct. 8, 1955

Benny Goodman Story (1955)
America 94:648, Mar. 10, 1956
Catholic World 182:383, Feb. 17, 1956
Commonweal 63:516, Feb. 17, 1956
Library Journal 81:360, Feb. 1, 1956
Look 20:103-4, Feb. 21, 1956
Nation 182:126, Feb. 11, 1956
National Parent-Teacher 50:38, Feb., 1956
New York Times p. 22, Feb. 22, 1956; II, p. 1, Feb. 26,
    1956
New York Times Magazine p. 44, Nov. 27, 1955
Newsweek 47:86, Feb. 6, 1956
Saturday Review 39:27, Feb. 25, 1956
Scholastic 68:39, Feb. 9, 1956
Time 67:108, Mar. 19, 1956

Berkeley Square (1933)
Canadian Magazine 80:34-5, Nov., 1933
Commonweal 19:103, Nov. 24, 1933
Literary Digest 116:32, Sep. 30, 1933
Nation 137:363-4, Sep. 27, 1933
New Outlook 162:48, Oct., 1933
New York Times p. 26, Sep. 14, 1933; X, p. 3, Sep. 24,
    1933
Newsweek 2:32, Sep. 23, 1933
Photoplay 44:11+, Oct., 1933
Vanity Fair 41:56, Nov., 1933

Berlin Correspondent (1942)
New York Times p. 19, Sep. 4, 1942

Berlin Express (1948)
Life 24:6, Mar. 22, 1948
New Republic 118:37, May 31, 1948
New York Times p. 19, May 21, 1948; II, p. 1, May 23,
    1948

Berlin Express (1948) (Continued)
Newsweek 31:72, May 31, 1948
Time 51:93, May 3, 1948

*Berliner
Commonweal 57:142, Nov. 14, 1952
New York Times p. 37, Oct. 28, 1952
Newsweek 40:108, Nov. 10, 1952
Theatre Arts 36:86, Dec., 1952

Bermuda Mystery (1944)
New York Times p. 17, May 13, 1944
New Yorker 20:38, Jul. 22, 1944

Bernadine (1957)
America 97:472, Aug. 3, 1957
National Parent-Teacher 52:32, Sep., 1957
New York Times p. 28, Jul. 25, 1957
Newsweek 50:94, Aug. 5, 1957

Bespoke Overcoat (1957)
Catholic World 184:143, Nov., 1956
National Parent-Teacher 51:39, Dec., 1956
New York Times p. 31, Oct. 8, 1956

Best Foot Forward (1943)
Commonweal 38:322, Jul. 16, 1943
Cosmopolitan 115:84, Oct., 1943
New York Times p. 25, Jun. 30, 1943
Newsweek 22:68, Jul. 12, 1943
Photoplay 23:32, Sep., 1943
Time 42:94+, Jul. 19, 1943
Woman's Home Companion 70:2, Aug. 1943

Best Man (1963)
Commonweal 80:147, Apr. 24, 1964
Esquire 61:18+, Jun., 1964
Life 56:15, Apr. 17, 1964
New Republic 150:24+, Apr. 18, 1964
New York Times II, p. 9, Oct. 6, 1963; II, p. 7, Apr.
    5, 1964; p. 29, Apr. 7, 1964; II, p. 1, Apr. 12, 1964
New Yorker 40:118+, Apr. 18, 1964
Saturday Review 47:36, Apr. 4, 1964
Vogue 143:52, Apr. 15, 1964

Best Man Wins (1935)
New York Times p. 22, Jan. 2, 1935

Best of Enemies (1933)
New York Times p. 9, Jul. 17, 1933
Newsweek 1:31, Jul. 22, 1933

Best of Enemies (1962)
America 107:572, Aug. 4, 1962
Commonweal 76:498, Sep. 7, 1962
New Republic 147:29, Sep. 10, 1962
New York Times p. 35, Aug. 7, 1962; II, p. 1, Aug. 26,
   1962
New Yorker 38:69, Aug. 18, 1962
Newsweek 60:82, Aug. 18, 1962
Saturday Review 45:16, Jul. 14, 1962
Time 80:68, Aug. 10, 1962

Best of Everything (1962)
America 102:111-12, Oct. 24, 1959
Commonweal 71:185, Nov. 6, 1959
New Republic 141:22, Nov. 2, 1959
New York Times p. 24, Oct. 9, 1959; II, p. 1, Oct. 18,
   1959
Newsweek 54:108, Oct. 19, 1959
Saturday Review 42:24, Oct. 31, 1959
Time 74:59, Oct. 26, 1959

Best of the Badmen (1951)
New York Times p. 13, Aug. 10, 1952
Newsweek 37:87, Jun. 4, 1951

Best Things in Life Are Free (1956)
America 96:112, Oct. 27, 1956
Catholic World 184:145, Nov., 1956
Life 41:79-80+, Sep. 10, 1956
National Parent-Teacher 51:39, Dec., 1956
New York Times p. 12, Sep. 29, 1956
New Yorker 32:182, Oct. 13, 1956
Newsweek 48:91, Oct. 8, 1956
Time 68:74, Oct. 29, 1956

Best Years of Our Lives (1946)
Catholic World 178:381, Feb., 1954
Commonweal 45:230, Dec. 13, 1946; 59:554, Mar. 5, 1954
Cosmopolitan 122:67+, Jan., 1947
Hollywood Quarterly 2:257-60, Apr., 1947
Life 21:16-17, Oct. 21, 1946; 21:71-3, Dec. 16, 1946
Musical Quarterly 33:517-32, Oct., 1947
Nation 163:672-3, 708-10, Dec. 7-14, 1946

Best Years of Our Lives (1946) (Continued)
New Republic 115:723, Dec. 2, 1946
New York Times p. 27, Nov. 22, 1946; II, p. 1, Nov. 24,
1946; II, p. 5, Mar. 7, 1954; II, p. 1, Mar. 14, 1954
New York Times Magazine p. 26-7, Nov. 17, 1946
New Yorker 22:75, Nov. 23, 1946
Newsweek 28:104+, Nov. 25, 1946
Photoplay 30:31, Mar., 1947
Saturday Review 37:38, Mar. 13, 1954
Scholastic 49:27, Jan. 20, 1947
Theatre Arts 31:38-40, Jan., 1947
Time 48:2-3, Oct. 28, 1946; 48:103, Nov. 25, 1946
Woman's Home Companion 74:11, Mar., 1947

Betrayal (1929)
New York Times IX, p. 8, Feb. 10, 1929; p. 23, Apr.
29, 1929; p. 30, May 6, 1929; IX, p. 5, May 12, 1929

Betrayal (1939)
New York Times p. 20, Sep. 16, 1939

Betrayal From the East (1945)
Nation 160:257, Mar. 3, 1945
New York Times p. 27, Apr. 25, 1945
Newsweek 25:102, Apr. 16, 1945
Time 45:91, Mar. 19, 1945

Betrayed (1954)
America 91:574, Sep. 11, 1954
Commonweal 60:632, Oct. 1, 1954
Farm Journal 78:137, Oct., 1954
National Parent-Teacher 49:38, Sep., 1954
New York Times p. 36, Sep. 9, 1954
Newsweek 44:98, Sep. 27, 1954
Time 64:111, Sep. 20, 1954

Between Heaven and Hell (1956)
Commonweal 65:207, Nov. 23, 1956
Library Journal 81:2548, Nov. 1, 1956
National Parent-Teacher 51:39, Dec., 1956
New York Times p. 33, Oct. 12, 1956

Between Midnight and Dawn (1950)
Commonweal 53:41, Oct. 20, 1950
New York Times p. 19, Oct. 20, 1950
Newsweek 36:90, Oct. 9, 1950

Between Two Women (1937)
New York Times p. 21, Aug. 6, 1937

Between Two Women (1944)
New York Times p. 18, Mar. 29, 1945; II, p. 1, Apr. 1,
1945

Between Two Worlds (1944)
Commonweal 40:156-7, Jun. 2, 1944
Nation 158:549, May 6, 1944
New York Times p. 11, May 6, 1944
Newsweek 23:80, May 15, 1944
Time 43:56+, May 15, 1944

Between Us Girls (1942)
Commonweal 36:520, Sep. 18, 1942
New York Times p. 25, Sep. 25, 1942
New Yorker 18:52, Sep. 19, 1942
Newsweek 20:80, Sep. 7, 1942
Time 40:84+, Oct. 5, 1942

Beware (1946)
Newsweek 28:85, Jul. 8, 1946

Beware, My Lovely (1952)
Christian Century 69:1302, Nov. 5, 1952
Commonweal 56:316, Jul. 4, 1952
New York Times p. 10, Sep. 13, 1952
Newsweek 40:94, Sep. 29, 1952
Saturday Review 35:36, Jun. 14, 1952
Theatre Arts 36:88, Jul., 1952
Time 60:104+, Sep. 22, 1952

Beware of Blondie (1950)
New York Times II, p. 5, Jun. 25, 1950

Beware of Married Men (1928)
New York Times p. 33, Apr. 10, 1928

*Beware of Pity
Canadian Forum 27:63-4, Jun., 1947
New York Times p. 11, Nov. 1, 1947
New Yorker 23:113, Nov. 8, 1947
Newsweek 30:81, Nov. 10, 1947
Time 50:105, Nov. 17, 1947

Beware, Spooks (1939)
New York Times p. 17, Nov. 3, 1939

Bewitched (1945)
Nation 161:190, Aug. 25, 1945
New York Times p. 20, Aug. 17, 1945
Time 46:96, Sep. 3, 1945

Beyond A Reasonable Doubt (1956)
National Parent-Teacher 51:39, Nov., 1956
New York Times p. 27, Sep. 14, 1956
Newsweek 48:104, Sep. 10, 1956
Saturday Review 39:22, Sep. 29, 1956
Scholastic 69:21, Oct. 18, 1956

Beyond Bengal (1934)
New York Times p. 27, May 18, 1934

Beyond Glory (1948)
Commonweal 48:454, Aug. 20, 1948
New York Times p. 18, Aug. 4, 1948
Newsweek 32:76, Aug. 16, 1948
Time 52:74, Aug. 9, 1948

Beyond Mombasa (1957)
Commonweal 66:232, May 31, 1957
National Parent-Teacher 51:37, Apr., 1957
New York Times p. 14, May 31, 1957
Time 69:86, Jun. 24, 1957

Beyond the Blue Horizon (1942)
New York Times p. 27, Jun. 25, 1942
Newsweek 19:64, Jun. 29, 1942

Beyond the Forest (1949)
New York Times p. 11, Oct. 22, 1949; II, p. 1, Oct. 30,
  1949
New Yorker 25:100, Oct. 29, 1949
Newsweek 34:67, Oct. 31, 1949
Rotarian 76:38, Feb., 1950
Scholastic 55:29, Nov. 9, 1949
Time 54:76, Oct. 31, 1949

Beyond Tomorrow (1940)
Commonweal 32:63, May 10, 1940
New York Times p. 27, Sep. 27, 1940
Photoplay 54:68, Jun., 1940

Beyond Victory (1930)
New York Times p. 24, Apr. 6, 1931

Bhowani Junction (1956)
    America 95:272, Jun. 9, 1956
    Catholic World 183:223, Jun., 1956
    Commonweal 64:251, Jun. 8, 1956
    Library Journal 81:1437, Jun. 1, 1956
    Life 40:125-6+, May 21, 1956
    National Parent-Teacher 50:37, Jun., 1956
    New York Times II, p. 5, May 15, 1955; p. 26, May 25,
        1956; II, p. 1, Jun. 3, 1956
    New Yorker 32:130, Jun. 2, 1956
    Newsweek 47:118, Jun. 11, 1956
    Saturday Review 39:25, Jun. 2, 1956
    Scholastic 68:35, May 17, 1956
    Time 67:109, Jun. 4, 1956

Bicycle Thief (1948)
    Christian Century 67:351, Mar. 15, 1950
    Commonweal 51:319, Dec. 23, 1949
    Hollywood Quarterly 4:28-33, Fall, 1949
    Library Journal 75:503, Mar. 15, 1949
    Life 28:43-4+, Jan. 9, 1950
    New Republic 121:23, Dec. 19, 1949
    New York Times p. 44, Dec. 13, 1949; II, p. 3, Dec.
        18, 1949
    New York Times Magazine p. 24-5, Dec. 4, 1949
    New Yorker 25:139, Dec. 10, 1949
    Newsweek 34:56, Dec. 26, 1949
    Rotarian 76:40, May, 1950
    Saturday Review 33:30-2, Jan. 7, 1950
    Theatre Arts 34:38-9, Feb., 1950
    Time 54:98, Dec. 12, 1949; 55:86, Jan. 16, 1950
    Vogue 114:87, Aug. 1, 1949

Big Attraction (1933)
    Commonweal 18:349, Aug. 4, 1933

Big Bluff (1955)
    National Parent-Teacher 50:38, Oct., 1955

Big Boodle (1957)
    National Parent-Teacher 51:37, Apr., 1957
    New York Times p. 38, Mar. 12, 1957
    Newsweek 49:118, Mar. 18, 1957

Big Boy (1930)
    Life (NY) 96:20, Oct. 17, 1930
    New York Times p. 9, Sep. 13, 1930; IX, p. 5, Sep. 21,
        1930

111

Big Brain (1933)
New Outlook 162:44, Sep., 1933
New York Times p. 9, Aug. 5, 1933

Big Broadcast (1932)
New York Times p. 13, Oct. 15, 1932

Big Broadcast of 1936 (1936)
Canadian Magazine 84:40, Nov., 1935
New York Times p. 15, Sep. 16, 1935
Newsweek 6:17, Sep. 21, 1935
Time 26:45, Sep. 23, 1935

Big Broadcast of 1937 (1936)
Commonweal 25:104, Nov. 20, 1936
New Republic 88:351, Oct. 28, 1936
New York Times p. 31, Oct. 22, 1936
Stage 14:14, Dec., 1936
Time 28:67, Oct. 19, 1936

Big Broadcast of 1938 (1938)
New York Times p. 16, Mar. 10, 1938; XI, p. 5, Mar.
    13, 1938
Scholastic 32:35, Apr. 2, 1938

Big Brown Eyes (1936)
New York Times p. 11, May 2, 1936
Time 27:32, Apr. 13, 1936

Big Business Girl (1931)
Life (NY) 98:18, Jul. 3, 1931
New York Times p. 27, Jun. 12, 1931

Big Cage (1933)
New York Times p. 20, May 9, 1933; IX, p. 3, May 14,
    1933
Stage 10:43-4, Jun., 1933

Big Caper (1957)
New York Times p. 16, Mar. 29, 1957

Big Carnival (1950) (see also ACE IN THE HOLE)
Christian Century 68:1207, Oct. 17, 1951

Big Cat (1949)
New York Times p. 12, Jul. 29, 1949
Newsweek 34:69, Jul. 11, 1949

Big Chief (1960)
New York Times p. 32, Apr. 27, 1960
Newsweek 55:89, May 2, 1960

Big Circus (1959)
America 101:559, Jul. 25, 1959
New York Times p. 6, Jul. 13, 1959
New Yorker 35:46, Jul. 25, 1959
Newsweek 54:94, Jul. 20, 1959
Time 74:65, Aug. 3, 1959

Big City (1937)
New York Times p. 29, Sep. 17, 1937; XI, p. 5, Sep. 26, 1937

Big City (1947)
New York Times p. 23, May 17, 1948
Newsweek 31:72, May 31, 1948
Woman's Home Companion 75:11, Aug., 1948

Big City Blues (1932)
New York Times p. 18, Sep. 10, 1932; IX, p. 3, Sep. 18, 1932

Big Clock (1948)
Life 24:133-4+, Apr. 19, 1948
New Republic 118:30, May 3, 1948
New York Times p. 34, Apr. 22, 1948; II, p. 1, May 2, 1948
New Yorker 24:83, May 1, 1948
Newsweek 31:91, Apr. 19, 1948
Scholastic 52:35, May 10, 1948
Time 51:92, Apr. 19, 1948

Big Combo (1954)
New York Times p. 13, Mar. 26, 1955
Newsweek 45:95, Mar. 28, 1955

Big Country (1958)
America 100:87+, Oct. 18, 1958
Catholic World 188:62, Oct., 1958
Commonweal 69:48, Oct. 10, 1958
Library Journal 83:2667, Oct. 1, 1958
Life 45:82-4, Sep. 29, 1958
New York Times p. 44, Oct. 2, 1958
New Yorker 34:93, Oct. 11, 1958
Newsweek 52:95, Sep. 8, 1958

Big Country (1958) (Continued)
Saturday Review 41:25, Aug. 23, 1958
Senrio Scholastic 73:29, Nov. 7, 1958
Time 72:96+, Sep. 8, 1958

*Big Day
Christian Century 69:791, Jul. 2, 1952
National Parent-Teacher 49:38, May, 1955

Big Deal on Madonna Street (1961)
Nation 192:20, Jan. 7, 1961
New Republic 143:27-8, Dec. 12, 1960
New York Times p. 20, Nov. 23, 1960; II, p. 1, Dec. 4,
1960
New Yorker 36:108, Dec. 3, 1960
Newsweek 56:83, Nov. 28, 1960
Time 76:96, Dec. 12, 1960

Big Drive (1933)
New York Times p. 21, Jan. 20, 1933; IX, p. 5, Jan. 29,
1933

Big Fight (1930)
Life (NY) 95:17, Jul. 18, 1930
New York Times p. 9, Jun. 28, 1930

Big Fisherman (1959)
America 101:656+, Aug. 29, 1959
Good Housekeeping 149:28, Sep., 1959
New York Times p. 18, Aug. 6, 1959; II, p. 1, Aug. 9,
1959
Newsweek 54:85, Aug. 10, 1959
Senior Scholastic 75:53, Sep. 30, 1959
Time 74:78, Aug. 17, 1959

Big Fix (1946)
New York Times p. 10, May 3, 1947

Big Frame (1953)
National Parent-Teacher 47:37, Jun., 1953

Big Gamble (1931)
New York Times p. 20, Sep. 21, 1931

Big Gamble (1961)
America 105:779, Sep. 16, 1961
New York Times p. 19, Sep. 2, 1961

Big Gamble (1961) (Continued)
New Yorker 37:112, Sep. 9, 1961
Time 78:103, Sep. 15, 1961

Big Game (1936)
New York Times p. 23, Oct. 24, 1936

Big Guy (1939)
New York Times p. 29, Jan. 1, 1940

Big Hangover (1950)
Christian Century 67:775, Jun. 21, 1950
New York Times p. 20, May 26, 1950
Newsweek 35:91, Jun. 12, 1950
Rotarian 77:43, Aug., 1950
Time 55:93, Jun. 19, 1950

Big-Hearted Herbert (1934)
New Outlook 163:49, Feb., 1934
New York Times p. 23, Nov. 14, 1934
Theatre Arts 18:171, Mar., 1934

*Big Heat
America 90:159, Nov. 7, 1953
Catholic World 178:63, Oct., 1953
Farm Journal 77:73, Dec., 1953
Library Journal 78:1677, Oct. 1, 1953
Nation 177:434, Nov. 21, 1953
National Parent-Teacher 48:36, Nov., 1953
Newsweek 42:90-1, Nov. 2, 1953
Time 62:112, Nov. 2, 1953
New York Times p. 43, Oct. 15, 1953

Big House (1930)
Life (NY) 95:17, Jul. 11, 1930
Literary Digest 106:15, Aug. 2, 1930
New York Times VIII, p. 4, Jun. 22, 1930; p. 31, Jun.
    25, 1930; VIII, p. 3, Jun. 29, 1930
Outlook 155:390, Jul. 9, 1930
Theatre Magazine 52:48, Aug.-Sep., 1930

Big House U.S.A. (1955)
National Parent-Teacher 49:38, May, 1955
New York Times p. 11, Mar. 12, 1955

Big Jack (1949)
New York Times p. 27, May 23, 1949

Big Jim McLain (1952)
National Parent-Teacher 47:37, Nov., 1952
New York Times p. 35, Sep. 18, 1952
Newsweek 40:104, Nov. 3, 1952
Time 60:93, Sep. 29, 1952

Big Knife (1955)
America 94:224, Nov. 19, 1955
Catholic World 181:58, Oct., 1955
Commonweal 63:225+, Dec. 2, 1955
Library Journal 80:2230, Oct. 15, 1955
Nation 181:427, Nov. 12, 1955
National Parent-Teacher 50:38, Dec., 1955
New Republic 134:19-20, Jan. 9, 1956
New York Times II, p. 5, Nov. 6, 1955; p. 41, Nov. 9,
   1955
New York Times Magazine p. 25, Oct. 16, 1955
New Yorker 31:194, Nov. 19, 1955
Newsweek 46:114, Nov. 21, 1955
Saturday Review 38:38, Nov. 19, 1955
Time 66:106+, Oct. 24, 1955

Big Land (1957)
America 96:686, Mar. 16, 1957
National Parent-Teacher 51:38, Apr., 1957
New York Times p. 18, Mar. 2, 1957
New Yorker 33:76+, Mar. 9, 1957
Time 69:96, Apr. 1, 1957

Big Leaguer (1953)
National Parent-Teacher 48:35, Nov., 1953
Saturday Review 36:29, Aug. 29, 1953
Scholastic 63:38, Sep. 23, 1953
Time 62:86, Sep. 28, 1953

Big Lift (1950)
Christian Century 67:743, Jun. 14, 1950
Commonweal 52:98, May 5, 1950
Good Housekeeping 130:275, May, 1950
New Republic 122:23, May 15, 1950
New York Times p. 37, Apr. 27, 1950; II, p. 1, Apr. 30,
   1950
New Yorker 26:96, Apr. 29, 1950
Newsweek 35:75, May 1, 1950
Rotarian 77:43, Aug., 1950
Scholastic 56:30, May 10, 1950
Time 55:90+, May 8, 1950

Big Money (1930)
New York Times p. 21, Nov. 22, 1930

Big News (1929)
New York Times p. 22, Oct. 7, 1929

Big Night (1952)
Christian Century 69:175, Feb. 6, 1952
Commonweal 55:593, Mar. 21, 1952
Holiday 11:19, Mar., 1952
Library Journal 77:713, Apr. 15, 1952
New York Times p. 21, Aug. 20, 1952; II, p. 1, Aug.
24, 1952
Newsweek 38:100+, Nov. 26, 1951
Saturday Review 34:31, Dec. 8, 1951
Time 58:112+, Nov. 12, 1951

Big Night (1960)
New York Times p. 37, Feb. 18, 1960

Big Noise (1936)
New York Times p. 18, Jul. 4, 1936

Big Noise (1944)
New York Times p. 16, Sep. 23, 1944

Big Operator (1959)
America 101:778, Sep. 26, 1959
Commonweal 71:21, Oct. 2, 1959
Saturday Review 42:36, Sep. 26, 1959

Big Pond (1930)
New York Times VIII, p. 5, Jan. 5, 1930; p. 21, May
19, 1930; IX, p. 5, May 25, 1930

Big Red (1962)
Commonweal 77:18, Sep. 28, 1962
New York Times p. 11, Sep. 3, 1962

Big Shakedown (1934)
New York Times p. 19, Feb. 12, 1934

Big Shot (1931)
New York Times p. 14, Jan. 2, 1932

Big Shot (1937)
New York Times p. 13, Aug. 13, 1937

117

Big Shot (1942)
New York Times p. 8, Jul. 18, 1942

Big Show (1961)
Commonweal 74:278, Jun. 9, 1961
New York Times p. 42, May 11, 1961

Big Sky (1952)
Catholic World 175:465, Sep., 1952
Christian Century 69:1046, Sep. 19, 1952
Commonweal 56:535, Sep. 5, 1952
Library Journal 77:1605, Oct. 1, 1952
Life 33:59, Sep. 8, 1952
Nation 175:283, Sep. 27, 1952
National Parent-Teacher 47:38, Sep., 1952
Natural History 61:381, Oct., 1952
New York Times p. 21, Aug. 20, 1952; II, p. 1, Aug.
   24, 1952
New Yorker 28:91, Sep. 6, 1952
Newsweek 40:85, Aug. 25, 1952
Saturday Review 35:28-9, Aug. 16, 1952
Scholastic 61:37, Sep. 17, 1952
Time 60:88+, Aug. 11, 1952

Big Sleep (1946)
Commonweal 44:504, Sep. 6, 1946
Harpers Bizarre 79:74, Apr., 1945
Hollywood Quarterly 2:161-3, Jan., 1947
Life 21:82, Oct. 28, 1946
Nation 163:250, Aug. 31, 1946
New Republic 115:351, Sep. 23, 1946
New York Times p. 6, Aug. 24, 1946; II, p. 1, Sep. 1,
   1946
New Yorker 22:48, Sep. 7, 1946
Newsweek 28:78, Sep. 2, 1946
Theatre Arts 30:520, Sep., 1946
Time 48:95, Aug. 26, 1946

Big Steal (1949)
Christian Century 66:879, Jul. 20, 1949
Commonweal 50:368, Jul. 22, 1949
New Republic 121:23, Jul. 25, 1949
New York Times p. 13, Jul. 11, 1949
Newsweek 34:76+, Jul. 25, 1949
Rotarian 75:36, Sep., 1949
Theatre Arts 33:6, Sep., 1949
Time 54:80, Jul. 25, 1949

Big Store (1941)
  Commonweal 34:258, Jul. 4, 1941
  New York Times p. 14, Jun. 27, 1941
  Newsweek 17:56, Jun. 30, 1941
  Scribner's Commentator 10:106, Sep., 1941
  Time 38:68, Jul. 14, 1941

Big Street (1942)
  Commonweal 36:449, Aug. 28, 1942
  New York Times p. 13, Aug. 14, 1942
  Newsweek 20:60, Aug. 24, 1942
  Time 40:104+, Sep. 7, 1942

Big Time (1929)
  New York Times p. 30, Sep. 9, 1929; IX, p. 4, Sep. 22, 1929

Big Tip-Off (1955)
  National Parent-Teacher 49:38, Jun., 1955

Big Town (see So This Is New York)

Big Town Czar (1939)
  New York Times p. 27, May 4, 1939; X, p. 5, May 7, 1939

Big Town Girl (1937)
  New York Times p. 23, Dec. 13, 1937

Big Trail (1930)
  Life (NY) 96:18, Nov. 14, 1930
  Literary Digest 107:34, Nov. 22, 1930
  Motion Picture Classic 32:59, Sep., 1930
  National Magazine 59:144, Dec., 1930
  New York Times VIII, p. 5, Aug. 3, 1930; VIII, p. 6, Oct. 26, 1930; VIII, p. 5, Nov. 2, 1930
  Outlook 156:393, Nov. 5, 1930
  Photoplay 38:32-4+, Oct., 1930; 39:98-9, Dec., 1930
  Theatre Magazine 53:48, Jan., 1931

Big Trees (1952)
  New York Times p. 24, Feb. 6, 1952
  Newsweek 39:100+, Feb. 25, 1952

Big Wheel (1949)
  Newsweek 35:84, Feb. 6, 1950
  Rotarian 76:38, Feb., 1950
  Time 54:105, Nov. 21, 1949

Bigamist (1953)
New York Times p. 10, Dec. 26, 1953
Newsweek 43:61, Jan. 4, 1954

Bigamist (1958)
New York Times p. 25, May 12, 1958

Bigger Than Life (1956)
America 95:452, Aug. 11, 1956
Commonweal 64:466, Aug. 10, 1956
National Parent-Teacher 51:37, Oct., 1956
New York Times p. 11, Aug. 3, 1956; II, p. 1, Aug. 5,
   1956
New Yorker 32:58, Aug. 11, 1956
Saturday Review 39:24, Jul. 28, 1956
Time 68:53, Aug. 6, 1956

Bill and Coo (1948)
Life 23:14-16, Jul. 28, 1947
New York Times p. 17, Mar. 29, 1948
New Yorker 24:103, Apr. 10, 1948
Time 51:104, Apr. 12, 1948

Bill of Divorcement (1933)
Commonweal 32:170, Jun. 14, 1940
Nation 135:409, Oct. 26, 1932
New York Times p. 15, Oct. 3, 1932; IX, p. 5, Oct. 9,
   1932; p. 11, Jul. 12, 1940; IX, p. 3, Jul. 21, 1940
Newsweek 15:48, Apr. 22, 1940
Photoplay 54:69, Jun., 1940
Scholastic 36:36, Apr. 15, 1940
Time 35:92, Apr. 22, 1940
Vanity Fair 39:58, Nov., 1932

Billion Dollar Scandal (1933)
New York Times p. 23, Jan. 9, 1933

Billy Budd (1962)
America 107:1279, Dec. 22, 1962
Commonweal 77:202-3, Nov. 16, 1962
Life 53:128+, Dec. 7, 1962
Nation 195:412, Dec. 8, 1962
New Republic 147:25, Nov. 10, 1962
New York Times p. 32, Oct. 31, 1962; II, p. 1, Nov. 18,
   1962
New Yorker 38:116, Nov. 3, 1962
Newsweek 60:112, Nov. 5, 1962

Billy Budd (1962) (Continued)
Reporter 27:42, Dec. 6, 1962
Saturday Review 45:27, Nov. 10, 1962
Senior Scholastic 81:24, Oct. 24, 1962
Time 80:99, Nov. 9, 1962

Billy Liar (1963)
America 110:202-3, Feb. 8, 1964
Commonweal 79:314, Dec. 6, 1963
New Republic 149:27, Dec. 14, 1963
New York Times p. 49, Dec. 17, 1963
New Yorker 39:88-9, Dec. 21, 1963
Newsweek 62:74+, Dec. 23, 1963

*Billy Rose's Diamond Horseshoe
Commonweal 42:119, May 18, 1945
Cosmopolitan 118:92, May, 1945
New York Times p. 27, May 3, 1945; II, p. 1, May 6,
   1945
Newsweek 25:109, May 14, 1945
Time 45:96, May 14, 1945

Billy the Kid (1930, 1941)
Commonweal 34:186, Jun. 13, 1941
Life 11:65-9, Aug. 4, 1941
Life (NY) 96:18, Nov. 7, 1930
New York Times VIII, p. 2, Jul. 6, 1930; p. 23, Oct. 8,
   1930; VIII, p. 5, Oct. 26, 1930; p. 28, Jun. 20, 1941;
   IX, p. 3, Jun. 22, 1941
Newsweek 17:51-3, Jun. 2, 1941
Outlook 156:353, Oct. 29, 1930
Scribner's Commentator 10:107-8, Sep., 1941

Bimbo the Great (1961)
New York Times p. 26, Jun. 29, 1961

Biography of a Bachelor Girl (1935)
New York Times p. 18, May 2, 1935
Time 25:32, Jan. 21, 1935

Bird Man of Alcatraz (1962)
America 107:552, Jul. 28, 1962
Commonweal 76:446, Aug. 10, 1962
Life 53:39+, Aug. 24, 1962
New Republic 147:28+, Aug. 13, 1962
New York Times p. 19, Jul. 19, 1962
Newsweek 60:72-3, Jul. 9, 1962

121

Bird Man of Alcatraz (1962) (Continued)
Saturday Review 45:31, May 19, 1962
Time 80:79, Jul. 20, 1962

Bird of Paradise (1932)
Literary Digest 114:17-19, Oct. 1, 1932
New Outlook 161:39, Oct., 1932
New York Times VIII, p. 4, Feb. 28, 1932; p. 18, Sep.
10, 1932; IX, p. 3, Sep. 18, 1932
Vanity Fair 39:44+, Oct., 1932

Bird of Paradise (1951)
Christian Century 68:599, May 9, 1951
New York Times p. 37, Mar. 15, 1951; II, p. 1, Mar.
18, 1951
New Yorker 27:95, Mar. 24, 1951
Newsweek 37:88, Mar. 12, 1951
Time 57:106+, Mar. 19, 1951

Birds (1963)
America 108:589, Apr. 20, 1963
Commonweal 78:73-4, Apr. 12, 1963
Esquire 60:36+, Oct., 1963
Look 26:52-4+, Dec. 4, 1962
New Republic 148:34-5, Apr. 13, 1963
New York Times p. 5, Mar. 29, 1963; p. 54, Apr. 1,
1963
New Yorker 39:177, Apr. 6, 1963
Newsweek 61:92, Apr. 8, 1963
Saturday Review 46:39, Apr. 6, 1963
Time 81:103, Apr. 5, 1963

Birds and the Bees (1956)
Catholic World 183:142, May, 1956
Coronet 40:10, May, 1956
National Parent-Teacher 50:36, Jun., 1956
New York Times p. 22, Apr. 23, 1956
New Yorker 32:147, May 5, 1956
Newsweek 47:100, May 7, 1956
Scholastic 68:35, May 17, 1956
Time 67:106, Apr. 30, 1956

Birth of a Baby (1938)
Life 4:336, Apr. 11, 1938
New Republic 94:179, Mar. 23, 1938
New York Times p. 31, Dec. 8, 1938
Newsweek 11:26, Mar. 21, 1938
Time 31:29-30, Apr. 4, 1938

Birth of the Blues (1941)
Commonweal 35:199, Dec. 12, 1941
Life 11:96-7, Nov. 17, 1941
New Republic 105:437, Oct. 6, 1941
New York Times IX, p. 4, Oct. 19, 1941; p. 39, Dec.
11, 1941; IX, p. 7, Dec. 14, 1941
Newsweek 18:69, Nov. 10, 1941
Scholastic 39:28, Nov. 17, 1941
Theatre Arts 25:885, Dec., 1941

Biscuit Eater (1940)
Life 8:71-2+, May 6, 1940
New Republic 102:536, Apr. 22, 1940
New York Times p. 28, May 23, 1940; IX, p. 3, May 26,
1940
Newsweek 15:32, May 6, 1940
Photoplay 54:68, Jun., 1940
Scholastic 36:36, Apr. 15, 1940

Bishop Misbehaves (1936)
Time 26:26, Sep. 30, 1935

Bishop Murder Case (1930)
New York Times p. 15, Feb. 1, 1930

Bishop's Wife (1948)
Commonweal 47:303, Jan. 2, 1948
Cosmopolitan 123:13+, Dec., 1947
Ladies Home Journal 65:225, Feb., 1948
Life 24:71-2, Jan. 12, 1948
New Republic 117:31, Dec. 15, 1947
New York Times p. 44, Dec. 10, 1947; II, p. 3, Dec.
14, 1947
Newsweek 30:81-2, Dec. 22, 1947
Scholastic 51:29, Dec. 15, 1947
Theatre Arts 31:48-50, Dec., 1947
Time 50:104, Dec. 8, 1947
Woman's Home Companion 75:8, Jan., 1948

Bitter Rice (1950)
Catholic World 176:461, Mar., 1953
Commonweal 52:632, Oct. 6, 1950
Life 27:108-9, Nov. 7, 1949
New Republic 123:30, Oct. 9, 1950
New York Times p. 39, Sep. 19, 1950; II, p. 1, Sep. 24,
1950
New Yorker 26:60, Sep. 30, 1950

123

Bitter Rice (1950) (Continued)
Newsweek 36:92, Sep. 18, 1950
Rotarian 78:36, Mar., 1951
Time 56:104, Nov. 6, 1950

Bitter Sweet (1933)
New York Times p. 18, Aug. 24, 1933
Newsweek 2:30, Sep. 2, 1933

Bitter Tea of General Yen (1933)
New York Times p. 20, Jan. 12, 1933;   p. 5, Jan.
22, 1933

Bitter Victory (1958)
Library Journal 83:835, Mar. 15, 1958
National Parent-Teacher 52:38, Jan., 1958

Bizarre Bizarre (1939)
New York Times p. 27, Mar. 21, 1939

Black Angel (1946)
Commonweal 44:504, Sep. 6, 1946
Nation 163:305, Sep. 14, 1946
New York Times II, p. 6, Dec. 15, 1946
New Yorker 22:83, Oct. 5, 1946
Newsweek 28:108+, Sep. 9, 1946
Time 48:92, Sep. 2, 1946

Black Arrow (1948)
Commonweal 49:95, Nov. 5, 1948
New York Times p. 14, Oct. 4, 1948

Black Bart (1948)
New York Times p. 30, Mar. 4, 1948
New Yorker 24:81, Mar. 13, 1948
Newsweek 31:88, Mar. 15, 1948

Black Beauty (1946)
New York Times p. 13, Aug. 30, 1946
Newsweek 28:111, Sep. 9, 1946
Scholastic 49:37, Oct. 14, 1946

Black Book (1949)
New Yorker 25:126, Oct. 15, 1949
Newsweek 34:82, Dec. 5, 1949

Black Camel (1931)
New York Times VIII, p. 5, Jun. 21, 1931; p. 11, Jul. 4,

Black Camel (1931) (Continued)
1931; VIII, p. 3, Jul. 12, 1931

Black Castle (1952)
Christian Century 69:1391, Nov. 26, 1952
National Parent-Teacher 47:37, Dec., 1952
New York Times p. 20, Dec. 26, 1952
Time 60:100, Dec. 8, 1952

Black Cat (1934)
New York Times p. 18, May 19, 1934

Black Dakotas (1954)
National Parent-Teacher 49:39, Nov., 1954
New York Times p. 21, Oct. 2, 1954

Black Diamonds (1940)
New York Times p. 26, Sep. 10, 1940

Black Doll (1938)
New York Times p. 10, Feb. 7, 1938

Black Fox (1963)
Commonweal 78:248, May 24, 1963
New York Times p. 26, Apr. 30, 1963
Newsweek 61:95, May 6, 1963
Time 81:117+, May 17, 1963

Black Friday (1940)
New York Times IX, p. 5, Jan. 28, 1940; p. 23, Mar.
22, 1940

Black Fury (1935)
Canadian Magazine 83:32, Jun., 1935
Literary Digest 119:34, Apr. 27, 1935
Nation 140:491-2, Apr. 24, 1935
New Republic 82:313, Apr. 24, 1935
New York Times IX, p. 3, Apr. 7, 1935; p. 27, Apr. 11,
1935
Newsweek 5:25, Apr. 13, 1935
Theatre Arts 19:408, Jun., 1935
Time 25:60, Apr. 22, 1935
Vanity Fair 44:47, Apr., 1935

Black Gold (1947)
Cosmopolitan 123:111+, Sep., 1947
New York Times II, p. 5, Jan. 12, 1947; II, p. 3, Aug.
31, 1947; p. 16, Sep. 5, 1947

Black Gold (1947) (Continued)
Woman's Home Companion 74:11, Oct., 1947

Black Hand (1950)
Christian Century 67:447, Apr. 5, 1950
Commonweal 51:630, Mar. 24, 1950
New Republic 122:23, Mar. 20, 1950
New York Times p. 15, Mar. 13, 1950
New Yorker 26:110, Mar. 25, 1950
Newsweek 35:84+, Mar. 27, 1950
Rotarian 76:37, Jun., 1950
Time 55:92, Mar. 20, 1950

Black Horse Canyon (1954)
Catholic World 179:304, Jul., 1954
Library Journal 79:1168, Jun. 15, 1954

Black Knight (1954)
America 92:259, Nov. 27, 1954
Commonweal 61:188, Nov. 19, 1954
National Parent-Teacher 49:38, Jan., 1955
New York Times p. 27, Oct. 29, 1954
Newsweek 44:112, Nov. 15, 1954
Time 64:110, Nov. 8, 1954

Black Legion (1937)
Commonweal 25:360, Jan. 22, 1937
Literary Digest 123:23, Jan. 16, 1937
Nation 144:137, Jan. 30, 1937
New Republic 90:47-8, Feb. 17, 1937
New York Times p. 21, Jan. 18, 1937; X, p. 5, Jan. 24,
    1937
Scholastic 30:22, Feb. 6, 1937
Time 29:46, Jan. 25, 1937
Fortune 16:113, Dec., 1937

Black Limelight (1939)
New York Times p. 12, Jun. 26, 1939

Black Magic (1949)
Commonweal 51:342, Dec. 30, 1949
Good Housekeeping 129:161, Aug., 1949
New Republic 121:31, Dec. 12, 1949
New York Times p. 37, Nov. 9, 1949
Newsweek 34:69, Aug. 8, 1949
Time 54:62, Sep. 5, 1949

Black Market Babies (1945)
New York Times p. 23, Apr. 1, 1946

Black Moon (1934)
New York Times p. 26, Jun. 28, 1934

Black Narcissus (1947)
Canadian Forum 27:232, Jan., 1948
Commonweal 46:455, Aug. 22, 1947
Life 23:55-6, Sep. 1, 1947
Nation 165:209, Aug. 30, 1947
New Republic 117:37, Sep. 15, 1947
New York Times p. 29, Aug. 14, 1947; II, p. 1, Aug.
   17, 1947
New Yorker 23:42, Aug. 23, 1947
Newsweek 30:77-8, Aug. 18, 1947
Photoplay 31:60-61, Oct., 1947
Theatre Arts 31:51-2, Oct., 1947
Time 50:88+, Aug. 25, 1947
Vogue 110:181, Sep. 1, 1947

Black Orchid (1959)
America 100:643, Feb. 28, 1959
Catholic World 189:54-5, Apr., 1959
Commonweal 69:600-1, Mar. 6, 1959
Life 46:73-4, Feb. 23, 1959
New Republic 140:23, Mar. 9, 1959
New York Times p. 33, Feb. 13, 1959
Newsweek 53:101-2, Feb. 16, 1959
Time 73:68, Mar. 2, 1959

Black Orpheus (1959)
America 102:537, Jan. 30, 1960
Commonweal 71:396, Jan. 1, 1960
Dance Magazine 33:16-17, Dec., 1959
McCalls 87:8, Feb., 1960
Nation 190:59-60, Jan. 16, 1960
New Republic 142:21, Jan. 4, 1960
New York Times p. 41, Dec. 22, 1959
New Yorker 35:47, Jan. 2, 1960
Saturday Review 42:12-13, Dec. 19, 1959
Time 74:114+, Nov. 16, 1959

Black Patch (1957)
National Parent-Teacher 52:33, Oct., 1957
New York Times p. 38, Apr. 24, 1958

Black Rose (1950)
  Christian Century 67:1215, Oct. 11, 1950
  Commonweal 52:581, Sep. 22, 1950
  Good Housekeeping 131:16-17, Aug., 1950
  Holiday 8:16-17, Dec., 1950
  Library Journal 75:1677, Oct. 1, 1950
  New York Times p. 11, Sep. 2, 1950
  New Yorker 26:111, Sep. 9, 1950
  Newsweek 36:87, Sep. 11, 1950
  Rotarian 77:37, Dec., 1950
  Scholastic 57:37, Oct. 11, 1950
  Time 56:102+, Sep. 11, 1950

Black Scorpion (1957)
  New York Times p. 23, Oct. 12, 1957
  Senior Scholastic 71:37, Dec. 6, 1957

Black Sea Fighters (1943)
  New York Times p. 18, Jul. 28, 1943

Black Shadows (1949)
  New York Times p. 33, Nov. 7, 1949

Black Sheep (1935)
  New York Times p. 34, Jun. 28, 1935

Black Shield of Falworth (1954) (see also Men of Iron)
  America 92:110, Oct. 23, 1954
  Farm Journal 78:140, Sep., 1954
  Library Journal 79:1485, Sep. 1, 1954
  National Parent-Teacher 49:38, Dec., 1954
  New York Times p. 16, Oct. 7, 1954
  Scholastic 65:29, Oct. 27, 1954
  Time 64:88+, Oct. 25, 1954

Black Sleep (1956)
  National Parent-Teacher 51:39, Sep., 1956
  Newsweek 48:96+, Jul. 9, 1956

Black Sunday (1961)
  New York Times p. 23, Mar. 9, 1961

Black Swan (1942)
  Commonweal 37:280, Jan. 1, 1943
  Cosmopolitan 113:68, Nov., 1942
  New York Times p. 18, Dec. 24, 1942
  Newsweek 20:86, Dec. 7, 1942

Black Swan (1942) (Continued)
Photoplay 22:4, Jan., 1943
Scholastic 41:33, Jan. 18, 1943
Time 40:109, Dec. 7, 1942

Black Tights (1962)
Commonweal 75:645, Mar. 16, 1962
Dance Magazine 36:20-1, Mar., 1962
New York Times p. 54, Feb. 21, 1962
Saturday Review 45:37, Feb. 24, 1962

Black Tuesday (1954)
Commonweal 61:656, Mar. 25, 1955
National Parent-Teacher 49:39, Feb., 1955
New York Times p. 16, Jan. 1, 1953
Newsweek 45:45, Jan. 3, 1955
Time 65:75, Jan. 24, 1955

Black Watch (1929)
New York Times IX, p. 4, May 19, 1929; p. 26, May
    23, 1929; IX, p. 7, May 26, 1929
Outlook 152:272, Jun. 12, 1929

Black Whip (1956)
National Parent-Teacher 51:38, Feb., 1957

Black Widow (1954)
America 92:194, Nov. 13, 1954
Catholic World 180:220, Dec., 1954
Commonweal 61:255, Dec. 3, 1954
Library Journal 79:2182, Nov. 15, 1954
National Parent-Teacher 49:39, Jan., 1955
New York Times p. 46, Oct. 28, 1954
New Yorker 30:211, Nov. 13, 1954
Newsweek 44:100, Nov. 8, 1954
Saturday Review 37:27, Nov. 13, 1954
Time 64:110+, Nov. 8, 1954

Blackbeard, the Pirate (1952)
National Parent-Teacher 47:37, Feb., 1953
New York Times p. 20, Dec. 26, 1952
Newsweek 41:98, Jan. 19, 1953
Theatre Arts 37:84, Feb., 1953
Time 60:66, Dec. 22, 1952

Blackboard Jungle (1955)
America 92:686-7, Mar. 26, 1955

Blackboard Jungle (1955) (Continued)
Catholic World 181:63, Apr. 1955
Commonweal 61:630-1, Mar. 18, 1955
Farm Journal 79:89, Apr., 1955
Library Journal 89:642, Mar. 15, 1955
Life 38:49-50+, Mar. 28, 1955
Look 19:31-2, May 3, 1955
Nation 180:294-5, Apr. 2, 1955
National Parent-Teacher 49:15, May, 1955
New Republic 132:29-30, Apr. 11, 1955
New York Times p. 21, Mar. 21, 1955; II, p. 1, Mar. 27, 1955
New Yorker 31:120, Mar. 26, 1955
Newsweek 45:94, Mar. 28, 1955
Saturday Review 38:31, Apr. 2, 1955
Scholastic 66:19, Mar. 23, 1955
School and Society 85:57-9, Feb. 16, 1957
Time 65:98, Mar. 21, 1955

Blackjack Ketchum, Desperado (1956)
National Parent-Teacher 50:39, May, 1956
New York Times p. 26, Apr. 5, 1956

Blackmail (1929)
Life (NY) 94:28, Oct. 18, 1929
New York Times IX, p. 4, Jul. 14, 1929; VIII, p. 5, Aug. 1, 1929; p. 22, Aug. 14, 1929; IX, p. 5, Sep. 15, 1929; p. 22, Oct. 7, 1929; IX, p. 6, Oct. 13, 1929

Blackmail (1939)
New York Times p. 26, Sep. 15, 1939

Blackout (1940)
New Republic 103:835, Dec. 16, 1940
New York Times p. 19, Dec. 2, 1940
Newsweek 16:48, Dec. 2, 1940
Time 36:52+, Nov. 25, 1940

Blackwells Island (1939)
New York Times p. 19, Mar. 2, 1939
Newsweek 13:34, Mar. 13, 1939
Photoplay 53:48, Feb., 1939

Blame the Woman (1932)
New York Times p. 24, Oct. 25, 1932

Blanche Fury (1948)
New Republic 119:38, Dec. 6, 1948

Blarney Kiss (1933)
New York Times p. 14, Aug. 19, 1933

Blast of Silence (1961)
New York Times p. 12, Dec. 30, 1961
Saturday Review 44:36, Jun. 3, 1961

Blaze of Noon (1947)
Commonweal 45:567, Mar. 21, 1947
Flying 40:48-50+, Apr., 1947
Nation 164:340, Mar. 22, 1947
New Republic 116:41, Mar. 24, 1947
New York Times p. 31, Mar. 5, 1947
New Yorker 23:68, Mar. 15, 1947
Newsweek 29:103, Mar. 17, 1947
Time 49:100, Mar. 24, 1947

Blazing Forest (1952)
National Parent-Teacher 47:36, Nov., 1952

Blessed Event (1932)
New York Times p. 16, Sep. 3, 1932; IX, p. 3, Sep. 18, 1932

Blind Adventure (1933)
New York Times p. 24, Oct. 31, 1933; IX, p. 5, Nov. 5, 1933
Newsweek 2:28, Nov. 11, 1933

Blind Alibi (1938)
New York Times p. 17, May 20, 1938

Blind Alley (1939)
New York Times X, p. 5, Apr. 9, 1939; p. 15, May 22, 1939
Photoplay 53:63, Jul., 1939

*Blind Desire
New Republic 118:29, Jun. 28, 1948
New York Times p. 28, Jun. 10, 1948
New Yorker 24:86, Jun. 12, 1948

Blind Goddess (1948)
New Republic 121:23, Jul. 4, 1949
New York Times p. 33, Jun. 23, 1949
New Yorker 25:33, Jul. 2, 1949

Blithe Spirit (1945)
 Commonweal 42:624, Oct. 12, 1945
 Cosmopolitan 119:96, Nov., 1945
 Life 19:77-80, Oct. 22, 1945; 20:77, Jan. 14, 1946
 Nation 161:441, Oct. 27, 1945
 New Republic 113:573-4, Oct. 29, 1945
 New York Times p. 27, Oct. 4, 1945; II, p. 1, Oct. 7, 1945
 New Yorker 21:95, Oct. 6, 1945
 Newsweek 26:102, Oct. 15, 1945
 Photoplay 28:22, Feb., 1946
 Scholastic 47:23, Oct. 29, 1945
 Theatre Arts 29:639-40, Nov., 1945
 Time 46:54, Oct. 15, 1945

Blob (1958)
 Commonweal 69:127, Oct. 31, 1958
 New York Times p. 25, Nov. 7, 1958

Blockade (1928) (see Q Ships)

Blockade (1938)
 Commonweal 28:273, Jul. 1, 1938
 Life 4:60-62, Jun. 13, 1938
 Nation 146:688, Jun. 18, 1938
 New Republic 95:217, Jun. 29, 1938
 New York Times p. 25, Jun. 17, 1938
 Newsweek 11:23, Jun. 20, 1938
 Time 31:37-8, Jun. 20, 1938

Blonde Captive (1931)
 New York Times p. 21, Feb. 29, 1932

Blonde Crazy (1931)
 New York Times p. 28, Dec. 4, 1931; VIII, p. 4, Dec. 20, 1931

Blonde Fever (1945)
 Canadian Forum 25:189, Nov., 1945

Blonde Savage (1947)
 New York Times p. 9, Oct. 4, 1947

Blonde Sinner (1956)
 New York Times p. 34, Jan. 24, 1957

Blonde Trouble (1937)
 New York Times p. 7, Aug. 7, 1937

Blonde Venus (1932)
 New Outlook 161:47, Nov., 1932
 New York Times p. 18, Sep. 24, 1932; IX, p. 5, Oct. 2,
   1932
 Vanity Fair 39:58, Nov., 1932

Blondie (1938)
 New York Times p. 25, Dec. 22, 1938
 Photoplay 53:45, Jan., 1939

Blondie Goes Latin (1941)
 New York Times p. 17, Feb. 26, 1941

Blondie Has Servant Trouble (1940)
 Photoplay 54:44, Aug., 1940

Blondie Hits the Jackpot (1949)
 New York Times p. 28, Sep. 9, 1949

Blondie in Society (1941)
 Child Life 20:364, Aug., 1941

Blondie Johnson (1933)
 New York Times p. 11, Feb. 27, 1933

Blondie Meets the Boss (1939)
 New York Times p. 31, Apr. 27, 1939
 Photoplay 53:62, May, 1939

Blondie of the Follies (1932)
 Fortune 6:56, Dec., 1932
 New York Times p. 19, Sep. 2, 1932

Blood Alley (1955)
 America 94:84, Oct. 15, 1955
 Commonweal 63:64, Oct. 21, 1955
 Library Journal 80:2230, Oct. 15, 1955
 National Parent-Teacher 50:38, Nov., 1955
 New York Times p. 25, Oct. 6, 1955
 Newsweek 46:117, Oct. 10, 1955
 Time 66:112, Oct. 17, 1955

Blood and Roses (1961)
 National Review 12:138, Feb. 27, 1962
 New York Times p. 41, Oct. 12, 1961
 New Yorker 37:179, Oct. 14, 1961
 Newsweek 58:77, Oct. 30, 1961

Blood and Sand (1941)
Commonweal 34:160, Jun. 6, 1941
Nation 152:677, Jun. 7, 1941
New York Times p. 25, May 23, 1941
Newsweek 17:51, Jun. 2, 1941
Scribner's Commentator 10:108, Aug., 1941
Time 37:88+, Jun. 9, 1941

Blood Money (1933)
New York Times p. 30, Nov. 16, 1933
Vanity Fair 41:46, Jan., 1931

Blood of the Vampire (1958)
Commonweal 69:127, Oct. 31, 1958

Blood on the Moon (1948)
Life 25:5, Oct. 4, 1948; 25:71, Nov. 15, 1948
New Republic 119:30, Nov. 29, 1948
New York Times p. 30, Nov. 12, 1948
Newsweek 32:92, Nov. 22, 1948
Rotarian 74:38, Mar., 1949
Time 52:100, Nov. 22, 1948

Blood on the Sun (1945)
Commonweal 42:209, Jul. 13, 1945
Cosmopolitan 118:105, Jun., 1945
Hollywood Quarterly 1:80-84, Oct., 1945
Life 18:49-50+, Jun. 18, 1945
Nation 161:67, Jul. 21, 1945
New York Times p. 12, Jun. 24, 1945
New Yorker 21:37, Jul. 7, 1945
Newsweek 26:101, Jul. 9, 1945
Photoplay 27:20, Apr., 1945
Time 45:88, Jun. 25, 1945
Woman's Home Companion 72:9, Jul., 1945

Bloodhounds of Broadway (1952)
Library Journal 77:2066, Dec. 1, 1952
National Parent-Teacher 47:37, Dec., 1952
New York Times p. 15, Nov. 15, 1952; p. 34, Nov. 25, 1952
Newsweek 40:102, Dec. 15, 1952
Time 60:64, Dec. 1, 1952

Blossoms in the Dust (1941)
Commonweal 34:278, Jul. 11, 1941
New Republic 105:155, Aug. 4, 1941

Blossoms in the Dust (1941) (Continued)
New York Times p. 14, Jun. 27, 1941; IX, p. 3, Jul. 6,
1941
Newsweek 18:51, Jul. 7, 1941
Photoplay 19:24, Sep., 1941
Scribner's Commentator 10:105-6, Sep., 1941
Time 38:66, Jul. 7, 1941

Blossoms on Broadway (1937)
New York Times p. 29, Dec. 3, 1937

Blowing Wild (1953)
Catholic World 178:141, Nov., 1953
National Parent-Teacher 48:36, Nov., 1953
New York Times p. 37, Oct. 8, 1953
New Yorker 29:108, Oct. 17, 1953
Scholastic 63:41, Nov. 11, 1953

Blue Angel (1931)
Canadian Forum 11:357-8, Jun., 1931
Commonweal 13:242, Dec. 31, 1930
Life (NY) 97:20, Jan. 2, 1931
New York Times p. 21, Dec. 26, 1930; IX, p. 4, Dec.
14, 1930
Outlook 156:630, Dec. 17, 1930

Blue Angel (1950)
Commonweal 53:198, Dec. 1, 1950
New Republic 123:21, Nov. 20, 1950
Saturday Review 33:50, Dec. 2, 1950; 35:57, Apr. 12,
1952

Blue Angel (1959)
America 101:678-9, Sep. 5, 1959
Commonweal 70:543, Sep. 25, 1959
New York Times p. 11, Sep. 5, 1959; II, p. 1, Sep. 13,
1959
Newsweek 53:118+, May 25, 1959; 54:118, Sep. 14, 1959
Saturday Review 42:28, Sep. 19, 1959
Time 74:78, Sep. 7, 1959

Blue Bird (1940)
Child Life 19:268, Jun., 1940
Commonweal 31:328, Feb. 2, 1940
Etude 58:207, Mar., 1940
New York Times p. 11, Jan. 20, 1940
Newsweek 15:35, Feb. 5, 1940

Blue Bird (1940) (Continued)
Photoplay 54:68, Apr., 1940
Scholastic 36:36, Feb. 12, 1940
Time 35:60, Feb. 5, 1940

Blue Dahlia (1946)
Commonweal 44:143, May 24, 1946
Cosmopolitan 120:61+, Apr., 1946
Life 21:82, Oct. 28, 1946
Nation 162:701, Jun. 8, 1946
New Republic 114:806, Jun. 3, 1946
New York Times p. 27, May 9, 1946; II, p. 1, May 12, 1946
New Yorker 22:91, May 18, 1946
Newsweek 27:98+, Apr. 22, 1946
Photoplay 28:26, Apr., 1946
Scholastic 48:33, Apr. 15, 1946
Time 47:98+, May 13, 1946

Blue Danube (1928)
New York Times p. 18, Apr. 30, 1928

Blue Danube (1934)
New York Times p. 27, Nov. 8, 1934

Blue Denim (1959)
America 101:638-9, Aug. 22, 1959
Life 47:69-70, Aug. 24, 1959
New York Times p. 12, Jul. 31, 1959
New Yorker 35:86+, Aug. 8, 1959
Newsweek 54:85, Aug. 10, 1959
Saturday Review 42:24, Aug. 15, 1959
Time 74:59, Aug. 10, 1959

Blue Gardenia (1953)
National Parent-Teacher 47:37, May, 1953
New York Times p. 31, Apr. 28, 1953
Time 61:108, Mar. 23, 1953

Blue Hawaii (1961)
Commonweal 75:121, Oct. 27, 1961
New York Times p. 20, Feb. 22, 1962
Seventeen 20:22, Nov., 1961
Senior Scholastic 80:43, Apr. 4, 1962

Blue Lagoon (1949)
Canadian Forum 29:41, May, 1949
Commonweal 50:608, Sep. 30, 1949

Blue Lagoon (1949) (Continued)
New Republic 121:22, Oct. 31, 1949
New York Times p. 13, Oct. 3, 1949
Newsweek 34:80, Aug. 15, 1949
Photoplay 36:25, Aug., 1949
Time 54:100, Sep. 26, 1949

Blue Lamp (1950)
Christian Century 68:511, Apr. 18, 1951
Commonweal 53:376, Jan. 19, 1951
New Republic 124:23, Jan. 29, 1951
New York Times p. 25, Jan. 9, 1951
New Yorker 26:84, Jan. 20, 1951
Newsweek 37:83, Jan. 22, 1951
Time 57:78+, Feb. 5, 1951

Blue Light (1933)
New York Times p. 23, May 9, 1934

Blue Murder at St. Trinian's (1958)
Commonweal 68:404, Jul. 18, 1958
New York Times p. 27, May 27, 1958

Blue Skies (1946)
Commonweal 44:597, Oct. 4, 1946
Cosmopolitan 121:66+, Sep., 1946
Life 21:116-19, Oct. 7, 1946
New York Times p. 28, Oct. 2, 1946; II, p. 1, Oct. 20,
  1946
New Yorker 22:66+, Oct. 12, 1946
Newsweek 28:90, Sep. 30, 1946
Photoplay 29:24, Oct., 1946; 32:42, Mar., 1948
Scholastic 49:37, Sep. 23, 1946
Theatre Arts 30:602, Oct., 1946
Time 48:103, Oct. 14, 1946
Woman's Home Companion 73:11, Nov., 1946

Blue Veil (1951)
Catholic World 174:144, Nov., 1951
Christian Century 68:1391, Nov. 28, 1951
Commonweal 55:118-19, Nov. 9, 1951
Life 31:116, Dec. 10, 1951
New Republic 125:21, Dec. 3, 1951
New York Times p. 10, Oct. 27, 1951
New Yorker 27:152, Nov. 10, 1951
Newsweek 38:94-6, Nov. 5, 1951
Saturday Review 34:28, Nov. 3, 1951
Time 58:122+, Nov. 5, 1951

Bluebeard's Eighth Wife (1938)
New Republic 94:275, Apr. 6, 1938
New York Times p. 21, Mar. 24, 1938
Newsweek 11:25-6, Mar. 28, 1938
Photoplay 52:46-7, Mar., 1938
Stage 15:27, May, 1938
Time 31:38, Mar. 28, 1938

Bluebeard's Ten Honeymoons (1960)
New York Times p. 32, Nov. 8, 1960

Blueprint for Murder (1953)
America 89:467, Aug. 8, 1953
Commonweal 58:467, Aug. 14, 1953
Farm Journal 77:161, Nov., 1953
Holiday 14:99, Nov., 1953
National Parent-Teacher 48:38, Oct., 1953
New York Times p. 8, Jul. 25, 1953
Newsweek 42:76, Aug. 3, 1953
Time 62:96, Aug. 10, 1953

Blueprint for Robbery (1961)
New York Times p. 24, Feb. 2, 1961

Blues in the Night (1941)
Commonweal 35:199, Dec. 12, 1941
Etude 59:811, Dec., 1941
New York Times p. 35, Dec. 12, 1941; IX, p. 7, Dec. 14, 1941

Bob Mathias Story (1954)
America 92:110, Oct. 23, 1954
Farm Journal 78:141, Dec., 1954
National Parent-Teacher 49:38, Dec., 1954
New York Times p. 14, Oct. 16, 1954
Time 64:100, Nov. 1, 1954

Bob, Son of Battle (see Thunder in the Valley)

Boccaccio '70 (1961)
America 107:697-8, Sep. 8, 1962
Catholic World 195:319-20, Aug., 1962
Commonweal 76:401, Jul. 13, 1962
New Republic 147:28-9, Jul. 16, 1962
New York Times p. 40, Jun. 27, 1962; II, p. 1, Jul. 8, 1962
New Yorker 38:64, Jul. 7, 1962
Newsweek 60:73, Jul. 9, 1962

Boccaccio '70 (1961) (Continued)
Saturday Review 45:16, Jul. 7, 1962
Time 79:75, Mar. 23, 1962; 79:60, Jun. 29, 1962

Body and Soul (1931)
Fortune 4:114+, Aug., 1931
Life (NY) 97:21, Apr. 3, 1931
New York Times p. 23, Mar. 14, 1931; VIII, p. 5, Mar. 22, 1931

Body and Soul (1947)
Cosmopolitan 123:168+, Oct., 1947
Good Housekeeping 125:11, Oct., 1947
Hollywood Quarterly 3:63-5, Fall, 1947
Life 23:141-2+, Sep. 29, 1947; 24:58, Mar. 8, 1948
Nation 165:511, Nov. 8, 1947
New Republic 117:35, Dec. 1, 1947
New York Times p. 21, Nov. 10, 1947
New Yorker 23:118, Nov. 15, 1947
Newsweek 30:94, Sep. 29, 1947
Opportunity 26:20-1, Jan., 1948
Photoplay 31:24, Nov., 1947
Scholastic 51:35, Oct. 20, 1947
Theatre Arts 31:52-4, Oct., 1947
Time 50:101, Oct. 20, 1947
Woman's Home Companion 74:10, Oct., 1947

The Body Disappears (1941)
New York Times p. 13, Jan. 31, 1942

Body Snatcher (1945)
Commonweal 42:214, Jun. 15, 1945
New York Times p. 18, May 26, 1945
Newsweek 25:96, Apr. 30, 1945
Time 45:94, May 21, 1945

The Bohemian Girl (1936)
New York Times p. 21, Feb. 17, 1936

Bold and the Brave (1956)
American Magazine 161:8, May, 1956
Commonweal 64:151, May 11, 1956
Life 40:75, Apr. 30, 1956
National Parent-Teacher 50:39, Apr., 1956
New York Times p. 15, May 26, 1956
Newsweek 47:118-19, Apr. 9, 1956
Saturday Review 39:27, Mar. 17, 1956

Bold and the Brave (1956) (Continued)
    Scholastic 68:46, Mar. 1, 1956
    Time 67:104, Apr. 16, 1956

Bolero (1934)
    Canadian Magazine 81:45, May, 1934
    New York Times p. 20, Feb. 17, 1934

Bolshoi Ballet (1957)
    Commonweal 67:312, Dec. 20, 1957
    Dance Magazine 32:36-7, Jan., 1958
    Nation 186:39, Jan. 11, 1958
    New York Times p. 45, Dec. 18, 1957
    Reporter 18:37-8, Feb. 20, 1958
    Theatre Arts 42:81, Feb., 1958

Bomba, the Jungle Boy (1948)
    New York Times p. 11, Apr. 16, 1949
    Rotarian 74:34, Jun., 1949

Bombardier (1943)
    Cosmopolitan 115:66, Aug., 1943
    New York Times p. 15, Jul. 2, 1943
    Newsweek 21:102, Jun. 21, 1943
    Time 41:54+, Jun. 21, 1943

Bombay Clipper (1941)
    New York Times p. 23, Jan. 12, 1942

Bombay Mail (1934)
    New York Times p. 18, Jan. 6, 1934

Bombers B-52 (1957)
    America 98:328, Dec. 7, 1957
    Library Journal 82:3096, Dec. 1, 1957
    National Parent-Teacher 52:33, Dec., 1957
    New York Times p. 11, Nov. 23, 1957
    New Yorker 33:100, Dec. 7, 1957
    Time 70:108, Dec. 9, 1957

Bomber's Moon (1943)
    Commonweal 38:514, Sep. 10, 1943
    New York Times p. 8, Jul. 31, 1943
    Time 42:94, Aug. 16, 1943

Bombs Over Burma (1942)
    New York Times p. 15, Aug. 10, 1942

140

Bombshell (1933)
   Literary Digest 116:35, Nov. 4, 1933
   New York Times p. 11, Oct. 21, 1933; IX, p. 3, Oct. 29,
   1933
   Newsweek 2:28, Oct. 28, 1933

Bon Voyage! (1962)
   America 107:390, Jun. 9, 1962
   Commonweal 76:230, May 25, 1962
   New York Times p. 34, May 18, 1962
   New Yorker 38:133, May 26, 1962
   Newsweek 59:96, May 21, 1962
   Time 79:89-90, May 25, 1962

Bond Street (1950)
   New Republic 122:29, Apr. 17, 1950
   New York Times p. 40, Mar. 30, 1950
   Newsweek 35:96+, Apr. 17, 1950

Bondage (1933)
   New York Times p. 11, Apr. 24, 1933

Bonjour Tristesse (1958)
   America 98:496, Jan. 25, 1958
   Commonweal 67:457, Jan. 31, 1958
   Library Journal 83:396, Feb. 1, 1958
   Nation 186:108, Feb. 1, 1958
   New York Times p. 32, Jan. 16, 1958; II, p. 1, Jan. 19,
   1958
   New Yorker 33:106, Jan. 25, 1958
   Newsweek 51:89, Jan. 20, 1958
   Saturday Review 41:30, Feb. 15, 1958
   Time 71:86, Jan. 20, 1958

*Bonnie Prince Charlie
   Christian Century 69:263, Feb. 27, 1952
   Commonweal 55:375, Jan. 18, 1952
   New York Times p. 14, Jan. 7, 1952
   New Yorker 27:50, Jan. 12, 1952
   Newsweek 39:90, Jan. 21, 1952

Bonzo Goes to College (1952)
   National Parent-Teacher 47:36, Oct., 1952
   Time 60:114+, Oct. 20, 1952

Boogie Man Will Get You (1942)
   New York Times p. 12, Oct. 12, 1942

141

Booloo (1938)
New York Times IX, p. 3, Jun. 19, 1938; p. 10, Jul. 30, 1938

Boom Town (1940)
Commonweal 32:429, Sep. 13, 1940
Cosmopolitan 117:49, Aug., 1944
New Republic 103:246, Aug. 19, 1940
New York Times p. 25, Sep. 6, 1940; IX, p. 3, Sep. 8, 1940
Newsweek 16:62, Sep. 9, 1940
Photoplay 54:67, Oct., 1940
Time 36:48, Aug. 26, 1940

Boomerang (1947)
Commonweal 45:566, Mar. 21, 1947; 24:60, Mar. 8, 1949
Cosmopolitan 122:67+, Apr., 1947
Holiday 2:174, May, 1947
Life 22:87-8+, Mar. 24, 1947
Nation 164:340, Mar. 22, 1947
New Republic 116:39, Feb. 17, 1947
New York Times p. 36, Mar. 6, 1947; II, p. 1, Mar. 9, 1947
New Yorker 23:64+, Mar. 15, 1947
Newsweek 29:100, Mar. 17, 1947
Photoplay 32:41, Mar., 1948
Scholastic 50:37, Mar. 17, 1947
Time 49:97, Mar. 10, 1947

Boot Polish (1959)
New York Times p. 15, Aug. 18, 1958
Time 72:90+, Sep. 15, 1958

Boots and Saddles (1937)
New York Times p. 19, Nov. 8, 1937

Boots Malone (1951)
Nation 174:332-3, Apr. 5, 1952
New York Times p. 26, Mar. 13, 1952; II, p. 1, Mar. 16, 1952
New Yorker 28:115, Mar. 22, 1952
Newsweek 39:78, Feb. 4, 1952
Saturday Review 35:24, Jan. 26, 1952
Theatre Arts 36:90, Feb., 1952
Time 59:72+, Feb. 4, 1952

Border Cafe (1937)
Literary Digest 123:22, Jun. 12, 1937

Border Cafe (1937) (Continued)
New York Times p. 30, Jun. 8, 1937

Border Flight (1936)
New York Times p. 22, Jun. 2, 1936

Border Incident (1949)
New York Times p. 29, Nov. 21, 1949

Border Legion (1930)
Life (NY) 96:17, Aug. 1, 1930
New York Times p. 9, Jun. 28, 1930; VIII, p. 3, Jul. 16,
1930

Border Patrolman (1936)
New York Times p. 11, Jun. 29, 1936

Border River (1954)
National Parent-Teacher 48:39, Mar., 1954

Border Romance (1930)
New York Times p. 25, May 26, 1930

*Border Street
New Republic 122:21, May 1, 1950
New York Times p. 35, Apr. 26, 1950
New Yorker 26:70+, May 6, 1950

Borderline (1950)
Christian Century 67:255, Feb. 22, 1950
Commonweal 51:630, Mar. 24, 1950
New York Times p. 17, Mar. 6, 1950
Time 55:104, Mar. 27, 1950

Bordertown (1935)
New York Times p. 22, Jan. 24, 1935; VIII, p. 5, Feb.
3, 1935
Newsweek 5:32, Jan. 12, 1935

Born for Glory (1935)
New York Times p. 22, Oct. 21, 1935

Born Reckless (1930)
Life (NY) 95:17, Jun. 27, 1930
New York Times p. 10, Jun. 7, 1930; VIII, p. 5, Jun.
15, 1930

Born Reckless (1937)
New York Times p. 22, Jul. 30, 1937

Born to Be Bad (1934)
New York Times p. 22, May 31, 1934

Born to Be Bad (1950)
Library Journal 75:1843, Oct. 15, 1950
New York Times p. 31, Sep. 29, 1950
New Yorker 26:125, Oct. 7, 1950
Newsweek 36:86, Oct. 2, 1950
Time 56:103, Sep. 18, 1950

Born to Dance (1936)
New York Times p. 16, Dec. 5, 1936
Newsweek 8:32+, Dec. 12, 1936
Time 28:26, Dec. 7, 1936

Born to Kill (1947)
New York Times p. 34, May 1, 1947; p. 41, Oct. 9, 1957
New Yorker 33:88, Oct. 19, 1957
Newsweek 29:103, May 12, 1947

Born to Love (1931)
New York Times p. 23, Apr. 25, 1931; VIII, p. 5, May
    3, 1931

Born to Sing (1941)
Commonweal 35:489, Mar. 6, 1942
New York Times p. 23, Feb. 19, 1942

Born Yesterday (1951)
Christian Century 68:191, Feb. 7, 1951
Commonweal 53:301-2, Dec. 29, 1950
Library Journal 76:124, Jan. 15, 1951
Nation 172:114, Feb. 3, 1951
New Republic 124:31, Jan. 15, 1951
New York Times II, p. 6, Sep. 10, 1950; II, p. 7, Jan.
    15, 1950; p. 30, Dec. 27, 1950; II, p. 1, Jan. 7, 1951
New Yorker 26:51, Dec. 23, 1950
Newsweek 37:57, Jan. 1, 1951
Rotarian 78:40, Apr., 1951
Saturday Review 34:26, Jan. 6, 1951
Time 56:56-7, Dec. 25, 1950

Borneo (1937)
New York Times p. 8, Sep. 4, 1937

Boss (1956)
    National Parent-Teacher 51:39, Nov., 1956
    New York Times p. 18, Sep. 1, 1956
    Saturday Review 39:38, Oct. 6, 1956

Botany Bay (1953)
    America 90:186, Nov. 14, 1953
    Farm Journal 78:83, Jan., 1954
    Library Journal 78:2009, Nov. 15, 1953
    New York Times p. 27, Oct. 30, 1953
    New Yorker 29:171, Nov. 7, 1953
    Newsweek 42:98, Nov. 9, 1953
    Saturday Review 36:37, Nov. 7, 1953
    Time 62:110+, Nov. 9, 1953

Both Sides of the Law (1954)
    Catholic World 178:383, Feb., 1954
    Commonweal 59:525, Feb. 26, 1954
    National Parent-Teacher 48:39, Feb., 1954
    New York Times p. 19, Jan. 12, 1954
    Saturday Review 37:28, Mar. 13, 1954

Bottom of the Bottle (1956)
    America 94:543, Feb. 11, 1956
    Catholic World 182:463, Mar., 1956
    Commonweal 63:516, Feb. 17, 1956
    Library Journal 81:523, Feb. 15, 1956
    National Parent-Teacher 50:39, Apr., 1956
    New York Times p. 19, Feb. 2, 1956
    Newsweek 47:108, Feb. 20, 1956
    Time 67:94+, Feb. 20, 1956

Bottoms Up (1934)
    New York Times p. 29, Mar. 23, 1934; X, p. 3, Apr. 1,
        1934
    Newsweek 3:34, Mar. 31, 1934

The Boudoir Diplomat (1930)
    New York Times p. 26, Dec. 8, 1930

Bought (1931)
    New York Times p. 18, Aug. 15, 1931

Boulder Dam (1936)
    New York Times p. 17, Mar. 30, 1936
    Scholastic 28:26, Mar. 28, 1936

Bounty Hunter (1954)
 Farm Journal 78:137, Oct., 1954
 National Parent-Teacher 49:39, Nov., 1954

Bouquets from Nicholas (1939)
 New York Times p. 19, Mar. 2, 1939

Bowery (1933)
 New Outlook 162:42, Nov., 1933
 New York Times IX, p. 3, Jul. 23, 1933; IX, p. 4, Oct.
  1, 1933; p. 24, Oct. 5, 1933; IX, p. 3, Oct. 15, 1933

Bowery Blitzkrieg (1941)
 New York Times p. 24, Oct. 1, 1941

Bowery to Broadway (1944)
 Commonweal 41:231, Dec. 15, 1944
 New York Times p. 19, Nov. 30, 1944; II, p. 5, Dec. 10,
  1944
 Newsweek 24:111, Nov. 13, 1944

Boy and the Pirates (1960)
 New York Times p. 48, Nov. 24, 1960
 Saturday Review 43:36, Apr. 9, 1960

Boy from Indiana (1950)
 Rotarian 78:38, May, 1951

Boy from Oklahoma (1954)
 Commonweal 59:600, Mar. 19, 1954
 National Parent-Teacher 48:38, Jan., 1954
 Time 63:100, Mar. 8, 1954

Boys in Brown (1949)
 Library Journal 75:991, Jun. 1, 1950

Boy Meets Girl (1938)
 Commonweal 28:505, Sep. 9, 1938
 New York Times p. 7, Aug. 27, 1938; X, p. 3, Sep. 4,
  1938
 Newsweek 12:22-3, Sep. 5, 1938
 Time 32:32, Sep. 5, 1938

Boy of the Streets (1937)
 Literary Digest p. 34, Dec. 25, 1937
 New Republic 93:256-7, Jan. 5, 1938
 New York Times p. 17, Jan. 24, 1938
 Scholastic 31:36, Dec. 18, 1937

Boy of the Streets (1937) (Continued)
    Theatre Arts 22:417, Jan., 1938
    Time 30:51, Dec. 20, 1937

Boy on a Dolphin (1957)
    America 97:180, May 4, 1957
    Commonweal 66:127, May 3, 1957
    Library Journal 82:1193, May 1, 1957
    National Parent-Teacher 51:37, Jun., 1957
    Natural History 66:332, Jun., 1957
    New York Times p. 21, Apr. 20, 1957
    New Yorker 33:68, Apr. 27, 1957
    Newsweek 49:122, Apr. 22, 1957
    Saturday Review 40:27, May 11, 1957
    Time 69:108, Apr. 22, 1957

Boy Slaves (1939)
    Commonweal 29:413, Feb. 3, 1939
    Nation 148:159, Feb. 4, 1939
    New Republic 98:129-30, Mar. 8, 1939
    New York Times p. 17, Feb. 9, 1939
    Photoplay 53:53, Apr., 1939
    Scholastic 34:33, Feb. 11, 1939

Boy Who Stole a Million (1960)
    New York Times p. 18, Dec. 22, 1960

Boy With Green Hair (1949)
    Collier's 123:36, Jan. 15, 1949
    Commonweal 49:378, Jan. 21, 1949
    Life 25:3, Jul. 12, 1948; 25:82-4, Dec. 6, 1948
    New Republic 120:29, Jan. 17, 1949
    New York Times p. 26, Jan. 13, 1949; II, p. 1, Jan. 16,
        1949
    New Yorker 24:55, Jan. 15, 1949
    Newsweek 33:74, Jan. 17, 1949
    Photoplay 34:21, Feb., 1949
    Rotarian 74:36, Apr., 1949
    Scholastic 53:25, Jan. 19, 1949
    Time 53:84, Jan. 10, 1949

Boys from Syracuse (1940)
    Commonweal 32:331, Aug. 9, 1940
    Etude 58:519, Aug., 1940
    Life 5:43-4, Dec. 12, 1938; 6:30, Feb. 6, 1939
    Nation 147:638, Dec. 10, 1938
    New Republic 97:173, Dec. 14, 1938
    New York Times p. 25, Aug. 1, 1940

Boys from Syracuse (1940) (Continued)
  Newsweek 12:24, Dec. 5, 1938; 16:35, Aug. 5, 1940
  Stage 16:16-17, Nov., 1938; 16:41, Dec., 1938
  Theatre Arts 23:7-8+, Jan., 1939; 23:197, Mar., 1939;
    23:398, Jun., 1939
  Time 32:35, Dec. 5, 1938; 36:56, Aug. 5, 1940
  Vogue 93:52-3, Jan. 1, 1939

Boys' Night Out (1961)
  America 107:470, Jul. 7, 1962
  Commonweal 76:377, Jul. 6, 1962
  New Republic 146:28, Jun. 25, 1962
  New York Times p. 15, Jun. 22, 1962
  New Yorker 38:68, Jun. 30, 1962
  Newsweek 59:88, Jun. 25, 1962
  Saturday Review 45:31, Jun. 30, 1962

Boys' Ranch (1946)
  Commonweal 44:479, Aug. 30, 1946
  New York Times p. 12, Aug. 19, 1946

Boy's School (1939)
  New York Times p. 26, Jun. 26, 1939

Boys' Town (1938)
  Canadian Magazine 90:55, Oct., 1938
  Commonweal 28:561, Sep. 23, 1938
  New Republic 96:188, Sep. 21, 1938
  New York Times p. 25, Sep. 9, 1938; X, p. 3, Sep. 11,
    1938
  Newsweek 12:23, Sep. 19, 1938
  Photoplay 52:22-3+, Nov., 1938
  Scholastic 33:13, Oct. 1, 1938
  Time 32:45, Sep. 12, 1938

Bramble Bush (1960)
  America 102:623, Feb. 20, 1960
  Commonweal 71:595, Feb. 26, 1960
  McCalls 87:6, Mar., 1960
  New York Times p. 34, Feb. 25, 1960
  Saturday Review 43:29, Feb. 20, 1960

Branded (1951)
  Christian Century 68:254, Feb. 21, 1951
  Commonweal 53:399, Jan. 26, 1951
  Nation 172:114, Feb. 3, 1951
  New York Times p. 28, Jan. 11, 1955

Branded (1951) (Continued)
Saturday Review 34:30, Feb. 17, 1951
Time 57:78, Jan. 15, 1951

Branded Men (1931)
New York Times p. 23, Dec. 12, 1931

Brandy for the Parson (1952)
New York Times p. 13, Apr. 18, 1952
New Yorker 28:53, Aug. 30, 1952
Newsweek 40:95, Sep. 8, 1952
Theatre Arts 36:96, Oct., 1952

Brasher Doubloon (1947)
New Republic 116:32, Jun. 16, 1947
New York Times p. 34, May 22, 1947
Newsweek 29:96, Apr. 21, 1947
Scholastic 50:43, May 12, 1947
Time 49:97, Jun. 2, 1947

Brass Bottle (1963)
Commonweal 80:91, Apr. 10, 1964
New York Times p. 42, May 21, 1964

Brat (1931)
New York Times p. 13, Aug. 24, 1931

Bravados (1958)
America 99:378, Jun. 28, 1958
Catholic World 187:383, Aug., 1958
Commonweal 68:351, Jul. 4, 1958
New York Times p. 23, Jun. 26, 1958; II, p. 1, Jun. 29,
1958
Saturday Review 41:31, Jun. 21, 1958
Time 72:66, Jul. 28, 1958

Brave Bulls (1951)
Christian Century 68:927, Aug. 8, 1951
Commonweal 54:90, May 4, 1951
Library Journal 76:785, May 1, 1951
Nation 172:497, May 26, 1951
New York Times p. 39, Apr. 19, 1951; II, p. 1, Apr. 22,
1951
New Yorker 27:118+, Apr. 21, 1951
Saturday Review 34:26-7, May 5, 1951
Scholastic 58:29, May 9, 1951
Time 57:106, Apr. 23, 1951

149

Brave Don't Cry (1952)
Christian Century 70:335, Mar. 18, 1953
National Parent-Teacher 47:37, Jan., 1953
New York Times p. 37, Nov. 6, 1952
Newsweek 40:92+, Dec. 8, 1952
Time 60:112, Nov. 24, 1952

Brave One (1956)
America 96:360, Dec. 22, 1956
Catholic World 183:465, Sep., 1956
Commonweal 65:254, Dec. 7, 1956
Holiday 20:197, Nov., 1956
National Parent-Teacher 51:38, Sep., 1956
New York Times p. 26, Mar. 22, 1957
New Yorker 33:128, Mar. 30, 1957
Newsweek 48:132+, Oct. 15, 1956
Saturday Review 39:59, Oct. 20, 1956
Time 69:104+, Mar. 18, 1957

Brazil (1944)
Commonweal 41:231, Dec. 15, 1944
New York Times p. 25, Nov. 20, 1944; II, p. 5, Dec. 10,
1944

Bread, Love and Dreams (1954)
Commonweal 60:557, Sep. 10, 1954
Life 37:125, Sep. 20, 1954
National Parent-Teacher 49:39, Nov., 1954
New York Times p. 24, Sep. 21, 1954; II, p. 1, Sep. 26,
1954
New York Times Magazine p. 54, Aug. 15, 1954
New Yorker 30:131, Oct. 2, 1954
Newsweek 44:85-6, Oct. 4, 1954
Reporter 11:42, Oct. 21, 1954
Saturday Review 37:26, Sep. 4, 1954; 38:63, Jan. 1, 1955
Time 64:100+, Oct. 4, 1954

Break of Hearts (1935)
Literary Digest 119:25, Jun. 1, 1935
New York Times p. 24, May 17, 1935
Newsweek 5:34, May 25, 1935
Time 25:34, May 27, 1935

Break the News (1941)
Nation 160:314, Mar. 17, 1945
New York Times p. 24, Jan. 2, 1941

Break to Freedom (1955)
National Parent-Teacher 50:39, Sep., 1955

Breakfast at Tiffany's (1961)
America 106:310-11, Nov. 25, 1961
Commonweal 75:93, Oct. 20, 1961
Esquire 56:64+, Dec., 1961
Life 51:133-6+, Sep. 8, 1961
New Republic 145:28, Sep. 18, 1961
New York Times II, p. 7, Oct. 9, 1960; p. 28, Oct. 6, 1961
New Yorker 37:198-9, Oct. 16, 1961
Newsweek 58:114, Oct. 16, 1961
Saturday Review 44:28, Sep. 30, 1961
Time 78:94, Oct. 20, 1961

Breakfast for Two (1937)
New York Times p. 21, Nov. 20, 1937

Breakfast in Hollywood (1946)
Commonweal 44:16, Apr. 19, 1946
New York Times p. 21, Jul. 15, 1946
Newsweek 27:92, Feb. 11, 1946

Breaking Point (1950)
Commonweal 53:14, Oct. 13, 1950
Library Journal 75:1677, Oct. 1, 1950
New York Times p. 10, Oct. 7, 1950
New Yorker 26:129, Oct. 21, 1950
Newsweek 36:92, Oct. 16, 1950
Time 56:96, Sep. 25, 1950

Breaking the Ice (1938)
New York Times IX, p. 3, Jul. 31, 1938; p. 35, Sep. 23, 1938

Breaking Through the Sound Barrier (1952)
American Photographer 47:15, Mar., 1953
Catholic World 176:222-3, Dec., 1952
Christian Century 69:1487, Dec. 17, 1952
Commonweal 57:141, Nov. 14, 1952
National Parent-Teacher 47:37, Jan., 1953
New York Times II, p. 5, Aug. 24, 1952; p. 19, Nov. 7, 1952; II, p. 1, Nov. 16, 1952
New Yorker 28:68, Aug. 30, 1952; 28:107, Nov. 22, 1952
Newsweek 40:82, Dec. 1, 1952
Saturday Review 35:38, Nov. 22, 1952

Breaking Through the Sound Barrier (1952) (Continued)
    Scholastic 61:25, Dec. 10, 1952
    Time 60:120+, Nov. 10, 1952

Breakout (1960)
    New York Times p. 44, May 19, 1960

Breakthrough (1950)
    Christian Century 68:95, Jan. 17, 1951
    Commonweal 53:232, Dec. 8, 1950
    Good Housekeeping 131:17+, Dec., 1950
    New Republic 123:29, Dec. 11, 1950
    New York Times p. 10, Nov. 18, 1950
    Newsweek 36:84, Nov. 27, 1950
    Rotarian 78:36, Mar., 1951
    Saturday Review 33:28-9, Dec. 9, 1950
    Time 56:101, Dec. 11, 1950

Breath of Scandal (1960)
    Commonweal 73:437, Jan. 20, 1961
    Life 49:129-30, Nov. 14, 1960
    New York Times p. 19, Dec. 17, 1960
    Newsweek 56:57, Dec. 26, 1960
    Time 77:42, Jan. 6, 1961

Breathless (1961)
    Commentary 30:230-2, Sep., 1960
    Commonweal 73:533, Feb. 17, 1961
    Esquire 56:20+, Jul., 1961
    Mademoiselle 52:52, Apr., 1961
    Nation 192:223, Mar. 11, 1961
    New Republic 144:20, Feb. 13, 1961
    New York Times p. 26, Feb. 8, 1961; II, p. 1, Feb. 12,
        1961
    New Yorker 36:102-4, Feb. 11, 1961
    Newsweek 57:84, Feb. 6, 1961
    Time 77:62, Feb. 17, 1961

Breezing Home (1937)
    New York Times p. 23, Mar. 20, 1937

Brewster's Millions (1933)
    New York Times IX, p. 4, Mar. 31, 1935; p. 23, Apr. 8,
        1935

Brewster's Millions (1945)
    Commonweal 42:94, May 11, 1945

Brewster's Millions (1945) (Continued)
    Musician 50:28, Feb., 1945
    New York Times p. 23, Apr. 27, 1945
    New Yorker 21:48, May 5, 1945
    Newsweek 25:113, Mar. 26, 1945

Bribe (1949)
    New Republic 120:31, Feb. 21, 1949
    New York Times p. 31, Feb. 4, 1949
    New Yorker 24:70, Feb. 12, 1949
    Newsweek 33:78, Feb. 14, 1949
    Rotarian 74:34, Jun., 1949
    Time 53:84, Feb. 7, 1949

Bridal Path (1959)
    America 102:537, Jan. 30, 1960
    New York Times p. 34, Dec. 21, 1959
    Time 74:44, Dec. 28, 1959

Bridal Suite (1939)
    New York Times p. 20, May 26, 1939
    Photoplay 53:62, Jul., 1939

Bride by Mistake (1944)
    Commonweal 40:615, Oct. 13, 1944
    New York Times p. 20, Sep. 16, 1944
    Time 44:96, Oct. 9, 1944

Bride Came C.O.D. (1941)
    Commonweal 34:352, Aug. 1, 1941
    New Republic 105:85, Jul. 21, 1941
    New York Times p. 18, Jul. 26, 1941
    Newsweek 18:53, Jul. 21, 1941
    Scribner's Commentator 10:105-6, Oct., 1941
    Time 38:74, Jul. 28, 1941

Bride Comes Home (1936)
    Canadian Magazine 85:38, Feb., 1936
    Commonweal 23:244, Dec. 27, 1935
    New York Times p. 30, Dec. 25, 1935
    Time 27:28, Jan. 6, 1936

Bride Comes to Yellow Sky (see Face to Face)

Bride for Sale (1949)
    New York Times p. 29, Nov. 21, 1949
    Newsweek 34:83, Dec. 5, 1949

Bride for Sale (1949) (Continued)
Rotarian 76:38, Feb., 1950
Time 54:53, Dec. 26, 1949

Bride Goes Wild (1948)
Commonweal 48:675, Apr. 30, 1948
New York Times p. 27, Jun. 4, 1948
Photoplay 33:20, Jun., 1948
Time 51:96, Jun. 21, 1948

Bride of Frankenstein (1935)
New Republic 83:75, May 29, 1935
New York Times VIII, p. 4, Feb. 3, 1935
Newsweek 5:25, May 4, 1935
Time 25:52, Apr. 29, 1935

Bride of the Lake (1934)
New York Times p. 24, Sep. 11, 1934

Bride of the Regiment (1930)
New York Times p. 32, May 22, 1930
Theatre Magazine 52:47, Jul., 1930

Bride of Vengeance (1949)
Good Housekeeping 128:267, May, 1949
New York Times p. 38, Apr. 7, 1949; II, p. 1, Apr. 10, 1949
Newsweek 33:91, Apr. 25, 1949
Time 53:100, Apr. 25, 1949

Bride Walks Out (1936)
New York Times p. 15, Jul. 10, 1936
Time 28:36, Jul. 20, 1936

Bride Wore Boots (1946)
Commonweal 44:167, May 31, 1946
Life 21:81, Oct. 28, 1946
New York Times p. 16, Jun. 6, 1946
Newsweek 27:93, Jun. 10, 1946
Time 47:98+, Jun. 3, 1946

Bride Wore Crutches (1941)
New York Times p. 15, May 26, 1941

Bride Wore Red (1937)
Commonweal 26:580, Oct. 15, 1937
New York Times p. 18, Oct. 15, 1937; X, p. 5, Oct. 31, 1937

Bride Wore Red (1937) (Continued)
Scholastic 31:37, Oct. 23, 1937
Time 30:29, Oct. 18, 1937

Brides Are Like That (1936)
New York Times p. 22, Mar. 23, 1936
Time 27:34, Mar. 30, 1936

The Brides of Dracula (1960)
New York Times p. 41, Sep. 6, 1960

Bridge (1961)
America 105:493, Jul. 1, 1961
Commonweal 74:128, Apr. 28, 1961
Coronet 50:14, Jul., 1961
Modern Photographer 25:25-6, May, 1961
Nation 192:420, May 13, 1961
New Republic 144:20, May 15, 1961
New York Times p. 42, May 2, 1961; II, p. 1, May 14,
    1961
New Yorker 37:167, May 13, 1961
Newsweek 57:94+, May 8, 1961
Saturday Review 44:37, May 20, 1961
Time 77:78, May 12, 1961

Bridge of San Luis Rey (1930)
New York Times p. 22, May 20, 1929; IX, p. 7, May 26,
    1929
Outlook 152:235, Jun. 5, 1929

Bridge of San Luis Rey (1944)
Cosmopolitan 116:112, Mar., 1944
New York Times p. 19, Mar. 3, 1944
New Yorker 20:46+, Mar. 4, 1944
Scholastic 44:38, Mar. 27, 1944

Bridge on the River Kwai (1957)
America 98:403, Jan. 4, 1958
Commonweal 67:311, Dec. 20, 1957
Coronet 43:14, Feb., 1958
Cosmopolitan 144:78, Jan., 1958
Library Journal 82:3199, Dec. 15, 1957
Life 43:109-10+, Dec. 9, 1957
Look 21:41-2, Dec. 24, 1957
Nation 186:38, Jan. 11, 1958
National Parent-Teacher 52:39, Feb., 1958
New Republic 138:22, Jan. 27, 1958

Bridge on the River Kwai (1957) (Continued)
New York Times II, p. 7, Jan. 6, 1957; VI, p. 44-5,
    Nov. 24, 1957; II, p. 7, Dec. 15, 1957; p. 39, Dec.
    19, 1957; II, p. 3, Dec. 22, 1957; II, p. 1, Jan. 12,
    1958
New Yorker 33:48, Dec. 28, 1957
Newsweek 50:77, Dec. 23, 1957
Reporter 18:36-7, Feb. 6, 1958
Saturday Review 40:23, Dec. 14, 1957
Senior Scholastic 71:27, Jan. 14, 1958
Time 70:70+, Dec. 23, 1957

Bridge to the Sun (1961)
America 106:104-5, Oct. 21, 1961
Commonweal 75:70-1, Oct. 13, 1961
New York Times p. 50, Oct. 18, 1961
Redbook 118:24+, Nov., 1961
Saturday Review 44:31, Oct. 28, 1961
Senior Scholastic 79:32, Sep. 20, 1961
Time 78:56, Oct. 27, 1961

Bridges at Toko-Ri (1954)
America 92:463, Jan. 29, 1955
Catholic World 180:381, Feb., 1955
Commonweal 61:477, Feb. 4, 1955
Farm Journal 79:149, Feb., 1955
Library Journal 80:150, Jan. 15, 1955
Life 38:91-2+, Feb. 7, 1955
Look 19:92+, Feb. 8, 1955
National Parent-Teacher 49:39, Jan., 1955
New Republic 132:28-9, Mar. 14, 1955
New York Times p. 20, Jan. 21, 1953; II, p. 1, Jan. 23,
    1953
New Yorker 30:82+, Jan. 29, 1955
Newsweek 45:86, Jan. 17, 1955
Saturday Review 38:43, Jan. 22, 1955
Time 65:75, Jan. 24, 1955

Brief Encounter (1946)
Commonweal 44:526-7, Sep. 13, 1946
Life 22:94, Mar. 10, 1947
Nation 163:249, Aug. 31, 1946
New Republic 115:518-19, Oct. 21, 1946
New York Times p. 21, Aug. 21, 1946; II, p. 21, Sep.
    15, 1946; II, p. 1, Nov. 17, 1946
New Yorker 22:48, Sep. 7, 1946
Newsweek 28:76, Sep. 2, 1946

Brief Encounter (1946) (Continued)
Saturday Review 29:36-7, Oct. 12, 1946
Theatre Arts 30:596, 604, Oct., 1946
Time 48:102+, Sep. 9, 1946

Brief Moment (1933)
New York Times p. 18, Sep. 30, 1933; X, p. 3, Oct. 8, 1933

Brigadoon (1954)
America 91:600, Sep. 18, 1954
Catholic World 180:66, Oct., 1954
Commonweal 61:37-8, Oct. 15, 1954
Farm Journal 78:137, Oct., 1954
Library Journal 79:1755, Oct. 1, 1954
Look 18:74-5, Oct. 5, 1954
National Parent-Teacher 49:38, Oct., 1954
New York Times p. 18, Sep. 17, 1954
New Yorker 30:61, Sep. 25, 1954
Newsweek 44:108-9, Sep. 13, 1954
Saturday Review 37:26, Sep. 25, 1954
Scholastic 65:45, Sep. 29, 1954
Time 64:103, Oct. 4, 1954
Woman's Home Companion 81:10-11, Aug., 1954

Brigand (1952)
Christian Century 69:1239, Oct. 22, 1952
New York Times p. 9, Jul. 26, 1952

Brigham Young (1940)
Commonweal 32:449, Sep. 20, 1940
Life 9:59-62, Sep. 23, 1940
New York Times p. 13, Sep. 21, 1940
Newsweek 16:51-2, Sep. 23, 1940
Photoplay 54:68, Nov., 1940
Theatre Arts 24:728, Oct., 1940
Time 36:63, Oct. 7, 1940

Bright Eyes (1934)
New York Times p. 31, Dec. 21, 1934; VIII, p. 4, Feb. 3,
    1935; X, p. 4, Apr. 28, 1935

Bright Leaf (1950)
Christian Century 67:903, Jul. 26, 1950
Good Housekeeping 130:143, Jun., 1950
Library Journal 75:885, May 15, 1950
New York Times p. 7, Jun. 17, 1950
New Yorker 26:76, Jun. 24, 1950

Bright Leaf (1950) (Continued)
Newsweek 36:69, Jul. 3, 1950
Rotarian 77:38, Sep., 1950
Time 55:94, Jun. 26, 1950

Bright Lights (1935)
Literary Digest 120:26, Aug. 24, 1935
New York Times p. 15, Aug. 15, 1935
Time 26:27, Aug. 26, 1935

Bright Road (1953)
America 89:175, May 9, 1953
Catholic World 177:145, May, 1953
Commonweal 58:73, Apr. 24, 1953
Library Journal 78:806, May 1, 1953
Nation 176:461, May 30, 1953
National Parent-Teacher 47:37, May, 1953
New York Times p. 33, Apr. 29, 1953
Newsweek 41:108, Apr. 27, 1953
Saturday Review 36:29, Apr. 25, 1953
Time 61:114+, Apr. 20, 1953

Bright Victory (1951)
Christian Century 68:1263, Oct. 31, 1951
Commonweal 54:454, Aug. 17, 1951
Life 31:77-8, Sep. 3, 1951
Nation 173:118, Aug. 11, 1951
New Republic 125:21, Aug. 27, 1951
New York Times p. 19, Aug. 1, 1951; II, p. 1, Aug. 12,
    1951
New Yorker 27:62, Aug. 4, 1951
Newsweek 38:84, Jul. 23, 1951
Saturday Review 34:26, Jul. 21, 1951
Scholastic 59:35, Sep. 19, 1951
Time 58:98+, Aug. 13, 1951

Brighton Strangler (1944)
New York Times p. 15, May 19, 1945
New Yorker 21:39, May 26, 1945

Brimstone (1949)
New York Times p. 35, Oct. 7, 1949

Bring 'Em Back Alive (1932)
Commonweal 16:351, Aug. 3, 1932
Nation 135:18, Jul. 6, 1932
New York Times p. 9, Jun. 18, 1932; IX, p. 3, Jun. 26,
    1932

Bring on the Girls (1945)
Cosmopolitan 118:95, Apr., 1945
Nation 160:257, Mar. 3, 1945
New Republic 113:287, Sep. 3, 1945
New York Times p. 25, Mar. 1, 1945
New Yorker 21:48, Mar. 10, 1945
Newsweek 25:106, Mar. 12, 1945
Time 45:92, Mar. 5, 1945

Bring Your Smile Along (1955)
National Parent-Teacher 50:38, Sep., 1955

Bringing Up Baby (1938)
Commonweal 27:524, Mar. 4, 1938
Good Housekeeping 106:52-3, Jun., 1938
Life 4:22-3, Feb. 28, 1938
New Republic 94:165, Mar. 16, 1938
New York Times p. 17, Mar. 4, 1938; XI, p. 5, Mar. 13, 1938
Saint Nicholas 65:42, Apr., 1938
Stage 15:27, May, 1938
Theatre Arts 22:417, Jun., 1938
Time 31:38, Mar. 7, 1938

Brink of Life (1959)
Nation 189:408, Nov. 28, 1959
New York Times p. 36, Nov. 9, 1959
New Yorker 35:172-3, Nov. 21, 1959
Newsweek 54:116, Nov. 23, 1959
Reporter 21:33, Dec. 24, 1959
Saturday Review 42:32, Nov. 14, 1959

British Agent (1934)
Canadian Magazine 82:36, Nov., 1934
Literary Digest 118:29, Sep. 29, 1934
New York Times p. 20, Sep. 20, 1934
Photoplay 46:40-41, Oct., 1934

British Intelligence (1940)
New York Times p. 14, Feb. 12, 1940

Broad Minded (1931)
Life (NY) 98:18, Jul. 24, 1931
New York Times p. 24, Jul. 6, 1931

Broadway (1929, 1942)
Commonweal 36:207, Jun. 19, 1942
Life (NY) 93:27, Jun. 14, 1929

Broadway (1929, 1942) (Continued)
New York Times p. 23, Jun. 5, 1942
Outlook 152:435, Jul. 10, 1929
Time 39:50, May 25, 1942

Broadway Babies (1929)
Life (NY) 94:28, Jul. 12, 1929
New York Times VIII, p. 3, Jun. 30, 1929

Broadway Bill (1934)
Literary Digest 118:36, Dec. 15, 1934
New Republic 81:167, Dec. 19, 1934
New York Times p. 22, Nov. 30, 1934
Newsweek 4:26, Dec. 8, 1934
Time 24:28, Dec. 10, 1934

Broadway Gondolier (1935)
New York Times p. 15, Jul. 18, 1935; IX, p. 3, Jul. 21, 1935
Time 26:42, Jul. 29, 1935

Broadway Hostess (1935)
New York Times p. 23, Dec. 16, 1935

Broadway Limited (1941)
New York Times IX, p. 3, Oct. 6, 1940; p. 11, Jun. 16, 1941

The Broadway Melody (1929)
Life (NY) 93:21, Mar. 22, 1929
New York Times p. 15, Feb. 9, 1929; IX, p. 7, Feb. 17, 1929; VIII, p. 3, Jun. 30, 1929; X, p. 8, Dec. 1, 1929
Outlook 151:382, Mar. 6, 1929

Broadway Melody of 1936 (1935)
Canadian Magazine 84:41, Nov., 1935
New Republic 84:216, Oct. 2, 1935
New York Times p. 28, Sep. 19, 1935
Stage 13:6, Oct., 1935
Time 26:46, Sep. 23, 1935

Broadway Melody of 1938 (1937)
New York Times p. 12, Sep. 3, 1937
Time 30:23-4, Aug. 30, 1937

Broadway Melody of 1940 (1940)
Commonweal 31:413, Mar. 1, 1940
New York Times p. 25, Mar. 29, 1940

160

Broadway Melody of 1940 (1940) (Continued)
Photoplay 54:68, Apr., 1940
Time 35:69, Mar. 4, 1940

Broadway Musketeers (1938)
New York Times p. 27, Oct. 14, 1938

Broadway Rhythm (1944)
Commonweal 39:521, Mar. 10, 1944
New York Times p. 24, Apr. 14, 1944; II, p. 3, Apr.
23, 1944
Photoplay 24:19, Apr., 1944
Time 43:54, May 8, 1944

Broadway Scandals (1929)
Life (NY) 94:22, Nov. 29, 1929
New York Times p. 35, Oct. 29, 1929; IX, p. 6, Nov. 3,
1929

Broadway Serenade (1939)
New York Times p. 25, Apr. 7, 1939
Photoplay 53:59, Jun., 1939

Broadway Through a Keyhole (1933)
New York Times p. 18, Nov. 2, 1933; IX, p. 4, Nov. 12,
1933
Newsweek 2:29, Nov. 11, 1933

Broadway to Hollywood (1933)
New York Times p. 14, Sep. 2, 1933
Newsweek 2:31, Sep. 9, 1933

Broken Arrow (1950)
Christian Century 67:1087, Sep. 13, 1950
Commonweal 52:413, Aug. 4, 1950
Good Housekeeping 131:16, Sep., 1950
Library Journal 75:991, Jun. 1, 1950
New Republic 123:23, Jul. 31, 1950
New York Times p. 15, Jul. 21, 1950
New Yorker 26:63, Jul. 22, 1950
Newsweek 36:76, Aug. 7, 1950
Rotarian 77:36, Nov., 1950
Saturday Review 33:30-1, Aug. 5, 1950
Time 56:62+, Jul. 31, 1950

Broken Blossoms (1936)
New York Times p. 16, Jan. 14, 1937

Broken Dreams (1933)
New York Times p. 23, Nov. 21, 1933

*Broken Journey
New Republic 120:31, Jun. 20, 1949
New York Times p. 34, May 26, 1949
Newsweek 33:82, Jun. 6, 1949
Photoplay 36:23, Sep., 1949
Theatre Arts 33:106, Aug., 1949

Broken Lance (1954)
America 91:486, Aug. 14, 1954
Catholic World 179:464, Sep., 1954
Commonweal 60:513, Aug. 27, 1954
National Parent-Teacher 49:39, Oct., 1954
New York Times p. 9, Jul. 30, 1954
Newsweek 44:82, Aug. 16, 1954
Time 64:72+, Aug. 23, 1954

Broken Lullaby (see Fifth Commandment)

Broken Melody (1934)
New York Times p. 17, Oct. 31, 1934

Broken Shoes (1934)
Nation 138:454, Apr. 18, 1934
New Republic 78:272, Apr. 18, 1934
New York Times p. 8, Mar. 31, 1934

Broken Star (1956)
National Parent-Teacher 50:39, May, 1956

Broken Wing (1932)
New York Times p. 17, Mar. 26, 1932

Bronco Buster (1952)
Christian Century 69:959, Aug. 20, 1952

Broth of a Boy (1959)
New York Times p. 18, Dec. 28, 1959
New Yorker 35:74, Jan. 9, 1960

Brother Orchid (1940)
Commonweal 32:170, Jun. 14, 1940
New York Times p. 18, Jun. 8, 1940
Newsweek 15:40+, Jun. 10, 1940
Time 35:86-7, Jun. 17, 1940

Brother Rat (1939)
 Commonweal 29:105, Nov. 18, 1938
 New York Times p. 15, Nov. 5, 1938
 Newsweek 12:33, Oct. 24, 1938
 Photoplay 53:81, Jan., 1939
 Scholastic 33:38, Nov. 5, 1938

Brother Rat and a Baby (1940)
 New York Times p. 9, Jan. 27, 1940
 Photoplay 54:62, Mar., 1940

*Brotherhood of Man
 Commonweal 45:446, Feb. 14, 1947
 New York Times p. 16, May 23, 1946
 Theatre Arts 31:6, Feb., 1947

Brothers (1930)
 Life (NY) 96:44, Dec. 5, 1930

Brothers (1948)
 Commonweal 48:140, May 21, 1948
 New Republic 118:38, May 31, 1948
 New Yorker 24:91, May 8, 1948
 Newsweek 31:98+, May 17, 1948
 Time 51:99, May 24, 1948

Brothers in Law (1956)
 Commonweal 66:523, Aug. 23, 1957
 New York Times p. 22, Aug. 20, 1957
 Saturday Review 40:30, Sep. 14, 1957

Brothers Karamazov (1958)
 America 98:643, Mar. 1, 1958
 Catholic World 187:66, Apr., 1958
 Christian Century 75:410-11, Apr. 2, 1958
 Commonweal 67:568, Feb. 28, 1958
 Library Journal 83:748, Mar. 1, 1958
 Life 44:60-6, Mar. 10, 1958
 Nation 186:216, Mar. 8, 1958
 New Republic 138:21, April 21, 1958
 New York Times p. 18, Feb. 21, 1958; II, p. 1, Feb. 23, 1958
 New York Times Magazine p. 78, Nov. 3, 1957
 New Yorker 34:104+, Mar. 1, 1958
 Newsweek 51:102+, Feb. 24, 1958
 Reporter 18:34-5, Apr. 3, 1958
 Saturday Review 41:27, Feb. 22, 1958
 Time 71:98+, Feb. 24, 1958

Brothers Rico (1957)
National Parent-Teacher 51:36, May, 1957
Newsweek 50:120, Sep. 16, 1957
Time 70:115+, Sep. 16, 1957

*Brought to Action
New Yorker 20:55, Jan. 13, 1945
Time 45:96, Jan. 29, 1945

Brown on Resolution (see Sailor of the King)

Browning Version (1951)
Christian Century 69:175, Feb. 6, 1952
Commonweal 55:144, Nov. 16, 1951
Library Journal 76:1818, Nov. 1, 1951
New Republic 125:21, Nov. 19, 1951
New York Times p. 33, Oct. 30, 1951; II, p. 1, Nov. 4, 1951
New Yorker 27:141, Nov. 3, 1951

Brute Force (1947)
Commonweal 46:405, Aug. 8, 1947
Cosmopolitan 123:59+, Jul., 1947
Hollywood Quarterly 3:63-5, Fall, 1947
Life 23:69-70+, Aug. 11, 1947
Nation 165:264, Sep. 13, 1947
New Republic 117:38, Aug. 18, 1947
New York Times p. 16, Jul. 17, 1947; II, p. 1, Jul. 20, 1947
Newsweek 30:84, Jul. 28, 1947
Photoplay 31:4, Sep., 1947
Time 50:76, Aug. 4, 1947

Buccaneer (1938, 1959)
America 100:532, Jan. 31, 1959
Canadian Magazine 89:28-9, Feb., 1938
Catholic World 188:416, Feb., 1959
Commonweal 27:414, Feb. 4, 1938
Library Journal 83:3507, Dec. 15, 1958
Life 4:54-7, Jan. 10, 1938
Literary Digest 125:22, Jan. 29, 1938
New York Times p. 17, Feb. 17, 1938
Newsweek 53:68, Jan. 5, 1959
St. Nicholas 65:37+, Jan., 1938
Scholastic 32:27S, Feb. 12, 1938
Stage 15:10, Feb., 1938
Time 31:44, Jan. 17, 1938; 73:90, Jan. 19, 1959

Buccaneer's Girl (1950)
Christian Century 67:479, Apr. 12, 1950
Commonweal 52:46, Apr. 21, 1950
New York Times p. 19, Mar. 27, 1950
Newsweek 38:99, Nov. 12, 1951
Saturday Review 34:27, Nov. 10, 1951
Scholastic 59:26, Nov. 14, 1951
Time 58:110+, Nov. 12, 1951

Buck Benny Rides Again (1940)
New York Times p. 28, Apr. 25, 1940; IX, p. 5, Apr.
28, 1940
Photoplay 54:69, Jan., 1940
Time 35:85, May 6, 1940

Buck Privates (1941)
Commonweal 33:498, Mar. 7, 1941
New York Times IX, p. 5, Feb. 2, 1941; p. 15, Feb. 14,
1941
Newsweek 17:62, Feb. 10, 1941
Time 37:89, Mar. 24, 1941

Buck Privates Come Home (1947)
New York Times p. 11, Apr. 12, 1947; II, p. 5, Apr. 13,
1947

Buddha (1963)
Time 82:95, Jul. 12, 1963

Buffalo Bill (1944)
Collier's 113:18-19, Mar. 18, 1944
Commonweal 40:62, May 5, 1944
Life 16:109-12+, Apr. 10, 1944
New York Times p. 22, Apr. 20, 1944; II, p. 3, Apr. 23,
1944
Newsweek 23:84+, Apr. 24, 1944
Time 43:94+, Aug. 24, 1944

Bugle Sounds (1942)
Commonweal 35:562, May 27, 1942
New York Times p. 25, Apr. 3, 1942

Bugles in the Afternoon (1951)
Library Journal 77:586, Apr. 1, 1952
New York Times p. 32, Mar. 5, 1952
Newsweek 39:102, Mar. 10, 1952
Time 59:97, Feb. 11, 1952

165

Bulldog Drummond (1930)
  Creative Art 5:729-34, Oct., 1929
  Life (NY) 93:24, May 24, 1929
  New York Times IX, p. 5, May 12, 1929; p. 23, May 3,
    1929
  Outlook 152:155, May 22, 1929
  Vogue 73:55+, Jun. 22, 1929

Bulldog Drummond at Bay (1937)
  New York Times p. 23, Oct. 25, 1937

Bulldog Drummond Comes Back (1937)
  New York Times p. 8, Sep. 4, 1937

Bulldog Drummond in Africa (1938)
  New York Times p. 15, Aug. 25, 1938

Bulldog Drummond Strikes Back (1934)
  Golden Book 20:378, Oct., 1934
  Literary Digest 118:26, Sep. 1, 1934
  Nation 139:336, Sep. 19, 1934
  New York Times p. 20, Aug. 16, 1934; IX, p. 3, Aug.
    26, 1934
  Vanity Fair 42:45, Jul., 1934

Bulldog Drummond's Bride (1939)
  New York Times p. 17, Jul. 13, 1939
  Photoplay 53:62, Sep., 1939

Bulldog Drummond's Peril (1938)
  New York Times p. 23, Mar. 18, 1938

Bulldog Drummond's Secret Police (1939)
  New York Times p. 19, Mar. 30, 1939

Bullet for Joey (1955)
  National Parent-Teacher 49:38, Jun., 1955
  New York Times p. 12, Apr. 16, 1955

Bullet is Waiting (1954)
  America 92:222, Nov. 20, 1954
  Catholic World 180:65, Oct., 1954
  National Parent-Teacher 49:39, Oct., 1954
  New Republic 132:22, Jun. 27, 1955
  New York Times p. 17, Nov. 12, 1954
  Time 64:114+, Dec. 6, 1954

Bullet Scars (1942)
New York Times p. 21, Apr. 24, 1942

Bullets for O'Hara (1941)
New York Times p. 16, Jul. 28, 1941

Bullets or Ballots (1936)
New York Times p. 27, May 27, 1936
Time 27:26, Jun. 1, 1936

*Bullfight
Dance Magazine 30:9, Aug., 1956
Holiday 20:139+, Nov., 1956
Nation 183:106, Aug. 4, 1956
National Parent-Teacher 51:37, Oct., 1956
New York Times p. 15, Jul. 4, 1956; II, p. 1, Jul. 15,
   1956
Newsweek 48:76-7, Jul. 23, 1956
Saturday Review 39:24, Jul. 28, 1956
Time 68:74, Jul. 30, 1956

Bullfighter and the Lady (1951)
Christian Century 68:751, Jun. 20, 1951
Commonweal 54:91, May 4, 1951
Nation 172:498, May 26, 1951
New York Times p. 19, Apr. 27, 1951
New Yorker 27:68, May 5, 1951
Newsweek 37:100, May 14, 1951
Saturday Review 34:26, May 5, 1951
Time 57:106+, Apr. 23, 1951

Bullfighters (1945)
New York Times p. 10, May 12, 1945

Bundle of Joy (1956)
America 96:379, Dec. 29, 1956
National Parent-Teacher 51:38, Feb., 1957
New York Times p. 36, Dec. 20, 1956
New Yorker 32:60, Dec. 29, 1956
Newsweek 48:61, Dec. 31, 1956
Time 69:72, Jan. 7, 1957

Bunker Bean (1936)
New York Times p. 21, Jun. 27, 1936
Time 28:48, Jul. 6, 1936

Bureau of Missing Persons (1933)
New Outlook 162:49, Oct., 1933

167

Bureau of Missing Persons (1933) (Continued)
    New York Times p. 9, Sep. 9, 1933; X, p. 3, Sep. 17,
    1933
    Newsweek 2:38, Sep. 16, 1933

Burglar (1957)
    National Parent-Teacher 52:32, Sep., 1957

Burma Convoy (1941)
    New York Times p. 26, Oct. 7, 1941

Burma Victory (1945)
    Theatre Arts 30:98+, Feb., 1946

Burn, Witch, Burn (1962)
    New York Times p. 21, Jul. 5, 1962
    Time 79:98+, Apr. 20, 1962

The Burning Court (1963)
    New York Times p. 17, Aug. 1, 1963

The Burning Cross (1947)
    New York Times II, p. 5, Jun. 1, 1947; p. 31, Nov. 4,
    1947; p. 19, Feb. 20, 1948

Burning Hills (1956)
    Catholic World 184:66, Oct., 1956
    National Parent-Teacher 51:37, Oct., 1956
    New York Times p. 15, Aug. 24, 1956
    Newsweek 48:116, Sep. 24, 1956
    Saturday Review 39:26, Aug. 25, 1956
    Time 68:74, Sep. 3, 1956

Burning Up (1930)
    New York Times p. 12, Feb. 8, 1930

Bury Me Dead (1947)
    New York Times p. 13, Oct. 25, 1947

Bus Stop (1956)
    America 95:576, Sep. 15, 1956
    Catholic World 184:66, Oct., 1956
    Commonweal 64:561, Sep. 7, 1956
    Coronet 40:8, Aug., 1956
    Library Journal 81:2174, Oct. 1, 1956
    Life 41:79-80+, Aug. 27, 1956
    Nation 183:294, Oct. 6, 1956

Bus Stop (1956) (Continued)
National Parent-Teacher 51:37, Oct., 1956
New York Times p. 19, Sep. 1, 1956; II, p. 1, Sep. 2,
1956; II, p. 1, Sep. 9, 1956
New Yorker 32:76, Sep. 15, 1956
Newsweek 48:90, Aug. 27, 1956
Saturday Review 39:37, Sep. 15, 1956
Theatre Arts 40:57-9, Oct., 1956
Time 68:74+, Sep. 3, 1956

Bush Christmas (1947)
Commonweal 47:228, Dec. 12, 1947
New Republic 117:31, Dec. 15, 1947
New York Times p. 50, Nov. 27, 1947
Time 50:104+, Dec. 15, 1947

Business and Pleasure (1932)
New York Times p. 13, Feb. 13, 1932; VIII, p. 4, Feb.
21, 1932

Busses Roar (1942)
New York Times p. 25, Sep. 25, 1942

Buster Keaton Story (1956)
America 97:180, May 4, 1957
National Parent-Teacher 51:37, Jun., 1957
New York Times p. 31, Apr. 22, 1957
New Yorker 33:163, May 4, 1957
Newsweek 49:110, Apr. 29, 1957
Time 69:104+, May 6, 1957

But Not For Me (1959)
America 102:27, Oct. 3, 1959
Commonweal 71:20, Oct. 2, 1959
Life 47:108, Oct. 12, 1959
New York Times p. 14, Oct. 3, 1959; II, p. 1, Oct. 11,
1959
New Yorker 35:172-3, Oct. 10, 1959
Newsweek 54:118, Oct. 12, 1959
Saturday Review 42:31, Sep. 5, 1959
Time 74:62, Oct. 5, 1959

But the Flesh Is Weak (1932)
New York Times p. 11, Apr. 16, 1932

Butch Minds the Baby (1942)
Commonweal 36:15, Apr. 24, 1942
New York Times p. 23, May 1, 1942

Butch Minds the Baby (1942) (Continued)
Newsweek 19:66, Apr. 13, 1942
Time 39:88, Apr. 27, 1942

Butterfield 8 (1960)
America 104:350, Dec. 3, 1960
Commonweal 73:179, Nov. 11, 1960
New York Times p. 46, Nov. 17, 1960; II, p. 1, Nov. 27,
1960
New Yorker 36:152, Nov. 19, 1960
Newsweek 56:121, Nov. 7, 1960
Saturday Review 43:39, Nov. 19, 1960
Time 76:89, Nov. 21, 1960

Buy Me That Town (1940)
New York Times p. 27, Oct. 23, 1941

Bwana Devil (1952)
America 88:633, Mar. 7, 1953
Christian Century 70:207, Feb. 18, 1953
Commonweal 57:575, Mar. 13, 1953
National Parent-Teacher 47:37, May, 1953
Natural History 62:188, Apr., 1953
New York Times p. 22, Nov. 28, 1952; p. 20, Feb. 19,
1953; II, p. 1, Feb. 22, 1953
Newsweek 41:86, Mar. 9, 1953
Time 61:90, Mar. 2, 1953

By Candlelight (1934)
Literary Digest 117:32, Jan. 20, 1934
New York Times p. 18, Jan. 6, 1934; IX, p. 5, Jan. 14,
1934
Newsweek 3:33, Jan. 13, 1934

By Love Possessed (1961)
Commonweal 74:378, Jul. 7, 1961
New Republic 145:26, Jul. 24, 1961
New York Times p. 32, Jul. 20, 1961; II, p. 1, Aug. 6,
1961
New Yorker 37:54-5, Jul. 22, 1961
Newsweek 58:68, Jul. 10, 1961
Saturday Review 44:33, Jul. 15, 1961
Time 78:61, Jul. 7, 1961

By Rocket to the Moon (1931)
New York Times p. 11, Feb. 7, 1931

By the Light of the Silvery Moon (1953)
America 89:62, Apr. 11, 1953
Commonweal 58:73, Apr. 24, 1953
National Parent-Teacher 48:37, Sep., 1953
New York Times p. 28, Mar. 27, 1953
Newsweek 41:90-1, Apr. 6, 1953
Scholastic 62:30, Apr. 29, 1953
Time 61:106+, Apr. 13, 1953

By Your Leave (1934)
Movie Classic 7:43-7+, Dec., 1934

Bye Bye Birdie (1963)
America 108:590-1, Apr. 20, 1963
Commonweal 78:107, Apr. 19, 1963
New York Times p. 27, Apr. 5, 1963
Newsweek 61:103, Apr. 15, 1963
Saturday Review 46:26, Apr. 27, 1963

C-Man (1949)
New York Times p. 11, May 28, 1949

Cabin in the Cotton (1932)
Nation 135:409, Oct. 26, 1932
New Outlook 161:47, Nov., 1932
New York Times p. 17, Sep. 30, 1932

Cabin in the Sky (1942)
Commonweal 38:225, Jun. 18, 1943
New Republic 109:20, Jul. 5, 1943
New York Times VIII, p. 3, Sep. 13, 1942; p. 19, May
    28, 1943
New Yorker 19:39, May 29, 1943
Newsweek 21:88, Apr. 26, 1943
Photoplay 22:22, May, 1943
Time 41:96, Apr. 12, 1943

Cabinet of Caligari (1962)
Esquire 58:32+, Oct., 1962
New Republic 146:28, Jun. 25, 1962
New York Times p. 13, May 26, 1962
Newsweek 59:99, Jun. 11, 1962
Saturday Review 45:23, Jun. 2, 1962

Cabinet of Dr. Caligari (1952)
Canadian Forum 27:280, Mar., 1948
Saturday Review 35:57, Apr. 12, 1952

171

Cabiria (1957)
Commonweal 67:202-4, 209, Nov. 22, 1957
Nation 185:396, Nov. 23, 1957
National Parent-Teacher 52:38, Jan., 1958
New York Times p. 34, Oct. 29, 1957; II, p. 1, Nov. 3,
   1957
New Yorker 33:109, Nov. 9, 1957
Newsweek 50:114-15, Nov. 4, 1957
Saturday Review 40:28-9, Nov. 9, 1957

Caddy (1953)
Farm Journal 77:161, Nov., 1953
Holiday 14:99, Nov., 1953
McCalls 81:10, Oct., 1953
National Parent-Teacher 48:38, Oct., 1953
New York Times p. 16, Sep. 18, 1953
Newsweek 42:88, Oct. 5, 1953
Time 62:84, Sep. 28, 1953

Cadet Girl (1941)
New York Times p. 39, Dec. 11, 1941

Caesar and Cleopatra (1946)
Commonweal 44:433-4, Aug. 16, 1946
Harper 194:382, Apr., 1947
Harper's Bazaar 80:89, Jan., 1946
Life 21:44-6, Jul. 29, 1946
Modern Music 23 no4:313-14, Oct., 1946
Nation 163:193, Aug. 17, 1946; 163:251, Aug. 31, 1946
New York Times II, p. 3, Oct. 29, 1944; II, p. 3, Mar.
   25, 1945; II, p. 3, Jul. 29, 1945; VI, p. 13, Oct. 21,
   1945; II, p. 3, Jun. 16, 1946; VI, p. 18, Jul. 21, 1946;
   II, p. 3, Sep. 1, 1946; p. 18, Sep. 6, 1946; II, p. 1,
   Sep. 8, 1946; II, p. 1, Nov. 17, 1946
New York Times Magazine p. 18-19, Jul. 21, 1946
New Yorker 22:48, Sep. 7, 1946
Newsweek 28:77, Aug. 26, 1946
Scholastic 49:36-7, Sep. 23, 1946
Theatre Arts 30:97, Feb., 1946; 30:517-18, Sep., 1946
Time 46:88, Dec. 31, 1945; 48:98, Aug. 19, 1946
Vogue 105:64-5, Jan. 15, 1945

Cafe Metropole (1937)
Canadian Magazine 87:51, Jun., 1937
Literary Digest 123:20, May 15, 1937
New York Times p. 17, Apr. 29, 1937
Time 29:69, May 10, 1937

172

Cafe Society (1939)
Canadian Magazine 91:46, Apr., 1939
Commonweal 29:525, Mar. 3, 1939
Life 6:47-51, Mar. 6, 1939
New York Times IX, p. 5, Nov. 6, 1938; p. 19, Feb. 23,
1939; IX, p. 5, Feb. 26, 1939
Photoplay 53:52, Apr., 1939
Time 33:31, Mar. 6, 1939

*Cage of Nightingales
Commonweal 45:648, Apr. 11, 1947
Nation 164:340, Mar. 22, 1947
New Republic 116:42, Apr. 28, 1947
New York Times p. 31, Apr. 3, 1947
New Yorker 23:82, Apr. 5, 1947
Newsweek 29:94, Mar. 31, 1947
Theatre Arts 31:46, Jun., 1947
Time 49:100+, Apr. 28, 1947

Caged (1950)
Commonweal 52:221, Jun. 9, 1950
Good Housekeeping 131:98, Jul., 1950
New York Times p. 8, May 20, 1950; II, p. 1, May 28,
1950
Newsweek 35:90, Jun. 19, 1950
Time 55:96, Jun. 19, 1950

Cain (1932)
New York Times p. 18, Jan. 18, 1932; VIII, p. 4, Jan.
31, 1932

Cain and Mabel (1936)
New York Times p. 22, Oct. 19, 1936
Stage 14:24, Oct., 1936
Time 28:70, Oct. 26, 1936

Caine Mutiny (1954)
America 91:367, Jul. 3, 1954
Catholic World 179:221-2, Jun., 1954
Collier's 132:50-3, Nov. 13, 1953
Commonweal 60:293-4, Jun. 25, 1954
Farm Journal 78:92, Jul., 1954
Library Journal 79:1304, Jul., 1954
Life 36:67-70, May 3, 1954
Look 18:84-5+, Jun. 29, 1954
National Parent-Teacher 48:39, Jun., 1954
New York Times II, p. 5, Oct. 11, 1953; p. 17, Jun. 25,

173

Caine Mutiny (1954) (Continued)
1954; II, p. 1, Jul. 4, 1954; II, p. 5, Jul. 4, 1954
New Yorker 30:48-9, Jul. 3, 1954
Newsweek 43:72, Jun. 28, 1954
Saturday Review 37:28+, Jun. 26, 1954
Scholastic 64:29, May 12, 1954
Time 63:90, Jun. 28, 1954

Cairo (1942)
New York Times p. 27, Nov. 6, 1942

Cairo (1963)
Commonweal 77:542, Feb. 15, 1963

Calaboose (1943)
New York Times p. 19, Jul. 30, 1943

Calamity Jane (1953)
America 90:305, Dec. 12, 1953
Catholic World 178:224, Dec., 1953
Farm Journal 78:83, Jan., 1954
Library Journal 78:2098, Dec. 1, 1953
National Parent-Teacher 48:38, Dec., 1953
New York Times p. 40, Nov. 5, 1953
Newsweek 42:100, Nov. 23, 1953
Saturday Review 36:40, Nov. 14, 1953
Time 62:120, Nov. 23, 1953

Calamity Jane and Sam Bass (1949)
Commonweal 50:367, Jul. 22, 1949
New York Times p. 14, Jul. 18, 1949
Newsweek 34:65, Aug. 1, 1949

Calcutta (1947)
New York Times II, p. 4, Apr. 20, 1947; p. 30, Apr. 24, 1947
Newsweek 29:94, May 5, 1947
Time 49:99, Apr. 28, 1947

California (1947)
Commonweal 45:376, Jan. 24, 1947
New Republic 116:42, Feb. 3, 1947
New York Times II, p. 5, Jan. 12, 1947; p. 31, Jan. 15, 1947
New Yorker 22:71, Jan. 25, 1947
Newsweek 29:91, Jan. 27, 1947
Time 49:104, Feb. 17, 1947

California Conquest (1952)
New York Times p. 22, Jun. 7, 1952
Newsweek 39:100+, Jun. 30, 1952
Time 59:101, Jun. 23, 1952

California Passage (1950)
New York Times p. 10, Dec. 16, 1950

Call (1938)
Commonweal 27:666, Apr. 8, 1938
New York Times p. 18, Mar. 29, 1938

Call a Messenger (1939)
New York Times p. 12, Nov. 11, 1939

Call Her Savage (1932)
New York Times p. 19, Nov. 25, 1932

Call It a Day (1937)
Canadian Magazine 87:52, Jun., 1937
Literary Digest 123:20+, Apr. 24, 1937
New York Times p. 29, May 7, 1937
Newsweek 9:30, May 1, 1937
Scholastic 30:27, Apr. 17, 1937
Stage 14:60, Mar., 1937
Time 29:58, May 17, 1937

Call It Luck (1934)
New York Times p. 24, Jul. 10, 1934; X, p. 3, Jul. 15, 1934

Call Me Bwana (1963)
New York Times p. 9, Jul. 4, 1963
Time 82:95, Jul. 12, 1963

Call Me Genius (1961)
New York Times p. 47, Oct. 17, 1961
Saturday Review 44:35, Oct. 21, 1961

Call Me Madam (1953)
America 89:25, Apr. 4, 1953
Catholic World 177:142, May, 1953
Commonweal 57:649, Apr. 3, 1953
Library Journal 78:588, Apr. 1, 1953
Look 17:100+, May 5, 1953
National Parent-Teacher 47:37, May, 1953
New York Times VI, p. 40, Mar. 15, 1953; p. 37, Mar. 26, 1953

Call Me Madam (1953) (Continued)
New York Times Magazine p. 40-1, Mar. 15, 1953
New Yorker 29:74+, Mar. 28, 1953
Newsweek 41:91, Mar. 30, 1953
Saturday Review 36:43, Apr. 4, 1953
Theatre Arts 37:82, May, 1953
Time 61:108+, Mar. 23, 1953

Call Me Mister (1951)
Christian Century 68:479, Apr. 11, 1951
Commonweal 53:544, Mar. 9, 1951
Library Journal 76:418, Mar. 1, 1951
New York Times p. 21, Feb. 1, 1951
Newsweek 37:80, Feb. 5, 1951
Saturday Review 34:26, Feb. 24, 1951
Time 57:78, Feb. 5, 1951

Call Northside 777 (1948)
Commonweal 47:495, Feb. 27, 1948
Life 24:57-9, Mar. 1, 1948
New York Times p. 29, Feb. 19, 1948; II, p. 1, Feb. 22, 1948
New Yorker 24:62, Feb. 28, 1948
Newsweek 31:90, Feb. 23, 1948
Photoplay 32:23, Apr., 1948
Scholastic 52:29, Feb. 9, 1948
Time 51:99, Feb. 16, 1948

Call of the Flesh (1930)
New York Times p. 9, Sep. 13, 1930; IX, p. 5, Sep. 21, 1930

Call of the Mesquiteers (1938)
New York Times p. 11, Mar. 19, 1938

Call of the Wild (1935)
Literary Digest 120:26, Aug. 24, 1935
New York Times p. 15, Aug. 15, 1935; IX, p. 3, Aug. 18, 1935
Time 26:26, Aug. 26, 1935
Vanity Fair 44:39, Jul., 1935

Call of the Yukon (1938)
New York Times p. 27, May 6, 1938

Call Out the Marines (1942)
New York Times p. 18, Jan. 26, 1942

Call to Arms (1937)
  New York Times p. 23, May 3, 1937

*Callaway Went Thataway
  Catholic World 174:221, Dec., 1951
  Christian Century 69:87, Jan. 16, 1952
  New York Times p. 42, Dec. 6, 1951
  New Yorker 27:148, Dec. 15, 1951
  Newsweek 38:100, Dec. 17, 1951
  Theatre Arts 36:29+, Jan., 1952
  Time 58:104+, Dec. 10, 1951

Calling All Marines (1939)
  New York Times p. 27, Oct. 26, 1939

Calling Bulldog Drummond (1951)
  Library Journal 77:140, Jan. 15, 1952

Calling Dr. Death (1943)
  New York Times p. 11, Feb. 12, 1944

Calling Dr. Gillespie (1942)
  New York Times p. 17, Jul. 9, 1942

Calling Dr. Kildare (1939)
  New York Times p. 25, May 12, 1939

Calling of Dan Matthews (1936)
  New York Times p. 18, Jan. 25, 1936

Calling Philo Vance (1940)
  New York Times p. 15, Feb. 9, 1940

Calypso Heat Wave (1957)
  National Parent-Teacher 52:32, Sep., 1957

Cameo Kirby (1929)
  Life (NY) 95:20, Feb. 28, 1930
  New York Times p. 12, Feb. 8, 1930; IX, p. 5, Feb. 16,
    1930

Camille (1936)
  Commonweal 25:388, Jan. 29, 1937
  Indian Woman 16:1+, Jan., 1937
  Literary Digest 123:23, Jan. 2, 1937
  Look 19:99-101, May 3, 1955
  Nation 180:167, Feb. 19, 1955

Camille (1936) (Continued)
New Republic 90:211-12, Mar. 24, 1937
New York Times p. 13, Jan. 23, 1937; XI, p. 5, Jan.
31, 1937; II, p. 1, Mar. 13, 1955
Newsweek 9:32, Jan. 9, 1937
Photoplay 50:48-9, Dec., 1936
Time 29:25, Jan. 18, 1937
Vogue 88:70-71, Nov. 15, 1936

Camp on Blood Island (1957)
New York Times p. 37, Sep. 18, 1958

Campbell's Kingdom (1958)
Commonweal 67:617, Mar. 14, 1958
Library Journal 83:748, Mar. 1, 1958
New York Times p. 35, Jan. 11, 1960
Newsweek 51:104, Feb. 24, 1958

Campus Confessions (1938)
New York Times IX, p. 3, Jul. 24, 1938; p. 35, Sep.
23, 1938
School and Society 48:755-6, Dec. 10, 1938

Canadian Pacific (1948)
Good Housekeeping 128:11+, May, 1949
New York Times II, p. 5, Oct. 3, 1948; p. 32, May 20,
1949
Newsweek 33:85, May 16, 1949
Rotarian 74:34, Jun., 1949
Time 53:102, Jun. 13, 1949

Canadians (1961)
New York Times p. 31, Jun. 1, 1961

Canal Zone (1942)
New York Times p. 21, Mar. 30, 1942

Canary Murder Case (1929)
Life (NY) 93:32, Apr. 12, 1929
New York Times p. 22, Mar. 11, 1929; X, p. 7, Mar.
24, 1929

Can-Can (1960)
America 102:773+, Mar. 26, 1960
Commonweal 72:16-17, Apr. 1, 1960
Dance Magazine 34:14, Apr., 1960
Life 48:72-5+, Mar. 14, 1960

Can-Can (1960) (Continued)
New York Times p. 36, Mar. 10, 1960; II, p. 1, Mar.
20, 1960
New Yorker 36:170+, Mar. 19, 1960
Newsweek 55:120, Mar. 21, 1960
Time 75:83, Mar. 21, 1960

*Candide
New Republic 147:26, Dec. 15, 1962
New York Times p. 39, Nov. 20, 1962
New Yorker 38:205, Nov. 24, 1962
Newsweek 60:92, Nov. 26, 1962
Saturday Review 45:75, Dec. 1, 1962

Candlelight in Algeria (1944)
Commonweal 40:302, Jul. 14, 1944
Nation 159:108, Jul. 22, 1944
New York Times p. 10, Jul. 31, 1944
Time 44:87, Jul. 24, 1944

*Cangaceiro
Commonweal 60:582, Sep. 17, 1954
National Parent-Teacher 49:39, Nov., 1954
New York Times p. 13, Sep. 3, 1954; II, p. 1, Sep. 5,
1954
Newsweek 44:77, Sep. 6, 1954
Saturday Review 37:45, Sep. 11, 1954

Cannibal Attack (1954)
National Parent-Teacher 49:39, Jan., 1955

Canon City (1948)
Life 25:72-4, Aug. 2, 1948
New Republic 119:29, Jul. 26, 1948
New York Times p. 19, Jul. 8, 1948; II, p. 1, Jul. 11,
1948
New Yorker 24:57, Jul. 17, 1948
Newsweek 32:82, Jul. 12, 1948
Photoplay 33:23, Sep., 1948
Time 52:93, Aug. 16, 1948

Can't Help Singing (1944)
New York Times p. 22, Dec. 26, 1944
New Yorker 20:39, Dec. 30, 1944
Newsweek 25:66, Jan. 1, 1945
Time 45:92, Jan. 15, 1945

Canterbury Tale (1944)
Canadian Forum 25:23, Apr., 1945
Life 16:75-6+, Jun. 26, 1944
New York Times II, p. 7, Dec. 5, 1943; p. 21, May 15,
1944; p. 16, Jan. 24, 1949
Time 53:96, Feb. 14, 1949

Canterville Ghost (1944)
Commonweal 40:400, Aug. 11, 1944
Nation 159:108, Jul. 22, 1944
New York Times II, p. 3, Aug. 22, 1943; p. 16, Jul. 29,
1944
New Yorker 20:32, Aug. 5, 1944
Newsweek 24:82, Jul. 31, 1944
Time 44:96, Aug. 14, 1944

Cantor's Son (1937)
New York Times p. 11, Dec. 27, 1937

Canyon Crossroads (1955)
National Parent-Teacher 49:38, May, 1955

Canyon Passage (1946)
Commonweal 44:479, Aug. 30, 1946
Cosmopolitan 121:66+, Sep., 1946
New York Times II, p. 3, Sep. 2, 1945; II, p. 3, Aug.
4, 1946; p. 18, Aug. 8, 1946
New Yorker 22:86, Aug. 17, 1946
Newsweek 28:77, Jul. 29, 1946
Time 48:98, Aug. 5, 1946
Woman's Home Companion 73:11, Sep., 1946

Cape Fear (1962)
America 107:85, Apr. 21, 1962
Commonweal 76:179, May 11, 1962
Esquire 58:59+, Nov., 1962
New York Times p. 35, Apr. 19, 1962
Newsweek 59:98, Apr. 30, 1962
Saturday Review 45:28, May 5, 1962
Time 79:87, Apr. 27, 1962

Captain Blood (1936)
Canadian Magazine 85:33, Jan., 1936; 85:36, Feb., 1936
Commonweal 23:272, Jan. 3, 1936
Fortune 16:112, Dec., 1937
Motion Picture 51:50, Feb., 1936
New York Times IX, p. 3, Aug. 18, 1935; p. 14, Dec.
27, 1935

180

Captain Blood (1936) (Continued)
Newsweek 6:24-5, Dec. 28, 1935
Scholastic 27:28, Jan. 25, 1936
Stage 13:32, Jan., 1936
Time 26:16, Dec. 30, 1935

Captain Boycott (1947)
New Republic 117:33, Dec. 22, 1947
New York Times p. 11, Dec. 6, 1947; II, p. 9, Dec. 7,
1947; II, p. 3, Dec. 14, 1947
New Yorker 23:95, Dec. 13, 1947
Newsweek 30:68, Dec. 29, 1947

Captain Carey, U.S.A. (1950)
Christian Century 67:599, May 10, 1950
Commonweal 51:677, Apr. 7, 1950
Good Housekeeping 130:257, May, 1950
Library Journal 75:503, Mar. 15, 1950
New York Times p. 40, Mar. 30, 1950
Newsweek 35:83, Apr. 10, 1950
Rotarian 77:37, Jul., 1950
Time 55:92, May 1, 1950

Captain Caution (1940)
Commonweal 32:391, Aug. 30, 1940
New York Times p. 21, Oct. 21, 1940
Photoplay 54:67, Oct., 1940

Captain China (1950)
New York Times p. 33, Mar. 2, 1950
Rotarian 76:40, May, 1950
Time 55:94, Apr. 3, 1950

Captain Eddie (1945)
Commonweal 42:431, Aug. 17, 1945
Cosmopolitan 119:136, Aug., 1945
Life 19:47-8+, Aug. 20, 1945
New York Times p. 24, Aug. 9, 1945; II, p. 1, Aug. 19,
1945
New Yorker 21:57, Aug. 18, 1945
Newsweek 26:86, Aug. 13, 1945
Scholastic 47:32, Sep. 17, 1945
Time 46:98, Aug. 6, 1945

Captain From Castile (1948)
Commonweal 47:256, Dec. 19, 1947
New Republic 118:32, Jan. 5, 1948

181

Captain From Castile (1948) (Continued)
New York Times II, p. 5, Dec. 21, 1947; p. 22, Dec.
26, 1947
Newsweek 31:68, Jan. 5, 1948
Scholastic 51:36, Jan. 12, 1948
Time 51:71, Jan. 5, 1948

Captain From Koepenick (1958)
New York Times p. 6, Jul. 26, 1958
Newsweek 52:69, Aug. 4, 1958
Saturday Review 41:20, Aug. 2, 1958
Time 72:66+, Aug. 4, 1958

Captain Fury (1939)
New York Times p. 20, May 26, 1939; X, p. 3, May 28,
1939
Photoplay 53:63, Jul., 1939

Captain Grant's Children (1939)
New York Times p. 23, Jan. 12, 1939

Captain Hates the Sea (1934)
Nation 139:750, Dec. 26, 1934
New Republic 85:313-14, Jan. 22, 1936
New York Times p. 33, Nov. 29, 1934

Captain Horatio Hornblower (1951)
Catholic World 174:64, Oct., 1951
Christian Century 68:1087, Sep. 19, 1951
Library Journal 76:1344, Sep. 1, 1951
New York Times II, p. 5, Apr. 23, 1950; p. 21, Sep. 14,
1951
New Yorker 27:107, Sep. 22, 1951
Newsweek 38:87, Sep. 24, 1951
Time 58:96+, Sep. 10, 1951

Captain January (1936)
New York Times p. 21, Apr. 25, 1936
Scholastic 28:26, Apr. 4, 1936
Time 27:36, Apr. 27, 1936

Captain John Smith and Pocahontas (1953)
National Parent-Teacher 48:38, Feb., 1954
Natural History 62:476, Dec., 1953

Captain Kidd (1945)
Commonweal 43:117, Nov. 16, 1945
New York Times p. 26, Nov. 23, 1945

Captain Kidd (1945) (Continued)
Newsweek 26:104, Oct. 22, 1945
Time 46:54+, Oct. 15, 1945

Captain Lash (1929)
Life (NY) 93:23, Mar. 1, 1929
New York Times p. 20, Feb. 4, 1929; IX, p. 7, Feb. 10, 1929

Captain Lightfoot (1954)
Catholic World 180:464-5, Mar., 1955
Commonweal 61:656, Mar. 25, 1955
Library Journal 80:555, Mar. 1, 1955
National Parent-Teacher 49:38, Apr., 1955
New Republic 132:21, Jun. 27, 1955
New York Times II, p. 5, Aug. 1, 1954
Newsweek 45:92, Apr. 4, 1955
Scholastic 66:23, Apr. 13, 1955

Captain Newman, M.D. (1963)
America 110:295, Feb. 29, 1964
Commonweal 79:694, Mar. 6, 1964
Look 28:92-4, Apr. 7, 1964
New York Times II, p. 7, May 19, 1963; p. 36, Feb. 21, 1964
New Yorker 40:122, Feb. 29, 1964
Newsweek 63:84, Mar. 2, 1964
Saturday Review 47:33, Feb. 15, 1964
Time 83:105, Feb. 28, 1964
Vogue 143:42, Apr. 1, 1964

Captain of Koepenick (Der Hauptmann Von Kopenick) (1931)
New York Times IX, p. 5, Nov. 33, 1941

Captain of the Guard (1930)
Commonweal 12:670, Oct. 29, 1930
Life (NY) 95:20, Apr. 18, 1930
New York Times p. 23, Mar. 29, 1930

Captain Pirate (1952)
Christian Century 69:1143, Oct. 1, 1952

Captain Sindbad (1963)
New York Times p. 9, Jul. 4, 1963
Newsweek 62:80, Jul. 15, 1963

Captain Swagger (1928)
New York Times p. 17, Dec. 24, 1928

Captain Thunder (1930)
New York Times p. 15, May 11, 1931

Captains Courageous (1937)
Canadian Magazine 87:46, Jun., 1937
Child Life 16:310, Jul., 1937
Commonweal 25:726, Apr. 23, 1937
Independent Woman 16:178, Jun., 1937
Life 2:32-5, Apr. 26, 1937
Literary Digest 123:28, May 22, 1937
Motion Picture 53:56-7+, Mar., 1937
Nation 144:685, Jun. 12, 1937
New Republic 91:160, Jun. 16, 1937
New York Times p. 27, May 12, 1937; X, p. 3, May 16, 1937
Newsweek 9:23, Apr. 24, 1937
Photoplay 52:28, May, 1938
Saint Nicholas 64:52, Dec., 1936
Stage 14:53, Jun., 1937
Time 29:65, Apr. 19, 1937
Woman's Home Companion 64:13-14+, Apr., 1937

Captains Courageous (1962)
Senior Scholastic 81:25, Oct. 10, 1962

Captain's Daughter (1959)
Life 46:40-5, Mar. 30, 1959
New York Times p. 41, Nov. 23, 1959

Captains of the Clouds (1942)
Commonweal 35:438, Feb. 20, 1942
Nation 154:320, Mar. 14, 1942
New York Times p. 24, Feb. 13, 1942; VIII, p. 5, Feb. 15, 1942
Newsweek 19:54, Feb. 23, 1942
Scholastic 40:29, Mar. 2, 1942
Time 39:74, Mar. 2, 1942

Captain's Paradise (1953)
Commonweal 58:610, Sep. 25, 1953
Farm Journal 78:83, Jan., 1954
National Parent-Teacher 48:39, Dec., 1953
New York Times VI, p. 36, Aug. 30, 1953; p. 25, Sep. 29, 1953; II, p. 1, Oct. 4, 1953
New York Times Magazine p. 36, Aug. 30, 1953
New Yorker 29:127, Oct. 10, 1953
Newsweek 42:100, Oct. 12, 1953

184

Captain's Paradise (1953) (Continued)
Saturday Review 36:34, Sep. 26, 1953
Time 62:110+, Oct. 12, 1953

Captain's Table (1960)
New York Times p. 40, Sep. 27, 1960
Newsweek 56:80, Aug. 15, 1960
Time 76:88, Sep. 19, 1960

Captive City (1952)
Christian Century 69:1015, Sep. 3, 1952
Commonweal 56:14, Apr. 11, 1952
New York Times p. 34, Mar. 27, 1952
Newsweek 39:101, Apr. 7, 1952
Saturday Review 35:41, Apr. 12, 1952

Captive Heart (1947)
Nation 164:553, May 10, 1947
New York Times p. 27, Apr. 28, 1947; II, p. 5, May 4, 1947
New Yorker 23:62, May 10, 1947
Newsweek 29:103, May 12, 1947
Theatre Arts 30:649, Nov., 1946
Time 49:102+, May 12, 1947

Captive Wild Woman (1943)
New York Times p. 9, Jun. 7, 1943
New Yorker 19:58, Jun. 12, 1943

*Capture
Commonweal 52:221, Jun. 9, 1950
New York Times p. 8, May 20, 1950
Time 55:94+, Jun. 19, 1950

Captured (1933)
Canadian Magazine 80:34, Sep., 1933
New York Times p. 18, Aug. 18, 1933
Newsweek 2:31, Aug. 26, 1933
Vanity Fair 41:45, Sep., 1933

Car Ninety Nine (1935)
New York Times p. 14, Feb. 23, 1935

Caravan (1934)
New York Times p. 27, Sep. 28, 1934
Vanity Fair 43:53, Nov., 1934
Vogue 84:18, Jul. 15, 1934

185

Caravan (1947)
New York Times p. 30, Apr. 21, 1949
Newsweek 30:90+, Sep. 22, 1947

Carbine Williams (1952)
Christian Century 69:687, Jun. 4, 1952
Commonweal 56:174, May 23, 1952
Library Journal 77:970, Jun. 1, 1952
New York Times p. 37, May 8, 1952
Newsweek 39:92, May 26, 1952
Saturday Review 35:31, May 3, 1952
Theatre Arts 36:96, Jun., 1952
Time 59:108, May 12, 1952

Cardinal (1963)
America 110:27, Jan. 4, 1964
Catholic World 198:327-8, Feb., 1964; 198:365-71-2, Mar.,
    1964
Commonweal 79:371-2, Dec. 20, 1963
Ebony 19:126-8+, Dec., 1963
Esquire 61:24+, Mar., 1964
National Review 16:77-9, Jan. 28, 1964
New Republic 149:29, Dec. 21, 1963
New York Times II, p. 9, Nov. 25, 1962; p. 41, Dec.
    13, 1963; II, p. 3, Dec. 15, 1963
New Yorker 39:198, Dec. 14, 1963
Newsweek 62:90, Dec. 16, 1963
Reporter 30:44, Feb. 13, 1964
Saturday Review 46:32, Dec. 7, 1963
Senior Scholastic 83:24, 17T, Dec. 13, 1963
Time 82:97-8, Dec. 13, 1963

Cardinal Richelieu (1935)
Canadian Magazine 83:33, Jun., 1935
Commonweal 22:20, May 3, 1935
Literary Digest 119:24, May 4, 1935
New York Times p. 24, Apr. 19, 1935
Theatre Arts 19:407, Jun., 1935
Time 25:53-4, Apr. 29, 1935

Career (1939)
Commonweal 30:320, Jul. 21, 1939
New York Times p. 14, Jul. 28, 1949
Newsweek 14:23-4, Jul. 24, 1939
Photoplay 53:55, Aug., 1939

Career (1959)
America 102:90-1, Oct. 17, 1959

Career (1959) (Continued)
Commonweal 71:185, Nov. 6, 1959
New York Times p. 24, Oct. 9, 1959; II, p. 1, Oct. 18, 1959
New Yorker 35:197, Oct. 17, 1959
Newsweek 54:108, Oct. 19, 1959
Saturday Review 42:32, Oct. 10, 1959
Time 74:106, Oct. 19, 1959

Careers (1929)
New York Times p. 23, Jun. 10, 1929

Carefree (1938)
Commonweal 28:505, Sep. 9, 1938
Life 5:28-30, Aug. 22, 1938
New York Times X, p. 3, Jun. 12, 1938; p. 35, Sep. 23, 1938; IX, p. 5, Sep. 25, 1938
Newsweek 12:20-1, Sep. 12, 1938
Time 32:32, Sep. 5, 1938

Careless Age (1929)
New York Times p. 17, Sep. 21, 1929

Careless Lady (1932)
New York Times p. 19, Apr. 18, 1932

Careless Years (1957)
Catholic World 185:464, Sep., 1957
National Parent-Teacher 52:34, Dec., 1957
New York Times p. 57, Nov. 28, 1957
Newsweek 50:120, Sep. 16, 1957

Caretakers (1963)
Commonweal 79:46+, Oct. 4, 1963
New York Times p. 19, Aug. 22, 1963
Saturday Review 46:34, Aug. 10, 1963
Time 82:84, Sep. 6, 1963

Cargo to Capetown (1950)
New York Times p. 36, Mar. 31, 1950

Caribbean (1952)
National Parent-Teacher 47:37, Oct., 1952
Newsweek 40:107, Nov. 3, 1952

Caribbean Mystery (1945)
New York Times p. 22, Aug. 20, 1945

Cariboo Trail (1950)
New York Times p. 17, Sep. 1, 1950

Carmen (1946)
New Republic 115:932, Dec. 30, 1946
New York Times II, p. 5, Nov. 24, 1946; p. 20, Nov.
27, 1946
Newsweek 28:101, Dec. 9, 1946
Time 48:104, Dec. 2, 1946

Carmen Comes Home (1960)
New York Times p. 22, Dec. 23, 1959

Carmen Jones (1954)
America 92:165, Nov. 6, 1954
Catholic World 180:221, Dec., 1954
Commentary 19:74-7, Jan., 1955
Commonweal 61:188, Nov. 19, 1954
Farm Journal 78:141, Dec., 1954
Harper 210:87, Jan., 1955
Library Journal 79:2182, Nov. 15, 1954
Life 37:87-90, Nov. 1, 1954
Nation 179:430, Nov. 13, 1954
National Parent-Teacher 49:39, Dec., 1954
New York Times VI, p. 64, Oct. 17, 1954; II, p. 5, Oct.
24, 1954; p. 29, Oct. 29, 1954; II, p. 1, Oct. 31,
1954
New York Times Magazine p. 64-5, Oct. 17, 1954
New Yorker 30:181, Nov. 6, 1954
Newsweek 44:102, Oct. 25, 1954
Saturday Review 38:63, Jan. 1, 1955; 37:39-40, Nov. 6,
1954
Time 64:98, Nov. 1, 1954

Carnation Kid (1929)
Life (NY) 93:32, Apr. 12, 1939
New York Times p. 16, Feb. 25, 1929

Carnegie Hall (1947)
Commonweal 44:118, May 16, 1947
Holiday 2:140, Jul., 1947
Musician 51:106-7, Aug., 1946
Musical Courier 135:20, May 15, 1947
Nation 164:553, May 10, 1947
New Republic 116:34, May 19, 1947
New York Times p. 27, Aug. 6, 1946; II, p. 3, Aug. 11,
1946; VI, p. 48, Sep. 1, 1946; II, p. 5, Dec. 22,
1946; II, p. 5, Apr. 27, 1947; p. 10, May 3, 1947

Carnegie Hall (1947) (Continued)
II, p. 1, May 4, 1947; II, p. 7, May 25, 1947
New York Times Magazine p. 48-9, Sep. 1, 1946
New Yorker 23:62, May 10, 1947
Newsweek 29:88, May 5, 1947
Scholastic 50:45, Apr. 14, 1947
Theatre Arts 30:669, Nov., 1946; 31:51-2, May, 1947
Time 49:101, May 12, 1947
Woman's Home Companion 74:10-11, Jul., 1947

Carnet De Bal (see Life Dances On)

Carnival (1935)
New York Times p. 9, Feb. 16, 1935
Newsweek 5:26, Feb. 23, 1935
Time 25:53, Feb. 25, 1935

Carnival Boat (1932)
New York Times p. 19, Mar. 21, 1932

Carnival in Costa Rica (1947)
Nation 164:553, May 10, 1947
New York Times II, p. 5, Mar. 23, 1947; p. 21, Mar.
29, 1947
Time 49:100, Apr. 14, 1947

Carnival in Flanders (1936)
Commonweal 25:52, Nov. 6, 1936
Nation 143:428-9, Oct. 10, 1936
New Republic 88:281, Oct. 14, 1936
New York Times IX, p. 5, Sep. 20, 1936; p. 29, Sep. 23,
1936; p. 19, Jan. 5, 1937; X, p. 5, Jan. 10, 1937
Newsweek 8:34, Oct. 3, 1936
Stage 14:42-3, Jun., 1937
Theatre Arts 25:657, Sep., 1941
Time 28:30, Oct. 5, 1936

Carnival of Crime (1929)
New York Times p. 17, Jul. 8, 1929

Carnival Story (1954)
America 91:203, May 15, 1954
Commonweal 60:118, May 7, 1954
National Parent-Teacher 48:38, May, 1954
New York Times p. 8, Apr. 17, 1954
New Yorker 30:81, Apr. 24, 1954
Newsweek 43:81, Apr. 5, 1954

Carnival Story (1954) (Continued)
Saturday Review 37:26, May 8, 1954
Time 63:100, Apr. 19, 1954

Carolina (1934)
New York Times p. 17, Feb. 16, 1934; IX, p. 5, Feb.
25, 1934
Time 23:20, Feb. 19, 1934

Carolina Blues (1944)
New York Times p. 26, Dec. 8, 1944; II, p. 5, Dec. 10,
1944
New Yorker 20:61, Dec. 16, 1944

Caroline Cherie (1954)
New York Times p. 23, May 25, 1954; II, p. 1, May 30,
1958
Saturday Review 37:27, Jun. 5, 1954

Carousel (1956)
America 94:620, Mar. 3, 1956
Catholic World 183:59, Apr., 1956
Commonweal 63:592, Mar. 9, 1956
Library Journal 81:821, Apr. 1, 1956
Life 40:90-2+, Feb. 6, 1956
National Parent-Teacher 50:38, Apr., 1956
New York Times II, p. 7, Sep. 11, 1955; VI, p. 68, Jan.
8, 1956; VI, p. 69, Jan. 8, 1956; p. 13, Feb. 17,
1956; II, p. 1, Feb. 19, 1956
New York Times Magazine p. 68-9, Jan. 8, 1956
New Yorker 32:68, Mar. 3, 1956
Newsweek 47:90, Mar. 5, 1956
Saturday Review 39:23, Mar. 3, 1956
Scholastic 68:4, Apr. 12, 1956
Time 67:108, Mar. 19, 1956

Carpetbaggers (1963)
Commonweal 80:514, Jul. 24, 1964
Life 56:12+, Jun. 26, 1964
New York Times p. 24, Jul. 2, 1964; II, p. 1, Jul. 5,
1964
Saturday Review 47:29, Jun. 20, 1964
Time 84:86, Jul. 3, 1964

Carrie (1952)
Catholic World 175:383-4, Aug., 1952
Christian Century 69:1175, Oct. 8, 1952

190

Carrie (1952) (Continued)
Commonweal 56:412, Aug. 1, 1952
Holiday 12:20+, Aug., 1952
Library Journal 77:1185, Jul., 1952
Nation 174:485, May 17, 1952
New York Times p. 20, Jul. 17, 1952; II, p. 1, Jul. 20, 1952
New Yorker 28:50, Jul. 26, 1952
Newsweek 40:81, Jul. 28, 1952
Saturday Review 35:25, Jul. 12, 1952
Theatre Arts 36:44, May, 1952
Time 59:59, Jun. 30, 1952

Carry on Nurse (1960)
New York Times p. 11, Sep. 10, 1960
New Yorker 36:168, Sep. 24, 1960
Time 76:94, Sep. 26, 1960

Carry on, Sergeant (1959)
New York Times p. 40, Oct. 28, 1959

Carson City (1952)
New York Times p. 12, Jun. 14, 1952
Newsweek 40:79, Jul. 7, 1952

Carthage in Flames (1960)
New York Times p. 32, Jan. 26, 1961

Casablanca (1943)
Commonweal 37:207, Dec. 11, 1942
Nation 156:283, Feb. 20, 1943
New Republic 107:793, Dec. 14, 1942
New York Times p. 27, Nov. 27, 1942; VIII, p. 3, Nov. 29, 1942; p. 17, Mar. 3, 1944; VI, p. 15, Mar. 12, 1944
Newsweek 20:78, Nov. 30, 1942
Photoplay 22:4, Feb., 1943
Theatre Arts 27:7, Jan., 1943
Time 40:94+, Nov. 30, 1942

Casanova Brown (1944)
Commonweal 40:547-8, Sep. 22, 1944
Cosmopolitan 117:85, Oct., 1944
Life 17:87-8, Sep. 18, 1944
Nation 159:334, Sep. 16, 1944
New York Times p. 16, Sep. 15, 1944
New Yorker 20:54, Sep. 23, 1944

Casanova Brown (1944) (Continued)
Newsweek 24:97-9, Aug. 28, 1944
Theatre Arts 28:597, Oct., 1944
Time 44:92+, Sep. 18, 1944

Casanova's Big Night (1954)
America 91:147, May 1, 1954
Farm Journal 78:137, May, 1954
National Parent-Teacher 48:39, May, 1954
New York Times p. 19, Apr. 19, 1954
New Yorker 30:110, May 1, 1954
Newsweek 43:80, Apr. 5, 1954
Saturday Review 37:36, Apr. 10, 1954
Scholastic 64:30, Apr. 21, 1954
Time 63:110+, Apr. 26, 1954

Casbah (1948)
Commonweal 48:675, Apr. 30, 1948
New York Times p. 27, May 3, 1948; II, p. 5, May 22,
1949
Newsweek 31:96, May 17, 1948
Time 51:98, Jun. 14, 1948

Case Against Mrs. Ames (1936)
Literary Digest 121:20+, May 16, 1936
New York Times p. 19, May 28, 1936
Newsweek 7:42, May 16, 1936
Time 27:62, May 18, 1936

Case of Dr. Laurent (1958)
Commonweal 68:376, Jul. 11, 1958
Look 22:86-7, Aug. 5, 1958
Nation 187:40, Jul. 19, 1958
New Republic 139:21, Jul. 21, 1958
New York Times p. 23, Jun. 26, 1958
New Yorker 34:60, Jul. 5, 1958
Time 72:60, Sep. 1, 1958

Case of Sergeant Grischa (1930)
Life (NY) 95:22, Apr. 11, 1930
New York Times p. 22, Feb. 26, 1930; p. 21, Mar. 8,
1930; IX, p. 5, Mar. 16, 1930
Outlook 154:471, Mar. 19, 1930

Case of the Black Parrot (1941)
New York Times p. 23, Jan. 10, 1941

Case of the Curious Bride (1935)
New York Times p. 21, Apr. 5, 1935
Time 25:38, Apr. 15, 1935

Case of the Howling Dog (1934)
Canadian Magazine 82:40, Dec., 1934
New York Times p. 26, Oct. 18, 1934

Case of the Lucky Legs (1935)
New York Times p. 25, Nov. 1, 1935

Case of the Missing Man (1936)
New York Times p. 23, Nov. 23, 1935

*Case of the Mukkinese Battle-Horn
Commonweal 76:497, Sep. 7, 1962
Newsweek 60:86, Aug. 20, 1962
Time 80:75, Aug. 17, 1962

Case of the Velvet Claws (1936)
New York Times p. 16, Aug. 29, 1936

Cash McCall (1960)
Commonweal 71:573, Feb. 19, 1960
New York Times p. 26, Jan. 28, 1960
Newsweek 55:91, Jan. 18, 1960
Time 75:76, Feb. 1, 1960

Cash on Delivery (1954)
Commonweal 63:643, Mar. 23, 1956
National Parent-Teacher 50:38, Mar., 1956
New York Times p. 19, Sep. 1, 1956

Cash on Demand (1962)
New York Times p. 31, May 17, 1962

Casino Murder Case (1935)
New York Times p. 26, Apr. 17, 1935

*Casque D'Or
Commonweal 56:559, Sep. 12, 1952
New York Times p. 19, Aug. 19, 1952; II, p. 1, Sep. 14,
1952
New Yorker 28:52, Aug. 30, 1952
Newsweek 40:64, Sep. 1, 1952
Theatre Arts 36:96, Oct., 1952

Cass Timberlane (1947)
Commonweal 47:145, Nov. 21, 1947
Cosmopolitan 124:10-11+, Jan., 1948
New Republic 117:34, Nov. 24, 1947
New York Times II, p. 5, Jan. 19, 1947; II, p. 3, Jul.
 20, 1947; II, p. 5, Nov. 2, 1947; p. 20, Nov. 7, 1947;
 II, p. 1, Nov. 9, 1947
New Yorker 23:118, Nov. 15, 1947
Newsweek 30:98-9, Nov. 17, 1947
Photoplay 32:21, Feb., 1948
Time 50:104, Nov. 24, 1947
Woman's Home Companion 75:10-11, Feb., 1948

Cassidy of Bar 20 (1938)
New York Times p. 19, Mar. 28, 1938

Cassino to Korea (1950)
New York Times p. 38, Oct. 4, 1950

Cast a Dark Shadow (1958)
New York Times p. 57, Nov. 28, 1957
New Yorker 33:99, Dec. 7, 1957

Castilian (1963)
New York Times p. 31, Oct. 3, 1963

Castle in the Air (1952)
National Parent-Teacher 47:26, Mar., 1953
New York Times p. 19, Jan. 5, 1953
New Yorker 28:75, Jan. 10, 1953
Time 61:96+, Jan. 26, 1953

Castle on the Hudson (1940)
New York Times p. 11, Mar. 4, 1940

Cat (1959)
New York Times p. 35, Apr. 13, 1959
New Yorker 35:97-8, Apr. 18, 1959

Cat and the Canary (1939)
Commonweal 31:119, Nov. 24, 1939
New York Times p. 38, Nov. 23, 1939; IX, p. 5, Nov.
 26, 1939
Newsweek 14:37, Nov. 20, 1939
Photoplay 53:62, Dec., 1939
Time 34:82, Nov. 27, 1939

Cat and the Fiddle (1934)
New York Times p. 20, Feb. 17, 1934; IX, p. 5, Feb.
25, 1934; X, p. 4, Apr. 28, 1935
Vanity Fair 42:49, Apr., 1934

Cat Creeps (1930)
New York Times p. 21, Nov. 8, 1930

Cat Creeps (1946)
New York Times p. 12, May 18, 1946

Cat on a Hot Tin Roof (1958)
America 99:679, Sep. 27, 1958
Catholic World 188:153, Nov., 1958
Commonweal 68:637, Sep. 26, 1958
Cosmopolitan 145:18, Sep., 1958
Library Journal 83:2667, Oct. 1, 1958
Nation 187:220, Oct. 11, 1958
New Republic 139:21-3, Sep. 29, 1958
New York Times VI, p. 34, Aug. 31, 1958; p. 24, Sep.
19, 1958; II, p. 1, Sep. 21, 1958
New Yorker 34:163-4, Sep. 27, 1958
Newsweek 52:56, Sep. 1, 1958
Saturday Review 41:58, Sep. 13, 1958
Time 72:92, Sep. 15, 1958

Cat People (1943)
New York Times p. 22, Dec. 7, 1942
Time 41:86, Jan. 4, 1943

Cat Women of the Moon (1953)
New York Times p. 10, Mar. 20, 1954
Time 62:112, Oct. 19, 1953

Catered Affair (1956)
America 95:312, Jun. 23, 1956
Catholic World 183:222, Jun., 1956
Commonweal 64:300, Jun. 22, 1956
Library Journal 81:705, Mar. 15, 1956
Library Journal 81:1609, Jun. 15, 1956
National Parent-Teacher 50:37, Jun., 1956
New York Times p. 32, Jun. 15, 1956; II, p. 1, Jun. 24,
1956
New Yorker 32:71, Jun. 23, 1956
Newsweek 47:94+, Jun. 25, 1956
Saturday Review 39:25, Jun. 2, 1956
Time 68:78, Jul. 2, 1956

Catherine the Great (1934)
Canadian Magazine 81:44-5, Apr., 1934
Literary Digest 117:40, Mar. 3, 1934
Nation 138:285-6, Mar. 7, 1934
New Outlook 163:33, Mar., 1934
New York Times p. 13, Jan. 20, 1934; p. 15, Feb. 15, 1934; IX, p. 5, Feb. 25, 1934
New Republic 78:102-3, Mar. 7, 1934
Newsweek 3:34, Feb. 24, 1934
Pictorial Review 35:78, May, 1934
Review of Reviews 89:58, Apr., 1934
Time 23:20-22, Feb. 19, 1934

Catman of Paris (1946)
New York Times p. 12, Jul. 13, 1946

Cat's Paw (1934)
New York Times p. 12, Aug. 17, 1934; IX, p. 3, Aug. 26, 1934
Newsweek 4:24, Aug. 25, 1934

Cattle Drive (1950)
Christian Century 68:1175, Oct. 10, 1951
New York Times p. 17, Aug. 19, 1951
Newsweek 38:80, Aug. 13, 1951

Cattle Queen of Montana (1954)
National Parent-Teacher 49:39, Jan., 1955
New York Times p. 22, Jan. 26, 1955; II, p. 1, Jan. 30, 1955

Cattle Town (1952)
National Parent-Teacher 47:36, Feb., 1953

Caucasian Love (1929)
New York Times p. 28, Dec. 3, 1929

Caught (1948)
Commonweal 49:521, Mar. 4, 1949
New Republic 120:30, Mar. 7, 1949
New York Times p. 26, Feb. 18, 1949
New Yorker 25:73, Feb. 26, 1949
Newsweek 33:79, Feb. 28, 1949
Theatre Arts 33:93, May, 1949
Time 53:103, Mar. 7, 1949

Caught in the Draft (1941)
Commonweal 34:278, Jul. 11, 1941

Caught in the Draft (1941) (Continued)
New York Times IX, p. 5, Feb. 2, 1941; p. 27, Jun. 26, 1941
Newsweek 18:50, Jul. 7, 1941
Scribner's Commentator 10:105, Sep., 1941
Time 38:64+, Jul. 7, 1941

Caught in the Fog (1928)
New York Times p. 30, Dec. 3, 1928; X, p. 7, Dec. 9, 1929

Caught Plastered (1931)
New York Times p. 15, Sep. 12, 1931

Caught Short (1930)
Life (NY) 95:17, Jul. 18, 1930
New York Times p. 20, Jun. 21, 1930; VIII, p. 3, Jun. 29, 1930

Cause for Alarm (1951)
Christian Century 68:383, Mar. 21, 1951
Commonweal 53:470, Feb. 16, 1951
New York Times p. 28, Mar. 30, 1951
Rotarian 78:38, May, 1951
Time 57:100+, Feb. 26, 1951

Cavalcade (1933)
Canadian Magazine 78:37, Dec., 1932
Catholic World 137:206-7, May, 1933
Commonweal 17:357, Jan. 25, 1933
Literary Digest 115:15-16, Jan. 28, 1933; 115:12, Apr. 8, 1933
Motion Picture 45:40-41+, Feb., 1933
Nation 136:130-1, Feb. 1, 1933
New Republic 74:282, Apr. 19, 1933
New York Times IX, p. 4, Sep. 25, 1932; p. 23, Jan. 6, 1933; p. 20, Jan. 12, 1933; IX, p. 5, Jan. 15, 1933; p. 10, Mar. 17, 1934
Saturday Review 9:527, Apr. 8, 1933
Stage 10:40, Feb., 1933
Time 21:19, Jan. 16, 1933
Vanity Fair 40:48, Mar., 1933

Cavalier (1928)
New York Times p. 28, Oct. 31, 1928; IX, p. 7, Nov. 4, 1928

Cavalry Scout (1951)
   Christian Century 68:975, Aug. 22, 1951
   New York Times p. 32, Jun. 8, 1951

Cease Fire (1953)
   America 90:304, Dec. 12, 1953
   Commonweal 59:226, Dec. 4, 1953
   Farm Journal 78:108, Feb., 1954
   Look 17:38, Dec. 29, 1953
   National Parent-Teacher 48:39, Jan., 1954
   New York Times II, p. 5, Sep. 27, 1953; p. 17, Nov. 25,
      1953; II, p. 1, Nov. 29, 1953
   New Yorker 29:141, Dec. 5, 1953
   Newsweek 42:90-1, Dec. 14, 1953
   Saturday Review 36:52, Dec. 5, 1953
   Time 62:114, Dec. 14, 1953

Ceiling Zero (1936)
   New Republic 85:369, Feb. 5, 1936
   New York Times p. 22, Jan. 20, 1936; IX, p. 5, Jan.
      26, 1936
   Newsweek 7:41, Jan. 18, 1936
   Time 27:46, Jan. 27, 1936

Cell 2455, Death Row (1955)
   Library Journal 80:775, Apr. 1, 1955
   National Parent-Teacher 49:38, May, 1955
   Newsweek 45:109, Apr. 25, 1955
   Saturday Review 38:26, Jun. 11, 1955
   Scholastic 66:30, May 11, 1955

Centennial Summer (1946)
   Commonweal 44:384, Aug. 2, 1946
   Cosmopolitan 121:66+, Jul., 1946
   Liberty 23:68-9, Aug. 24, 1946
   New York Times II, p. 3, Sep. 2, 1945; II, p. 3, Oct.
      14, 1945; II, p. 3, Jul. 14, 1946; p. 20, Jul. 18, 1946
   New Yorker 22:49, Jul. 27, 1946
   Newsweek 28:78-9, Jul. 29, 1946
   Photoplay 29:22, Sep., 1946
   Time 48:88+, Jul. 29, 1946

Central Airport (1933)
   New Outlook 162:47, May, 1933
   New York Times IX, p. 3, Apr. 2, 1933; p. 20, May 4,
      1933

Central Park (1932)
New York Times p. 29, Dec. 7, 1932; IX, p. 5, Dec.
  25, 1932

Ceremony (1963)
America 110:749-50, May 23, 1964
New York Times p. 39, May 14, 1964
Newsweek 63:89, Feb. 24, 1964
Saturday Review 47:27, Jan. 18, 1964

Certain Smile (1958)
America 99:539, Aug. 23, 1958
Commonweal 68:496, Aug. 15, 1958
Library Journal 83:2278, Sep. 1, 1958
New York Times p. 13, Aug. 1, 1958; II, p. 1, Aug. 3,
  1958
New Yorker 34:58+, Aug. 9, 1958
Newsweek 52:87, Aug. 11, 1958
Time 72:70, Aug. 11, 1958

Certain Young Man (1928)
New York Times p. 27, Jun. 11, 1928

Chad Hanna (1940)
New York Times IX, p. 3, Oct. 6, 1940; IX, p. 6, Oct.
  20, 1940; X, p. 8, Dec. 8, 1940; p. 23, Dec. 26,
  1940
Newsweek 17:53: Jan. 6, 1941
Time 37:48, Jan. 6, 1941

Chain Lightning (1950)
Christian Century 67:383, Mar. 22, 1950
Commonweal 51:582, Mar. 10, 1950
New York Times p. 21, Feb. 20, 1950
New Yorker 26:85, Mar. 4, 1950
Newsweek 35:84, Mar. 6, 1950
Rotarian 76:40, May, 1950
Scholastic 55:25, Jan. 11, 1950
Time 55:92, Mar. 6, 1950

Chained (1934)
New York Times p. 16, Sep. 1, 1934; IX, p. 3, Sep. 9,
  1934

Chalk Garden (1963)
America 110:805, Jun. 6, 1964
Commonweal 80:298, May 29, 1964

Chalk Garden (1963) (Continued)
Life 56:21, Jun. 12, 1964
New Republic 150:25-6, May 30, 1964
New York Times p. 42, May 22, 1964; II, p. 1, May 31, 1964
New Yorker 40:112+, May 30, 1964
Newsweek 63:84, Jun. 1, 1964
Saturday Review 47:50, Jun. 27, 1964
Senior Scholastic 84:11T, May 15, 1964; 84:32, May 8, 1964
Time 83:85, May 29, 1964

Challenge (1939)
New York Times p. 15, Oct. 2, 1939
Photoplay 53:90, Dec., 1939

Challenge to Lassie (1949)
Christian Century 67:159, Feb. 1, 1950
New York Times p. 22, Apr. 7, 1950
Newsweek 35:78, Jan. 16, 1950
Rotarian 76:38, Apr., 1950

Challenge to Live (1961)
New York Times p. 33, Apr. 8, 1964

Champ (1931)
Life (NY) 98:21, Nov. 27, 1931
Nation 133:652, Dec. 9, 1931
New York Times p. 29, Nov. 10, 1931; VIII, p. 5, Nov. 15, 1931
Outlook 159:406, Nov. 25, 1931

Champ for a Day (1953)
National Parent-Teacher 48:36, Nov., 1953

Champagne Charlie (1936)
New York Times p. 21, May 7, 1936
Time 27:62, May 18, 1936

Champagne for Caesar (1950)
Christian Century 67:800, Jun. 28, 1950
Commonweal 52:172, May 26, 1950
Good Housekeeping 130:139, Mar., 1950
Life 28:119-22, Apr. 10, 1950
New Republic 122:23, May 29, 1950
New York Times II, p. 5, Sep. 25, 1949; p. 33, May 12, 1950
New Yorker 26:106, May 20, 1950
Newsweek 35:87-8, May 8, 1950
Rotarian 77:43, Aug., 1950
Time 55:94+, May 8, 1950

Champagne Waltz (1937)
Commonweal 25:418, Feb. 5, 1937
Harper's Bazaar 79:64, Jan., 1945
New York Times X, p. 4, Jan. 24, 1937; XI, p. 4, Jan.
31, 1937; p. 17, Feb. 4, 1937
Time 29:45, Jan. 25, 1937

Champion (1948)
Commonweal 50:69, Apr. 29, 1949
Cosmopolitan 126:12+, May, 1949
Good Housekeeping 128:231, Jun., 1949
Life 26:68-70+, Apr. 11, 1949
Nation 168:538-9, May 7, 1949
New Republic 120:30, Apr. 25, 1949
New York Times II, p. 5, Apr. 10, 1949; p. 29, Apr.
11, 1949
New Yorker 25:60, Apr. 9, 1949
Newsweek 33:89, Apr. 11, 1949
Photoplay 36:31, Jun., 1949
Rotarian 75:36, Sep., 1949
Theatre Arts 33:92, May, 1949
Time 53:102+, Apr. 11, 1949

Champs Elysses (1939)
New York Times p. 17, Feb. 28, 1939

Chance at Heaven (1933)
New York Times p. 19, Dec. 26, 1933

Chance Meeting (1954)
America 93:139, Apr. 30, 1955
Catholic World 181:61, Apr., 1955
Commonweal 62:77, Apr. 22, 1955
Nation 180:411, May 7, 1955
National Parent-Teacher 49:39, Apr., 1955
New York Times p. 38, Apr. 20, 1955; II, p. 1, Apr.
24, 1955
New Yorker 31:117, Apr. 30, 1955
Newsweek 45:88, Feb. 28, 1955
Scholastic 66:19, Mar. 23, 1955

Chance Meeting (1960)
Commonweal 71:655, Mar. 11, 1960
New Republic 142:30, Apr. 4, 1960
New York Times p. 45, Oct. 27, 1960
Saturday Review 43:26, Feb. 27, 1960

Chance of a Lifetime (1950)
New Republic 124:22, Mar. 26, 1951
New York Times p. 37, Mar. 15, 1951
New Yorker 27:118, Mar. 17, 1950
Newsweek 37:87, Mar. 5, 1951
Saturday Review 34:25, Mar. 10, 1951
Time 55:90, May 8, 1950

Chance of a Night Time (1931)
New York Times VIII, p. 6, Jun. 7, 1931

Chances (1931)
Life (NY) 98:18, Jul. 17, 1931
New York Times p. 27, Jun. 12, 1931; VIII, p. 3, Jun.
21, 1931

Chandu, the Magician (1932)
New York Times p. 10, Oct. 1, 1932

Change of Heart (1934)
New York Times p. 24, May 11, 1934; IX, p. 3, May 20,
1934

Channel Crossing (1934)
New York Times p. 28, May 24, 1934; IX, p. 3, Jun. 3,
1934
Newsweek 3:36, Jun. 2, 1934

*Chapayev
Nation 140:140, Jan. 30, 1935
New Republic 81:360, Feb. 6, 1935
New York Times X, p. 3, Jun. 30, 1935; IX, p. 4, Sep.
8, 1935
Time 25:32-3, Jan. 28, 1935

Chapman Report (1962)
America 107:1012, Nov. 3, 1962
Commonweal 77:315, Dec. 14, 1962
New York Times II, p. 7, Oct. 15, 1961; p. 49, Oct. 18,
1962
New Yorker 38:205, Oct. 27, 1962
Newsweek 60:88, Oct. 29, 1962
Redbook 120:36+, Nov., 1962
Time 80:101, Nov. 2, 1962

Charade (1963)
America 109:810, Dec. 21, 1963
Commonweal 79:349, Dec. 13, 1963

Charade (1963) (Continued)
New Republic 149:29, Dec. 21, 1963
New York Times p. 40, Dec. 6, 1963
New Yorker 39:196, Dec. 14, 1963
Newsweek 62:90, Dec. 16, 1963
Saturday Review 46:24, Dec. 14, 1963
Time 82:63, Dec. 20, 1963
Vogue 143:24, Jan. 1, 1964

Charge at Feather River (1953)
America 89:366, Jul. 4, 1953
Farm Journal 77:118, Sep., 1953
National Parent-Teacher 48:38, Oct., 1953
New York Times p. 17, Jul. 16, 1953
New Yorker 29:47, Jul. 25, 1953
Newsweek 42:76, Aug. 3, 1953
Saturday Review 36:36, Jul. 11, 1953
Time 62:97, Jul. 13, 1953

Charge of the Lancers (1953)
National Parent-Teacher 48:39, Mar., 1954

Charge of the Light Brigade (1936)
Canadian Magazine 86:46, Oct., 1936
Commonweal 25:76, Nov. 13, 1936
Literary Digest 122:30, Oct. 17, 1936
Movie Classic 11:12, Jan., 1937
New York Times IX, p. 3, Mar. 22, 1936; X, p. 3, May
   3, 1936; X, p. 4, Oct. 25, 1936; p. 24, Nov. 2, 1936;
   X, p. 5, Nov. 8, 1936
Newsweek 8:24-5, Oct. 31, 1936
Scholastic 29:29-36, Sep. 19, 1936
Stage 14:69, Nov., 1936; 14:14, Dec., 1936
Time 28:21, Nov. 2, 1936

Charlatan (1929)
New York Times p. 22, Apr. 15, 1929

Charley's Aunt (1930)
New York Times p. 18, Dec. 26, 1930; VIII, p. 5, Jan.
   11, 1931

Charley's Aunt (1942)
Commonweal 34:448, Aug. 29, 1941
New York Times p. 18, Aug. 2, 1941
Newsweek 18:60, Aug. 11, 1941
Scribner's Commentator 10:106, Oct., 1941
Time 38:71, Aug. 18, 1941

Charlie Chan at Monte Carlo (1938)
New York Times p. 18, Dec. 18, 1937

Charlie Chan at the Circus (1936)
New York Times p. 22, Mar. 19, 1936
Newsweek 7:26, Mar. 28, 1936

Charlie Chan at the Olympics (1937)
New York Times p. 23, May 24, 1937

Charlie Chan at the Opera (1937)
New York Times p. 16, Dec. 5, 1936

Charlie Chan at the Race Track (1937)
New York Times p. 6, Aug. 15, 1936
Time 28:44, Aug. 17, 1936

Charlie Chan at the Wax Museum (1940)
New York Times p. 9, Sep. 28, 1940

Charlie Chan at Treasure Island (1939)
New York Times p. 15, Sep. 1, 1939

Charlie Chan Carries On (1931)
New York Times p. 15, Mar. 21, 1931; VIII, p. 6, Mar.
22, 1931; VIII, p. 5, Mar. 29, 1931

Charlie Chan in Egypt (1935)
New York Times p. 12, Jun. 24, 1935
Time 26:35, Jul. 1, 1935

Charlie Chan in Honolulu (1939)
New York Times IX, p. 7, Dec. 18, 1938; p. 7, Dec. 31,
1938
Photoplay 53:53, Mar., 1939

Charlie Chan in London (1934)
New York Times p. 26, Sep. 13, 1934

Charlie Chan in Panama (1940)
New York Times p. 19, Feb. 23, 1940

Charlie Chan in Paris (1935)
New York Times p. 23, Jan. 22, 1935
Time 25:40-41, Feb. 4, 1935

Charlie Chan in Reno (1939)
New York Times p. 27, May 31, 1939

Charlie Chan in Reno (1939) (Continued)
   Photoplay 53:54, Aug., 1939

Charlie Chan in Shanghai (1935)
   New York Times p. 21, Oct. 14, 1935

Charlie Chan on Broadway (1937)
   New York Times p. 19, Sep. 20, 1937

Charlie Chan's Chance (1931)
   New York Times p. 18, Jan. 23, 1932; VIII, p. 4, Jan.
   31, 1932

Charlie Chan's Courage (1934)
   New York Times p. 16, Aug. 25, 1934; IX, p. 3, Sep. 2,
   1934

Charlie Chan's Greatest Case (1933)
   New York Times p. 18, Oct. 7, 1933

Charlie Chan's Murder Cruise (1940)
   New York Times p. 17, May 3, 1940

Charlie McCarthy, Detective (1939)
   New York Times p. 29, Dec. 25, 1939

Charm of La Boheme (1938)
   New York Times p. 11, Mar. 19, 1938

Charming Deceiver (1933)
   New York Times p. 18, Dec. 9, 1933; IX, p. 7, Dec. 17,
   1933

Charming Sinners (1929)
   Life (NY) 94:27, Aug. 2, 1929
   New York Times p. 17, Jul. 8, 1929; IX, p. 3, Jul. 14,
   1929

Chase (1946)
   Commonweal 45:168, Nov. 29, 1946
   Life 21:137-8+, Nov. 11, 1946
   New York Times II, p. 6, Nov. 10, 1946; p. 31, Nov.
   18, 1946
   Newsweek 28:106, Nov. 25, 1946
   Time 48:101, Nov. 18, 1946

Chase a Crooked Shadow (1957)
   America 99:28, Apr. 5, 1958

Chase a Crooked Shadow (1957) (Continued)
Commonweal 67:661, Mar. 28, 1958
New York Times p. 28, Mar. 25, 1958
Time 71:101, Apr. 28, 1958

Chaser (1938)
New York Times p. 15, Aug. 2, 1938

*Chasers
Commonweal 71:698-9, Mar. 25, 1960
Nation 190:430-1, May 14, 1960
New York Times p. 43, May 3, 1960
Newsweek 55:89, May 2, 1960
Saturday Review 43:28, Mar. 19, 1960

Chasing Rainbows (1930)
Life (NY) 95:28, Mar. 28, 1930
New York Times p. 13, Feb. 22, 1930

Chatterbox (1936)
New York Times p. 18, Feb. 15, 1936
Scholastic 27:28, Jan. 25, 1936

Cheaper by the Dozen (1950)
Christian Century 67:575, May 3, 1950
Commonweal 52:17, Apr. 14, 1950
Library Journal 75:708, Apr. 15, 1950
New York Times p. 12, Apr. 1, 1950; II, p. 1, Apr. 9,
    1950
New Yorker 26:112, Apr. 8, 1950
Newsweek 35:82, Apr. 10, 1950
Parents Magazine 25:34-5+, May, 1950
Rotarian 76:37, Jun., 1950
Scholastic 56:23+, Apr. 26, 1950
Time 55:90, Apr. 10, 1950

Cheat (see Story of a Cheat)

Cheaters (1934)
New York Times p. 12, May 12, 1934

Cheaters (1945)
Commonweal 42:406, Aug. 10, 1945
New York Times p. 7, Jul. 21, 1945
Newsweek 26:85, Jul. 30, 1945

Cheaters (1961)
Commonweal 74:326-7, Jun. 23, 1961
New Republic 144:29, Jun. 19, 1961
New York Times p. 37, Jun. 5, 1961
New Yorker 37:58+, Jun. 24, 1961
Time 77:53, Jun. 23, 1961

Cheaters at Play (1932)
New York Times p. 21, Feb. 27, 1932

Cheating Blondes (1933)
New York Times p. 11, May 20, 1933

Check and Double Check (1930)
New York Times p. 16, Jul. 12, 1930; p. 23, Nov. 1,
    1930; IX, p. 5, Nov. 9, 1930

Checkpoint (1957)
New York Times p. 25, Sep. 19, 1957
New Yorker 33:90, Sep. 28, 1957

Cheers for Miss Bishop (1941)
Commonweal 33:543-4, Mar. 21, 1941
New Republic 104:372, Mar. 17, 1941
New York Times IX, p. 5, Feb. 2, 1941; IX, p. 4, Mar.
    9, 1941; p. 17, Mar. 14, 1941; IX, p. 5, Mar. 16,
    1941
Newsweek 17:47-8, Jan. 27, 1941
Photoplay 18:6, Apr., 1941
Scholastic 38:36, Feb. 10, 1941; 38:17-19+, Mar. 3, 1941
Scribner's Commentator 10:107, May, 1941
Time 37:70, Feb. 3, 1941

Cherokee Strip (1940)
New York Times p. 23, Nov. 4, 1940

Chetniks (1943)
New York Times p. 15, Mar. 19, 1943

Cheyenne (1947)
Commonweal 46:262, Jun. 27, 1947
Cosmopolitan 122:90, Jun., 1947
New York Times II, p. 3, May 12, 1946; p. 9, Jun. 7,
    1947; II, p. 5, Jun. 8, 1947
Newsweek 29:95, May 26, 1947
Time 49:97, Jun. 30, 1947

Chicago (1928)
Life (NY) 91:26, Feb. 16, 1928
New York Times p. 9, Dec. 24, 1927; VIII, p. 7, Dec.
25, 1927; IX, p. 7, Feb. 17, 1929

Chicago After Midnight (1928)
New York Times p. 20, Mar. 6, 1928

Chicago Calling (1952)
Christian Century 69:231, Feb. 20, 1952

Chicago Confidential (1957)
National Parent-Teacher 52:37, Nov., 1957
New York Times p. 19, Aug. 31, 1957

Chicago Deadline (1949)
Commonweal 51:294, Dec. 16, 1949
Good Housekeeping 129:238, Dec., 1949
New York Times p. 37, Nov. 3, 1949
Newsweek 34:93, Nov. 21, 1949
Photoplay 26:20, Nov., 1949
Rotarian 76:40, Jan., 1950
Time 54:102+, Nov. 21, 1949

Chicago Kid (1945)
New York Times p. 24, Feb. 12, 1945

Chicago Syndicate (1955)
National Parent-Teacher 49:38, Jun. 1955
New York Times p. 37, Jun. 21, 1955

Chicken A La King (1928)
New York Times p. 27, Jun. 11, 1928; VIII, p. 5, Jun.
17, 1928

Chicken Every Sunday (1949)
New York Times p. 34, Jan. 19, 1949
Newsweek 33:75, Jan. 31, 1949
Photoplay 34:21, May, 1949
Rotarian 74:34, May, 1949
Scholastic 53:37, Jan. 12, 1949
Time 53:86, Jan. 24, 1949

Chief (1933)
New York Times p. 9, Dec. 2, 1933

Chief Crazy Horse (1955)
National Parent-Teacher 49:38, Apr., 1955

Chief Crazy Horse (1955) (Continued)
New York Times p. 25, Apr. 28, 1955
Saturday Review 38:28, Mar. 5, 1955
Scholastic 66:27, Apr. 6, 1955
Time 65:86, May 30, 1955

Child is Born (1940)
New York Times p. 19, Jan. 11, 1940

Child is Waiting (1962)
America 108:275, Feb. 23, 1963
Catholic World 196:387-9, Mar., 1963
Commonweal 77:494, Feb. 1, 1963
New Republic 148:28+, Jan. 26, 1963
New York Times II, p. 9, Feb. 18, 1962; p. 5, Feb. 14, 1963
New Yorker 39:126, Feb. 23, 1963
Newsweek 61:78, Feb. 4, 1963
Saturday Review 46:31, Jan. 26, 1963

*Child of Man
Commonweal 51:488, Feb. 10, 1950
New Republic 122:23, Feb. 20, 1950
New York Times p. 25, Feb. 1, 1950
New Yorker 25:81, Feb. 11, 1950

Child of Manhattan (1933)
New York Times p. 11, Feb. 13, 1933

Childhood of Maxim Gorky (1938)
New York Times p. 29, Sep. 28, 1938

Children (see Marriage Playground)

Children of Dreams (1931)
New York Times p. 20, Jul. 20, 1931

Children of Montmarte (see Maternelle, La)

Children of Paradise (see Enfants Du Paradis)

Children of the Revolution (1936)
New York Times p. 18, Apr. 6, 1936

Children of the Ritz (1929)
New York Times p. 28, Apr. 2, 1929

Children's Hour (1962)
America 107:360, Jun. 2, 1962
Commonweal 75:598, Mar. 2, 1962
New Republic 146:28, Apr. 16, 1962
New York Times p. 28, Mar. 15, 1962; II, p. 1, Mar. 18, 1962
New Yorker 38:123-4, Mar. 17, 1962
Newsweek 59:101, Mar. 12, 1962
Redbook 118:20+, Apr., 1962
Saturday Review 45:37, Feb. 24, 1962
Time 79:83, Feb. 9, 1962

China (1943)
Commonweal 38:74, May 7, 1943
Cosmopolitan 115:66, Jul., 1943
New York Times p. 31, Apr. 22, 1943
New Yorker 19:36+, May 1, 1943
Newsweek 21:84+, May 3, 1943
Photoplay 23:38-40+, Jun., 1943
Time 41:96, May 3, 1943

China Clipper (1936)
Canadian Magazine 86:46, Oct., 1936
Literary Digest 122:24, Aug. 22, 1936
New York Times p. 14, Aug. 12, 1936
Scholastic 29:32, Oct. 3, 1936
Time 28:32, Aug. 24, 1936

China Doll (1958)
New York Times p. 52, Dec. 4, 1958

China Gate (1957)
New York Times p. 40, May 23, 1957

China Girl (1942)
Commonweal 37:350, Jan. 22, 1943
New York Times p. 27, Jan. 21, 1943
Scholastic 42:36, Feb. 1, 1943

China Passage (1937)
New York Times p. 27, Apr. 16, 1937

China Seas (1935)
Literary Digest 120:28, Aug. 17, 1935
New York Times IX, p. 3, Apr. 21, 1935; p. 16, Aug. 10, 1935
Time 26:26, Aug. 19, 1935

China Sky (1945)
Commonweal 42:240, Jun. 22, 1945
New York Times II, p. 1, Sep. 24, 1944; p. 22, May 25,
1945

China Venture (1953)
National Parent-Teacher 48:36, Nov., 1953

Chinatown at Midnight (1949)
New York Times p. 35, May 18, 1949

Chinatown Nights (1929)
New York Times p. 22, Apr. 1, 1929

Chinatown Squad (1935)
New York Times p. 21, May 30, 1935

Chinese Den (1941)
New York Times p. 27, Mar. 26, 1941

Chip of the Flying "U" (1939)
New York Times p. 11, Jan. 22, 1939

Chip Off the Old Block (1943)
New Republic 110:471, Apr. 3, 1944
New York Times p. 14, Mar. 17, 1944

Chips are Down (1949)
Nation 168:193, Feb. 12, 1949
New Republic 120:29, Feb. 14, 1949
New York Times p. 36, Feb. 2, 1949; II, p. 5, Feb. 13,
1949
Newsweek 33:78, Feb. 14, 1949
Theatre Arts 33:88, Apr., 1949
Vogue 112:129, Nov. 1, 1948

Chocolate Soldier (1942)
Commonweal 35:94, Nov. 14, 1941
New York Times p. 20, Nov. 1, 1941; IX, p. 5, Nov. 19,
1941
Newsweek 18:68, Nov. 10, 1941
Time 38:92, Nov. 17, 1941

Christina (1929)
New York Times p. 22, Apr. 1, 1929; X, p. 7, Apr. 7,
1929

Christmas Carol (1938)
Commonweal 29:273, Dec. 30, 1938
Life 5:17, Dec. 26, 1938
New York Times IX, p. 7, Dec. 18, 1938; p. 16, Dec.
23, 1938; IX, p. 7, Dec. 25, 1938
Photoplay 53:74, Jan., 1939
Saint Nicholas 66:35, Jan., 1939
Scholastic 33:32, Jan. 7, 1939
Time 32:21, Dec. 19, 1938

*Christmas Carol
Christian Century 68:1495, Dec. 19, 1951
Commonweal 55:278, Dec. 21, 1951
Library Journal 76:2110, Dec. 15, 1951
New Republic 125:20, Dec. 17, 1951
New York Times p. 41, Nov. 9, 1951; II, p. 1, Dec. 2,
1951
New Yorker 27:67, Dec. 8, 1951
Newsweek 38:98, Dec. 10, 1951
Scholastic 59:26, Dec. 12, 1951
Time 58:104, Dec. 3, 1951

Christmas Eve (1947)
New York Times II, p. 5, Nov. 23, 1947; p. 30, Nov.
28, 1947
Newsweek 30:90, Aug. 4, 1947
Time 50:105, Dec. 8, 1947

Christmas Holiday (1944)
Commonweal 40:280, Jul. 7, 1944
Life 17:53-4, Jul. 3, 1944
Nation 159:24, Jul. 1, 1944
New York Times II, p. 3, Jan. 2, 1944; p. 16, Jun. 29,
1944; II, p. 3, Jul. 2, 1944
New Yorker 20:46, Jul. 1, 1944
Newsweek 24:86, Jul. 10, 1944
Time 44:88, Jul. 3, 1944
Woman's Home Companion 71:10, Aug., 1944

Christmas in Connecticut (1945)
Commonweal 42:335, Jul. 20, 1945
Nation 161:67, Jul. 21, 1945
New York Times p. 7, Jul. 28, 1945
Newsweek 26:86, Aug. 6, 1945
Time 46:96+, Jul. 23, 1945

Christmas in July (1940)
Commonweal 33:104, Nov. 15, 1940

Christmas in July (1940) (Continued)
New Republic 104:85, Jan. 20, 1941
New York Times IX, p. 5, Oct. 20, 1940; p. 35, Nov. 6,
1940; IX, p. 5, Nov. 10, 1940
Newsweek 16:73, Oct. 14, 1940
Photoplay 54:62, Dec., 1940
Scholastic 37:33, Nov. 18, 1940
Time 36:91, Oct. 21, 1940

Christopher Bean (1933) (see also Her Sweetheart)
New York Times p. 10, Nov. 25, 1933; p. 9, Dec. 3,
1933
Newsweek 2:33, Dec. 2, 1933

Christopher Columbus (1949)
Commonweal 51:36, Oct. 21, 1949
Coronet 26:61-8, Oct., 1949
New York Times II, p. 5, Apr. 4, 1948; II, p. 5, Oct.
9, 1949; p. 33, Oct. 13, 1949; II, p. 1, Oct. 16, 1949
Newsweek 34:94, Oct. 17, 1949
Rotarian 75:38, Dec., 1949
Scholastic 55:35, 37T, Sep. 28, 1949
Time 54:98, Nov. 7, 1949

Christopher Strong (1933)
Nation 136:354, Mar. 29, 1933
New York Times p. 19, Mar. 10, 1933; IX, p. 3, Mar.
19, 1933
Newsweek 1:28, Mar. 18, 1933
Vanity Fair 40:49-50, May, 1933

Chu Chin Chow (1934)
New York Times p. 12, Sep. 22, 1934

Chump at Oxford (1940)
New York Times p. 17, Feb. 20, 1940

Chushingura (1963)
New York Times p. 26, Oct. 4, 1963; II, p. 1, Oct. 20,
1963
Newsweek 62:115, Oct. 14, 1963

El Cid (1961)
America 106:405, Dec. 16, 1961
Commonweal 75:340, Dec. 22, 1961
National Review 12:103, Feb. 13, 1962
New Republic 146:22, Jan. 8, 1962

213

El Cid (1961) (Continued)
New York Times II, p. 5, Jan. 1, 1961; p. 49, Dec. 15,
    1961; II, p. 3, Dec. 17, 1961
Newsweek 58:98, Dec. 18, 1961
Redbook 118:29, Feb., 1962
Saturday Review 44:39, Dec. 23, 1961
Senior Scholastic 79:25, Jan. 10, 1962
Time 78:45, Dec. 22, 1961

Cimarron (1931)
Commonweal 13:440-1, Feb. 18, 1931
Life (NY) 97:23, Mar. 27, 1931
Literary Digest 108:28, Feb. 21, 1931
Nation 132:199-200, Feb. 18, 1931
New York Times p. 20, Jan. 27, 1931; VIII, p. 5, Feb. 1,
    1931
Outlook 157:233, Feb. 11, 1931
Photoplay 42:66-7+, Jul., 1932
Theatre Magazine 53:48, Jan., 1931

Cimarron (1960)
America 104:768-9, Mar. 11, 1961
Commonweal 73:587, Mar. 3, 1961
Life 50:81-2, Feb. 10, 1961
McCalls 88:181, Mar., 1961
New York Times II, p. 7, Jan. 10, 1960; p. 21, Feb. 17,
    1961; II, p. 1, Feb. 26, 1961
New Yorker 37:126+, Feb. 25, 1961
Newsweek 57:79-80, Jan. 16, 1961
Redbook 116:12-13, Feb., 1961
Saturday Review 44:31, Feb. 18, 1961
Senior Scholastic 78:22, Mar. 22, 1961
Time 77:38, Feb. 24, 1961

Cinderella (1949)
Christian Century 67:351, Mar. 15, 1950
Commonweal 51:607, Mar. 17, 1950; 58:298, Jun. 26,
    1953
Library Journal 75:410, Mar. 1, 1950
New York Times p. 30, Feb. 14, 1949; p. 33, Feb. 23,
    1949; II, p. 1, Feb. 26, 1949; p. 20, May 15, 1953
Newsweek 35:84+, Feb. 13, 1950
Rotarian 76:40, May, 1950
Saturday Review 33:28-30, Jun. 3, 1950
Scholastic 56:29, Apr. 5, 1950
Time 55:88+, Feb. 20, 1950

Cinderella (1960)
Dance Magazine 35:29, Dec., 1961
New York Times p. 30, Dec. 21, 1961

Cinderella Jones (1946)
New York Times II, p. 3, Mar. 10, 1946; p. 9, Mar. 16,
1946

Cinderfella (1959)
Commonweal 73:341, Dec. 23, 1960
New York Times p. 19, Dec. 17, 1960
Senior Scholastic 78:24, Feb. 15, 1961

*Cinerama Holiday
America 92:575, Feb. 26, 1955
Catholic World 180:463, Mar., 1955
Commonweal 61:582, Mar. 4, 1955
Dance Magazine 29:9, Mar., 1955
Nation 180:186, Feb. 26, 1955
National Parent-Teacher 49:38, Apr., 1955
Natural History 64:221, Apr., 1955
New York Times p. 31, Feb. 9, 1955; II, p. 1, Feb. 13,
1955; II, p. 5, Nov. 20, 1955
New Yorker 31:125, Feb. 19, 1955
Newsweek 45:88, Feb. 28, 1955
Scholastic 66:46, Mar. 16, 1955
Time 65:86, Feb. 28, 1955

Cinerama South Seas Adventure (1958)
New York Times p. 26, Jul. 16, 1958; II, p. 1, Jul. 20,
1958

Cipher Bureau (1938)
New York Times p. 32, Dec. 14, 1938

Circle (1959)
New York Times p. 29, Aug. 16, 1959
Newsweek 53:114, Apr. 27, 1959

Circle of Danger (1951)
Christian Century 68:671, May 30, 1951
Commonweal 54:38, Apr. 20, 1951
New Republic 125:23, Jul. 30, 1951
New York Times p. 21, Jul. 12, 1951
New Yorker 27:79, May 26, 1951; 27:74, Jul. 21, 1951
Newsweek 38:68, Jul. 30, 1951
Time 58:69, Jul. 30, 1951

Circle of Deception (1961)
America 104:676, Feb. 18, 1961
Commonweal 73:533, Feb. 17, 1961
New York Times p. 12, Feb. 18, 1961
Newsweek 57:89, Feb. 13, 1961
Time 77:38, Jan. 27, 1961

Circumstantial Evidence (1945)
New York Times p. 18, Apr. 21, 1945

Circus (1928)
Dial 84:257-9, Mar., 1928
Life (NY) 91:26, Jan. 26, 1928
Literary Digest 96:36, Mar. 24, 1928
Motion Picture Classic 26:28-9+, Oct., 1927
New York Times VIII, p. 5, Jan. 1, 1928; VIII, p. 3,
    Jan. 8, 1928; p. 20, Jan. 9, 1928; VIII, p. 7, Jan.
    15, 1928; II, p. 6, Feb. 12, 1928; p. 26, Mar. 16,
    1928; IX, p. 6, Apr. 1, 1928
Theatre Arts 32:50, Fall, 1948
Vanity Fair 30:68-9+, Mar., 1928

Circus Clown (1934)
New York Times p. 18, Jun. 30, 1934

Circus Kid (1928)
New York Times p. 23, Dec. 17, 1928; VIII, p. 7, Dec.
    23, 1928

Circus of Horrors (1960)
New York Times p. 31, Sep. 1, 1960

Circus of Love (1958)
New York Times p. 10, Aug. 16, 1958

Circus Queen Murder (1933)
New York Times p. 10, May 8, 1933

Circus Stars (1960)
New York Times p. 19, Jul. 28, 1960

Cisco Kid (1931)
New York Times p. 20, Oct. 24, 1931; VIII, p. 6, Oct.
    25, 1931; VIII, p. 5, Nov. 1, 1931

Citadel (1938)
Commonweal 29:77, Nov. 11, 1938
Education 59:157-63, Nov., 1938

Citadel (1938) (Continued)
Life 5:35-6, Nov. 7, 1938
Nation 147:516, Nov. 12, 1938
New Republic 97:46, Nov. 16, 1938
New York Times IX, p. 4, Oct. 30, 1938; p. 27, Nov.
4, 1938; IX, p. 5, Nov. 6, 1938; IX, p. 5, Nov. 13,
1938; p. 11, Dec. 17, 1938; p. 18, Jan. 3, 1939; IX,
p. 5, Jan. 8, 1939
Newsweek 12:28, Oct. 31, 1938
Scholastic 33:8-9, Oct. 22, 1938
Stage 16:57, Dec., 1938
Theatre Arts 23:188, Mar., 1939
Time 32:41, Nov. 7, 1938

Citadel of Silence (1939)
New York Times p. 29, Dec. 25, 1939

Citizen Kane (1941)
Commonweal 34:65, May 9, 1941
Life 10:53-6, Mar. 17, 1941; 10:108-16, May 26, 1941
Nation 152:508, Apr. 26, 1941
New Republic 104:760-1, Jun. 2, 1941; 104:824-5, Jun.
16, 1941
New York Times IX, p. 5, Jan. 19, 1941; p. 25, May 2,
1941; IX, p. 4, May 4, 1941; IX, p. 5, May 4, 1941;
p. 25, Dec. 22, 1941; p. 22, Dec. 31, 1941
New Yorker 17:79, May 3, 1941
Newsweek 17:60, Mar. 17, 1941
Photoplay 19:24, Jul., 1941
Scholastic 38:33, May 5, 1941
Scribner's Commentator 10:103-4, Jul., 1941
Stage 1:54-5, Dec., 1940
Theatre Arts 25:427-9, 431-2, Jun., 1941
Time 37:69, Jan. 27, 1941; 37:90+, Mar. 17, 1941

City (1939)
American City 54:129, Jun., 1939
Commonweal 30:218, Jun. 16, 1939
Life 6:64-5, Jun. 5, 1939
Nation 148:654, Jun. 3, 1939
New York Times X, p. 3, May 21, 1939
Theatre Arts 23:552-3, Aug., 1939
Time 33:66, Jun. 5, 1939

City Across the River (1949)
Good Housekeeping 128:265, May, 1949
New Republic 120:30, Apr. 25, 1949

217

City Across the River (1949) (Continued)
New York Times II, p. 5, Apr. 3, 1949; p. 31, Apr. 8,
1949; p. 38, Apr. 12, 1949
New Yorker 25:95, Apr. 16, 1949
Rotarian 75:36, Jul., 1949
Time 53:96+, Apr. 25, 1949

City Beneath the Sea (1953)
Commonweal 57:626, Mar. 27, 1953
Library Journal 78:516, Mar. 15, 1953
National Parent-Teacher 47:27, Mar., 1953
Natural History 62:139, Mar., 1953
New York Times p. 24, Mar. 12, 1953
Theatre Arts 37:89, Mar., 1953
Time 61:102+, Feb. 23, 1953

City for Conquest (1940)
Commonweal 32:492, Oct. 4, 1940
New York Times IX, p. 4, May 19, 1940; p. 9, Sep. 28,
1940
Newsweek 16:56, Sep. 30, 1940
Time 36:63, Oct. 7, 1940

City Girl (1938)
New York Times p. 17, Feb. 4, 1938

*City is Dark
National Parent-Teacher 48:39, Sep., 1953
Time 62:97, Jul. 13, 1953

City Lights (1931, 1950, 1963)
Bookman 73:184-5, Apr., 1931
Commonweal 13:553, Mar. 18, 1931; 52:15+, Apr. 14,
1950
Life 27:76, Sep. 5, 1949; 28:81-2+, May 8, 1950
Life (NY) 97:20, Feb. 27, 1931
Literary Digest 108:28, Feb. 28, 1931
Nation 132:250-1, Mar. 4, 1931
New Republic 66:46-7, Feb. 25, 1931; 122:21, May 1,
1950; 149:29, Dec. 21, 1963
New York Times VIII, p. 5, Jan. 12, 1930; VIII, p. 3,
Jul. 6, 1930; p. 11, Feb. 7, 1931; II, p. 5, Mar. 19,
1950; II, p. 1, Apr. 16, 1950; p. 56, Dec. 4, 1963
Newsweek 35:75, May 1, 1950
Outlook 157:271, Feb. 18, 1931
Time 55:105, Apr. 17, 1950

City of Bad Men (1953)
New York Times p. 37, Oct. 21, 1953

City of Chance (1939)
New York Times p. 11, Jan. 22, 1940

City of Fear (1959)
Commonweal 69:624, Mar. 13, 1959
Saturday Review 42:27, Jan. 31, 1959

City Streets (1931)
Life (NY) 97:20, May 8, 1931
New York Times p. 17, Apr. 18, 1931; VIII, p. 5, Apr. 26, 1931

City Streets (1938)
New York Times p. 18, Jul. 25, 1938

City That Never Sleeps (1953)
National Parent-Teacher 48:39, Sep., 1953
New York Times p. 14, Aug. 8, 1953

City That Stopped Hitler (1943)
Nation 157:360, Sep. 25, 1943
New Republic 109:487, Oct. 11, 1943
New York Times II, p. 4, Aug. 29, 1943; p. 21, Sep. 6, 1943
Newsweek 22:107, Oct. 4, 1943
Time 42:94, Oct. 18, 1943

Clairvoyant (1935)
Canadian Forum 15:15, Jan., 1936
New York Times p. 12, Jun. 8, 1935

Clancy in Wall Street (1930)
New York Times p. 23, May 3, 1930

Clandestine (1947)
New Republic 118:29, Jun. 7, 1948
New York Times p. 23, May 24, 1948

Clash By Night (1952)
Catholic World 175:307, Jul., 1952
Library Journal 77:1071, Jun. 15, 1952
Nation 175:77, Jul. 26, 1952
National Parent-Teacher 47:38, Sep., 1952
New York Times p. 32, Jun. 19, 1952

219

Clash By Night (1952) (Continued)
New Yorker 28:62, Jun. 28, 1952
Newsweek 39:84, Jun. 2, 1952
Saturday Review 35:35, Jun. 14, 1952
Theatre Arts 36:36, Jul., 1952
Time 59:104+, Jun. 9, 1952

Claudelle Inglish (1961)
America 105:811, Sep. 23, 1961
New York Times p. 40, Sep. 21, 1961
Newsweek 58:102-3, Sep. 11, 1961
Time 78:89, Sep. 8, 1961

Claudia (1943)
Commonweal 39:145, Nov. 26, 1943
Cosmopolitan 115:84, Oct., 1943
Nation 157:275, Sep. 4, 1943
New York Times p. 23, Nov. 5, 1943
Newsweek 22:98, Sep. 27, 1943
Scholastic 43:35, Oct. 4, 1943
Theatre Arts 28:28, Jan., 1944
Time 42:96+, Sep. 13, 1943

Claudia and David (1946)
Commonweal 44:457, Aug. 23, 1946
New York Times II, p. 3, Aug. 11, 1946; p. 19, Aug. 15,
    1946
New Yorker 22:42, Aug. 24, 1946
Newsweek 28:105, Aug. 12, 1946
Scholastic 49:40, Sep. 16, 1946
Time 48:105, Sep. 9, 1946
Woman's Home Companion 73:10, Nov., 1946

Claudine (1940)
Commonweal 31:534, Apr. 12, 1940
New York Times p. 15, Apr. 1, 1940

Clear All Wires (1933)
New York Times p. 11, Mar. 4, 1933; IX, p. 3, Mar.
    12, 1933

Cleo From 5 to 7 (1962)
Commonweal 76:474, Aug. 24, 1962
Esquire 59:116, Jan., 1963
Nation 195:228, Oct. 13, 1962
New Republic 147:28-9, Sep. 10, 1962
New York Times p. 43, Sep. 5, 1962; II, p. 1, Sep. 9,
    1962

Cleo From 5 to 7 (1962) (Continued)
New Yorker 38:95, Sep. 15, 1962
Newsweek 60:106, Sep. 10, 1962
Saturday Review 45:14, Aug. 4, 1962; 45:22, Sep. 29, 1962
Time 80:103, Sep. 14, 1962

Cleopatra (1934)
Canadian Magazine 82:36, Nov., 1934
Golden Book 20:378, Oct., 1934
New York Times p. 12, Aug. 17, 1934; IX, p. 3, Aug. 26, 1934; VIII, p. 4, Feb. 10, 1935
Newsweek 4:25, Aug. 25, 1934
Pictorial Review 36:78, Nov., 1934
Scholastic 25:29, Oct. 6, 1934
Time 24:36, Aug. 27, 1934

Cleopatra (1963)
America 108:910+, Jun. 29, 1963
Business World p. 34, Jun. 15, 1963
Commonweal 78:398, Jul. 5, 1963
Life 54:30, Jun. 21, 1963
McCalls 91:136-7, Oct., 1963
Nation 197:19, Jul. 6, 1963
National Review 15:114+, Aug. 13, 1963
New Republic 148:27-8, Jun. 29, 1963
New York Times II, p. 9, Jan. 7, 1962; p. 29, Jun. 13, 1963; II, p. 1, Jun. 16, 1963; II, p. 1, Jun. 23, 1963
New Yorker 39:61-2+, Jun. 22, 1963
Newsweek 61:110-12, Jun. 24, 1963; 62:78+, Jul. 8, 1963
Saturday Evening Post 236:28-38+, Jun. 1, 1963
Saturday Review 46:20, Jun. 29, 1963
Senior Scholastic 83:6T, Sep. 27, 1963; 83:22T-23T+, Oct. 4, 1963
Time 81:90, Jun. 21, 1963

Climax (1944)
Commonweal 40:614, Oct. 13, 1944
Cosmopolitan 117:90, Sep., 1944
New York Times II, p. 3, Feb. 27, 1944; p. 28, Dec. 14, 1944
Newsweek 24:111, Nov. 13, 1944

Clive of India (1935)
Nation 140:139-40, Jan. 30, 1935
New York Times p. 29, Jan. 18, 1935; VIII, p. 5, Jan. 27, 1935
Newsweek 5:27, Jan. 26, 1935

Clive of India (1935) (Continued)
  Scholastic 26:29, Feb. 9, 1935
  Time 25:33, Jan. 28, 1935

Cloak and Dagger (1946)
  Commonweal 45:17, Oct. 18, 1946
  New York Times II, p. 1, Nov. 25, 1945; p. 13, Oct. 5,
    1946; II, p. 5, Oct. 6, 1946
  New Yorker 22:66, Oct. 12, 1946
  Newsweek 28:94+, Oct. 7, 1946
  Scholastic 49:35, Oct. 28, 1946
  Theatre Arts 30:670-1, Nov., 1946
  Time 48:102, Oct. 21, 1946

Clock (1945)
  Commonweal 42:48, Apr. 27, 1945
  Life 18:75-6+, May 28, 1945
  Nation 160:608-9, May 26, 1945
  New Republic 112:709, May 21, 1945
  New York Times II, p. 3, Jun. 18, 1944; p. 23, May 4,
    1945
  New Yorker 21:77-8, May 12, 1945
  Newsweek 25:110-11, May 14, 1945
  Photoplay 27:20, Jun., 1945
  Theatre Arts 29:278, May, 1945
  Time 45:93-4+, May 14, 1945

Cloistered (1936)
  Commonweal 24:218, Jun. 19, 1936; 26:573, Oct. 15, 1937
  Nation 142:754, Jun. 10, 1936
  New York Times p. 25, May 20, 1936
  Newsweek 7:42, Jun. 6, 1936
  Time 27:27, Jun. 1, 1936

Close Harmony (1928)
  New York Times p. 23, Apr. 29, 1929
  Outlook 152:112, May 15, 1929

Close to My Heart (1951)
  Christian Century 69:351, Mar. 19, 1952

Close-Up (1948)
  New York Times p. 16, Aug. 9, 1947; II, p. 5, Nov. 30,
    1947; p. 24, Apr. 5, 1948

Cloudburst (1952)
  National Parent-Teacher 47:37, Oct., 1952

Clouded Yellow (1951)
Commonweal 55:200, Nov. 30, 1951
New Republic 125:22, Dec. 3, 1951
New York Times p. 33, Nov. 13, 1951
New Yorker 27:146, Nov. 24, 1951
Newsweek 38:100, Nov. 26, 1951
Scholastic 59:22, Nov. 28, 1951

Clouds Over Europe (1939)
Commonweal 30:259, Jun. 30, 1939
Nation 149:25, Jul. 1, 1939
New Republic 99:252, Jul. 5, 1939
New York Times IX, p. 4, Jun. 11, 1939; p. 27, Jun.
   16, 1939; IX, p. 3, Jun. 18, 1939
Time 33:45, Jun. 26, 1939

Clown (1952)
Christian Century 70:303, Mar. 11, 1953
National Parent-Teacher 47:27, Mar., 1953
New York Times p. 25, Jan. 29, 1952
Newsweek 41:83, Feb. 9, 1953
Time 61:98, Jan. 19, 1953

Clown Must Laugh (1938)
New York Times p. 35, Oct. 12, 1938

Club De Femmes (1937)
Nation 145:486, Oct. 30, 1937
New York Times XI, p. 5, Oct. 17, 1937; p. 27, Oct.
   20, 1937; XI, p. 5, Oct. 24, 1937
Time 30:26+, Oct. 25, 1937

Club Havanna (1945)
Cosmopolitan 120:162, Jan., 1946

Cluny Brown (1946)
Commonweal 44:216, Jun. 14, 1946
Cosmopolitan 120:69+, Jun., 1946
Forum 106:177, Aug., 1946
Life 20:125-8, May 27, 1946
Nation 162:701, Jun. 8, 1946
New Republic 115:103, Jul. 29, 1946
New York Times II, p. 3, Dec. 16, 1945; II, p. 3, May
   26, 1946; p. 27, Jun. 3, 1946; II, p. 1, Jun. 9, 1946
New Yorker 22:59, Jun. 15, 1946
Newsweek 27:90, May 6, 1946
Photoplay 29:4, Aug., 1946

Cluny Brown (1946) (Continued)
Theatre Arts 30:349-50, Jun., 1946
Time 47:90, May 20, 1946

Coast Guard (1939)
New York Times p. 17, Aug. 28, 1939

Coastal Command (1942)
New York Times p. 26, Apr. 19, 1944
Newsweek 23:76, Jan. 24, 1944

Cobra Woman (1943)
New York Times p. 17, May 18, 1944
Newsweek 23:72, May 29, 1944
Time 43:96, May 29, 1944

Cobweb (1955)
America 93:493, Aug. 20, 1955
Catholic World 181:221, Jun., 1955
Commonweal 62:495-6, Aug. 19, 1955
Library Journal 80:1576, Jul., 1955
National Parent-Teacher 50:39, Sep., 1955
New York Times p. 13, Aug. 6, 1955
New Yorker 31:49, Aug. 13, 1955
Newsweek 45:94, Jun. 20, 1955
Saturday Review 38:36, Jul. 16, 1955
Time 66:88, Jul. 25, 1955

Cock of the Air (1931)
New York Times p. 20, Jan. 25, 1932; VIII, p. 4, Jan.
31, 1932

Cock O' The Walk (1930)
New York Times p. 23, Apr. 12, 1930; VIII, p. 5, Apr.
20, 1930

Cockeyed Cavaliers (1934)
New York Times p. 22, Jul. 25, 1934; IX, p. 3, Jul. 29,
1934

Cockeyed Miracle (1946)
Commonweal 45:95, Nov. 8, 1946
New York Times II, p. 3, Oct. 20, 1946; p. 28, Oct. 25,
1946; II, p. 5, Jan. 5, 1947
Newsweek 28:113, Oct. 14, 1946
Time 48:104, Oct. 14, 1946

Cockeyed World (1929)
Life (NY) 94:26, Sep. 6, 1929
New York Times VIII, p. 4, Jul. 21, 1929; p. 25, Aug.
5, 1929; VIII, p. 4, Aug. 18, 1929
Outlook 152:713, Aug. 28, 1929
Theatre Arts 33:36, Sep., 1949

Cockleshell Heroes (1956)
America 95:272, Jun. 9, 1956
Commonweal 64:300, Jun. 22, 1956
Library Journal 81:705, Mar. 15, 1956
National Parent-Teacher 50:39, May, 1956
New York Times p. 25, Jun. 4, 1956
Newsweek 47:104+, Apr. 30, 1956
Saturday Review 39:27, Mar. 17, 1956

Cocktail Hour (1933)
Nation 136:707, Jun. 21, 1933
New Outlook 162:43, Jul., 1933
New York Times p. 22, Jun. 2, 1933
Newsweek 1:29, Jun. 10, 1933

Cocoanut Grove (1938)
New York Times p. 21, Jun. 16, 1938; IX, p. 3, Jun. 19,
1938

Cocoanuts (1929)
Life (NY) 93:25, Jun. 21, 1929
New York Times IX, p. 3, May 19, 1929; p. 17, May 25,
1929
Outlook 152:272, Jun. 12, 1929

Cohens and Kellys in Africa (1930)
New York Times p. 20, Dec. 20, 1930

Cohens and Kellys in Atlantic City (1929)
New York Times p. 30, Mar. 18, 1929; X, p. 7, Mar.
24, 1929

Cohens and Kellys in Hollywood (1932)
New York Times p. 23, Apr. 22, 1932

Cohens and Kellys in Paris (1928)
New York Times p. 12, Feb. 6, 1928

Cohens and Kellys in Scotland (1930)
New York Times p. 24, Mar. 10, 1930; IX, p. 5, Mar.
16, 1930

Cohens and Kellys in Trouble (1933)
New York Times p. 16, Apr. 17, 1933

Cold Wind in August (1961)
Esquire 57:30+, Jan., 1962
New Republic 145:19+, Sep. 11, 1961
New York Times p. 23, Jul. 27, 1961
New Yorker 37:37-8, Aug. 5, 1961
Newsweek 58:69, Aug. 14, 1961
Saturday Review 43:32, Aug. 20, 1960
Time 78:47, Aug. 11, 1961

Colditz Story (1954)
America 98:228, Nov. 16, 1957
Commonweal 67:234, Nov. 29, 1957
National Parent-Teacher 52:38, Jan., 1958
New York Times p. 23, Oct. 25, 1957
New Yorker 33:167, Nov. 2, 1957
Newsweek 50:120, Nov. 11, 1957

Colleen (1936)
New York Times p. 20, Mar. 9, 1936

College Coach (1933)
New York Times p. 10, Nov. 11, 1933

College Confidential (1960)
New York Times p. 23, Aug. 22, 1960

College Coquette (1929)
New York Times p. 17, Aug. 26, 1929; VIII, p. 4, Sep.
1, 1929

College Holiday (1936)
New York Times p. 21, Dec. 24, 1936
Time 29:22, Jan. 4, 1937

College Humor (1933)
New York Times IX, p. 3, Apr. 30, 1933; p. 15, Jun.
23, 1933
Newsweek 1:31, Jul. 1, 1933

College Love (1929)
New York Times p. 25, Aug. 5, 1929

College Rhythm (1934)
New York Times p. 19, Nov. 24, 1934; IX, p. 5, Dec.
23, 1934

College Swing (1938)
New York Times X, p. 3, May 1, 1938

Collegiate (1935)
New York Times p. 25, Jan. 23, 1936
Time 27:57, Feb. 3, 1936

Colonel Blimp (1945)
Canadian Forum 27:232, Jan., 1948
Commonweal 41:590, Mar. 30, 1945
Life 18:61-5, Apr. 16, 1945
Nation 160:370, Mar. 31, 1945
New Republic 112:587, Apr. 30, 1945
New York Times p. 18, Mar. 30, 1945; II, p. 1, Apr. 1,
    1945; II, p. 1, Jun. 22, 1947
New Yorker 21:65, Apr. 7, 1945
Newsweek 25:114-15, Mar. 26, 1945
Nineteenth Century 134:90, Aug., 1943
Saturday Review 28:22-3, Apr. 21, 1945
Scholastic 46:28, Apr. 23, 1945
Time 41:31, Jun. 21, 1943; 45:90, Apr. 2, 1945

Colonel Effingham's Raid (1946)
Commonweal 43:458, Feb. 15, 1946
New York Times p. 21, Apr. 5, 1946
New Yorker 22:104, Apr. 13, 1946
Newsweek 27:86, Mar. 4, 1946
Scholastic 47:31, Jan. 7, 1946
Time 47:98+, Feb. 18, 1946

Colorado Territory (1949)
Commonweal 50:367, Jul. 22, 1949
New York Times p. 8, Jun. 25, 1949
Newsweek 33:88, Jun. 27, 1949
Rotarian 75:36, Sep., 1949
Time 53:84, Jun. 20, 1949

Colossus of Rhodes (1961)
New York Times p. 55, Dec. 14, 1961

Colt .45 (1949)
Commonweal 52:151, May 19, 1950
New York Times p. 8, May 6, 1950

Column South (1953)
National Parent-Teacher 48:39, Oct., 1953
Newsweek 41:90, Jun. 22, 1953

Comanche (see Tonka)

Comanche Territory (1950)
Commonweal 52:46, Apr. 21, 1950
New York Times p. 9, Apr. 8, 1950

Comancheros (1962)
America 106:228, Nov. 11, 1961
New York Times p. 42, Nov. 2, 1961
New Yorker 37:235, Dec. 9, 1961
Newsweek 58:107, Nov. 13, 1961
Time 78:59, Nov. 17, 1961

Combat Squad (1953)
National Parent-Teacher 48:36, Nov., 1953

Come and Get It (1936)
New York Times p. 31, Nov. 12, 1936; XI, p. 5, Nov.
15, 1936
Newsweek 8:60, Nov. 14, 1936
Stage 14:14, Dec., 1936
Time 28:37, Nov. 16, 1936

*Come Back, Africa
Commonweal 72:95, Apr. 22, 1960
New Republic 142:22, May 16, 1960
New York Times p. 45, Apr. 5, 1960; II, p. 1, Apr. 10,
1960
New Yorker 36:149, Apr. 16, 1960
Saturday Review 43:26, Apr. 2, 1960; 43:28, Apr. 2, 1960
Time 75:92, Apr. 25, 1960

Come Back, Little Sheba (1952)
Catholic World 176:302, Jan., 1953
Christian Century 70:271, Mar. 4, 1953
Commonweal 57:308, Dec. 26, 1952
Harper 206:94, Jan., 1953
Holiday 13:22-3+, Feb., 1953
Library Journal 78:141, Jan. 15, 1953
McCall's 89:9, Feb., 1953
Nation 175:434, Nov. 8, 1952
National Parent-Teacher 47:37, Jan., 1953
New York Times VI, p. 58-9, Nov. 16, 1952; II, p. 5,
Dec. 14, 1952; p. 13, Dec. 24, 1952; II, p. 1, Jan.
11, 1953
New Yorker 28:59, Dec. 27, 1952
Newsweek 40:64, Dec. 29, 1952

Come Back, Little Sheba (1952) (Continued)
Saturday Review 35:26, Dec. 27, 1952
Theatre Arts 36:29+, Dec. , 1952; 37:15, Feb. , 1953
Time 60:66, Dec. 29, 1952

Come Blow Your Horn (1962)
America 108:872, Jun. 15, 1963
Commonweal 78:356, Jun. 21, 1963
New York Times p. 37, Jun. 7, 1963
New Yorker 39:54+, Jun. 15, 1963
Newsweek 61:104, Jun. 10, 1963
Saturday Review 46:45, Jun. 15, 1963
Time 81:99, Jun. 14, 1963

Come Closer, Folks (1936)
New York Times p. 17, Nov. 23, 1936

Come Dance With Me (1960)
Commonweal 72:519, Sep. 23, 1960
New York Times p. 32, Nov. 8, 1960
New Yorker 36:205, Nov. 12, 1960
Newsweek 56:72, Sep. 5, 1960
Time 76:45, Aug. 29, 1960

Come Fill the Cup (1952)
Christian Century 68:1495, Dec. 19, 1951
Commonweal 55:119, Nov. 9, 1951
Library Journal 76:1818, Nov. 1, 1951
New Republic 125:21, Dec. 17, 1951
New York Times p. 47, Nov. 22, 1951; II, p. 1, Nov.
    25, 1951
New Yorker 27:155, Dec. 1, 1951
Newsweek 38:102-3, Nov. 26, 1951
Time 58:118+, Nov. 5, 1951

Come Fly With Me (1960)
New York Times p. 40, May 2, 1963
Saturday Review 46:16, Jun. 1, 1963
Time 81:117, May 17, 1963

Come Live With Me (1941)
New York Times p. 17, Feb. 28, 1941
Newsweek 17:59, Feb. 3, 1941
Photoplay 18:44-5+, Apr. , 1941

Come Next Spring (1956)
America 95:292, Jun. 16, 1956
Catholic World 182:462, Mar. , 1956

229

Come Next Spring (1956) (Continued)
Commonweal 64:49, Apr. 13, 1956
National Parent-Teacher 50:38, Feb., 1956

Come On (1956)
New York Times p. 13, Apr. 7, 1956

Come On, Leathernecks (1938)
New York Times p. 29, Sep. 15, 1938

Come On, Marines (1934)
New York Times p. 20, Mar. 24, 1934; X, p. 3, Apr. 1, 1934

Come Out of the Pantry (1935)
Canadian Magazine 85:38, Feb., 1936

Come September (1961)
America 105:778-9, Sep. 16, 1961
Commonweal 74:519, Sep. 22, 1961
New Republic 145:28-9, Sep. 4, 1961
New York Times II, p. 7, Nov. 27, 1960; p. 34, Sep. 8, 1961; II, p. 1, Sep. 17, 1961
New Yorker 37:88, Sep. 16, 1961
Saturday Review 44:25, Aug. 26, 1961
Time 78:104, Sep. 15, 1961

Come to the Stable (1949)
Catholic World 169:387-8, Aug., 1949
Commonweal 50:415, Aug. 5, 1949
Cosmopolitan 127:12+, Jul., 1949
Life 27:48-50, Aug. 8, 1949
New Republic 121:29, Aug. 1, 1949
New York Times p. 19, Jul. 28, 1949; II, p. 1, Jul. 31, 1949
New Yorker 25:38, Aug. 6, 1949
Newsweek 34:68, Aug. 8, 1949
Rotarian 76:40, Jan., 1950
Theatre Arts 33:106, Aug., 1949
Time 54:64, Aug. 1, 1949
Vogue 114:87, Aug. 1, 1949
Woman's Home Companion 76:10-11, Aug., 1949

Comet Over Broadway (1938)
New York Times X, p. 3, Apr. 24, 1938; p. 33, Dec. 16, 1938

Coming Out Party (1934)
New York Times p. 11, Mar. 17, 1934; X, p. 3, Mar. 25, 1934

Coming-Out Party (1962)
Commonweal 76:497, Sep. 7, 1962
New York Times p. 19, Jul. 31, 1962
New Yorker 38:69, Aug. 18, 1962

Comin' Round the Mountain (1940)
New York Times p. 27, Sep. 26, 1940

Comin' 'Round the Mountain (1951)
Christian Century 68:975, Aug. 22, 1951
New York Times p. 15, Jul. 27, 1951

Command (1955)
America 90:491, Feb. 6, 1954
Catholic World 178:460, Mar., 1954
Commonweal 59:525, Feb. 26, 1954
Farm Journal 78:165, Apr., 1954
National Parent-Teacher 48:39, Mar., 1954
New York Times p. 10, Jan. 16, 1954
Newsweek 43:76, Feb. 1, 1954
Time 63:74, Feb. 1, 1954

Command Decision (1949)
Commonweal 49:400, Jan. 28, 1949
Cosmopolitan 126:15+, Mar., 1949
Good Housekeeping 128:10-11+, Apr., 1949
New Republic 120:30, Feb. 7, 1949
New York Times p. 34, Jan. 20, 1949; II, p. 1, Jan. 23, 1949; p. 14, Aug. 22, 1949
Newsweek 33:73, Jan. 24, 1949; 34:67, Sep. 5, 1949
Photoplay 34:23, Apr., 1949
Player's Magazine 26:46, Nov., 1949
Rotarian 74:34, May, 1949
Scholastic 54:27, Feb. 9, 1949
Theatre Arts 33:86, Apr., 1949
Time 53:82, Jan. 24, 1949
Woman's Home Companion 76:10, Apr., 1949

Commandos Strike at Dawn (1943)
Commonweal 37:374, Jan. 29, 1943
Life 14:43-4+, Jan. 11, 1943
New York Times p. 25, Jan. 14, 1943
New Yorker 18:45, Jan. 16, 1943

Commandos Strike at Dawn (1943) (Continued)
Newsweek 21:64, Jan. 18, 1943
Photoplay 22:24, Mar., 1943
Scholastic 42:17, Feb. 15, 1943
Time 41:97, Jan. 18, 1943

Common Clay (1931)
Life (NY) 96:18, Aug. 29, 1930
New York Times p. 16, Aug. 2, 1930; VIII, p. 3, Aug.
10, 1930
Theatre Magazine 52:47, Oct., 1930

Common Law (1931)
Life (NY) 98:18, Aug. 14, 1931
Nation 133:192, Aug. 19, 1931
New York Times p. 20, Jul. 20, 1931; VIII, p. 3, Jul.
26, 1931

Company She Keeps (1950)
Commonweal 53:448, Feb. 9, 1951
New York Times p. 14, Jan. 29, 1951
Time 57:100, Feb. 19, 1951

Compromised (1931)
New York Times p. 16, Nov. 7, 1931

Conclusion (1959)
America 101:257, Apr. 25, 1959
Catholic World 189:154, May, 1959
Commonweal 70:130, May 1, 1959
Library Journal 84:1119, Apr. 1, 1959
Life 46:60+, Apr. 13, 1959
Nation 188:395, Apr. 25, 1959
New Republic 140:20, Apr. 20, 1959
New York Times p. 26, Apr. 2, 1959; II, p. 1, Apr. 5,
1959
New Yorker 35:163, Apr. 11, 1959
Newsweek 53:118, Apr. 13, 1959
Saturday Review 42:27, Mar. 28, 1959
Time 73:98+, Apr. 13, 1959

Comrade X (1940)
New Republic 104:54, Jan. 13, 1941
New York Times IX, p. 4, Nov. 10, 1940; p. 23, Dec.
26, 1940
Newsweek 16:51, Dec. 23, 1940
Time 37:48, Jan. 6, 1941

Comrades of 1918 (1931)
Nation 132:306, Mar. 18, 1931
New York Times p. 18, Feb. 20, 1931; VIII, p. 5, Mar.
1, 1931

Concentration Camp (1939)
New York Times p. 13, Mar. 20, 1939

Concrete Jungle (1962)
Newsweek 59:87, Jun. 18, 1962
Time 80:66, Jul. 13, 1962

Condemned (1929)
Life (NY) 94:51, Dec. 6, 1929
New York Times VIII, p. 5, Jun. 9, 1929; VIII, p. 5,
Aug. 25, 1929; X, p. 8, Nov. 24, 1929
Outlook 153:471, Nov. 20, 1929

Condemned of Altona (1963)
New Republic 149:28, Sep. 28, 1963
New York Times II, p. 9, Oct. 27, 1963; p. 26, Oct. 31,
1963
New Yorker 39:209, Nov. 9, 1963
Newsweek 62:110, Oct. 7, 1963
Saturday Review 46:46, Oct. 19, 1963
Time 82:83, Sep. 27, 1963

Condemned to Death (1932)
New York Times p. 24, Jul. 14, 1932

Condemned Women (1938)
New York Times X, p. 5, Feb. 6, 1938; p. 15, Apr. 22,
1938

Coney Island (1928)
New York Times p. 27, Feb. 14, 1928

Coney Island (1943)
Commonweal 38:302, Jul. 9, 1943
New York Times p. 17, Jun. 17, 1943; II, p. 3, Jun. 20,
1943
Newsweek 21:86, Jun. 14, 1943
Photoplay 23:24, Jul., 1943
Time 41:54, Jun. 21, 1943

Confession (1937)
New York Times p. 23, Aug. 19, 1937
Time 30:24, Aug. 30, 1937

Confession of Boston Blackie (1942)
New York Times p. 31, Dec. 8, 1941

Confession of a Co-Ed (1931)
Life (NY) 98:22, Jul. 10, 1931
New York Times p. 20, Jun. 20, 1931; VIII, p. 3, Jun. 28, 1931

Confessions of a Nazi Spy (1939)
Commonweal 30:106, May 19, 1939
Nation 148:595-6, May 20, 1939
New Republic 99:20, May 10, 1939
New York Times IX, p. 5, Feb. 5, 1939; IX, p. 4, Feb. 19, 1939; X, p. 5, Apr. 2, 1939; X, p. 6, Apr. 23, 1939; p. 13, Apr. 29, 1939; X, p. 5, May 7, 1939; p. 28, Dec. 25, 1939; IX, p. 3, May 26, 1940; IX, p. 4, Jun. 2, 1940; p. 11, Jun. 3, 1940; IX, p. 3, Jun. 16, 1940
Newsweek 13:23, May 8, 1939
North America 247 no2:384-5, Jun., 1939
Scholastic 34:31, May 27, 1939
Stage 16:36-7, Apr. 15, 1939
Time 33:58, May 15, 1939

Confessions of Felix Krull (1958)
New York Times p. 38, Mar. 5, 1958
Saturday Review 41:55, Mar. 15, 1958
Time 71:102+, Mar. 24, 1958

Confidence Girl (1952)
New York Times p. 12, Jun. 21, 1952

Confidential Agent (1945)
Nation 161:506, Nov. 10, 1945
New York Times p. 11, Nov. 3, 1945
New Yorker 21:59, Nov. 10, 1945
Newsweek 26:100, Nov. 12, 1945
Scholastic 47:35, Dec. 3, 1945
Time 46:98, Nov. 19, 1945

Confirm or Deny (1941)
New York Times IX, p. 3, Sep. 14, 1941; IX, p. 5, Oct. 5, 1941; p. 35, Dec. 19, 1941

Conflict (1936)
New York Times p. 21, Jan. 18, 1937

Conflict (1945)
Commonweal 42:239, Jun. 22, 1945
New York Times p. 10, Jun. 16, 1945
New Yorker 21:40, Jun. 23, 1945
Newsweek 25:99, Jun. 25, 1945
Time 45:90, Jun. 18, 1945
Woman's Home Companion 72:11, Aug., 1945

Conga Nights (1940)
New York Times p. 33, Jun. 5, 1940
Newsweek 15:46, Jun. 3, 1940

Congo Crossing (1956)
National Parent-Teacher 51:39, Sep., 1956
New York Times p. 13, Jul. 14, 1956

Congo Maisie (1940)
New York Times p. 18, Feb. 8, 1940
Photoplay 54:62, Mar., 1940

Congorilla (1932)
Commonweal 16:371, Aug. 10, 1932
New York Times IX, p. 3, Jul. 17, 1932; p. 18, Jul. 22,
    1932; IX, p. 3, Jul. 31, 1932

Congress Dances (1932)
Canadian Magazine 78:27, Aug., 1932
New York Times p. 23, May 12, 1932; VIII, p. 3, May
    22, 1932

Connecticut Yankee (1931)
New York Times VIII, p. 7, Mar. 29, 1931; p. 17, Apr.
    11, 1931; VIII, p. 5, Apr. 19, 1931
Outlook 157:539, Apr. 15, 1931

Connecticut Yankee in King Arthur's Court (1949)
Collier's 123:36+, Mar. 19, 1949
Commonweal 50:48, Apr. 22, 1949
Cosmopolitan 126:12-13+, Apr., 1949
Good Housekeeping 128:303, Apr., 1949
New Republic 120:31, Apr. 18, 1949
New York Times p. 31, Apr. 8, 1949
New Yorker 25:95, Apr. 16, 1949
Newsweek 33:89, Apr. 18, 1949
Photoplay 34:22, Apr., 1949
Publisher's Weekly 153:1907, May 1, 1948
Rotarian 75:42, Aug., 1949

Connecticut Yankee in King Arthur's Court (1949) (Continued)
Scholastic 54:25, Apr. 13, 1949
Time 53:99, Apr. 25, 1949
Woman's Home Companion 76:10-11, Apr., 1949

Connection (1962)
Nation 192:526-7, Jun. 17, 1961
New Republic 147:29-31, Oct. 27, 1962
New York Times II, p. 7, Nov. 6, 1960; VI, p. 46, Aug.
    26, 1961; p. 44, Oct. 4, 1961
New York Times Magazine p. 46+, Aug. 26, 1962
New Yorker 38:210, Nov. 17, 1962
Newsweek 60:60, Sep. 17, 1962
Reporter 27:50, Nov. 8, 1962
Saturday Review 45:20+, Apr. 7, 1962
Time 80:M18, Oct. 5, 1962

Conquering Horde (1931)
New York Times p. 25, Mar. 30, 1931; VIII, p. 5, Apr.
    5, 1931

Conqueror (1955)
America 95:72, Apr. 14, 1956
Catholic World 183:61, Apr., 1956
Commonweal 64:96, Apr. 27, 1956
Life 40:161-2+, May 7, 1956
Nation 182:246, Mar. 24, 1956
National Parent-Teacher 50:39, Apr., 1956
New York Times p. 13, Mar. 31, 1956; II, p. 1, Apr. 1,
    1956
New Yorker 32:112, Apr. 7, 1956
Newsweek 47:118, Apr. 9, 1956
Time 67:112, Apr. 9, 1956

Conquerors (1932)
New York Times p. 21, Nov. 21, 1932; IX, p. 5, Nov.
    27, 1932

Conquerors of the Arctic (1937)
New York Times p. 15, Nov. 22, 1937

Conquest (1928)
New York Times p. 26, Feb. 11, 1929

Conquest (1937)
Commonweal 27:78, Nov. 12, 1937
Independent Woman 16:398, Dec., 1937

Conquest (1937) (Continued)
  Life 3:40-43, Nov. 8, 1937
  Literary Digest 1:34, Nov. 20, 1937
  New York Times p. 19, Nov. 5, 1937; XI, p. 5, Nov. 7,
    1937
  Newsweek 10:22, Nov. 8, 1937
  Scholastic 31:10, Dec. 4, 1937
  Stage 15:50-52, Oct., 1937
  Time 30:48, Nov. 8, 1937

Conquest of Cochise (1953)
  National Parent-Teacher 48:39, Oct., 1953

Conquest of Everest (1954)
  America 90:346, Dec. 26, 1953
  Catholic World 178:462-3, Mar., 1954
  Commonweal 59:331, Jan. 1, 1954
  National Parent-Teacher 48:38, Feb., 1954
  Natural History 63:44, Jan., 1954
  New York Times p. 64, Dec. 10, 1953; II, p. 9, Dec.
    13, 1953; II, p. 3, Dec. 20, 1953
  New Yorker 29:91-2, Dec. 12, 1953
  Newsweek 42:90, Dec. 21, 1953
  Saturday Review 37:32-3, Jan. 9, 1954
  Scholastic 63:29, Jan. 13, 1954
  Time 62:90+, Dec. 21, 1963

Conquest of Space (1955)
  National Parent-Teacher 49:39, Apr., 1955
  New York Times p. 7, May 28, 1955

Conquest of Peter the Great (1939)
  New York Times IX, p. 4, Aug. 20, 1939; p. 17, Aug.
    24, 1939

Consolation Marriage (1931)
  New York Times VIII, p. 5, Nov. 8, 1931

Conspiracy (1939)
  New York Times p. 19, Aug. 23, 1939

Conspiracy of Hearts (1960)
  America 103:54, Apr. 9, 1960
  Commonweal 72:40, Apr. 8, 1960
  McCalls 87:180, Jun., 1960
  New York Times p. 24, Apr. 8, 1960
  Newsweek 55:121, Apr. 11, 1960

Conspiracy of Hearts (1960) (Continued)
    Saturday Review 43:27, May 7, 1960
    Time 75:81, Apr. 18, 1960

Conspirator (1950)
    Christian Century 67:599, May 10, 1950
    Commonweal 52:127, May 12, 1950
    Good Housekeeping 130:139, Mar., 1950
    Library Journal 75:181, Feb. 1, 1950
    New York Times p. 26, Apr. 28, 1950
    Newsweek 35:83, Apr. 10, 1950
    Rotarian 77:37, Jul., 1950
    Scholastic 56:36, Mar. 15, 1950
    Time 55:104+, May 22, 1950

Conspirators (1944)
    Commonweal 41:125, Nov. 17, 1944
    New Republic 111:627, Nov. 13, 1944
    New York Times p. 15, Oct. 21, 1944
    Newsweek 24:110, Oct. 30, 1944
    Time 44:96, Nov. 13, 1944
    Woman's Home Companion 71:11, Oct., 1944

Constant Husband (1957)
    New York Times p. 10, Jul. 26, 1957

Constant Nymph (1928)
    Life (NY) 93:37, Jul. 7, 1929
    New York Times p. 23, Jun. 10, 1929; VIII, p. 3, Jun.
        16, 1929

Constant Nymph (1934)
    Canadian Magazine 82:42, Jul., 1934
    New Republic 78:338, May 2, 1934
    New York Times p. 19, Apr. 7, 1934; X, p. 3, Apr. 15,
        1934

Constant Nymph (1943)
    Commonweal 38:421, Aug. 13, 1943
    Life 15:38+, Aug. 2, 1943
    New Republic 109:255, Aug. 23, 1943
    New York Times p. 8, Jul. 24, 1943
    Newsweek 22:85, Aug. 9, 1943
    Photoplay 23:28, Sep., 1943
    Scholastic 43:34, Sep. 13, 1943
    Time 42:96, Aug. 9, 1943

Constantine and the Cross (1962)
New York Times p. 8, Mar. 14, 1963
Newsweek 61:89, Feb. 11, 1963

Continental Express (1942)
New York Times p. 26, Apr. 7, 1942

Convention City (1933)
New York Times p. 28, Dec. 25, 1933
Vanity Fair 41:46, Feb., 1934

Convicted (1938)
New York Times p. 9, Aug. 23, 1938

Convicted (1950)
Christian Century 67:1031, Aug. 30, 1950
Library Journal 75:1915, Nov. 1, 1950
Rotarian 77:36, Oct., 1950

Convicted Woman (1940)
New York Times p. 11, Feb. 26, 1940

Convicts 4 (1962)
America 107:1012, Nov. 3, 1962
Commonweal 76:446, Aug. 10, 1962
New York Times p. 44, Oct. 4, 1962
Newsweek 59:110, May 14, 1962
Saturday Review 45:31, May 19, 1962

Convoy (1941)
Commonweal 33:352, Jan. 24, 1941
Life 11:24, Sep. 22, 1941
New York Times p. 21, Jan. 17, 1941
Time 37:70, Jan. 27, 1941

Cop (1928)
New York Times p. 35, Nov. 6, 1928

Cop Hater (1957)
New York Times p. 44, Oct. 2, 1958

Copacabana (1947)
Commonweal 46:241, Jun. 20, 1947
Holiday 2:141, Jul., 1947
New Republic 117:31, Jul. 28, 1947
New York Times p. 7, Jul. 12, 1947
Newsweek 29:85, Jun. 2, 1947
Time 49:64, Jun. 16, 1947

Copper Canyon (1949)
Commonweal 53:173, Nov. 24, 1950
New York Times p. 39, Nov. 16, 1950
Newsweek 36:84, Nov. 27, 1950
Time 56:98, Dec. 4, 1950

Coquette (1929)
New York Times X, p. 7, Dec. 2, 1928; VIII, p. 3, Jan.
6, 1929; p. 14, Apr. 5, 1929; X, p. 7, Apr. 14, 1929;
VIII, p. 7, Jun. 2, 1929; VIII, p. 4, Sep. 1, 1929
Outlook 151:671, Apr. 24, 1929

Corbeau (see The Raven and The Thirteenth Letter)

Corn is Green (1946)
Commonweal 41:626-7, Apr. 6, 1945
Cosmopolitan 119:98, Jul., 1945
Nation 160:425, Apr. 14, 1945
New York Times p. 18, Mar. 30, 1945; II, p. 1, Apr. 1,
1945
New Yorker 21:76, Mar. 24, 1945
Newsweek 25:91-3, Apr. 9, 1945
Photoplay 27:19, Jul., 1945
Scholastic 46:30, Apr. 16, 1945
Time 45:89, Apr. 30, 1945

Cornered (1945)
Commonweal 43:383, Jan. 25, 1946
Life 19:71-2+, Dec. 10, 1945
Nation 162:206, Feb. 16, 1946
New York Times p. 15, Dec. 16, 1945
New Yorker 21:59, Dec. 29, 1945
Newsweek 26:114+, Dec. 17, 1945
Saturday Review 29:18, Feb. 2, 1946
Theatre Arts 30:102-3, Feb., 1946
Time 46:93, Dec. 17, 1945

Coronado (1936)
New York Times p. 33, Dec. 19, 1935

Coroner Creek (1948)
Newsweek 32:86, Jul. 26, 1948
Time 52:88, Sep. 6, 1948

Corpse Came C.O.D. (1947)
New Republic 117:38, Sep. 15, 1947
New York Times p. 27, Aug. 19, 1947

Corregidor (1943)
New York Times p. 19, May 28, 1943

Corridor of Mirrors (1948)
New Republic 120:31, Apr. 4, 1949
New York Times p. 35, Mar. 23, 1949

Corridors of Blood (1963)
New York Times p. 39, Jun. 6, 1963

Corsair (1931)
New York Times p. 27, Nov. 19, 1931

Corsican Brothers (1941)
Commonweal 35:249-50, Dec. 26, 1941
New York Times p. 25, Jan. 16, 1942; IX, p. 5, Jan.
   25, 1942
Newsweek 18:71+, Dec. 15, 1941
Time 39:66, Jan. 5, 1942

Corvette K-225 (1943)
Commonweal 39:97, Nov. 12, 1943
New Republic 109:687, Nov. 15, 1943
New York Times II, p. 3, Jul. 4, 1943; p. 30, Oct. 21,
   1943
New Yorker 19:83, Oct. 30, 1943
Newsweek 22:110, Oct. 18, 1943
Scholastic 43:34, Nov. 15, 1943

Cosmic Monsters (1959)
New York Times p. 38, Jan. 1, 1959

Cossacks (1928)
Life (NY) 92:23, Jul. 12, 1928
New York Times VIII, p. 4, Jun. 24, 1928; p. 27, Jun.
   25, 1928
Outlook 149:427, Jul. 11, 1928

Cossacks (1960)
Commonweal 72:328, Jun. 24, 1960
New York Times p. 41, Sep. 6, 1960

Cossacks in Exile (1939)
New York Times p. 19, Jan. 28, 1939

Cossacks of the Don (1932)
New York Times p. 11, Mar. 19, 1932

Costello Case (1930)
New York Times p. 36, Nov. 4, 1930

Couch (1962)
Commonweal 75:645, Mar. 16, 1962
New York Times p. 20, Feb. 22, 1962
Newsweek 59:84, Mar. 5, 1962

Cougar (1933)
New York Times p. 18, May 22, 1933

Counsel for Crime (1937)
New York Times p. 16, Oct. 9, 1937

Counsellor-At-Law (1933)
Literary Digest 116:31, Dec. 23, 1933
Nation 137:744, Dec. 27, 1933
New Outlook 163:43, Jan., 1934
New York Times p. 31, Dec. 8, 1933; IX, p. 7, Dec. 17, 1933
Newsweek 2:30, Dec. 16, 1933

Count Five and Die (1958)
Catholic World 186:464, Mar., 1958
New York Times p. 25, May, 15, 1958

Count of Monte Cristo (1934)
New Republic 80:311, Oct. 24, 1934
New York Times p. 25, Sep. 27, 1934

Count of Ten (1928)
New York Times p. 23, Mar. 13, 1928

Count the Hours (1953)
National Parent-Teacher 47:37, May, 1953
New York Times p. 30, Jun. 24, 1953

Count Three and Pray (1955)
National Parent-Teacher 50:38, Oct., 1955
Newsweek 46:110, Sep. 12, 1955

Count Your Blessings (1959)
America 101:314, May 9, 1959
Catholic World 189:236-7, Jun., 1959
Commonweal 70:130, May 1, 1959
Library Journal 84:1221, Apr. 15, 1959
New York Times p. 23, Apr. 24, 1959

Count Your Blessings (1959) (Continued)
New Yorker 35:154+, May 2, 1959
Newsweek 53:114, Apr. 27, 1959
Saturday Review 42:24, May 23, 1959
Time 73:79, Apr. 27, 1959

Counter-Attack (1945)
Hollywood Quarterly 1:37-8, Oct., 1945
Life 18:69, Apr. 2, 1945
Nation 160:554, May 12, 1945
New Republic 112:815, Jun. 11, 1945
New York Times p. 15, May 17, 1945; II, p. 1, May 27, 1945
New Yorker 21:38, May 26, 1945
Newsweek 25:112, May 28, 1945
Time 45:89, Apr. 30, 1945

Counter Espionage (1942)
New York Times p. 13, Sep. 28, 1942

Counterfeit (1935)
New York Times p. 11, Jul. 20, 1936

Counterfeit Coin (1960)
New York Times p. 39, May 16, 1960

Counterfeit Lady (1936)
New York Times p. 15, Jan. 11, 1937

Counterfeit Plan (1957)
National Parent-Teacher 51:37, Jun., 1957

Counterfeit Traitor (1962)
America 107:276, May 19, 1962
Commonweal 76:211, May 18, 1962
Life 52:57, Apr. 27, 1962
New York Times p. 28, Apr. 18, 1962
Newsweek 59:96, Apr. 23, 1962
Saturday Review 45:37, Apr. 28, 1962
Time 79:65, May 4, 1962

Countess of Monte Cristo (1934)
New York Times p. 13, Apr. 2, 1934

Country Beyond (1936)
New York Times p. 17, Apr. 30, 1936
Time 27:58, May 11, 1936

Country Bride (1938)
New York Times p. 18, Jun. 4, 1938

Country Doctor (1936)
Canadian Magazine 85:56, Apr., 1936
Collier's 97:17+, Apr. 4, 1936
Hygeia 14:518-19, Jun., 1936
Literary Digest 120:21, Dec. 14, 1935; 121:22, Mar. 14, 1936
Motion Picture 51:30-31+, Mar., 1936
Movie Classic 10:31+, Mar., 1936
New York Times IX, p. 5, Dec. 29, 1935; p. 37, Mar. 13, 1936; XI, p. 3, Mar. 22, 1936
Newsweek 7:22-4, Mar. 21, 1936
Photoplay 49:21-3+, Mar., 1936
Scholastic 28:26, Mar. 28, 1936
Time 27:57, Mar. 16, 1936

Country Doctor (1963)
New York Times p. 28, Aug. 14, 1963

Country Fair (1937)
New York Times p. 11, Dec. 27, 1937

Country Girl (1954)
America 92:366-7, Jan. 1, 1955
Catholic World 180:222, Dec., 1954
Commonweal 61:312, Dec. 17, 1954
Farm Journal 79:70, Jan., 1955
Library Journal 79:2438, Dec. 15, 1954
Life 37:106, Dec. 6, 1954
Look 18:163-5, Dec. 14, 1954
Nation 179:518, Dec. 11, 1954
National Parent-Teacher 49:39, Jan., 1955
New Republic 132:21, Apr. 4, 1955
New York Times VI, p. 39, Nov. 14, 1954; II, p. 7, Dec. 12, 1954; p. 51, Dec. 16, 1954; II, p. 3, Dec. 19, 1954
New York Times Magazine p. 39, Nov. 14, 1954
New Yorker 30:60, Dec. 25, 1954
Newsweek 44:107, Dec. 6, 1954
Reporter 12:47, Feb. 24, 1955
Saturday Review 37:27, Dec. 18, 1954
Time 64:96, Dec. 13, 1954
Woman's Home Companion 82:12-13, Jan., 1955

County Chairman (1935)
New York Times p. 8, Jan. 19, 1935

244

County Chairman (1935) (Continued)
Scholastic 26:29, Feb. 9, 1935
Time 25:32, Jan. 28, 1935

Courage (1930)
New York Times p. 21, May 23, 1930

Courage of Lassie (1946)
Commonweal 44:479, Aug. 30, 1946
New York Times p. 18, Jul. 25, 1946; II, p. 3, Jul. 28, 1946
Photoplay 29:22, Sep., 1946

Courageous Dr. Christian (1940)
New York Times p. 25, Mar. 29, 1940

Courier of Lyons (1938)
New York Times p. 17, Jun. 3, 1938

Court Jester (1956)
America 94:542, Feb. 11, 1956
Catholic World 182:220, Dec., 1955
Commonweal 63:544, Feb. 24, 1956
Life 40:93-4+, Jan. 30, 1956
National Parent-Teacher 50:38, Mar., 1956
New Republic 134:21, Mar. 5, 1956
New York Times VI, p. 20-21, Jan. 1, 1956; p. 19, Feb. 2, 1956; II, p. 1, Feb. 5, 1956
New Yorker 31:117, Feb. 11, 1956
Newsweek 47:86, Feb. 6, 1956
Reporter 14:44, Mar. 22, 1956
Saturday Review 39:21, Feb. 4, 1956
Time 67:92, Feb. 6, 1956

Court Martial (1955)
America 93:479, Aug. 13, 1955
Catholic World 181:222, Jun., 1955
Commonweal 62:183, May 20, 1955
National Parent-Teacher 50:39, Sep., 1955
New Yorker 31:49, Aug. 13, 1955
Newsweek 46:76, Aug. 8, 1955
Time 66:84, Aug. 22, 1955

Courtmartial of Billy Mitchell (1955)
America 94:384, Dec. 31, 1955
Commonweal 63:332, Dec. 30, 1955
Library Journal 81:74, Jan. 1, 1956
National Parent-Teacher 50:38, Feb., 1956

245

Courtmartial of Billy Mitchell (1955) (Continued)
New York Times p. 17, Aug. 2, 1955; p. 14, Dec. 23,
1955
New Yorker 31:36, Dec. 31, 1955
Newsweek 47:71, Jan. 9, 1956
Saturday Review 39:21, Jan. 14, 1956
Time 66:59-61, Dec. 26, 1955

Courtship of Andy Hardy (1942)
Commonweal 35:649, Apr. 17, 1942
New York Times p. 21, Apr. 10, 1942
Time 39:92, Apr. 13, 1942

Courtship of Eddie's Father (1962)
Commonweal 77:665, Mar. 22, 1963
New York Times p. 8, Mar. 28, 1963
Newsweek 61:93, Apr. 8, 1963
Time 81:103-4, Apr. 5, 1963

Cousins (1959)
Commonweal 71:351, Dec. 18, 1959
Nation 189:474, Dec. 19, 1959
New York Times p. 44, Nov. 24, 1959
New Yorker 35:126, Dec. 19, 1959
Saturday Review 42:27, Sep. 19, 1959
Time 75:93, Jan. 25, 1960

Cover Girl (1943)
Commonweal 40:16, Apr. 21, 1944
Cosmopolitan 116:112, Mar., 1944
Life 14:74-81, Jan. 18, 1943
Musician 49:96, May, 1944
Nation 158:428, Apr. 8, 1944
New York Times II, p. 3, Nov. 7, 1943; II, p. 3, Mar.
19, 1944; p. 26, Mar. 31, 1944; II, p. 3, Apr. 23,
1944
Newsweek 23:79, Apr. 10, 1944
Theatre Arts 28:362, Jun., 1944
Time 43:94+, Apr. 10, 1944

Cover Up, (1948)
Newsweek 33:87, Mar. 28, 1949
Time 53:90, Feb. 28, 1949

*Cow and I
Commonweal 74:327, Jun. 23, 1961
New York Times p. 42, Jun. 6, 1961
Newsweek 57:97, Jun. 19, 1961

*Cow and I (Continued)
Time 77:53, Jun. 23, 1961

Cowboy (1954)
Catholic World 179:223, Jun., 1954
Commonweal 60:513, Aug. 27, 1954
Farm Journal 78:141, Jun., 1954
National Parent-Teacher 48:38, Jun., 1954
New York Times II, p. 5, Mar. 28, 1954; p. 14, Aug. 3, 1954
Newsweek 43:102, Apr. 26, 1954
Saturday Review 37:30, Aug. 21, 1954
Scholastic 65:35, Sep. 15, 1954

Cowboy (1958)
America 98:643, Mar. 1, 1958
Commonweal 67:593, Mar. 7, 1958
Library Journal 83:748, Mar. 1, 1958
New York Times p. 29, Feb. 20, 1958
New Yorker 34:107, Mar. 1, 1958
Newsweek 51:106, Feb. 17, 1958
Saturday Review 41:26, Mar. 1, 1958
Time 71:64+, Feb. 17, 1958

Cowboy and the Lady (1938)
Commonweal 29:161, Dec. 2, 1938
Life 5:38-40, Nov. 21, 1938
New Republic 97:174, Dec. 14, 1938
New York Times IX, p. 4, Nov. 20, 1938; p. 19, Nov. 25, 1938; IX, p. 5, Nov. 27, 1938
Newsweek 12:19, Nov. 28, 1938
Stage 15:26, Sep., 1938
Time 32:53, Nov. 21, 1938

Cowboy from Brooklyn (1938)
New York Times p. 17, Jul. 14, 1938

Cowboy in Manhattan (1943)
New York Times p. 19, May 28, 1943

Cowboy Serenade (1942)
New York Times X, p. 9, Dec. 7, 1941

Crack in the Mirror (1960)
America 103:342+, Jun. 4, 1960
Commonweal 72:279, Jun. 10, 1960
Life 48:81-2, May 23, 1960

Crack in the Mirror (1960) (Continued)
New York Times II, p. 7, Nov. 15, 1959; p. 26, May 20,
1960
Newsweek 55:116, May 23, 1960
Saturday Review 43:29, May 14, 1960
Time 75:46, May 30, 1960

Crack Up (1937)
New York Times p. 20, Jan. 4, 1937

Cracked Nuts (1931)
Life (NY) 97:22, May 1, 1931
New York Times p. 24, Apr. 6, 1931; IX, p. 5, Apr. 12,
1931

Cracked Nuts (1941)
New York Times IX, p. 5, Mar. 23, 1941

Crackup (1946)
New York Times p. 11, Sep. 7, 1946; II, p. 3, Sep. 8,
1946
New Yorker 22:105, Sep. 14, 1946
Time 48:106, Sep. 16, 1946

Cradle Song (1933)
Literary Digest 116:38, Dec. 2, 1933
Nation 137:631, Nov. 29, 1933
New York Times p. 18, Nov. 18, 1933; IX, p. 5, Nov.
26, 1933
Newsweek 2:30, Nov. 4, 1933

Craig's Wife (1936)
Canadian Magazine 86:37, Nov., 1936
Literary Digest 122:28, Oct. 10, 1936
Nation 143:502, Oct. 24, 1936
New York Times p. 29, Oct. 2, 1936
Newsweek 8:27, Sep. 26, 1936
Stage 14:24, Oct., 1936
Time 28:32, Oct. 12, 1936

Cranes Are Flying (1960)
Commonweal 71:351, Dec. 18, 1959
Nation 190:324, Apr. 9, 1960
New York Times p. 31, May 22, 1960; II, p. 1, Mar. 27,
1960
New Yorker 36:88+, Apr. 2, 1960
Newsweek 54:112-13, Dec. 7, 1959
Time 75:87, Feb. 22, 1960

Crash (1932)
New York Times p. 17, Sep. 9, 1932

Crash Dive (1943)
Commonweal 38:100, May 14, 1943
New York Times p. 25, Apr. 29, 1943; II, p. 3, May 2, 1943
New Yorker 19:36, May 1, 1943
Time 41:98, May 10, 1943

Crash Donovan (1936)
New York Times p. 10, Aug. 10, 1936

Crashout (1955)
New York Times p. 9, Jul. 9, 1955
Newsweek 45:89, Feb. 28, 1955
Time 65:106, Mar. 7, 1955

Crawling Eye (1958)
Commonweal 69:127, Oct. 31, 1958
New York Times p. 38, Jan. 1, 1959

Crazy for Love (1960)
New York Times p. 13, Nov. 26, 1960

Crazy House (1943)
New York Times p. 33, Dec. 16, 1943

Crazylegs (1953)
America 90:305, Dec. 12, 1953
Catholic World 178:141, Nov., 1953
Commonweal 59:142, Nov. 13, 1953
Farm Journal 77:73, Dec., 1953
National Parent-Teacher 48:38, Dec., 1953
Newsweek 42:104+, Nov. 16, 1953
Saturday Review 36:52, Nov. 21, 1953
Scholastic 63:28, Jan. 6, 1954
Time 62:108+, Dec. 7, 1953

Creature from the Black Lagoon (1954)
Commonweal 60:145, May 14, 1954
National Parent-Teacher 48:38, Apr., 1954
New York Times p. 13, May 1, 1954; II, p. 1, May 9, 1954

Creature Walks Among Us (1956)
American Magazine 161:9, Apr., 1956
National Parent-Teacher 50:39, Apr., 1956

Creature Walks Among Us (1956) (Continued)
New York Times p. 21, Apr. 27, 1956; II, p. 1, May 6, 1956
Newsweek 47:126, May 14, 1956

Creature with the Atom Brain (1955)
National Parent-Teacher 49:39, May, 1955

Creeping Unknown (1956)
National Parent-Teacher 51:39, Sep., 1956

Crest of the Wave (1954)
America 92:222, Nov. 20, 1954
Farm Journal 79:70, Jan., 1955
Library Journal 79:2438, Dec. 15, 1954
National Parent-Teacher 49:39, Jan., 1955
New York Times p. 43, Nov. 11, 1954
New Yorker 30:82, Nov. 20, 1954
Newsweek 45:45, Jan. 3, 1955
Saturday Review 37:28, Nov. 27, 1954
Time 64:113, Nov. 15, 1954

Crime and Punishment (1935)
Canadian Magazine 85:32, Jan., 1936
Commonweal 23:162, Dec. 6, 1935
Nation 141:659, Dec. 4, 1935
New Republic 118:27, Mar. 15, 1948
New York Times IX, p. 4, Sep. 15, 1935; X, p. 5, Nov.
    3, 1935; p. 25, Nov. 13, 1935; p. 18, Nov. 22, 1935;
    IX, p. 5, Nov. 24, 1935; p. 17, Mar. 1, 1948
Newsweek 6:27, Nov. 30, 1935
Stage 13:64-5, Nov., 1935
Time 26:39, Dec. 2, 1935

Crime and Punishment (1958)
Commonweal 69:16, Oct. 3, 1958
Library Journal 83:2825, Oct. 15, 1958
New York Times p. 23, Sep. 16, 1958
Newsweek 52:94, Sep. 29, 1958
Saturday Review 41:26, Sep. 27, 1958
Time 72:73, Sep. 22, 1958

Crime and Punishment, U.S.A. (1959)
Commonweal 70:232, May 29, 1959
Library Journal 84:2171, Jul., 1959
Nation 189:20, Jul. 4, 1959
New Republic 140:22, Jun. 15, 1959

250

Crime and Punishment, U. S. A. (1959) (Continued)
New York Times p. 39, Jun. 17, 1959
Newsweek 53:95, Jun. 1, 1959
Saturday Review 42:23, May 9, 1959

Crime Doctor (1934)
Literary Digest 117:32, May 26, 1934
New Outlook 163:44, Jun., 1934
New York Times p. 24, May 11, 1934; IX, p. 3, May 20,
1934
Vanity Fair 42:54, May, 1934

Crime Doctor (1943)
New York Times p. 11, Jul. 5, 1943

Crime Doctor's Courage (1945)
New York Times II, p. 11, Mar. 3, 1945

Crime Does Not Pay (1962)
Commonweal 77:154, Nov. 2, 1962
New York Times p. 35, Oct. 17, 1962
Newsweek 60:112, Nov. 5, 1962
Time 80:99, Nov. 9, 1962

Crime Et Chatiment (see Crime and Punishment, 1935)

Crime in the Streets (1956)
America 95:252, Jun. 2, 1956
Catholic World 183:143, May, 1956
Commonweal 64:179, May 18, 1956
National Parent-Teacher 50:39, May, 1956
New York Times VI, p. 34, Apr. 15, 1956; p. 27, May
24, 1956; II, p. 1, May 27, 1956
Newsweek 47:106, May, 1956
Saturday Review 39:47, May 19, 1956
Time 67:100, May 28, 1956

Crime Inc. (1945)
New York Times II, p. 3, Nov. 19, 1944; p. 9, Jun. 23,
1945

Crime Nobody Saw (1937)
New York Times p. 17, Apr. 5, 1937

Crime of Doctor Crespi (1935)
New York Times p. 14, Jan. 13, 1936

251

Crime of Dr. Forbes (1936)
  New York Times IX, p. 4, Jul. 5, 1936; p. 11, Jul. 6,
    1936

Crime of Dr. Hallet (1938)
  New York Times p. 21, Mar. 24, 1938

Crime of Passion (1957)
  National Parent-Teacher 51:38, Mar., 1957
  New York Times p. 25, Jan. 10, 1957

Crime of the Century (1933)
  New York Times p. 18, Mar. 13, 1933
  Newsweek 1:28, Mar. 18, 1933

Crime Ring (1938)
  New York Times p. 10, Jul. 22, 1938

Crime School (1938)
  Commonweal 28:133, May 27, 1938
  New Republic 95:76, May 25, 1938
  New York Times p. 17, May 11, 1938; X, p. 3, May 15,
    1938

Crime Takes a Holiday (1938)
  New York Times p. 11, Nov. 28, 1938

Crime Wave (1954)
  Farm Journal 78:165, Apr., 1954
  New York Times p. 26, Jan. 13, 1954

Crime Without Passion (1934)
  Literary Digest 118:30, Sep. 15, 1934
  New Republic 80:184, Sep. 26, 1934
  New York Times IX, p. 4, Jun. 10, 1934; p. 16, Sep. 1,
    1934; IX, p. 3, Sep. 9, 1934
  Vanity Fair 43:48, Oct., 1934

Criminal at Large (1934)
  New York Times p. 27, Dec. 20, 1933
  Newsweek 2:30, Dec. 30, 1933

Criminal Code (1930)
  Nation 132:80, Jan. 21, 1931
  New York Times p. 21, Jan. 5, 1931; VIII, p. 5, Jan. 11,
    1931
  Outlook 157:113, Jan. 21, 1931

Criminal Court (1946)
New York Times p. 15, Nov. 16, 1946

Criminal Lawyer (1937)
New York Times p. 17, Jan. 27, 1937

Criminal Lawyer (1951)
New York Times p. 11, Aug. 24, 1951

*Criminal Life of Archibaldo De La Cruz
New Republic 147:26, Dec. 1, 1962
New York Times p. 44, Nov. 28, 1962
Newsweek 60:100+, Dec. 3, 1962

Criminals of the Air (1937)
New York Times p. 29, Oct. 28, 1937

Crimson Circle (1930)
New York Times p. 11, Dec. 28, 1929

Crimson Circle (1937)
New York Times p. 12, Dec. 28, 1936

Crimson Key (1947)
New York Times p. 9, Oct. 18, 1947

Crimson Pirate (1952)
Catholic World 176:63, Oct., 1952
Commonweal 56:559, Sep. 12, 1952
National Parent-Teacher 47:37, Nov., 1952
New York Times II, p. 5, Aug. 19, 1951; p. 21, Aug.
28, 1952
Newsweek 40:97-8, Sep. 8, 1952
Saturday Review 35:29, Aug. 2, 1952
Time 60:106+, Sep. 15, 1952

Crimson Romance (1934)
New York Times p. 10, Oct. 13, 1934

Cripple Creed (1952)
National Parent-Teacher 47:37, Sep., 1952

Crisis (1939)
Commonweal 29:640, Mar. 31, 1939
Nation 148:301, Mar. 11, 1939
New Republic 98:194, Mar. 22, 1939
New York Times XI, p. 5, Mar. 12, 1939; p. 12, Mar.
13, 1939; X, p. 4, Apr. 2, 1939

Crisis (1939) (Continued)
Scholastic 34:34, Apr. 15, 1939

Crisis (1950)
Christian Century 67:983, Aug. 16, 1950
Commonweal 52:346, Jul. 14, 1950
New Republic 123:22-3, Jul. 24, 1950
New York Times p. 10, Jul. 4, 1950
New Yorker 26:63, Jul. 15, 1950
Newsweek 36:85, Jul. 10, 1950
Rotarian 77:36, Oct., 1950
Time 56:92, Jul. 17, 1950

Criss Cross (1949)
Good Housekeeping 128:212, Mar., 1949
New Republic 120:30, Mar. 28, 1949
New York Times p. 10, Mar. 12, 1949
Time 53:89, Feb. 28, 1949

Critic's Choice (1963)
America 108:692, May 11, 1963
Commonweal 78:106, Apr. 19, 1963
New York Times p. 40, May 2, 1963
Newsweek 61:104, Apr. 15, 1963
Saturday Review 46:31, Mar. 2, 1963

Crooked Road (1940)
New York Times p. 33, Jun. 11, 1940

Crooked Way (1949)
Commonweal 50:438, Aug. 12, 1949
New York Times p. 13, Sep. 5, 1949
Newsweek 33:83, May 2, 1949
Rotarian 75:39, Oct., 1949

Crooked Web (1955)
National Parent-Teacher 50:39, Dec., 1955

Crooner (1932)
New York Times p. 7, Aug. 20, 1932; IX, p. 3, Aug.
28, 1932

Cross Country Cruise (1934)
New York Times p. 12, Jan. 20, 1934

Cross Country Romance (1940)
New York Times p. 22, Jul. 19, 1940

Cross Country Romance (1940) (Continued)
Newsweek 16:43, Jul. 8, 1940
Photoplay 54:66, Sep., 1940

Cross Examination (1932)
New York Times p. 21, Feb. 27, 1932

Cross My Heart (1947)
New York Times p. 42, Dec. 19, 1946
Time 49:100, Jan. 13, 1947

Cross of Lorraine (1943)
Commonweal 39:176, Dec. 3, 1943
New Republic 109:885-6, Dec. 20, 1943
New York Times p. 27, Dec. 3, 1943
New Yorker 19:82, Dec. 4, 1943
Newsweek 22:102, Dec. 13, 1943
Photoplay 24:22, Feb., 1944
Time 42:55+, Dec. 6, 1943

Crossed Swords (1953)
National Parent-Teacher 49:39, Nov., 1954

Crossfire (1947)
Canadian Forum 28:39, May, 1948
Commonweal 46:386, Aug. 1, 1947
Hollywood Quarterly 3:63-5, Fall, 1947
Life 22:4, Jun. 16, 1947; 22:71-2+, Jun. 30, 1947
Nation 165:129, Aug. 2, 1947
New Republic 117:34, Aug. 11, 1947
New York Times II, p. 5, Mar. 16, 1947; II, p. 3, Jul.
    6, 1947; II, p. 3, Jul. 20, 1947; p. 19, Jul. 23, 1947;
    II, p. 1, Jul. 27, 1947; p. 27, Sep. 26, 1947
New Yorker 23:46, Jul. 19, 1947
Newsweek 30:84, Jul. 28, 1947
Photoplay 31:4, Oct., 1947
Saturday Review 30:69-70, Dec. 6, 1947
Scholastic 51:31, Sep. 29, 1947
Theatre Arts 31:15, Sep., 1947
Time 50:76, Aug. 4, 1947

Crossroads (1938)
New York Times p. 17, Mar. 14, 1939

Crossroads (1942)
Commonweal 36:374, Aug. 7, 1942
Good Housekeeping 115:2, Jul., 1942

Crossroads (1942) (Continued)
New York Times p. 23, Jul. 24, 1942
New Yorker 18:41, Aug. 1, 1942
Time 40:86, Jul. 13, 1942
Woman's Home Companion 69:2, Jul., 1942

Crosswinds (1951)
New York Times p. 35, Dec. 7, 1951

Couching Beast (1936)
New York Times p. 6, Aug. 22, 1936

Crowd Roars (1932)
Nation 134:444-5, Apr. 13, 1932
New York Times p. 25, Mar. 23, 1932; VIII, p. 4, Apr.
4, 1932

Crowd Roars (1938)
Canadian Magazine 90:58, Sep., 1938
Commonweal 28:430, Aug. 19, 1938
New York Times p. 11, Aug. 5, 1938
Newsweek 12:27, Aug. 15, 1938
Time 32:35, Aug. 15, 1938

Crowded Paradise (1956)
Catholic World 183:143, May, 1956
New York Times p. 5, Jun. 22, 1956
Time 68:78, Jul. 9, 1956

Crowded Sky (1960)
Good Housekeeping 151:26, Sep., 1960
New York Times p. 27, Feb. 11, 1961

Crowning Experience (1960)
America 104:284+, Nov. 26, 1960; 110:831, Jun. 13, 1964
New York Times p. 25, Oct. 24, 1960

Cruel Sea (1952)
America 89:506, Aug. 22, 1953
Commonweal 58:520, Aug. 28, 1953
Farm Journal 77:107, Aug., 1953
Library Journal 78:1321, Aug., 1953
Life 35:73-4, Sep. 21, 1953
Nation 177:178, Aug. 29, 1953
National Parent-Teacher 48:39, Oct., 1953
New York Times p. 1, Aug. 11, 1953; II, p. 1, Aug. 16,
1953

Cruel Sea (1952) (Continued)
New York Times Magazine p. 42, Apr. 26, 1953
New Yorker 29:56, Aug. 15, 1953
Newsweek 42:88+, Aug. 17, 1953
Saturday Review 36:26, Aug. 22, 1953; 38:29, Jan. 8, 1955
Scholastic 63:38, Sep. 23, 1953
Time 62:64+, Aug. 24, 1953

Crusader (1932)
New York Times p. 15, Oct. 8, 1932

Crusades (1935)
Catholic World 142:83-8, Oct., 1935
Commonweal 22:472, Sep. 13, 1935
Literary Digest 120:29, Aug. 31, 1935
Motion Picture 50:34-5+, Sep., 1935
Nation 141:391-2, Oct. 2, 1935
New York Times X, p. 4, May 12, 1935; IX, p. 2, Aug. 4, 1935; IX, p. 2, Aug. 18, 1935; p. 21, Aug. 22, 1935; X, p. 3, Aug. 25, 1935; IX, p. 4, Sep. 8, 1935
Newsweek 6:26-7, Aug. 31, 1935
Photoplay 48:94, Jul., 1935; 48:35, Nov., 1935
Scientific America 153:61-3, Aug., 1935
Stage 13:8, Oct., 1935
Time 26:38, Sep. 2, 1935
Vanity Fair 45:46, Oct., 1935

Cry Danger (1950)
Commonweal 53:448, Feb. 9, 1951
Christian Century 68:351, Mar. 14, 1951
New York Times p. 27, Feb. 22, 1951
Newsweek 37:86-7, Mar. 5, 1951
Rotarian 78:38, May, 1951
Time 57:103, Feb. 26, 1951

Cry for Happy (1961)
America 104:800, Mar. 18, 1961
Commonweal 74:103, Apr. 21, 1961
New York Times p. 16, Mar. 4, 1961
Time 77:70, Mar. 17, 1961

Cry from the Streets (1959)
Commonweal 69:601, Mar. 6, 1959
New York Times p. 32, Feb. 24, 1959
New Yorker 35:92+, Mar. 7, 1959

Cry Havoc (1944)
   Commonweal 39:206, Dec. 10, 1943
   New York Times p. 16, Nov. 24, 1943
   Newsweek 22:96, Dec. 6, 1943
   Time 42:56, Dec. 6, 1943

Cry in the Night (1956)
   National Parent-Teacher 51:39, Nov., 1956
   New York Times p. 19, Sep. 1, 1956

Cry of the City (1948)
   Commonweal 49:13, Oct. 15, 1948
   New York Times p. 32, Sep. 30, 1948
   Newsweek 32:94-5, Oct. 11, 1948
   Rotarian 74:11+, Jan., 1949
   Time 52:105, Oct. 18, 1948

Cry of the Hunted (1953)
   National Parent-Teacher 47:37, May, 1953

Cry of the Werewolf (1944)
   New York Times p. 16, Aug. 12, 1944

Cry of the World (1932)
   New York Times p. 23, May 5, 1932

Cry Terror (1958)
   America 99:271, May 24, 1958
   Commonweal 67:660, Mar. 28, 1958
   New York Times p. 25, May 15, 1958
   New Yorker 34:74, May 24, 1958
   Newsweek 51:113, May 5, 1958
   Time 71:84, Jun. 2, 1958

Cry, the Beloved Country (1952)
   Catholic World 174:457, Mar., 1952
   Christian Century 69:1207, Oct. 15, 1952
   Commonweal 55:446, Feb. 8, 1952
   Holiday 11:105, May, 1952
   Library Journal 77:311, Feb. 15, 1952
   New Republic 126:21-2, Feb. 11, 1952
   New York Times II, p. 5, Apr. 22, 1951; p. 22, Jan.
      20, 1952; p. 23, Jan. 24, 1952; II, p. 1, Jan. 27,
      1952; II, p. 4, Feb. 3, 1952; II, p. 5, Apr. 13, 1952
   New Yorker 27:68, Feb. 2, 1952
   Newsweek 39:89, Jan. 28, 1952
   Saturday Review 35:31, Feb. 2, 1952
   Time 59:86, Feb. 18, 1952

Cry Tough (1959)
New York Times p. 48, Sep. 17, 1959
Time 74:76, Sep. 28, 1959

Cry Vengeance (1954)
New York Times p. 18, Feb. 19, 1955

Cry Wolf (1947)
Commonweal 46:406, Aug. 8, 1947
New York Times p. 10, Jul. 19, 1947; II, p. 4, Jul. 20, 1947
Newsweek 30:78, Jul. 21, 1947
Woman's Home Companion 74:11, Sep., 1947

Crystal Ball (1943)
New York Times p. 22, Feb. 19, 1943
Time 41:46, Feb. 1, 1943

Cuban Love Song (1931)
New York Times p. 21, Dec. 5, 1931

Cuban Rebel Girl (1960)
New York Times p. 7, Dec. 26, 1959

Cuckoos (1930)
New York Times p. 11, Apr. 26, 1930

Cult of the Cobra (1955)
Library Journal 80:865, Apr. 15, 1955
National Parent-Teacher 49:39, May, 1955

Curley (1947)
New York Times p. 12, Sep. 20, 1947; p. 26, Oct. 6, 1947; II, p. 5, Jun. 6, 1948

*Curly Top
Commonweal 22:387, Aug. 16, 1935
Literary Digest 120:29, Aug. 10, 1935
New York Times p. 22, Aug. 2, 1935
Time 26:32, Aug. 12, 1935

Curse of Frankenstein (1957)
National Parent-Teacher 52:33, Oct., 1957
New York Times p. 15, Aug. 8, 1957

Curse of the Cat People (1944)
Nation 158:401, Apr. 1, 1944

Curse of the Cat People (1944) (Continued)
New Republic 110:380-1, Mar. 20, 1944
New York Times p. 11, Mar. 4, 1944

Curse of the Werewolf (1961)
New York Times p. 40, Jun. 8, 1961

Curtain Call (1940)
New York Times IX, p. 5, Feb. 11, 1940; p. 25, Apr.
19, 1940

Curtain Call at Cactus Creek (1950)
New York Times p. 35, Sep. 22, 1950
Newsweek 35:91, Jun. 19, 1950

Curtain Rises (1939)
New York Times p. 15, Apr. 22, 1939

Curtain Up (1952)
Catholic World 176:303, Jan., 1953
Commonweal 57:378, Jan. 16, 1953
Library Journal 78:516, Mar. 15, 1953
Nation 176:153, Feb. 14, 1953
National Parent-Teacher 47:38, Apr., 1953
New York Times p. 17, Feb. 2, 1953
Saturday Review 35:28, Dec. 20, 1952
Theatre Arts 37:84, Jan., 1953
Time 61:108, Feb. 16, 1953

Curucu, Beast of the Amazon (1956)
National Parent-Teacher 51:39, Dec., 1956

Cyclops (1957)
National Parent-Teacher 51:38, Mar., 1957

Cynara (1932)
New York Times p. 26, Dec. 26, 1932
Vanity Fair 39:48, Jan., 1933

Cynthia (1947)
Commonweal 46:599, Oct. 3, 1947
New York Times II, p. 5, Sep. 14, 1947; p. 27, Sep. 19,
1947
Time 50:104, Oct. 6, 1947
Woman's Home Companion 74:10-11, Aug., 1947

Cyrano De Bergerac (1950)
Christian Century 68:191, Feb. 7, 1951

Cyrano De Bergerac (1950) (Continued)
Commonweal 53:172, Nov. 24, 1950
Harper 202:103-4, Jan., 1951
Library Journal 75:2086, Dec. 1, 1950
Life 29:73-5, Nov. 20, 1950
New Republic 123:22, Dec. 4, 1950
New York Times II, p. 5, Sep. 17, 1950; VI, p. 24, Nov.
   12, 1950; p. 31, Nov. 17, 1950; II, p. 1, Nov. 19,
   1950
New Yorker 26:176, Nov. 18, 1950
Newsweek 36:84, Nov. 27, 1950
Rotarian 78:40, Apr., 1951
Saturday Review 33:32, Nov. 18, 1950
Scholastic 57:22, Dec. 13, 1950
Theatre Arts 34:32-5, Nov., 1950
Time 56:103, Nov. 20, 1950

Czar of Broadway (1930)
Life (NY) 96:17, Aug. 1, 1930
New York Times p. 9, Jun. 28, 1930; VIII, p. 3, Jul. 6,
   1930

D-Day, the Sixth of June (1956)
America 95:292, Jun. 16, 1956
Commonweal 64:274, Jun. 15, 1956
Library Journal 81:1609, Jun. 15, 1956
National Parent-Teacher 51:39, Sep., 1956
New York Times p. 13, May 30, 1956; II, p. 1, Jun. 3,
   1956
New Yorker 32:54, Jun. 9, 1956
Newsweek 47:124+, Jun. 18, 1956
Saturday Review 39:33, Jun. 16, 1956
Time 67:98+, Jun. 18, 1956

D. I. (1957)
American 97:352, Jun. 22, 1957
Commonweal 66:308, Jun. 21, 1957
National Parent-Teacher 52:33, Sep., 1957
New York Times p. 35, Jun. 6, 1957
New Yorker 33:72, Jun. 15, 1957
Newsweek 49:114, Jun. 10, 1957
Saturday Review 40:30, Jun. 8, 1957
Time 69:96, Jun. 17, 1957

D. O. A. (1950)
Commonweal 52:45, Apr. 21, 1950

D. O. A. (1950) (Continued)
Good Housekeeping 130:328, Apr., 1950
New York Times p. 15, May 1, 1950
New Yorker 26:72, May 6, 1950
Newsweek 35:87, May 8, 1950
Time 55:96, May 15, 1950

Daddy Long Legs (1931, 1955)
America 93:223, May 21, 1955
American Magazine 159:14, May, 1955
Catholic World 181:223, Jun., 1955
Commonweal 62:207, May 27, 1955
Library Journal 80:1321, Jun. 1, 1955
Life 38:78-82, May 23, 1955
Life (NY) 97:18, Jun. 26, 1931
Look 19:92-3, May 17, 1955
National Parent-Teacher 50:38, Sep., 1955
New York Times p. 15, Jun. 6, 1931; VIII, p. 5, Jun.
    14, 1931; p. 17, May 6, 1955; p. 18, May 6, 1955
New Yorker 31:145, May 14, 1955
Newsweek 45:113, May 16, 1955
Saturday Review 38:45, May 21, 1955
Time 65:106, May 9, 1955
Woman's Home Companion 82:12, Jul., 1955

Daisy Kenyon (1947)
New York Times p. 32, Dec. 25, 1947
Newsweek 31:78, Jan. 12, 1948
Time 50:62, Dec. 29, 1947

Dakota (1945)
Commonweal 43:310, Jan. 4, 1946
New York Times VI, p. 17, Aug. 19, 1945; p. 17, Dec.
    17, 1945

Dakota Incident (1956)
New York Times p. 14, Nov. 10, 1956

Dakota Lil (1950)
New York Times p. 21, Mar. 3, 1950

Dallas (1950)
Christian Century 68:287, Feb. 28, 1951
Commonweal 53:399, Jan. 26, 1951
New York Times p. 10, Jan. 13, 1951
Rotarian 78:36, Mar., 1951
Saturday Review 34:31, Feb. 17, 1951
Time 57:92, Jan. 22, 1951

Dalton Gang (1949)
    New York Times p. 27, Nov. 25, 1949

Daltons Ride Again (1945)
    New York Times p. 21, Dec. 8, 1945

Dam Busters (1954)
    America 93:603, Sep. 17, 1955
    Aviation Week 63:138, Dec. 5, 1955
    Catholic World 181:383, Aug., 1955
    Commonweal 62:647, Sep. 30, 1955
    National Parent-Teacher 50:38, Oct., 1955
    New York Times II, p. 5, Nov. 21, 1955
    Time 66:82+, Aug. 22, 1955

Damaged Lives (1935)
    New York Times p. 26, Jun. 14, 1937

Damaged Love (1931)
    New York Times p. 25, Jan. 19, 1931

Dames (1934)
    Movie Classic 7:34-5, Sep., 1934
    New York Times p. 20, Aug. 16, 1934; IX, p. 3, Aug.
    26, 1934

Dames Ahoy (1930)
    New York Times p. 23, Mar. 29, 1930

Damn Citizen (1957)
    Catholic World 186:464, Mar., 1958
    Commonweal 67:660, Mar. 28, 1958

Damn the Defiant! (1962)
    America 107:823-4, Sep. 29, 1962
    New York Times p. 29, Sep. 20, 1962; II, p. 1, Nov. 18,
    1962
    New Yorker 38:141, Sep. 29, 1962
    Newsweek 60:92, Sep. 24, 1962
    Reporter 27:43, Dec. 6, 1962
    Senior Scholastic 81:44, Sep. 26, 1962

Damn Yankees (1958)
    America 100:119, Oct. 25, 1958
    Catholic World 188:154, Nov., 1958
    Commonweal 69:73, Oct. 17, 1958
    Dance Magazine 32:13-14, Oct., 1958

Damn Yankees (1958) (Continued)
Library Journal 83:2825, Oct. 15, 1958
New York Times p. 12, Sep. 27, 1958; II, p. 1, Oct. 5,
1958
New Yorker 34:158, Oct. 4, 1958
Newsweek 52:94, Sep. 29, 1958
Saturday Review 41:26, Sep. 27, 1958
Senior Scholastic 73:27, Oct. 17, 1958
Time 72:69, Sep. 29, 1958

Damned Don't Cry (1950)
Christian Century 67:687, May 31, 1950
Commonweal 52:127, May 12, 1950
New York Times p. 9, Apr. 8, 1950
New Yorker 26:75, Apr. 15, 1950
Newsweek 35:96, Apr. 17, 1950
Rotarian 77:43, Aug., 1950
Time 55:106, Apr. 17, 1950

Damon and Pythia (1962)
America 107:795, Sep. 22, 1962
Commonweal 77:18, Sep. 28, 1962
New York Times p. 37, Sep. 6, 1962
Senior Scholastic 81:44, Sep. 26, 1962

Damsel in Distress (1937)
Commonweal 27:160, Dec. 3, 1937
Life 3:74-5, Nov. 29, 1937
Literary Digest 124:34, Dec. 11, 1937
Nation 145:697, Dec. 18, 1937
New York Times X, p. 3, Aug. 29, 1937; XI, p. 6, Nov.
21, 1937; p. 37, Nov. 25, 1937
Newsweek 10:33, Dec. 6, 1937
Scholastic 31:19E, Dec. 11, 1937
Time 30:49, Dec. 6, 1937

Dance Band (1935)
New York Times p. 19, Jan. 4, 1935

Dance, Charlie, Dance (1937)
New York Times p. 25, Aug. 26, 1937

Dance Fools, Dance (1931)
Life (NY) 97:23, Mar. 27, 1931
New York Times p. 15, Mar. 21, 1931; VIII, p. 5, Mar.
29, 1931; VIII, p. 6, Feb. 14, 1931
Outlook 157:475, Apr. 1, 1931

Dance, Girl, Dance (1933)
New York Times p. 23, Oct. 25, 1933

Dance, Girl, Dance (1940)
Commonweal 32:470, Sep. 27, 1940
New York Times IX, p. 3, Jun. 30, 1940; p. 25, Oct.
11, 1940

Dance Hall (1929)
Life (NY) 95:22, Feb. 14, 1930
New York Times p. 34, Dec. 16, 1929

Dance Hall (1941)
New York Times p. 16, Jul. 19, 1941
Scribner's Commentator 10:107, Oct., 1941

Dance, Little Lady (1955)
National Parent-Teacher 50:39, Mar., 1956
New York Times p. 23, Dec. 26, 1955
New Yorker 31:55, Jan. 7, 1956

Dance of Life (1929)
Life (NY) 94:23, Sep. 27, 1929
New York Times p. 5, Aug. 17, 1929
Outlook 153:32, Sep. 4, 1929
Vogue 74:180+, Oct. 12, 1929

Dance Team (1932)
New York Times p. 13, Jan. 16, 1932

Dance with Me, Henry (1956)
National Parent-Teacher 51:37, Feb., 1957
New York Times p. 8, Dec. 24, 1956

Dancers (1930)
New York Times p. 15, Nov. 15, 1930; IX, p. 5, Nov.
23, 1930
Outlook 156:512, Nov. 26, 1930

Dancers in the Dark (1932)
New York Times p. 11, Mar. 19, 1932; VIII, p. 4, Mar.
27, 1932

Dancing Coed (1939)
New York Times IX, p. 4, Nov. 5, 1939; p. 27, Nov. 10,
1939

Dancing Feet (1936)
New York Times p. 11, Mar. 28, 1936

Dancing Heart (1959)
New York Times p. 10, Jan. 18, 1958

Dancing in the Dark (1950)
Christian Century 67:191, Feb. 8, 1950
New Republic 121:31, Dec. 12, 1949
New York Times p. 8, Dec. 3, 1949
Newsweek 34:90, Dec. 12, 1949
Time 54:90, Dec. 19, 1949

Dancing Lady (1933)
Literary Digest 116:47, Dec. 16, 1933
New York Times p. 23, Dec. 1, 1933; X, p. 7, Dec. 1,
1933
Newsweek 2:33, Dec. 9, 1933

Dancing Masters (1943)
New York Times p. 30, Dec. 2, 1943

Dancing on a Dime (1940)
New York Times IX, p. 3, May 12, 1940

Dancing Pirate (1936)
Canadian Magazine 86:32, Jul., 1936
Commonweal 24:104, May 22, 1936
Literary Digest 121:20, May 23, 1936
New York Times p. 19, Jun. 18, 1936; IX, p. 3, Jun. 21,
1936
Time 27:24+, Jun. 1, 1936

Dancing Sweeties (1930)
Life (NY) 96:17, Sep. 12, 1930
New York Times p. 8, Aug. 16, 1930

Danger Lights (1930)
New York Times p. 29, Dec. 15, 1930; VIII, p. 5, Dec.
21, 1930

Danger, Love at Work (1937)
New York Times p. 22, Dec. 11, 1937
Time 30:42+, Nov. 15, 1937

Danger Patrol (1937)
New York Times p. 27, Nov. 19, 1937

Danger Signal (1945)
New York Times p. 39, Nov. 22, 1945
Time 46:94, Dec. 17, 1945

Danger Street (1928)
New York Times p. 29, Sep. 25, 1928

Dangerous (1936)
New York Times p. 14, Dec. 27, 1935
Newsweek 7:25, Jan. 4, 1936
Time 27:28, Jan. 6, 1936

Dangerous Affair (1931)
New York Times p. 22, Nov. 23, 1931

Dangerous Crossing (1953)
Commonweal 58:537, Sep. 4, 1953
Library Journal 78:1677, Oct. 1, 1953
National Parent-Teacher 48:39, Sep., 1953
New York Times p. 37, Sep. 30, 1953
Newsweek 42:98+, Sep. 28, 1953
Saturday Review 36:29, Aug. 29, 1953

Dangerous Curves (1929)
Life (NY) 94:26, Aug. 9, 1929
New York Times p. 25, Jul. 15, 1929; VIII, p. 5, Sep. 1, 1929

Dangerous Exile (1958)
Commonweal 68:376, Jul. 11, 1958
Library Journal 83:1913, Jun. 15, 1958
New York Times p. 18, Oct. 11, 1958

Dangerous Game (1941)
New York Times p. 20, Mar. 4, 1941

Dangerous Journey (1944)
New York Times p. 22, Oct. 2, 1944
New Yorker 20:61, Oct. 14, 1944
Newsweek 24:91, Sep. 25, 1944
Time 44:54, Sep. 25, 1944

Dangerous Millions (1946)
New York Times p. 10, Mar. 15, 1947

Dangerous Mission (1954)
America 90:694, Mar. 27, 1954

Dangerous Mission (1954) (Continued)
  National Parent-Teacher 48:39, May, 1954
  New York Times p. 13, Mar. 6, 1954
  New Yorker 30:124, Mar. 13, 1954
  Time 63:113, Mar. 22, 1954

Dangerous Moonlight (1941)
  New York Times IX, p. 4, Jan. 26, 1941

Dangerous Nan McGrew (1930)
  Life (NY) 95:17, Jul. 18, 1930
  New York Times p. 20, Jun. 21, 1930

Dangerous Number (1937)
  New York Times p. 19, Mar. 12, 1937

Dangerous Paradise (1930)
  New York Times p. 15, Feb. 15, 1930

Dangerous Partners (1945)
  New York Times p. 22, Nov. 2, 1945

Dangerous Profession (1949)
  Commonweal 51:294, Dec. 16, 1949
  New York Times p. 29, Dec. 12, 1949

Dangerous to Know (1938)
  New York Times p. 15, Mar. 11, 1938
  Time 31:53, Mar. 14, 1938

Dangerous Waters (1936)
  New York Times p. 15, Jan. 22, 1936

Dangerous When Wet (1953)
  America 89:425, Jul. 25, 1953
  Catholic World 177:304, Jul., 1953
  Commonweal 58:323, Jul. 3, 1953
  Farm Journal 77:107, Aug., 1953
  McCalls 80:10, Jul., 1953
  National Parent-Teacher 48:38, Sep., 1953
  New York Times p. 18, Jun. 19, 1953; II, p. 1, Jun.
    28, 1953
  Newsweek 42:94, Jul. 20, 1953
  Saturday Review 36:31, Jul. 4, 1953
  Time 61:92, Jun. 29, 1953

Dangerous Woman (1929)
  Life (NY) 93:29, Jun. 7, 1929

Dangerous Woman (1929) (Continued)
New York Times p. 22, May 20, 1929

Dangerously They Live (1942)
Commonweal 35:650, Apr. 17, 1942
New York Times p. 9, Apr. 11, 1942

Dangerously Yours (1933)
New York Times p. 20, Feb. 23, 1933

Dangerously Yours (1937)
New York Times p. 14, Oct. 18, 1937

Dangers of the Arctic (1932)
New York Times p. 26, Jun. 30, 1932

Daniel Boone (1936)
New York Times p. 23, Oct. 24, 1936
Time 28:28, Oct. 5, 1936

Dante's Inferno (1935)
New York Times VIII, p. 3, Mar. 3, 1935
Newsweek 6:27-8, Aug. 10, 1935
Photoplay 54:42, Mar., 1940
Time 26:32-3, Aug. 12, 1935

*Darby O'Gill and the Little People
America 101:618, Aug. 15, 1959
Catholic World 189:318, Jul., 1959
Commonweal 70:327, Jun. 26, 1959
Dance Magazine 33:14-15, Jun., 1959
Good Housekeeping 148:24, Jun., 1959
Library Journal 84:1801, Jun. 1, 1959
New York Times p. 26, Jul. 1, 1959

Darby's Rangers (1958)
America 98:578, Feb. 15, 1958
New York Times p. 23, Feb. 13, 1958
Newsweek 51:87, Feb. 3, 1958

Daredevil Drivers (1938)
New York Times p. 27, Feb. 23, 1938

Daring Young Man (1935)
New York Times p. 15, Jul. 18, 1935

Dark Angel (1935)
Canadian Magazine 84:41, Oct., 1935; 84:43, Dec., 1935

Dark Angel (1935) (Continued)
Commonweal 22:499, Sep. 20, 1935
Literary Digest 120:33, Sep. 14, 1935
New York Times IX, p. 2, Aug. 18, 1935; p. 12, Sep. 6, 1935
Newsweek 6:22, Sep. 7, 1935
Stage 13:6, Oct., 1935
Time 26:61, Sep. 16, 1935
Vanity Fair 45:47, Oct., 1935

Dark at the Top of the Stairs (1960)
America 104:56+, Oct. 8, 1960
Commonweal 73:73-4, Oct. 14, 1960
New York Times p. 33, Sep. 23, 1960; II, p. 1, Sep. 25, 1960
New Yorker 36:167, Oct. 1, 1960
Newsweek 56:119, Sep. 26, 1960
Saturday Review 43:44, Sep. 17, 1960
Time 76:80, Sep. 12, 1960

Dark City (1950)
Commonweal 53:122, Nov. 10, 1950
Good Housekeeping 131:16-17, Nov., 1950
New York Times p. 40, Oct. 19, 1950
Newsweek 36:82, Oct. 30, 1950
Time 56:106+, Nov. 6, 1950

Dark Command (1940)
Commonweal 32:20, Apr. 26, 1940
New York Times p. 15, May 11, 1940
Newsweek 15:30, Apr. 15, 1940
Photoplay 54:69, Jun., 1940
Scholastic 36:36, Apr. 22, 1940

Dark Corner (1946)
Commonweal 44:144, May 24, 1946
Nation 163:305, Sep. 14, 1946
New York Times p. 27, May 9, 1946; II, p. 1, May 12, 1946
Newsweek 27:90, May 6, 1946
Time 47:101, Jun. 3, 1946

Dark Delusion (1947)
New York Times p. 19, Jun. 26, 1947

Dark Eyes (1938)
Commonweal 28:21, Apr. 29, 1938
New York Times p. 24, Apr. 19, 1938

Dark Hazard (1934)
New York Times p. 23, Feb. 23, 1934; X, p. 5, Mar. 11, 1934

Dark Horse (1932)
New York Times p. 27, Jun. 9, 1932; IX, p. 3, Jun. 19, 1932

Dark is the Night (1946)
New York Times p. 24, Mar. 18, 1946

Dark Journey (1937)
New York Times p. 22, Aug. 23, 1937

Dark Mirror (1946)
Commonweal 45:71, Nov. 1, 1946
Cosmopolitan 121:73+, Nov., 1946
Harper's Bazaar 80:256, Sep., 1946
Life 21:131-3+, Oct. 21, 1946
Nation 163:536, Nov. 9, 1946
New Republic 115:661, Nov. 18, 1946
New York Times p. 15, Oct. 19, 1946; II, p. 3, Oct. 20, 1946
New Yorker 22:109, Oct. 26, 1946
Newsweek 28:92, Nov. 4, 1946
Scholastic 49:36, Nov. 11, 1946
Theatre Arts 30:714, Dec., 1946
Time 48:99, Oct. 21, 1946

Dark Passage (1947)
Commonweal 46:574, Sep. 26, 1947
Good Housekeeping 125:11, Oct., 1947
New Republic 117:37, Sep. 29, 1947
New York Times II, p. 3, Aug. 31, 1947; p. 11, Sep. 6, 1947
New Yorker 23:113, Sep. 13, 1947
Newsweek 30:90, Sep. 15, 1947
Time 50:97, Sep. 22, 1947

Dark Past (1949)
Commonweal 49:378, Jan. 21, 1949
New Republic 120:29, Jan. 17, 1949
New York Times p. 25, Dec. 23, 1948
Newsweek 32:69, Dec. 27, 1948
Photoplay 34:21, Mar., 1949
Rotarian 74:36, Apr., 1949
Time 53:84, Jan. 10, 1949

Dark Rapture (1938)
Commonweal 28:645, Oct. 14, 1938
New York Times p. 14, Oct. 10, 1938; IX, p. 5, Oct.
16, 1938
Newsweek 12:23, Oct. 3, 1938
Theatre Arts 23:59, Jan., 1939
Time 32:32, Oct. 17, 1938

Dark River (1956)
New York Times p. 19, Feb. 27, 1956

Dark Sands (1938)
New York Times p. 23, Aug. 17, 1938

Dark Streets of Cairo (1940)
New York Times p. 19, Dec. 2, 1940

Dark Victory (1939)
Canadian Magazine 91:46, Apr., 1939
Commonweal 30:48, May 5, 1939
Harper 179:217-19, Jul., 1939
Life 6:31-2+, Apr. 24, 1939
Nation 148:540, May 6, 1939
New Republic 99:252, Jul. 5, 1939
New York Times IX, p. 5, Nov. 6, 1938; p. 27, Apr. 21,
1939
Newsweek 13:33, Apr. 24, 1939
Photoplay 53:62, May, 1939
Stage 16:20+, Apr. 1, 1939
Time 33:68, May 1, 1939

Dark Waters (1944)
Commonweal 41:152, Nov. 24, 1944
New York Times p. 25, Nov. 22, 1944
New Yorker 20:85, Dec. 2, 1944
Newsweek 24:104, Dec. 4, 1944
Time 44:92, Dec. 11, 1944
Woman's Home Companion 71:11, Dec., 1944

Darling, How Could You (1951)
Catholic World 174:145, Nov., 1951
New York Times p. 22, Nov. 9, 1951

Date with Judy (1948)
Commonweal 48:402, Aug. 6, 1948
New York Times p. 22, Aug. 6, 1948
New Yorker 24:71, Aug. 14, 1948

272

Date with Judy (1948) (Continued)
Newsweek 32:81, Jul. 19, 1948
Photoplay 33:22, Sep., 1948
Time 52:86, Sep. 6, 1948

Date with the Falcon (1941)
New York Times p. 33, Nov. 25, 1941; IX, p. 5, Nov. 30, 1941

Daughter of Israel (1928)
New York Times p. 25, May 21, 1928

Daughter of Rosie O'Grady (1949)
New York Times p. 36, Mar. 31, 1950; II, p. 1, Apr. 9, 1950
New Yorker 26:112, Apr. 8, 1950
Newsweek 35:83, Apr. 10, 1950
Time 55:110, Apr. 17, 1950

Daughter of Shanghai (1937)
New York Times p. 21, Dec. 24, 1937

Daughter of the Dragon (1931)
New York Times p. 7, Aug. 22, 1931; VIII, p. 5, Aug. 30, 1931

Daughters Courageous (1939)
Commonweal 30:259, Jun. 30, 1939
New York Times p. 14, Jun. 24, 1939; IX, p. 3, Jun. 25, 1939
Newsweek 14:28, Jul. 3, 1939
Photoplay 53:45, Aug., 1939
Time 34:35, Jul. 3, 1939

Daughters of Destiny (1954)
New York Times p. 19, Jul. 6, 1954

David and Bathsheba (1951)
Catholic World 174:68-9, Oct., 1951
Christian Century 68:1111, Sep. 26, 1951
Commonweal 54:501, Aug. 31, 1951
Life 31:77+, Aug. 27, 1951
New York Times II, p. 7, Dec. 17, 1950; II, p. 5, Feb. 4, 1951; p. 23, Aug. 15, 1951; II, p. 1, Aug. 19, 1951; II, p. 1, Sep. 9, 1951
New Yorker 27:66, Aug. 25, 1951
Newsweek 38:90-1, Aug. 20, 1951
Saturday Review 34:36, Sep. 8, 1951

David and Bathsheba (1951) (Continued)
Time 58:86, Aug. 20, 1951

David and Goliath (1961)
New York Times p. 14, Oct. 7, 1961

David and Lisa (1962)
America 108:154, Jan. 26, 1963
Commonweal 77:389, Jan. 4, 1963
Nation 196:216, Mar. 9, 1963
New Republic 148:20, Jan. 5, 1963
New York Times p. 5, Dec. 27, 1962
New Yorker 38:100-1, Jan. 12, 1963
Newsweek 60:57, Dec. 31, 1962
Saturday Evening Post 236:56+, Mar. 16, 1963
Saturday Review 46:30, Jan. 5, 1963
Time 80:60, Dec. 28, 1962

David Copperfield (1934)
Canadian Magazine 83:41, Apr., 1935
Commonweal 21:403, Feb. 1, 1935; 21:470, Feb. 22, 1935
Library Journal 76:418, Mar. 1, 1951
Literary Digest 119:30, Feb. 2, 1935
Motion Picture 49:22-3, Feb., 1935
Movie Classic 7:40-42+, Feb., 1935
Nation 140:168, Feb. 6, 1935
New York Times IX, p. 4, Sep. 2, 1934; IX, p. 4, Oct.
    21, 1934; p. 8, Jan. 19, 1935; VIII, p. 5, Jan. 27,
    1935; p. 5, Feb. 3, 1935
Newsweek 5:27, Jan. 26, 1935
Photoplay 47:52-3, Mar., 1935
Scholastic 25:9-10+, Jan. 26, 1935; 26:27, Mar. 30, 1935
Time 25:32, Jan. 28, 1935

David Golder (1932)
New York Times p. 24, Oct. 20, 1932

David Harum (1934)
Canadian Magazine 81:44, May, 1934
New Outlook 163:45, Apr., 1934
New York Times p. 23, Mar. 2, 1934; X, p. 5, Mar. 11,
    1934
Newsweek 3:33, Mar. 10, 1934
Time 23:28, Mar. 12, 1934

*Davy Crockett
National Parent-Teacher 50:38, Oct., 1955

*Davy Crockett (Continued)
New York Times p. 36, May 26, 1955; II, p. 1, May 29, 1955
Newsweek 45:106, Jun. 13, 1955
Time 65:102+, Jun. 13, 1955

Davy Crockett and the River Pirates (1955)
Commonweal 64:514, Aug. 24, 1956
National Parent-Teacher 51:37, Oct., 1956
Newsweek 48:88, Aug. 20, 1956

Davy Crockett, Indian Scout (1950)
New York Times p. 28, Mar. 17, 1950
Newsweek 35:72, Jan. 30, 1950
Rotarian 76:40, May, 1950

Dawn at Sorocco (1954)
Catholic World 180:65, Oct., 1954
National Parent-Teacher 49:38, Sep., 1954
New York Times p. 8, Aug. 28, 1954

Dawn Patrol (1930)
Canadian Magazine 91:44, Feb., 1939
Commonweal 12:345, Jul. 30, 1930; 29:273, Dec. 30, 1938
Life 5:33-5, Dec. 26, 1938
Life (NY) 96:17, Aug. 8, 1930
Nation 131:209, Aug. 20, 1930
New York Times p. 22, Jul. 11, 1930; VIII, p. 4, Jul. 20, 1930; p. 12, Dec. 24, 1938; IX, p. 7, Dec. 25, 1938
Newsweek 12:25, Dec. 12, 1938
Photoplay 53:48, Feb., 1939
Outlook 155:510, Jul. 30, 1930
Stage 16:42, Jan., 1939
Time 33:17, Jan. 2, 1939

Day and the Hour (1963)
New York Times p. 22, Feb. 20, 1964
Time 83:84, Mar. 6, 1964

Day at the Races (1937)
Life 2:30-33, Jun. 21, 1937
Literary Digest 123:22-3, Jun. 26, 1937
Nation 145:53, Jul. 10, 1937
New Republic 91:222, Jun. 30, 1937
New York Times p. 25, Jun. 18, 1937
Newsweek 9:20, Jun. 19, 1937
Time 29:45-6, Jun. 21, 1937

Day Mars Invaded the Earth (1963)
New York Times p. 28, Apr. 2, 1964

Day of Fury (1956)
National Parent-Teacher 50:39, May, 1956

Day of Reckoning (1933)
New York Times p. 18, Nov. 4, 1933; IX, p. 4, Nov.
12, 1933
Newsweek 2:29, Nov. 11, 1933

Day of the Bad Man (1957)
Catholic World 186:466-7, Mar., 1958
New York Times p. 19, Jan. 30, 1958

Day of the Outlaw (1959)
Library Journal 84:2171, Jul., 1959

Day of the Triffids (1963)
Commonweal 78:283-4, May 31, 1963
New York Times p. 15, May 11, 1963
Newsweek 61:107, May 13, 1963

Day of Triumph (1954)
Catholic World 180:462, Mar., 1955
Commonweal 62:15, Apr. 8, 1955
Farm Journal 79:89, Apr., 1955
Library Journal 80:865, Apr. 15, 1955
Life 38:113-14+, Mar. 21, 1955
National Parent-Teacher 49:39, Mar., 1955
Newsweek 44:50, Dec. 20, 1954

*Day of Wrath
Life 25:61-2+, Sep. 6, 1948; 26:45, Mar. 14, 1949
Nation 166:584, May 22, 1948
New York Times p. 27, Apr. 26, 1948; II, p. 1, May 9,
1948
New Yorker 24:82, May 1, 1948
Rotarian 74:36, Apr., 1949
Saturday Review 31:35, Aug. 14, 1948; 36:39, May 9, 1953
Time 51:96+, May 24, 1948
Vogue 110:110, Aug. 15, 1947

Day the Bookies Wept (1939)
New York Times p. 18, Sep. 14, 1939

Day the Earth Caught Fire (1962)
America 106:840, Mar. 24, 1962

Day the Earth Caught Fire (1962) (Continued)
Commonweal 76:39, Apr. 6, 1962
New Republic 146:26, Apr. 9, 1962
New York Times p. 25, Mar. 16, 1962
New Yorker 38:149, Mar. 24, 1962
Newsweek 59:84, Mar. 5, 1962
Redbook 118:20, Apr., 1962
Saturday Review 45:35, Feb. 10, 1962
Seventeen 21:42, Apr., 1962
Time 79:96, Apr. 6, 1962

Day the Earth Stood Still (1951)
Christian Century 68:1263, Oct. 31, 1951
Nation 174:19, Jan. 5, 1952
New York Times p. 37, Sep. 19, 1951
New Yorker 27:107, Sep. 22, 1951
Newsweek 38:90, Oct. 1, 1951
Saturday Review 34:35, Oct. 6, 1951
Scholastic 59:30, Oct. 31, 1951
Time 58:98+, Oct. 1, 1951

Day They Robbed the Bank of England (1960)
America 103:563, Aug. 20, 1960
New York Times p. 11, Sep. 5, 1960
Newsweek 56:80, Aug. 1, 1960

Day to Remember (1952)
Library Journal 80:1576, Jul., 1955
National Parent-Teacher 50:38, Oct., 1955

Daybreak (1931)
New York Times VIII, p. 5, May 24, 1931; p. 15, Jun.
1, 1931; VIII, p. 5, Jun. 7, 1931

Daybreak (1940)
Commonweal 32:352, Aug. 16, 1940; 50:391, Jul. 29, 1949
New York Times p. 16, Jul. 30, 1940; p. 9, Jul. 4, 1949
Time 36:79, Aug. 19, 1940

Daybreak in Udi (1949)
New Republic 122:22-3, Jun. 12, 1950
New York Times p. 26, Jun. 2, 1950
Saturday Review 33:27, Jul. 22, 1950

Days and Nights (1946)
Nation 162:581, May 11, 1946
New York Times p. 24, Apr. 29, 1946
Time 47:97, May 27, 1946

Days of Glory (1941)
Nation 159:24, Jul. 1, 1944
New York Times II, p. 3, Oct. 3, 1943; p. 10, Jun. 17, 1944
New Yorker 20:60, Jun. 10, 1944
Newsweek 23:97, Jun. 19, 1944
Photoplay 25:19, Jun., 1944
Time 44:87, Jul. 3, 1944

Days of Thrills and Laughter (1961)
New York Times p. 37, Mar. 22, 1961
New Yorker 37:165, Apr. 8, 1961
Time 77:72, Apr. 14, 1961

Days of Wine and Roses (1962)
America 108:238, Feb. 16, 1963
Commonweal 77:493-4, Feb. 1, 1963
New Republic 148:31, Feb. 2, 1963
New York Times II, p. 7, Apr. 8, 1962; p. 7, Jan. 18, 1963; p. 5, Jan. 26, 1963
New Yorker 38:121-2, Jan. 26, 1963
Newsweek 61:88, Jan. 28, 1963
Saturday Review 46:19+, Feb. 2, 1963
Time 81:M17+, Feb. 1, 1963

Day-Time Wife (1939)
New York Times p. 29, Nov. 24, 1939

Dead End (1937)
Commonweal 26:406, Aug. 20, 1937
Life 2:40, Jan. 11, 1937; 3:62-4, Aug. 30, 1937
Literary Digest 124 (Digest 1): 30, Sep. 4, 1937
New Republic 92:103, Sep. 1, 1937
New York Times X, p. 3, May 30, 1937; X, p. 3, Aug. 22, 1937; p. 25, Aug. 25, 1937; X, p. 3, Aug. 29, 1937; XI, p. 3, Sep. 12, 1937
Newsweek 10:24, Aug. 28, 1937
Scholastic 31:36, Sep. 25, 1937
Stage 14:41, Sep., 1937
Time 30:61, Sep. 6, 1937
Vogue 90:91, Nov. 1, 1937

Dead Man's Eyes (1944)
New York Times p. 11, Oct. 7, 1944

Dead Men Tell (1941)
New York Times p. 29, Apr. 17, 1941

278

Dead Men Tell No Tales (1939)
New York Times p. 9, Jul. 24, 1939

Dead of Night (1945)
Commonweal 44:335, Jul. 19, 1946
Nation 163:194, Aug. 17, 1946
New York Times p. 22, Jun. 29, 1946; II, p. 3, Jul. 14, 1946; II, p. 5, Mar. 9, 1947; II, p. 7, Dec. 21, 1947
New Yorker 22:77, Jul. 13, 1946
Newsweek 28:98, Jul. 15, 1946
Theatre Arts 30:441, Aug., 1946
Time 48:98, Jul. 15, 1946

Dead Reckoning (1947)
Commonweal 45:399, Jan. 31, 1947
New Republic 116:44, Feb. 10, 1947
New York Times II, p. 5, Jan. 26, 1947
New Yorker 22:56, Feb. 1, 1947
Newsweek 29:73, Feb. 3, 1947
Time 49:95, Feb. 3, 1947

Deadlier Than the Male (see Born to Kill)

Deadline at Dawn (1946)
Commonweal 43:480, Feb. 22, 1946
Cosmopolitan 120:71+, Mar., 1946
Nation 162:516, Apr. 27, 1946
New York Times p. 33, Apr. 4, 1946; II, p. 3, Apr. 7, 1946
New Yorker 22:99, Apr. 6, 1946
Newsweek 27:94+, Mar. 25, 1946
Time 47:100, Feb. 18, 1946

Deadline for Murder (1946)
New York Times p. 22, Jun. 29, 1946

Deadline U. S. A. (1952)
Christian Century 69:711, Jun. 11, 1952
New York Times p. 8, Mar. 15, 1952; II, p. 1, Mar. 16, 1952
New Yorker 28:114, Mar. 22, 1952
Newsweek 39:87, Mar. 31, 1952
Saturday Review 35:27, Mar. 29, 1952
Time 59:100, Mar. 31, 1952

Deadly Companions (1961)
New York Times p. 41, Apr. 12, 1962

Deadly Decision (1958)
New York Times p. 26, Apr. 29, 1958

Deadly is the Female (1948)
Commonweal 52:46, Apr. 21, 1950
Library Journal 75:180, Feb. 1, 1950; 75:411, Mar. 1, 1950
Newsweek 35:70, Jan. 9, 1950

Deadly Mantis (1957)
National Parent-Teacher 51:36, May, 1957

Dealers in Death (1934)
New York Times p. 9, Dec. 15, 1934

Dear Brat (1951)
New York Times p. 21, Jul. 5, 1951
Newsweek 38:84, Jul. 16, 1951
Time 58:68, Jul. 30, 1951

Dear Mr. Prohack (1949)
Christian Century 68:951, Aug. 15, 1951
New York Times p. 7, Jul. 15, 1950

Dear Murderer (1947)
New Republic 118:37, May 18, 1947
New York Times p. 12, May 8, 1948
New Yorker 24:78, May 15, 1948
Newsweek 31:96, May 24, 1948

Dear Ruth (1947)
Commonweal 46:240, Jun. 20, 1947
Cosmopolitan 123:55+, Aug., 1947
New Republic 116:35, Jun. 30, 1947
New York Times II, p. 5, Jun. 8, 1947; p. 33, Jun. 11, 1947
New Yorker 23:88+, Jun. 14, 1947
Newsweek 29:98, Jun. 16, 1947
Photoplay 32:41, Mar., 1948
Time 49:63, Jun. 16, 1947
Woman's Home Companion 74:10, Aug., 1947

Dear Wife (1950)
Commonweal 51:511, Feb. 17, 1950
Good Housekeeping 130:92, Feb., 1950
New York Times p. 31, Feb. 2, 1950
Newsweek 35:83, Feb. 6, 1950

Dear Wife (1950) (Continued)
Scholastic 56:29, Feb. 8, 1950
Time 55:93, Feb. 20, 1950

Death of a Champion (1939)
New York Times p. 17, Aug. 24, 1939

Death of a Salesman (1951)
Catholic World 174:386, Feb., 1952
Christian Century 69:231, Feb. 20, 1952
Commonweal 55:300, Dec. 28, 1951
Holiday 11:14+, Mar., 1952
Library Journal 77:140, Jan. 15, 1952
Life 32:63-4+, Jan. 14, 1952
New Republic 125:22, Dec. 31, 1951
New York Times II, p. 9, Dec. 9, 1951; p. 21, Dec. 21,
    1951; II, p. 3, Dec. 23, 1951; p. 24, Jan. 9, 1952
New Yorker 27:70, Dec. 22, 1951
Newsweek 38:56-7, Dec. 31, 1951
Saturday Review 34:34, Dec. 22, 1951
Time 56:60, Dec. 31, 1951

Death of a Scoundrel (1956)
Catholic World 184:142-3, Nov., 1956
National Parent-Teacher 51:36, Jan., 1957
New York Times p. 30, Nov. 6, 1956
Time 68:106, Nov. 19, 1956

Death on the Diamond (1934)
New York Times p. 14, Sep. 24, 1934

Death Takes a Holiday (1934)
American Review 3:153-4, May, 1934
Canadian Magazine 81:43, Jun., 1934
Literary Digest 117:38, Mar. 10, 1934
Nation 138:342, Mar. 21, 1934
New York Times p. 18, Feb. 24, 1934; IX, p. 5, Mar.
    4, 1934
Newsweek 3:34, Mar. 3, 1934
Vanity Fair 42:49, Apr., 1934

Decameron Nights (1952)
Catholic World 178:223, Dec., 1953
Commonweal 59:258, Dec. 11, 1953
Library Journal 78:2098, Dec. 1, 1953
National Parent-Teacher 48:39, Dec., 1953
New York Times p. 38, Nov. 17, 1953

281

Decameron Nights (1952) (Continued)
New Yorker 29:134, Nov. 21, 1953
Newsweek 42:114+, Oct. 26, 1953
Saturday Review 36:37, Oct. 17, 1953
Time 62:111, Nov. 16, 1953

Deceiver (1931)
New York Times p. 22, Nov. 23, 1931; VIII, p. 5, Nov.
29, 1931

Deception (1932)
New York Times p. 26, Jan. 10, 1933

Deception (1946)
Commonweal 45:71, Nov. 1, 1946
New York Times p. 15, Oct. 19, 1946; II, p. 1, Oct. 27,
1946
New Yorker 22:108, Oct. 26, 1946
Newsweek 28:93, Oct. 28, 1946
Photoplay 30:4, Jan., 1947
Scholastic 49:27, Nov. 25, 1946
Theatre Arts 30:715, Dec., 1946
Time 48:104+, Nov. 4, 1946
Woman's Home Companion 74:8, Jan., 1947

Decision Against Time (1956)
Commonweal 66:523, Aug. 23, 1957
National Parent-Teacher 52:32, Sep., 1957

Decision Before Dawn (1951)
Catholic World 174:143, Nov., 1951
Christian Century 69:143, Jan. 30, 1952
Commonweal 55:350, Jan. 11, 1952
Library Journal 77:44, Jan. 1, 1952
Life 31:118+, Dec. 17, 1951
New Republic 126:21, Jan. 14, 1952
New York Times II, p. 9, Dec. 10, 1950; p. 12, Dec.
22, 1951; II, p. 3, Dec. 23, 1951; II, p. 1, Jan. 13,
1952
New Yorker 27:66, Jan. 5, 1952
Newsweek 38:56, Dec. 31, 1951
Saturday Review 34:6+, Nov. 17, 1951; 34:20-2, Dec. 29,
1951
Time 58:59, Dec. 24, 1951

Decision of Christopher Blake (1948)
Good Housekeeping 128:10, Jan., 1949

Decision of Christopher Blake (1948) (Continued)
New Republic 119:30, Dec. 27, 1948
New York Times p. 12, Dec. 11, 1948
Newsweek 32:78, Dec. 20, 1948
Time 52:107, Dec. 13, 1948

Decks Ran Red (1958)
America 100:119, Oct. 25, 1958
New York Times p. 18, Oct. 11, 1958
Newsweek 52:94, Oct. 27, 1958
Time 72:42, Oct. 27, 1958

*Declaration of Independence
Saint Nicholas 66:39, Feb., 1939
Scholastic 33:32, Dec. 3, 1938

Decoy (1946)
New York Times p. 12, Nov. 2, 1946

Dedee (1949)
New Republic 120:30, Apr. 25, 1949
New York Times p. 9, Apr. 9, 1949
Newsweek 33:83, May 2, 1949
Theatre Arts 33:97, Jun., 1949

Deep Blue Sea (1955)
America 94:112, Oct. 22, 1955
Catholic World 182:136, Nov., 1955
Commonweal 63:118, Nov. 4, 1955
Nation 181:369, Oct. 29, 1955
National Parent-Teacher 50:39, Dec., 1955
New Republic 134:20, Apr. 23, 1956
New York Times II, p. 5, Mar. 13, 1955; p. 35, Oct. 13,
    1955; II, p. 1, Oct. 23, 1955
Time 66:53, Oct. 31, 1955

Deep in My Heart (1954)
America 92:326, Dec. 18, 1954
Catholic World 180:305, Jan., 1955
Colliers 135:26-7, Jan. 7, 1955
Commonweal 61:334, Dec. 24, 1954
Dance Magazine 29:9, Jan., 1955
Farm Journal 79:70, Jan., 1955
Library Journal 80:150, Jan. 15, 1955
National Parent-Teacher 49:39, Feb., 1955
New York Times p. 35, Dec. 10, 1954; II, p. 7, Dec.
    12, 1954; II, p. 3, Dec. 19, 1954

Deep in My Heart (1954) (Continued)
New Yorker 30:67, Dec. 18, 1954
Newsweek 44:83, Dec. 20, 1954
Saturday Review 38:26, Jan. 8, 1955
Time 65:74+, Jan. 17, 1955

Deep Six (1958)
Commonweal 57:432, Jan. 24, 1958
Library Journal 83:396, Feb. 1, 1958
New York Times II, p. 5, Jul. 7, 1957; p. 32, Jan. 16, 1958
Newsweek 51:88, Jan. 13, 1958

Deep Valley (1947)
Commonweal 46:574, Sep. 26, 1947
Life 24:56, Feb. 23, 1948
New York Times II, p. 3, Aug. 17, 1947; p. 7, Aug. 23, 1947
Newsweek 30:77, Sep. 1, 1947
Time 50:104, Sep. 15, 1947

Deep Waters (1948)
New York Times p. 12, Jul. 23, 1948
Newsweek 32:82, Jul. 12, 1948
Time 52:82, Jul. 12, 1948

Deerslayer (1943)
Nation 157:593, Nov. 20, 1943
New York Times II, p. 3, Jul. 4, 1943

Deerslayer (1957)
Library Journal 82:2525, Oct. 15, 1957
Senior Scholastic 71:33, Nov. 15, 1957

Defense of Volchayevsk (1938)
New York Times p. 13, Aug. 11, 1938; IX, p. 3, Aug. 14, 1938

Defense Rests (1934)
New York Times p. 20, Aug. 16, 1934

Defiant Ones (1958)
America 99:679, Sep. 27, 1958
Catholic World 188:65, Oct., 1958
Commonweal 68:637-8, Sep. 26, 1958
Life 45:51-2+, Aug. 11, 1958
Nation 187:219, Oct. 11, 1958
New Republic 139:22-3, Sep. 1, 1958

Defiant Ones (1958) (Continued)
New York Times p. 29, Sep. 25, 1958; II, p. 1, Oct. 5,
1958; II, p. 1, Dec. 31, 1958
New Yorker 34:159, Oct. 4, 1958
Newsweek 52:77, Aug. 25, 1958
Saturday Review 41:22-3, Jul. 26, 1958
Time 72:78, Aug. 25, 1958

Delicate Delinquent (1957)
America 97:432, Jul. 20, 1957
Commonweal 66:376, Jul. 12, 1957
National Parent-Teacher 51:37, Jun., 1957
New York Times p. 16, Jul 4, 1957
Newsweek 49:108, Jun. 24, 1957

Delicious (1932)
New York Times p. 15, Dec. 26, 1931
Outlook 160:55, Jan. 13, 1932

Delightfully Dangerous (1945)
New York Times p. 17, Jun. 9, 1945
Newsweek 25:103, Apr. 23, 1945

Delinquents (1957)
National Parent-Teacher 51:38, Mar., 1957

Deluge (1933)
New York Times p. 22, Oct. 9, 1933

Demetrius and the Gladiators (1954)
America 91:345, Jun. 26, 1954
Catholic World 179:301-2, Jul., 1954
Commonweal 60:344, Jul. 9, 1954
Farm Journal 78:101, Aug., 1954
National Parent-Teacher 49:33, Sep., 1954
New York Times p. 9, Jun. 19, 1954; II, p. 1, Jun. 27,
1954
Newsweek 44:79, Jul. 5, 1954
Time 64:77, Jul. 5, 1954

Demoniaque (1958)
New York Times p. 34, Mar. 4, 1958
New Yorker 34:94, Mar. 15, 1958
Newsweek 51:106, Mar. 17, 1958

Denver and Rio Grande (1952)
Christian Century 69:863, Jul. 23, 1952

Denver and Rio Grande (1952) (Continued)
New York Times II, p. 3, Jul. 29, 1951; p. 22, May 17, 1952
Newsweek 39:91, May 26, 1952
Time 59:96, Jun. 2, 1952

Deported (1950)
Christian Century 68:127, Jan. 24, 1951
Commonweal 53:198, Dec. 1, 1950
New York Times p. 39, Nov. 2, 1950
Newsweek 36:94, Nov. 6, 1950
Rotarian 78:38, Feb., 1951

Deputy Marshall (1949)
New York Times p. 31, Nov. 11, 1949

Derelict (1930)
Life (NY) 96:20, Dec. 12, 1930
New York Times p. 21, Nov. 22, 1930; IX, p. 5, Nov. 30, 1930

*Dernier Milliardaire, Le
Nation 141:548, Nov. 6, 1935
New York Times p. 16, Oct. 30, 1935
Time 26:28, Nov. 11, 1935

Desert Attack (1960)
New York Times p. 28, Mar. 23, 1961

Desert Fox (1951)
Christian Century 68:1327, Nov. 14, 1951
Commonweal 55:94, Nov. 2, 1951
Library Journal 76:1722, Oct. 15, 1951
Life 31:78-9+, Oct. 8, 1951
New Republic 125:21, Nov. 19, 1951
New York Times II, p. 5, Feb. 25, 1951; p. 32, Oct. 18, 1951; II, p. 5, Nov. 4, 1951
New Yorker 27:81, Oct. 27, 1951
Newsweek 38:92, Oct. 29, 1951
Saturday Review 34:28, Oct. 20, 1951
Scholastic 59:45, Sep. 26, 1951
Time 58:117-18, Oct. 15, 1951

Desert Fury (1947)
Commonweal 46:574, Sep. 26, 1947
New York Times II, p. 5, Sep. 21, 1947; p. 35, Sep. 25, 1947; II, p. 1, Oct. 5, 1947

Desert Fury (1947) (Continued)
Newsweek 30:92, Sep. 15, 1947
Time 50:80, Sep. 1, 1947

Desert Hawk (1950)
New York Times p. 9, Aug. 26, 1950

Desert Legion (1953)
America 89:201, May 16, 1953
Library Journal 78:588, Apr. 1, 1953
National Parent-Teacher 47:38, May, 1953
New York Times p. 13, May 9, 1953
Newsweek 41:109, Apr. 27, 1953
Time 61:107, Apr. 6, 1953

Desert Nights (1929)
New York Times p. 30, May 6, 1929; IX, p. 5, May 12,
1929

Desert Patrol (1962)
New York Times p. 23, Jan. 18, 1962

Desert Rats (1953)
America 89:200, May 16, 1953
Catholic World 177:142-3, May, 1953
Commonweal 58:122, May 8, 1953
National Parent-Teacher 47:37, Jun., 1953
New York Times p. 13, May 9, 1953
New Yorker 29:131, May 16, 1953
Newsweek 41:101, May 25, 1953
Saturday Review 36:32, May 16, 1953
Scholastic 62:30, May 13, 1953
Time 61:114+, May 18, 1953

Desert Sands (1955)
National Parent-Teacher 50:39, Jan., 1956
New York Times p. 22, Nov. 19, 1955

Desert Song (1929)
New York Times p. 20, May 2, 1929; VIII, p. 5, Aug. 4,
1929

Desert Song (1943, 1953)
America 89:200, May 16, 1953
Commonweal 39:305, Jan. 7, 1944; 58:249, Jun. 12, 1953
National Parent-Teacher 47:39, Apr., 1953
New York Times p. 10, Dec. 18, 1943; p. 39, May 21,
1953

Desert Song (1943, 1953) (Continued)
Newsweek 22:82, Dec. 27, 1943
Time 43:94+, Jan. 10, 1944; 61:104, May 25, 1953

Desert Victory (1943)
Commonweal 38:41+, Apr. 30, 1943
Harper's Bazaar 77:94-5, May, 1943
Nation 156:642, May 1, 1943
New Republic 108:476, Apr. 12, 1943
New Yorker 19:39, Apr. 17, 1943
Newsweek 21:81-2, Mar. 22, 1943
Saturday Review 26:16, May 15, 1943
Theatre Arts 27:286, May, 1943; 27:546, Sep., 1943
Time 41:95-6, Apr. 12, 1943

Deserter (1934)
New York Times p. 10, Oct. 13, 1934

Design for Death (1948)
Life 24:21, May 10, 1948
New York Times II, p. 5, Jan. 18, 1948; p. 27, Jun. 11, 1948

Design for Living (1933)
Literary Digest 116:29, Dec. 9, 1933
Nation 137:660-1, Dec. 6, 1933
New Outlook 163:43, Jan., 1934
New York Times p. 24, Nov. 23, 1933; IX, p. 9, Dec. 3, 1933
Newsweek 2:33, Dec. 2, 1933
Vanity Fair 41:45-6, Jan., 1934

Design for Scandal (1941)
New York Times p. 23, Feb. 6, 1942
Time 39:75, Mar. 2, 1942

Designing Woman (1957)
America 97:244, May 18, 1957
Commonweal 66:183, May 17, 1957
Coronet 42:10, May, 1957
Life 42:79-80, May 20, 1957
National Parent-Teacher 51:36, May, 1957
New York Times p. 20, May 27, 1957
New York Times Magazine p. 24, Apr. 14, 1957
New Yorker 33:129, May 25, 1957
Newsweek 49:115, Apr. 8, 1957
Saturday Review 40:26, Apr. 13, 1957

Designing Woman (1957) (Continued)
Senior Scholastic 70:34, Apr. 5, 1957
Time 69:94, Apr. 1, 1957

Desirable (1934)
New York Times p. 20, Sep. 15, 1934

Desire (1936)
Literary Digest 121:21, Mar. 7, 1936
New Republic 86:222, Apr. 1, 1936
New York Times X, p. 5, Feb. 9, 1936; p. 15, Apr. 13,
    1936; IX, p. 3, Apr. 19, 1936
Newsweek 7:32, Mar. 7, 1936
Time 27:47, Mar. 9, 1936

Desire Me (1947)
Commonweal 46:623, Oct. 10, 1947
Life 24:62, Mar. 8, 1948
New York Times II, p. 5, Sep. 21, 1947; p. 28, Sep. 26,
    1947; II, p. 1, Oct. 5, 1947
New Yorker 23:105, Sep. 27, 1947
Newsweek 30:80, Oct. 6, 1947
Time 50:105, Oct. 13, 1947
Woman's Home Companion 74:10-11, Dec., 1947

Desire Under the Elms (1958)
America 98:734, Mar. 22, 1958
Catholic World 187:65, Apr., 1958
Commonweal 67:639, Mar. 21, 1958
Cosmopolitan 144:16, Mar., 1958
Library Journal 83:835, Mar. 15, 1958
Life 44:69-70, Feb. 17, 1958
Nation 186:304, Apr. 5, 1958
New Republic 138:22-3, Apr. 7, 1958
New York Times VI, p. 27, Aug. 11, 1957; II, p. 5,
    Mar. 2, 1958; p. 24, Mar. 13, 1958
New York Times Magazine p. 30+, Dec. 22, 1957
New Yorker 34:95, Mar. 22, 1958
Newsweek 51:106-7, Mar. 17, 1958
Saturday Review 41:55, Mar. 15, 1958
Theatre Arts 42:79-81, Apr., 1958
Time 71:106+, Mar. 17, 1958

Désirée (1954)
America 92:259, Nov. 27, 1954
Catholic World 180:304, Jan., 1955
Commonweal 61:255, Dec. 3, 1954
Library Journal 79:2315, Dec. 1, 1954

Désirée (1954) (Continued)
Life 37:197-200, Nov. 22, 1954
National Parent-Teacher 49:39, Jan., 1955
New York Times p. 42, Nov. 18, 1954; II, p. 1, Nov. 21,
1954
New Yorker 30:189, Nov. 27, 1954
Newsweek 44:97-8, Nov. 29, 1954
Saturday Review 37:38-9, Dec. 4, 1954
Time 64:75, Nov. 29, 1954

*Desires
Catholic World 179:467, Sep., 1954
New York Times p. 10, Jul. 2, 1954
Time 64:74, Aug. 2, 1954

Desk Set (1947)
America 97:292, Jun. 1, 1957
Catholic World 185:306, Jul., 1957
Commonweal 66:257, Jun. 7, 1957
Library Journal 82:1456, Jun. 1, 1957
National Parent-Teacher 52:33, Sep., 1957
New York Times p. 23, May 16, 1957
New Yorker 33:129, May 25, 1957
Newsweek 49:118, May 27, 1957
Saturday Review 40:23, Jun. 1, 1957
Time 69:101, May 27, 1957

Desperadoes (1943)
New York Times p. 13, Aug. 7, 1942; p. 17, May 13,
1943

Desperados Are in Town (1956)
National Parent-Teacher 51:36, Jan., 1957

Desperadoes' Outpost (1952)
National Parent-Teacher 47:36, Dec., 1952

Desperate Hours (1955)
America 94:56, Oct. 8, 1955
Catholic World 182:136, Nov., 1955
Commonweal 63:63-4, Oct. 21, 1955
Library Journal 80:2230, Oct. 15, 1955
Life 39:111-12+, Oct. 10, 1955
Look 19:124-8, Nov. 15, 1955
McCalls 82:36-8, Sep., 1955
Nation 181:369, Oct. 29, 1955
National Parent-Teacher 50:39, Nov., 1955

Desperate Hours (1955) (Continued)
New York Times p. 25, Oct. 6, 1955; II, p. 1, Oct. 9,
    1955; II, p. 5, Oct. 16, 1955; II, p. 5, Oct. 30, 1955
New Yorker 31:182, Oct. 15, 1955
Newsweek 46:86-7, Oct. 3, 1955
Saturday Review 38:30, Oct. 22, 1955
Scholastic 67:35, Dec. 1, 1955
Time 66:116+, Oct. 10, 1955

Desperate Journey (1942)
Commonweal 36:473, Sep. 4, 1942
Musician 47:145, Sep., 1942
New York Times p. 11, Sep. 26, 1942
New Yorker 18:74, Sep. 26, 1942
Newsweek 20:80+, Sep. 21, 1942; 22:104, Nov. 15, 1943
Time 40:44, Aug. 17, 1942

Desperate Moment (1953)
Catholic World 178:64, Oct., 1953
Commonweal 59:62, Oct. 23, 1953
Library Journal 78:1677, Oct. 1, 1953
National Parent-Teacher 48:36, Nov., 1953
New York Times p. 19, Sep. 1, 1953
Newsweek 42:98+, Sep. 21, 1953
Time 62:106, Sep. 21, 1953

Desperate Search (1952)
Christian Century 70:335, Mar. 18, 1953
Library Journal 78:50, Jan. 1, 1953
National Parent-Teacher 47:27, Mar., 1953

Destination Big House (1950)
New York Times p. 32, Jun. 28, 1950; II, p. 1, Jul. 9,
    1950

Destination Gobi (1953)
America 88:662, Mar. 14, 1953
Commonweal 57:625, Mar. 27, 1953
Nation 176:313, Apr. 11, 1953
National Parent-Teacher 47:36, May, 1953
New York Times p. 17, May 22, 1953; p. 7, May 30,
    1953
Saturday Review 36:43, Apr. 4, 1953
Time 61:104+, Apr. 6, 1953

Destination Moon (1950)
Commonweal 52:367, Jul. 21, 1950

Destination Moon (1950) (Continued)
  Holiday 10:26, Nov., 1951
  Library Journal 75:1677, Oct. 1, 1950
  Life 28:107-10, Apr. 24, 1950
  New Republic 123:22, Jul. 10, 1950
  New York Times II, p. 4, May 21, 1950; p. 32, Jun. 28,
    1950; II, p. 1, Jul. 9, 1950
  New York Times Magazine p. 46-7, Feb. 19, 1950
  Newsweek 36:86, Jul. 10, 1950
  Rotarian 78:38, Jan., 1951
  Scholastic 57:38, Sep. 20, 1950
  Time 56:76, Jul. 10, 1950

Destination Tokyo (1944)
  Commonweal 39:352, Jan. 21, 1944
  Life 16:38-40+, Jan. 24, 1944
  Nation 158:23, Jan. 1, 1944
  New York Times II, p. 3, Aug. 1, 1943; p. 9, Jan. 1,
    1944; II, p. 3, Jan. 9, 1944
  New Yorker 19:53, Jan. 1, 1944
  Newsweek 23:82, Jan. 10, 1944
  Theatre Arts 28:101, Feb., 1944

Destination Unknown (1933)
  New York Times p. 16, Apr. 8, 1933; IX, p. 3, Apr. 16,
    1933
  Newsweek 1:27, Apr. 15, 1933

Destination Unknown (1942)
  New York Times p. 19, Oct. 29, 1942

Destiny (1944)
  New York Times p. 16, Feb. 3, 1945

Destroyer (1943)
  New York Times p. 15, Sep. 2, 1943
  New Yorker 19:68, Sep. 11, 1943

Destry (1954)
  Catholic World 180:303, Jan., 1955
  Colliers 134:26-7, Oct. 1, 1954
  National Parent-Teacher 49:39, Jan., 1955

Destry Rides Again (1932)
  New York Times VIII, p. 4, Feb. 21, 1932

Destry Rides Again (1939)
  Commonweal 31:187, Dec. 15, 1939

Destry Rides Again (1939) (Continued)
Nation 149:662, Dec. 9, 1939
New York Times p. 25, Nov. 30, 1939; IX, p. 8, Dec. 3,
1939; X, p. 7, Dec. 10, 1939; IX, p. 7, Dec. 17, 1939
Newsweek 14:33, Dec. 11, 1939
Time 34:76, Dec. 18, 1939

Detective (1954)
America 91:480, Aug. 14, 1954; 92:194, Nov. 13, 1954
Catholic World 180:64, Oct., 1954
Commonweal 61:167, Nov. 12, 1954
Farm Journal 78:141, Dec., 1954
Library Journal 79:2315, Dec. 1, 1954
Nation 179:429, Nov. 13, 1954
National Parent-Teacher 49:39, Oct., 1954
New York Times p. 25, Nov. 2, 1954; II, p. 1, Nov. 7,
1954
New York Times Magazine p. 40, Oct. 24, 1954
New Yorker 30:210, Nov. 13, 1954
Newsweek 44:76, Sep. 6, 1954
Reporter 11:42, Dec. 2, 1954
Saturday Review 37:26, Sep. 18, 1954
Scholastic 65:37, Nov. 17, 1954
Time 64:110, Nov. 15, 1954

Detective Story (1951)
Catholic World 174:142, Nov., 1951
Christian Century 69:87, Jan. 16, 1952
Commonweal 55:144, Nov. 16, 1951
Library Journal 76:1818+, Nov. 1, 1951
Life 31:169-70+, Nov. 19, 1951
Nation 173:457, Nov. 24, 1951
New Republic 125:21, Dec. 3, 1951
New York Times II, p. 5, Mar. 11, 1951; p. 35, Nov.
7, 1951; II, p. 1, Nov. 11, 1951
New Yorker 27:120, Nov. 17, 1951
Newsweek 38:98-9, Nov. 5, 1951
Saturday Review 34:27, Nov. 10, 1951
Time 58:83, Oct. 29, 1951

Deuxieme Bureau (Second Bureau) (1935)
Canadian Forum 15:15, Jan., 1936
New York Times p. 21, Feb. 17, 1935

*Devi
Commonweal 77:342-3, Dec. 21, 1962
Nation 195:316, Nov. 10, 1962

*Devi (Continued)
New York Times p. 19, Oct. 8, 1962
Saturday Review 45:24, May 26, 1962
Time 80:102, Oct. 12, 1962

Devil and Daniel Webster (1952)
Saturday Review 36:39, May 9, 1953

Devil and Miss Jones (1941)
Child Life 20:268, Jun., 1941
Commonweal 34:39, May 2, 1941
Life 10:53-4+, Apr. 28, 1941
New Republic 104:665, May 12, 1941
New York Times IX, p. 5, Jan. 12, 1941; p. 21, May
16, 1941; IX, p. 3, May 18, 1941; IX, p. 4, May 18,
1941
Newsweek 17:60, Apr. 21, 1941
Scholastic 38:34, Apr. 28, 1941
Time 37:98, Apr. 21, 1941

Devil and the Deep (1932)
New Outlook 161:39, Oct., 1932
New York Times p. 7, Aug. 20, 1932; IX, p. 3, Aug.
28, 1932

Devil at 4 O'Clock (1961)
America 106:104, Oct. 21, 1961
Commonweal 75:175, Nov. 10, 1961
New York Times II, p. 7, Oct. 23, 1960; p. 39, Oct.
19, 1961
Newsweek 58:101, Oct. 23, 1961
Saturday Review 44:37, Nov. 4, 1961
Time 78:55, Oct. 27, 1961

Devil Commands (1940)
New York Times p. 15, Feb. 15, 1941

Devil Dogs of the Air (1935)
New York Times p. 23, Feb. 7, 1935; VIII, p. 4, Feb.
10, 1935; VIII, p. 5, Feb. 24, 1935
Time 25:71, Feb. 18, 1935

Devil Doll (1936)
Canadian Magazine 86:36, Aug., 1936
Commonweal 24:347, Jul. 31, 1936
Literary Digest 122:19, Jul. 18, 1936
New York Times p. 5, Aug. 8, 1936
Time 28:36, Jul. 20, 1936

Devil in the Flesh (1948)
 Christian Century 67:1343, Nov. 8, 1950
 Commonweal 49:567, Mar. 18, 1949
 Nation 168:313, Mar. 12, 1949; 168:690, Jun. 18, 1949
 New Republic 120:30-1, May 23, 1949
 New York Times II, p. 4, Mar. 20, 1949; p. 29, May
   10, 1949; II, p. 1, May 15, 1949
 New Yorker 25:105, May 14, 1949
 Newsweek 33:83, May 30, 1949
 Rotarian 77:37, Dec., 1950
 Time 53:98, Mar. 21, 1949
 Vogue 113:117, Feb. 15, 1949

Devil is a Sissy (1936)
 Canadian Magazine 86:38, Nov., 1936
 Commonweal 24:504, Sep. 25, 1936
 Literary Digest 122:24, Sep. 26, 1936
 New Republic 88:310, Oct. 21, 1936
 New York Times p. 21, Oct. 17, 1936; X, p. 5, Oct. 25,
   1936
 Stage 14:24, Oct., 1936
 Time 28:31, Sep. 28, 1936

Devil is a Woman (1935)
 New York Times VIII, p. 3, Mar. 3, 1935; p. 17, May
   4, 1935
 Time 25:38, May 13, 1935
 Vanity Fair 44:48, Jun., 1935

Devil is an Empress (1939)
 New York Times p. 18, Dec. 4, 1939

Devil is Driving (1932)
 New York Times p. 25, Dec. 16, 1932; IX, p. 5, Dec.
   25, 1932

Devil is Driving (1937)
 New York Times p. 22, Jul. 16, 1937

Devil Makes Three (1952)
 Catholic World 176:63, Oct., 1952
 Christian Century 69:1423, Dec. 3, 1952
 Commonweal 56:583, Sep. 19, 1952
 National Parent-Teacher 47:38, Sep., 1952
 New York Times p. 6, Aug. 30, 1952
 Newsweek 40:103, Sep. 15, 1952
 Saturday Review 35:34, Sep. 20, 1952
 Time 60:106, Sep. 8, 1952

Devil May Care (1930)
Life (NY) 95:22, Jan. 31, 1930
New York Times p. 18, Dec. 23, 1929; VIII, p. 6, Dec. 29, 1929
Outlook 154:74, Jan. 8, 1930

Devil on Wheels (1947)
Commonweal 45:446, Feb. 14, 1947

Devil Strikes at Night (1959)
New York Times p. 31, Jan. 30, 1959
New Yorker 34:121, Feb. 7, 1959
Reporter 20:40-1, Mar. 5, 1959
Saturday Review 42:32, Feb. 21, 1959
Time 73:70, Mar. 2, 1959

Devil Thumbs a Ride (1947)
New Republic 116:40, Apr. 14, 1947
New York Times p. 10, Mar. 22, 1947

Devil Tiger (1934)
New York Times p. 23, Feb. 9, 1934; IX, p. 5, Feb. 18, 1934

Devil with Hitler (1942)
New York Times p. 15, Oct. 19, 1942

Devil with Women (1930)
New York Times p. 28, Oct. 20, 1930

Devil's Brother (Fra Diavolo) (1933)
Commonweal 18:214, Jun. 23, 1933
Literary Digest 116:25, Jul. 8, 1933
New Outlook 162:43, Jul., 1933
New York Times p. 16, Jun. 10, 1933; X, p. 3, Jun. 18, 1933
Newsweek 1:31, Jun. 17, 1933
Vanity Fair 40:37, Aug., 1933

Devil's Canyon (1953)
Farm Journal 77:161, Nov., 1953
National Parent-Teacher 48:36, Nov., 1953
New York Times p. 14, Oct. 3, 1953

Devil's Disciple (1955)
America 101:658, Aug. 29, 1959
Commonweal 70:496, Sep. 11, 1959

Devil's Disciple (1955) (Continued)
Life 47:68-70, Aug. 31, 1959
New Republic 141:21-2, Sep. 14, 1959
New York Times p. 12, Aug. 21, 1959; II, p. 1, Aug. 23, 1959
New Yorker 35:68, Aug. 29, 1959
Newsweek 54:82-3, Aug. 24, 1959
Saturday Review 42:24, Aug. 15, 1959
Time 74:46, Aug. 31, 1959

Devil's Doorway (1949)
Commonweal 53:173, Nov. 24, 1950
New York Times p. 35, Nov. 10, 1950
Time 56:118, Oct. 9, 1950

*Devil's Envoys
Nation 165:264, Sep. 13, 1947
New York Times p. 8, Aug. 30, 1947; II, p. 4, Aug. 31, 1947
Newsweek 30:90, Sep. 15, 1947
Time 50:98+, Sep. 29, 1947

Devil's Eye (1961)
Commonweal 75:210, Nov. 17, 1961
Esquire 56:64, Dec., 1961
Nation 193:439-40, Nov. 25, 1961
New Republic 145:29-30, Sep. 25, 1961
New York Times p. 47, Oct. 18, 1960; p. 27, Oct. 31, 1961; II, p. 1, Nov. 5, 1961
New Yorker 37:207-8, Nov. 4, 1961
Newsweek 58:77, Oct. 30, 1961
Saturday Review 44:26, Sep. 23, 1961
Time 78:116, Sep. 22, 1961

Devil's General (1957)
Commonweal 65:568, Mar. 1, 1957
Nation 184:487, Jun. 1, 1957
National Parent-Teacher 51:37, Jun., 1947
New York Times p. 38, Apr. 16, 1957
Time 69:106+, May 13, 1957

Devil's Hairpin (1957)
National Parent-Teacher 52:33, Oct., 1957

Devil's Holiday (1930)
Life (NY) 95:20, May 30, 1930
New York Times p. 25, May 10, 1930; VIII, p. 5, May 18, 1930

Devil's in Love (1933)
New York Times p. 18, Jul. 28, 1933

Devil's Island (1939)
New York Times p. 17, Feb. 28, 1939; p. 31, Apr. 6,
1939

Devil's Lottery (1932)
New York Times p. 13, Apr. 2, 1932; VIII, p. 4, Apr.
10, 1932

Devil's Mate (1933)
New York Times p. 11, Sep. 23, 1933

Devil's Party (1938)
New York Times p. 8, May 30, 1938

Devil's Pipeline (1940)
New York Times p. 22, Nov. 11, 1940

Devil's Pit (1930)
New York Times p. 20, Oct. 14, 1929

Devil's Pitchfork (1954)
Commonweal 60:198, May 28, 1954
New York Times p. 38, May 18, 1954
New Yorker 30:53, May 29, 1954
Newsweek 43:80, Mar. 1, 1954
Saturday Review 37:29, May 22, 1954

Devil's Playground (1933)
New York Times p. 26, Dec. 26, 1932

Devil's Playground (1937)
New York Times p. 2, Feb. 15, 1937
Time 29:58, Feb. 15, 1937

Devil's Squadron (1936)
New York Times p. 16, May 11, 1936

Devil's Wanton (1962)
Commonweal 76:230, May 25, 1962
New Republic 146:28, May 28, 1962
New York Times p. 21, Jul. 5, 1962; II, p. 1, Jul. 15,
1962
New Yorker 38:60-1, Jul. 14, 1962
Newsweek 59:96-7, May 21, 1962

Devotion (1931)
  Life (NY) 98:18, Oct. 23, 1931
  New York Times p. 20, Oct. 3, 1931; VIII, p. 5, Oct. 11, 1931

Devotion (1946)
  Commonweal 44:96, May 10, 1946
  Nation 162:516, Apr. 27, 1946
  New York Times p. 10, Apr. 6, 1946; II, p. 1, Apr. 7, 1946; II, p. 3, Apr. 7, 1946; p. 24, Apr. 29, 1946
  New Yorker 22:100, Apr. 6, 1946
  Newsweek 27:92, Apr. 15, 1946
  Scholastic 48:28, Apr. 1, 1946; 48:16-17, Apr. 22, 1946
  Time 47:98, Apr. 15, 1946

Diabolique (1955)
  Catholic World 182:382, Feb., 1956
  Commonweal 63:286, Dec. 16, 1955; 75:414, Jan. 12, 1962
  Library Journal 80:2763, Dec. 1, 1955
  Life 40:127-8+, Mar. 19, 1956
  Nation 181:524, Dec. 10, 1955
  National Parent-Teacher 50:39, Jan., 1956
  New York Times p. 41, Nov. 22, 1955
  New Yorker 30:111, Feb. 12, 1955; 31:96, Nov. 26, 1955
  Newsweek 46:116, Nov. 28, 1955
  Saturday Review 38:39, Dec. 3, 1955
  Time 66:109, Dec. 5, 1955

Dial M for Murder (1954)
  America 91:287, Jun. 5, 1954
  Catholic World 179:222-3, Jun., 1954
  Colliers 133:90-1, Jun. 11, 1954
  Commonweal 60:197, May 28, 1954
  New York Times II, p. 5, Oct. 11, 1953; p. 13, May 29, 1954; II, p. 1, Jun. 13, 1954

Dial Nine Nine Nine (see Way Out)

Dial 1119 (1950)
  Commonweal 53:232, Dec. 8, 1950
  New York Times p. 32, Dec. 4, 1950
  Newsweek 36:93, Nov. 6, 1950

Diamond Frontier (1940)
  New York Times p. 29, Oct. 4, 1940

Diamond Head (1962)
  Commonweal 77:599, Mar. 1, 1963

Diamond Head (1962) (Continued)
New York Times II, p. 7, Apr. 29, 1962; p. 5, Feb. 21,
1963
New Yorker 39:146-7, Mar. 9, 1963
Saturday Review 46:31, Jan. 26, 1963
Time 81:93, Feb. 22, 1963

Diamond Jim (1935)
Canadian Magazine 84:38, Nov., 1935
Literary Digest 120:30, Sep. 7, 1935
New York Times p. 18, Aug. 24, 1935; X, p. 3, Aug.
25, 1935
Newsweek 6:26, Aug. 31, 1935
Stage 12:3, Sep., 1935
Time 26:32, Aug. 12, 1935

Diamond Wizard (1954)
New York Times p. 7, Jul. 17, 1954

Diane (1956)
America 94:459, Jan. 21, 1956
Commonweal 63:459, Feb. 3, 1956
Harper 212:91-3, Mar., 1956
Library Journal 81:74, Jan. 1, 1956
National Parent-Teacher 50:39, Feb., 1956
New York Times p. 18, Jan. 13, 1956
Newsweek 47:80, Jan. 16, 1956
Saturday Review 39:42, Jan. 21, 1956
Time 67:96, Jan. 16, 1956

Diary of a Bad Girl (1958)
New York Times p. 13, May 30, 1958

Diary of a Chambermaid (1946)
Commonweal 43:526, Mar. 8, 1946
New York Times II, p. 1, Jul. 22, 1945; p. 28, Jun. 24,
1946
Newsweek 27:102, Mar. 18, 1946
Theatre Arts 30:159-60, Mar., 1946
Time 47:97, Mar. 11, 1946
Woman's Home Companion 73:10, Apr., 1946

Diary of a Country Priest (1954)
America 91:80, Apr. 17, 1954
Catholic World 179:221, Jun., 1954
Commonweal 60:69, Apr. 23, 1954
Library Journal 79:852, May 1, 1954

Diary of a Country Priest (1954) (Continued)
National Parent-Teacher 48:39, Jun., 1954
New York Times p. 35, Apr. 6, 1954; II, p. 1, Apr. 11, 1954
New Yorker 30:123, Apr. 17, 1954
Saturday Review 37:25, Mar. 27, 1954
Time 63:108+, May 10, 1954

Diary of a Madman (1963)
New York Times p. 39, Jun. 6, 1963
Newsweek 61:90, Apr. 29, 1963

Diary of a Nazi (1943)
New York Times p. 25, Mar. 25, 1943

Diary of a Revolutionist (1932)
New York Times p. 27, Jun. 9, 1932

Diary of Anne Frank (1959)
America 101:52-4, Apr. 4, 1959
Catholic World 189:236, Jun., 1959
Commonweal 70:58-9, Apr. 10, 1959
Library Journal 84:1221, Apr. 15, 1959
Life 45:44-51, Dec. 22, 1958
Look 23:105-6, May 26, 1959
McCalls 86:6+, Jun., 1959
New Republic 140:22, Apr. 6, 1959
New York Times VI, p. 14, Aug. 3, 1958; VI, p. 34-5, Mar. 8, 1959; p. 40, Mar. 19, 1959; II, p. 1, Mar. 22, 1959
New Yorker 35:95, Mar. 28, 1959
Newsweek 53:98, Mar. 30, 1959
Reporter 20:36, Apr. 16, 1959
Saturday Review 42:29, Apr. 4, 1959
Senior Scholastic 74:35, Apr. 10, 1959
Time 73:75-6, Mar. 30, 1959

Dick Tracy (1945)
Commonweal 43:481, Feb. 22, 1946
New York Times p. 10, Jan. 12, 1946

Dick Tracy and Gruesome (1947)
New York Times p. 11, Sep. 27, 1947

Dick Tracy Versus Cueball (1946)
New York Times p. 12, Nov. 23, 1946

Dictator (1935)
New York Times VIII, p. 3, Mar. 24, 1935

*Difficult Years
Commonweal 52:559, Sep. 15, 1950
Library Journal 75:1677, Oct. 1, 1950
New Republic 123:21, Sep. 11, 1950
New York Times II, p. 3, Aug. 6, 1960; p. 31, Aug. 22,
    1950; II, p. 1, Sep. 10, 1950
New Yorker 26:66, Sep. 2, 1950
Newsweek 36:70, Sep. 4, 1950
Saturday Review 33:32-3, Sep. 16, 1950
Theatre Arts 34:8-9, Oct., 1950
Time 56:72+, Aug. 28, 1950

Dillinger (1945)
New Republic 112:753, May 28, 1945
New York Times p. 26, Apr. 26, 1945
New Yorker 21:48, May 5, 1945
Newsweek 25:98, May 7, 1945
Time 45:94, May 7, 1945

Dime with a Halo (1963)
New York Times p. 23, Jun. 27, 1963

Dimples (1936)
Child Life 15:567, Dec., 1936
New York Times p. 21, Oct. 10, 1936
Time 28:64, Oct. 19, 1936

Dinner at Eight (1933)
Canadian Magazine 80:34, Nov., 1933; 81:28, Mar., 1934
Commonweal 18:509, Sep. 29, 1933
Literary Digest 116:35, Sep. 9, 1933
Motion Picture 46:54-5+, Sep., 1933
New Outlook 162:48, Oct., 1933
New York Times IX, p. 3, Aug. 20, 1933; p. 18, Aug.
    24, 1933; IX, p. 3, Sep. 3, 1933
Newsweek 2:30, Sep. 2, 1933
Vanity Fair 41:39, Oct., 1933

Dinner at the Ritz (1937)
New York Times XI, p. 6, Nov. 21, 1937; p. 21, Dec.
    4, 1937

Dino (1957)
Commonweal 66:376, Jul. 12, 1957

Dino (1957) (Continued)
National Parent-Teacher 52:33, Sep., 1957
New York Times p. 9, Jun. 22, 1957

Dinosaurus (1960)
America 103:603, Sep. 3, 1960
New York Times p. 36, Sep. 9, 1960

Diplomaniacs (1933)
New York Times p. 14, Apr. 29, 1933

Diplomatic Courier (1952)
Catholic World 175:305, Jul., 1952
Commonweal 56:291, Jun. 27, 1952
Library Journal 77:1071, Jun. 15, 1952
New York Times p. 12, Jun. 14, 1952
Newsweek 39:103, Jun. 30, 1952
Theatre Arts 36:88, Aug., 1952
Time 59:59, Jun. 30, 1952

Dirigible (1931)
Life (NY) 97:22, Apr. 24, 1931
New York Times p. 24, Apr. 6, 1931; IX, p. 5, Apr. 12,
   1931; VIII, p. 6, Feb. 14, 1932
Outlook 157:539, Apr. 15, 1931

Dirty Hands (1954)
New York Times p. 25, May 11, 1954
New Yorker 30:113, May 22, 1954
Newsweek 43:94, May 24, 1954
Saturday Review 37:29, May 22, 1954
Twentieth Century 152:362-4, Oct., 1952

Disbarred (1939)
New York Times p. 17, Jan. 19, 1939

Disgraced (1933)
New Outlook 162:45, Aug., 1933
New York Times p. 14, Jul. 15, 1933

Dishonored (1931)
Life (NY) 97:22, Apr. 17, 1931
New York Times p. 26, Mar. 6, 1931; IX, p. 5, Mar.
   15, 1931
Outlook 157:412, Mar. 18, 1931

Dishonored Lady (1947)
Commonweal 46:190, Jun. 6, 1947

Dishonored Lady (1947) (Continued)
New Republic 116:37, Jun. 9, 1947
New York Times II, p. 1, Feb. 3, 1946; p. 10, May 24,
1947; II, p. 5, May 25, 1947; II, p. 1, Jun. 1, 1947
New Yorker 23:112, Jun. 7, 1947
Newsweek 29:94, Jun. 9, 1947
Time 49:102, Jun. 9, 1947
Woman's Home Companion 74:10, Jul., 1947

Disorderly Conduct (1932)
New York Times p. 19, Apr. 11, 1932; VIII, p. 4, Apr.
17, 1932

Dispatch from Reuter's (1940)
Commonweal 33:128, Nov. 22, 1940
New Republic 103:662, Nov. 11, 1940
New York Times p. 37, Dec. 12, 1940
Newsweek 16:58, Oct. 28, 1940
Photoplay 54:63, Dec., 1940
Scholastic 37:37, Nov. 4, 1940
Theatre Arts 24:788, Nov., 1940
Time 36:78, Nov. 4, 1940

Disputed Passage (1939)
New York Times p. 27, Oct. 26, 1939; IX, p. 5, Oct.
29, 1939
Photoplay 53:63, Dec., 1939
Time 34:85-6, Nov. 13, 1939

Disraeli (1929)
Commonweal 11:399, Feb. 5, 1930
Life (NY) 94:24, Oct. 25, 1929
Literary Digest 105:19, Apr. 12, 1930
Nation 129:562, Nov. 13, 1929
New York Times p. 24, Oct. 3, 1939; IX, p. 9, Oct. 6,
1939; X, p. 5, Dec. 15, 1939; p. 23, Nov. 14, 1930;
p. 19, Jan. 11, 1934
Outlook 153:273, Oct. 16, 1929
Photoplay 39:56-7, Dec., 1930

Distant Drums (1951)
Christian Century 69:111, Jan. 23, 1952
Commonweal 55:374, Jan. 18, 1952
Holiday 11:19, Mar., 1952
Library Journal 77:140, Jan. 15, 1952
New York Times II, p. 5, May 20, 1951; p. 19, Dec. 26,
1951

Distant Drums (1951) (Continued)
Newsweek 39:82, Jan. 14, 1952
Saturday Review 35:28, Jan. 12, 1952
Time 59:94, Jan. 21, 1952

Distant Journey (1950)
New Republic 123:30, Sep. 25, 1950
New York Times p. 13, Aug. 28, 1950; II, p. 1, Sep. 10, 1950

Dive Bomber (1941)
Commonweal 34:497, Sep. 12, 1941
New Republic 105:405, Sep. 29, 1941
New York Times p. 10, Aug. 30, 1941
New Yorker 17:49, Aug. 30, 1941
Newsweek 18:48, Sep. 1, 1941
Scholastic 39:30, Sep. 22, 1941
Time 38:67, Sep. 8, 1941

Divided Heart (1955)
America 93:479, Aug. 13, 1955
Catholic World 181:463, Sep., 1955
Commonweal 62:445, Aug. 5, 1955
Life 39:79-80+, Aug. 15, 1955
National Parent-Teacher 50:39, Oct., 1955
New York Times p. 16, Aug. 4, 1955; II, p. 1, Aug. 7, 1955
New Yorker 31:69, Aug. 20, 1955
Newsweek 46:90, Aug. 22, 1955
Saturday Review 38:34, Sep. 17, 1955
Time 66:84, Aug. 22, 1955

Divine Lady (1929)
New York Times VIII, p. 2, Jul. 1, 1928; p. 22, Mar. 23, 1929; VIII, p. 7, Mar. 31, 1929
Outlook 151:592, Apr. 10, 1929

Divine Woman (1929)
New York Times p. 24, Jan. 16, 1928; VIII, p. 7, Jan. 22, 1928
Outlook 148:228, Feb. 8, 1928

Divorce Among Friends (1932)
New York Times p. 30, Apr. 2, 1931

Divorce in the Family (1930)
New York Times p. 18, Oct. 31, 1932

Divorce--Italian Style (1962)
America 107:1011, Nov. 3, 1962
Commonweal 77:73, Oct. 12, 1962
Nation 195:412, Dec. 8, 1962
New Republic 147:26+, Oct. 8, 1962
New York Times p. 34, Sep. 18, 1962; II, p. 1, Sep. 23, 1962
New Yorker 38:139, Sep. 29, 1962
Newsweek 60:60-1, Oct. 1, 1962
Saturday Review 45:22, Sep. 22, 1962
Time 80:103, Sep. 28, 1962

Divorce of Lady X (1939)
Literary Digest p. 34, Dec. 11, 1937
New York Times p. 17, Apr. 1, 1938
Newsweek 11:25, Feb. 14, 1938
Time 31:23, Apr. 11, 1938

Divorcee (1930)
New York Times p. 25, May 10, 1930; p. 5, May 18, 1930

Dixiana (1930)
New York Times p. 21, Sep. 5, 1930; VIII, p. 5, Sep. 14, 1930
Photoplay 38:102, Sep., 1930

Dixie (1943)
Commonweal 38:302, Jul. 9, 1943
Cosmopolitan 115:66, Aug., 1943
Life 15:80, Jul. 5, 1943
New York Times p. 26, Jun. 24, 1943
New Yorker 19:38, Jul. 3, 1943
Newsweek 22:108, Jul. 5, 1943
Photoplay 23:32, Sep., 1943
Time 42:94, Jul. 12, 1943

Dixie Dugan (1943)
New York Times p. 25, Apr. 9, 1943

Do You Love Me? (1946)
Commonweal 44:384, Aug. 2, 1946
New York Times p. 12, May 25, 1946; II, p. 3, May 26, 1946
New Yorker 22:101, Jun. 8, 1946
Newsweek 27:89, Jun. 3, 1946
Time 47:98+, Jun. 10, 1946

Docks of Hamburg (1930)
New York Times p. 22, Jul. 7, 1930

Docks of New York (1928)
Life (NY) 92:25, Oct. 12, 1928
New York Times p. 28, Sep. 17, 1928
Vanity Fair 31:75, Nov., 1928

Doctor and the Girl (1949)
New York Times p. 20, Oct. 31, 1949
Newsweek 3:87, Oct. 24, 1949
Rotarian 76:40, Jan., 1950
Scholastic 55:30, Dec. 7, 1949
Time 54:102, Dec. 12, 1949

Doctor at Large (1957)
Commonweal 66:523, Aug. 23, 1957
Library Journal 82:1994, Sep. 1, 1957
National Parent-Teacher 52:32, Oct., 1957
New York Times p. 15, Jul. 29, 1957

Doctor at Sea (1955)
Catholic World 182:464, Mar., 1956
Library Journal 81:627, Mar. 1, 1956
National Parent-Teacher 50:39, Mar., 1956
New York Times p. 37, Mar. 1, 1956; II, p. 1, Mar. 4, 1956
Newsweek 47:90, Mar. 5, 1956
Saturday Review 39:27, Feb. 25, 1956
Scholastic 68:46, Mar. 1, 1956
Time 67:104+, Mar. 26, 1956

Dr. Broadway (1942)
Commonweal 36:207, Jun. 19, 1942
New York Times p. 27, Jun. 25, 1942

Doctor Christian Meets the Women (1940)
New York Times p. 12, Aug. 2, 1940

Dr. Cyclops (1940)
New York Times IX, p. 4, Jan. 28, 1940; p. 32, Apr. 11, 1940; IX, p. 5, Apr. 14, 1940
Newsweek 15:35, Apr. 8, 1940
Photoplay 54:73, May, 1940
Time 35:83, Apr. 8, 1940

Dr. Ehrlich's Magic Bullet (1940)
Commonweal 31:412, Mar. 1, 1940

307

Dr. Ehrlich's Magic Bullet (1940) (Continued)
Hygeia 18:138-9, Feb., 1940
Life 8:74-7, Mar. 4, 1940
Nation 150:346, Mar. 9, 1940
New Republic 102:409, Mar. 25, 1940
New York Times IX, p. 4, Jan. 14, 1940; IX, p. 5, Feb.
    13, 1940; p. 9, Feb. 24, 1940; IX, p. 5, Feb. 25,
    1940
New Yorker 16:67, Feb. 24, 1940
Newsweek 15:30+, Feb. 26, 1940
Photoplay 54:69, May, 1940
Scholastic 36:38, Feb. 19, 1940
Time 35:80+, Feb. 19, 1940

Doctor in Love (1962)
New York Times p. 27, Apr. 27, 1962

Doctor in the House (1954)
America 92:630, Mar. 12, 1955
Catholic World 180:383, Feb., 1955
Commonweal 61:551, Feb. 25, 1955
Mademoiselle 41:124, May, 1955
Nation 180:206, Mar. 5, 1955
National Parent-Teacher 49:39, Jan., 1955
New York Times p. 18, Feb. 18, 1955; II, p. 1, Feb.
    27, 1955
New Yorker 31:89, Feb. 26, 1955; 32:72, Mar. 10, 1956
Newsweek 45:88, Feb. 28, 1955
Saturday Review 38:27, Mar. 12, 1955
Time 65:106, Mar. 7, 1955

Dr. Jekyll and Mr. Hyde (1932)
Nation 134:82, Jan. 20, 1932
New York Times p. 14, Jan. 2, 1932; VIII, p. 6, Jan. 3,
    1932; VIII, p. 4, Jan. 10, 1932
Outlook 160:23, Jan. 6, 1932

Dr. Jekyll and Mr. Hyde (1941)
Commonweal 34:473-4, Sep. 5, 1941
Life 11:14-16, Aug. 25, 1941
New York Times p. 13, Aug. 13, 1941; IX, p. 3, Aug.
    17, 1941
New Yorker 17:63, Aug. 23, 1941
Newsweek 18:53, Aug. 25, 1941
Time 38:86, Sep. 1, 1941

Dr. Kildare Goes Home (1940)
Commonweal 32:470, Sep. 27, 1940

Dr. Kildare Goes Home (1940) (Continued)
New York Times p. 27, Sep. 19, 1940
Time 36:74-5, Sep. 30, 1940

Dr. Kildare's Crisis (1940)
New York Times p. 33, Dec. 19, 1940; IX, p. 5, Dec.
22, 1940

Dr. Kildare's Strange Case (1940)
New York Times p. 19, Apr. 12, 1940

Dr. Kildare's Victory (1942)
New York Times p. 25, Feb. 5, 1942

Dr. Kildare's Wedding Day (1941)
New York Times p. 31, Sep. 18, 1941; IX, p. 3, Sep.
21, 1941

Doctor Knock (1937)
New York Times p. 16, May 1, 1937

Dr. Monica (1934)
New York Times p. 28, Jun. 21, 1934; X, p. 3, Jul. 1,
1934; p. 20, Jul. 31, 1934

Dr. No (1963)
Commonweal 78:355, Jun. 21, 1963
New Republic 148:36, Jun. 15, 1963
New York Times II, p. 11, Mar. 25, 1962; p. 20, May
30, 1963
New Yorker 39:65-6, Jun. 1, 1963
Newsweek 61:106, May 13, 1962
Saturday Review 46:16, Jun. 1, 1963
Time 80:63, Oct. 19, 1962; 81:80, May 31, 1963

Doctor Rhythm (1938)
Commonweal 28:161, Jun. 3, 1938
New York Times X, p. 4, May 1, 1938; p. 25, May 19,
1938; XI, p. 3, May 22, 1938
Newsweek 11:23, May 9, 1938
Time 31:44, May 9, 1938

Dr. Socrates (1935)
Canadian Magazine 84:40, Oct., 1935; 84:39, Nov., 1935
New York Times p. 29, Oct. 3, 1935

Dr. Strangelove, or How I Learned to Stop Worrying and
Love the Bomb (1963)
   America 110:462+, Mar. 28, 1964
   Commentary 37:75-7, May, 1964
   Commonweal 79:632, Feb. 21, 1964
   Esquire 61:26+, Feb., 1964
   Life 56:15, Mar. 13, 1964
   Nation 198:127-8, Feb. 3, 1964
   National Review 16:203-4, Mar. 10, 1964
   New Republic 150:28, Mar. 21, 1964; 150:26-8, Feb. 1,
     1964
   New York Times II, p. 7, Apr. 21, 1963; II, p. 13, Jan.
     26, 1964; p. 24, Jan. 30, 1964; II, p. 1, Feb. 2, 1964;
     p. 29, Feb. 5, 1964; p. 21, Feb. 10, 1964; II, p. 1,
     Feb. 16, 1964; p. 44, May 1, 1964; II, p. 1, Sep. 27,
     1964
   New Yorker 39:75-6, Feb. 1, 1964
   Newsweek 63:79, Feb. 3, 1964
   Reporter 30:48+, Feb. 27, 1964
   Saturday Review 47:24, Jan. 25, 1964
   Senior Scholastic 84:10T, Feb. 21, 1964
   Time 83:69, Jan. 31, 1964

Doctor Syn (1937)
   Literary Digest 124:34, Nov. 13, 1937
   New York Times p. 15, Nov. 15, 1937
   Scholastic 31:36, Nov. 6, 1937
   Time 30:44, Nov. 15, 1937

Doctor Takes a Wife (1940)
   Commonweal 32:83, May 17, 1940
   Etude 58:420, Jun., 1940
   New York Times p. 12, Jun. 15, 1940
   Photoplay 54:68, Jun., 1940
   Time 35:86, May 20, 1940

Doctor X (1933)
   Commonweal 16:411, Aug. 24, 1932
   New Outlook 161:39, Oct., 1932
   New York Times p. 17, Aug. 4, 1932; IX, p. 3, Aug. 14,
     1932

Doctors (1956)
   Commonweal 64:539, Aug. 31, 1956
   National Parent-Teacher 51:38, Oct., 1956
   New York Times p. 19, Aug. 7, 1956
   New Yorker 32:62, Aug. 18, 1956

Doctors (1956) (Continued)
Newsweek 48:95, Aug. 13, 1956
Time 68:74, Aug. 13, 1956

Doctor's Diary (1937)
New York Times p. 16, Feb. 17, 1937
Time 29:45, Feb. 1, 1937

Doctor's Dilemma (1959)
America 100:437, Jan. 10, 1959
Catholic World 188:415-16, Feb., 1959
Commonweal 69:413, Jan. 16, 1959
Library Journal 84:70, Jan. 1, 1959
New Republic 139:22, Dec. 29, 1958
New York Times p. 2, Dec. 18, 1958
New Yorker 34:60, Dec. 27, 1958
Reporter 20:35-6, Feb. 19, 1959
Saturday Review 41:21, Dec. 27, 1958
Time 73:72, Jan. 12, 1959

Doctors Don't Tell (1941)
New York Times X, p. 5, May 5, 1940

Doctor's Secret (1929)
Life (NY) 93:23, Mar. 1, 1929
New York Times p. 20, Feb. 4, 1929; IX, p. 7, Feb.
10, 1929
Outlook 151:300, Feb. 20, 1929

Doctor's Wives (1931)
New York Times p. 23, Apr. 25, 1931; VIII, p. 5, May
3, 1931
Outlook 158:27, May 6, 1931

Dodge City (1939)
Commonweal 29:693, Apr. 14, 1939
Life 6:68-71, Apr. 17, 1939
New York Times IX, p. 5, Nov. 6, 1938; IX, p. 7, Dec.
25, 1938; p. 19, Apr. 8, 1939
Newsweek 13:26, Apr. 17, 1939
North American Review 247 no2:384, Jun., 1939
Photoplay 53:59, Jun., 1939
Time 33:50, Apr. 17, 1939

Dodsworth (1936)
Canadian Magazine 86:44, Oct., 1936; 86:36, Nov., 1936
Commonweal 24:532, Oct. 2, 1936

Dodsworth (1936) (Continued)
Literary Digest 122:20, Oct. 3, 1936
Nation 143:502, Oct. 24, 1936
New York Times IX, p. 3, Jun. 7, 1936; p. 29, Sep. 24, 1936
Newsweek 8:34, Oct. 3, 1936
Time 28:31, Sep. 28, 1936

Dog of Flanders (1960)
McCalls 87:6, Mar., 1960
New York Times p. 37, Apr. 1, 1960
New Yorker 36:108, Apr. 9, 1960
Saturday Review 43:36, Apr. 9, 1960

Dog's Life (see Mondo Cane)

Dolce Vita, La (1960)
America 105:410-11, Jun. 3, 1961; 106:13-15, Oct. 7, 1961
American Record Guide 28:160-1, Oct., 1961
Catholic World 194:14-19, Oct., 1961
Christian Century 78:488-90, Apr. 19, 1961
Commonweal 74:177, May 12, 1961; 74:221, May 26, 1961
Esquire 55:18+, Apr., 1961
Harper 221:65-66+, Sep., 1960
Horizon 4:110-12, Sep., 1961
Nation 192:379-80, Apr. 29, 1961
National Review 10:392+, Jun. 17, 1961
New Republic 144:22-3, May 1, 1961
New York Times II, p. 7, Apr. 16, 1961; p. 30, Apr. 20, 1961; II, p. 1, Apr. 23, 1961
New Yorker 37:126-8, Apr. 29, 1961
Newsweek 57:98, Apr. 24, 1961
Reporter 24:40+, Mar. 30, 1961
Saturday Review 44:33, Apr. 22, 1961; 44:37, May 20, 1961; 46:22, Mar. 9, 1963; 46:30, Mar. 30, 1963
Time 77:72, Apr. 21, 1961

Doll Face (1946)
Commonweal 43:358, Jan. 18, 1946
New York Times p. 35, Mar. 28, 1946

Dolly Sisters (1945)
Commonweal 43:170, Nov. 30, 1945
Cosmopolitan 119:96, Nov., 1945
New York Times II, p. 5, Dec. 24, 1944; p. 24, Nov. 15, 1945

Dolly Sisters (1945) (Continued)
Newsweek 26:109-10, Nov. 26, 1945
Scholastic 47:29, Oct. 15, 1945
Time 46:98, Oct. 29, 1945
Woman's Home Companion 72:10, Dec., 1945

*Dolwyn
New Republic 121:21, Sep. 5, 1949
New York Times II, p. 1, Sep. 4, 1949; p. 18, Aug. 30, 1949
New Yorker 25:61, Sep. 3, 1949
Newsweek 34:67, Sep. 5, 1949

Domino Kid (1957)
National Parent-Teacher 52:33, Oct., 1957

Don Bosco (1936)
New York Times p. 27, May 27, 1936

Don Giovanni (1956)
Nation 182:265-6, Mar. 31, 1956
New York Times II, p. 9, Mar. 11, 1956; p. 22, Dec. 22, 1956
New Yorker 32:96, Jan. 19, 1957
Newsweek 47:103, Mar. 26, 1956
Theatre Arts 40:85, Apr., 1956

Don Juan (1927)
Life (NY) 88:26, Aug. 20, 1926
Motion Picture Magazine 31:62, Feb., 1926
New Republic 48:44, Sep. 1, 1926
Newsweek 4:22, Dec. 1, 1934

*Don Juan
Catholic World 183:62, Apr., 1956
National Parent-Teacher 50:39, Apr., 1956
New York Times p. 26, Mar. 6, 1956; II, p. 9, Mar. 11, 1956
New Yorker 32:78, Mar. 17, 1956

Don Juan Quilligan (1945)
New York Times p. 16, Jul. 30, 1945
Newsweek 26:84, Aug. 13, 1945
Time 46:98+, Jul. 30, 1945

Don Quixote (1933)
Arts and Decoration 39:32-3, Jun., 1933

Don Quixote (1933) (Continued)
Literary Digest 119:31, Jan. 12, 1935
Living Age 343:555, Feb., 1933
Nation 140:27-8, Jan. 2, 1935
New Republic 81:246, Jan. 9, 1935
New York Times p. 17, Dec. 24, 1934
Newsweek 4:21, Dec. 29, 1934
Time 24:14, Dec. 31, 1934

Don Quixote (1948)
New York Times p. 29, May 13, 1948

Don Quixote (1961)
Commonweal 73:508, Feb. 10, 1961
New Republic 144:21, Feb. 13, 1961
New York Times p. 18, Jan. 21, 1961; p. 30, Feb. 7,
1961
New Yorker 36:88, Jan. 21, 1961

*Don Quixote De La Mancha
Christian Century 67:287, Mar. 1, 1950
Commonweal 50:202, Jun. 3, 1949
New York Times p. 39, May 13, 1949
Rotarian 76:38, Apr., 1950

Dondi (1961)
Commonweal 74:103, Apr. 21, 1961
Senior Scholastic 78:38, Apr. 26, 1961

Donovan Affair (1929)
New York Times p. 23, Apr. 29, 1929; IX, p. 7, May
19, 1929

Donovan's Brain (1953)
National Parent-Teacher 48:39, Dec., 1953
New York Times p. 28, Jan. 21, 1954

Donovan's Kid (1931)
New York Times p. 28, May 22, 1931

Donovan's Reef (1962)
New York Times p. 14, Jul. 25, 1963; II, p. 1, Jul. 28,
1963
New Yorker 39:50, Aug. 3, 1963
Time 82:50, Aug. 2, 1963

Don't Bet on Blondes (1935)
New York Times p. 16, Jul. 20, 1935

Don't Bet on Blondes (1935) (Continued)
Time 26:42, Jul. 29, 1935

Don't Bet on Love (1933)
New York Times p. 16, Jul. 31, 1933

Don't Bet on Women (1931)
New York Times p. 17, Mar. 7, 1931; IX, p. 5, Mar. 15, 1931

Don't Bother to Knock (1952)
Catholic World 175:383, Aug., 1952
Christian Century 69:1079, Sep. 17, 1952
Library Journal 77:1801, Oct. 15, 1952
Nation 175:138, Aug. 16, 1952
National Parent-Teacher 47:38, Sep., 1952
New York Times p. 8, Jul. 19, 1952
Newsweek 40:81, Jul. 28, 1952
Time 60:88, Aug. 11, 1952

Don't Gamble with Love (1936)
New York Times p. 13, Mar. 2, 1936

Don't Get Personal (1936)
New York Times p. 12, Feb. 22, 1936

Don't Give Up the Ship (1959)
Catholic World 189:395, Aug., 1959
Commonweal 70:308, Jun. 19, 1959
New York Times p. 22, Jul. 9, 1959

Don't Go Near the Water (1957)
America 98:256, Nov. 23, 1957
Commonweal 67:234, Nov. 29, 1957
Library Journal 82:3096, Dec. 1, 1957
Life 43:121+, Nov. 4, 1957
New York Times p. 37, Nov. 15, 1957; II, p. 1, Nov. 24, 1957
New Yorker 33:84, Nov. 23, 1957
Newsweek 50:132, Nov. 18, 1957
Saturday Review 40:22, Nov. 30, 1957
Time 70:120, Nov. 25, 1957

Don't Knock the Rock (1957)
National Parent-Teacher 51:38, Mar., 1957
New York Times p. 13, Feb. 23, 1957

Don't Take It to Heart (1948)
New York Times p. 10, Dec. 25, 1948
Rotarian 75:34, Nov., 1949

Don't Tell the Wife (1937)
New York Times p. 15, Feb. 19, 1937

Don't Trust Your Husband (see Innocent Affair)

Don't Turn 'Em Loose (1936)
Literary Digest 122:23, Sep. 5, 1936
New York Times p. 20, Sep. 25, 1936

Doomed Batallion (1932)
New York Times p. 19, Jun. 13, 1932; IX, p. 3, Jun. 19, 1932
Stage 10:34, Jul., 1933

Doomed to Die (1940)
New York Times p. 16, Jul. 30, 1940

Doorway to Hell (1930)
Life (NY) 96:20, Nov. 28, 1930
New York Times p. 23, Nov. 1, 1930; IX, p. 5, Nov. 23, 1930
Outlook 156:473, Nov. 19, 1930

Double Alibi (1940)
New York Times p. 11, Mar. 11, 1940

Double Bunk (1961)
New York Times p. 41, Nov. 17, 1961

Double Cross Roads (1930)
New York Times p. 31, Apr. 29, 1930; XI, p. 5, May 4, 1930

Double Crossbones (1949)
New York Times p. 19, Apr. 27, 1951

Double Danger (1938)
New York Times p. 17, Feb. 10, 1938

Double Door (1934)
Literary Digest 117:36, May 19, 1934
New York Times p. 22, May 5, 1934; IX, p. 3, May 13, 1934

Double Dynamite (1951)
New York Times p. 19, Dec. 26, 1951
Time 58:106, Nov. 26, 1951

Double Harness (1933)
New Outlook 162:44, Sep., 1933
New York Times p. 20, Jul. 21, 1933

Double Indemnity (1945)
Commonweal 40:132-3, May 26, 1944
Life 17:55+, Jul. 10, 1944
Nation 159:445, Oct. 14, 1944
New Republic 111:103, Jul. 24, 1944
New York Times p. 21, Sep. 7, 1944; II, p. 3, Apr. 21,
   1946
New Yorker 20:53, Sep. 16, 1944
Newsweek 23:70, May 29, 1944
Photoplay 25:24, Aug., 1944
Scholastic 45:36, Sep. 25, 1944
Time 44:94, Jul. 10, 1944
Woman's Home Companion 71:10, Aug., 1944

Double Jeopardy (see Murder Without Tears)

Double Life (1948)
Commonweal 47:546, Mar. 12, 1948
New Republic 118:27, Mar. 15, 1948
New York Times p. 19, Feb. 20, 1948; II, p. 1, Feb.
   22, 1948
New Yorker 24:62, Feb. 28, 1948
Newsweek 31:74, Feb. 9, 1948
Photoplay 32:23, Apr., 1948
Theatre Arts 31:30-5, Dec., 1947
Time 51:99-101, Feb. 23, 1948
Woman's Home Companion 75:10-11, Apr., 1948

Double or Nothing (1937)
New York Times p. 17, Sep. 2, 1937

Double Wedding (1937)
New York Times p. 27, Oct. 22, 1937; X, p. 5, Oct. 31,
   1937
Time 30:25-6, Oct. 25, 1937

Doubting Thomas (1935)
New York Times p. 24, Jul. 11, 1935; IX, p. 3, Jul. 21,
   1935
Time 25:24, Jun. 10, 1935

Dough Boys (1930)
    Life (NY) 96:18, Oct. 10, 1930
    New York Times p. 23, Sep. 22, 1930; VIII, p. 5, Sep.
        28, 1930

Doughgirls (1944)
    Commonweal 40:494, Sep. 8, 1944
    New York Times II, p. 5, Dec. 12, 1943; II, p. 3, Mar.
        5, 1944; p. 14, Aug. 31, 1944
    New Yorker 20:50, Sep. 2, 1944
    Newsweek 24:101, Sep. 4, 1944
    Time 44:94+, Oct. 16, 1944

Dove (1928)
    Life (NY) 91:26, Jan. 19, 1928
    New York Times p. 28, Jan. 3, 1928; VIII, p. 7, Jan. 8,
        1928

Down Among the Sheltering Palms (1953)
    New York Times p. 11, Jun. 13, 1953

Down Argentine Way (1940)
    Commonweal 33:81, Nov. 8, 1940
    New York Times IX, p. 3, Jun. 16, 1940; IX, p. 3, Jul.
        7, 1940; p. 25, Oct. 18, 1940
    Newsweek 16:59, Oct. 28, 1940
    Photoplay 54:62, Dec., 1940

Down Dakota Way (1949)
    Photoplay 36:19, Dec., 1949

Down Mexico Way (1941)
    New York Times IX, p. 4, Jul. 6, 1941

Down Three Dark Streets (1954)
    National Parent-Teacher 49:39, Oct., 1954
    New York Times p. 6, Sep. 4, 1954
    Time 64:98+, Sep. 27, 1954

Down to Earth (1947)
    Commonweal 46:554, Sep. 19, 1947
    Cosmopolitan 122:120, May, 1947
    Good Housekeeping 125:13, Aug., 1947
    Harper 195:189-90, Aug., 1947
    New Republic 117:33, Oct. 6, 1947
    New York Times p. 18, Sep. 12, 1947
    New Yorker 23:53, Sep. 20, 1947

318

Down to Earth (1947) (Continued)
Newsweek 30:81, Aug. 25, 1947
Publisher's Weekly 156:221, Jul. 16, 1949
Theatre Arts 31:50-1, Jun., 1947
Time 50:80, Sep. 1, 1947

Down to the Sea in Ships (1949)
Commonweal 49:543, Mar. 11, 1949
Life 26:81-2+, Mar. 28, 1949
New York Times II, p. 5, Feb. 20, 1949; p. 31, Feb.
23, 1949
New Yorker 25:60, Mar. 5, 1949
Newsweek 33:91, Mar. 7, 1949
Photoplay 35:33, May, 1949
Rotarian 75:36, Jul., 1949
Scholastic 54:28, Mar. 23, 1949
Time 53:98+, Mar. 7, 1949

Down to Their Last Yacht (1934)
New York Times p. 14, Sep. 23, 1934

Downstairs (1932)
New Outlook 161:47, Nov., 1932
New York Times p. 15, Oct. 8, 1932; IX, p. 5, Oct. 16,
1932

Dracula (1931)
New York Times p. 21, Feb. 13, 1931; VIII, p. 6, Feb.
15, 1931; VIII, p. 5, Feb. 22, 1931

Dracula's Daughter (1936)
New York Times IX, p. 3, May 17, 1936; p. 14, May 18,
1936

Drag (1929)
Life (NY) 94:28, Jul. 12, 1929
New York Times p. 17, Jun. 21, 1929; VIII, p. 3, Jun.
23, 1929
Outlook 152:516, Jul. 24, 1929

Drag Net (1928)
Life (NY) 92:23, Jul. 12, 1928
New York Times p. 13, Jun. 4, 1928; VIII, p. 5, Jun.
10, 1928

Dragnet (1954)
America 92:26, Oct. 2, 1954

Dragnet (1954) (Continued)
Commonweal 60:557, Sep. 10, 1954
Farm Journal 78:137, Oct., 1954
Life 37:50-2, Aug. 30, 1954
National Parent-Teacher 49:39, Oct., 1954
New York Times II, p. 5, Aug. 8, 1954; p. 10, Aug. 21, 1954
Newsweek 44:107, Sep. 13, 1954
Scholastic 65:25, Oct. 13, 1954
Time 64:87, Sep. 6, 1954

Dragon Murder Case (1934)
New York Times p. 13, Aug. 23, 1934; IX, p. 3, Sep. 2, 1934

Dragon Seed (1944)
Asia 44:424, Sep., 1944
Commonweal 40:400, Aug. 11, 1944
Cosmopolitan 117:90, Sep., 1944
Nation 159:165, Aug. 5, 1944
New Republic 111:161, Aug. 7, 1944
New York Times II, p. 3, Aug. 22, 1943; VI, p. 18, Nov. 28, 1943; p. 16, Jul. 21, 1944
New Yorker 20:42, Jul. 29, 1944
Newsweek 24:106, Jul. 24, 1944
Saturday Review 27:16, Jul. 29, 1944
Scholastic 45:33, Sep. 11, 1944; 45:22-3, Sep. 25, 1944
Theatre Arts 28:594, Oct., 1944
Time 44:50+, Jul. 21, 1944
Woman's Home Companion 71:10, Oct., 1944

Dragon Wells Massacre (1957)
New York Times p. 25, May 6, 1957

Dragon's Gold (1954)
National Parent-Teacher 48:39, Mar., 1954

Dragonwyck (1946)
Commonweal 43:623, Apr. 5, 1946
Cosmopolitan 120:70+, May, 1946
Life 20:121-2+, Mar. 18, 1946
New York Times II, p. 1, Mar. 4, 1945; II, p. 3, Apr. 7, 1946; p. 35, Apr. 11, 1946
New Yorker 22:107, Apr. 13, 1946
Newsweek 27:94+, Apr. 22, 1946
Photoplay 28:22, May, 1946
Scholastic 48:27, Apr. 8, 1946
Time 47:96, Apr. 1, 1946

Drake Case (1929)
New York Times p. 30, Sep. 16, 1929

Dramatic School (1938)
Commonweal 29:245, Dec. 23, 1938
New York Times p. 31, Dec. 9, 1938
Time 32:39, Dec. 12, 1938

Drango (1957)
Catholic World 184:466, Mar., 1957
Commonweal 65:512, Feb. 15, 1957
National Parent-Teacher 51:38, Mar., 1957
Saturday Review 40:29, Feb. 9, 1957

Dream Girl (1948)
Commonweal 48:356, Jul. 23, 1948
Life 25:84, Jul. 12, 1948
New York Times p. 29, Jun. 17, 1948; II, p. 1, Jun. 20, 1948
New Yorker 24:55, Jun. 26, 1948
Newsweek 31:88-90, Jun. 28, 1948
Photoplay 33:20, Aug., 1948
Time 52:62, Jul. 5, 1948
Woman's Home Companion 75:10-11, Mar., 1948

Dream No More (1950)
New Republic 122:21, Jan. 23, 1950
New York Times II, p. 4, Jan. 1, 1950; p. 25, Jan. 6, 1950

Dream of Love (1928)
New York Times p. 11, Dec. 24, 1928; VIII, p. 7, Dec. 30, 1928

Dream of the Butterfly (1941)
New York Times p. 25, Feb. 13, 1941

Dream Wife (1953)
America 89:467, Aug. 8, 1953
Commonweal 58:395, Jul. 24, 1953
National Parent-Teacher 47:38, May, 1953
New York Times p. 20, Jul. 30, 1953
Newsweek 42:76, Jul. 27, 1953
Time 62:90+, Aug. 17, 1953

Dreamboat (1952)
Christian Century 69:1175, Oct. 8, 1952

Dreamboat (1952) (Continued)
Commonweal 56:462, Aug. 15, 1952
National Parent-Teacher 47:37, Sep., 1952
New York Times p. 9, Jul. 26, 1952
New Yorker 28:56, Aug. 2, 1952
Newsweek 40:86, Aug. 11, 1952
Saturday Review 35:24, Aug. 30, 1952
Time 60:92, Aug. 11, 1952

*Dreaming Lips
New York Times X, p. 5, Feb. 21, 1937; p. 17, May 20, 1937
Scholastic 30:29, Apr. 24, 1937
Time 29:30+, May 31, 1937

Dreaming Lips (1958)
New York Times p. 14, Nov. 1, 1958

Dreams (1960)
Commonweal 72:328, Jun. 24, 1960
Nation 190:540, Jun. 18, 1960
New York Times p. 42, Jun. 1, 1960
New Yorker 36:66+, Jun. 11, 1960
Newsweek 55:102, Jun. 13, 1960
Saturday Review 43:26, Jun. 4, 1960
Time 75:67, Jun. 13, 1960

Dreams That Money Can Buy (1948)
Life 21:86-8, Dec. 2, 1946
Nation 167:108, Jul. 24, 1948
New York Times II, p. 5, Apr. 11, 1948; p. 11, Apr. 24, 1948; II, p. 1, May 9, 1948
Newsweek 31:91+, Apr. 26, 1948
Saturday Review 35:59, Apr. 12, 1952
Theatre Arts 32:39-40, Feb., 1948
Time 51:99, Apr. 26, 1948

Dress Parade (1928)
New York Times p. 22, Oct. 31, 1927

Dressed to Kill (1928)
New York Times p. 26, Mar. 12, 1928; IX, p. 7, Mar. 18, 1928
Outlook 148:505, Mar. 28, 1928

Dressed to Kill (1941)
New York Times p. 19, Aug. 22, 1941

Dressed to Kill (1946)
New York Times p. 12, May 25, 1946

*Dreyfus Case
Commonweal 14:556, Oct. 7, 1931
New Republic 68:128, Sep. 16, 1931
New York Times p. 11, Aug. 31, 1931; VIII, p. 5, Sep. 6, 1931
Outlook 159:87, Sep. 16, 1931

Drive a Crooked Road (1954)
Commonweal 60:144, May 14, 1954
Farm Journal 78:137, May, 1954
National Parent-Teacher 48:39, May, 1954
Newsweek 43:103, Mar. 22, 1954
New York Times p. 19, Apr. 3, 1954
Time 63:106+, Apr. 12, 1954

Drum Beat (1954)
America 92:259, Nov. 27, 1954
Commonweal 61:188, Nov. 19, 1954
National Parent-Teacher 49:39, Jan., 1955
New York Times p. 42, Nov. 18, 1954; II, p. 1, Nov. 28, 1954
Newsweek 44:98+, Dec. 13, 1954
Time 64:105, Nov. 22, 1954

Drums (1938)
Commonweal 28:645, Oct. 14, 1938
New Republic 96:363, Nov. 2, 1938
New York Times p. 24, Sep. 30, 1938; IX, p. 5, Oct. 2, 1938; IX, p. 5, Oct. 16, 1938
Newsweek 12:22-3, Sep. 19, 1938
Scholastic 33:29, Sep. 24, 1938
Time 32:24, Sep. 19, 1938

Drums Across the River (1954)
National Parent-Teacher 48:39, Jun., 1954

Drums Along the Mohawk (1939)
Life 7:74-7, Nov. 13, 1939
New Republic 101:142, Nov. 22, 1939
New York Times p. 11, Nov. 4, 1939; IX, p. 5, Nov. 12, 1939
Photoplay 54:58, Jan., 1940
Scholastic 35:33-4, Nov. 20, 1939
Time 34:80, Nov. 20, 1939
World Horizons 4:22-3, Nov., 1939

Drums in the Deep South (1952)
Christian Century 69:207, Feb. 13, 1952

Drums of Africa (1963)
New York Times p. 9, Jul. 4, 1963

Drums of Tahiti (1953)
National Parent-Teacher 48:39, Mar., 1954
New York Times p. 14, Apr. 24, 1954

Drums of the Congo (1942)
New York Times p. 16, Jul. 20, 1942

Drunken Angel (1960)
New York Times p. 12, Dec. 31, 1959

Dry Martini (1928)
New York Times p. 26, Nov. 5, 1928; X, p. 7, Nov. 11,
1928

Dubarry Was a Lady (1943)
American Mercury 135:2, Apr., 1943
Cosmopolitan 114:2, Apr., 1943; 114:66, Jun., 1943
Good Housekeeping 116:2, Mar., 1943
Life 13:104+, Nov. 16, 1942
New York Times p. 13, Aug. 20, 1943
New Yorker 19:58+, Aug. 21, 1943
Newsweek 21:108, Jun. 28, 1943
Photoplay 23:24, Jul., 1943
Theatre Arts 27:220, Apr., 1943
Time 41:94, May 31, 1943
Woman's Home Companion 70:2, Mar., 1943

Dubarry, Woman of Passion (1930)
New York Times p. 19, Nov. 3, 1930; IX, p. 5, Nov. 9,
1930

Dubrovsky (1936)
Nation 142:492, Apr. 15, 1936
New York Times p. 17, Mar. 30, 1936

Duchess of Idaho (1950)
Christian Century 67:903, Jul. 26, 1950
New York Times p. 15, Jul. 21, 1950
Newsweek 36:78, Jul. 31, 1950
Rotarian 77:38, Sep., 1950
Time 56:62, Jul. 31, 1950

Duck Soup (1933)
Nation 137:688, Dec. 13, 1933
New York Times p. 24, Nov. 23, 1933; X, p. 7, Dec. 10, 1933
Newsweek 2:33, Dec. 2, 1933

Dude Goes West (1948)
New York Times II, p. 3, Jul. 4, 1948

Dude Ranch (1931)
New York Times p. 23, Apr. 25, 1931; VIII, p. 5, Mar. 8, 1931

Dude Ranger (1934)
New York Times p. 18, Oct. 2, 1934

Duel at Silver Creek (1952)
National Parent-Teacher 47:37, Sep., 1952
New York Times p. 7, Aug. 2, 1952
Newsweek 40:84, Aug. 4, 1952
Saturday Review 35:26, Jul. 26, 1952
Theatre Arts 36:34, Aug., 1952

Duel in the Jungle (1954)
America 91:527, Aug. 28, 1954
National Parent-Teacher 49:39, Oct., 1954
Natural History 63:380, Oct., 1954
New York Times p. 13, Aug. 9, 1954
Time 64:110, Sep. 13, 1954

Duel in the Sun (1946)
American Home 36:84+, Sep., 1946
Commonweal 46:142, May 23, 1947
Cosmopolitan 122:67+, Jan., 1947
Harper's Bazaar 80:123, May, 1946; 80:206, Sep., 1946
Life 22:68-71, Feb. 10, 1947
New Republic 116:33, May 19, 1947
New York Times II, p. 1, Apr. 8, 1945; II, p. 1, May 27, 1945; VI, p. 16, Aug. 19, 1945; II, p. 1, Dec. 2, 1945; II, p. 1, Jan. 27, 1946; II, p. 3, Nov. 3, 1946; p. 30, May 8, 1947; II, p. 5, Jan. 19, 1947; II, p. 2, May 11, 1947
Newsweek 29:81-2, Mar. 3, 1947
Photoplay 30:38-9+, May, 1947; 31:4, Jun., 1947
Theatre Arts 31:49, Jun., 1947
Time 49:86, Jan. 27, 1947; 49:99-100, Mar. 17, 1947
Woman's Home Companion 74:11, Apr., 1947

Duel of the Titans (1963)
New York Times p. 19, Aug. 8, 1963

Duffy of San Quentin (1954)
National Parent-Teacher 48:39, Apr., 1954
New York Times p. 38, Feb. 10, 1954

Duffy's Tavern (1945)
Commonweal 42:502-3, Sep. 7, 1945
Nation 161:441, Oct. 27, 1945
New York Times II, p. 1, Oct. 8, 1944; II, p. 5, Dec.
10, 1944; p. 23, Sep. 6, 1945
New Yorker 21:70, Sep. 15, 1945
Newsweek 26:98, Sep. 17, 1945
Time 46:56+, Sep. 24, 1945

Duke of West Point (1938)
Commonweal 29:330, Jan. 13, 1939
New York Times IX, p. 5, Nov. 13, 1938; p. 33, Dec.
16, 1938; IX, p. 7, Dec. 18, 1938
Photoplay 53:48, Feb., 1939

Duke Steps Out (1929)
Life (NY) 93:25, May 10, 1929
New York Times p. 22, Apr. 15, 1929; IX, p. 7, Apr.
21, 1929

Dulcimer Street (1948)
Commonweal 49:198, Dec. 3, 1948
New Republic 119:30, Nov. 29, 1948
New York Times p. 24, Nov. 8, 1948
New Yorker 24:107, Nov. 20, 1948
Rotarian 74:34, May, 1949
Time 52:108, Dec. 6, 1948

Dulcy (1940)
New York Times p. 28, Nov. 28, 1940
Photoplay 54:66, Oct., 1940

Dumbells in Ermine (1930)
New York Times p. 22, Jan. 28, 1930

Dumbo (1941)
Commonweal 35:72, Nov. 7, 1941
Etude 59:741, Nov., 1941
Life 11:72-3, Dec. 8, 1941

Dumbo (1941) (Continued)
Nation 153:463, Nov. 8, 1941
New Republic 105:537, Oct. 27, 1941
New York Times IX, p. 3, Sep. 14, 1941; IX, p. 4, Sep.
    21, 1941; p. 27, Sep. 26, 1941; p. 27, Oct. 24, 1941
Newsweek 18:61, Oct. 27, 1941
Scholastic 39:30, Nov. 3, 1941
Theatre Arts 25:907, Dec., 1941
Time 38:97-8, Oct. 27, 1941; 38:27-8, Dec. 29, 1941

Dummy (1928)
Life (NY) 93:32, Mar. 29, 1929
New York Times p. 20, Mar. 4, 1929; X, p. 7, Mar.
    10, 1929

Dunkirk (1958)
America 99:650-1, Sep. 20, 1958
Commonweal 69:99, Oct. 24, 1958
Library Journal 83:2278, Sep. 1, 1958
New York Times p. 42, Sep. 11, 1958; II, p. 1, Sep. 14,
    1958
New Yorker 34:84+, Sep. 20, 1958
Newsweek 52:107, Sep. 22, 1958
Saturday Review 41:30, Sep. 20, 1958
Senior Scholastic 73:27, Oct. 17, 1958
Time 72:90, Sep. 15, 1958

Dust Be My Destiny (1939)
New York Times IX, p. 3, Jun. 4, 1939; IX, p. 4, Aug.
    27, 1939; p. 11, Oct. 7, 1939
Photoplay 53:65, Nov., 1939

Dybbuk (1938)
New York Times p. 17, Jan. 28, 1938
Time 31:58, Feb. 7, 1938

Dynamite (1929)
New York Times VIII, p. 5, Sep. 1, 1929; p. 11, Dec.
    28, 1929

Each Dawn I Die (1939)
Commonweal 30:359, Aug. 4, 1939
New Republic 100:20, Aug. 9, 1939
New York Times p. 12, Jul. 22, 1939
Newsweek 14:30, Jul. 31, 1939
Time 34:22, Jul. 31, 1939

Eagle and the Hawk (1933)
New Outlook 161:49, Jun., 1933
New York Times p. 16, May 13, 1933; IX, p. 3, May 21, 1933

Eagle and the Hawk (1950)
New York Times p. 31, Jul. 6, 1950; II, p. 1, Jul. 16, 1950

Eagle Has Two Heads (1948)
New York Times II, p. 9, Dec. 7, 1947; II, p. 6, Dec. 19, 1948; p. 24, Dec. 30, 1948
New Yorker 24:49, Jan. 1, 1948

Eagle Squadron (1942)
Commonweal 36:304, Jul. 17, 1942
Life 12:62-4, Jun. 29, 1942
New York Times IX, p. 3, Sep. 14, 1941; p. 12, Jul. 3, 1942
Newsweek 20:59, Jul. 6, 1942
Photoplay 21:42-4+, Jun., 1942; 21:24, Sep., 1942
Time 40:86-7, Jul. 13, 1942

Earl Carroll Sketchbook (1946)
New York Times p. 13, Aug. 30, 1946

Earl Carroll Vanities (1945)
New York Times II, p. 3, Nov. 19, 1944; p. 15, Apr. 2, 1945

Earl of Chicago (1940)
Commonweal 31:307, Jan. 26, 1940
New York Times IX, p. 3, Jul. 30, 1939; IX, p. 5, Nov. 5, 1939; p. 29, Mar. 14, 1940; X, p. 5, Mar. 17, 1940
Newsweek 15:33, Jan. 15, 1940
Time 35:73+, Feb. 12, 1940

Early to Bed (1936)
Literary Digest 121:21, Jun. 6, 1936
New York Times p. 20, Jul. 16, 1936
Time 27:40, Jun. 8, 1936

Earrings of Madame De (1954)
Mademoiselle 40:143, Nov., 1954
New Republic 131:21, Aug. 16, 1954
New York Times p. 15, Jul. 20, 1954

Earrings of Madame De (1954) (Continued)
Newsweek 44:80, Aug. 9, 1954
Saturday Review 37:26, Sep. 4, 1954
Time 64:77, Jul. 26, 1954

*Earth Cries Out
Commonweal 50:536, Sep. 9, 1949
New Republic 121:22, Sep. 19, 1949
New York Times p. 26, Aug. 31, 1949; II, p. 1, Sep. 4,
   1949

Earth Vs. the Flying Saucers (1956)
National Parent-Teacher 50:37, Jun., 1956
New York Times p. 21, Aug. 2, 1956; II, p. 1, Aug. 5,
   1956

Earthworm Tractors (1936)
New York Times p. 16, Jul. 25, 1936
Time 28:41, Jul. 27, 1936

Easiest Profession (1960)
New York Times p. 15, Mar. 26, 1960
New Yorker 36:90, Apr. 2, 1960

Easiest Way (1931)
New York Times p. 15, Feb. 28, 1931; VIII, p. 5, Mar.
   8, 1931

East Is West (1930)
New York Times p. 23, Nov. 1, 1930

East Lynne (1931)
New York Times p. 15, Feb. 21, 1931; VIII, p. 5, Mar.
   1, 1931; VIII, p. 7, Mar. 1, 1931
Outlook 157:348, Mar. 4, 1931

East Meets West (1936)
Canadian Magazine 86:37, Nov., 1936
Commonweal 25:104, Nov. 20, 1936
New York Times p. 24, Oct. 31, 1936; X, p. 5, Nov. 8,
   1936

East of Borneo (1931)
Life (NY) 98:18, Oct. 16, 1931
New York Times p. 25, Sep. 26, 1931; VIII, p. 5, Oct.
   4, 1931

East of Eden (1955)
American Magazine 159:16, Apr., 1955
America 92:659, Mar. 19, 1955
Catholic World 181:60, Apr., 1955
Commonweal 61:604, Mar. 11, 1955
Farm Journal 79:89, Apr., 1955
Library Journal 80:555, Mar. 1, 1955
Look 19:100-1, Apr. 5, 1955
Nation 180:294, Apr. 2, 1955
National Parent-Teacher 49:39, Apr., 1955
New Republic 132:22, Apr. 25, 1955
New York Times p. 32, Mar. 10, 1955; p. 33, Mar. 10,
    1955; II, p. 1, Mar. 20, 1955
New Yorker 31:140-1, Mar. 19, 1955
Newsweek 45:90, Mar. 7, 1955
Saturday Review 38:25, Mar. 19, 1955
Scholastic 66:46, Mar. 16, 1955
Time 65:98+, Mar. 21, 1955

East of Java (1935)
Time 26:44, Dec. 9, 1935

East of Sumatra (1952)
National Parent-Teacher 48:36, Nov., 1953
Time 62:108, Nov. 2, 1953

East of the River (1940)
New York Times p. 21, Oct. 28, 1940
Scholastic 37:33, Nov. 18, 1940

East River (1949)
New York Times II, p. 5, Feb. 1, 1948

East Side Kids (1940)
New York Times p. 21, Feb. 19, 1940

East Side of Heaven (1939)
Commonweal 30:49, May 5, 1939
New York Times p. 29, May 5, 1939; X, p. 5, May 7,
    1939
Newsweek 13:33-4, Apr. 24, 1939
Photoplay 53:59, Jun., 1939

East Side, West Side (1927)
Life (NY) 90:26, Nov. 10, 1927
Motion Picture Magazine 34:59, Jan., 1928
New York Times p. 33, Oct. 18, 1927; VIII, p. 7, Oct.
    23, 1927

East Side, West Side (1950)
Christian Century 67:319, Mar. 8, 1950
Commonweal 51:415, Jan. 20, 1950
Library Journal 75:180, Feb. 1, 1950
Nation 170:162, Feb. 18, 1950
New York Times p. 17, Dec. 23, 1949
Newsweek 34:57, Dec. 26, 1949
Time 55:86+, Jan. 30, 1950

Easter Parade (1948)
Commonweal 48:260, Jun. 25, 1948
Life 24:71, Jun. 21, 1948
New Republic 118:30, Jul. 12, 1948
New York Times II, p. 5, Apr. 20, 1947; II, p. 5, Nov.
    30, 1947; p. 19, Jul. 1, 1948; II, p. 1, Jul. 4, 1948
New York Times Magazine p. 54-5, Jun. 6, 1948
New Yorker 24:39, Jul. 10, 1948
Newsweek 32:70, Jul. 5, 1948
Photoplay 33:20, Aug., 1948
Time 52:60, Jul. 5, 1948

Easy Come, Easy Go (1947)
New York Times II, p. 5, Feb. 2, 1947; p. 29, Feb. 26,
    1947; II, p. 1, Feb. 16, 1947
New Yorker 22:86, Feb. 15, 1947
Newsweek 29:101-2, Feb. 17, 1947
Time 49:82, Mar. 3, 1947

Easy Living (1937)
New York Times p. 20, Jul. 8, 1937; X, p. 3, Jul. 11,
    1937

Easy Living (1949)
Commonweal 51:69, Oct. 28, 1949
New York Times p. 33, Oct. 13, 1949; II, p. 1, Oct. 23,
    1949
Newsweek 34:82+, Sep. 12, 1949
Rotarian 75:38, Dec., 1949
Time 54:103, Sep. 19, 1949
Woman's Home Companion 76:11, Oct., 1949

Easy Money (1949)
New York Times p. 15, Feb. 14, 1949
Newsweek 33:80, Feb. 28, 1949
Rotarian 76:40, Jan., 1950

Easy to Love (1934)
New York Times p. 12, Jan. 15, 1934

Easy to Love (1953)
America 90:305, Dec. 12, 1953
Catholic World 178:303-4, Jan. 1954
Commonweal 59:281, Dec. 18, 1953
Life 36:72-3, Jan. 18, 1954
National Parent-Teacher 48:39, Jan., 1954
New Yorker 29:97, Dec. 19, 1953
Newsweek 42:104-5, Nov. 30, 1953
Saturday Review 36:30, Dec. 19, 1953
Time 62:90, Dec. 21, 1953

Easy to Wed (1946)
Commonweal 44:73, May 3, 1946
Life 21:64-6, Jul. 8, 1946
New York Times II, p. 3, Jul. 7, 1946; p. 12, Jul. 12, 1946; II, p. 1, Jul. 21, 1946
New Yorker 22:52, Jul. 20, 1946
Time 48:97, Jul. 15, 1946
Woman's Home Companion 73:11, Jul., 1946

Ebb Tide (1937)
Literary Digest 124:34, Dec. 11, 1937
Motion Picture 54:42-3+, Nov., 1937
New York Times X, p. 3, Jun. 20, 1937; X, p. 3, Jul. 4, 1937; XI, p. 4, Nov. 14, 1937; p. 27, Nov. 18, 1937; IX, p. 5, Nov. 21, 1937
Saint Nicholas 65:41, Nov., 1937
Saturday Review 17:21, Feb. 12, 1938
Scholastic 31:10, Dec. 4, 1937
Time 30:42, Nov. 29, 1937

Eclipse (1962)
America 108:181, Feb. 2, 1963
Christian Century 80:1137-8, Sep. 18, 1963
Commonweal 77:367-8, Dec. 28, 1962
Esquire 59:20+, May, 1963
Nation 196:59, Jan. 19, 1963
New Republic 147:26+, Dec. 29, 1962; 148:27, May 11, 1963
New York Times p. 5, Dec. 21, 1962
New Yorker 38:60+, Dec. 29, 1962
Newsweek 60:87-8, Oct. 29, 1962
Saturday Review 45:27+, Oct. 27, 1962; 45:41, Nov. 3, 1962
Theatre Arts 46:6-9, Jul., 1962
Time 81:89, Jan. 11, 1963

Ecstasy (Extase) (1933)
Newsweek 5:26, Jan. 19, 1935; 6:18, Jul. 6, 1935

Eddie Cantor Story (1954)
America 90:386, Jan. 9, 1954
Catholic World 178:302, Jan., 1954
Farm Journal 78:94, Mar., 1954
National Parent-Teacher 48:38, Jan., 1954
New York Times p. 10, Dec. 26, 1953
New Yorker 29:55, Dec. 26, 1953
Newsweek 42:94+, Dec. 7, 1953
Time 63:64, Jan. 4, 1954

Eddie Duchin Story (1956)
American Magazine 162:8-9, Jul., 1956
America 95:332, Jun. 30, 1956
Catholic World 183:305, Jul., 1956
Commonweal 64:348, Jul. 6, 1956
Look 20:55+, Jun. 26, 1956
National Parent-Teacher 51:39, Sep., 1956
New York Times p. 15, Jun. 22, 1956; II, p. 1, Jul. 1,
    1956; II, p. 1, Jul. 15, 1956
New Yorker 32:53, Jun. 30, 1956
Newsweek 48:72-3, Jul. 2, 1956
Saturday Review 39:18, Jul. 7, 1956
Time 67:58, Jun. 25, 1956

Edge of Darkness (1943)
Commonweal 37:617, Apr. 9, 1943
Cosmopolitan 115:66, Jul., 1943
New York Times VIII, p. 3, Sep. 27, 1942; p. 12, Apr.
    10, 1943; II, p. 3, Apr. 11, 1943
New Yorker 19:40, Apr. 17, 1943
Newsweek 21:74, Apr. 19, 1943
Theatre Arts 27:115-17, Feb., 1943

*Edge of Divorce
Commonweal 60:388, Jul. 23, 1954
National Parent-Teacher 49:38, Sep., 1954
New York Times p. 10, Jul. 2, 1954
Newsweek 44:83, Jul. 26, 1954

Edge of Doom (1950)
Christian Century 67:1343, Nov. 8, 1950
Commonweal 52:532-2, Sep. 8, 1950
Library Journal 75:1201, Jul., 1950
New Republic 123:23, Aug. 14, 1950

Edge of Doom (1950) (Continued)
New York Times II, p. 6, Feb. 5, 1950; p. 13, Aug. 4,
1950; II, p. 1, Aug. 6, 1950; II, p. 4, Oct. 29, 1950
New Yorker 26:46, Aug. 12, 1950
Newsweek 36:82+, Aug. 14, 1950
Rotarian 78:38, Jan., 1951
Time 56:74+, Aug. 28, 1950

Edge of Eternity (1959)
New York Times p. 34, Feb. 25, 1960

Edge of Hell (1956)
National Parent-Teacher 51:39, Sep., 1956
Scholastic 69:51, Sep. 27, 1956

Edge of the City (1957)
America 96:512, Feb. 2, 1957
Commonweal 65:434, Jan. 25, 1957
Coronet 41:10, Dec., 1956
Library Journal 82:528, Feb. 15, 1957
Nation 184:125, Feb. 9, 1957
National Parent-Teacher 51:38, Feb., 1957
New Republic 136:22, Mar. 4, 1957
New York Times II, p. 5, Apr. 15, 1956; p. 33, Jan. 30,
1957; p. 20, Jan. 31, 1957; II, p. 1, Feb. 3, 1957
New York Times Magazine p. 71, Jan. 20, 1957
New Yorker 32:107, Feb. 9, 1957
Newsweek 49:68, Jan. 7, 1957
Reporter 16:41-2, Mar. 7, 1957
Saturday Review 40:59, Jan. 12, 1957
Time 69:100, Jan. 14, 1957

Edge of the World (1938)
Commonweal 28:590, Sep. 30, 1938
Nation 147:278, Sep. 17, 1938
New Republic 96:160, Sep. 14, 1938
New York Times X, p. 4, Sep. 4, 1938; p. 13, Sep. 12,
1938; X, p. 3, Sep. 18, 1938
Scholastic 33:29, Oct. 29, 1938

Edison, the Man (1940)
Child Life 19:316+, Jul., 1940
Commonweal 32:130, May 31, 1940
Etude 58:157, Mar., 1940
Nation 150:763, Jun. 22, 1940
New York Times IX, p. 5, Feb. 18, 1940; X, p. 5, Mar.
17, 1940; p. 27, Jun. 7, 1940; IX, p. 3, Jun. 9, 1940

Edison, the Man (1940) (Continued)
Newsweek 15:48, May 27, 1940
Photoplay 54:74, Aug., 1940
Popular Science 137:102-5, Jul., 1940
Time 35:100+, Jun. 10, 1940

Educating Father (1936)
New York Times p. 22, Jun. 20, 1936

*Edward and Caroline
Commonweal 56:140, May 16, 1952
New York Times p. 33, Apr. 30, 1952
Saturday Review 35:33, May 24, 1952

Edward, My Son (1948)
Commonweal 50:245, Jun. 17, 1949
Good Housekeeping 129:10-11, Jul., 1949
New Republic 120:20-1, Jun. 13, 1949
New York Times p. 21, Jun. 3, 1949; II, p. 1, Jun. 12, 1949
New Yorker 25:84, Jun. 11, 1949
Newsweek 33:84, May 23, 1949
Rotarian 75:36, Sep., 1949
Theatre Arts 33:9, Jul., 1949
Time 53:98+, Jun. 13, 1949
Woman's Home Companion 76:4, Jul., 1949

Egg and I (1947)
Commonweal 46:142, May 23, 1947
Holiday 2:141, Jul., 1947
Nation 164:553, May 10, 1949
New Republic 116:39, May 12, 1947
New York Times II, p. 9, Dec. 8, 1946; II, p. 5, Apr. 20, 1947; p. 29, Apr. 25, 1947
New Yorker 23:95, May 3, 1947
Newsweek 29:96, Apr. 21, 1947
Photoplay 32:42, Mar., 1948
Scholastic 50:29, Apr. 28, 1947
Time 49:99, Apr. 28, 1947
Woman's Home Companion 74:11, Jun., 1947

Egyptian (1954)
America 91:553-4, Sep. 4, 1954
Catholic World 180:66, Oct., 1954
Commonweal 60:537, Sep. 3, 1954
Library Journal 79:1755, Oct. 1, 1954
Life 37:102-3+, Sep. 6, 1954

Egyptian (1954) (Continued)
National Parent-Teacher 49:39, Oct., 1954
Natural History 63:379, Oct., 1954
New York Times p. 23, Aug. 25, 1954; II, p. 1, Aug. 29,
1954; II, p. 7, Sep. 12, 1954
New Yorker 30:42-3, Sep. 4, 1954
Newsweek 44:76, Sep. 6, 1954
Saturday Review 37:26, Sep. 4, 1954
Scholastic 65:25, Oct. 13, 1954
Time 64:76, Aug. 30, 1954

8 1/2 (1963)
America 109:61-2, Jul. 13, 1963
Catholic World 197:395-6, Sep., 1963
Commonweal 78:425, Jul. 12, 1963
Mademoiselle 57:62, Sep., 1963
Nation 197:59-60, Jul. 27, 1963
New Republic 149:28-9, Jul. 13, 1963
New York Times II, p. 7, Aug. 26, 1962; II, p. 7, Jun.
23, 1963; p. 36, Jun. 26, 1963; II, p. 1, Jun. 30,
1963; VI, p. 20-21, Jul. 21, 1963
New Yorker 39:62, Jun. 29, 1963; 39:19-20, Jul. 6, 1963
Newsweek 61:112+, Jun. 24, 1963
Saturday Review 46:20, Jun. 29, 1963
Senior Scholastic 83:6T, Sep. 27, 1963
Time 81:82, Jun. 28, 1963

Eight Girls in a Boat (1934)
New York Times p. 16, Jan. 13, 1934; X, p. 5, Jan. 21,
1934

Eight Iron Men (1952)
Catholic World 176:144, Nov., 1952
Christian Century 69:1391, Nov. 26, 1952
Commonweal 57:425, Jan. 30, 1953
National Parent-Teacher 47:37, Oct., 1952
New York Times p. 11, Jan. 2, 1953; II, p. 1, Jan. 11,
1953
Newsweek 41:60, Jan. 5, 1953
Theatre Arts 36:84, Dec., 1952
Time 60:104, Dec. 8, 1952

Eight O'Clock Walk (1955)
Nation 180:450, May 21, 1955
New York Times p. 10, Apr. 30, 1955
New Yorker 31:131, May 7, 1955

Eighteen and Anxious (1957)
New York Times p. 16, Dec. 14, 1957

*1812
New York Times p. 14, Sep. 11, 1944
New Yorker 20:55, Sep. 23, 1944
Time 44:92+, Oct. 16, 1944

Eighth Day of the Week (1959)
Commonweal 70:23, Apr. 3, 1959
New Republic 140:19, Mar. 30, 1959
New York Times II, p. 10, Mar. 22, 1959; p. 45, Mar.
24, 1959
Newsweek 53:99, Mar. 30, 1959
Saturday Review 42:24, Jan. 24, 1959

El Paso (1948)
New York Times p. 35, Mar. 24, 1949
Newsweek 33:80+, Apr. 4, 1949
Rotarian 75:42, Aug., 1949
Time 53:104+, Apr. 18, 1949

Electra (1963)
America 108:122-3+, Jan. 19, 1963
Esquire 59:34, Feb., 1963
New Republic 148:28-9, Jan. 19, 1963
New York Times p. 5, Dec. 18, 1962
New York Times Magazine p. 92+, Nov. 25, 1962
New Yorker 38:78, Dec. 22, 1962
Newsweek 60:57, Dec. 31, 1962
Saturday Review 45:29, Dec. 15, 1962
Time 81:58, Jan. 4, 1963

Elephant Boy (1937)
Asia 36:799-800, Dec. 1936; 37:463, Jun., 1937
Canadian Magazine 87:42-3, Jan., 1937
Commonweal 26:20, Apr. 30, 1937
Life 2:32-8, Apr. 12, 1937
Literary Digest 123:21, Apr. 17, 1937
Nation 144:489, Apr. 24, 1937
New Republic 90:323, Apr. 21, 1937
New York Times p. 20, Apr. 6, 1937
Scholastic 30:20, Apr. 3, 1937
Time 29:48+, Apr. 12, 1937
Vogue 89:56, Jun. 15, 1937

Elephant Gun (1959)
New York Times p. 11, Jun. 20, 1959

337

Elephant Walk (1954)
America 91:172+, May 8, 1954
Catholic World 179:623, Apr., 1954
Commonweal 60:117, May 7, 1954
Farm Journal 78:137, May, 1954
Library Journal 79:766, Apr. 15, 1954
Look 18:72+, May 4, 1954
National Parent-Teacher 48:39, Apr., 1954
Natural History 63:189, Apr., 1954
New York Times p. 37, Apr. 22, 1954
New Yorker 30:109, May 1, 1954
Saturday Review 37:23, Apr. 17, 1954
Scholastic 64:30, Apr. 21, 1954
Time 63:100+, Apr. 19, 1954

Ellery Queen and the Murder Ring (1941)
New York Times p. 29, Oct. 21, 1941

Ellery Queen and the Perfect Crime (1941)
New York Times p. 17, Aug. 11, 1941

Ellery Queen, Master Detective (1940)
New York Times p. 33, Dec. 19, 1940

Ellery Queen's Penthouse Mystery (1941)
New York Times p. 17, Mar. 7, 1941

Elmer and Elsie (1934)
New York Times p. 14, Aug. 4, 1934; IX, p. 3, Aug. 12, 1934

Elmer Gantry (1960)
America 103:463, Jul. 16, 1960; 78:592-3, May 10, 1961
Commonweal 72:402, Aug. 5, 1960
Esquire 56:114+, Aug., 1961
Life 49:81, Jul. 18, 1960
Mademoiselle 51:57, Sep., 1960
Nation 191:78, Aug. 6, 1960
New Republic 143:20, Aug. 15, 1960
New York Times II, p. 9, Oct. 11, 1959; II, p. 5, Jul. 3, 1960; p. 16, Jul. 8, 1960; II, p. 1, Jul. 10, 1960
New Yorker 36:57, Jul. 16, 1960
Newsweek 56:90-1, Jul. 11, 1960
Saturday Review 43:28, Jun. 25, 1960
Time 76:76, Jul. 18, 1960

Elmer the Great (1933)
New York Times IX, p. 4, Apr. 30, 1933; p. 24, May 26, 1933

Elopement (1951)
Catholic World 174:304, Jan., 1952
Christian Century 69:295, Mar. 5, 1952
New York Times p. 21, Dec. 21, 1951
Newsweek 38:57, Dec. 31, 1951
Time 58:60, Dec. 31, 1951

Elsa Maxwell's Hotel for Women (1939)
Commonweal 30:400, Aug. 18, 1939
Time 34:33, Aug. 14, 1939

Elusive Corporal (1963)
Commonweal 77:620, Mar. 8, 1963
Esquire 59:22+, May, 1963
New Republic 148:26, Mar. 9, 1963
New York Times p. 5, Feb. 19, 1963; p. 5, Feb. 27, 1963
New Yorker 39:135, Mar. 2, 1963
Newsweek 61:94+, Feb. 25, 1963
Time 81:E5, Mar. 8, 1963

Embezzled Heaven (1959)
America 101:284+, May 2, 1959
Catholic World 189:155, May, 1959
Commonweal 70:82, Apr. 17, 1959
Good Housekeeping 148:25, Apr., 1959
Library Journal 84:1119, Apr. 1, 1959
New York Times p. 23, Apr. 24, 1959
New Yorker 35:106, May 16, 1959
Newsweek 53:115, Apr. 27, 1959
Saturday Review 42:31, May 2, 1959
Time 73:86, May 11, 1959

Embraceable You (1948)
Time 52:86+, Sep. 6, 1948

Emergency Call (1933)
New York Times p. 16, Jun. 24, 1933
Newsweek 1:30, Jul. 1, 1933

Emergency Hospital (1956)
National Parent-Teacher 51:39, Sep., 1956

Emergency Wedding (1950)
Christian Century 68:63, Jan. 10, 1951
New York Times II, p. 5, Nov. 12, 1950; p. 19, Dec. 22, 1950
Rotarian 78:38, Feb., 1951

Emil (1938)
New York Times p. 23, Apr. 15, 1938

Emil and the Detectives (1931)
New York Times p. 28, Dec. 21, 1931

Emma (1932)
New York Times p. 14, Feb. 6, 1932; VIII, p. 4, Feb. 14, 1932

Emperor Jones (1933)
Canadian Magazine 80:35, Nov., 1933
Commonweal 18:532, Oct. 6, 1933
Nation 137:419, Oct. 11, 1933
New York Times p. 42, May 26, 1933; IX, p. 3, Jun. 11, 1933; IX, p. 2, Jul. 16, 1933; p. 26, Sep. 20, 1933; X, p. 3, Sep. 24, 1933
Newsweek 2:32, Sep. 23, 1933
Stage 10:40, Aug., 1933
Vanity Fair 41:47+, Nov., 1933

Emperor Waltz (1946)
Collier's 121:20-1, Jan. 24, 1948
Commonweal 48:260, Jun. 25, 1948
Cosmopolitan 124:13+, Jun., 1948
Life 24:44-5, Jan. 12, 1948; 24:72, Jun. 21, 1948
Nation 167:108, Jul. 24, 1948
New Republic 118:29, Jun. 28, 1948
New York Times II, p. 5, Nov. 10, 1946; p. 19, Jun. 18, 1948; II, p. 1, Jun. 27, 1948
New Yorker 24:55, Jun. 26, 1948
Newsweek 31:88, Jun. 28, 1948
Time 52:98+, Jul. 19, 1948
Woman's Home Companion 75:10-11, Jul., 1948

Emperor's Candlesticks (1937)
New York Times p. 18, Jul. 9, 1937
Newsweek 10:38, Jul. 17, 1937

Emperor's Nightingale (1951)
Christian Century 69:87, Jan. 16, 1952
Commonweal 54:166, May 25, 1951
House Beautiful 97:43, Jul., 1955
Library Journal 76:972, Jun. 1, 1951
New Republic 124:23, May 21, 1951
New York Times II, p. 5, Apr. 29, 1951; p. 29, May 14, 1951; II, p. 1, May 27, 1951

340

Emperor's Nightingale (1951) (Continued)
New Yorker 27:79, May 26, 1951
Newsweek 37:97, May 14, 1951
Saturday Review 34:26, May 12, 1951; 35:42, May 10,
1952
Scholastic 59:37, Nov. 7, 1951
Theatre Arts 35:86+, Jun., 1951
Time 57:116, May 21, 1951

Employee's Entrance (1932)
New York Times p. 10, Jan. 21, 1933; IX, p. 5, Jan. 29,
1933

Enamorada (1949)
New York Times p. 8, Dec. 3, 1949

Enchanted April (1935)
New York Times p. 19, Mar. 9, 1935

Enchanted Cottage (1945)
Commonweal 41:567, Mar. 23, 1945
Cosmopolitan 118:90, Mar., 1945
Life 18:49-50+, Apr. 9, 1945
Nation 160:425, Apr. 14, 1945
New Republic 112:753, May 28, 1945
New York Times II, p. 3, Aug. 20, 1944; p. 19, Apr.
28, 1945
New Yorker 21:63, Apr. 28, 1945
Newsweek 25:102, Apr. 23, 1945
Photoplay 26:18, May, 1945
Theatre Arts 29:232, Apr., 1945
Time 45:94, Apr. 16, 1945
Woman's Home Companion 72:10, Apr., 1945

Enchanted Forest (1945)
Commonweal 43:288, Dec. 28, 1945
New York Times p. 17, Dec. 17, 1945
New Yorker 21:50, Dec. 22, 1945

Enchanted Island (1958)
Library Journal 83:3418, Dec. 1, 1958

Enchantment (1949)
Collier's 122:46+, Dec. 11, 1948
Commonweal 49:282, Dec. 24, 1948
Good Housekeeping 128:11+, Feb., 1949
New Republic 120:23, Jan. 10, 1949

Enchantment (1949) (Continued)
New York Times p. 16, Dec. 27, 1948
New York Times Magazine p. 66-7, Dec. 5, 1948
New Yorker 24:37, Dec. 25, 1948
Newsweek 33:57, Jan. 3, 1949
Photoplay 34:20, Feb., 1949
Rotarian 74:34, May, 1949
Time 52:58, Dec. 27, 1948
Woman's Home Companion 76:10-11, Feb., 1949

Encore (1951)
Catholic World 175:142, May, 1952
Christian Century 69:1111, Sep. 24, 1952
Commonweal 56:94, May 2, 1952
Holiday 11:128-30, Jun., 1952
Library Journal 77:713, Apr. 15, 1952
New York Times p. 45, Apr. 3, 1952
New Yorker 28:119, Apr. 12, 1952
Newsweek 39:96, Mar. 17, 1952
Saturday Review 35:28, Apr. 5, 1952
Theatre Arts 36:104, May, 1952
Time 59:106+, Apr. 7, 1952

End of Desire (1962)
Commonweal 76:498, Sep. 7, 1962
New York Times p. 29, Jul. 10, 1962
New Yorker 38:60, Jul. 14, 1962
Newsweek 60:71, Jul. 23, 1962

End of Innocence (1961)
Commonweal 72:497, Sep. 16, 1960
New York Times p. 25, Aug. 30, 1960
New Yorker 36:80, Sep. 10, 1960
Saturday Review 43:30, Sep. 24, 1960
Time 76:44, Sep. 5, 1960

End of the Affair (1955)
America 93:167, May 7, 1955
Catholic World 181:141, May, 1955
Commonweal 62:105, Apr. 29, 1955
Library Journal 80:775, Apr. 1, 1955
National Parent-Teacher 49:39, May, 1955
New York Times p. 28, Apr. 29, 1955
New Yorker 31:131, May 7, 1955
Time 65:98+, May 2, 1955

End of the Day (1939)
Commonweal 30:481, Sep. 15, 1939

End of the Day (1939) (Continued)
    Nation 149:329, Sep. 23, 1939
    New York Times IX, p. 4, Sep. 10, 1939; p. 28, Sep.
    12, 1939; X, p. 3, Sep. 17, 1939
    Time 34:33, Sep. 25, 1939

End of the River (1948)
    New Republic 119:28, Jul. 5, 1948
    New York Times p. 18, Jun. 21, 1948

Enemies of the Law (1931)
    New York Times p. 13, Jul. 13, 1931

Enemy (1928)
    New York Times p. 26, Dec. 28, 1927; VIII, p. 7, Jan.
    1, 1928

Enemy Agent (1940)
    New York Times p. 13, Apr. 22, 1940

Enemy Agents Meet Ellery Queen (1942)
    New York Times p. 16, Aug. 22, 1942

Enemy Below (1957)
    America 98:404, Jan. 4, 1958
    Catholic World 186:380, Feb., 1958
    Commonweal 67:432, Jan. 24, 1958
    Library Journal 83:71, Jan. 1, 1958
    Nation 186:38, Jan. 11, 1958
    National Parent-Teacher 52:38, Feb., 1958
    New Republic 138:21-2, Mar. 3, 1958
    New York Times p. 23, Dec. 26, 1957
    New Yorker 33:95, Jan. 18, 1958
    Newsweek 51:69, Jan. 6, 1958
    Saturday Review 41:24, Jan. 18, 1958
    Senior Scholastic 72:42, Feb. 14, 1958
    Time 71:92, Jan. 13, 1958

Enemy General (1960)
    New York Times p. 42, Oct. 20, 1960

Enemy of Women (1944)
    New York Times p. 23, Sep. 12, 1944

Enfants Du Paradis, Les (1946)
    Canadian Forum 28:112, Aug., 1948
    Commonweal 45:304, Jan. 3, 1947

343

Enfants Du Paradis, Les (1946) (Continued)
Hollywood Quarterly 1:420-21, Jul., 1946
Life 18:113-15, May 14, 1945
Nation 164:433, Apr. 12, 1947
New Republic 116:39, Mar. 3, 1947
New York Times p. 32, Feb. 20, 1947; p. 1, Mar. 2,
    1947; II, p. 6, Mar. 16, 1947
New York Times Magazine p. 22-3, Dec. 1, 1946
New Yorker 22:86, Feb. 15, 1947
Newsweek 28:101, Dec. 9, 1946
Theatre Arts 30:713-14, Dec., 1946
Time 48:103+, Nov. 25, 1946
Vogue 108:318, Sep. 15, 1946

Enforcer (1951)
Commonweal 53:448, Feb. 9, 1951
New Republic 124:23, Feb. 12, 1951
New York Times p. 19, Jan. 26, 1951
New Yorker 26:86+, Feb. 3, 1950
Newsweek 37:81, Feb. 5, 1951
Time 57:90+, Feb. 12, 1951

Englishman's Home (1939)
New York Times p. 29, Oct. 1, 1939

Entente Cordiale (1939)
Life 8:36-7, Jan. 15, 1940
Nation 150:25, Jan. 6, 1940
New York Times p. 23, Dec. 26, 1939; XI, p. 4, Dec.
    31, 1939

Enter Arsene Lupin (1944)
New York Times p. 17, Dec. 2, 1944

Enter Madame (1934)
New York Times p. 12, Jan. 12, 1935

Entertainer (1960)
Commonweal 73:97, Oct. 21, 1960
McCalls 88:220, Nov., 1960
Nation 191:355, Nov. 5, 1960
New Republic 143:20-1, Oct. 17, 1960
New York Times II, p. 7, Nov. 23, 1959; p. 49, Oct. 4,
    1960; II, p. 1, Oct. 9, 1960
New Yorker 36:134, Oct. 15, 1960
Newsweek 56:104, Oct. 10, 1960
Time 76:73, Oct. 3, 1960

Episode (1937)
New York Times p. 23, May 17, 1937

Errand Boy (1962)
New York Times p. 25, Feb. 8, 1962

Escapade (1935)
Commonweal 22:307, Jul. 19, 1935
Literary Digest 120:24, Jul. 20, 1935
Nation 141:112, Jul. 24, 1935
New York Times p. 16, Jul. 6, 1935
Time 26:40, Jul. 15, 1935

Escapade (1955)
New York Times p. 30, Aug. 6, 1957
Newsweek 50:94, Aug. 12, 1957
Time 70:82, Aug. 26, 1957

Escapade in Japan (1957)
America 98:328, Dec. 7, 1957
Commonweal 67:288, Dec. 13, 1957
Library Journal 82:2351, Oct. 1, 1957
National Parent-Teacher 52:37, Nov., 1957
New York Times p. 11, Dec. 24, 1957
New Yorker 33:103, Jan. 11, 1958
Senior Scholastic 71:25, Nov. 8, 1957

Escape (1928)
New York Times p. 29, May 7, 1928
Outlook 149:145, May 23, 1928

Escape (1930)
New York Times p. 23, Nov. 1, 1930; IX, p. 5, Nov. 9,
    1930

Escape (1939)
Life 11:23, Sep. 22, 1941
New York Times p. 17, Nov. 4, 1939
Newsweek 16:58, Nov. 11, 1940
Photoplay 54:44, Aug., 1940
Time 36:86, Nov. 18, 1940

Escape (1940)
Commonweal 33:104, Nov. 15, 1940
Life 11:23, Sep. 22, 1941
New Republic 103:724, Nov. 25, 1940
New York Times p. 33, Nov. 1, 1940

345

Escape (1940) (Continued)
Newsweek 16:58, Nov. 11, 1940
Photoplay 54:44, Aug., 1940
Scholastic 37:34, Nov. 11, 1940
Scribner's Commentator 9:106-7, Jan., 1941
Time 36:86, Nov. 18, 1940

Escape (1948)
Canadian Forum 28:163, Oct., 1948
New York Times p. 12, Aug. 16, 1948
Newsweek 32:81, Jul. 19, 1948
Time 52:85, Jul. 12, 1948

Escape from Devil's Island (1935)
New York Times p. 22, Nov. 25, 1935

Escape from East Berlin (1962)
New York Times p. 55, Dec. 6, 1962

Escape from Fort Bravo (1953)
America 90:327, Dec. 19, 1953
Commonweal 59:307, Dec. 25, 1953
National Parent-Teacher 48:39, Jan., 1954
New York Times p. 11, Jan. 23, 1954
New Yorker 29:87, Jan. 30, 1954
Newsweek 42:98, Dec. 7, 1953
Saturday Review 36:49, Dec. 12, 1953
Time 62:108+, Dec. 14, 1953

Escape from San Quentin (1957)
National Parent-Teacher 52:38, Jan., 1958

Escape from Yesterday (1939)
New York Times X, p. 3, Sep. 4, 1938; p. 27, May 3,
1939

Escape from Zahrain (1962)
New York Times p. 19, Jul. 12, 1962

Escape in the Desert (1945)
New York Times p. 10, May 12, 1945

*Escape into Dreams
New York Times p. 34, Apr. 13, 1950
New Yorker 26:113, Apr. 22, 1950
Newsweek 35:76, May 1, 1950

Escape Me Never (1935)
Commonweal 22:160, Jun. 7, 1935
Literary Digest 119:26, Jun. 8, 1935
Nation 140:668, Jun. 5, 1935
New York Times p. 24, May 24, 1935; XI, p. 3, May 26, 1935
Newsweek 5:24, Jun. 1, 1935
Stage 12:60, Jun., 1935
Time 25:50, Jun. 3, 1935
Vanity Fair 44:39, Jul., 1935

Escape Me Never (1947)
Commonweal 47:256, Dec. 19, 1947
Good Housekeeping 124:12, Mar., 1947
New York Times p. 11, Nov. 8, 1947; II, p. 5, Nov. 9, 1947
Newsweek 30:100, Nov. 17, 1947
Woman's Home Companion 74:11, Nov., 1947

Escape to Burma (1955)
National Parent-Teacher 49:39, May, 1955
New York Times II, p. 2, May 21, 1955

Escape to Glory (see Submarine Zone)

Eskimo (1933)
Movie Classic 5:34-5, Nov., 1933
Nation 137:631, Nov. 29, 1933
New Outlook 162:47, Dec., 1933
New York Times IX, p. 4, Nov. 5, 1933; IX, p. 4, Nov. 12, 1933; p. 25, Nov. 15, 1933; IX, p. 9, Dec. 3, 1933
Newsweek 2:32, Nov. 25, 1933

Espionage (1937)
New York Times p. 27, Mar. 9, 1937

Espionage Agent (1937)
Nation 149:422, Oct. 14, 1939
New Republic 100:301, Oct. 18, 1939
New York Times p. 22, Sep. 23, 1939; IX, p. 5, Oct. 8, 1939
Time 34:49, Oct. 2, 1939

Esther and the King (1960)
Commonweal 73:280, Dec. 9, 1960
New York Times p. 13, Nov. 19, 1960
Newsweek 56:103, Dec. 5, 1960

Eternal Husband (1948)
New Republic 120:28, Jan. 24, 1949
New York Times p. 19, Jan. 10, 1949

Eternal Love (1929)
Life (NY) 93:31, May 31, 1929
New York Times p. 27, May 13, 1929; IX, p. 7, May 19, 1929
Outlook 152:235, Jun. 5, 1929

Eternal Mask (1937)
Literary Digest 123:24, Jan. 16, 1937
New York Times X, p. 5, Jan. 10, 1937; p. 20, Jan. 13, 1937; X, p. 5, Jan. 17, 1937
Scholastic 30:22, Feb. 6, 1937
Time 29:45, Jan. 25, 1937

Eternal Return (1948)
Christian Century 67:543, Apr. 26, 1950
Commonweal 47:448, Feb. 13, 1948
New York Times p. 15, Jan. 5, 1948; p. 18, Mar. 29, 1948; p. 11, Jul. 19, 1948
New Yorker 23:62, Jan. 17, 1948
Newsweek 31:89, Jan. 19, 1948
Rotarian 76:37, Jun., 1950
Theatre Arts 32:44, Feb., 1948
Time 51:102, Jan. 19, 1948

Eternal Sea (1955)
National Parent-Teacher 49:38, May, 1955
New York Times p. 16, Jun. 10, 1955
Newsweek 45:91, May 2, 1955
Saturday Review 38:26, May 14, 1955

Eternal Waltz (1959)
New York Times p. 22, Jul. 9, 1959

Eternally Yours (1939)
New York Times p. 11, Oct. 7, 1939
Photoplay 53:64, Nov., 1939
Time 34:101-2, Oct. 16, 1939

Eugene Onegin (1959)
New York Times p. 33, Sep. 14, 1959

*Europe '51
New York Times II, p. 5, Dec. 16, 1951; IV, p. 34, Jun. 29, 1952

*Europe '51 (Continued)
New York Times Magazine p. 34-5, Jun. 29, 1952
New Yorker 28:109, Sep. 6, 1952

Evangeline (1929)
Motion Picture 37:42+, Jun., 1929
New York Times VIII, p. 4, Jul. 7, 1929; p. 23, Jul.
29, 1929; VIII, p. 4, Aug. 4, 1929
Outlook 152:633, Aug. 14, 1929
Woman's Home Companion 56:130, Nov., 1929

Eve of St. Mark (1944)
Commonweal 40:205, Jun. 16, 1944
Nation 158:661, Jun. 3, 1944
New Republic 110:816, Jun. 19, 1944
New York Times p. 22, May 31, 1944; II, p. 3, Jun. 4,
1944
New Yorker 20:61, Jun. 3, 1944
Newsweek 23:72, Jun. 12, 1944

Eve Wants to Sleep (1961)
New York Times p. 42, Jun. 6, 1961
Newsweek 57:94, Jun. 12, 1961
Saturday Review 44:37, Jun. 10, 1961
Time 77:76, Jun. 16, 1961

Evelyn Prentice (1934)
New York Times p. 19, Nov. 10, 1934; IX, p. 5, Dec.
23, 1934

Evenings for Sale (1932)
New York Times p. 20, Nov. 12, 1932

Evensong (1934)
Literary Digest 118:30, Dec. 1, 1934
New York Times p. 12, Nov. 17, 1934

Ever in My Heart (1933)
New York Times p. 25, Oct. 13, 1933

Ever Since Eve (1934)
New York Times p. 27, Mar. 28, 1934
Time 30:20, Jul. 5, 1937

Ever Since Eve (1937)
New York Times p. 25, Jun. 25, 1937
Time 30:20, Jul. 5, 1937

Evergreen (1934)
Canadian Magazine 82:38, Oct., 1934
New York Times p. 29, Jan. 11, 1935
Time 25:32, Jan. 21, 1935
Vanity Fair 43:43, Feb., 1935

Every Day's a Holiday (1938)
Life 4:2-3, Jan. 10, 1938
New York Times p. 17, Jan. 27, 1938; X, p. 5, Jan. 30, 1938
Newsweek 11:24-5, Jan. 31, 1938
Time 31:35, Jan. 24, 1938

Every Girl Should Be Married (1948)
Life 25:11, Nov. 15, 1948
New York Times p. 14, Dec. 24, 1948
Newsweek 33:76, Jan. 10, 1949
Rotarian 74:38, Mar., 1949
Scholastic 53:27, Dec. 15, 1948
Time 53:60, Jan. 3, 1949

Every Night at Eight (1935)
New York Times p. 16, Aug. 3, 1935
Time 26:34-5, Aug. 12, 1935

Every Saturday Night (1936)
New York Times p. 10, Mar. 14, 1936
Scholastic 28:26, Feb. 22, 1936
Time 27:25, Mar. 2, 1936

Everybody Does It (1949)
Good Housekeeping 129:239, Dec., 1949
Life 27:117, Oct. 10, 1949
New Republic 121:38, Nov. 14, 1949
New York Times p. 32, Oct. 26, 1949; II, p. 1, Oct. 30, 1949
New Yorker 25:110, Nov. 5, 1949
Newsweek 34:88-90, Nov. 7, 1949
Photoplay 36:20, Nov., 1949
Rotarian 76:40, Jan., 1950
Scholastic 55:29, Nov. 9, 1949
Time 54:106+, Nov. 14, 1949
Woman's Home Companion 76:10-11, Dec., 1949

Everybody Go Home (1961)
New Republic 147:23+, Dec. 15, 1962
New York Times p. 38, Nov. 6, 1962

Everybody Go Home (1961) (Continued)
New Yorker 38:204, Nov. 24, 1962
Newsweek 60:118+, Nov. 19, 1962
Time 80:51, Dec. 7, 1962

Everybody Sing (1938)
Canadian Magazine 89:33, Mar., 1938
New York Times p. 15, Mar. 11, 1938

Everybody's Old Man (1936)
New York Times p. 27, Mar. 26, 1936
Time 27:34+, Mar. 30, 1936

Everything but the Truth (1956)
Catholic World 184:299, Jan., 1957
National Parent-Teacher 51:36, Jan., 1957

Everything Happens at Night (1939)
New York Times p. 12, Dec. 16, 1939; IX, p. 3, Dec. 24, 1939
Photoplay 54:26, Apr., 1940

Everything I Have Is Yours (1952)
Catholic World 176:144, Nov., 1952
Christian Century 69:1367, Nov. 19, 1952
Commonweal 57:120, Nov. 7, 1952
National Parent-Teacher 47:37, Nov., 1952
New York Times p. 40, Oct. 30, 1952
Newsweek 40:106, Nov. 3, 1952
Time 60:104, Nov. 3, 1952

Everything Is Thunder (1936)
Canadian Magazine 86:38, Nov., 1936

Everything's Lucky (1961)
New York Times p. 30, Dec. 21, 1961

Everything's on Ice (1939)
New York Times p. 31, Oct. 6, 1939

Everything's Rosie (1931)
New York Times p. 28, May 22, 1931

Evidence (1929)
New York Times p. 22, Oct. 5, 1929

Ex-Flame (1931)
New York Times p. 15, Jan. 24, 1931

Ex-Lady (1933)
New York Times p. 16, May 15, 1933

Ex-Mrs. Bradford (1936)
Literary Digest 121:20-1, Jun. 6, 1936
New York Times p. 19, May 28, 1936
Time 27:50, May 25, 1936

Excess Baggage (1928)
New York Times p. 25, Sep. 24, 1928; IX, p. 7, Sep. 30, 1928

Exchamp (1939)
New York Times p. 25, May 12, 1939

Exclusive (1937)
New York Times p. 15, Jul. 22, 1937
Time 30:26, Jul. 26, 1937

Exclusive Story (1936)
New York Times p. 19, Jan. 18, 1936
Time 27:46, Jan. 27, 1936

Excuse My Dust (1951)
Christian Century 68:879, Jul. 25, 1951
Commonweal 54:380, Jul. 27, 1951
Library Journal 76:972, Jun. 1, 1951
New York Times p. 21, Jun. 28, 1951
Newsweek 37:87, Jun. 25, 1951
Saturday Review 34:22, Jun. 30, 1951

Executive Suite (1954)
America 91:201+, May 15, 1954
Catholic World 179:142, May, 1954
Commonweal 60:96-7, Apr. 30, 1954
Farm Journal 78:137, May, 1954
Fortune 51:108-9+, Jan., 1955
Library Journal 79:766, Apr. 15, 1954
Life 36:85+, Apr. 19, 1954
Look 18:117-19, May 18, 1954
National Parent-Teacher 48:39, Apr., 1954
New York Times p. 19, May 7, 1954; II, p. 1, May 16, 1954
New Yorker 30:74, May 15, 1954
Newsweek 43:102, Apr. 26, 1954; 43:90-4, May 3, 1954
Saturday Review 37:33-4, May 1, 1954; 38:63, Jan. 1, 1955
Time 63:108, May 10, 1954

352

Exile (1947)
New York Times II, p. 5, Dec. 21, 1947; p. 22, Dec.
26, 1947
Photoplay 32:21, Feb., 1948
Time 50:103, Dec. 8, 1947

Exile Express (1939)
New York Times IX, p. 5, Nov. 25, 1938; p. 21, Aug.
16, 1939
Photoplay 53:79, Aug., 1939

Exodus (1960)
America 104:451, Jan. 7, 1961
Commonweal 73:316, Dec. 16, 1960
Life 49:70-7, Dec. 12, 1960
McCalls 88:168, Feb., 1961
National Review 10:89-90, Feb. 11, 1961
New Republic 143:21-2, Dec. 19, 1960
New York Times II, p. 5, Apr. 17, 1960; II, p. 1, May
15, 1960; VI, p. 22, May 29, 1960; VI, p. 64, Dec.
4, 1960
New Yorker 36:136-7, Dec. 17, 1960
Newsweek 56:87-8, Dec. 19, 1960
Saturday Review 43:30, Dec. 17, 1960
Senior Scholastic 77:23, Jan. 25, 1961
Seventeen 20:20, Feb., 1961
Time 76:69, Dec. 19, 1960

Expensive Husbands (1937)
New York Times p. 19, Jan. 8, 1938

Expensive Women (1931)
New York Times p. 15, Nov. 14, 1931

Experiment in Terror (1962)
America 107:187, Apr. 28, 1962
Commonweal 76:86, Apr. 20, 1962
Esquire 58:56+, Nov., 1962
New York Times p. 14, Apr. 14, 1962
New Yorker 38:171, Apr. 21, 1962
Newsweek 59:110, Apr. 16, 1962
Senior Scholastic 80:40, May 9, 1962

Experiment Perilous (1944)
New York Times p. 15, Dec. 30, 1944
Newsweek 25:94, Jan. 15, 1945
Time 44:44+, Dec. 25, 1944

353

Expert (1932)
New York Times p. 21, Feb. 27, 1932

Explorers of the World (1931)
New York Times VIII, p. 5, Dec. 6, 1931; p. 32, Dec.
15, 1931; VIII, p. 4, Dec. 20, 1931

Explosive Generation (1961)
Commonweal 75:121, Oct. 27, 1961
New York Times p. 24, Feb. 15, 1962
Newsweek 58:93, Dec. 11, 1961
Saturday Review 44:36, Sep. 16, 1961

Exposed (1938)
New York Times p. 41, Nov. 21, 1938

Expresso Bongo (1960)
Commonweal 72:127, Apr. 29, 1960
McCalls 87-8+, Jun., 1960
Nation 190:392, Apr. 30, 1960
New Republic 142:20-1, Apr. 11, 1960
New York Times p. 44, Apr. 13, 1960
Newsweek 55:97, Mar. 28, 1960
Saturday Review 43:70, Mar. 12, 1960
Time 75:92, Apr. 25, 1960

Extase (see Ecstasy)

Extravagance (1930)
New York Times p. 31, Dec. 9, 1930

Eye for an Eye (1959)
Commonweal 73:559, Feb. 24, 1961
New York Times p. 19, Feb. 10, 1961

Eye Witness (1950)
Christian Century 67:1407, Nov. 22, 1950
New Republic 123:22, Sep. 11, 1950
New York Times p. 13, Aug. 28, 1950
Newsweek 36:89, Sep. 11, 1950
Rotarian 78:38, Jan., 1951
Time 56:98, Sep. 25, 1950

Eyes in the Night (1942)
Commonweal 37:44, Oct. 30, 1942
New York Times VIII, p. 3, Jun. 7, 1942; p. 23, Oct.
16, 1942
Scholastic 41:35, Nov. 9, 1942

Eyes of the Underworld (1942)
New York Times p. 15, Oct. 5, 1942

Eyes of the World (1930)
New York Times p. 20, Aug. 15, 1930

F. B. I. (1933)
New York Times IX, p. 4, Mar. 12, 1933

F. B. I. Story (1959)
America 101:778-9, Sep. 26, 1959
Commonweal 70:543, Sep. 25, 1959
McCalls 87:6, Nov., 1959
New York Times p. 31, Nov. 27, 1958; p. 23, Sep. 25,
  1959; II, p. 1, Oct. 4, 1959
New Yorker 35:145-6, Oct. 3, 1959
Newsweek 54:118, Sep. 28, 1959
Saturday Review 42:30, Sep. 12, 1959
Time 74:115, Oct. 12, 1959

F Man (1936)
New York Times p. 16, May 4, 1936

F. P. One (1933)
New York Times p. 9, Sep. 16, 1933

Fabiola (1951)
Christian Century 68:854, Jul. 18, 1951
Commonweal 54:238, Jun. 15, 1951
Library Journal 76:59, Jan. 1, 1951
Nation 173:178, Sep. 1, 1951
New Republic 124:22, Jun. 18, 1951
New York Times II, p. 3, Sep. 3, 1950; p. 14, May 30,
  1951
New Yorker 27:96, Jun. 9, 1951
Newsweek 37:86, Jun. 4, 1951
Saturday Review 34:30, May 26, 1951
Time 57:92, Jun. 25, 1951

Fabulous Dorseys (1947)
Commonweal 45:492, Feb. 28, 1947
New Republic 116:32-3, Jun. 16, 1947
New York Times p. 25, May 30, 1947; II, p. 5, Jun. 1,
  1947
New Yorker 23:112, Jun. 7, 1947
Newsweek 29:98+, Feb. 24, 1947
Time 49:98, Mar. 10, 1947

Fabulous Suzanee (1946)
Commonweal 45:492, Feb. 28, 1947

Fabulous Texan (1947)
New York Times p. 22, Dec. 26, 1947

Fabulous World of Jules Verne (1961)
New Republic 144:28, Jun. 26, 1961
New York Times p. 26, Jun. 29, 1961

Face Behind the Mask (1941)
New York Times p. 23, Feb. 7, 1941

Face in the Crowd (1957)
America 97:332, Jun. 15, 1957
Commonweal 66:277-8, Jun. 14, 1957
Coronet 42:10, May, 1957
Good Housekeeping 145:70, Aug., 1957
Library Journal 82:1665, Jun. 15, 1957
Life 42:68+, May 27, 1957
Nation 184:533-4, Jun. 15, 1957
National Parent-Teacher 52:33, Sep., 1957
New York Times II, p. 7, Sep. 30, 1956; II, p. 5, May
    26, 1957; p. 33, May 29, 1957; II, p. 1, Jun. 2, 1957;
    VI, p. 17, Jun. 2, 1957
New York Times Magazine p. 72, Jan. 13, 1957
New Yorker 33:86+, Jun. 8, 1957
Newsweek 49:101, Jun. 3, 1957
Reporter 17:45-7, Aug. 8, 1957
Saturday Review 40:23, May 25, 1957
Time 69:92, Jun. 3, 1957

Face in the Sky (1933)
New York Times p. 11, Feb. 20, 1933; IX, p. 5, Feb.
    26, 1933

Face to Face (1953)
Catholic World 176:223-4, Dec., 1952
Christian Century 70:95, Jan. 21, 1953
Commonweal 57:474, Feb. 13, 1953
Holiday 13:28, Mar., 1953
Library Journal 77:1981, Nov. 15, 1952
National Parent-Teacher 47:27, Mar., 1953
New York Times p. 27, Jan. 14, 1953
New Yorker 28:62, Jan. 24, 1953
Newsweek 41:60, Jan. 5, 1953
Saturday Review 35:27, Dec. 20, 1952

356

Face to Face (1953) (Continued)
Scholastic 61:28, Oct. 29, 1952
Theatre Arts 37:82-3, Jan., 1953
Time 60:108+, Dec. 15, 1952

*Face to the Wind
Commonweal 53:495, Feb. 23, 1951
New York Times p. 34, Jan. 16, 1951
New Yorker 26:69, Jan. 27, 1951
Newsweek 37:82, Jan. 15, 1951
Time 57:80, Feb. 5, 1951

Facts of Life (1960)
America 104:605, Feb. 4, 1961
Commonweal 73:463, Jan. 27, 1961
Esquire 55:56, Jun., 1961
Nation 192:223, Mar. 11, 1961
New Republic 144:21, Feb. 27, 1961
New York Times II, p. 5, Jul. 31, 1960; p. 27, Feb. 11,
    1961; II, p. 1, Feb. 19, 1961
New Yorker 37:98, Feb. 18, 1961
Newsweek 57:80, Jan. 16, 1961
Time 77:38, Jan. 27, 1961

Facts of Love (1949)
New York Times p. 20, Oct. 31, 1949

Fail Safe (1963)
America 111:464-5, Oct. 17, 1964
Catholic World 200:195-6, Dec., 1964
Commonweal 81:72, Oct. 9, 1964
Life 57:12, Oct. 30, 1964
National Review 16:1026-7, Nov. 17, 1964
New Republic 151:26-7, Sep. 12, 1964
New York Times p. 36, Sep. 16, 1964; II, p. 1, Sep.
    27, 1964; p. 48, Oct. 8, 1964
New Yorker 40:200-1, Oct. 10, 1964
Newsweek 64:114+, Oct. 12, 1964
Senior Scholastic 85:10T, Oct. 7, 1964; 85:52, Oct. 7,
    1964
Vogue 144:100, Oct. 15, 1964

Fair Wind to Java (1953)
New York Times p. 13, Aug. 28, 1953

Faithful City (1952)
New York Times p. 35, Aug. 8, 1952
Saturday Review 35:28, Mar. 29, 1952

357

Faithful Heart (1932)
New York Times p. 20, Aug. 15, 1933

Faithless (1932)
New York Times p. 20, Nov. 19, 1932

Falcon in Hollywood (1944)
New York Times p. 21, Dec. 9, 1944

Falcon in Mexico (1945)
New York Times p. 16, Aug. 5, 1944

Falcon in San Francisco (1945)
New York Times p. 7, Jul. 21, 1945

Falcon Out West (1944)
New York Times p. 18, Mar. 18, 1944

Falcon Strikes Back (1943)
New York Times p. 17, Apr. 2, 1943

Falcon Takes Over (1942)
New York Times p. 9, May 30, 1942

Falcon's Brother (1942)
New York Times p. 9, Oct. 3, 1942

Fall Guy (1930)
Life (NY) 95:20, Jun. 13, 1930
New York Times p. 27, May 27, 1930

Fall In (1942)
New York Times p. 13, May 15, 1943

Fall of Berlin (1945)
New Yorker 21:56, Sep. 29, 1945
Time 46:56, Oct. 15, 1945

Fall of Eve (1929)
Life (NY) 94:25, Jul. 5, 1929
New York Times p. 29, Jun. 18, 1929
Outlook 152:555, Jul. 31, 1929

Fall of the House of Usher (1952)
America 103:522, Aug. 6, 1960

Fallen Angel (1946)
Commonweal 43:206, Dec. 7, 1945

Fallen Angel (1946) (Continued)
New York Times II, p. 3, Feb. 3, 1946; p. 29, Feb. 7,
1946
New Yorker 22:87, Feb. 16, 1946
Newsweek 26:116+, Dec. 17, 1945
Photoplay 28:19, Jan., 1946
Time 46:98, Nov. 12, 1945

Fallen Idol (1948)
Canadian Forum 29:161, Oct., 1949
Commonweal 51:238+, Dec. 2, 1949
Good Housekeeping 129:11, Aug., 1949
Library Journal 75:181, Feb. 1, 1950
Life 25:105-8, Dec. 13, 1948
New Republic 121:22, Nov. 21, 1949
New York Times p. 39, Nov. 16, 1949; II, p. 1, Nov.
20, 1949; II, p. 5, Dec. 11, 1949
New Yorker 25:110, Nov. 19, 1949
Newsweek 34:66, Oct. 31, 1949
Rotarian 76:38, Feb., 1950
Theatre Arts 33:97, Aug., 1949
Time 53:98+, Apr. 4, 1949
Vogue 113:118, Feb. 15, 1949

Fallen Sparrow (1943)
Nation 157:275, Sep. 4, 1943
New York Times p. 13, Aug. 20, 1943
New Yorker 19:58, Aug. 21, 1943
Newsweek 22:82, Aug. 30, 1943
Scholastic 43:31, Sep. 20, 1943

False Faces (1932)
New York Times p. 19, Nov. 25, 1932

Fame is the Spur (1948)
Christian Century 67:95, Jan. 18, 1950
Commonweal 51:180, Nov. 18, 1949
New Republic 121:22, Nov. 21, 1949
New York Times p. 34, Nov. 8, 1949
New Yorker 25:86, Nov. 26, 1949
Newsweek 34:90, Nov. 7, 1949
Rotarian 76:36, Mar., 1950
Scholastic 55:22, Dec. 14, 1949
School and Society 70:361-2, Dec. 3, 1949

Family Affair (1937)
New York Times p. 29, Apr. 20, 1937

Family Honeymoon (1949)
   Commonweal 49:592, Mar. 25, 1949
   Good Housekeeping 128:303, Apr., 1949
   New York Times II, p. 5, May 16, 1948; p. 28, Feb. 25,
      1949
   Newsweek 33:90, Mar. 21, 1949
   Photoplay 34:20, Mar., 1949
   Time 53:92, Feb. 14, 1949

Family Next Door (1939)
   New York Times p. 31, Apr. 28, 1939

Family Secret (1951)
   Catholic World 174:223, Dec., 1951
   Christian Century 69:415, Apr. 2, 1952
   Commonweal 55:424, Feb. 1, 1952
   Theatre Arts 36:84, Jan., 1952

Famous Ferguson Case (1932)
   New York Times p. 18, Apr. 25, 1932

Fan (1949)
   Commonweal 50:46+, Apr. 22, 1949
   Good Housekeeping 128:10, May, 1949
   New Republic 120:31, Apr. 18, 1949
   New York Times p. 12, Apr. 2, 1949; II, p. 1, Apr. 10,
      1949
   Newsweek 33:90, Apr. 18, 1949
   Photoplay 34:22, Apr., 1949
   Rotarian 75:50, Jul., 1949
   Time 53:102, Apr. 11, 1949
   Woman's Home Companion 76:10-11, May, 1949

Fancy Pants (1950)
   Christian Century 67:1119, Sep. 20, 1950
   Commonweal 52:605, Sep. 29, 1950
   Good Housekeeping 131:17, Sep., 1950
   New Republic 123:21, Sep. 11, 1950
   New York Times II, p. 5, Oct. 2, 1949; p. 21, Aug. 31,
      1950
   Newsweek 36:87, Sep. 11, 1950
   Rotarian 77:36, Nov., 1950
   Time 56:82, Sep. 4, 1950

Fanfan the Tulip (1952)
   Commonweal 58:180, May 22, 1953
   New York Times p. 34, May 5, 1953
   New Yorker 29:130, May 16, 1953

Fanfan the Tulip (1952) (Continued)
Newsweek 41:100, May 25, 1953
Saturday Review 36:36, May 2, 1953
Theatre Arts 37:88, Jul., 1953
Time 61:110+, May 11, 1953

Fang and Claw (1935)
New York Times p. 10, Dec. 28, 1935

*Fanny
Commonweal 47:448, Feb. 13, 1948
New Republic 118:34, Feb. 2, 1948
New York Times p. 26, Feb. 13, 1948
Newsweek 31:73, Feb. 2, 1948

Fanny (1961)
America 105:616, Aug. 12, 1961
Commonweal 74:403, Jul. 14, 1961
Life 50:97-9, Jun. 30, 1961
New Republic 145:26, Jul. 24, 1961
New York Times p. 48, May 18, 1960; p. 16, Jul. 7,
    1961; II, p. 1, Jul. 16, 1961
New Yorker 37:58, Jul. 8, 1961
Newsweek 58:84, Jul. 17, 1961
Saturday Review 44:29, Jul. 8, 1961
Time 78:92, Jul. 14, 1961

Fanny by Gaslight (1944)
Canadian Forum 25:94, Jul., 1945
New York Times II, p. 3, Jul. 16, 1944

Fanny Foley Herself (1931)
New York Times p. 22, Oct. 26, 1931

Fanny Hawthorne (1929)
New York Times p. 20, Nov. 11, 1929

Fantasia (1940)
Child Life 20:21, Jan., 1941
Commonweal 33:152, Nov. 29, 1940
Etude 58:805+, Dec., 1940
Independent Woman 20:15, Jan., 1941
Musician 45:217, Dec., 1940
Nation 151:513+, Nov. 23, 1940; 151:543, Nov. 30, 1940;
    152:53-4, Jan. 11, 1941; 152:566, May 10, 1941
New Republic 103:724, Nov. 25, 1940
New York Times IX, p. 7, Jan. 21, 1940; XI, p. 5, Mar.

Fantasia (1940) (Continued)
  10, 1940; IX, p. 3, Aug. 25, 1940; IX, p. 5, Oct. 20,
  1940; IX, p. 4, Oct. 27, 1940; VII, p. 6, Nov. 3,
  1940; p. 27, Nov. 14, 1940; p. 28, Nov. 14, 1940;
  p. 20, Nov. 15, 1940; IX, p. 4, Nov. 17, 1940; IX,
  p. 5, Nov. 17, 1940; IX, p. 7, Nov. 17, 1940; IX,
  p. 2, Nov. 24, 1940; X, p. 13, Dec. 8, 1940
  New Yorker 16:63-4+, Nov. 23, 1940
  Newsweek 16:50-51, Nov. 25, 1940
  Popular Science 138:65-67, Jan., 1941
  Scholastic 37:34, Dec. 9, 1940
  Scientific America 164:28-30, Jan., 1940
  Scribner's Commentator 9:105-6, Jan., 1941
  Stage 1:78-81, Nov., 1940
  Theatre Arts 24:870-71, Dec., 1940; 25:55-61, Jan., 1941
  Time 36:52-55, Nov. 18, 1940

Far Country (1955)
  America 92:602, Mar. 5, 1955
  Commonweal 61:582, Mar. 4, 1955
  Farm Journal 79:149, Feb., 1955
  Library Journal 80:555, Mar. 1, 1955
  Nation 179:558, Dec. 25, 1954
  National Parent-Teacher 49:39, Jan., 1955
  New York Times p. 24, Feb. 14, 1955
  Scholastic 66:14, Feb. 16, 1955

Far Frontier (1948)
  Photoplay 34:23, Apr., 1949

Far Horizons (1955)
  America 93:339, Jun. 25, 1955
  Commonweal 62:256, Jun. 10, 1955
  New York Times p. 11, May 21, 1955
  Newsweek 45:98, Jun. 6, 1955
  Time 65:110, Jun. 6, 1955

Farewell Again (1937)
  Literary Digest 124:34, Nov. 13, 1937

Farewell, My Lovely (see Murder, My Sweet)

Farewell to Arms (1933)
  Nation 136:28, Jan. 4, 1933
  New Outlook 161:47, Jan., 1933
  New York Times p. 26, Dec. 9, 1932; X, p. 7, Dec. 18,
    1932; X, p. 3, May 29, 1938

Farewell to Arms (1933) (Continued)
    Stage 10:42, Jan., 1933
    Vanity Fair 39:62, Jan., 1933

Farewell to Arms (1958)
    America 98:495-6, Jan. 25, 1958
    Commonweal 67:488, Feb. 7, 1958
    Coronet 43:14, Jan., 1958
    Cosmopolitan 143:12, Dec., 1957
    Library Journal 83:174, Jan. 15, 1958
    National Parent-Teacher 52:39, Feb., 1958
    New Republic 138:22, Feb. 17, 1958
    New York Times II, p. 5, May 12, 1957; VI, p. 66, May
        26, 1957; VI, p. 27, Aug. 11, 1957; p. 14, Jan. 25,
        1958; II, p. 1, Feb. 2, 1958
    New Yorker 33:65, Feb. 1, 1958
    Newsweek 50:61, Dec. 30, 1957
    Saturday Review 41:27, Feb. 1, 1958
    Time 71:80, Feb. 3, 1958

Farewell to Love (1933)
    New York Times p. 10, Nov. 25, 1933
    Vanity Fair 44:46, May, 1935

Farewell to Yesterday (1950)
    Christian Century 67:1279, Oct. 25, 1950
    Rotarian 77:37, Dec., 1950
    New York Times II, p. 5, Jun. 25, 1950; p. 31, Dec. 1,
        1950

Farmer in the Dell (1936)
    Canadian Magazine 85:59, Apr., 1936
    New York Times p. 11, Mar. 7, 1936
    Scholastic 28:26, Apr. 4, 1936

Farmer Takes a Wife (1935)
    Commonweal 22:427, Aug. 30, 1935
    Literary Digest 120:28, Aug. 17, 1935
    Movie Classic 9:18+, Sep., 1935
    New York Times p. 21, Aug. 9, 1935
    Time 26:27, Aug. 19, 1935

Farmer Takes a Wife (1953)
    Library Journal 78:985, Jun. 1, 1953
    New York Times p. 11, Jun. 13, 1953

Farmer's Daughter (1940)
    New York Times p. 23, Feb. 16, 1940

Farmer's Daughter (1940) (Continued)
  Photoplay 54:72, May, 1940
  Time 35:82, Mar. 11, 1940

Farmer's Daughter (Katie for Congress) (1947)
  Commonweal 45:614, Apr. 4, 1947
  Cosmopolitan 122:66+, Apr., 1947
  Life 21:85, Dec. 9, 1946; 22:67-8+, May 5, 1947
  Nation 164:433, Apr. 12, 1947
  New Republic 116:40, Apr. 14, 1947
  New York Times II, p. 5, Mar. 23, 1947; p. 31, Mar.
    26, 1947; II, p. 5, May 25, 1947
  New Yorker 23:83, Apr. 5, 1947
  Newsweek 29:87, Apr. 7, 1947
  Photoplay 32:42, Mar., 1948
  Scholastic 50:31, Apr. 7, 1947
  Theatre Arts 31:52, May, 1947
  Time 49:100+, Apr. 7, 1947

Farrebique (1948)
  Commonweal 47:522, Mar. 5, 1948
  Nation 166:312-13, Mar. 13, 1948
  New Republic 118:26-7, Mar. 1, 1948
  New York Times p. 21, Feb. 24, 1948; II, p. 1, Feb.
    29, 1948
  New Yorker 24:74, Mar. 6, 1948
  Newsweek 31:83, Mar. 8, 1948
  Time 51:100+, Mar. 15, 1948
  Vogue 110:53, Jul. 1, 1947

Fashions in Love (1929)
  New York Times p. 31, Jul. 1, 1929; VIII, p. 5, Jul. 28,
    1929; VIII, p. 4, Sep. 1, 1929

Fashions of 1934 (1934)
  New York Times p. 25, Jan. 19, 1934; p. 14, Jan. 20,
    1934; X, p. 4, Jan. 21, 1934; IX, p. 5, Jan. 28,
    1934
  Newsweek 3:34, Jan. 20, 1934

Fast and Furious (1939)
  New York Times p. 33, Oct. 12, 1939
  Photoplay 53:63, Dec., 1939

Fast and Loose (1930)
  Life (NY) 96:21, Dec. 26, 1930
  New York Times p. 21, Dec. 1, 1930

Fast and Loose (1939)
New York Times p. 18, Mar. 9, 1939
Time 33:30, Feb. 27, 1939

Fast and Sexy (1960)
New York Times p. 51, Oct. 6, 1960

Fast Company (1929)
New York Times p. 22, Oct. 5, 1929
Outlook 153:315, Oct. 23, 1929

Fast Company (1938)
New York Times p. 21, Jul. 6, 1938

Fast Company (1953)
National Parent-Teacher 47:37, Jun., 1953
Time 61:114, May 18, 1953

Fast Life (1929)
Life (NY) 94:27, Sep. 13, 1929
New York Times p. 18, Aug. 16, 1929; VIII, p. 4, Aug.
25, 1929

Fast Life (1932)
New York Times p. 11, Dec. 24, 1932

Fast Workers (1933)
New York Times p. 18, Mar. 20, 1933

Fastest Gun Alive (1956)
America 95:412, Jul. 28, 1956
Commonweal 64:492, Aug. 17, 1956
National Parent-Teacher 51:39, Sep., 1956
New York Times p. 23, Jul. 13, 1956
New Yorker 32:44, Jul. 21, 1956
Newsweek 48:98, Jul. 9, 1956
Time 68:74, Jul. 30, 1956

Fatal Hour (1940)
New York Times p. 11, Jan. 13, 1940

Fatal Lady (1936)
New York Times p. 11, 1956

Fate of a Man (1962)
America 105:811, Sep. 23, 1961
New Republic 145:27, Aug. 7, 1961

Fate of a Man (1962) (Continued)
New York Times p. 28, Jul. 11, 1961
New Yorker 37:51, Jul. 29, 1961
Newsweek 58:71, Jul. 24, 1961
Saturday Review 44:31, Jul. 22, 1961
Time 78:60, Jul. 28, 1961

Father and Son (1929)
New York Times p. 29, Jun. 4, 1929; VIII, p. 5, Jun. 9,
1929

Father is a Bachelor (1950)
Christian Century 67:351, Mar. 15, 1950
New York Times p. 33, Feb. 23, 1950
Rotarian 76:40, May, 1950

Father O'Flynn (1938)
New York Times p. 29, Dec. 26, 1938

Father of the Bride (1950)
Christian Century 67:855, Jul. 12, 1950
Commonweal 52:173, May 26, 1950
Good Housekeeping 130:16, Jun., 1950
Library Journal 75:1058, Jun. 15, 1950
New Republic 122:23, Jun. 12, 1950
New York Times p. 31, May 19, 1950; II, p. 1, Jun. 4,
1950
New Yorker 26:63, May 27, 1950
Newsweek 35:83, May 29, 1950
Rotarian 77:38, Sep., 1950
Time 55:87-8+, May 29, 1950

Father Takes a Wife (1941)
New York Times IX, p. 5, Apr. 20, 1941; p. 19, Sep. 5,
1941
Time 38:83, Sep. 29, 1941

Father Was a Fullback (1949)
Commonweal 51:70, Oct. 28, 1949
New York Times p. 33, Oct. 13, 1949; II, p. 1, Oct. 23,
1949
Newsweek 34:88, Oct. 24, 1949
Rotarian 75:38, Dec., 1949
Scholastic 55:19, Oct. 12, 1949
Time 54:76+, Oct. 31, 1949

Fathers and Sons (1960)
New York Times p. 27, Dec. 26, 1960

Father's Dilemma (1952)
Catholic World 176:224, Dec., 1952
New York Times p. 25, Sep. 23, 1952
New Yorker 28:74, Oct. 4, 1952
Saturday Review 35:30, Oct. 18, 1952

*Father's Little Dividend
Christian Century 68:623, May 16, 1951
Commonweal 54:59, Apr. 27, 1951
New York Times p. 18, Apr. 13, 1951
Newsweek 37:83, Apr. 30, 1951
Saturday Review 34:47, Apr. 14, 1951
Time 57:104+, Apr. 23, 1951

Father's Son (1931)
Life (NY) 97:24, Mar. 20, 1931
New York Times p. 15, Feb. 21, 1931; VIII, p. 5, Mar. 1, 1931

Father's Son (1941)
New York Times p. 25, Feb. 13, 1941

Faust (1963)
New York Times p. 31, Apr. 16, 1963

Faust and the Devil (1950)
Christian Century 67:743, Jun. 14, 1950
Etude 68:20-2, Oct., 1950
Library Journal 75:786, May 1, 1950
Musical America 70:26, Jun., 1950
New York Times p. 18, May 1, 1950
Rotarian 77:43, Aug., 1950

Fazil (1928)
Life (NY) 91:23, Jun. 28, 1928
New York Times p. 21, Jun. 5, 1928; VIII, p. 5, Jun. 10, 1928
Outlook 149:307, Jun. 20, 1928

Fear and Desire (1953)
Commonweal 58:73, Apr. 24, 1953
New York Times p. 35, Apr. 1, 1953
New Yorker 29:128, Apr. 11, 1953
Newsweek 41:106+, Apr. 13, 1953
Saturday Review 39:51, May 19, 1956
Theatre Arts 37:82-3, May, 1953

Fear in the Night (1947)
New York Times p. 11, Apr. 19, 1947
Newsweek 29:104+, May 12, 1947

Fear Strikes Out (1957)
America 96:743, Mar. 30, 1957
Commonweal 65:661, Mar. 29, 1957
Coronet 41:10, Apr., 1957
Cosmopolitan 142:22, Mar., 1957
Library Journal 82:974, Apr. 1, 1957
Life 42:54+, Apr. 1, 1957
National Parent-Teacher 51:38, Apr., 1957
New York Times p. 37, Mar. 21, 1957; II, p. 1, Mar.
   24, 1957
New Yorker 33:128, Mar. 30, 1957
Newsweek 49:109, Mar. 25, 1957
Saturday Review 40:25, Mar. 23, 1957
Senior Scholastic 70:35, Apr. 12, 1957
Time 69:100+, Mar. 18, 1957

Fearful Decision (see Ransom)

Fearless Fagan (1952)
National Parent-Teacher 47:36, Sep., 1952
Newsweek 40:86, Aug. 25, 1952
Saturday Review 35:26, Sep. 6, 1952
Time 60:78, Aug. 4, 1952

Feather in Her Hat (1935)
New York Times p. 24, Oct. 25, 1935

Federal Bullets (1937)
New York Times p. 11, Dec. 27, 1937

Federal Manhunt (1938)
New York Times p. 17, Feb. 2, 1939

Fedra, the Devil's Daughter (1957)
New York Times p. 19, Oct. 26, 1957

Feet First (1930)
Life (NY) 96:20, Nov. 28, 1930
New York Times p. 20, Oct. 31, 1930; IX, p. 5, Nov.
   9, 1930

Female (1933)
Canadian Magazine 80:38, Dec., 1933
Literary Digest 116:37, Nov. 18, 1933

Female (1933)
New York Times p. 18, Nov. 4, 1933; IX, p. 4, Nov.
12, 1933

Female Animal (1957)
Catholic World 186:465, Mar., 1958
New York Times p. 24, Jan. 23, 1958

Female Fugitive (1938)
New York Times p. 12, Apr. 11, 1938

Female on the Beach (1955)
America 93:519, Aug. 27, 1955
Commonweal 62:566, Sep. 9, 1955
National Parent-Teacher 50:39, Sep., 1955
New York Times p. 20, Aug. 20, 1955
Newsweek 46:67, Sep. 5, 1955
Time 66:108+, Sep. 19, 1955

Feminine Touch (1941)
Commonweal 35:125, Nov. 21, 1941
New York Times p. 35, Dec. 12, 1941; IX, p. 7, Dec.
14, 1941

Fernandel the Dressmaker (1957)
New York Times p. 19, Jul. 1, 1957

Ferry to Hong Kong (1961)
New York Times p. 27, Apr. 27, 1961

Fever in the Blood (1961)
New York Times p. 30, Apr. 20, 1961

Fiend Who Walked the West (1958)
Catholic World 188:63, Oct., 1958
Newsweek 52:77, Aug. 25, 1958
Time 72:96, Sep. 8, 1958

Fiend Without a Face (1957)
New York Times p. 15, Jul. 4, 1958

Fiercest Heart (1961)
New York Times p. 13, Aug. 3, 1961
Time 78:47, Aug. 25, 1961

Fiesta (1947)
Commonweal 46:333, Jul. 18, 1947
Cosmopolitan 122:64-5+, Jun., 1947

Fiesta (1947) (Continued)
New Republic 117:30, Jul. 7, 1947
New York Times I, p. 5, Jun. 22, 1947; p. 17, Jun. 27, 1947
New Yorker 23:66, Jun. 28, 1947
Newsweek 29:76, Jun. 30, 1947
Time 49:97, Jun. 30, 1947
Woman's Home Companion 74:10-11, Sep., 1947

15 Maiden Lane (1936)
New York Times p. 21, Oct. 17, 1936

Fifth Avenue Girl (1939)
Commonweal 30:439, Sep. 1, 1939
New Republic 100:132, Sep. 6, 1939
New York Times IX, p. 3, Jul. 9, 1939; p. 12, Aug. 25, 1939
Photoplay 53:65, Nov., 1939
Time 34:47, Aug. 28, 1939

Fifth Commandment (1932)
Nation 134:212, Feb. 17, 1932
New York Times p. 17, Jan. 20, 1932; VIII, p. 4, Jan. 24, 1932; p. 25, Feb. 4, 1932
Outlook 160:150, Feb. 3, 1932

Fifty Fathoms Deep (1931)
New York Times p. 10, Sep. 19, 1931

55 Days at Peking (1962)
America 109:26, Jul. 6, 1963
National Review 15:72, Jul. 30, 1963
New York Times II, p. 11, Dec. 9, 1962; p. 20, May 30, 1963
New Yorker 39:68, Jun. 1, 1963
Newsweek 61:83-4, Jun. 3, 1963
Time 81:80, May 31, 1963

Fifty Million Frenchmen (1931)
Life (NY) 97:20, Apr. 10, 1931
New York Times p. 31, Mar. 26, 1931

Fifty Roads to Town (1937)
New York Times p. 21, Jun. 5, 1937
Scholastic 30:28, Apr. 24, 1937
Time 29:46, Apr. 12, 1937

52nd Street (1937)
  Life 3:64-7, Nov. 29, 1937
  New York Times p. 15, Nov. 15, 1937; XI, p. 5, Nov.
    21, 1937
  Time 30:52, Nov. 22, 1937

Fight for Life (1940)
  Life 8:98-101, Mar. 18, 1940
  Magazine of Art 33:243-4, Apr., 1940
  Nation 150:372, Mar. 16, 1940
  New Republic 102:409, Mar. 25, 1940
  New York Times IX, p. 7, Dec. 17, 1939; p. 19, Mar.
    7, 1940; XI, p. 5, Mar. 10, 1940; IX, p. 4, Apr. 7,
    1940
  New Yorker 16:84, Mar. 9, 1940
  Scholastic 36:34, Apr. 1, 1940
  Time 35:92, Mar. 25, 1940

Fight for Peace (1938)
  Nation 146:595-6, May 21, 1938
  New York Times p. 18, May 14, 1938; X, p. 3, May 15,
    1938
  Scholastic 32:33, May 28, 1938
  Time 31:40, May 23, 1938; 34:40, Oct. 9, 1939

Fight for Your Lady (1937)
  New York Times p. 21, Nov. 20, 1937

Fighter (1952)
  Commonweal 56:291, Jun. 27, 1952
  Library Journal 77:970, Jun. 1, 1952
  Nation 174:410, Apr. 26, 1952
  New York Times p. 12, May 31, 1952
  Newsweek 39:103, May 12, 1952
  Saturday Review 35:25, May 17, 1952
  Theatre Arts 36:95, Jun., 1952
  Time 59:92+, Jun. 2, 1952

Fighter Squadron (1948)
  Commonweal 49:259, Dec. 17, 1948
  Good Housekeeping 128:111, Feb., 1949
  New York Times II, p. 4, Jun. 20, 1948; II, p. 4, Nov.
    14, 1948; p. 9, Nov. 20, 1948
  Newsweek 32:94+, Dec. 6, 1948
  Rotarian 74:35, Feb., 1949
  Time 52:107, Dec. 6, 1948

Fighting Caravans (1931)
Life (NY) 97:20, Feb. 20, 1931
Motion Picture 40:78, Dec., 1930; 40:36, Jan., 1931
New York Times p. 21, Jan. 26, 1931; VIII, p. 5, Feb.
1, 1931
Theatre Magazine 53:48, Mar., 1931

Fighting Coast Guard (1951)
Commonweal 54:214, Jun. 8, 1951
New York Times p. 14, Mar. 12, 1951

Fighting Father Dunne (1948)
Commonweal 48:235, Jun. 18, 1948
Life 23:6, Dec. 1, 1947; 24:15, Feb. 9, 1948
New York Times p. 26, Jun. 25, 1948
New Yorker 24:58, Jul. 3, 1948
Time 52:74, Aug. 2, 1948

Fighting for the Fatherland (1930)
New York Times p. 25, Jul. 15, 1929

Fighting Guardsman (1945)
New York Times p. 9, Oct. 6, 1945

Fighting Kentuckian (1949)
Commonweal 50:632, Oct. 7, 1949
New York Times p. 18, Sep. 19, 1949

Fighting Lady (1945)
Collier's 115:8+, Mar. 31, 1945
Commonweal 41:426, Feb. 9, 1945
Life 18:76-8, Mar. 5, 1945
New Republic 112:227, Feb. 12, 1945
New Yorker 20:55, Jan. 13, 1945
Newsweek 25:86, Jan. 22, 1945
Saturday Review 28:22-3, Jan. 27, 1945
Scholastic 46:27, Feb. 12, 1945
Theatre Arts 29:174+, Mar., 1945
Time 45:91, Jan. 22, 1945

Fighting Man of the Plains (1949)
New York Times p. 35, Nov. 17, 1949

Fighting O'Flynn (1948)
Commonweal 49:543, Mar. 11, 1949
New York Times II, p. 5, Feb. 16, 1949; p. 16, Feb.
28, 1949

Fighting O'Flynn (1948) (Continued)
Photoplay 34:16, Jan., 1949
Rotarian 74:34, May, 1949
Time 53:105, Feb. 21, 1949

Fighting Seabees (1943)
Commonweal 39:471, Feb. 25, 1944
Cosmopolitan 116:112, Apr., 1944
New York Times p. 14, Mar. 20, 1944; II, p. 3, Mar.
   26, 1944
Newsweek 23:80, Mar. 6, 1944
Scholastic 44:38, Mar. 27, 1944

Fighting 69th (1939)
Commonweal 31:348, Feb. 9, 1940
Life 8:32-4, Jan. 29, 1940
Nation 150:262, Feb. 17, 1940
New York Times p. 9, Jan. 27, 1940; IX, p. 5, Feb. 4,
   1940
Photoplay 54:62, Mar., 1940
Time 35:73, Feb. 12, 1940

Fighting Youth (1935)
New York Times p. 13, Nov. 2, 1935

*Film Without a Name
New York Times p. 32, Oct. 20, 1950
New Republic 123:22, Nov. 6, 1950
Saturday Review 38:30, Jan. 8, 1955

Final Edition (1932)
New York Times p. 23, Feb. 22, 1932

Final Hour (1936)
New York Times p. 16, Aug. 1, 1936

Final Test (1954)
America 90:610, Mar. 6, 1954
National Parent-Teacher 48:38, Apr., 1954
New York Times p. 21, Jan. 26, 1954
New Yorker 29:100, Feb. 6, 1954
Newsweek 43:77, Feb. 1, 1954
Saturday Review 37:29, Feb. 6, 1954
Time 63:102, Feb. 22, 1954

Finders Keepers (1928)
New York Times p. 21, Mar. 5, 1928

Finger Man (1955)
New York Times p. 12, Jul. 16, 1955

Finger of Guilt (1956)
National Parent-Teacher 51:39, Dec., 1956

Finger Points (1931)
Life (NY) 97:22, May 1, 1931
New York Times p. 15, Mar. 28, 1931; VIII, p. 5, Apr.
5, 1931
Outlook 157:539, Apr. 15, 1931

Fingers at the Window (1942)
New York Times p. 19, Apr. 17, 1942; p. 27, Apr. 23,
1942

Finishing School (1934)
New York Times p. 11, Apr. 30, 1934

Finn and Hattie (1931)
Life (NY) 97:18, Feb. 13, 1931
New York Times p. 15, Jan. 31, 1931; VIII, p. 5, Apr.
5, 1931
Photoplay 40:124, Nov., 1931

Fire Down Below (1957)
America 97:532, Aug. 24, 1957
Catholic World 185:304, Jul., 1957
Commonweal 66:542, Aug. 30, 1957
Library Journal 82:1665+, Jun. 15, 1957
National Parent-Teacher 51:37, Jun., 1957
New York Times II, p. 5, May 27, 1956; p. 11, Aug. 9,
1957
Newsweek 50:102-3, Jul. 15, 1957
Time 70:78, Jul. 22, 1957

Fire Over Africa (1954)
National Parent-Teacher 49:39, Dec., 1954
New York Times p. 29, Nov. 22, 1954

Fire Over England (1937)
Canadian Magazine 87:31, May, 1937
Life 2:46-9, Feb. 1, 1937
Literary Digest 123:24, Mar. 13, 1937
New York Times X, p. 4, Feb. 21, 1937; p. 16, Mar. 5,
1937; XI, p. 3, Mar. 14, 1937
Newsweek 9:22, Feb. 27, 1937

Fire Over England (1937) (Continued)
Photoplay 51:78, Jan., 1937
Scholastic 30:21, Apr. 3, 1937
Stage 14:58-9, Apr., 1937
Time 29:36+, Mar. 15, 1937

Fire Under Her Skin (1959)
New York Times p. 13, Jun. 28, 1958

Fireball (1950)
New York Times p. 35, Nov. 10, 1950
Newsweek 36:93, Oct. 16, 1950
Rotarian 78:38, Jan., 1951

Firebird (1934)
New York Times p. 25, Nov. 15, 1934

Fired Wife (1943)
New York Times p. 15, Oct. 1, 1943

Firefly (1937)
New York Times X, p. 4, Aug. 29, 1937; p. 17, Sep. 2,
1937; X, p. 3, Sep. 5, 1937
Saint Nicholas 64:37, Jul., 1937
Time 30:50, Aug. 23, 1937

Fireman, Save My Child (1932)
New York Times p. 33, Feb. 18, 1932

Fireman Save My Child (1954)
National Parent-Teacher 48:38, Jun., 1954
Newsweek 43:103, Apr. 26, 1954

Fires of Fate (1932)
New York Times p. 13, Apr. 3, 1933

First a Girl (1935)
Canadian Magazine 85:37, Feb., 1936
Literary Digest 120:22, Dec. 28, 1935
New York Times p. 19, Jan. 4, 1936
Time 27:43, Jan. 13, 1936

First Auto (1927)
Life (NY) 90:26, Aug. 4, 1927
New York Times p. 21, Jul. 2, 1927; VII, p. 3, Jul. 3,
1927

First Comes Courage (1943)
Commonweal 38:514, Sep. 10, 1943
New York Times p. 15, Sep. 3, 1943

First Front (1949)
New York Times p. 19, Nov. 14, 1949

First Hundred Years (1938)
New York Times p. 17, May 13, 1938

First Kiss (1928)
New York Times p. 21, Aug. 20, 1928

First Lady (1937)
New York Times p. 25, Dec. 23, 1937
Newsweek 10:30, Dec. 13, 1937
Scholastic 31:19E, Dec. 11, 1937
Time 30:24, Dec. 13, 1937

First Legion (1951)
Commonweal 54:117, May 11, 1951
Library Journal 76:59, Jan. 1, 1951
New Republic 124:23, May 14, 1951
New York Times p. 9, Apr. 28, 1951
Newsweek 37:89, May 7, 1951

First Love (1939)
New York Times IX, p. 4, Nov. 5, 1939; p. 27, Nov. 9,
    1939
Newsweek 14:33, Nov. 13, 1939
Photoplay 54:58, Jan., 1940
Scholastic 35:33, Nov. 20, 1939
Time 34:80, Nov. 20, 1939

First Mrs. Fraser (1932)
New York Times VIII, p. 4, May 29, 1932

First of the Few (1942)
New York Times IX, p. 3, Jul. 20, 1941; IX, p. 7, Dec.
    14, 1941

First Texan (1956)
National Parent-Teacher 51:38, Sep., 1956
New York Times p. 20, Jun. 23, 1956

First Time (1952)
Christian Century 69:839, Jul. 16, 1952

376

First Traveling Saleslady (1956)
American Magazine 162:6, Aug., 1956
National Parent-Teacher 51:38, Oct., 1956
Saturday Review 39:29, Aug. 18, 1956
Scholastic 69:41, Sep. 20, 1956

First World War (1934)
Literary Digest 118:28, Nov. 24, 1934
Nation 139:602, Nov. 21, 1934
New York Times IX, p. 4, Nov. 4, 1934; p. 27, Nov. 8, 1934; IX, p. 5, Nov. 11, 1934; IX, p. 5, Nov. 18, 1934
Newsweek 4:27, Nov. 17, 1934
Time 24:28-9, Nov. 19, 1934

First Yank into Tokyo (1945)
Commonweal 42:577, Sep. 28, 1945
New York Times II, p. 1, Feb. 11, 1945
Time 46:56, Sep. 24, 1945

First Year (1932)
New York Times p. 20, Aug. 22, 1932; IX, p. 3, Aug. 28, 1932

Fisherman's Wharf (1939)
New York Times IX, p. 7, Dec. 18, 1938; p. 15, Feb. 24, 1939
World Horizons 3:34-5, Apr., 1939

Fit for a King (1937)
New York Times p. 18, Oct. 15, 1937

Five (1951)
Christian Century 68:751, Jun. 20, 1951
Commonweal 54:143, May 18, 1951
New Republic 124:23, May 14, 1951
New York Times II, p. 4, Dec. 31, 1950; p. 34, Apr. 26, 1951; II, p. 1, Apr. 29, 1951
New Yorker 27:68, May 5, 1951
Newsweek 37:90, May 7, 1951
Saturday Review 34:26, May 5, 1951
Time 57:120, May 21, 1951

Five Against the House (1955)
Catholic World 181:143, May, 1955
Commonweal 62:279, Jun. 17, 1955
National Parent-Teacher 49:39, May, 1955
New York Times p. 8, Jun. 11, 1955

Five Against the House (1955) (Continued)
New Yorker 31:65, Jun. 18, 1955
Newsweek 45:88+, Jun. 27, 1955
Time 65:91, Jun. 20, 1955

Five and Ten (1931)
New York Times p. 7, Jul. 11, 1931; VIII, p. 3, Jul. 19, 1931

Five Branded Women (1960)
New York Times p. 27, Jun. 2, 1960
Time 75:88, May 9, 1960

Five Came Back (1939)
New York Times p. 20, Jul. 5, 1939; IX, p. 3, Jul. 9, 1939
Time 33:45, Jun. 26, 1939

Five-Day Lover (1961)
Commonweal 75:366, Dec. 29, 1961
New Republic 146:20+, Jan. 1, 1962
New York Times p. 55, Dec. 14, 1961
New Yorker 37:111-12, Dec. 16, 1961
Saturday Review 44:27, Sep. 2, 1961
Time 78:66, Nov. 24, 1961

Five Finger Exercise (1962)
America 107:212, May 5, 1962
Commonweal 76:114, Apr. 27, 1962
New Republic 146:28-9, Apr. 16, 1962
New York Times II, p. 7, Aug. 13, 1961; p. 20, Apr. 20, 1962; II, p. 1, Apr. 22, 1962
New Yorker 38:141, Apr. 28, 1962
Newsweek 59:99, Apr. 30, 1962
Saturday Review 45:37, Apr. 28, 1962
Time 79:87, Apr. 27, 1962

Five Fingers (1952)
Catholic World 175:62, Apr., 1952
Christian Century 69:543, Apr. 30, 1952
Holiday 11:6+, May, 1952
Library Journal 77:522, Mar. 15, 1952
Life 32:139-40+, Apr. 7, 1952
New Republic 126:22, Mar. 10, 1952
New York Times p. 7, Feb. 23, 1952; II, p. 1, Mar. 2, 1952
New Yorker 28:76, Mar. 1, 1952

Five Fingers (1952) (Continued)
Newsweek 39:90-1, Mar. 3, 1952
Saturday Review 35:32-3, Mar. 8, 1952
Theatre Arts 36:41, Apr., 1952
Time 59:100+, Mar. 10, 1952

Five from Barska Street (1955)
New York Times p. 29, Mar. 14, 1955

Five Gates to Hell (1959)
New York Times p. 51, Dec. 10, 1959

Five Golden Hours (1961)
New York Times p. 39, Oct. 19, 1961
Saturday Review 44:36, Jun. 3, 1961

Five Graves to Cairo (1943)
Commonweal 38:203, Jun. 11, 1943
Life 14:47-8+, Jun. 14, 1943
New York Times p. 21, May 27, 1943; II, p. 3, May 30, 1943
New Yorker 19:48, Jun. 5, 1943
Newsweek 21:87-8, May 31, 1943
Time 41:98, May 24, 1943

Five Miles to Midnight (1963)
America 108:590, Apr. 20, 1963
Commonweal 77:599, Mar. 1, 1963
New York Times II, p. 7, Feb. 25, 1962; p. 8, Mar. 21, 1963
Newsweek 61:99, Mar. 11, 1963
Saturday Review 46:82, Mar. 16, 1963
Time 81:M29, Apr. 12, 1963

Five of a Kind (1938)
New York Times p. 12, Oct. 31, 1938
Time 32:26+, Oct. 31, 1938

Five Pennies (1959)
America 101:458, Jun. 20, 1959
Catholic World 189:316-17, Jul., 1959
Commonweal 70:327-8, Jun. 26, 1959
Coronet 46:18, Aug., 1959
Good Housekeeping 148:24, Jun., 1959
Life 46:106, May 25, 1959
New York Times p. 30, Jun. 19, 1959
New Yorker 35:54, Jun. 27, 1959
Time 74:66, Aug. 3, 1959

Five Star Final (1932)
Life (NY) 98:18, Oct. 2, 1931
New York Times p. 24, Sep. 11, 1931; VIII, p. 5, Sep. 20, 1931

Five Steps to Danger (1957)
National Parent-Teacher 51:39, Mar., 1957
New York Times p. 21, Jan. 31, 1957

5000 Fingers of Dr. T (1953)
America 89:345, Jun. 27, 1953
American Photographer 47:8, May, 1953
Commonweal 58:322, Jul. 3, 1953
Farm Journal 77:107, Aug., 1953
Musical America 73:9, May, 1953
National Parent-Teacher 47:26, Mar., 1953
New York Times p. 8, Jun. 20, 1953; II, p. 1, Jun. 28, 1953
New Yorker 29:58, Jun. 27, 1953
Newsweek 41:100-1, Jun. 15, 1953
Photography 33:98+, Jul., 1953
Saturday Review 36:30, Jun. 13, 1953
Theatre Arts 37:82, May, 1953
Time 61:84, Jun. 22, 1953

Five Weeks in a Baloon (1962)
Commonweal 77:18, Sep. 28, 1962
New York Times p. 18, Aug. 27, 1962
Newsweek 60:70-1, Sep. 3, 1962
Time 80:66, Aug. 31, 1962

*Five-Year Plan
Commonweal 14:159-60, Jun. 10, 1931
Nation 132:687, Jun. 24, 1931
New York Times p. 35, Jun. 2, 1931
Outlook 158:181, Jun. 10, 1931

Fixed Bayonets (1951)
Christian Century 69:31, Jan. 2, 1952
Commonweal 55:255, Dec. 14, 1951
Holiday 11:19, Mar., 1952
Library Journal 77:44, Jan. 1, 1952
Nation 174:18, Jan. 5, 1952
New York Times p. 20, Nov. 21, 1951
Newsweek 38:94, Dec. 3, 1951

Fixer Dugan (1939)
New York Times p. 21, May 6, 1939

Flame (1947)
New York Times p. 19, Feb. 20, 1948

Flame and the Arrow (1950)
Christian Century 67:1007, Aug. 23, 1950
Commonweal 52:392, Jul. 28, 1950
Life 29:51, Aug. 14, 1950
New York Times p. 7, Jul. 8, 1950; II, p. 1, Jul. 16, 1950
New Yorker 26:63, Jul. 15, 1950
Rotarian 77:35, Oct., 1950
Time 56:65, Jul. 31, 1950

Flame and the Flesh (1954)
America 91:203, May 15, 1954
Commonweal 60:176, May 21, 1954
Library Journal 79:953, May 15, 1954
New York Times p. 21, May 3, 1954; II, p. 1, May 9, 1954
Newsweek 43:102, May 10, 1954
Saturday Review 37:23, May 29, 1954
Time 63:106, May 24, 1954

Flame in the Streets (1962)
New York Times p. 32, Sep. 13, 1962
Newsweek 60:92, Sep. 24, 1962
Time 80:103, Sep. 14, 1962

Flame of Araby (1952)
New York Times p. 41, Dec. 20, 1951

Flame of Barbary Coast (1945)
New York Times p. 22, May 28, 1945
Newsweek 25:112, Jun. 11, 1945

Flame of New Orleans (1941)
Commonweal 34:86, May 16, 1941
New York Times IX, p. 5, Jan. 19, 1941; p. 20, Apr. 26, 1941
Newsweek 17:66, May 5, 1941
Scribner's Commentator 10:106, Jul., 1941
Time 37:54, May 12, 1941

Flame of the Islands (1955)
National Parent-Teacher 50:39, Feb., 1956
New York Times p. 12, Feb. 25, 1956

Flame Over India (1960)
America 103:265, May 14, 1960
Commonweal 72:257, Jun. 3, 1960
New York Times p. 14, Apr. 30, 1960
Newsweek 55:112, May 9, 1960
Time 75:87, May 16, 1960

Flame Within (1935)
New York Times p. 18, Jun. 1, 1935

Flaming Star (1960)
Commonweal 73:414, Jan. 13, 1961
New York Times p. 19, Dec. 17, 1960
Saturday Review 44:32, Jan. 7, 1961
Senior Scholastic 78:54, Feb. 8, 1961

Flamingo Road (1949)
Commonweal 50:69, Apr. 29, 1949
Good Housekeeping 128:10-11, Jun., 1949
New Republic 120:22, May 16, 1949
New York Times II, p. 5, Sep. 19, 1948; p. 10, May 7,
    1949; II, p. 1, May 8, 1949
Newsweek 33:84, May 16, 1949
Photoplay 36:30, Jun., 1949
Rotarian 75:36, Jul., 1949
Time 53:90, May 2, 1949
Woman's Home Companion 76:10-11, Jun., 1949

Flat Top (1952)
New York Times p. 17, Dec. 6, 1952

Flash Gordon's Trip to Mars (see Mars Attacks the World)

Flaxy Martin (1949)
Newsweek 33:92, Mar. 7, 1949
Photoplay 34:22, Apr., 1949
Rotarian 74:36, Apr., 1949
Time 53:92+, Feb. 14, 1949

*Fleet That Came to Stay
New York Times
Newsweek 26:85, Jul. 30, 1945
Time 46:94, Aug. 13, 1945

Fleet's In (1942)
Commonweal 35:562, Mar. 27, 1942
New York Times p. 24, Mar. 12, 1942; VIII, p. 3, Mar.
    22, 1942

Fleet's In (1942) (Continued)
Newsweek 19:58, Mar. 23, 1942
Time 39:74, Mar. 23, 1942

Flesh (1932)
New York Times p. 19, Dec. 10, 1932

Flesh and Fantasy (1943)
Commonweal 39:144, Nov. 26, 1943
Life 15:69-70+, Oct. 25, 1943
New Republic 109:622, Nov. 1, 1943
New York Times VIII, p. 3, Nov. 29, 1942; p. 29, Nov. 18, 1943
Newsweek 22:89-90, Nov. 1, 1943
Photoplay 24:22, Dec., 1943
Scholastic 43:31, Dec. 6, 1943
Time 42:56, Nov. 1, 1943

Flesh and Fury (1952)
Christian Century 69:631, May 21, 1952
Commonweal 56:117, May 9, 1952
New York Times p. 27, Mar. 28, 1952

Flesh is Weak (1958)
New York Times p. 31, Nov. 9, 1957

Flight (1929)
Canadian Forum 10:273, May, 1930
Life (NY) 94:28, Oct. 18, 1929
New York Times p. 17, Sep. 14, 1929
Outlook 153:193, Oct. 2, 1929

Flight at Midnight (1939)
New York Times p. 29, Sep. 7, 1939

Flight Command (1940)
Commonweal 33:352, Jan. 24, 1941
New Republic 104:307, Mar. 3, 1941
New York Times IX, p. 3, Oct. 6, 1940; p. 21, Jan. 17, 1941
Newsweek 17:52, Jan. 6, 1941
Photoplay 18:6, Mar., 1941

Flight Commander (see Dawn Patrol)

Flight for Freedom (1943)
Commonweal 37:643, Apr. 16, 1943

Flight for Freedom (1943) (Continued)
Cosmopolitan 114:76, Apr., 1943
New York Times p. 24, Apr. 16, 1943
New Yorker 19:41, Apr. 17, 1943
Newsweek 21:74, Apr. 19, 1943
Photoplay 22:22, May, 1943
Time 41:56, Apr. 5, 1943

Flight from Destiny (1941)
Commonweal 33:424, Feb. 14, 1941
New York Times p. 26, Mar. 28, 1941
Newsweek 17:63, Jan. 20, 1941
Photoplay 18:6, Mar., 1941
Time 37:78, Jan. 20, 1941

Flight from Glory (1937)
New York Times p. 20, Sep. 11, 1937

Flight into France (1949)
New York Times p. 16, Jul. 22, 1949
New Yorker 25:63, Jul. 30, 1949

Flight into Nowhere (1938)
New York Times p. 13, May 2, 1938

Flight Nurse (1953)
National Parent-Teacher 48:39, Jan., 1954
New York Times p. 9, Jan. 30, 1954

Flight of the Lost Baloon (1962)
New York Times p. 29, May 24, 1962

Flight to Hong Kong (1956)
National Parent-Teacher 51:39, Dec., 1956
New York Times p. 28, Jan. 3, 1957

Flight to Tangier (1953)
National Parent-Teacher 48:39, Dec., 1953
New York Times p. 50, Nov. 26, 1953
Newsweek 42:107, Nov. 16, 1953

Flipper (1962)
New York Times p. 23, Sep. 19, 1963

Flirtation Walk (1934)
New York Times p. 33, Nov. 29, 1934; X, p. 4, Dec. 2,
1934
Time 24:28, Dec. 10, 1934

Flirting Widow (1930)
New York Times p. 16, Aug. 2, 1930

Flirting with Fate (1938)
New York Times p. 35, Dec. 15, 1938

Flood (1931)
New York Times p. 25, Apr. 27, 1931

Flood Tide (1958)
National Parent-Teacher 52:38, Jan., 1958

Floods of Fear (1959)
Commonweal 70:206, May 22, 1959
Library Journal 84:1593, May 15, 1959

Floradora Girl (1930)
Life (NY) 95:20, Jun. 20, 1930
New York Times p. 19, May 31, 1930; VIII, p. 5, Jun.
    1, 1930; IX, p. 5, Jun. 8, 1930; VIII, p. 6, Jun. 15,
    1930
Outlook 155:229, Jun. 11, 1930

Florentine Dagger (1935)
New York Times p. 20, Apr. 27, 1935

Florian (1940)
Commonweal 31:555, Apr. 19, 1940
Etude 58:157, Mar., 1940
New York Times p. 33, Jun. 6, 1940
Newsweek 15:30+, Apr. 15, 1940

Flower Drum Song (1961)
America 106:375, Dec. 9, 1961
Commonweal 75:259, Dec. 1, 1961
New York Times II, p. 9, Apr. 30, 1961; p. 40, Nov. 10,
    1961; II, p. 1, Nov. 19, 1961
New Yorker 37:207, Nov. 18, 1961
Newsweek 58:89, Nov. 27, 1961
Time 78:66, Nov. 24, 1961

Flowers of St. Francis (1953)
Catholic World 176:224, Dec., 1952
Commonweal 57:101-2, Oct. 31, 1952
New York Times p. 26, Oct. 7, 1952
New Yorker 28:152, Oct. 18, 1952
Newsweek 40:122+, Oct. 20, 1952
Time 60:102+, Oct. 6, 1952

Flowing Gold (1940)
Commonweal 32:429, Sep. 13, 1940
New York Times p. 19, Sep. 2, 1940
Time 36:75, Sep. 23, 1940

Flute and the Arrow (1960)
New York Times p. 55, Oct. 11, 1960

Flute Concert of Sans Souci (1931)
New York Times p. 17, Dec. 20, 1930; VIII, p. 6, Feb.
8, 1931; p. 20, Oct. 17, 1931

Fly (1958)
America 99:537, Aug. 23, 1958
Commonweal 68:472, Aug. 8, 1958
New York Times p. 6, Aug. 30, 1958

Fly Away Baby (1937)
New York Times p. 18, Jul. 9, 1937

Flying Cadets (1941)
New York Times p. 29, Oct. 14, 1941

Flying Carpet (1960)
New York Times p. 31, Feb. 29, 1960

Flying Deuces (1939)
New York Times IX, p. 4, Sep. 24, 1939; p. 29, Nov.
24, 1939

Flying Devils (1933)
New York Times p. 14, Aug. 26, 1933

Flying Down to Rio (1933)
Movie Classic 5:38-9, Jan., 1934
New York Times p. 25, Dec. 22, 1933
Newsweek 2:31, Dec. 30, 1933
Vanity Fair 41:46, Feb., 1934

Flying Fleet (1929)
Life (NY) 93:25, Mar. 8, 1929
New York Times p. 26, Feb. 11, 1929; IX, p. 7, Feb.
17, 1929
Outlook 151:344, Feb. 27, 1929

Flying Fontaines (1959)
New York Times p. 13, Dec. 24, 1959
Senior Scholastic 76:59, Feb. 10, 1960

Flying Fortress (1942)
New York Times p. 22, Dec. 19, 1942

Flying High (1931)
New York Times p. 23, Dec. 12, 1931; VIII, p. 4, Dec.
20, 1931

Flying Hostess (1936)
Literary Digest 122:22+, Nov. 23, 1936
New York Times p. 29, Dec. 14, 1936

Flying Irishman (1939)
New York Times p. 27, Apr. 12, 1939
Newsweek 13:29, Mar. 27, 1939
Photoplay 53:62, May, 1939
Time 33:67, Mar. 27, 1939

Flying Leathernecks (1951)
Christian Century 68:1111, Sep. 26, 1951
Commonweal 55:94, Nov. 2, 1951
New York Times p. 37, Sep. 20, 1951
Time 58:114+, Oct. 8, 1951

Flying Missile (1951)
Commonweal 53:376, Jan. 19, 1951
New York Times p. 25, Dec. 25, 1950
Newsweek 37:82, Jan. 15, 1951
Scholastic 57:30, Jan. 10, 1951
Time 57:80, Jan. 15, 1951

Flying Saucer (1950)
New York Times p. 28, Jan. 5, 1950

Flying Tigers (1942)
New York Times VIII, p. 3, Jun. 14, 1942; p. 25, Oct.
23, 1942
Newsweek 20:72, Oct. 5, 1942
Photoplay 21:47-8+, Sep., 1942; 22:6, Dec., 1942
Time 40:96+, Oct. 12, 1942

Flying Wild (1941)
New York Times p. 19, Apr. 12, 1941

Flying with Music (1942)
New York Times VIII, p. 3, Jul. 5, 1942

Fog Over Frisco (1934)
New York Times p. 26, Jun. 7, 1934

Follies Bergere (1935)
New York Times X, p. 5, Jan. 20, 1935; p. 13, Feb. 25,
1935

Follies Bergere (1958)
New York Times p. 37, May 28, 1958

*Follow a Star
New York Times p. 34, Apr. 26, 1961
New Yorker 37:159, May 6, 1961
Time 77:78, May 12, 1961

Follow Me Quietly (1949)
New York Times p. 14, Jul. 8, 1949

Follow That Dream (1962)
Commonweal 76:114+, Apr. 27, 1962
New York Times p. 17, Aug. 9, 1962
Newsweek 59:111, May 14, 1962
Time 79:65, May 4, 1962

Follow the Boys (1944)
Commonweal 40:17, Apr. 21, 1944
Cosmopolitan 116:102, May, 1944
New York Times II, p. 3, Apr. 2, 1944; p. 24, Apr. 26,
1944
New Yorker 20:50+, Apr. 29, 1944
Newsweek 23:93, May 1, 1944
Photoplay 25:19, Jun., 1944
Time 43:94, Apr. 24, 1944

Follow the Fleet (1936)
Canadian Magazine 85:57, Apr., 1936
Literary Digest 121:20, Feb. 29, 1936
New York Times p. 21, Feb. 21, 1936
Time 27:26, Mar. 2, 1936

Follow the Leader (1930)
New York Times p. 21, Dec. 6, 1930; IX, p. 4, Dec. 14,
1930

Follow the Sun (1951)
Christian Century 68:879, Jul. 25, 1951
Commonweal 54:117, May 11, 1951
Library Journal 76:608, Apr. 1, 1951
New York Times p. 34, Apr. 26, 1951
Newsweek 37:105, Apr. 16, 1951

Follow the Sun (1951) (Continued)
  Scholastic 58:31, Apr. 4, 1951
  Time 57:106+, Apr. 30, 1951

Follow Thru (1930)
  Life (NY) 96:20, Oct. 3, 1930
  New York Times p. 9, Sep. 13, 1930; IX, p. 5, Sep. 21,
    1930

Follow Your Heart (1936)
  Commonweal 24:428, Aug. 28, 1936
  New York Times p. 31, Oct. 22, 1936
  Time 28:31, Sep. 14, 1936

Folly to be Wise (1952)
  New York Times p. 17, Dec. 28, 1953
  New Yorker 29:73, Jan. 9, 1954
  Time 63:100, Jan. 18, 1954

Fools for Scandal (1938)
  New York Times p. 15, Mar. 25, 1938
  Newsweek 11:24, Apr. 4, 1938
  Stage 15:26, May, 1938
  Time 31:29, Apr. 4, 1938

Footlight Parade (1933)
  Literary Digest 116:31, Oct. 21, 1933
  New Outlook 162:43, Nov., 1933
  New York Times p. 21, Oct. 6, 1933; IX, p. 3, Oct. 15,
    1933

Footlight Serenade (1942)
  Commonweal 36:400, Aug. 14, 1942
  New York Times p. 30, Sep. 10, 1942
  Newsweek 20:54, Aug. 10, 1942

Footlights and Fools (1929)
  New York Times p. 22, Nov. 9, 1929

Footloose Heiress (1937)
  New York Times p. 16, Oct. 9, 1937

Footsteps in the Dark (1941)
  Commonweal 33:520, Mar. 14, 1941
  New York Times p. 13, Mar. 15, 1941
  Scholastic 38:46, Mar. 24, 1941

Footsteps in the Fog (1955)
   Commonweal 62:647, Sep. 30, 1955
   Library Journal 80:2080, Oct. 1, 1955
   National Parent-Teacher 50:39, Sep., 1955
   New York Times p. 39, Sep. 15, 1955
   Time 66:111+, Sep. 19, 1955

For Freedom (1940)
   New York Times IX, p. 5, Mar. 31, 1940

For Heaven's Sake (1950)
   Christian Century 68:95, Jan. 17, 1951
   Good Housekeeping 131:254, Dec., 1950
   Library Journal 75:2163, Dec. 15, 1950
   New York Times p. 10, Dec. 16, 1950; II, p. 3, Dec.
      24, 1950
   New Yorker 26:52, Dec. 23, 1950
   Newsweek 36:92+, Dec. 11, 1950
   Rotarian 78:36, Mar., 1951
   Scholastic 57:24, Jan. 3, 1951
   Time 56:92, Dec. 18, 1950

For Love or Money (1962)
   New York Times p. 19, Aug. 8, 1963

For Me and My Gal (1942)
   Commonweal 37:72-3, Nov. 6, 1942
   Good Housekeeping 115:2, Nov., 1942
   New York Times p. 25, Oct. 22, 1942; VIII, p. 3, Oct.
      25, 1942
   Newsweek 20:75, Oct. 26, 1942
   Time 40:98, Nov. 16, 1942
   Woman's Home Companion 69:2, Nov., 1942

For Men Only (1951)
   Commonweal 55:472, Feb. 15, 1952
   New York Times p. 21, Jan. 16, 1952
   Newsweek 39:90, Jan. 28, 1952

For the Defense (1930)
   Life (NY) 96:17, Aug. 8, 1930
   New York Times p. 7, Jul. 19, 1930; VIII, p. 3, Jul.
      27, 1930

For the First Time (1959)
   America 101:619, Aug. 15, 1959
   Commonweal 70:471, Sep. 4, 1959

For the First Time (1959) (Continued)
New York Times II, p. 7, Nov. 9, 1958; p. 8, Aug. 15,
1959
Newsweek 54:83, Aug. 24, 1959
Time 74:46, Aug. 31, 1959

For the Love of Mary (1948)
Commonweal 48:572, Sep. 24, 1948
New York Times p. 37, Sep. 23, 1948
Newsweek 32:101, Sep. 20, 1948
Time 52:106, Oct. 11, 1948

For Them That Trespass (1950)
New Republic 123:23, Oct. 23, 1950
New York Times p. 37, Sep. 27, 1950

For Whom the Bell Tolls (1943)
Atlantic 172:109+, Dec., 1943
Catholic World 157:637, Sep., 1943
Commonweal 38:371-2, Jul. 30, 1943
Cosmopolitan 115:84, Oct., 1943
Life 10:52-7, Jan. 6, 1941; 15:96-7, Jul. 26, 1943
Nation 155:668, Dec. 19, 1942; 157:108, Jul. 24, 1943
New Republic 109:77, Jul. 19, 1943
New York Times IX, p. 3, Aug. 24, 1941; IX, p. 3, Sep.
14, 1941; VIII, p. 3, Sep. 6, 1942; VIII, p. 35, Sep.
20, 1942; VIII, p. 5, Oct. 18, 1942; II, p. 3, Feb. 14,
1943; II, p. 3, May 30, 1943; II, p. 3, Jul. 4, 1943;
p. 25, Jul. 15, 1943; II, p. 3, Jul. 18, 1943; VI, p.
15, Dec. 16, 1945
Newsweek 22:66+, Jul. 26, 1943
Photoplay 23:34-5, Aug., 1943; 23:26, Oct., 1943
Saturday Review 26:18, Jul. 31, 1943
Theatre Arts 27:568, Oct., 1943
Time 42:55-6+, Aug. 2, 1943
Vogue 101:65, Feb. 15, 1943

Forbidden (1932)
New York Times p. 28, Jan. 11, 1932
Outlook 160:87, Jan. 20, 1932

Forbidden (1954)
National Parent-Teacher 48:39, Feb., 1954
New York Times p. 11, Jan. 23, 1954
Newsweek 43:81, Jan. 11, 1954
Time 63:114, Mar. 22, 1954

Forbidden Fruit (1959)
Nation 188:284, Mar. 28, 1959
New Republic 140:21, Mar. 23, 1959
New York Times p. 19, Feb. 23, 1959
New Yorker 35:92, Mar. 7, 1959

Forbidden Games (1953)
American Photographer 47:15, Mar., 1953
Catholic World 176:385-6, Feb., 1953
Christian Century 70:271, Mar. 4, 1953
Commonweal 57:260, Dec. 12, 1952
Life 34:41-4, Jan. 12, 1953
Nation 175:586, Dec. 20, 1952
National Parent-Teacher 47:37, Dec., 1952
New Republic 128:21-3, Feb. 9, 1953
New York Times p. 43, Dec. 9, 1952; II, p. 3, Dec. 14,
    1952
New Yorker 28:118, Oct. 25, 1952; 28:152, Dec. 13, 1952
Newsweek 40:72-3, Dec. 22, 1952
Saturday Review 35:43, Dec. 6, 1952
Theatre Arts 37:82-3, Feb., 1953
Time 60:100+, Dec. 8, 1952

Forbidden Love (1928)
New York Times p. 20, Jan. 14, 1929

Forbidden Music (1938)
New York Times p. 13, Dec. 27, 1938

Forbidden Planet (1956)
America 94:724, Mar. 31, 1956
National Parent-Teacher 50:39, May, 1956
New York Times p. 21, May 4, 1956; II, p. 1, May 6,
    1956
New Yorker 32:171, May 12, 1956
Newsweek 47:98, Jun. 4, 1956
Saturday Review 39:23, Apr. 7, 1956
Scholastic 68:29, Apr. 26, 1956
Time 67:112+, Apr. 9, 1956

Forbidden Street (1948)
New York Times p. 9, May 14, 1949
Newsweek 33:83, May 30, 1949
Rotarian 75:38, Oct., 1949
Time 53:82, May 30, 1949

Force of Arms (1951)
Commonweal 54:501, Aug. 31, 1951

Force of Arms (1951) (Continued)
Nation 173:218, Sep. 15, 1951
New York Times p. 20, Aug. 14, 1951
New Yorker 27:67, Aug. 25, 1951
Newsweek 38:72, Sep. 3, 1951
Saturday Review 34:36+, Sep. 8, 1951
Time 58:100, Sep. 10, 1951

Force of Evil (1949)
Good Housekeeping 128:11+, Jan., 1949
New Republic 120:23, Jan. 10, 1949
New York Times p. 16, Dec. 27, 1948
Newsweek 33:57, Jan. 3, 1949
Time 53:84, Jan. 10, 1949

Foreign Affair (1948)
Canadian Forum 28:137, Sep., 1948
Commonweal 48:401, Aug. 6, 1948
Cosmopolitan 125:13+, Aug., 1948
Independent Woman 28:40+, Feb., 1949
Life 25:59-60, Aug. 9, 1948
New Republic 119:29, Jul. 12, 1948
New York Times p. 19, Jul. 1, 1948; II, p. 1, Jul. 4, 1948
New Yorker 24:39, Jul. 10, 1948
Newsweek 32:82, Jul. 12, 1948
Time 52:65-6, Jul. 26, 1948
Woman's Home Companion 75:10-11, Sep., 1948

Foreign Correspondent (1940)
American Mercury 51:358-62, Nov., 1940
Christian Century 57:1284-5, Oct. 16, 1940
Commonweal 32:390, Aug. 30, 1940
Life 9:42-5, Aug. 26, 1940
New Republic 103:385-6, Sep. 16, 1940
New York Times IX, p. 5, Apr. 14, 1940; IX, p. 5, Apr. 28, 1940; p. 15, Aug. 28, 1940; IX, p. 3, Sep. 1, 1940
New Yorker 16:51, Aug. 31, 1940
Newsweek 16:49, Aug. 26, 1940
Photoplay 54:66, Oct., 1940
Scholastic 37:38, Sep. 16, 1940
Theatre Arts 24:727, Oct., 1940; 25:628, Sep., 1941; 33:37, May, 1949
Time 36:31, Sep. 2, 1940

Foreign Intrigue (1956)
America 95:432, Aug. 4, 1956

Foreign Intrigue (1956) (Continued)
Catholic World 183:306, Jul., 1956
National Parent-Teacher 51:39, Sep., 1956
New York Times p. 23, Jul. 13, 1956
New Yorker 32:44, Jul. 21, 1956
Newsweek 48:88, Aug. 6, 1956
Saturday Review 39:47, May 19, 1956
Time 68:74, Aug. 13, 1956

Foreign Legion (1929)
New York Times p. 27, Jun. 25, 1928

Forest People of Siberia (1929)
New York Times p. 24, Oct. 8, 1929

Forest Rangers (1942)
Commonweal 36:594, Oct. 9, 1942
Cosmopolitan 113:68, Nov., 1942
New York Times p. 25, Oct. 22, 1942; VIII, p. 3, Oct.
25, 1942
Time 40:97, Nov. 2, 1942

Forever Amber (1947)
Commonweal 47:71, Oct. 31, 1947
Life 23:66-8+, Nov. 3, 1947; 24:56, Feb. 23, 1948
New Republic 117:36, Oct. 27, 1947
New York Times II, p. 1, Mar. 10, 1946; II, p. 3, Jul.
14, 1946; VI, p. 12, Aug. 4, 1946; II, p. 1, Nov. 3,
1946; II, p. 5, Feb. 9, 1947; VI, p. 12, Jul. 20, 1947;
II, p. 5, Oct. 19, 1947; p. 31, Oct. 23, 1947; II, p.
1, Oct. 26, 1947; p. 33, Dec. 5, 1947
New Yorker 23:95, Oct. 25, 1947
Newsweek 30:87, Nov. 3, 1947
Photoplay 31:38-41+, Jun., 1947; 32:26, Jan., 1948
Time 50:99, Nov. 3, 1947; 50:79, Dec. 22, 1947
Woman's Home Companion 75:8, Jan., 1948

Forever and a Day (1943)
Commonweal 37:544, Mar. 19, 1943
New York Times VIII, p. 3, Jul. 19, 1942; p. 9, Mar.
13, 1943
Newsweek 21:65, Mar. 29, 1943
Photoplay 22:62, Apr., 1943
Scholastic 42:32, Apr. 5, 1943
Time 41:40, Mar. 29, 1943

Forever, Darling (1956)
Look 19:57-8+, Nov. 15, 1955

Forever, Darling (1956) (Continued)
National Parent-Teacher 50:38, Mar., 1956
New York Times p. 18, Feb. 10, 1956
New Yorker 31:126, Feb. 18, 1956
Newsweek 47:100+, Feb. 13, 1956
Scholastic 68:39, Feb. 9, 1956
Time 67:116, Mar. 12, 1956

Forever Female (1953)
America 90:427, Jan. 23, 1954
Farm Journal 77:98, Oct., 1953
National Parent-Teacher 48:39, Jan., 1954
New York Times p. 26, Jan. 14, 1954
New Yorker 29:82, Jan. 23, 1954
Newsweek 43:91, Jan. 25, 1954
Saturday Review 37:28, Feb. 6, 1954
Scholastic 64:30, Feb. 17, 1954

Forever My Love (1962)
New York Times p. 36, May 28, 1962

Forever Yours (1937)
New York Times p. 22, Jun. 7, 1937
Time 29:55, May 24, 1937

Forgotten Commandments (1932)
Nation 134:708, Jun. 22, 1932
New York Times p. 25, Jun. 2, 1932

Forgotten Faces (1936)
New York Times p. 18, Jul. 4, 1936

Forgotten Men (1933)
New Republic 75:127, Jun. 14, 1933
New York Times p. 16, May 15, 1933; IX, p. 3, May 28,
    1933
Newsweek 1:31, May 20, 1933

Forgotten Village (1941)
Commonweal 35:198-9, Dec. 12, 1941
New Republic 105:763, Dec. 8, 1941
New York Times IX, p. 5, Jan. 26, 1941; IX, p. 4, Mar.
    23, 1941; p. 26, Nov. 19, 1941; p. 26, Nov. 20, 1941;
    IX, p. 5, Nov. 23, 1941
New Yorker 17:91, Nov. 29, 1941
Newsweek 18:70, Dec. 1, 1941
Saturday Review 35:58, Apr. 12, 1952

Forgotten Village (1941) (Continued)
Theatre Arts 25:336-43, May, 1941; 25:883, Dec., 1941
Time 38:96, Dec. 8, 1941

Forgotten Woman (1939)
New York Times p. 11, Aug. 4, 1939

Forsaking All Others (1934)
New Republic 82:132, Mar. 13, 1935
New York Times p. 18, Dec. 26, 1934
Time 25:55, Jan. 7, 1935

Fort Apache (1948)
Life 24:6, Mar. 22, 1948
Nation 167:109, Jul. 24, 1948
New Republic 119:29, Jul. 12, 1948
New York Times p. 26, Jun. 25, 1948; II, p. 1, Jun. 27,
1948
New Yorker 24:58, Jul. 3, 1948
Newsweek 31:95, May 17, 1948
Time 51:102+, May 10, 1948

Fort Dobbs (1958)
New York Times p. 10, Apr. 19, 1958

Fort Ti (1953)
America 89:366, Jul. 4, 1953
New York Times p. 7, May 30, 1953
Saturday Review 36:36, Jul. 11, 1953

Fort Worth (1951)
Commonweal 54:407, Aug. 3, 1951
New York Times p. 12, Jul. 13, 1951

Fort Yuma (1955)
National Parent-Teacher 50:39, Dec., 1955

Fortunes of Captain Blood (1950)
Christian Century 67:935, Aug. 2, 1950
Library Journal 75:992, Jun. 1, 1950
New York Times p. 11, Jun. 10, 1950

48 Hours (1944)
Commonweal 40:302, Jul. 14, 1944
Nation 159:81, Jul. 15, 1944
New Republic 111:44, Jul. 10, 1944
New York Times p. 21, Jun. 26, 1944

48 Hours (1944) (Continued)
Newsweek 24:83, Jul. 31, 1944
Time 44:96, Jul. 10, 1944

Forty-First (1959)
New York Times p. 10, Jun. 15, 1957
Newsweek 50:78, Jul. 1, 1957

45 Fathers (1937)
New York Times p. 22, Dec. 11, 1937

Forty Guns (1957)
National Parent-Teacher 52:37, Nov., 1957

40 Little Mothers (1940)
Nation 147:702, Dec. 24, 1938
New York Times p. 16, Dec. 23, 1938; IX, p. 5, Mar.
    24, 1940; p. 25, Apr. 19, 1940
Newsweek 15:44, Apr. 29, 1940
Photoplay 54:68, Jun., 1940

49th Parallel (1941)
New York Times IX, p. 4, Sep. 15, 1940; IX, p. 4, Jan.
    5, 1941

Forty-Ninth Man (1953)
National Parent-Teacher 47:38, May, 1953

40 Pounds of Trouble (1962)
America 108:316, Mar. 2, 1963
Commonweal 77:541, Feb. 15, 1963
New York Times II, p. 7, Jun. 10, 1962; p. 5, Jan. 24,
    1963; p. 5, Feb. 6, 1963
New Yorker 38:102, Feb. 2, 1963
Saturday Review 46:44, Feb. 2, 1963
Time 81:66, Feb. 8, 1963

42nd Street (1932)
Motion Picture 45:40-41+, Mar., 1933
Movie Classic 4:42-3, Mar., 1933
New York Times p. 19, Mar. 10, 1933; IX, p. 3, Mar.
    19, 1933
Newsweek 1:28, Mar. 18, 1933
Vanity Fair 40:43, Apr., 1933

Forward Pass (1929)
New York Times p. 25, Nov. 29, 1929

Found Alive (1934)
New York Times p. 19, Feb. 12, 1934

Fountain (1934)
Canadian Magazine 82:37, Nov., 1934
New York Times p. 14, Aug. 31, 1934; IX, p. 3, Sep. 9, 1934

Fountainhead (1949)
Canadian Forum 29:135, Sep., 1949
Commonweal 50:390, Jul. 29, 1949
Good Housekeeping 129:200, Jul., 1949
New Republic 121:22, Jul. 18, 1949
New York Times p. 8, Jul. 9, 1949; II, p. 1, Jul. 17, 1949; II, p. 4, Jul. 24, 1949
New Yorker 25:46, Jul. 16, 1949
Newsweek 34:76, Jul. 25, 1949
Rotarian 75:38, Oct., 1949
Scholastic 55:2, Oct. 26, 1949
Time 54:95, Jul. 11, 1949
Woman's Home Companion 76:4, Jul., 1949

Four Bags Full (1957)
National Parent-Teacher 52:37, Nov., 1957
New York Times p. 32, Sep. 5, 1957; II, p. 1, Sep. 8, 1957
New Yorker 33:94, Sep. 14, 1957
Newsweek 50:110, Sep. 9, 1957
Saturday Review 40:25, Aug. 24, 1957
Time 70:112+, Sep. 16, 1957

Four Boys and a Gun (1957)
Library Journal 82:528, Feb. 15, 1957
National Parent-Teacher 51:39, Mar., 1957

Four Daughters (1938)
Commonweal 28:477, Sep. 2, 1938
Life 5:62-3, Sep. 12, 1938
New York Times p. 13, Aug. 19, 1938; IX, p. 3, Aug. 21, 1938; IX, p. 3, Aug. 28, 1938
Newsweek 12:20-1, Aug. 29, 1938
Scholastic 33:12, Sep. 17, 1938
Time 32:23, Aug. 29, 1938

Four Days' Leave (1950)
Christian Century 67:719, Jun. 7, 1950
New York Times p. 29, Jun. 9, 1950
Rotarian 77:43, Aug., 1950

Four Days of Naples (1962)
　Commonweal 77:619-20, Mar. 8, 1963
　Nation 196:187-8, Mar. 2, 1963; 196:296, Apr. 6, 1963
　New Republic 148:27, Mar. 16, 1963
　New York Times p. 5, Mar. 20, 1963
　New Yorker 39:169-70, Mar. 23, 1963
　Newsweek 61:81, Apr. 1, 1963
　Saturday Review 46:82, Mar. 16, 1963
　Time 81:102+, Mar. 15, 1963

Four Devils (1928)
　Life (NY) 92:24, Oct. 26, 1928
　Literary Digest 99:28-9, Oct. 20, 1928
　New York Times p. 26, Oct. 4, 1928; IX, p. 7, Oct. 7,
　　1928
　Outlook 150:986, Oct. 17, 1928

Four Faces West (1948)
　New York Times p. 18, Aug. 4, 1948; II, p. 1, Aug. 8,
　　1948
　New Yorker 24:71, Aug. 14, 1948
　Newsweek 32:76, Aug. 16, 1948
　Photoplay 33:21, Jun., 1948
　Time 51:86+, May 31, 1948

Four Feathers (1930)
　Life (NY) 94:25, Jul. 5, 1929
　New York Times X, p. 8, Mar. 17, 1929; VIII, p. 6,
　　Jun. 9, 1929; p. 35, Jun. 13, 1929; VIII, p. 3, Jun.
　　16, 1929
　Outlook 152:435, Jul. 10, 1929

Four Feathers (1939)
　Commonweal 30:400, Aug. 18, 1939
　New Republic 100:20, Aug. 9, 1939
　New York Times IX, p. 4, Aug. 14, 1938; p. 11, Aug.
　　4, 1939; IX, p. 3, Aug. 6, 1939; IX, p. 4, Aug. 6,
　　1939
　Newsweek 14:40, Aug. 7, 1939
　North American Review no 1:195, Sep., 1939
　Photoplay 53:63, Sep., 1939
　Time 34:32, Aug. 14, 1939

Four Flights to Love (1942)
　New York Times p. 12, Apr. 13, 1942

Four Frightened People (1934)
　Literary Digest 117:27, Feb. 10, 1934

Four Frightened People (1934) (Continued)
New York Times p. 9, Jan. 27, 1934; IX, p. 5, Feb. 4,
1934
Newsweek 3:38, Feb. 3, 1934

Four Girls in Town (1956)
National Parent-Teacher 51:38, Feb., 1957
New York Times p. 34, Jan. 17, 1957

Four Girls in White (1939)
New York Times p. 19, Feb. 23, 1939
Photoplay 53:53, Apr., 1939

Four Guns to the Border (1954)
National Parent-Teacher 49:39, Nov., 1954
New York Times p. 15, Nov. 6, 1954

Four Hearts (1946)
New York Times p. 21, Feb. 25, 1946

Four Horsemen of the Apocalypse (1961)
America 106:801, Mar. 17, 1962
Commonweal 75:668, Mar. 23, 1962
National Review 12:333-4+, May 8, 1962
New York Times II, p. 5, Jan. 1, 1961; p. 10, Mar. 10,
1962; II, p. 1, Mar. 18, 1962
New Yorker 38:127-8, Mar. 31, 1962
Newsweek 59:116, Mar. 19, 1962
Saturday Review 45:26, Mar. 31, 1962
Time 79:67, Mar. 23, 1962

Four Hours to Kill (1935)
New York Times p. 27, Apr. 11, 1935

400 Blows (1959)
Commonweal 71:265, Nov. 27, 1959; 76:474, Aug. 24,
1962
Nation 189:407, Nov. 28, 1959
New Republic 141:21-2, Dec. 7, 1959
New York Times p. 41, Nov. 17, 1959
New Yorker 35:227-8, Nov. 28, 1959
Newsweek 54:122, Oct. 26, 1959
Saturday Review 42:29, Oct. 3, 1959
Time 74:96, Dec. 14, 1959

*Four Hundred Million
Commonweal 29:640, Mar. 31, 1939

400

*Four Hundred Million (Continued)
   Nation 148:358, Mar. 25, 1939
   New Republic 98:194, Mar. 22, 1939
   New York Times p. 19, Mar. 8, 1939; XI, p. 5, Mar.
      12, 1939

Four in a Jeep (1951)
   Christian Century 68:1063, Sep. 12, 1951
   Commonweal 54:310, Jul. 6, 1951
   New Republic 125:23, Jul. 2, 1951
   New York Times II, p. 6, Mar. 4, 1951; p. 35, Jun. 12,
      1951; II, p. 1, Jun. 24, 1951
   New Yorker 27:90, Jun. 16, 1951
   Newsweek 37:92+, Jun. 18, 1951
   Saturday Review 34:22, Jun. 30, 1951
   Time 57:100+, Jun. 18, 1951

Four Jills in a Jeep (1944)
   Commonweal 40:17, Apr. 21, 1944
   New York Times p. 27, Apr. 6, 1944
   Newsweek 23:79, Apr. 10, 1944
   Time 43:92+, Apr. 3, 1944

Four Men and a Prayer (1938)
   Commonweal 28:106, May 20, 1938
   New Republic 95:363, Aug. 3, 1938
   New York Times X, p. 4, Apr. 24, 1938; p. 18, May 7,
      1938; X, p. 3, May 15, 1938
   Newsweek 11:23, May 2, 1938
   Time 31:43, May 2, 1938

Four Mothers (1940)
   New York Times p. 12, Jan. 11, 1941
   Scribner's Commentator 9:108, Mar., 1941
   Time 37:71, Feb. 3, 1941

Four Sided Triangle (1952)
   New York Times p. 10, May 16, 1953

Four Sons (1928)
   Independent Woman 120:362, Apr. 14, 1928
   New York Times p. 27, Feb. 14, 1928; VIII, p. 7, Feb.
      19, 1928; VIII, p. 7, Feb. 26, 1928
   Outlook 148:384, Mar. 7, 1928
   Photoplay 37:34-5+, Jan., 1930

Four Sons (1940)
   Commonweal 32:192, Jun. 21, 1940

401

Four Sons (1940) (Continued)
New York Times p. 18, Jun. 8, 1940
Newsweek 15:50, Jun. 17, 1940
Time 35:90, Jun. 24, 1940

Four Steps in the Clouds (1948)
Commonweal 49:197, Dec. 3, 1948
Nation 167:648, Dec. 4, 1948
New Republic 119:30, Nov. 8, 1948
New York Times p. 25, Nov. 22, 1948; II, p. 5, Dec. 5, 1948
New Yorker 24:88, Dec. 11, 1948
Newsweek 32:87, Nov. 29, 1948
Rotarian 74:35, May, 1949

Four Wives (1939)
Canadian Forum 19:327, Jan., 1940
Commonweal 31:227, Dec. 29, 1939
New York Times p. 9, Dec. 23, 1939; IX, p. 4, Dec. 24, 1939
Newsweek 14:36, Dec. 18, 1939
Photoplay 54:63, Feb., 1940
Time 34:78, Dec. 18, 1939

Fourposter (1952)
Catholic World 176:62, Oct., 1952
Christian Century 70:207, Feb. 18, 1953
Commonweal 57:120, Nov. 7, 1952
Library Journal 77:1801, Oct. 15, 1952
National Parent-Teacher 47:38, Sep., 1952
New York Times II, p. 5, Oct. 7, 1951; p. 37, Oct. 16, 1952; II, p. 1, Oct. 19, 1952
New York Times Magazine p. 24-5, Aug. 24, 1952
New Yorker 28:151, Oct. 18, 1952
Newsweek 40:122, Oct. 20, 1952
Saturday Review 35:31, Oct. 18, 1952
Theatre Arts 36:73, Sep., 1952
Time 60:106+, Oct. 13, 1952

Four's a Crowd (1938)
Canadian Magazine 90:58, Sep., 1938
New York Times p. 11, Aug. 12, 1939; IX, p. 3, Aug. 14, 1938
Time 32:42, Aug. 22, 1938

Fourteen Hours (1951)
Christian Century 68:1031, Sep. 5, 1951

Fourteen Hours (1951)
Commonweal 53:589, Mar. 23, 1951
Library Journal 76:535, Mar. 15, 1951
Life 30:114-18, Mar. 12, 1951
Nation 172:306, Mar. 31, 1951
New Republic 124:22, Mar. 12, 1951
New Yorker 27:117, Mar. 17, 1951
New York Times II, p. 3, Jun. 11, 1950; p. 43, Mar. 7,
    1951; II, p. 1, Mar. 11, 1951; II, p. 1, Apr. 15,
    1951
Newsweek 37:94-5, Mar. 19, 1951
Saturday Review 34:27, Mar. 24, 1951
Time 57:96+, Mar. 12, 1951

Fourteenth of July (1933)
Literary Digest 116:31, Nov. 11, 1933
Nation 137:520, Nov. 1, 1933
New York Times IX, p. 4, Feb. 5, 1933; IX, p. 4, Mar.
    19, 1933; p. 14, Oct. 20, 1933; IX, p. 3, Oct. 29,
    1933
Newsweek 2:28, Oct. 28, 1933
Vanity Fair 40:45+, Jul., 1933

Foxes of Harrow (1947)
New York Times II, p. 5, May 4, 1947; II, p. 5, Sep.
    21, 1947; p. 35, Sep. 25, 1947; II, p. 1, Oct. 5, 1947
New Yorker 23:85, Oct. 4, 1947
Newsweek 30:80, Oct. 6, 1947
Time 50:105, Oct. 13, 1947

Foxfire (1955)
America 93:439, Jul. 30, 1955
Catholic World 181:223, Jun., 1955
Commonweal 62:371-2, Jul. 15, 1955
Library Journal 80:1576, Jul., 1955
National Parent-Teacher 50:39, Sep., 1955
New York Times p. 19, Jul. 14, 1955
Saturday Review 38:26, Jul. 30, 1955

Foxhole in Cairo (1961)
New York Times p. 25, Feb. 16, 1961

Foxiest Girl in Paris (1958)
New York Times p. 10, Sep. 20, 1958

Fra Diavolo (see Devil's Brother)

Frail Women (1932)
New York Times VIII, p. 6, Feb. 14, 1932

Frame-Up (1937)
New York Times p. 23, Aug. 9, 1937

Framed (1930)
New York Times p. 23, Mar. 29, 1930

Framed (1947)
New Republic 117:38, Sep. 15, 1947
New York Times II, p. 5, May 25, 1947; p. 24, May 26, 1947
Newsweek 29:94, Jun. 9, 1947
Photoplay 31:4, Jun., 1947

Franchise Affair (1952)
New York Times p. 19, Jun. 6, 1952
New Yorker 28:99, Jun. 14, 1952
Theatre Arts 36:88, Aug., 1952
Time 60:72, Jul. 28, 1952

Francis (1950)
Christian Century 67:575, May 3, 1950
Commonweal 51:607, Mar. 17, 1950
Library Journal 75:332, Feb. 15, 1950
New Republic 122:21, Apr. 3, 1950
New York Times II, p. 4, Mar. 12, 1950; p. 40, Mar. 16, 1950; II, p. 1, Mar. 26, 1950
New Yorker 26:114, Mar. 18, 1950
Newsweek 35:87, Feb. 20, 1950
Rotarian 76:37, Jun., 1950
Time 55:95, Mar. 20, 1950

Francis Covers the Big Town (1953)
Library Journal 78:1411, Sep. 1, 1953
National Parent-Teacher 48:37, Sep., 1953

Francis Goes to the Races (1951)
Christian Century 68:975, Aug. 22, 1951
New York Times p. 19, Jul. 25, 1951

Francis Goes to West Point (1952)
Christian Century 69:983, Aug. 27, 1952
National Parent-Teacher 47:36, Sep., 1952
New York Times p. 10, Aug. 23, 1952
Newsweek 40:85, Aug. 25, 1952
Time 60:84, Aug. 18, 1952

Francis in the Haunted House (1956)
  National Parent-Teacher 51:38, Sep., 1956
  New York Times p. 9, Jul. 21, 1956

Francis in the Navy (1955)
  National Parent-Teacher 50:38, Sep., 1955
  New York Times p. 13, Aug. 6, 1955

Francis Joins the Wacs (1954)
  Farm Journal 78:140, Sep., 1954
  National Parent-Teacher 49:37, Sep., 1954
  New York Times p. 6, Jan. 31, 1954

Francis of Assisi (1961)
  Commonweal 74:448, Aug. 11, 1961
  McCalls 88:6, Aug., 1961
  New York Times II, p. 7, Jan. 8, 1961; p. 8, Jul. 29,
    1961; II, p. 1, Aug. 6, 1961
  New Yorker 37:38, Aug. 5, 1961
  Newsweek 58:79, Jul. 31, 1961
  Saturday Review 44:24, Aug. 5, 1961
  Time 78:60, Jul. 28, 1961

Frankenstein (1931)
  New York Times VIII, p. 5, Oct. 11, 1931; p. 21, Dec.
    5, 1931; VIII, p. 6, Dec. 13, 1931; VIII, p. 4, Dec.
    20, 1931; IX, p. 4, Oct. 16, 1938

Frankenstein Meets the Wolf Man (1943)
  New York Times p. 8, Mar. 6, 1943
  Newsweek 21:74, Mar. 8, 1943

Frankenstein's Daughter (1959)
  New York Times p. 37, Nov. 17, 1958

Frankie and Johnny (1936)
  New York Times p. 23, May 25, 1936

Frantic (1961)
  Commonweal 74:404, Jul. 14, 1961
  New York Times p. 34, Jun. 12, 1961
  New Yorker 37:42, Jul. 1, 1961
  Time 77:53, Jun. 23, 1961

Frasquita (1936)
  New York Times p. 19, Jan. 18, 1936

Fraulein (1958)
America 99:320, Jun. 7, 1958
Catholic World 187:222, Jun., 1958
Commonweal 68:153, May 9, 1958
Library Journal 83:1389, May 1, 1958
New York Times p. 27, Jun. 9, 1958
Saturday Review 41:25, Jul. 12, 1958

Freaks (1932)
Motion Picture 43:30-32+, Apr., 1932
New York Times p. 7, Jul. 9, 1932; IX, p. 3, Jul. 17,
1932

Freckles (1935)
New York Times p. 12, Oct. 26, 1935

Free and Easy (1941)
New York Times p. 29, Apr. 8, 1941

Free Blonde and Twenty One (1940)
New York Times p. 25, Apr. 5, 1940
Photoplay 54:72, May, 1940

Free Love (1930)
New York Times p. 29, Dec. 15, 1930; VIII, p. 5, Dec.
21, 1930

Free Soul (1931)
Life (NY) 97:19, Jun. 19, 1931
New York Times VIII, p. 5, Jan. 7, 1931; VIII, p. 4,
May 24, 1931; p. 29, Jun. 3, 1931
Outlook 158:154, Jun. 3, 1931

French-Cancan (1956)
Commonweal 64:150, May 11, 1956
Nation 182:391, May 5, 1956
New York Times p. 26, Apr. 17, 1956
New Yorker 32:90, Apr. 28, 1956
Newsweek 47:100, May 7, 1956
Saturday Review 39:25, Apr. 21, 1956

French Dressing (1928)
New York Times p. 33, Dec. 13, 1927; IX, p. 7, Dec.
18, 1927

French Line (1953)
Look 17:106-9, Nov. 3, 1953

French Line (1953) (Continued)
 National Parent-Teacher 48:39, May, 1954
 New York Times p. 16, Dec. 30, 1953; p. 13, May 15,
  1954; II, p. 1, May 23, 1954
 New Yorker 30:112, May 22, 1954
 Newsweek 43:84, May 31, 1954
 Time 63:72, May 31, 1954

French Mistress (1960)
 Commonweal 73:365, Dec. 30, 1960
 New York Times p. 34, Dec. 19, 1960
 New Yorker 36:50, Dec. 31, 1960

French They Are a Funny Race (1957)
 Commonweal 66:205, May 24, 1957
 New York Times p. 41, May 21, 1957
 New Yorker 33:73, Jun. 1, 1957
 Newsweek 49:118, May 20, 1957
 Saturday Review 40:23, Jun. 1, 1957
 Time 69:102+, May 27, 1957

French Touch (1954)
 National Parent-Teacher 49:39, Nov., 1954
 New York Times p. 18, Sep. 2, 1954; II, p. 1, Sep. 5,
  1954
 Newsweek 44:76, Aug. 30, 1954

French Without Tears (1940)
 New York Times IX, p. 5, Jan. 21, 1940; IX, p. 5, Apr.
  28, 1940; p. 12, Apr. 29, 1940

Frenchie (1951)
 New York Times p. 19, Feb. 12, 1951
 Newsweek 37:83, Jan. 22, 1951
 Time 57:100+, Feb. 19, 1951

Frenchman's Creek (1944)
 Commonweal 40:614, Oct. 13, 1944
 Nation 159:445, Oct. 14, 1944
 New York Times p. 26, Sep. 21, 1944
 New Yorker 20:54, Sep. 30, 1944
 Newsweek 24:106, Oct. 2, 1944
 Scholastic 45:23, Oct. 16, 1944
 Time 44:94+, Oct. 9, 1944
 Woman's Home Companion 72:12, Jan., 1945

Freshman Love (1936)
 New York Times p. 18, Jan. 25, 1936

Freshman Year (1938)
New York Times IX, p. 3, Jul. 10, 1938

Freud (1962)
America 108:153, Jan. 26, 1963
Catholic World 196:327-8, Feb., 1963
Commonweal 77:389, Jan. 4, 1963
Life 54:51A-51B, Jan. 4, 1963
Nation 196:59, Jan. 19, 1963
New Republic 148:19-20, Jan. 5, 1963
New York Times II, p. 7, Oct. 29, 1961; p. 37, Nov. 12, 1962; II, p. 1, Dec. 9, 1962
New Yorker 38:77-8, Dec. 22, 1962
Newsweek 60:63, Dec. 24, 1962
Reporter 28:50, Jan. 31, 1963
Saturday Review 46:30, Jan. 5, 1963
Time 80:60, Dec. 28, 1962

Fric-Frac (1939)
New Republic 118:30, Jun. 14, 1948
New York Times p. 8, May 29, 1948
Rotarian 74:35, Feb., 1949

Friday the 13th (1934)
New York Times p. 18, May 15, 1934; IX, p. 3, May 20, 1934

Frieda (1947)
Commonweal 46:476, Aug. 29, 1947
Life 23:67-8+, Sep. 8, 1947
Nation 165:209, Aug. 30, 1947
New Republic 117:39, Sep. 22, 1947
New York Times II, p. 5, Oct. 20, 1946; II, p. 4, Aug. 10, 1947; p. 12, Aug. 15, 1947; II, p. 1, Aug. 17, 1947
New Yorker 23:38, Aug. 30, 1947
Newsweek 30:81-2, Aug. 25, 1947
Theatre Arts 31:52, Oct., 1947
Time 50:98+, Sep. 22, 1947
Woman's Home Companion 74:10, Nov., 1947

Friederike (1933)
New York Times p. 11, Feb. 27, 1933; p. 15, Feb. 28, 1933

Friendly Enemies (1942)
Commonweal 36:281, Jul. 10, 1942
New York Times p. 19, Jun. 22, 1942

Friendly Persuasion (1956)
America 96:212, Nov. 17, 1956
Catholic World 184:301-2, Jan., 1957
Commonweal 65:206, Nov. 23, 1956
Library Journal 81:2676, Nov. 15, 1956
Life 41:95-6+, Nov. 5, 1956
Look 20:63-5, Oct. 30, 1956
Nation 183:467, Nov. 24, 1956
National Parent-Teacher 51:38, Dec., 1956
New York Times VI, p. 22, Jul. 16, 1956; p. 30, Nov. 2,
    1956; II, p. 1, Nov. 4, 1956; VII, p. 6, Feb. 10, 1957
New Yorker 32:125, Nov. 10, 1956
Newsweek 48:88, Oct. 1, 1956
Saturday Review 39:28, Nov. 10, 1956
Scholastic 69:33, Nov. 15, 1956
Time 68:110+, Nov. 5, 1956

Friends (1939)
New York Times p. 28, Jan. 2, 1939

Friends and Lovers (1931)
Life (NY) 98:21, Nov. 27, 1931
New York Times p. 16, Nov. 7, 1931

Friends of Mr. Sweeney (1934)
New Republic 80:23, Aug. 15, 1934
New York Times IX, p. 3, Aug. 5, 1934; p. 20, Jul. 31,
    1934

Frightened Bride (1953)
New York Times p. 18, Aug. 20, 1953

Frightened City (1961)
Library Journal 75:1201, Jul., 1950

Frisco Kid (1935)
Literary Digest 120:24, Dec. 7, 1935
Motion Picture 50:50, Jan., 1936
Nation 141:724, Dec. 18, 1935
New York Times IX, p. 4, Nov. 24, 1935; p. 22, Nov.
    25, 1935
Newsweek 6:27, Nov. 30, 1935

Frisco Lil (1942)
New York Times p. 27, Feb. 12, 1942

Frisco Sal (1945)
New York Times p. 11, Feb. 17, 1945

Frisco Sal (1945) (Continued)
Newsweek 25:98+, Feb. 26, 1945

Frisky (1955)
National Parent-Teacher 50:39, Jan., 1956
New York Times p. 37, Oct. 25, 1955
Time 66:114, Nov. 21, 1955

Frogmen (1951)
Christian Century 68:903, Aug. 1, 1951
Commonweal 54:335, Jul. 13, 1951
Nation 173:37, Jul. 14, 1951
New Republic 125:23, Jul. 16, 1951
New York Times p. 8, Jun. 30, 1951; II, p. 1, Jul. 1,
    1951
New Yorker 27:72, Jul. 14, 1951
Newsweek 37:89, Jun. 25, 1951
Saturday Review 34:26, Jul. 21, 1951
Time 58:84+, Jul. 9, 1951

From a Roman Balcony (1961)
New York Times p. 33, Oct. 16, 1961
New Yorker 37:194-5, Oct. 28, 1961

From Headquarters (1933)
New York Times p. 22, Nov. 17, 1933

From Hell to Heaven (1933)
New York Times p. 9, Mar. 18, 1933; IX, p. 3, Mar. 26,
    1933

From Hell to Texas (1958)
Catholic World 187:307, Jul., 1958
New York Times p. 39, Jun. 5, 1958
Newsweek 51:105, Jun. 16, 1958

From Here to Eternity (1953)
America 89:486, Aug. 15, 1953
Catholic World 177:461, Sep., 1953
Colliers 132:38-9, Aug. 7, 1953
Commonweal 58:488-9, Aug. 21, 1953
Farm Journal 77:98, Oct., 1953
Harpers 207:92-3, Oct., 1953
Holiday 15:14, Jan., 1954
Library Journal 78:1411, Sep. 1, 1953
Life 35:81-3, Aug. 31, 1953
Look 17:41-3, Aug. 25, 1953

From Here to Eternity (1953) (Continued)
McCalls 81:8, Oct., 1953
Nation 177:178, Aug. 29, 1953
National Parent-Teacher 48:39, Oct., 1953
New York Times VII, p. 8, May 10, 1953; II, p. 5, Jun.
14, 1953; VI, p. 24, Jun. 14, 1953; p. 16, Aug. 6,
1953; II, p. 1, Aug. 9, 1953; II, p. 1, Sep. 20, 1953;
II, p. 5, Apr. 25, 1954
New Yorker 29:51, Aug. 8, 1953
Newsweek 42:82, Aug. 10, 1953
Saturday Review 36:25, Aug. 8, 1953
Time 62:94+, Aug. 10, 1953

From Russia with Love (1963)
America 110:580, Apr. 25, 1964
Life 56:51-2, Apr. 3, 1964
New Republic 150:26, Apr. 25, 1964
New York Times p. 25, Apr. 9, 1964
New Yorker 40:20+, Apr. 18, 1964
Newsweek 63:93-4, Apr. 13, 1964
Saturday Review 47:29, Apr. 18, 1964
Time 83:103+, Apr. 10, 1964

From Earth to the Moon (1958)
America 100:327, Dec. 6, 1958
Commonweal 69:293, Dec. 12, 1958
New York Times p. 52, Nov. 27, 1958

From the Terrace (1960)
America 103:522, Aug. 6, 1960
Commonweal 72:402, Aug. 5, 1960
New York Times II, p. 7, Jan. 3, 1960; p. 10, Jul. 16,
1960
New Yorker 36:72-3, Jul. 23, 1960
Newsweek 56:88, Jul. 18, 1960
Saturday Review 43:24, Jul. 30, 1960
Time 76:76, Jul. 18, 1960

From This Day Forward (1946)
Commonweal 44:47, Apr. 26, 1946
Cosmopolitan 120:132, Feb., 1946
Nation 162:516, Apr. 27, 1946
New York Times II, p. 3, Apr. 14, 1946; p. 16, Apr. 20,
1946; II, p. 1, Apr. 21, 1946
New Yorker 22:86, Apr. 20, 1946
Newsweek 27:89, Apr. 29, 1946
Scholastic 48:33, Apr. 15, 1946

From This Day Forward (1946) (Continued)
Theatre Arts 30:350, Jun., 1946
Time 47:96+, Apr. 22, 1946
Woman's Home Companion 73:11, Mar., 1946

Front Page (1931)
Commonweal 14:17, May 6, 1931
Life (NY) 97:20, Apr. 10, 1931
Nation 132:429-30, Apr. 15, 1931
New Republic 66:303, Apr. 29, 1931
New York Times p. 29, Mar. 20, 1931; VIII, p. 5, Mar.
29, 1931; VIII, p. 6, May 24, 1931
Outlook 157:475, Apr. 1, 1931

Front Page Story (1955)
Commonweal 62:184, May 20, 1955
Nation 180:382, Apr. 30, 1955
National Parent-Teacher 49:39, Jun., 1955
New York Times p. 28, Apr. 19, 1955; II, p. 1, Apr. 24,
1955
New Yorker 31:117, Apr. 30, 1955
Newsweek 45:103, May 9, 1955

Front Page Woman (1935)
Literary Digest 120:27, Jul. 27, 1935
New York Times p. 15, Jul. 12, 1935; IX, p. 3, Jul. 21,
1935
Newsweek 6:29, Jul. 20, 1935
Time 26:30, Jul. 22, 1935

Frontier Bad Men (1943)
New York Times II, p. 3, Jul. 4, 1943; p. 12, Aug. 14,
1943

Frontier Gal (1945)
New York Times p. 14, Dec. 15, 1945
Newsweek 26:90, Dec. 24, 1945
Time 47:52+, Jan. 7, 1946

Frontier Marshal (1934)
New York Times p. 20, Jan. 31, 1934

Frontier Town (1938)
New York Times p. 13, Mar. 12, 1938

Frozen Ghost (1945)
New York Times p. 7, Jul. 28, 1945

Frozen Justice (1929)
New York Times IX, p. 3, Jul. 14, 1929; IX, p. 5, Sep.
8, 1929; p. 15, Oct. 26, 1929; IX, p. 6, Nov. 3, 1929

Fugitive (1940)
Commonweal 32:331, Aug. 9, 1940
New York Times p. 22, Jul. 23, 1940

Fugitive (1947)
Commonweal 47:277-8, Dec. 26, 1947
Life 23:51, Oct. 6, 1947
New Republic 117:34, Dec. 29, 1947
New York Times II, p. 5, Feb. 16, 1947; VI, p. 17, Mar.
23, 1947; II, p. 5, Dec. 21, 1947; p. 22, Dec. 26,
1947; II, p. 1, Jan. 11, 1948; II, p. 3, Aug. 22, 1948
New Yorker 23:38, Dec. 27, 1947
Newsweek 31:78, Jan. 12, 1948
Scholastic 51:29, Dec. 15, 1947
Theatre Arts 31:48+, Nov., 1947
Time 50:105, Dec. 1, 1947
Woman's Home Companion 74:10-11, Dec., 1947

Fugitive at Large (1939)
New York Times p. 15, Nov. 13, 1939

Fugitive from Justice (1940)
New York Times p. 13, Jul. 8, 1940

Fugitive in the Sky (1936)
New York Times p. 21, Jan. 16, 1937

Fugitive Kind (1960)
America 103:201, Apr. 30, 1960
Commonweal 72:127, Apr. 29, 1960
McCalls 87:179, Jun., 1960
New Republic 142:21-2, May 2, 1960
New York Times II, p. 5, Jul. 5, 1959; p. 58, Dec. 8,
1959; p. 13, Apr. 15, 1960; II, p. 1, Apr. 24, 1960
New Yorker 36:147, Apr. 23, 1960
Newsweek 55:115, Apr. 25, 1960
Saturday Review 43:28, Apr. 23, 1960
Time 75:81, Apr. 18, 1960

Fugitive Lady (1951)
New York Times p. 7, Aug. 25, 1951

Fugitive Lovers (1934)
New York Times p. 16, Jan. 13; X, p. 5, Jan. 21, 1934

Fugitives for a Night (1938)
New York Times p. 30, Sep. 21, 1938

Full Confession (1939)
Commonweal 30:539, Oct. 6, 1939
New York Times IX, p. 3, Jul. 23, 1939; IX, p. 3, Aug.
20, 1939; p. 29, Sep. 28, 1939

Full of Life (1957)
America 96:632, Mar. 2, 1957
Commonweal 65:568, Mar. 1, 1957
Holiday 21:111, Mar., 1957
Library Journal 82:71, Jan. 1, 1957
Nation 184:194, Mar. 2, 1957
National Parent-Teacher 51:38, Feb., 1957
New York Times p. 38, Feb. 13, 1957; II, p. 1, Feb. 17,
1957
New Yorker 33:75, Feb. 23, 1957
Newsweek 49:110, Feb. 18, 1957
Saturday Review 40:27, Feb. 23, 1957
Time 69:98+, Feb. 18, 1957

Fuller Brush Girl (1950)
New York Times p. 23, Oct. 6, 1950

Fuller Brush Man (1948)
New York Times II, p. 5, Oct. 5, 1947; p. 18, May 15,
1948
Time 51:86, May 31, 1948

Fun in Acapulco (1963)
Commonweal 79:349, Dec. 13, 1963
New York Times p. 22, Feb. 20, 1964

Funny Face (1957)
America 97:83, Apr. 20, 1957
Catholic World 185:63, Apr., 1957
Commonweal 66:16, Apr. 5, 1957
Cosmopolitan 142:14, May, 1957
Dance Magazine 31:16-22, May, 1957
Good Housekeeping 144:273, Apr., 1957; 144:72, May, 1957
Holiday 21:113, May, 1957
Library Journal 82:1047, Apr. 15, 1957
Life 42:88-91, Apr. 15, 1957
Look 21:116+, May 14, 1957
National Parent-Teacher 51:38, Apr., 1957
New Republic 136:22-3, Jun. 10, 1957

Funny Face (1957) (Continued)
New York Times II, p. 5, Jul. 15, 1956; p. 16, Mar. 29,
1957; II, p. 1, Apr. 7, 1957
New York Times Magazine p. 16+, Mar. 17, 1957
New Yorker 33:76, Apr. 6, 1957
Newsweek 49:106, Apr. 1, 1957
Saturday Review 40:26, Apr. 13, 1957
Senior Scholastic 70:38, Mar. 22, 1957
Time 69:94+, Apr. 1, 1957

*Furia
Commonweal 47:448, Feb. 13, 1948
New York Times p. 30, Jan. 21, 1948; p. 34, Feb. 11,
1948
New Yorker 23:52, Jan. 31, 1948
Newsweek 31:72, Feb. 2, 1948
Theatre Arts 31:51, Dec., 1947

Furies (1929)
New York Times p. 15, Apr. 19, 1930

Furies (1950)
Christian Century 67:1063, Sep. 6, 1950
Commonweal 52:510, Sep. 1, 1950
Newsweek 36:70+, Sep. 4, 1950
New York Times p. 23, Aug. 17, 1950
Rotarian 77:36, Nov., 1950
Time 56:82, Aug. 21, 1950

Fury (1936)
Canadian Magazine 86:36, Aug., 1936
Commonweal 24:246, Jun. 26, 1936
Literary Digest 121:28, May 30, 1936
Nation 142:821, Jun. 24, 1936
New Republic 87:130-31, Jun. 10, 1936
New York Times p. 21, Jun. 6, 1936; IX, p. 3, Jun. 7,
1936; X, p. 2, Jun. 14, 1936
Newsweek 7:39-40, Jun. 13, 1936
Time 27:40+, Jun. 8, 1936

Fury and the Woman (1937)
New York Times p. 26, Jun. 22, 1937

Fury at Furnace Creek (1948)
Canadian Forum 28:112, Aug., 1948
New Republic 119:29, Jul. 26, 1948
New York Times p. 11, Jul. 12, 1948

415

Fury at Furnace Creek (1948) (Continued)
Newsweek 32:82, Jul. 19, 1948
Time 52:60, Jul. 5, 1948

Fury at Gunsight Pass (1956)
National Parent-Teacher 50:39, Mar., 1956

Fury at Showdown (1957)
National Parent-Teacher 52:33, Sep., 1957
New York Times p. 21, Apr. 20, 1957

Fury Over Spain (1937)
New York Times p. 19, Jul. 21, 1937

Fuzzy Pink Nightgown (1957)
Library Journal 82:2351, Oct. 1, 1957
National Parent-Teacher 52:33, Oct., 1957
New York Times p. 41, Oct. 31, 1957

G Men (1935)
Literary Digest 119:30, May 11, 1935
Nation 140:694+, Jun. 12, 1935
New Republic 83:19, May 15, 1935
New York Times X, p. 4, Apr. 28, 1935; p. 17, May 2, 1935
Newsweek 5:25, May 4, 1935
Theatre Arts 19:406, Jun., 1935
Vanity Fair 44:49, Jun., 1935

G. I. Blues (1960)
America 104:350, Dec. 3, 1960
New York Times p. 28, Nov. 5, 1960
Newsweek 56:110, Nov. 14, 1960
Time 76:64, Dec. 5, 1960

Gabriel Over the White House (1933)
Commonweal 18:20, May 5, 1933
Literary Digest 115:13, Apr. 22, 1933
Movie Classic 4:30-31+, May, 1933
Nation 136:482-3, Apr. 26, 1933
New Outlook 161:47, May, 1933
New Republic 74:280-2, Apr. 19, 1933
Newsweek 1:25, Apr. 8, 1933
Vanity Fair 40:37, Jun., 1933

Gaby (1956)
America 95:148, May 5, 1956

Gaby (1956) (Continued)
American Magazine 161:9, Apr., 1956
Catholic World 183:222, Jun., 1956
Commonweal 64:274, Jun. 15, 1956
Library Journal 81:1146, May 1, 1956
Nation 182:498, Jun. 9, 1956
National Parent-Teacher 50:39, May, 1956
New York Times p. 26, May 10, 1956; II, p. 1, May 13,
    1956
Newsweek 47:125, May 14, 1956
Saturday Review 39:25, May 12, 1956
Time 67:100, May 28, 1956

Gaiety Girls (1938)
New York Times p. 15, Mar. 31, 1938

Gal Who Took the West (1949)
Newsweek 34:80, Oct. 3, 1949
Photoplay 36:21, Nov., 1949

Gallant Bess (1947)
New York Times p. 27, Dec. 6, 1946

Gallant Blade (1948)
New York Times II, p. 5, Dec. 14, 1947; p. 31, Oct. 13,
    1948
Newsweek 32:81, Nov. 1, 1948
Rotarian 74:52, Jan., 1949

Gallant Hours (1959)
Commonweal 72:378, Jul. 22, 1960
New York Times p. 19, Jun. 23, 1960
Newsweek 55:116+, May 23, 1960

Gallant Journey (1946)
Commonweal 45:17, Oct. 18, 1946
New York Times II, p. 3, Mar. 24, 1946; II, p. 3, Sep.
    1, 1946; II, p. 5, Oct. 6, 1946; p. 33, Oct. 10, 1946
Newsweek 28:102, Oct. 21, 1946
Time 48:104, Oct. 7, 1946

Gallant Lady (1933)
New York Times p. 12, Jan. 22, 1934; IX, p. 5, Jan. 28,
    1934
Newsweek 3:34, Jan. 13, 1934
Vanity Fair 41:45, Feb., 1934

Gallant Sons (1940)
New York Times p. 37, Dec. 12, 1940

Gals Incorporated (1943)
New York Times p. 13, Aug. 13, 1943

Gambler from Natchez (1954)
National Parent-Teacher 49:39, Oct., 1954
New York Times p. 8, Aug. 14, 1954

Gamblers (1929)
New York Times p. 11, Aug. 24, 1929; VIII, p. 4, Sep. 1, 1929

Gambling (1934)
New York Times IX, p. 3, Sep. 2, 1934; p. 22, Dec. 4, 1934; X, p. 5, Dec. 9, 1934

Gambling House (1951)
New York Times p. 23, Mar. 10, 1951

Gambling Lady (1934)
New York Times p. 25, Apr. 5, 1934; X, p. 3, Apr. 15, 1934

Gambling Ship (1933)
New York Times p. 17, Jul. 13, 1933

Game of Death (1946)
New York Times p. 22, Nov. 24, 1945

Game of Love (1954)
Nation 179:557, Dec. 25, 1954
New York Times p. 41, Dec. 15, 1954
Newsweek 45:45, Jan. 3, 1955
Saturday Review 38:26, Jan. 8, 1955
Time 65:76, Jan. 24, 1955

Gamma People (1956)
National Parent-Teacher 50:37, Jun., 1956

Gang Bullets (1938)
New York Times IX, p. 7, Dec. 25, 1938

Gang Buster (1931)
New York Times p. 15, Jan. 24, 1931; VIII, p. 5, Feb. 1, 1931

Gang's All Here (1943)
Commonweal 39:206, Dec. 10, 1943
New York Times p. 26, Dec. 23, 1943

Gangs of Chicago (1940)
New York Times p. 29, Jun. 13, 1940

Gangs of New York (1938)
New York Times p. 9, May 28, 1938

Gangster (1947)
New York Times p. 29, Oct. 31, 1947

Gangster's Boy (1938)
New York Times p. 23, Nov. 7, 1938

Gangway (1937)
New York Times p. 7, Aug. 21, 1937
Time 30:23, Aug. 30, 1937

Garden Murder Case (1936)
New York Times p. 13, Mar. 2, 1936

Garden of Allah (1936)
Canadian Magazine 86:44-5, Oct., 1936
Commonweal 25:134, Nov. 27, 1936
Literary Digest 122:21, Nov. 14, 1936
New York Times p. 27, Nov. 20, 1936; XI, p. 5, Nov.
   22, 1936
Newsweek 8:20-2, Nov. 21, 1936
Stage 14:16, Dec., 1936
Time 28:39-40, Nov. 30, 1936

Garden of Evil (1954)
America 91:426, Jul. 24, 1954
Catholic World 179:305, Jul., 1954
Commonweal 60:413, Jul. 30, 1954
National Parent-Teacher 49:38, Sep., 1954
New Republic 131:20, Sep. 6, 1954
New York Times p. 7, Jul. 10, 1954
New Yorker 30:57, Jul. 17, 1954
Newsweek 44:83, Jul. 26, 1954
Time 64:76+, Jul. 19, 1964

Garden of the Moon (1938)
New York Times X, p. 4, Sep. 18, 1938; p. 13, Sep. 24,
   1938

419

Garment Jungle (1957)
Library Journal 82:1456, Jun. 1, 1957
National Parent-Teacher 52:33, Sep., 1957
New York Times p. 28, May 16, 1957
Saturday Review 40:36, May 18, 1957
Time 69:92+, Jun. 3, 1957

Gaslight (1944)
Collier's 113:4, Mar. 18, 1944
Commonweal 40:132, May 26, 1944
Life 16:75-8, May 22, 1944
Nation 158:605, May 20, 1944
New Republic 110:711, May 22, 1944
New York Times p. 17, May 5, 1944
New Yorker 20:66, May 13, 1944
Newsweek 23:102, May 22, 1944
Time 43:94+, May 22, 1944
Woman's Home Companion 71:2, Apr., 1944

Gate of Hell (1954)
America 92:407, Jan. 15, 1955
Catholic World 180:302, Jan., 1955
Commonweal 61:360, Dec. 31, 1954
Library Journal 80:63, Jan. 1, 1955
Life 37:90-1, Nov. 15, 1954
Nation 179:516, Dec. 11, 1954
National Parent-Teacher 49:39, Jan., 1955
New York Times p. 45, Dec. 14, 1954; II, p. 3, Dec. 19, 1954
New Yorker 30:77, Jan. 8, 1955
Newsweek 44:98, Dec. 13, 1954
Reporter 13:54, Aug. 11, 1955
Saturday Review 37:26, Dec. 11, 1954; 38:63, Jan. 1, 1955
Time 64:100+, Dec. 13, 1954

Gates of Paris (1958)
Commonweal 67:513, Feb. 14, 1958
Nation 186:108, Feb. 1, 1958
New York Times p. 24, Jan. 15, 1958; II, p. 1, Jan. 19, 1958
Newsweek 51:87, Feb. 3, 1958
Saturday Review 41:27, Jan. 25, 1958
Time 71:80, Feb. 3, 1958

Gateway (1938)
New York Times p. 9, Aug. 8, 1938; IX, p. 3, Aug. 14, 1938

420

Gateway of the Moon (1928)
New York Times p. 20, Jan. 9, 1928

Gathering of Eagles (1962)
America 109:124, Aug. 3, 1963
New York Times II, p. 7, Aug. 26, 1962; p. 21, Jul. 11, 1963
Newsweek 62:86, Jul. 22, 1963
Saturday Review 46:16, Jul. 6, 1963
Time 82:80, Jul. 26, 1963

Gay Adventure (1953)
National Parent-Teacher 49:39, Nov., 1954
New York Times p. 35, Sep. 16, 1954

Gay Bride (1934)
New York Times p. 27, Dec. 19, 1934

Gay Caballero (1932)
New York Times p. 17, Mar. 26, 1932

Gay Caballero (1940)
New York Times p. 25, Oct. 25, 1940

Gay Deception (1935)
New York Times p. 31, Oct. 11, 1935
Newsweek 6:17, Sep. 21, 1935
Time 26:63, Sep. 16, 1935

Gay Desperado (1936)
Commonweal 24:617, Oct. 23, 1936
New Republic 88:351, Oct. 28, 1936
New York Times p. 31, Oct. 9, 1936; X, p. 5, Oct. 18, 1936
Newsweek 8:30, Oct. 10, 1936
Time 28:66, Oct. 19, 1936

Gay Diplomat (1931)
New York Times p. 20, Oct. 10, 1931

Gay Divorcee (1934)
Literary Digest 118:30, Dec. 1, 1934
New Republic 81:46, Nov. 21, 1934
New York Times p. 27, Nov. 16, 1934
Vanity Fair 43:50, Dec., 1934

Gay Falcon (1941)
Scholastic 39:33, Oct. 27, 1941

Gay Intruders (1948)
New York Times p. 33, Jun. 28, 1949

Gay Purr-ee (1963)
New York Times II, p. 13, Dec. 10, 1961; p. 55, Dec.
6, 1962
Newsweek 60:92, Nov. 26, 1962
Time 80:77, Dec. 21, 1962

Gay Sisters (1942)
Commonweal 36:329, Jul. 24, 1942
Musican 47:116, Aug., 1942
New York Times p. 14, Aug. 15, 1942; VIII, p. 2, Aug.
23, 1942
Newsweek 20:53, Aug. 10, 1942
Photoplay 21:24, Sep., 1942
Time 40:44, Jul. 27, 1942

Gazebo (1960)
America 102:511, Jan. 23, 1960
Commonweal 71:470, Jan. 22, 1960
New York Times p. 14, Jan. 16, 1960
Newsweek 55:61, Jan. 4, 1960
Time 75:76, Feb. 1, 1960

Geisha Boy (1958)
Commonweal 69:340, Dec. 26, 1958
Newsweek 52:64, Dec. 29, 1958
Senior Scholastic 74:30, Feb. 6, 1959
Time 73:90, Jan. 19, 1959

Gene Krupa Story (1960)
New York Times p. 7, Dec. 26, 1959

General Crack (1930)
New York Times p. 37, Dec. 4, 1929; X, p. 6, Dec. 8,
1929

General Delia Rovere (1960)
America 104:739-40, Mar. 4, 1961
Commonweal 73:201, Nov. 18, 1960
Horizon 3:98-100, Mar., 1961
New Republic 143:27, Dec. 12, 1960
New York Times p. 41, Nov. 22, 1960; II, p. 1, Dec. 4,
1960
New Yorker 36:206-7, Nov. 26, 1960
Newsweek 56:108+, Nov. 14, 1960

General Delia Rovere (1960) (Continued)
  Reporter 23:42+, Nov. 10, 1960
  Saturday Review 43:39, Nov. 19, 1960
  Time 76:89, Nov. 21, 1960

General Died at Dawn (1936)
  Commonweal 24:504, Sep. 25, 1936
  Nation 143:375, Sep. 26, 1936
  New Republic 88:156-7, Sep. 16, 1936
  New York Times X, p. 4, Jul. 19, 1936; IX, p. 4, Aug.
    23, 1936; IX, p. 4, Aug. 30, 1936; IX, p. 5, Aug. 30,
    1936; p. 17, Sep. 3, 1936; IX, p. 3, Sep. 6, 1936
  Newsweek 8:42, Sep. 12, 1936
  Photoplay 50:10-11, Sep., 1936
  Scholastic 29:32, Oct. 3, 1936
  Stage 14:24, Oct., 1936; 14:42-3, Oct., 1936
  Time 28:28, Sep. 14, 1936

General Suvorov (1941)
  New York Times p. 11, Sep. 20, 1941

Generals Without Buttons (1938)
  Nation 146:366, Mar. 26, 1938
  New Republic 94:165-6, Mar. 16, 1938
  New York Times p. 23, Mar. 8, 1938; XI, p. 5, Mar. 13,
    1938
  Scholastic 32:23E, Mar. 5, 1938
  Stage 15:25, Apr., 1938
  Theatre Arts 22:422, Jun., 1938
  Time 31:40, Mar. 21, 1938

Genevieve (1953)
  America 90:582, Feb. 27, 1954
  Catholic World 178:226, Dec., 1953
  Collier's 133:6, Apr. 30, 1954
  Commonweal 59:577, Mar. 12, 1954
  Farm Journal 78:83, Jan., 1954
  Holiday 16:24, Jul., 1954
  Life 36:97-8, Mar. 8, 1954
  National Parent-Teacher 48:39, Jan., 1954
  New York Times p. 30, Feb. 16, 1954; II, p. 1, Feb. 28,
    1954
  New Yorker 30:105, Feb. 27, 1954
  Newsweek 42:104, Nov. 30, 1953
  Saturday Review 37:32, Feb. 13, 1954
  Time 62:100+, Nov. 30, 1953

Genghis Khan (1953)
   Commonweal 58:348, Jul. 10, 1953
   Natural History 62:285, Jun., 1953
   Saturday Review 36:29, Jun. 13, 1953; 39:28, Mar. 31,
      1956
   Theatre Arts 37:88, Jul., 1953
   Time 61:84+, Jun. 22, 1953

Gentle Annie (1944)
   New York Times p. 11, May 5, 1945

Gentle Gunman (1935)
   National Parent-Teacher 48:39, Sep., 1953
   New York Times p. 34, Oct. 1, 1953

Gentle Julia (1936)
   Canadian Magazine 85:59, Apr., 1936
   New York Times p. 19, Apr. 11, 1936
   Scholastic 28:30, Feb. 8, 1936
   Time 27:36, Apr. 27, 1936

Gentle Touch (1957)
   Commonweal 66:523, Aug. 23, 1957

Gentleman After Dark (1942)
   Commonweal 36:15, Apr. 24, 1942
   New York Times p. 21, Apr. 17, 1942

Gentleman at Heart (1942)
   New York Times p. 25, Feb. 23, 1942

Gentleman Jim (1942)
   Commonweal 37:231, Dec. 18, 1942
   New York Times p. 40, Nov. 26, 1942; VIII, p. 3, Nov.
      29, 1942
   Newsweek 20:68, Nov. 9, 1942
   Time 40:110+, Dec. 4, 1942

Gentleman's Agreement (1947)
   Canadian Forum 28:39, May, 1948
   Commentary 5:51-6, Jan., 1948; 7:278-80, Mar., 1949
   Commonweal 47:144, Nov. 21, 1947
   Cosmopolitan 124:10-11+, Jan., 1948
   Good Housekeeping 125:10, Nov., 1947
   Life 23:95-6+, Dec. 1, 1947; 24:59, Mar. 8, 1948
   New Republic 117:38, Nov. 17, 1947
   New York Times II, p. 5, Nov. 9, 1947; p. 36, Nov. 12,
      1947; II, p. 1, Nov. 16, 1947; p. 17, Dec. 30, 1947

Gentleman's Agreement (1947) (Continued)
New Yorker 23:117, Nov. 15, 1947
Newsweek 30:98, Nov. 17, 1947
Photoplay 32:20, Feb., 1948
Saturday Review 30:68-71, Dec. 6, 1947
Scholastic 51:32, Dec. 8, 1947
Theatre Arts 32:32-3, Jan., 1948
Time 50:105, Nov. 17, 1947; 51:101, Jan. 19, 1948
Woman's Home Companion 75:10-11, Feb., 1948

Gentleman's Fate (1931)
New York Times p. 20, Jun. 27, 1931

Gentlemen Are Born (1934)
Movie Classic 7:48-51+, Jan., 1935
New York Times p. 27, Nov. 22, 1934

Gentlemen Marry Brunettes (1955)
America 94:287, Dec. 3, 1955
National Parent-Teacher 50:39, Nov., 1955
New York Times p. 31, Oct. 31, 1955
Time 66:112+, Oct. 17, 1955

Gentlemen of the Press (1928)
New York Times p. 27, May 13, 1929; IX, p. 7, May 19,
1929; VIII, p. 5, Aug. 4, 1929

Gentlemen Prefer Blondes (1953)
America 89:446, Aug. 1, 1953
Catholic World 177:384, Aug., 1953
Commonweal 58:442, Aug. 7, 1953
Coronet 34:6, Aug., 1953
Library Journal 78:1321, Aug., 1953
Life 34:79-80+, May 25, 1953
National Parent-Teacher 48:39, Sep., 1953
New York Times II, p. 5, Jul. 12, 1953; p. 17, Jul. 16,
1953; II, p. 1, Jul. 19, 1953
New Yorker 29:46, Jul. 25, 1953
Newsweek 42:76-7, Jul. 27, 1953
Saturday Review 36:27, Aug. 1, 1953
Time 62:88, Jul. 27, 1953

George Raft Story (1961)
New York Times p. 40, Mar. 22, 1962
Newsweek 59:65, Jan. 8, 1962
Saturday Review 45:50, Jan. 13, 1962

George Washington Carver (1940)
New York Times p. 26, Apr. 17, 1940

George Washington Slept Here (1942)
Commonweal 37:97, Nov. 13, 1942
Life 13:57-9, Nov. 30, 1942
Musician 47:184, Jan., 1943
New York Times p. 11, Oct. 31, 1942; VIII, p. 4, Nov.
8, 1942
Newsweek 20:66, Nov. 9, 1942
Time 40:94, Nov. 30, 1942

George White's Scandals (1935)
Movie Classic 8:23, Apr., 1935
New York Times p. 24, Mar. 16, 1934; X, p. 3, Mar.
25, 1934; p. 12, Apr. 29, 1935
Newsweek 3:39, Mar. 24, 1934
Vanity Fair 44:45, May, 1935

George White's Scandals (1945)
New York Times p. 26, Oct. 11, 1945
Newsweek 26:90, Aug. 20, 1945
Time 46:98+, Oct. 27, 1945

Geraldine (1928)
New York Times p. 20, Mar. 4, 1929

Geraldine (1954)
National Parent-Teacher 48:39, Feb., 1954

Germany Year Zero (1949)
Christian Century 67:127, Jan. 25, 1950
Commonweal 50:632, Oct. 7, 1949
Harper 199:100-2, Oct., 1949
New Republic 121:22, Oct. 3, 1949
New York Times p. 35, Sep. 20, 1949; II, p. 1, Sep. 25,
1949
New Yorker 25:52+, Sep. 24, 1949
Newsweek 34:90, Sep. 26, 1949
Rotarian 76:36, Mar., 1950
Saturday Review 32:26, Oct. 15, 1949
Theatre Arts 33:7+, Oct., 1949
Time 54:96, Sep. 26, 1949

Geronimo (1940)
New York Times p. 13, Nov. 27, 1939; p. 18, Feb. 8,
1940

Geronimo (1940) (Continued)
Photoplay 54:63, Feb., 1940
Saint Nicholas 66:41+, Oct., 1939
Scholastic 35:37, Jan. 8, 1940

Geronimo (1962)
Newsweek 59:110-11, May 14, 1962

Gervaise (1957)
Commonweal 67:202-4, 210, Nov. 22, 1957
Library Journal 83:588, Feb. 15, 1958
Nation 185:396, Nov. 23, 1957
National Parent-Teacher 52:39, Jan., 1958
New York Times p. 46, Nov. 12, 1957; II, p. 1, Nov. 17,
    1957; II, p. 11, Dec. 8, 1957; II, p. 1, Jan. 19, 1958
New York Times Magazine p. 79, Nov. 3, 1957
New Yorker 33:83, Nov. 23, 1957
Newsweek 50:120, Nov. 11, 1957
Reporter 18:42-3, Jan. 23, 1958
Saturday Review 40:30, Nov. 16, 1957

Get Away (1941)
New York Times p. 23, Jul. 17, 1941

Get Hep to Love (1943)
New York Times p. 15, Oct. 19, 1942

Getting Gertie's Garter (1945)
Commonweal 43:406, Feb. 1, 1946
New York Times p. 21, Feb. 4, 1946

Ghost and Mrs. Muir (1947)
Commonweal 46:311, Jul. 11, 1947
New Republic 116:36, May 26, 1947
New York Times II, p. 5, Jun. 22, 1947; p. 17, Jun. 27,
    1947
New Yorker 23:42, Jul. 5, 1947
Newsweek 29:76, Jun. 30, 1947
Theatre Arts 31:28, Jul., 1947
Time 49:93, Jun. 23, 1947
Woman's Home Companion 74:10-11, Aug., 1947

Ghost Breakers (1940)
New York Times p. 12, Jul. 4, 1940; IX, p. 3, Jul. 21,
    1940
Newsweek 15:51, Jun. 24, 1940
Photoplay 54:61, Aug., 1940

Ghost Catchers (1944)
New York Times p. 22, May 31, 1944

Ghost Goes West (1936)
Commonweal 23:356, Jan. 24, 1936
Literary Digest 121:20, Jan. 18, 1936
Nation 142:138+, Jan. 29, 1936
New York Times IX, p. 4, Jan. 5, 1936; p. 33, Dec. 18,
1935; p. 9, Jan. 11, 1936
Newsweek 7:40, Jan. 18, 1936
Scholastic 28:26, Feb. 1, 1936
Stage 13:9, Feb., 1936
Time 27:57, Jan. 20, 1936

Ghost of Frankenstein (1942)
New York Times p. 19, Apr. 4, 1942

Ghost Ship (1943)
Life 15:18-20, Sep. 13, 1943
New York Times p. 19, Dec. 25, 1943

Ghost Town (1956)
National Parent-Teacher 50:39, Mar., 1956

Ghost Train (1931)
New York Times p. 13, Feb. 18, 1933

Ghoul (1931)
Canadian Magazine 81:42, Jun., 1934
New York Times p. 9, Jan. 27, 1934

Giant (1956)
Catholic World 184:221-2, Dec., 1956
Commonweal 65:102-3, Oct. 26, 1956
Library Journal 81:2548, Nov. 1, 1956
Life 41:68-70+, Oct. 15, 1956
Nation 183:334, Oct. 20, 1956
National Parent-Teacher 51:39, Dec., 1956
New York Times p. 51, Oct. 11, 1956; II, p. 1, Oct. 21,
1956
New Yorker 32:178, Oct. 20, 1956
Newsweek 48:112+, Oct. 22, 1956
Saturday Review 39:28-9, Oct. 13, 1956
Scholastic 69:33, Nov. 15, 1956
Time 68:108+, Oct. 22, 1956

Giant of Marathon (1960)
New York Times p. 37, May 26, 1960

Gideon of Scotland Yard (1959)
Library Journal 83:2278, Sep. 1, 1958
New York Times p. 38, May 20, 1959; II, p. 1, May 24, 1959
Time 73:91, Jun. 8, 1959

Gidget (1959)
Library Journal 84:1119, Apr. 1, 1959
New York Times p. 27, Apr. 23, 1959

Gidget Goes Hawaiian (1961)
America 105:811, Sep. 23, 1961
New York Times p. 17, Aug. 10, 1961

Gidget Goes to Rome (1963)
New York Times p. 32, Sep. 12, 1963
Time 82:74, Aug. 16, 1963

Gift of Gab (1934)
New York Times p. 17, Sep. 26, 1934

Gift of Love (1958)
America 98:707, Mar. 15, 1958
New York Times p. 32, Feb. 12, 1958
New Yorker 34:76, Feb. 22, 1958
Newsweek 51:108+, Mar. 10, 1958
Time 71:98, Feb. 24, 1958

*Gigi
Commonweal 51:511, Feb. 17, 1950
Life 28:71-2+, Apr. 3, 1950
New Republic 122:23, Feb. 20, 1950
New York Times p. 20, Jan. 31, 1950
Newsweek 35:85, Mar. 6, 1950

Gigi (1958)
America 99:298-9, May 31, 1958
Catholic World 187:223, Jun., 1958
Commonweal 68:183, May 16, 1958
Cosmopolitan 144:76-9, May, 1958
Dance Magazine 32:22, May, 1958
Library Journal 83:1389, May 1, 1958
Life 44:105-10, Apr. 28, 1958
Nation 186:551, Jun. 14, 1958
New Republic 138:22, Jun. 9, 1958
New York Times p. 21, May 16, 1958; II, p. 1, May 18, 1958

Gigi (1958) (Continued)
New Yorker 34:73, May 24, 1958
Newsweek 51:98, May 26, 1958
Saturday Review 41:28, May 17, 1958
Time 71:98+, May 19, 1958

Gigolette (1935)
New York Times p. 18, May 13, 1935; p. 20, Sep. 12, 1936

Gigot (1962)
America 107:967, Oct. 27, 1962
Good Housekeeping 155:26, Sep., 1962
New Republic 147:26, Oct. 8, 1962
New York Times II, p. 5, Jul. 2, 1961; p. 26, Sep. 28, 1962
New Yorker 38:158, Oct. 6, 1962
Newsweek 60:60, Oct. 1, 1962
Saturday Review 45:65, Oct. 27, 1962
Senior Scholastic 81:32, Sep. 12, 1962
Time 80:102, Oct. 12, 1962

Gilbert and Sullivan (1953)
America 90:139, Oct. 31, 1953
Catholic World 178:225, Dec., 1953
Commonweal 59:91, Oct. 30, 1953
Farm Journal 78:83, Jan., 1954
Library Journal 78:1927, Nov. 1, 1953
Life 33:49-52, Dec. 22, 1952
Musical America 73:8, Nov. 15, 1953
National Parent-Teacher 48:38, Dec., 1953
New York Times p. 36, Oct. 28, 1953; II, p. 1, Nov. 1, 1953
New York Times Magazine p. 34, Oct. 18, 1953
New Yorker 29:121, Oct. 31, 1953
Newsweek 42:88, Nov. 2, 1953
Saturday Review 36:31-2, Oct. 31, 1953
Scholastic 63:29, Jan. 13, 1954
Time 62:108, Oct. 26, 1953

Gilda (1946)
Commonweal 43:623, Apr. 5, 1946
Cosmopolitan 120:60+, Apr., 1946
New York Times II, p. 3, Sep. 16, 1945; p. 27, Mar. 15, 1946; II, p. 3, Mar. 17, 1946
New Yorker 22:77, Mar. 23, 1946
Newsweek 27:94, Mar. 25, 1946

Gilda (1946) (Continued)
Photoplay 28:22, May, 1946
Time 47:94, Apr. 1, 1946
Woman's Home Companion 73:11, May, 1946

Guilded Lily (1935)
Literary Digest 119:33, Feb. 23, 1935
New Republic 81:361, Feb. 6, 1935
New York Times p. 11, Feb. 9, 1935
Vanity Fair 44:54, Mar., 1935

Gildersleeve's Bad Day (1943)
New York Times p. 23, Jun. 11, 1943

Ginger (1935)
Commonweal 22:347, Aug. 2, 1935
Literary Digest 120:25, Aug. 3, 1935
New York Times p. 13, Jul. 19, 1935
Time 26:38, Jul. 15, 1935

Girl, a Guy and a Gob (1941)
Commonweal 34:39, May 2, 1941
New York Times p. 25, Apr. 24, 1941
Newsweek 17:62, Mar. 17, 1941
Time 37:92, Mar. 17, 1941

Girl and the Gambler (1939)
New York Times p. 17, Jun. 23, 1939

Girl Can't Help It (1956)
America 96:492, Jan. 26, 1957
National Parent-Teacher 51:38, Feb., 1957
New York Times p. 12, Feb. 9, 1957; II, p. 1, Feb. 10, 1957
Newsweek 48:61, Dec. 31, 1956
Time 69:100, Jan. 14, 1957

Girl Crazy (1932)
New York Times p. 23, Mar. 25, 1932

Girl Crazy (1943)
Commonweal 39:233, Dec. 17, 1943
Good Housekeeping 117:2, Oct., 1943
New York Times p. 27, Dec. 3, 1943
Photoplay 23:20, Nov., 1943
Time 42:90, Dec. 27, 1943
Woman's Home Companion 70:2, Oct., 1943

Girl Downstairs (1938)
New York Times p. 17, Jan. 26, 1939

Girl Friend (1935)
New York Times p. 12, Sep. 28, 1935

Girl from Alaska (1942)
New York Times VIII, p. 3, Mar. 1, 1942

Girl from Avenue A (1940)
Child Life 19:410, Sep., 1940

Girl from Brooklyn (1939)
New York Times XI, p. 5, Mar. 19, 1939

Girl from Chicago (1927)
Life (NY) 91:24, Jan. 5, 1928
New York Times p. 33, Dec. 20, 1927; VIII, p. 7, Dec.
25, 1927

Girl from God's Country (1940)
New York Times p. 18, Sep. 9, 1940

Girl from Havana (1929)
New York Times p. 16, Sep. 2, 1929; IX, p. 4, Sep. 8,
1929

Girl from Jones Beach (1949)
Commonweal 50:415, Aug. 5, 1949
New York Times p. 9, Jul. 30, 1949
Newsweek 34:66, Aug. 1, 1949
Rotarian 75:39, Oct., 1949
Time 54:79, Jul. 25, 1949

Girl from Maxim's (1933)
Vogue 81:43, Mar. 1, 1933

Girl from Maxim's (1936)
New York Times p. 29, Sep. 16, 1936

Girl from Mexico (1939)
New York Times p. 31, Jun. 8, 1939
Photoplay 53:79, Aug., 1939

Girl from Missouri (1934)
Literary Digest 118:27, Aug. 18, 1934
New York Times p. 14, Aug. 4, 1934; IX, p. 3, Aug. 12,
1934

Girl from Scotland Yard (1937)
    New York Times p. 11, May 31, 1937

Girl from Tenth Avenue (1935)
    New York Times p. 12, May 25, 1935

Girl Habit (1931)
    New York Times p. 11, Jul. 4, 1931

Girl He Left Behind (1956)
    Commonweal 65:207, Nov. 23, 1956
    National Parent-Teacher 51:36, Jan., 1957
    New York Times p. 17, Oct. 27, 1956; II, p. 1, Nov. 4,
        1956
    New Yorker 32:126, Nov. 10, 1956
    Newsweek 48:132, Nov. 12, 1956
    Time 68:100, Dec. 3, 1956

Girl in Black (1959)
    Commonweal 67:49, Oct. 11, 1957
    Library Journal 82:2525, Oct. 15, 1957
    National Parent-Teacher 52:37, Nov., 1957
    New York Times p. 39, Sep. 17, 1957
    New York Times Magazine p. 27, Jul. 21, 1957
    New Yorker 33:91, Sep. 28, 1957
    Saturday Review 40:23, Oct. 5, 1957
    Time 70:98+, Oct. 7, 1957

Girl in Every Port (1928)
    New York Times p. 14, Feb. 20, 1928; VIII, p. 7, Feb.
        26, 1928

Girl in Every Port (1952)
    New York Times p. 23, Feb. 14, 1952
    Time 59:71, Feb. 25, 1952

Girl in 419 (1933)
    New York Times p. 11, May 20, 1933; IX, p. 3, May 28,
        1933

Girl in Room 313 (1940)
    New York Times p. 25, Jun. 14, 1940

Girl in the Bikini (1958)
    New York Times p. 16, Oct. 25, 1958

Girl in the Kremlin (1957)
    National Parent-Teacher 51:37, Jun., 1957

433

Girl in the Kremlin (1957) (Continued)
New York Times p. 29, May 22, 1957

Girl in the News (1941)
New Republic 104:729, May 26, 1941
New York Times p. 13, May 5, 1941; IX, p. 3, May 11,
1941
Scribner's Commentator 10:105, Jul., 1941

Girl in the Painting (1949)
Commonweal 50:536, Sep. 9, 1949
New Republic 121:21, Sep. 5, 1949
New York Times p. 13, Aug. 22, 1949
Newsweek 34:69, Sep. 5, 1949
Rotarian 76:41, Jan., 1950
Theatre Arts 33:8, Nov., 1949
Time 54:76, Aug. 29, 1949

Girl in the Red Velvet Swing (1955)
Collier's 136:96, Nov. 11, 1955
Library Journal 80:2594, Nov. 15, 1955
Life 39:70-2+, Sep. 12, 1955
National Parent-Teacher 50:39, Dec., 1955
New York Times p. 41, Oct. 20, 1955; II, p. 1, Oct. 23,
1955
New Yorker 31:145, Oct. 29, 1955
Newsweek 46:118, Nov. 7, 1955
Time 66:116+, Nov. 7, 1955

Girl in White (1952)
Catholic World 175:223, Jun., 1952
Christian Century 69:983, Aug. 27, 1952
Commonweal 56:435, Aug. 8, 1952
Library Journal 77:873, May 15, 1952
New York Times p. 12, May 31, 1952
New Yorker 28:81, May 31, 1952
Newsweek 39:110, May 19, 1952
Saturday Review 35:31, May 3, 1952
Theatre Arts 36:96, Jun., 1952
Time 59:96, Jun. 16, 1952

Girl Loves Boy (1937)
Scholastic 30:28, Apr. 24, 1937

Girl Missing (1933)
New York Times p. 18, Apr. 1, 1933

Girl Most Likely (1958)
Catholic World 186:301, Jan., 1958
New York Times p. 47, Oct. 9, 1958
Senior Scholastic 72:28, Mar. 7, 1958

Girl Must Live (1941)
New York Times p. 25, Mar. 24, 1942

Girl Named Tamiko (1962)
New York Times p. 8, Mar. 15, 1963
Newsweek 61:81, Apr. 1, 1963
Time 81:E10, Mar. 22, 1963

Girl Next Door (1953)
National Parent-Teacher 47:36, Jun., 1953
New York Times p. 7, Sep. 5, 1953

Girl Number 217 (1945)
Nation 161:385, Oct. 13, 1945
New York Times p. 17, Sep. 3, 1945
Time 46:56, Sep. 24, 1945

Girl of the Golden West (1930)
New York Times p. 17, Oct. 27, 1930; VIII, p. 5, Nov.
2, 1930

Girl of the Golden West (1938)
Commonweal 27:636, Apr. 1, 1938
New York Times p. 15, Mar. 25, 1938
Saint Nicholas 65:37+, Apr., 1938

Girl of the Limberlost (1934)
New York Times p. 24, Nov. 9, 1934

Girl of the Night (1960)
Commonweal 73:179, Nov. 11, 1960
New York Times p. 15, Nov. 12, 1960; II, p. 1, Nov.
27, 1960
Saturday Review 43:87, Nov. 12, 1960

Girl of the Rio (1932)
New York Times p. 21, Jan. 9, 1932

Girl on the Barge (1928)
New York Times p. 31, Feb. 26, 1929

Girl on the Front Page (1936)
New York Times p. 15, Nov. 7, 1936

Girl on the Third Floor (1958)
New York Times p. 18, Oct. 11, 1958

Girl Overboard (1937)
New York Times p. 15, Mar. 1, 1937

Girl Rush (1955)
America 94:28, Oct. 1, 1955
National Parent-Teacher 50:39, Nov., 1955
New York Times II, p. 5, Jan. 9, 1955

Girl Said No (1930)
Life (NY) 95:18, Apr. 25, 1930
New York Times p. 23, Apr. 5, 1930; X, p. 4, Apr. 13, 1930

Girl Said No (1937)
New York Times XI, p. 3, Mar. 21, 1937; X, p. 4, Jun. 27, 1937; p. 14, Oct. 18, 1937; XI, p. 5, Oct. 24, 1937
Scholastic 31:36, Nov. 6, 1937
Time 29:45, Jun. 21, 1937

Girl Trouble (1942)
Commonweal 36:617, Oct. 16, 1942
New York Times p. 31, Oct. 8, 1942

Girl Was Young (1938)
Nation 146:193, Feb. 12, 1938
New York Times p. 27, Feb. 11, 1938; X, p. 4, Feb. 13, 1938; XI, p. 5, Feb. 20, 1938
Stage 15:38, Mar., 1938
Time 31:32, Feb. 14, 1938

Girl Who Had Everything (1953)
Library Journal 78:724, Apr. 15, 1953

Girl with a Suitcase (1961)
Commonweal 74:498, Sep. 8, 1961
New Republic 145:22, Sep. 11, 1961
New York Times p. 36, Sep. 12, 1961; II, p. 1, Sep. 17, 1961
New Yorker 37:86+, Sep. 16, 1961
Newsweek 58:105, Sep. 18, 1961
Saturday Review 44:32, Sep. 9, 1961
Time 78:89, Sep. 8, 1961

Girl with Ideas (1937)
New York Times p. 11, Jan. 1, 1938

*Girl with the Golden Eyes
Commonweal 76:498, Sep. 7, 1962
Esquire 59:114+, Jan., 1963
New York Times p. 36, Aug. 21, 1962; II, p. 1, Sep. 9,
1962
New Yorker 38:56, Sep. 1, 1962
Newsweek 60:77, Aug. 27, 1962
Reporter 27:46, Sep. 27, 1962
Saturday Review 45:19, Sep. 1, 1962
Time 80:81, Aug. 24, 1962

Girl with the Guitar (1960)
New York Times p. 22, Feb. 1, 1960

Girl without a Room (1933)
New York Times p. 26, Dec. 7, 1933; IX, p. 7, Dec. 17,
1933
Newsweek 2:30, Dec. 16, 1933

Girls, Les (1957)
America 98:92, Oct. 19, 1957
Commonweal 67:74, Oct. 18, 1957
Coronet 43:10, Nov., 1957
Dance Magazine 31:11+, Nov., 1957
Library Journal 82:2525, Oct. 15, 1957
Life 43:48-53, Sep. 30, 1957
Look 21:104-5, Sep. 17, 1957
National Parent-Teacher 52:38, Nov., 1957
New Republic 137:21, Dec. 23, 1957
New York Times p. 27, Oct. 4, 1957; II, p. 1, Oct. 14,
1957
New Yorker 33:108, Oct. 12, 1957
Newsweek 50:122+, Oct. 14, 1957
Saturday Review 40:54, Oct. 19, 1957
Time 70:112, Oct. 14, 1957

Girls About Town (1931)
New York Times p. 27, Nov. 2, 1931; VIII, p. 5, Nov.
8, 1931

Girls Demand Excitement (1931)
Life (NY) 97:22, Mar. 6, 1931
New York Times p. 11, Feb. 7, 1931

Girls Dormitory (1936)
  Canadian Magazine 86:36, Aug., 1936
  Literary Digest 122:20, Aug. 29, 1936
  New York Times p. 16, Aug. 29, 1936
  Newsweek 8:31, Aug. 8, 1936
  Time 28:30, Aug. 24, 1936

Girls Gone Wild (1929)
  New York Times p. 23, Apr. 22, 1929; IX, p. 7, Apr.
  28, 1929

Girls in the Night (1953)
  National Parent-Teacher 47:27, Mar., 1953
  New York Times p. 19, Jan. 6, 1953
  Time 61:96, Jan. 26, 1953

Girls of Pleasure Island (1953)
  Library Journal 78:806, May 1, 1953
  McCalls 80:10, Apr., 1953
  National Parent-Teacher 47:37, May, 1953
  New York Times p. 10, May 16, 1953
  Newsweek 41:104, Apr. 13, 1953
  Time 61:108, Apr. 6, 1953

Girls of the Night (1959)
  New York Times p. 13, Mar. 29, 1959

Girls of the Road (1940)
  New York Times p. 20, Jul. 23, 1940

Girls on Probation (1937)
  New York Times p. 27, Oct. 21, 1938

Girls' School (1938)
  New Republic 96:362, Nov. 2, 1938
  New York Times p. 27, Nov. 3, 1938

Girl's School (1950)
  New York Times p. 29, Feb. 3, 1950

Girls Under 21 (1940)
  New York Times p. 22, Nov. 11, 1940

Gitta Discovers Her Heart (1932)
  New York Times p. 17, Sep. 30, 1932

Give a Girl a Break (1953)
  Catholic World 178:64, Oct., 1953

Give a Girl a Break (1953) (Continued)
National Parent-Teacher 48:38, Oct., 1953
Saturday Review 36:30, Dec. 19, 1953

Give and Take (1928)
New York Times p. 27, Dec. 27, 1928

Give Me a Sailor (1938)
New York Times p. 13, Aug. 11, 1938; IX, p. 3, Aug. 14, 1938

Give Me Your Heart (1936)
Canadian Magazine 86:45, Oct., 1936
New York Times p. 18, Sep. 17, 1936
Newsweek 8:31, Aug. 8, 1936
Time 28:31, Sep. 28, 1936

Give My Regards to Broadway (1948)
New Republic 119:30, Jul. 12, 1948
New York Times p. 32, Jun. 23, 1948
Newsweek 31:92+, Jun. 14, 1948
Photoplay 33:21, Aug., 1948
Time 52:60+, Jul. 5, 1948

Give Out Sisters (1942)
New York Times p. 22, Aug. 28, 1942

Give Us This Day (1949)
Commonweal 51:391, Jan. 13, 1950
Library Journal 75:411, Mar. 1, 1950
New Republic 122:22, Jan. 9, 1950
New York Times p. 41, Dec. 21, 1949
New Yorker 25:55, Dec. 24, 1949
Newsweek 35:69, Jan. 9, 1950
Theatre Arts 34:92, Feb., 1950

Give Us This Night (1936)
New York Times p. 18, Apr. 6, 1936
Scholastic 28:26, Apr. 4, 1936
Stage 13:8, Feb., 1936
Time 27:46, Mar. 9, 1936

Give Us Wings (1940)
New York Times p. 43, Nov. 21, 1940

Gladiator (1938)
New York Times IX, p. 3, Jul. 3, 1938; p. 10, Aug. 29, 1938

Glamour (1934)
New York Times p. 12, May 12, 1934

Glamour for Sale (1940)
New York Times p. 33, Nov. 5, 1940

Glass Key (1935)
Literary Digest 119:28, Jun. 29, 1935
New York Times p. 20, Jun. 15, 1935

Glass Key (1942)
Commonweal 37:44, Oct. 30, 1942
New Republic 108:54, Jan. 11, 1943
New York Times p. 27, Oct. 15, 1942
Newsweek 20:78, Oct. 12, 1942

Glass Menagerie (1950)
Christian Century 67:1407, Nov. 22, 1950
Christian Science Monitor Magazine p. 8, Apr. 15, 1950
Commonweal 52:631-2, Oct. 6, 1950
Good Housekeeping 131:215, Aug., 1950
Holiday 8:14+, Aug., 1950
Library Journal 75:1843, Oct. 15, 1950
New Republic 123:22, Oct. 23, 1950
New York Times II, p. 5, Jan. 22, 1950; p. 31, Sep. 29,
    1950; II, p. 1, Oct. 8, 1950
New York Times Magazine p. 58, Jun. 4, 1950
New Yorker 26:60, Sep. 30, 1950
Newsweek 36:90, Oct. 9, 1950
Rotarian 78:38, Jan., 1951
Saturday Review 33:32, Oct. 14, 1950
Scholastic 57:28, Oct. 18, 1950
Time 56:74+, Oct. 2, 1950

Glass Mountain (1949)
New York Times p. 37, May 18, 1950
Newsweek 35:96, Apr. 24, 1950

Glass Slipper (1955)
America 93:26, Apr. 2, 1955
American Magazine 159:16, Apr., 1955
Catholic World 181:62, Apr., 1955
Commonweal 62:49, Apr. 15, 1955
Coronet 38:6, May, 1955
Library Journal 80:642, Mar. 15, 1955
National Parent-Teacher 49:38, Apr., 1955
New York Times p. 19, Mar. 25, 1955; II, p. 1, Apr. 3,
    1955

Glass Slipper (1955) (Continued)
New Yorker 31:117, Apr. 2, 1955
Newsweek 45:113, Apr. 11, 1955
Saturday Review 38:27, Apr. 16, 1955
Scholastic 66:23, Apr. 13, 1955
Time 65:98, Mar. 28, 1955

Glass Tower (1959)
New York Times p. 24, Apr. 27, 1959
New Yorker 35:123, Sep. 12, 1959
Time 74:107, Sep. 21, 1959

Glass Wall (1953)
National Parent-Teacher 47:39, Apr., 1953
Newsweek 41:106-7, Apr. 20, 1953
Time 61:112, Apr. 27, 1953

Glass Web (1953)
America 90:216, Nov. 21, 1953
Farm Journal 78:83, Jan., 1954
Library Journal 78:2009, Nov. 15, 1953
National Parent-Teacher 48:39, Dec., 1953
New York Times p. 37, Nov. 12, 1953
Newsweek 42:99, Nov. 23, 1953
Time 62:118+, Nov. 23, 1953

Glenn Miller Story (1954)
America 90:518, Feb. 13, 1954
Catholic World 178:382, Feb., 1954
Commonweal 59:449, Feb. 5, 1954
Coronet 35:6, Mar., 1954
Farm Journal 78:94, Mar., 1954
Life 36:74, Mar. 1, 1954
Look 18:84-6, Jan. 26, 1954
National Parent-Teacher 48:38, Mar., 1954
New York Times p. 33, Feb. 11, 1954; II, p. 1, Feb.
    14, 1954
New Yorker 30:103, Feb. 20, 1954
Newsweek 43:76, Feb. 1, 1954
Saturday Review 37:29, Feb. 27, 1954
Scholastic 64:37, Mar. 17, 1954
Time 63:90, Mar. 1, 1954

Gloria (1932)
New York Times p. 22, Oct. 28, 1932

Glorifying the American Girl (1929)
New York Times IX, p. 5, May 5, 1929; IX, p. 5, May

441

Glorifying the American Girl (1929) (Continued)
    26, 1929; p. 21, Jan. 11, 1930; VIII, p. 6, Jan. 19,
    1930
Vanity Fair 33:62, Sep., 1929

Glorious Betsy (1928)
    New York Times p. 16, Apr. 27, 1928; IX, p. 5, May 6,
    1928
Outlook 149:105, May 16, 1928

Glory (1955)
    National Parent-Teacher 50:38, Feb., 1956

Glory Alley (1952)
    Commonweal 56:316, Jul. 4, 1952
    Nation 175:138-9, Aug. 16, 1952
    New York Times p. 20, Jul. 30, 1952
    Newsweek 39:110-11, Jun. 16, 1952
    Time 59:106, Jun. 9, 1952

Glory at Sea (1953)
    America 88:662, Mar. 14, 1953
    Commonweal 57:626, Mar. 27, 1953
    National Parent-Teacher 47:38, May, 1953
    New York Times p. 36, Mar. 11, 1953
    New Yorker 29:73, Feb. 28, 1953
    Newsweek 41:86, Mar. 9, 1953
    Saturday Review 36:36, Mar. 7, 1953

Glory Brigade (1953)
    America 89:526, Aug. 29, 1953
    New York Times p. 8, Aug. 15, 1953

Go Chase Yourself (1938)
    New York Times p. 27, Jun. 15, 1938; IX, p. 3, Jun. 19,
    1938

Go for Broke (1951)
    Christian Century 68:777, Jun. 27, 1951
    Commonweal 54:214, Jun. 8, 1951
    New Republic 124:23, Jun. 4, 1951
    New York Times II, p. 5, Oct. 15, 1950; p. 31, May 25,
        1951; II, p. 3, Jun. 3, 1951; II, p. 1, Jun. 10, 1951
    New Yorker 27:93, Jun. 2, 1951
    Newsweek 37:89, May 28, 1951
    Saturday Review 34:30, May 26, 1951
    Scholastic 58:30, Apr. 25, 1951
    Time 57:106+, May 28, 1951

Go-Getter (1937)
New York Times p. 27, Jun. 4, 1937
Time 29:26+, Jun. 14, 1937

Go into Your Dance (1935)
New York Times p. 17, May 4, 1935
Time 25:56, Apr. 29, 1935

Go, Man, Go! (1954)
America 90:666, Mar. 20, 1954
National Parent-Teacher 48:38, Feb., 1954
New York Times II, p. 5, May 17, 1953; p. 29, Mar. 10, 1954
Newsweek 43:90, Jan. 25, 1954
Time 63:96, Feb. 8, 1954

Go Naked in the World (1961)
America 104:800, Mar. 18, 1961
New York Times p. 15, Mar. 11, 1961; II, p. 1, Mar. 19, 1961
New Yorker 37:137, Mar. 25, 1961
Newsweek 57:100, Mar. 27, 1961
Saturday Review 44:31, Feb. 18, 1961

Go West (1940)
Commonweal 33:498, Mar. 7, 1941
New Republic 104:117, Jan. 27, 1941
New York Times p. 16, Feb. 21, 1941; IX, p. 5, Feb. 23, 1941
Scribner's Commentator 10:106, May, 1941
Theatre Arts 25:90, Feb., 1941
Time 36:46, Dec. 23, 1940

Go West, Young Lady (1941)
New York Times p. 11, Nov. 24, 1941

Go West Young Man (1936)
Literary Digest 122:26, Nov. 21, 1936
New York Times IX, p. 4, Nov. 15, 1936; p. 31, Nov. 19, 1936; XI, p. 5, Nov. 22, 1936
Newsweek 8:20, Nov. 28, 1936
Time 28:25, Nov. 23, 1936

God Is My Co-Pilot (1945)
Nation 160:370-71, Mar. 31, 1945
New Yorker 21:76, Mar. 24, 1945
New York Times p. 22, Mar. 24, 1945

God Is My Co-Pilot (1945) (Continued)
Newsweek 25:78, Apr. 2, 1945
Scholastic 46:46, Mar. 26, 1945
Theatre Arts 29:228, Apr., 1945
Time 45:90+, Apr. 2, 1945

God Is My Partner (1957)
National Parent-Teacher 52:33, Oct., 1957
New York Times p. 39, Jun. 5, 1958

God Needs Men (1951)
Christian Century 68:1327, Nov. 14, 1951
Commonweal 53:647, Apr. 6, 1951
New Republic 124:22, Apr. 9, 1951
New York Times p. 35, Mar. 27, 1951; II, p. 1, Apr. 1,
1951; II, p. 5, Apr. 8, 1951
New Yorker 27:73, Mar. 31, 1951
Newsweek 37:82, Apr. 30, 1951
Saturday Review 34:30, Mar. 31, 1951; 38:43, Feb. 12,
1955
Time 57:106+, Apr. 16, 1951

Goddess (1958)
Catholic World 187:141, May, 1958
Commonweal 68:206, May 23, 1958
Nation 187:40, Jul. 19, 1958
New Republic 138:19-20, Jun. 2, 1958
New York Times II, p. 5, Aug. 18, 1957; p. 24, Jun. 25,
1958; II, p. 1, Jun. 29, 1958; II, p. 1, Aug. 24, 1958
New York Times Magazine p. 68, Sep. 22, 1957
New Yorker 34:60, Jul. 5, 1958
Newsweek 51:99, May 26, 1958
Saturday Review 41:21, May 10, 1958
Time 72:70, Jul. 7, 1958

Godless Girl (1928)
New York Times VIII, p. 7, Feb. 19, 1928; VIII, p. 3,
Mar. 11, 1928; p. 22, Apr. 1, 1929
Photoplay Magazine 34:29, Jun., 1928

God's Country and the Woman (1937)
New York Times X, p. 4, Jan. 10, 1937; p. 15, Jan. 11,
1937
Time 29:25, Jan. 18, 1937

God's Gift to Women (1931)
Life (NY) 97:20, May 8, 1931
New York Times p. 17, Apr. 18, 1931

God's Little Acre (1958)
　　Commonweal 68:280, Jun. 13, 1958
　　Cosmopolitan 144:22, Jun., 1958
　　Library Journal 83:2036, Jul., 1958
　　Life 44:93-4+, May 5, 1958
　　New Republic 138:21, Jun. 30, 1958
　　New York Times p. 11, Aug. 9, 1957; II, p. 5, Oct. 20,
　　　　1957; II, p. 7, May 4, 1958; p. 23, Aug. 24, 1958;
　　　　II, p. 1, Aug. 24, 1958
　　Newsweek 51:90, Jun. 2, 1958
　　Time 71:84, Jun. 2, 1958

Godzilla, King of the Monsters (1956)
　　New York Times p. 11, Apr. 28, 1956; II, p. 1, May 6,
　　　　1956
　　Newsweek 47:126, May 14, 1956

Gog (1954)
　　National Parent-Teacher 49:38, Sep., 1954
　　New Republic 131:21, Oct. 25, 1954
　　New York Times p. 8, Aug. 14, 1954
　　Time 62:112, Oct. 19, 1953; 64:78, Jul. 19, 1954

Going Hollywood (1933)
　　Literary Digest 117:31, Jan. 6, 1934
　　New York Times p. 19, Dec. 23, 1933

Going My Way (1944)
　　Catholic World 159:554, Sep., 1944
　　Christian Century 61:1132, Oct. 4, 1944
　　Commonweal 40:41, Apr. 28, 1944
　　Life 16:69-70+, May 1, 1944; 18:37-8+, Apr. 2, 1945
　　Nation 158:577, May 13, 1944
　　New Republic 110:629, May 8, 1944
　　New York Times p. 25, May 3, 1944; II, p. 3, May 7,
　　　　1944; p. 34, Dec. 28, 1944
　　New Yorker 20:66, May 13, 1944
　　Newsweek 23:78+, May 15, 1944
　　Photoplay 26:28-9, Mar., 1945
　　Time 43:90, May 1, 1944

Going Places (1938)
　　New York Times p. 6, Jan. 7, 1939

Goin' to Town (1935)
　　New York Times p. 21, May 11, 1935; IX, p. 3, May 19,
　　　　1935

Going Wild (1930)
New York Times p. 21, Jan. 26, 1931; VIII, p. 5, Feb.
1, 1931

Gold Diggers in Paris (1938)
New York Times p. 19, Jun. 2, 1938
Newsweek 31:24, Jun. 13, 1938
Time 31:24, Jun. 13, 1938

Gold Diggers of Broadway (1929)
Life (NY) 94:23, Sep. 27, 1929
New York Times p. 13, Aug. 31, 1929; IX, p. 4, Sep. 8,
1929

Gold Diggers of 1933 (1933)
Motion Picture 45:42-3+, Jul., 1933
Movie Classic 4:38-9, Jun., 1933
New Outlook 162:43, Jul., 1933
New York Times IX, p. 3, Jun. 4, 1933; p. 22, Jun. 8,
1933; X, p. 3, Jun. 18, 1933; VIII, p. 3, Mar. 10,
1935

Gold Diggers of 1935 (1935)
Literary Digest 119:32, Mar. 30, 1935
New York Times p. 25, Mar. 15, 1935
Time 25:46, Mar. 25, 1935

Gold Diggers of 1937 (1936)
New York Times XI, p. 6, Dec. 13, 1936; p. 19, Dec.
25, 1936
Newsweek 8:23, Dec. 19, 1936
Stage 14:15, Dec., 1936
Time 29:21, Jan. 4, 1937

Gold Dust Gertie (1931)
New York Times p. 9, May 30, 1931

Gold Is Where You Find It (1938)
New York Times X, p. 4, Feb. 6, 1938; p. 20, Feb. 14,
1938; XI, p. 5, Mar. 6, 1938
Scholastic 32:31-2, Feb. 5, 1938
Time 31:58, Feb. 21, 1938

Gold of Naples (1957)
Commonweal 65:539-40, Feb. 22, 1957
Nation 184:194, Mar. 2, 1957
National Parent-Teacher 51:38, Apr., 1957

446

Gold of Naples (1957) (Continued)
New York Times p. 30, Feb. 12, 1957; II, p. 1, Feb.
17, 1957
New Yorker 32:123-4, Feb. 16, 1957
Newsweek 49:110, Feb. 18, 1957
Saturday Review 40:27, Feb. 23, 1957
Time 69:96+, Feb. 25, 1957

Gold of the Seven Saints (1961)
Commonweal 73:559, Feb. 24, 1961
New York Times p. 30, Apr. 6, 1961

Gold Racket (1937)
New York Times p. 10, Aug. 2, 1937

Gold Rush (1942)
Commonweal 36:38, May 1, 1942
Life 12:49-50+, Mar. 30, 1942
Modern Music 19:275-6, May-Jun., 1942
Musician 47:58, Apr., 1942
Nation 154:553, May 9, 1942
New Republic 106:606, May 4, 1942
New York Times p. 17, Apr. 20, 1942; VIII, p. 3, Apr.
26, 1942
New Yorker 18:10, May 2, 1942
Newsweek 19:74, Apr. 20, 1942
Scholastic 40:36, May 18, 1942
Theatre Arts 26:399-40, Jun., 1942
Time 39:80+, Apr. 6, 1942

Gold Rush Maisie (1940)
New York Times X, p. 5, May 5, 1940; p. 19, Sep. 2,
1940

Gold Town Ghost Riders (1953)
National Parent-Teacher 47:39, Apr., 1953

*Goldbergs
Newsweek 37:83, Jan. 15, 1951
Time 57:100, Jan. 29, 1951

Golden Age of Comedy (1957)
New York Times p. 23, Dec. 27, 1957
Reporter 18:39-41, Mar. 6, 1958

Golden Arrow (1936)
New York Times p. 16, May 4, 1936
Time 27:58, May 11, 1936

Golden Blade (1953)
Catholic World 178:62, Oct., 1953
Farm Journal 77:161, Nov., 1953

Golden Boy (1939)
Commonweal 30:459, Sep. 8, 1939
Nation 149:301, Sep. 16, 1939
New York Times p. 28, Sep. 8, 1939; IX, p. 3, Sep. 10, 1939
Newsweek 14:28, Sep. 4, 1939
Time 34:51, Sep. 18, 1939

Golden Coach (1953)
America 90:464, Jan. 30, 1954
Catholic World 178:225-6, Dec., 1953
Commonweal 59:472-3, Feb. 12, 1954
Musical America 74:8, Jan. 15, 1954
National Parent-Teacher 48:39, Mar., 1954
New York Times II, p. 5, May 4, 1952; p. 30, Jan. 22, 1954; II, p. 1, Feb. 7, 1954
New Yorker 29:86, Jan. 30, 1954
Newsweek 43:90, Jan. 25, 1954
Saturday Review 37:62-3, Jan. 23, 1954
Time 63:72+, Feb. 1, 1954

Golden Dawn (1930)
New York Times p. 16, Jul. 26, 1930

Golden Demon (1956)
Catholic World 182:384, Feb., 1956
Commonweal 63:483, Feb. 10, 1956
Library Journal 81:175, Jan. 15, 1956
Life 37:89+, Nov. 15, 1954
Nation 182:126, Feb. 11, 1956
National Parent-Teacher 50:39, Feb., 1956
New York Times p. 34, Jan. 31, 1956; II, p. 1, Feb. 5, 1956
New Yorker 31:118, Feb. 11, 1956
Newsweek 47:98, Jan. 30, 1956
Saturday Review 39:38, Feb. 11, 1956
Time 67:64+, Jan. 30, 1956

Golden Earrings (1947)
Commonweal 47:256, Dec. 19, 1947
New York Times p. 41, Dec. 4, 1947; II, p. 5, Dec. 7, 1947
Newsweek 38:88+, Nov. 3, 1947

Golden Earrings (1947) (Continued)
  Photoplay 31:4, Oct., 1947
  Scholastic 51:35, Nov. 17, 1947
  Time 50:108, Dec. 15, 1947

Golden Fleecing (1940)
  New York Times p. 33, Nov. 7, 1940

Golden Girl (1951)
  Catholic World 174:220-1, Dec., 1951
  New York Times p. 20, Nov. 21, 1951
  Newsweek 38:95, Dec. 3, 1951
  Time 58:110+, Nov. 26, 1951

Golden Gloves (1940)
  New York Times p. 23, Aug. 21, 1940

Golden Gloves Story (1950)
  Christian Century 67:479, Apr. 12, 1950
  Rotarian 76:37, Jun., 1950

*Golden Goal (Das Lockende Ziel)
  Commonweal 18:269-70, Jul. 7, 1933
  Nation 137:55, Jul. 12, 1933
  New York Times p. 18, Jun. 19, 1933; IX, p. 5, Jun.
    25, 1933
  Newsweek 1:30, Jun. 24, 1933

Golden Hawk (1952)
  National Parent-Teacher 47:38, Oct., 1952
  New York Times p. 16, Oct. 18, 1952
  Newsweek 40:107, Nov. 3, 1952

Golden Hoofs (1941)
  Child Life 20:61, Feb., 1941
  Scholastic 38:37, Feb. 24, 1941

Golden Horde (1951)
  Commonweal 55:201, Nov. 30, 1951
  New York Times II, p. 5, Feb. 4, 1951

Golden Madona (1949)
  New York Times p. 13, Sep. 5, 1949

Golden Mask (1954)
  New York Times p. 10, Mar. 20, 1954

Golden Mistress (1954)
New York Times p. 15, Oct. 30, 1954

Golden Mountains (1932)
New York Times p. 25, Apr. 14, 1932

Golden Salamander (1950)
Library Journal 75:885, May 15, 1950
New York Times p. 8, Mar. 24, 1951

Golden Taiga (1935)
New York Times p. 22, Aug. 2, 1935

Golden Twenties (1950)
Commonweal 51:655, Mar. 31, 1950
Good Housekeeping 130:354, May, 1950
House Beautiful 95:185, Mar., 1953
Library Journal 75:885, May 15, 1950
Life 28:165, Apr. 17, 1950
New Republic 122:22, May 1, 1950
New York Times II, p. 5, Oct. 23, 1949; p. 15, Apr. 10,
    1950; II, p. 1, Apr. 16, 1950
New Yorker 26:111, Apr. 8, 1950
Rotarian 77:43, Aug., 1950
Saturday Review 36:39, May 9, 1953
Time 55:92+, Apr. 3, 1950

*Golden Virgin
Catholic World 186:64-5, Oct., 1957
Commonweal 67:50, Oct. 11, 1957
National Parent-Teacher 52:33, Sep., 1957
Saturday Review 40:25, Sep. 7, 1957

Goldie (1931)
New York Times p. 20, Jun. 29, 1931

Goldie Gets Along (1933)
New York Times p. 16, Jun. 3, 1933

Goldwyn Follies (1938)
Commonweal 27:468, Feb. 18, 1938
Life 4:20-3, Feb. 7, 1938
Literary Digest 125:23, Feb. 19, 1938
New York Times p. 15, Feb. 21, 1938; X, p. 5, Feb. 27,
    1938
Newsweek 11:25, Feb. 14, 1938
Stage 15:86, Dec., 1937
Time 31:58, Feb. 7, 1938

Golem (1937)
New York Times XI, p. 4, Mar. 21, 1937; p. 27, Mar.
22, 1937; XI, p. 3, Mar. 28, 1937
Time 29:48, Mar. 29, 1937

*Golgotha
Commonweal 22:76, May 17, 1935; 25:332-3, Jan. 15,
1937

Goliath and the Barbarians (1959)
New York Times p. 24, Jan. 7, 1960

Goliath and the Dragon (1960)
New York Times p. 27, Jan. 5, 1961

Gone Are the Days (1963)
America 109:494-6, Oct. 26, 1963
New Republic 149:28+, Sep. 27, 1963
New York Times p. 43, Sep. 24, 1963; II, p. 1, Oct. 6,
1963
New Yorker 39:178, Oct. 5, 1963
Newsweek 62:84, Sep. 30, 1963
Reporter 31:40, Jul. 16, 1964
Saturday Review 46:44, Sep. 28, 1963

Gone with the Wind (1939)
Catholic World 179:385, Aug., 1954
Collier's 104:20+, Dec. 16, 1939
Commonweal 31:246, Jan. 5, 1940
Esquire 56:62-3, Nov., 1961
Good Housekeeping 130:10, Jan., 1950
House & Garden 76:36-40+, Nov., 1939
Ladies Home Journal 57:25+, Jan., 1940
Life 7:9-13, Dec. 25, 1939; 27:54-5, Aug. 29, 1949
Nation 149:740, Dec. 30, 1939
New Republic 102:53, Jan. 8, 1940; 102:536, Apr. 22,
1940
New York Times IX, p. 5, Feb. 5, 1939; X, p. 5, Apr.
23, 1939; IX, p. 3, Jul. 16, 1939; p. 15, Sep. 1,
1939; VI, p. 2, Sep. 3, 1939; VI, p. 8, Dec. 10,
1939; VII, p. 6, Dec. 10, 1939; p. 31, Dec. 20, 1939;
IX, p. 5, Dec. 24, 1939; p. 17, Mar. 1, 1940; XI,
p. 5, Mar. 10, 1940; X, p. 8, Dec. 8, 1940; VI, p.
22, Oct. 26, 1947; VII, p. 2, Jun. 24, 1956; II, p. 1,
Aug. 26, 1956; p. 34, Apr. 25, 1961; II, p. 1, Apr.
30, 1961
New York Times Magazine p. 22-3+, Oct. 26, 1947

451

Gone with the Wind (1939) (Continued)
  Newsweek 14:26-9, Dec. 25, 1939; 30:77, Sep. 1, 1947;
    43:104, Jun. 14, 1954; 57:102+, Apr. 10, 1961
  Photoplay 51:21-3+, Mar., 1937; 54:68, May, 1940
  Saturday Review 21:10-12, Dec. 23, 1939
  Scholastic 35:32-3, Jan. 8, 1940
  Theatre Arts 24:128-9, Feb., 1940; 25:619, Sep., 1941
  Time 34:30-2, Dec. 25, 1939; 77:46-7, May 5, 1961
  Woman's Home Companion 67:17, Feb., 1940

Good Bad Girl (1931)
  New York Times p. 20, May 15, 1931

Good Companions (1933)
  New York Times p. 24, Oct. 10, 1933; IX, p. 3, Oct.
    15, 1933
  Newsweek 2:30, Oct. 21, 1933

Good Dame (1934)
  New York Times p. 11, Mar. 17, 1934

Good Die Young (1955)
  National Parent-Teacher 49:39, Feb., 1955
  Time 65:106, Mar. 14, 1955

Good Earth (1937)
  Asia 37:314-15, Apr., 1937
  Canadian Magazine 86:29, Sep., 1936
  Commonweal 25:472-3, Feb. 19, 1937
  Independent Woman 16:65+, Mar., 1937
  Life 2:50-56, Jan. 18, 1937
  Literary Digest 123:19-20, Feb. 13, 1937
  Motion Picture 52:40-41+, Oct., 1936
  Movie Classic 11:34-5+, Oct., 1936
  Nation 144:194, Feb. 13, 1937
  New Republic 90:167-8, Mar. 17, 1937
  New York Times XI, p. 6, Jan. 31, 1937; p. 27, Feb. 3,
    1937; X, p. 5, Feb. 7, 1937
  Newsweek 9:23-4, Feb. 13, 1937
  Photoplay 50:38-9, Aug., 1936
  Scholastic 30:22-3, Feb. 20, 1937
  Stage 14:54-6, Apr., 1937; 14:54-5, Jun., 1937
  Studio 17:196-7, May, 1939
  Time 29:55-6, Feb. 15, 1937

Good Fairy (1935)
  Literary Digest 119:22, Feb. 16, 1935

Good Fairy (1935) (Continued)
    New York Times p. 18, Feb. 1, 1935; VIII, p. 5, Feb.
    10, 1935
    Movie Classic 7:44-9+, Feb., 1935
    Time 25:48, Feb. 11, 1935

Good Girls Go to Paris (1939)
    Commonweal 30:278, Jul. 7, 1938
    New York Times p. 23, Jun. 23, 1939; IX, p. 3, Jun.
    25, 1939

Good Humor Man (1950)
    Christian Century 67:959, Aug. 9, 1950
    Library Journal 75:1058, Jun. 15, 1950
    New York Times p. 17, Jul. 14, 1950
    Rotarian 77:38, Sep., 1950

Good Intentions (1930)
    New York Times p. 16, Jul. 26, 1930; VIII, p. 5, Aug.
    3, 1930

Good Morning Judge (1943)
    New York Times p. 25, Apr. 30, 1943

Good Morning, Miss Dove (1955)
    America 94:314+, Dec. 10, 1955
    Catholic World 182:305-6, Jan., 1956
    Commonweal 63:258, Dec. 9, 1955
    Library Journal 80:2855, Dec. 15, 1955
    National Parent-Teacher 50:38, Dec., 1955; 50:11-12,
    Jan., 1956
    New York Times p. 41, Nov. 24, 1955
    New Yorker 31:186, Dec. 3, 1955
    Newsweek 46:98, Dec. 5, 1955
    Time 66:106+, Dec. 5, 1955

Good News (1930)
    Life (NY) 96:20, Oct. 3, 1930
    New York Times p. 9, Sep. 6, 1930

Good News (1947)
    Commonweal 47:304, Jan. 2, 1948
    New York Times p. 33, Dec. 5, 1947; II, p. 5, Dec. 7,
    1947
    Newsweek 30:88, Dec. 15, 1947
    Scholastic 51:36, Jan. 12, 1948
    Time 50:79, Dec. 22, 1947

Good Old Soak (1937)
Canadian Magazine 87:52, Jun., 1937
New York Times p. 25, Apr. 23, 1937
Time 29:32, May 3, 1937

Good Sam (1948)
Canadian Forum 28:183, Nov., 1948
Commonweal 48:573, Sep. 24, 1948
Good Housekeeping 127:10, Sep., 1948
New York Times p. 28, Sep. 17, 1948; II, p. 1, Sep. 26,
  1948
New Yorker 24:104, Sep. 25, 1948
Newsweek 32:92+, Sep. 13, 1948
Time 52:99, Sep. 20, 1948

Good Soldier Schwelk (1963)
Commonweal 78:458, Jun. 26, 1963
New Republic 149:28, Sep. 14, 1963
New York Times p. 38, Aug. 21, 1963
Newsweek 62:79, Sep. 2, 1963

Good Sport (1931)
New York Times p. 23, Dec. 12, 1931; VIII, p. 5, Dec.
  20, 1931

Good Time Charley (1927)
New York Times p. 20, Nov. 21, 1927

Good Time Girl (1950)
New York Times p. 18, Sep. 25, 1950

Goodbye Again (1933)
New Outlook 162:49, Oct., 1933
New York Times p. 15, Sep. 1, 1933
Vanity Fair 41:46+, Sep., 1933

Goodbye Again (1961)
America 105:616, Aug. 12, 1961
Commonweal 74:404, Jul. 14, 1961
New Republic 144:28, Jun. 26, 1961
New York Times II, p. 7, Jan. 8, 1961; II, p. 1, Jul. 9,
  1961; p. 32, Jun. 30, 1961
New Yorker 37:54-5, Jul. 15, 1961
Newsweek 58:72, Jul. 3, 1961
Saturday Review 44:33, Jul. 15, 1961
Time 77:50, Jun. 30, 1961

Goodbye Broadway (1938)
New York Times p. 18, May 14, 1938

Goodbye Kiss (1928)
New York Times p. 18, Nov. 12, 1928

Goodbye, Mr. Chips (1939)
New Republic 99:102, May 31, 1939
New York Times IX, p. 4, Jan. 1, 1939; IX, p. 4, Jan.
22, 1939; IX, p. 5, Feb. 12, 1939; XI, p. 4, May 14,
1939; p. 27, May 16, 1939; X, p. 3, May 21, 1939;
p. 11, Jan. 13, 1940; p. 17, Feb. 28, 1940
Newsweek 13:34-5, May 22, 1939
Scholastic 34:31, May 27, 1939
Theatre Arts 25:696, Sep., 1941
Time 33:56, May 22, 1939

Goodbye, My Fancy (1951)
Christian Century 68:831, Jul. 11, 1951
Commonweal 54:190, Jun. 1, 1951
Library Journal 76:535, Mar. 15, 1951
New York Times II, p. 5, Oct. 29, 1950; p. 14, May 30,
1951; II, p. 1, Jun. 10, 1951
New Yorker 27:96, Jun. 9, 1951
Newsweek 37:102-3, Jun. 11, 1951
Saturday Review 34:26, May 19, 1951
Scholastic 58:30, Apr. 25, 1951
Time 57:102, May 28, 1951

Goodbye, My Lady (1956)
American Magazine 161:8, May, 1956
Catholic World 183:145, May, 1956
Commonweal 64:204, May 25, 1956
Library Journal 81:1265, May 15, 1956
National Parent-Teacher 50:38, May, 1956

Goona Goona, Isle of Bali (1932)
Nation 135:338, Oct. 12, 1932
New York Times p. 18, Sep. 17, 1932

Goose and the Gander (1935)
New York Times p. 29, Sep. 12, 1935
Newsweek 6:18, Sep. 21, 1935
Time 26:47, Sep. 23, 1935

Gorgeous Hussy (1936)
Canadian Magazine 86:45, Oct., 1936
Commonweal 24:487, Sep. 18, 1936

455

Gorgeous Hussy (1936) (Continued)
Literary Digest 122:17, Sep. 12, 1936
New York Times IX, p. 4, Sep. 6, 1936
Stage 14:24, Oct., 1936
Time 28:19, Sep. 7, 1936

Gorgo (1961)
Commonweal 73:587, Mar. 3, 1961
New York Times p. 24, Mar. 30, 1961

Gorilla (1930)
New York Times p. 20, Feb. 23, 1931

Gorilla (1939)
New York Times III, p. 6, May 28, 1939
Newsweek 13:35, Jun. 5, 1939

Gorilla at Large (1954)
National Parent-Teacher 48:39, Jun., 1954
New York Times p. 13, Jun. 12, 1954
Time 62:112, Oct. 19, 1953

Gorilla Man (1943)
New York Times p. 21, Jan. 15, 1943

Government Girl (1943)
New York Times p. 13, Jan. 7, 1944
Newsweek 22:78, Nov. 29, 1943
Time 42:54, Dec. 6, 1943

Gracie Allen Murder Case (1939)
New York Times p. 31, Jun. 8, 1939
Newsweek 13:28, May 29, 1939
Photoplay 53:62, Jul., 1939
Stage 16:34-5, Jun., 1939

*Gran Varietà
Nation 180:383, Apr. 30, 1955
New York Times p. 29, Apr. 11, 1955
Newsweek 45:108, Apr. 25, 1955

Grand Canary (1934)
New York Times p. 11, Jul. 20, 1934

Grand Central Murder (1942)
New York Times p. 8, May 23, 1942

Grand Exit (1935)
New York Times p. 24, Nov. 4, 1935

Grand Hotel (1932)
Canadian Forum 12:399, Jul., 1932
Commonweal 16:351, Aug. 3, 1932
Literary Digest 113:15, May 7, 1932
Motion Picture 43:52-3+, May, 1932
Nation 134:498, Apr. 27, 1932
New Republic 70:301, Apr. 27, 1932
New York Times VIII, p. 4, Feb. 14, 1932; VIII, p. 5,
    Mar. 27, 1932; VIII, p. 5, Apr. 3, 1952; p. 23, Apr.
    13, 1932; VIII, p. 4, Apr. 17, 1932; IX, p. 2, Jun. 4,
    1933
Vanity Fair 38:24-5, Jun., 1932

Grand Illusion (1938)
Commonweal 28:590, Sep. 30, 1938
Current History 49:45-6, Dec., 1938
Life 5:35-6, Oct. 10, 1938
Nation 147:433-4, Oct. 22, 1938
New Republic 96:307, Oct. 19, 1938
New York Times X, p. 4, Sep. 11, 1938; p. 28, Sep. 13,
    1938; X, p. 3, Sep. 18, 1938; IX, p. 4, Oct. 23,
    1938; p. 11, Dec. 17, 1938; p. 18, Jan. 3, 1939; XI,
    p. 5, Jan. 8, 1939
Photoplay 58:45, Jan., 1939
Theatre Arts 25:656, Sep., 1941
Time 32:50, Sep. 26, 1938
Vogue 92:74, Oct. 1, 1938

Grand Jury (1936)
New York Times p. 16, Aug. 1, 1936

Grand Jury Secrets (1939)
New York Times p. 19, Jun. 29, 1939

Grand Maneuver (1956)
Commonweal 65:73, Oct. 19, 1956
National Parent-Teacher 51:39, Nov., 1956
New York Times II, p. 7, Sep. 23, 1956; p. 39, Oct. 2,
    1956
New Yorker 31:149, Nov. 19, 1955; 32:181, Oct. 13, 1956
Newsweek 48:114, Oct. 22, 1956
Time 68:112+, Oct. 15, 1956

Grand Old Girl (1934)
New York Times p. 16, Feb. 26, 1935

Grand Parade (1929)
New York Times p. 15, Feb. 1, 1930

Grand Slam (1933)
New York Times p. 25, Feb. 22, 1933

Granny Get Your Gun (1939)
Photoplay 54:63, Mar., 1940

Grapes of Wrath (1940)
Collier's 105:23+, Jan. 27, 1940
Commonweal 31:348, Feb. 9, 1940
Fortnightly 154(ns 148):409-16, Oct., 1940
Life 8:29-31, Jan. 22, 1940; 8:10-11, Feb. 19, 1940
Nation 150:137-8, Feb. 3, 1940
New Republic 102:212, Feb. 12, 1940
New York Times X, p. 7, Dec. 10, 1939; IX, p. 5, Dec. 24, 1939; p. 17, Jan. 25, 1940; IX, p. 5, Jan. 28, 1940; IX, p. 5, Feb. 4, 1940; p. 23, Dec. 23, 1940; p. 20, Dec. 30, 1940
Newsweek 15:37-8, Feb. 12, 1940
Photoplay 53:22-3+, Nov., 1939; 54:44-5, Mar., 1940; 54:68, Apr., 1940
Saturday Review 21:16, Feb. 10, 1940
Scholastic 36:36, Feb. 5, 1940
Theatre Arts 24:214, Mar., 1940; 25:619, Sep., 1941
Time 35:70+, Feb. 12, 1940

Grass Is Greener (1961)
America 104:480, Jan. 14, 1961
Commonweal 73:463, Jan. 27, 1961
Esquire 55:46, May, 1961
New Republic 143:21-2, Dec. 26, 1960
New York Times p. 8, Dec. 24, 1960
New Yorker 36:63, Jan. 7, 1961
Newsweek 57:66, Jan. 2, 1961
Redbook 116:13, Feb., 1961
Time 77:42, Jan. 6, 1961

Great Adventure (1955)
America 93:279, Jun. 4, 1955
Catholic World 181:305, Jul., 1955
Commonweal 62:231, Jun. 3, 1955
House Beautiful 99:100-1+, Feb., 1957
Life 38:71-2+, Jun. 13, 1955
Nation 180:510-11, Jun. 11, 1955
National Parent-Teacher 50:38, Sep., 1955; 51:39, Oct., 1956

Great Adventure (1955) (Continued)
  Natural History 64:334, Jun. , 1955
  New York Times p. 34, May 24, 1955; II, p. 1, May 29,
    1955
  New Yorker 31:123, Jun. 11, 1955
  Newsweek 45:112, May 16, 1955
  Saturday Review 38:27, Jun. 4, 1955; 39:32, Dec. 15,
    1956
  Scholastic 67:25, Jan. 12, 1956
  Time 65:91, Jun. 20, 1955

Great American Broadcast (1941)
  Commonweal 34:86, May 16, 1941
  New Republic 104:793, Jun. 9, 1941
  New York Times p. 25, May 2, 1941
  Newsweek 17:60, May 12, 1941
  Scribner's Commentator 10:104, Jul. , 1941
  Time 37:54+, May 19, 1941

Great American Pastime (1956)
  Commonweal 65:312, Dec. 21, 1956
  National Parent-Teacher 51:36, Jan. , 1957
  Newsweek 48:118, Dec. 10, 1956
  Scholastic 69:27, Jan. 18, 1957

Great Caruso (1951)
  Christian Century 68:695, Jun. 6, 1951
  Commonweal 54:117, May 11, 1951
  Library Journal 76:883, May 15, 1951
  New York Times II, p. 5, Sep. 10, 1950; II, p. 4, Oct.
    22, 1950; p. 32, May 11, 1951; II, p. 1, May 20,
    1951; II, p. 5, Jul. 8, 1951; p. 20, Jul. 19, 1951
  New Yorker 27:107, May 19, 1951
  Newsweek 37:98+, May 14, 1951
  Saturday Review 34:26, May 12, 1951
  Time 57:116+, May 21, 1951

Great Chase (1963)
  Commonweal 77:462+, Jan. 25, 1963
  New York Times p. 5, Dec. 21, 1962
  New Yorker 38:60, Dec. 29, 1962
  Newsweek 61:58, Jan. 7, 1963

Great Citizen (1939)
  New York Times p. 11, Jan. 16, 1939

Great Commandment (1939, 1941)
  New York Times X, p. 5, Mar. 3, 1940; p. 11, Oct. 17, 1942

Great Commandment (1939, 1941) (Continued)
  Time 34:77-8, Nov. 6, 1939

Great Dan Patch (1949)
  New York Times p. 37, Nov. 9, 1949
  Newsweek 34:78, Jul. 25, 1949
  Rotarian 75:39, Oct., 1949
  Time 54:66, Aug. 1, 1949

*Great Dawn
  Musician 52:76, Dec., 1947
  Nation 165:320, Sep. 27, 1947
  New York Times p. 28, Aug. 28, 1947

Great Day in the Morning (1956)
  Library Journal 81:898, Apr. 15, 1956
  National Parent-Teacher 50:39, May, 1956
  New York Times p. 12, May 19, 1956

Great Diamond Robbery (1954)
  National Parent-Teacher 48:39, Feb., 1954
  Newsweek 43:80, Jan. 11, 1954
  Time 63, 94+, Feb. 15, 1954

Great Dictator (1940)
  Canadian Forum 21:149-50, Aug., 1941
  Catholic World 152:333, Dec., 1940
  Christian Science Monitor Magazine p. 7+, Sep. 7, 1940
  Commonweal 33:80, Nov. 8, 1940
  Current History 51:52, Sep., 1939
  Etude 58:805, Dec., 1940
  Ladies Home Journal 57:18+, Jul., 1940
  Life 9:53-6, Sep. 2, 1940; 11:24-5, Sep. 22, 1941
  Living Age 360:53, Mar., 1941
  Modern Music 18:15-17, Nov.-Dec., 1940
  Nation 151:401, Oct. 26, 1940; 153:310, Oct. 4, 1941
  New Republic 103:629-30, Nov. 4, 1940; 150:30+, Mar.
    28, 1964
  New York Times IX, p. 5, Mar. 31, 1940; IX, p. 3,
    Aug. 18, 1940; VII, p. 8, Sep. 8, 1940; IX, p. 5,
    Oct. 13, 1940; p. 25, Oct. 14, 1940; p. 29, Oct. 16,
    1940; IX, p. 5, Oct. 20, 1940; IX, p. 5, Oct. 27,
    1940; p. 20, Dec. 30, 1940; VII, p. 18, May 18, 1941
  New Yorker 16:78, Oct. 26, 1940
  Newsweek 16:60, Oct. 28, 1940
  Photoplay 18:14, Jan., 1941
  Saturday Review 23:8+, Nov. 9, 1940; 23:9, Dec. 21,
    1940

Great Dictator (1940) (Continued)
Scholastic 37:32, Sep. 16, 1940; 37:39, Oct. 28, 1940
Scribner's Commentator 9:104-5, Dec., 1940
Theatre Arts 24:862-5, Dec., 1940
Time 34:24, Aug. 7, 1939; 36:76, Nov. 4, 1940

Great Divide (1930)
New York Times p. 17, Feb. 17, 1930

Great Escape (1963)
America 109:178-9, Aug. 17, 1963
Commonweal 78:458, Jul. 26, 1963
New York Times p. 19, Aug. 8, 1963; II, p. 1, Aug. 11, 1963
New Yorker 39:64, Aug. 24, 1963
Newsweek 62:79, Jul. 15, 1963
Saturday Review 46:16, Jul. 6, 1963
Time 82:78, Jul. 19, 1963

Great Expectations (1934)
Canadian Magazine 82:39, Dec., 1934
Movie Classic 7:48-51+, Dec., 1934
New York Times IX, p. 4, Aug. 26, 1934; IX, p. 4, Nov. 4, 1934; IX, p. 5, Dec. 23, 1934; VIII, p. 3, Mar. 24, 1935
Vanity Fair 43:51, Dec., 1934

Great Expectations (1947)
Canadian Forum 27:114, Aug., 1947
Commonweal 46:168, May 30, 1947
Harper's Bazaar 81:206-7, Apr., 1947
Hollywood Quarterly 2:408-11, Jul., 1947; 3:87-9, Fall, 1947
Life 22:61-4+, Jun. 2, 1947
Nation 165:79-81, Jul. 19, 1947
New Republic 116:41, Mar. 10, 1947; 116:38, Jun. 9, 1947
New York Times II, p. 5, Dec. 23, 1945; II, p. 3, Apr. 21, 1946; II, p. 5, May 18, 1947; p. 31, May 23, 1947; II, p. 1, May 25, 1947
New York Times Magazine p. 22-3, May 11, 1947
New Yorker 22:63, Jan. 4, 1947; 23:56, May 31, 1947
Newsweek 29:95, May 26, 1947
Photoplay 31:4, Jul., 1947; 31, 54-5, Oct., 1947
Scholastic 51:36, Sep. 15, 1947
Theatre Arts 31:48, Jun., 1947
Time 49:99-100+, May 26, 1947
Woman's Home Companion 74:11, Aug., 1947

Great Flamarion (1945)
  New York Times p. 15, Jan. 15, 1945

Great Flirtation (1934)
  Literary Digest 118:28, Jul. 7, 1934
  New York Times p. 16, Jun. 23, 1934; X, p. 3, Jul. 1,
    1934

Great Gabbo (1930)
  New York Times p. 33, Sep. 13, 1929; IX, p. 7, Sep.
    22, 1929; IX, p. 7, Sep. 29, 1929

Great Gambini (1937)
  New York Times p. 20, Jul. 12, 1937

Great Garrick (1937)
  Commonweal 27:20, Oct. 29, 1937
  New York Times X, p. 3, Jun. 27, 1937; XI, p. 4, Oct.
    10, 1937; XI, p. 6, Oct. 24, 1937; p. 23, Oct. 25,
    1937; X, p. 5, Oct. 31, 1937
  Scholastic 31:37, Oct. 23, 1937
  Stage 15:95, Oct., 1937
  Time 30:44, Nov. 1, 1937

Great Gatsby (1949)
  Commonweal 50:296, Jul. 1, 1949
  Good Housekeeping 129:10, Aug., 1949
  Nation 169:162, Aug. 13, 1949
  New Republic 121:22, Jul. 25, 1949
  New York Times p. 20, Jul. 14, 1949; II, p. 3, Jul. 24,
    1949
  New Yorker 25:69, Jul. 23, 1949
  Newsweek 34:64, Aug. 1, 1949
  Photoplay 36:24, Aug., 1949
  Rotarian 75:34, Nov., 1949
  Theatre Arts 33:9, Jul., 1949
  Time 54:78, Jul. 25, 1949
  Woman's Home Companion 76:10-11, Aug., 1949

Great Gildersleeve (1943)
  New Republic 108:85, Jan. 18, 1943
  New York Times p. 36, Dec. 18, 1942

Great God Gold (1935)
  New York Times p. 22, May 6, 1935

Great Guns (1941)
  New York Times p. 27, Oct. 3, 1941

Great Guy (1937)
Canadian Magazine 87:38, Apr., 1937
Literary Digest 123:23, Jan. 16, 1937
Nation 144:80, Jan. 16, 1937
New York Times XI, p. 5, Nov. 22, 1936; X, p. 4, Dec.
27, 1936; p. 19, Jan. 1, 1937
Newsweek 8:37, Dec. 26, 1936
Scholastic 29:24, Jan. 16, 1937
Time 29:56, Jan. 11, 1937

Great Hospital Mystery (1937)
New York Times p. 22, Jul. 16, 1937

Great Hotel Murder (1935)
New York Times p. 17, Feb. 28, 1935

Great Impersonation (1935)
New York Times p. 11, Dec. 14, 1935
Time 26:42+, Dec. 16, 1935

Great Imposter (1961)
America 105:26, Apr. 1, 1961
Commonweal 73:637, Mar. 17, 1961
New York Times p. 24, Mar. 30, 1961
Newsweek 57:92, Feb. 27, 1961
Saturday Review 44:36, Mar. 4, 1961

Great Jasper (1933)
New York Times p. 15, Feb. 17, 1933; IX, p. 5, Feb.
26, 1933

Great Jewel Robber (1950)
New York Times p. 13, Aug. 4, 1950

*Great John Ericsson
Newsweek 11:23, May 30, 1938
Time 31:49, May 30, 1938

Great John L. (1945)
Commonweal 42:213, Jun. 15, 1945
New York Times II, p. 3, Oct. 8, 1944; p. 14, Jul. 19,
1945
New Yorker 21:30, Jul. 21, 1945
Newsweek 26:85, Jul. 2, 1945
Time 45:54, May 28, 1945

Great Lie (1941)
Commonweal 34:16, Apr. 25, 1941

Great Lie (1941) (Continued)
New York Times p. 19, Apr. 12, 1941
New Yorker 17:78, Apr. 12, 1941
Newsweek 17:60, Apr. 21, 1941
Scribner's Commentator 10:105-6, Jul., 1941
Time 37:98+, Apr. 21, 1941

*Great Library Misery
Library Journal 63:871, Nov. 15, 1938; 64:571, Aug.,
1938
Wilson Library Bulletin 13:251, Dec., 1938

Great Locomotive Chase (1956)
America 95:352, Jul. 7, 1956
American Magazine 161:14, Jun., 1956
Catholic World 183:224, Jun., 1956
Commonweal 64:324, Jun. 29, 1956
Life 41:65-6, Jul. 9, 1956
National Parent-Teacher 51:38, Sep., 1956
New York Times p. 35, Jun. 27, 1956
New Yorker 32:63, Jul. 7, 1956
Newsweek 48:84, Jul. 16, 1956
Saturday Review 39:24, Jun. 30, 1956
Scholastic 68:37, May 10, 1956
Time 68:76+, Jul. 2, 1956

Great Lover (1931)
New York Times p. 13, Aug. 24, 1931; VIII, p. 5, Aug.
30, 1931

Great Lover (1948)
Christian Century 67:63, Jan. 11, 1950
New Republic 121:30, Dec. 12, 1949
New York Times p. 48, Nov. 24, 1949
New Yorker 25:74+, Dec. 3, 1949
Newsweek 34:83, Dec. 5, 1949
Rotarian 76:36, Mar., 1950
Time 54:90, Dec. 19, 1949

Great McGinty (1940)
Commonweal 32:352, Aug. 16, 1940; 33:58, Nov. 1, 1940
New Republic 103:448, Sep. 30, 1940
New York Times p. 23, Aug. 15, 1940; IX, p. 3, Aug.
18, 1940; IX, p. 3, Aug. 25, 1940; II, p. 1, Nov. 6,
1949
New Yorker 16:60, Aug. 24, 1940
Newsweek 16:44, Aug. 19, 1940

Great McGinty (1940) (Continued)
  Photoplay 54:66, Oct., 1940
  Time 36:48, Aug. 26, 1940

Great Man (1956)
  America 96:464, Jan. 19, 1957
  Catholic World 184:383, Feb., 1957
  Commonweal 65:435, Jan. 25, 1957
  Cosmopolitan 142:26, Feb., 1957
  Holiday 21:111+, Mar., 1957
  Library Journal 82:183, Jan. 15, 1957
  National Parent-Teacher 51:38, Feb., 1957
  New Republic 136:22, Feb. 4, 1957; 136:21, Mar. 11,
    1957
  New York Times p. 28, Jan. 2, 1957; II, p. 1, Jan. 13,
    1957
  New Yorker 32:80, Jan. 12, 1957
  Newsweek 49:86, Jan. 14, 1957
  Reporter 16:42, Mar. 7, 1957; 17:45-7, Aug. 8, 1957
  Saturday Review 40:49, Jan. 19, 1957
  Time 69:82, Jan. 21, 1957

Great Man Votes (1939)
  Commonweal 29:386, Jan. 27, 1939
  New York Times IX, p. 5, Oct. 30, 1938; p. 15, Jan.
    20, 1939
  Newsweek 13:26-7, Jan. 16, 1939
  Photoplay 53:52, Mar., 1939
  Scholastic 34:31, Feb. 4, 1939
  Time 33:26, Jan. 23, 1939

Great Manhunt (1950)
  Christian Century 68:222, Feb. 14, 1951
  Rotarian 78:40, Apr., 1951

Great Man's Lady (1942)
  Commonweal 36:63, May 8, 1942
  Nation 154:554, May 9, 1942
  New York Times p. 14, Apr. 30, 1942; VIII, p. 3, May
    3, 1942
  Time 39:50, May 25, 1942

Great Meadow (1931)
  Life (NY) 97:20, Apr. 10, 1931
  New York Times p. 23, Mar. 14, 1931; IX, p. 6, Mar.
    15, 1931; VIII, p. 5, Mar. 22, 1931

Great Missouri Raid (1951)
Commonweal 54:14, Apr. 13, 1951
New York Times p. 31, Apr. 9, 1951
Saturday Review 34:30, Feb. 17, 1951
Time 57:102, Feb. 19, 1951

Great Mr. Handel (1944)
Canadian Forum 24:259-60, Feb., 1945
Etude 62:196, 198-200, Apr., 1944
New York Times p. 29, Sep. 10, 1943

Great Moment (1944)
Commonweal 40:446, Aug. 25, 1944
New Republic 111:692, Nov. 27, 1944
New York Times p. 15, Nov. 13, 1944; II, p. 1, Nov.
    19, 1944
New Yorker 20:79, Nov. 25, 1944
Newsweek 24:109, Nov. 27, 1944
Time 44:94+, Dec. 4, 1944

Great O'Malley (1937)
New York Times p. 10, Mar. 6, 1937

Great Plane Robbery (1940)
New York Times p. 25, Nov. 15, 1940

Great Profile (1940)
New York Times IX, p. 3, Jun. 16, 1940; p. 25, Oct.
    18, 1940
Newsweek 16:49, Sep. 2, 1940
Photoplay 54:68, Nov., 1940

Great Rupert (1950)
Commonweal 51:655, Mar. 31, 1950
New York Times p. 27, Apr. 14, 1950
Newsweek 35:83, Feb. 6, 1950

Great St. Louis Bank Robbery (1959)
New York Times p. 34, Feb. 4, 1960

Great Sinner (1949)
Commonweal 50:342, Jul. 15, 1949
New York Times II, p. 5, Jan. 9, 1949; p. 19, Jun. 30,
    1949; II, p. 1, Jul. 10, 1949
New Yorker 25:38, Jul. 9, 1949
Newsweek 34:68, Jul. 11, 1949
Photoplay 36:22, Sep., 1949

Great Sinner (1949) (Continued)
Rotarian 75:38, Oct., 1949
Time 54:76+, Jul. 18, 1949

Great Sioux Uprising (1953)
National Parent-Teacher 48:37, Sep., 1953
Natural History 62:286, Jun., 1953
New York Times p. 6, Jul. 18, 1953

Great Swindle (1941)
New York Times p. 25, May 14, 1941

Great Victor Herbert (1939)
Commonweal 31:187, Dec. 15, 1939
Etude 58:14+, Jan., 1940
New York Times p. 35, Dec. 7, 1939; IX, p. 7, Dec. 17, 1939
Newsweek 14:35-6, Dec. 18, 1939
Photoplay 54:62, Feb., 1940
Time 34:78, Dec. 18, 1939

Great Waltz (1938)
Commonweal 29:133, Nov. 25, 1938
New York Times IX, p. 5, Oct. 30, 1938; p. 19, Nov. 25, 1938; IX, p. 5, Nov. 27, 1938
Newsweek 12:29, Nov. 14, 1938
Photoplay 53:45, Jan., 1939
Scholastic 33:32, Dec. 3, 1938
Time 32:42, Nov. 14, 1938

Great War (1961)
Commonweal 75:45, Oct. 6, 1961
New Republic 145:28+, Sep. 18, 1961
New York Times p. 22, Aug. 31, 1961; II, p. 1, Sep. 10, 1961
New Yorker 37:60+, Sep. 2, 1961
Newsweek 58:62, Sep. 4, 1961
Saturday Review 44:32, Sep. 9, 1961

Great Ziegfeld (1936)
Canadian Magazine 85:59, May, 1936; 85:40, Jun., 1936
Commonweal 23:698, Apr. 17, 1936
Literary Digest 121:22, Apr. 4, 1936
Motion Picture 51:28-9, Mar., 1936
New Republic 87:18, May 13, 1936
New York Times XI, p. 5, Oct. 6, 1935; p. 21, Apr. 9, 1936; IX, p. 3, Apr. 19, 1936; IX, p. 4, May 17, 1936; p. 17, Mar. 5, 1937

Great Ziegfeld (1936) (Continued)
Newsweek 7:29, Apr. 18, 1936
Photoplay 49:42-3, Feb., 1936
Scholastic 28:22, May 16, 1936
Stage 13:62, Mar., 1936
Time 27:47-8, Apr. 20, 1936

Greatest Love (1954)
Catholic World 179:64, Apr., 1954
New York Times p. 19, Jan. 12, 1954
Newsweek 43:90, Jan. 25, 1954

Greatest Show on Earth (1952)
Catholic World 174:384-5, Feb., 1952
Christian Century 69:655, May 28, 1952
Commonweal 55:399-400, Jan. 25, 1952
Holiday 11:19, Mar., 1952
New Republic 126:22, Feb. 11, 1952
New York Times p. 17, Jan. 11, 1952; II, p. 1, Jan. 20, 1952
New Yorker 27:83, Jan. 19, 1952
Newsweek 39:90, Jan. 21, 1952
Saturday Review 35:27, Jan. 12, 1952
Scholastic 60:29, Feb. 6, 1952
Theatre Arts 36:33, Feb., 1952
Time 59:90, Jan. 14, 1952

Greeks Had a Word for Them (1932)
New York Times p. 25, Feb. 4, 1932

Green Dolphin Street (1947)
Commonweal 47:71, Oct. 31, 1947
Cosmopolitan 123:13+, Dec., 1947
Life 24:56, Feb. 23, 1948
New Republic 117:36, Oct. 27, 1947
New York Times II, p. 3, Aug. 18, 1946; II, p. 5, Jun. 1, 1947; II, p. 5, Oct. 12, 1947; p. 34, Oct. 16, 1947; II, p. 1, Oct. 19, 1947
New Yorker 23:94, Oct. 25, 1947
Newsweek 30:96, Oct. 27, 1947
Photoplay 32:27, Jan., 1948
Scholastic 51:35, Nov. 3, 1947
Time 50:100+, Nov. 3, 1947
Woman's Home Companion 75:8, Jan., 1948

Green Fields (1937)
New York Times p. 31, Oct. 12, 1937

Green Fire (1954)
America 92:367, Jan. 1, 1955
Commonweal 61:455, Jan. 28, 1955
Farm Journal 79:149, Feb., 1955
National Parent-Teacher 49:40, Jan., 1955
New York Times p. 5, May 16, 1954; p. 7, Dec. 25,
1954
Newsweek 45:94, Jan. 24, 1955
Time 65:82, Jan. 10, 1955

Green for Danger (1946)
Commonweal 46:406, Aug. 8, 1947
Good Housekeeping 125:13, Jul., 1947
New Republic 117:38, Sep. 15, 1947
New York Times p. 10, Aug. 8, 1947; II, p. 1, Aug. 17,
1947
New Yorker 23:45, Aug. 9, 1947
Newsweek 30:81, Aug. 25, 1947
Theatre Arts 31:27, Jul., 1947
Time 50:92, Jul. 21, 1947

Green Glove (1952)
New York Times p. 38, Apr. 24, 1952
Newsweek 39:100, Feb. 25, 1952

Green Goddess (1930)
Life (NY) 95:20, Mar. 7, 1930
New York Times p. 20, Feb. 14, 1930; VIII, p. 5, Feb.
23, 1930
Outlook 154:355, Feb. 26, 1930

Green Grass of Wyoming (1948)
New York Times p. 28, Jun. 10, 1948; II, p. 1, Jun. 13,
1948
New Yorker 24:68, Jun. 19, 1948
Newsweek 31:96+, May 17, 1948
Time 51:100, Jun. 21, 1948

Green Hell (1940)
New York Times p. 15, Jan. 30, 1940; IX, p. 5, Feb. 4,
1940
Photoplay 54:63, Feb., 1940
Time 35:68, Jan. 29, 1940

Green Helmet (1961)
Commonweal 74:103, Apr. 21, 1961
New York Times p. 32, Jul. 20, 1961
Senior Scholastic 78:38, Apr. 26, 1961

Green Light (1937)
  Canadian Magazine 87:36-8, Apr., 1937
  Commonweal 25:528, Mar. 5, 1937
  New York Times p. 9, Feb. 13, 1937; X, p. 5, Feb. 21,
    1937
  Newsweek 9:21, Feb. 20, 1937
  Scholastic 30:22, Feb. 20, 1937
  Time 29:25, Feb. 22, 1937

Green Magic (1955)
  Catholic World 181:220, Jun., 1955
  Commonweal 62:231, Jun. 3, 1955
  Nation 180:511, Jun. 11, 1955
  National Parent-Teacher 49:39, Jun., 1955
  Natural History 64:334, Jun., 1955
  New York Times p. 32, May 17, 1955; II, p. 1, May 22,
    1955
  New Yorker 31:78, May 28, 1955
  Newsweek 45:98, Jun. 6, 1955
  Saturday Review 38:45, May 21, 1955

Green Man (1956)
  Library Journal 82:1874, Aug., 1957
  National Parent-Teacher 52:33, Sep., 1957
  New York Times p. 40, May 23, 1957
  New Yorker 33:72, Jun. 1, 1957

Green Mansions (1959)
  Commonweal 70:83, Apr. 17, 1959
  Good Housekeeping 148:24, May, 1959
  Library Journal 84:1221, Apr. 15, 1959
  New York Times II, p. 5, May 18, 1958; p. 26, Mar. 20,
    1959; II, p. 1, Mar. 22, 1959
  New Yorker 35:95, Mar. 28, 1959
  Newsweek 53:114, Apr. 6, 1959
  Saturday Review 42:28, Apr. 11, 1959
  Time 73:92, Apr. 6, 1959

Green Mare (1962)
  Commonweal 75:46, Oct. 6, 1961
  New York Times p. 41, Oct. 24, 1961
  New Yorker 37:195-6, Oct. 28, 1961

Green Pastures (1936)
  Canadian Magazine 86:34-5, Aug., 1936
  Commonweal 24:160, Jun. 5, 1936
  Good Housekeeping 103:28-9+, Aug., 1936

Green Pastures (1936) (Continued)
  Literary Digest 121:20, May 16, 1936
  Nation 143:110, Jul. 25, 1936
  New York Times IX, p. 4, Mar. 8, 1936; IX, p. 3, May
    24, 1936; IX, p. 3, Jun. 7, 1936; IX, p. 4, Jun. 28,
    1936; IX, p. 3, Jul. 12, 1936; p. 20, Jul. 17, 1936;
    IX, p. 3, Jul. 26, 1936; XI, p. 5, Jan. 31, 1937
  Newsweek 7:26-7, May 30, 1936
  Scholastic 29:17, Sep. 19, 1936
  Stage 13:37, Jun., 1936; 13:6, Jul., 1936
  Time 27:38-40, Jun. 29, 1936

Green Promise (1949)
  New York Times p. 29, Jun. 24, 1949
  Newsweek 33:87, Mar. 28, 1949
  Rotarian 75:36, Sep., 1949

Green Scarf (1954)
  Commonweal 61:478, Feb. 4, 1955
  Library Journal 80:436, Feb. 15, 1955
  Nation 180:85, Jan. 22, 1955
  National Parent-Teacher 49:39, Mar., 1955
  Newsweek 45:94, Jan. 24, 1955
  Time 65:106, Mar. 14, 1955

Green Years (1946)
  Catholic World 163:170, May, 1946
  Commonweal 43:653-5, Apr. 12, 1946
  Cosmopolitan 120:71+, May, 1946
  Life 20:71-4, Apr. 15, 1946
  Nation 162:516, Apr. 27, 1946
  New York Times II, p. 1, Aug. 12, 1945; p. 21, Apr.
    5, 1946; II, p. 1, Apr. 7, 1946; II, p. 3, Mar. 31,
    1946; II, p. 5, Dec. 29, 1946
  New Yorker 22:104, Apr. 13, 1946
  Newsweek 27:92, Apr. 15, 1946
  Photoplay 29:2, Jun., 1946; 29:21, Jul., 1946; 30:42,
    Feb., 1947
  Scholastic 48:35, May 6, 1946
  Theatre Arts 30:283-4, May, 1946
  Time 47:98+, Apr. 15, 1946
  Woman's Home Companion 73:10, Jun., 1946

Greene Murder Case (1929)
  New York Times p. 11, Aug. 10, 1929; VIII, p. 3, Aug.
    18, 1929

Greengage Summer (see Loss of Innocence)

Greenwich Village (1944)
    Commonweal 40:493, Sep. 8, 1944
    New York Times p. 26, Sep. 28, 1944
    New Yorker 20:54, Sep. 30, 1944
    Newsweek 24:91, Sep. 25, 1944
    Time 44:95, Sep. 11, 1944

Greenwich Village Story (1963)
    Nation 197:80, Aug. 10, 1963
    New York Times p. 14, Jul. 12, 1963
    New Yorker 39:96, Jul. 27, 1963
    Time 82:80+, Jul. 26, 1963

Greyfriars' Bobby (1961)
    America 106:228, Nov. 11, 1961
    Commonweal 75:176, Nov. 10, 1961
    New York Times p. 41, Oct. 12, 1961
    Senior Scholastic 79:28, Nov. 15, 1961
    Time 78:56, Oct. 27, 1961

*Grido, Il
    Esquire 55:57-8, Jun., 1961
    New Republic 147:26+, Dec. 28, 1962
    New York Times p. 42, Oct. 23, 1962
    Newsweek 60:87-8, Oct. 29, 1962
    Saturday Review 45:41+, Nov. 3, 1962
    Time 80:E9+, Nov. 16, 1962

Grisbi (1959)
    New York Times p. 23, Jul. 23, 1959
    New Yorker 35:50, Jul. 18, 1959

Groom Wore Spurs (1950)
    Library Journal 76:343, Feb. 15, 1951
    New York Times p. 41, Mar. 14, 1951
    New Yorker 27:95, Mar. 24, 1951
    Rotarian 78:38, May, 1951

Grounds for Marriage (1950)
    Christian Century 68:159, Jan. 31, 1951
    New York Times p. 24, Jan. 12, 1951
    Newsweek 37:81, Feb. 5, 1951
    Rotarian 78:36, Mar., 1951
    Time 57:104, Jan. 29, 1951

Grumpy (1930)
Commonweal 12:386, Aug. 13, 1930
Nation 131:209, Aug. 20, 1930
New York Times p. 16, Aug. 2, 1930; VIII, p. 3, Aug.
10, 1930

Guadalajara (1943)
New York Times p. 9, Jun. 12, 1943

Guadalcanal Diary (1943)
Commonweal 39:97, Nov. 12, 1943
Nation 157:565, Nov. 13, 1943
New York Times II, p. 3, Aug. 1, 1943; p. 29, Nov. 18,
1943
New Yorker 19:92-3, Nov. 27, 1943
Newsweek 22:85, Nov. 8, 1943
Saturday Review 26:30, Nov. 6, 1943
Scholastic 43:55, Jan. 10, 1944
Time 42:94+, Nov. 15, 1943

Guaglio (1949)
Commonweal 50:201, Jun. 3, 1949
New Republic 120:22, May 30, 1949
New York Times p. 35, May 19, 1949
Newsweek 33:87, Jun. 20, 1949
Theatre Arts 33:106, Aug., 1949

Guardsman (1931)
Commonweal 14:496-7, Sep. 23, 1931
Life (NY) 98:18, Sep. 25, 1931
New York Times p. 22, Sep. 10, 1931; VIII, p. 5, Sep.
20, 1931

Guendalina (1959)
New York Times p. 23, Jun. 30, 1958

Guerilla Brigade (1942)
Commonweal 36:230, Jun. 26, 1942
New York Times p. 17, Apr. 14, 1942
Newsweek 19:62, Apr. 27, 1942
Time 39:88-9, May 11, 1942

Guerrilla Girl (1953)
New York Times p. 23, Jul. 7, 1953

Guest (1963)
Commonweal 79:571, Feb. 7, 1964

Guest (1963) (Continued)
New Republic 150:26+, Jan. 25, 1964
New York Times p. 25, Jan. 21, 1964
Newsweek 63:84, Feb. 10, 1964
Saturday Review 47:33, Feb. 15, 1964
Time 83:52, Jan. 24, 1964

Guest in the House (1944)
Commonweal 41:398, Feb. 2, 1945
Nation 160:110, Jan. 27, 1945
New York Times p. 19, Feb. 16, 1945; II, p. 1, Feb.
18, 1945
New Yorker 21:71, Feb. 24, 1945
Newsweek 25:66, Jan. 1, 1945
Theatre Arts 29:40, Jan., 1945
Time 45:94, Jan. 29, 1945
Woman's Home Companion 71:11, Nov., 1944

Guest Wife (1945)
Commonweal 42:335, Jul. 20, 1945
New York Times p. 21, Oct. 18, 1945
Newsweek 26:84, Jul. 23, 1945
Woman's Home Companion 72:10, Oct., 1945

Guilt of Janet Ames (1947)
Commonweal 46:189, Jun. 6, 1947
Holiday 2:143, Jul., 1947
New York Times p. 31, May 23, 1947
Newsweek 29:85, Jun. 2, 1947

Guilty (1930)
New York Times p. 21, Apr. 7, 1930

Guilty (1947)
New York Times p. 27, May 19, 1947
New Yorker 23:84, May 24, 1947

Guilty As Hell (1932)
New York Times p. 14, Aug. 6, 1932; IX, p. 3, Aug. 14,
1932

Guilty Bystander (1950)
Commonweal 52:46, Apr. 21, 1950
New York Times p. 18, Apr. 21, 1950
Newsweek 35:75, May 1, 1950

Guilty Generation (1931)
New York Times p. 20, Nov. 21, 1931; VIII, p. 5, Nov.

Guilty Generation (1931) (Continued)
    29, 1931

Guilty Hands (1931)
    New York Times p. 16, Aug. 29, 1931; VIII, p. 5, Sep. 6,
    1931

Guilty of Treason (1950)
    Christian Century 67:287, Mar. 1, 1950
    Commonweal 51:152-5, Nov. 11, 1949; 51:557, Mar. 3, 1950
    New York Times II, p. 5, Nov. 27, 1949; p. 13, Dec. 28,
    1949; p. 26, Apr. 11, 1950
    Newsweek 35:96, Apr. 24, 1950
    Rotarian 76:38, Apr., 1950

Guinea Pig (1949)
    Commonweal 50:122, May 13, 1949
    Good Housekeeping 128:100, Jan., 1949
    New Republic 120:30, May 9, 1949
    New York Times p. 20, May 2, 1949
    New Yorker 25:104, May 7, 1949
    Newsweek 33:85, May 16, 1949
    Saturday Review 32:44-6, May 14, 1949
    Time 53:102+, May 16, 1949

Guitars of Love (1958)
    New York Times p. 18, Jul. 12, 1958

Gulliver's Travels (1939)
    Commonweal 31:227, Dec. 29, 1939
    Good Housekeeping 110:38-9+, Feb., 1940
    New York Times p. 29, Dec. 21, 1939; IX, p. 5, Dec.
    24, 1939
    Newsweek 15:30-31, Jan. 1, 1940
    Photoplay 54:19, Jan., 1940; 54:62, Feb., 1940
    Scholastic 35:37, Jan. 8, 1940
    Time 35:29, Jan. 1, 1940

Gun Belt (1953)
    New York Times p. 8, Aug. 1, 1953

Gun for a Coward (1957)
    Catholic World 185:63, Apr., 1957
    Commonweal 65:512, Feb. 15, 1957
    National Parent-Teacher 51:39, Mar., 1957
    New York Times p. 21, Jan. 31, 1957

Gun Fury (1953)
Commonweal 59:198, Nov. 27, 1953
National Parent-Teacher 48:39, Dec., 1953
Newsweek 42:116, Oct. 26, 1953
Time 62:110, Dec. 7, 1953

Gun Glory (1957)
America 97:492, Aug. 10, 1957
Catholic World 85:465, Sep., 1957
Commonweal 66:472, Aug. 9, 1957
New York Times p. 8, Jul. 20, 1957

Gun Law (1938)
New York Times p. 51, Jun. 24, 1938

Gun Smoke (1931)
New York Times p. 27, Apr. 24, 1931

Gun the Man Down (1956)
National Parent-Teacher 51:37, Jan., 1957

Gunfight at the O. K. Corral (1957)
America 97:292, Jun. 1, 1957
Life 42:80, Jun. 24, 1957
National Parent-Teacher 51:38, Apr., 1957
New York Times II, p. 5, May 20, 1956; p. 23, May 30,
    1957; II, p. 1, Jun. 9, 1957
New Yorker 33:88, Jun. 8, 1957
Newsweek 49:101, Jun. 3, 1957
Saturday Review 40:25, Jun. 22, 1957
Time 69:96+, Jun. 17, 1957

Gunfighter (1950)
Christian Century 67:903, Jul. 26, 1950
Commonweal 52:346, Jul. 14, 1950
Good Housekeeping 131:98, Jul., 1950
Life 29:67-8, Jul. 24, 1950
New York Times p. 7, Jun. 24, 1950; II, p. 1, Jul. 2,
    1950
New Yorker 26:76, Jun. 24, 1950
Newsweek 36:85, Jul. 10, 1950
Rotarian 77:38, Sep., 1950
Time 56:90+, Jul. 17, 1950

Gunfighters (1947)
New York Times p. 12, Jul. 25, 1947; II, p. 3, Jul. 27,
    1947

476

Gung Ho (1943)
Commonweal 39:353, Jan. 21, 1944
Life 16:77-8+, Feb. 7, 1944
New York Times p. 23, Jan. 26, 1944
New Yorker 19:46+, Jan. 29, 1944
Newsweek 23:68+, Jan. 17, 1944

Gunga Din (1939)
Commonweal 29:441, Feb. 10, 1939
Country Life 75:26, Apr., 1939
Life 6:26-8, Jan. 16, 1939
Nation 148:158, Feb. 4, 1939
New Republic 98:73, Feb. 22, 1939
New York Times IX, p. 3, Aug. 14, 1938; IX, p. 5, Oct.
    16, 1938; p. 17, Jan. 27, 1939; IX, p. 5, Jan. 29,
    1939; X, p. 4, Feb. 5, 1939
Newsweek 13:25, Feb. 6, 1939
Photoplay 53:38-9, Jan., 1939
Scholastic 34:33, Feb. 11, 1939
Stage 16:7, Mar. 15, 1939
Time 33:36, Feb. 6, 1939
World Horizons 3:14-15, Feb., 1939

Gunman's Walk (1958)
Commonweal 68:472, Aug. 8, 1958

Guns of Darkness (1962)
America 107:657, Aug. 25, 1962
Commonweal 76:497, Sep. 7, 1962
New York Times p. 10, Aug. 18, 1962
Saturday Review 45:26, Sep. 8, 1962
Time 80:76, Sep. 7, 1962

Guns of Fort Petticoat (1957)
National Parent-Teacher 51:38, Apr., 1957

Guns of Navarone (1961)
America 105:492-3, Jul. 1, 1961
Commonweal 74:353, Jun. 30, 1961
Coronet 50:12, Aug., 1961
Life 50:120-1, Jun. 9, 1961
New Republic 144:28, Jun. 26, 1961
New York Times II, p. 7, May 8, 1960; p. 19, Jun. 23,
    1961; II, p. 1, Jun. 25, 1961
New Yorker 37:41, Jul. 1, 1961
Newsweek 57:94, Jun. 26, 1961
Saturday Review 44:24, Jun. 24, 1961

Guns of Navarone (1961) (Continued)
Senior Scholastic 79:41, Sep. 13, 1961
Time 77:50, Jun. 30, 1961

*Gunsmoke
Library Journal 78:437, Mar. 1, 1953
National Parent-Teacher 47:39, Apr., 1953
Newsweek 41:8-, Mar. 9, 1953
Theatre Arts 37:90, Apr., 1953
Time 61:104, Feb. 23, 1953

Guv'nor (see Mister Hobo)

Guy Named Joe (1944)
American Mercury 137:2, Mar., 1944
Cosmopolitan 116:112, Mar., 1944
Life 16:39-40+, Jan. 17, 1944
Musician 49:96, May, 1944
Nation 158:52, Jan. 8, 1944; 158:549, May 6, 1944
New Republic 110:84, Jan. 17, 1944
New York Times p. 17, Dec. 24, 1943; II, p. 3, Jan. 9, 1944
New Yorker 19:53, Jan. 1, 1944
Newsweek 23:82, Jan. 10, 1944
Photoplay 24:24, Mar., 1944
Scholastic 44:31, Mar. 13, 1944
Time 43:92+, Jan. 10, 1944
Woman's Home Companion 71:2, Feb., 1944

Guy Who Came Back (1951)
Christian Century 68:1063, Sep. 12, 1951
New York Times p. 13, Aug. 17, 1951
Saturday Review 34:34, Jun. 23, 1951

Guys and Dolls (1955)
America 94:224, Nov. 19, 1955
Catholic World 182:217, Dec., 1955
Commonweal 63:165, Nov. 18, 1955
Dance Magazine 29:18-23, Nov., 1955; 29:9, Dec., 1955
Library Journal 80:2594, Nov. 15, 1955
Look 19:82+, Nov. 29, 1955
Nation 181:486, Dec. 3, 1955
National Parent-Teacher 50:39, Jan., 1956
New Republic 134:20, Apr. 23, 1956
New York Times II, p. 5, Mar. 13, 1955; II, p. 5, May 8, 1955; VI, p. 28, Oct. 9, 1955; II, p. 5, Oct. 23, 1955; p. 26, Nov. 4, 1955; II, p. 1, Nov. 6, 1955

478

Guys and Dolls (1955) (Continued)
New York Times Magazine p. 28-9, Apr. 17, 1955
New Yorker 31:131, Nov. 5, 1955
Newsweek 46:117, Nov. 7, 1955
Saturday Review 38:25, Nov. 12, 1955
Time 66:116+, Nov. 14, 1955; 66:34, Dec. 12, 1955

Gypsies (1936)
New York Times p. 22, Jul. 30, 1936

Gypsy (1962)
America 107:1104, Nov. 17, 1962
Commonweal 77:231, Nov. 23, 1962
Good Housekeeping 156:22, Jan., 1963
New York Times II, p. 7, Apr. 8, 1962; p. 24, Nov. 2,
    1962; II, p. 1, Nov. 11, 1962
New Yorker 38:235, Nov. 10, 1962
Newsweek 60:96, Nov. 12, 1962
Saturday Review 45:50, Dec. 8, 1962
Time 80:97, E9, Nov. 16, 1962

Gypsy Blood (1952) (see also Wild Heart)
Theatre Arts 36:73, Mar., 1952

Gypsy Colt (1954)
Catholic World 178:462, Mar., 1954
Farm Journal 78:165, Apr., 1954
Library Journal 79:618, Apr. 1, 1954
National Parent-Teacher 48:38, Mar., 1954

Gypsy Wildcat (1944)
Commonweal 40:471, Sep. 1, 1944
New York Times p. 18, Oct. 5, 1944
New Yorker 20:61, Oct. 14, 1944
Newsweek 24:97, Aug. 28, 1944
Time 44:92, Sep. 4, 1944

H. M. Pulham, Esq. (1941)
Commonweal 35:270, Jan. 2, 1942
Nation 154:19, Jan. 3, 1942
New Republic 105:892, Dec. 29, 1941
New York Times IX, p. 3, Sep. 7, 1941; p. 35, Dec. 19,
    1941; IX, p. 5, Dec. 21, 1941
New Yorker 17:90, Dec. 20, 1941
Newsweek 18:60, Dec. 22, 1941
Time 39:66, Jan. 5, 1942

Hail the Conquering Hero (1944)
  Canadian Forum 24:234-5, Jan., 1945
  Commonweal 40:446-7, Aug. 25, 1944
  Life 17:45-6, Aug. 28, 1944
  Nation 159:361-2, Sep. 23, 1944
  New Republic 111:220, Aug. 21, 1944
  New York Times p. 14, Aug. 10, 1944; II, p. 1, Aug. 13,
    1944
  New Yorker 20:34, Aug. 19, 1944
  Newsweek 24:98-9, Aug. 7, 1944
  Scholastic 45:33, Sep. 11, 1944
  Theatre Arts 28:595-6, Oct., 1944
  Time 44:94, Aug. 21, 1944

Hairy Ape (1944)
  Commonweal 40:256, Jun. 30, 1944
  Nation 158:716, Jun. 17, 1944
  New York Times p. 8, Jul. 3, 1944; II, p. 1, Jul. 9,
    1944
  New Yorker 20:44, Jul. 8, 1944
  Newsweek 24:82-3, Jul. 3, 1944
  Time 43:94, Jun. 19, 1944

Half a Hero (1953)
  National Parent-Teacher 48:36, Nov., 1953
  Newsweek 42:98, Sep. 28, 1953
  Saturday Review 36:30, Sep. 19, 1953
  Time 62:108+, Nov. 9, 1953

Half a Sinner (1934)
  New York Times p. 16, Jun. 23, 1934

Half Angel (1936)
  New York Times p. 7, May 30, 1936

*Half-Angel
  Christian Century 68:807, Jul. 4, 1951
  Commonweal 54:310, Jul. 6, 1951
  New York Times p. 9, Jun. 16, 1951
  New Yorker 27:53, Jun. 23, 1951
  Newsweek 37:100, May 14, 1951
  Time 57:90, Jun. 25, 1951

Half-Breed (1952)
  New York Times p. 7, Jun. 5, 1952
  Newsweek 40:90, Jul. 14, 1952

Half Marriage (1929)
New York Times p. 22, Aug. 19, 1929

Half Shot at Sunrise (1930)
New York Times p. 21, Oct. 11, 1930; IX, p. 5, Oct. 19, 1930
Theatre Magazine 52:50, Dec., 1930

Half Way to Heaven (1929)
New York Times p. 19, Dec. 7, 1929; X, p. 6, Dec. 15, 1929

Halfway House (1945)
New York Times p. 22, Aug. 13, 1945
New Yorker 21:34, Aug. 25, 1945

Halka (1938)
New York Times p. 11, Jan. 17, 1938

Hallelujah (1929)
Life (NY) 94:21, Sep. 20, 1929
Literary Digest 103:42-56, Oct. 5, 1929
New York Times VIII, p. 5, Jun. 2, 1929; p. 33, Aug. 21, 1929; VIII, p. 4, Aug. 25, 1929; VIII, p. 6, Aug. 25, 1929
Outlook 153:273, Oct. 16, 1929
Theatre Arts 13:634+, Sep., 1929; 26:511, Aug., 1942; 33:36, Sep., 1949
Vanity Fair 32:70, May, 1929
Woman's Home Companion 56:128, Nov., 1929

Hallelujah, I'm a Bum (1933)
New York Times p. 15, Feb. 12, 1933; IX, p. 4, Feb. 19, 1933; IX, p. 5, Feb. 19, 1933
Vanity Fair 40:43, Apr., 1933

Halliday Brand (1957)
Catholic World 185:64, Apr., 1957
National Parent-Teacher 51:39, Mar., 1957

Halls of Montezuma (1951)
Christian Century 68:254, Feb. 21, 1951
Commonweal 53:375, Jan. 19, 1951
New Republic 124:23, Jan. 29, 1951
New York Times p. 9, Jan. 6, 1951; II, p. 1, Jan. 21, 1951
New Yorker 26:74, Jan. 13, 1951

481

Halls of Montezuma (1951) (Continued)
　Newsweek 37:74, Jan. 8, 1951
　Rotarian 78:40, Apr., 1951
　Saturday Review 34:29-30, Jan. 20, 1951
　Time 57:78-80, Jan. 15, 1951

Hamlet (1948)
　Atlantic 183:30-3, May, 1949
　Canadian Forum 28:233, Jan., 1949; 28:255, Feb., 1949
　Catholic World 168:243-4, Dec., 1948
　Commonweal 48:596, Oct. 1, 1948
　Cosmopolitan 125:12-13+, Sep., 1948
　Good Housekeeping 127:117, Sep., 1948
　Harper 197:116-17, Sep., 1948
　Life 23:18-20, Nov. 24, 1947; 24:117-27, Mar. 15, 1948
　Musical Courier 138:21, Jul., 1948
　Nation 167:468, Oct. 23, 1948
　National Review 131:603-6, Dec., 1948
　New Republic 119:28-30, Oct. 4, 1948
　New York Times II, p. 5, Jun. 1, 1947; VI, p. 15, Aug.
　　10, 1947; II, p. 5, Sep. 14, 1947; p. 30, May 7,
　　1948; II, p. 3, Jul. 25, 1948; p. 20, Aug. 4, 1948;
　　II, p. 5, Sep. 19, 1948; p. 33, Sep. 30, 1948; II, p.
　　1, Oct. 3, 1948; VI, p. 10, Oct. 17, 1948; II, p. 5,
　　May 14, 1950
　New York Times Magazine p. 20-1, Aug. 15, 1948
　New Yorker 24:90-1, Oct. 2, 1948
　Newsweek 32:87, Sep. 27, 1948
　Photoplay 33:22, Oct., 1948; 33:54-5+, Nov., 1948
　Rotarian 74:52, Jan., 1949
　Saturday Review 31:26-8, Oct. 2, 1948
　Scholastic 53:37, Oct. 20, 1948
　School and Society 68:387-9, Dec. 4, 1948
　Theatre Arts 32:30-1, Aug., 1948
　Time 51:100, May 17, 1948; 51:54-6+, Jun. 28, 1948
　Vogue 112:158, Sep. 15, 1948
　Woman's Home Companion 75:10-11, Oct., 1948

Hand in Hand (1961)
　America 104:646, Feb. 11, 1961
　Commonweal 73:509, Feb. 10, 1961
　Life 50:41-2, Mar. 31, 1961
　New York Times p. 41, Feb. 7, 1961
　New Yorker 37:99, Feb. 18, 1961
　Newsweek 57:86, Feb. 20, 1961
　Saturday Review 44:26, Jan. 28, 1961
　Senior Scholastic 78:23, Mar. 1, 1961

Handle with Care (1932)
New York Times p. 11, Dec. 24, 1932

Handle with Care (1958)
Newsweek 51:116+, Apr. 21, 1958

Hands Across the Table (1935)
Literary Digest 120:24, Dec. 7, 1935
New Republic 85:18, Nov. 13, 1935
New York Times p. 13, Nov. 2, 1935
Time 26:54, Oct. 28, 1935
Vanity Fair 45:51, Dec., 1935

Handy Andy (1934)
Canadian Magazine 82:36, Oct., 1934
Commonweal 20:389, Aug. 17, 1934
New York Times p. 14, Aug. 4, 1934; IX, p. 3, Aug. 12, 1934

Hanging Tree (1959)
America 100:585+, Feb. 14, 1959
Catholic World 189:56, Apr., 1959
Commonweal 69:497, Feb. 6, 1959
Library Journal 84:589, Feb. 15, 1959
New Republic 140:21, Feb. 16, 1959
New York Times p. 23, Feb. 12, 1959; II, p. 1, Feb. 15, 1959
New Yorker 35:137, Feb. 21, 1959
Newsweek 53:102, Feb. 16, 1959
Saturday Review 42:31, Feb. 7, 1959
Time 73:101, Feb. 16, 1959

Hangman's Knot (1952)
National Parent-Teacher 47:38, Jan., 1953
New York Times p. 45, Dec. 11, 1952
Newsweek 40:72, Dec. 22, 1952

Hangmen Also Die (1943)
Commonweal 38:75, May 7, 1943
Nation 156:643, May 1, 1943
New Republic 108:595, May 3, 1943
New York Times II, p. 3, Mar. 7, 1943; p. 24, Apr. 16, 1943
New Yorker 19:40, Apr. 17, 1943
Newsweek 21:88, Apr. 26, 1943
Time 41:40, Mar. 29, 1943

Hangover Square (1945)
  Commonweal 41:476, Feb. 23, 1945
  Harper's Bazaar 79:75, Apr., 1945
  New Republic 112:296, Feb. 26, 1945
  New York Times p. 15, Feb. 8, 1945; II, p. 1, Feb. 18,
    1945
  Newsweek 25:98+, Feb. 19, 1945
  Time 45:52, Feb. 12, 1945

*Hannah Lee
  Farm Journal 77:161, Nov., 1953
  Time 62:114, Sep. 14, 1953

Hannibal (1960)
  New York Times p. 17, Aug. 4, 1960

Hans Christian Andersen (1952)
  Catholic World 176:301, Jan., 1953
  Christian Century 70:271, Mar. 4, 1953
  Commonweal 57:199-200, Nov. 28, 1952
  Cosmopolitan 134:24, Jan., 1953
  Library Journal 77:2170, Dec. 15, 1952
  Life 33:84-9, Nov. 3, 1952
  McCalls 80:12-13, Jan., 1953
  Musical America 73:9, Jan. 15, 1953
  National Parent-Teacher 47:36, Jan., 1953; 50:40, Jan.,
    1956
  New York Times II, p. 5, May 18, 1952; II, p. 3, Jun.
    29, 1952; II, p. 5, Nov. 16, 1952; p. 34, Nov. 25,
    1952; p. 20, Nov. 26, 1952; II, p. 1, Nov. 30, 1952;
    p. 20, Aug. 10, 1953; p. 14, Sep. 7, 1953
  New York Times Magazine p. 62-3, Nov. 2, 1952
  New Yorker 28:73, Dec. 6, 1952
  Newsweek 40:92, Dec. 8, 1952
  Saturday Review 35:28, Nov. 29, 1952
  Scholastic 61:34, Dec. 3, 1952
  Theatre Arts 37:82, Jan., 1953
  Time 60:62+, Dec. 1, 1952

Hansel and Gretel (1954)
  America 92:110, Oct. 23, 1954
  Catholic World 180:139-40, Nov., 1954
  Commonweal 61:37, Oct. 15, 1954
  Farm Journal 78:141, Dec., 1954
  Library Journal 79:1755, Oct. 15, 1954
  National Parent-Teacher 49:38, Oct., 1954
  New York Times II, p. 5, Oct. 18, 1953; p. 33, Oct. 11,
    1954

Hansel and Gretel (1954) (Continued)
Newsweek 44:110, Oct. 11, 1954
Saturday Review 37:28, Nov. 13, 1954
Scholastic 65:25, Dec. 8, 1954
Time 64:88, Oct. 25, 1954

Happiest Days of Your Life (1949)
Christian Century 68:447, Apr. 4, 1951
New York Times p. 19, Sep. 18, 1950
Rotarian 78:38, May, 1951

*Happiest Years of Your Life
New Republic 123:30, Oct. 9, 1950
New Yorker 26:58+, Sep. 23, 1950
Newsweek 36:85, Oct. 2, 1950
Scholastic 57:20, Oct. 25, 1950
Time 56:112+, Oct. 9, 1950

Happiness Ahead (1928)
New York Times p. 31, Jun. 19, 1928

Happiness Ahead (1934)
Canadian Magazine 82:38, Nov., 1934
New York Times p. 28, Oct. 11, 1934
Vanity Fair 43:54, Nov., 1934

Happiness C.O.D. (1935)
Scholastic 27:12, Dec. 7, 1935

Happiness of Us Alone (1963)
New York Times p. 31, Apr. 10, 1963
New Yorker 39:166, Apr. 27, 1963

Happy Anniversary (1960)
Commonweal 71:290, Dec. 4, 1959
New Yorker 53:196, Dec. 12, 1959
Reporter 21:32, Dec. 24, 1959
Time 74:114, Nov. 16, 1959

Happy Days (1930)
Life (NY) 95:20, Mar. 7, 1930
Nation 130:280, Mar. 5, 1930
New York Times p. 20, Feb. 14, 1930; IX, p. 5, Feb.
16, 1930; VIII, p. 5, Feb. 23, 1930

Happy Go Lovely (1951)
New York Times p. 17, Jul. 26, 1951
Newsweek 38:81, Aug. 13, 1951

Happy Go Lovely (1951) (Continued)
    Saturday Review 34:27, Jul. 21, 1951

Happy Go Lucky (1943)
    Commonweal 37:591, Apr. 2, 1943
    New York Times p. 25, Mar. 25, 1943; II, p. 3, Apr.
       11, 1943
    Newsweek 21:66, Mar. 29, 1943
    Time 41:38, Mar. 29, 1943

Happy Is the Bride (1959)
    Library Journal 84:1445, May 1, 1959
    New York Times p. 27, Jun. 30, 1959

Happy Land (1943)
    Commonweal 39:253, Dec. 24, 1943
    Cosmopolitan 116:134, Jan., 1944
    Nation 157:741, Dec. 18, 1943; 158:549, May 6, 1944
    New Republic 109:851-2, Dec. 13, 1943
    New York Times p. 33, Dec. 9, 1943
    Newsweek 22:84+, Dec. 20, 1943
    Scholastic 43:35, Jan. 10, 1944
    Time 42:92+, Dec. 13, 1943

Happy Landing (1938)
    New York Times p. 19, Jan. 22, 1938
    Time 31:35, Jan. 31, 1938

Happy Road (1956)
    America 97:351, Jun. 22, 1957
    Catholic World 184:382-3, Feb., 1957
    Commonweal 65:614, Mar. 15, 1957
    Coronet 41:14, Mar., 1957
    Good Housekeeping 144:37, Mar., 1957
    National Parent-Teacher 51:37, Feb., 1957
    New York Times p. 20, Jun. 21, 1957
    New York Times Magazine p. 37, Apr. 7, 1957
    New Yorker 33:72, Jun. 29, 1957
    Saturday Review 40:23, Jul. 6, 1957
    Scholastic 69:24, Jan. 11, 1957
    Time 70:80, Jul. 1, 1957

Happy Thieves (1962)
    New York Times p. 19, Feb. 5, 1962
    Time 79:63, Feb. 2, 1962

Happy Time (1952)
    Catholic World 175:381-2, Aug., 1952

Happy Time (1952) (Continued)
Christian Century 70:63, Jan. 14, 1953
Commonweal 56:607, Sep. 26, 1952
Library Journal 77:1299, Aug., 1952
Nation 175:338, Oct. 11, 1952
National Parent-Teacher 47:38, Sep., 1952
New York Times p. 30, Oct. 31, 1952
New Yorker 28:74, Nov. 15, 1952
Newsweek 40:100+, Oct. 13, 1952
Saturday Review 35:26, Sep. 6, 1952
Theatre Arts 36:34, Aug., 1952
Time 60:90+, Sep. 29, 1952

Happy Years (1950)
Christian Century 67:1311, Nov. 1, 1950
Commonweal 52:437, Aug. 11, 1950
Library Journal 75:1059, Jun. 15, 1950
Newsweek 36:68, Jul. 24, 1950
Rotarian 76:38, Apr., 1950

Harbor Lights (1963)
New York Times p. 25, Feb. 13, 1964

Hard Boiled Canary (see There's Magic in Music)

Hard, Fast, and Beautiful (1951)
Commonweal 54:380, Jul. 27, 1951
New York Times p. 16, Jul. 2, 1951
Newsweek 37:94-5, Jun. 18, 1951
Saturday Review 34:23, Jun. 30, 1951
Time 57:93, Jun. 25, 1951

Hard Man (1957)
National Parent-Teacher 52:39, Jan., 1958

Hard Rock Harrigan (1935)
New York Times p. 16, Jul. 30, 1935

Hard to Get (1929)
New York Times p. 17, Sep. 28, 1929

Hard to Get (1938)
New York Times p. 15, Nov. 14, 1938
Photoplay 53:44, Jan., 1939

Hard to Handle (1933)
New York Times p. 21, Feb. 2, 1933; III, p. 5, Feb. 12,
1933

Hard Way (1943)
 Commonweal 37:471, Feb. 26, 1943
 Nation 156:283, Feb. 20, 1943
 New Republic 108:414, Mar. 29, 1943
 New York Times p. 9, Mar. 13, 1943
 Photoplay 21:45-6+, Oct., 1942
 Time 41:46+, Mar. 1, 1943

Harder They Fall (1956)
 America 95:209+, May 19, 1956
 American Magazine 161:8, May, 1956
 Catholic World 183:144, May, 1956
 Commonweal 64:227, Jun. 1, 1956
 Coronet 40:12, May, 1956
 Library Journal 81:898, Apr. 15, 1956
 Life 40:103-4+, Apr. 16, 1956
 Look 20:101-3+, May 15, 1956
 National Parent-Teacher 50:37, Jun., 1956
 New York Times p. 26, May 10, 1956; II, p. 1, May 13,
  1956
 New York Times Magazine p. 62, Apr. 8, 1956
 New Yorker 32:138, May 19, 1956
 Newsweek 47:99, May 7, 1956
 Saturday Review 39:25, May 12, 1956
 Time 67:114, May 21, 1956

Hardys (Hardy Family Series)
 New York Times X, p. 8, Dec. 4, 1938

Hardys Ride High (1939)
 New York Times p. 28, Apr. 14, 1939

Harlem Globetrotters (1951)
 Christian Century 69:263, Feb. 27, 1952

Harlem on the Prairie (1938)
 Time 30:24, Dec. 13, 1937

Harmon of Michigan (1941)
 New York Times p. 29, Oct. 2, 1941

Harmony Lane (1935)
 New York Times p. 19, Oct. 24, 1935
 Vanity Fair 45:49, Nov., 1935

Harold Lloyd's World of Comedy (1962)
 America 107:408, Jun. 16, 1962

Harold Lloyd's World of Comedy (1962) (Continued)
Commonweal 76:86, Apr. 20, 1962
Nation 194:544, Jun. 16, 1962
New Republic 146:28+, Mar. 19, 1962
New York Times p. 36, Jun. 5, 1962; II, p. 1, Jun. 10, 1962
New Yorker 38:117, Jun. 9, 1962
Newsweek 59:98-9, Jun. 4, 1962

Harpoon (1948)
New York Times II, p. 5, May 9, 1948; p. 48, Dec. 9, 1948

Harriet Craig (1950)
Christian Century 68:30, Jan. 3, 1951
Commonweal 53:141, Nov. 17, 1950
Library Journal 75:2021, Nov. 15, 1950
New York Times p. 31, Nov. 3, 1950
New Yorker 26:133, Nov. 4, 1950
Rotarian 78:38, Feb., 1951
Saturday Review 33:32, Nov. 18, 1950
Time 56:104+, Nov. 6, 1950

Harry Black and the Tiger (1958)
Catholic World 188:152, Nov., 1958
Commonweal 69:49, Oct. 10, 1958
Library Journal 83:2667+, Oct. 1, 1958
New York Times p. 24, Sep. 19, 1958
Newsweek 52:95, Sep. 29, 1958
Time 72:64, Oct. 13, 1958

Harvest (1939)
Nation 149:154, Aug. 5, 1939
New Republic 100:75, Aug. 23, 1939
New York Times IX, p. 4, Oct. 1, 1939; p. 16, Dec. 28, 1939; p. 19, Oct. 3, 1939; IX, p. 5, Mar. 24, 1940; IX, p. 4, May 12, 1940
Time 34:52-3, Oct. 23, 1939

Harvester (1936)
New York Times p. 18, Jul. 4, 1936

Harvey (1951)
Christian Century 68:95, Jan. 17, 1951
Commonweal 53:301-2, Dec. 29, 1950
Library Journal 75:2021, Nov. 15, 1950
New Republic 124:31, Jan. 15, 1951

Harvey (1951) (Continued)
  New York Times II, p. 5, Mar. 19, 1950; II, p. 3, Jun.
    4, 1950; II, p. 4, Jul. 2, 1950; II, p. 5, Nov. 26,
    1950; p. 19, Dec. 22, 1950; II, p. 3, Dec. 24, 1950
  New Yorker 26:51, Dec. 23, 1950
  Newsweek 36:64, Dec. 25, 1950
  Rotarian 78:36, Mar., 1951
  Saturday Review 34:26, Jan. 6, 1951
  Scholastic 58:23, Feb. 14, 1951
  Time 57:60-1, Jan. 1, 1951

Harvey Girls (1946)
  Collier's 116:20+, Nov. 17, 1945
  Commonweal 43:358, Jan. 18, 1946
  Life 19:82-6, Dec. 3, 1945
  New York Times II, p. 3, Jan. 20, 1946; p. 26, Jan. 25,
    1946
  Newsweek 27:93, Feb. 4, 1946
  Saturday Review 29:19, Feb. 2, 1946
  Scholastic 47:25, Jan. 21, 1946
  Time 47:99, Jan. 28, 1946
  Woman's Home Companion 73:8, Jan., 1946

Has Anybody Seen My Gal? (1952)
  Library Journal 77:1893, Nov. 1, 1952
  New York Times p. 7, Jul. 5, 1952
  Newsweek 40:84, Aug. 4, 1952
  Time 60:74, Jul. 28, 1952

Hasty Heart (1950)
  Christian Century 67:191, Feb. 8, 1950
  Commonweal 51:464, Feb. 3, 1950
  Good Housekeeping 130:11, Feb., 1950
  Library Journal 75:181, Feb. 1, 1950
  New Republic 122:22, Feb. 6, 1950
  New York Times II, p. 9, Dec. 4, 1949; p. 10, Jan. 21,
    1950; II, p. 1, Jan. 22, 1950
  New Yorker 25:74, Jan. 28, 1950
  Newsweek 35:72, Jan. 30, 1950
  Rotarian 77:37, Dec., 1950
  Scholastic 55:25, Jan. 11, 1950
  Time 55:88+, Feb. 13, 1950

Hat Check Girl (1932)
  New York Times p. 15, Oct. 8, 1932; IX, p. 5, Oct. 16,
    1932

Hat, Coat and Glove (1934)
Literary Digest 118:29, Aug. 11, 1934
Golden Book 20:248, Sep., 1934
New York Times p. 21, Jul. 27, 1934; IX, p. 3, Aug. 5,
1934

Hatari (1962)
America 107:512, Jul. 14, 1962
Commonweal 76:351, Jun. 29, 1962
National Review 13:237-8, Sep. 25, 1962
New York Times II, p. 7, Jan. 22, 1961; p. 19, Jul. 12,
1962
New Yorker 38:39, Jul. 21, 1962
Newsweek 60:72, Jul. 23, 1962
Seventeen 21:22, May, 1962
Senior Scholastic 80:34, May 16, 1962
Time 80:69, Jul. 27, 1962

Hatchet Man (1932)
New York Times p. 25, Feb. 4, 1932; VIII, p. 4, Feb.
14, 1932

Hate Ship (1930)
New York Times p. 15, Nov. 15, 1930

Hatful of Rain (1957)
America 97:471, Aug. 3, 1957
Catholic World 185:464, Sep., 1957
Commonweal 66:425, Jul. 26, 1957
Cosmopolitan 143:72, Jul., 1957
Look 21:91, Aug. 20, 1957
Nation 185:78, Aug. 17, 1957
National Parent-Teacher 52:33, Sep., 1957
New York Times II, p. 5, Feb. 3, 1957; p. 18, Jul. 18,
1957; II, p. 1, Jul. 21, 1957
New York Times Magazine p. 60, May 19, 1957
New Yorker 33:67-8, Jul. 27, 1957
Newsweek 50:84, Jul. 22, 1957
Saturday Review 40:23-4, Jul. 27, 1957
Time 70:76, Aug. 5, 1957

Hatred (1941)
New York Times p. 11, Jan. 27, 1941

Hatter's Castle (1948)
New York Times p. 8, Jul. 3, 1948
Newsweek 31:93-4, Jun. 21, 1948
Time 52:66, Jul. 26, 1948

491

Haunted Honeymoon (1940)
New Republic 104:307, Mar. 3, 1941
New York Times IX, p. 5, Apr. 21, 1940; p. 28, Oct.
31, 1940
Theatre Arts 24:787, Nov., 1940
Time 36:85, Nov. 18, 1940

Haunted House (1928)
New York Times p. 23, Dec. 17, 1928; VIII, p. 7, Dec.
23, 1928

Haunted Palace (1963)
New York Times p. 24, Jan. 30, 1964
Newsweek 62:86+, Sep. 16, 1963

Haunted Strangler (1957)
New York Times p. 15, Jul. 4, 1958

Haunting (1963)
Commonweal 79:16, Sep. 27, 1963
Life 55:35-6+, Aug. 30, 1963
New York Times p. 23, Sep. 19, 1963
New Yorker 39:108, Sep. 28, 1963
Newsweek 62:101, Sep. 23, 1963
Saturday Review 46:44, Sep. 28, 1963
Time 82:122+, Oct. 4, 1963

Havana Widows (1933)
New York Times p. 24, Nov. 23, 1933

Have a Heart (1934)
New York Times p. 20, Oct. 20, 1934

Having Wonderful Crime (1945)
New York Times p. 15, Apr. 13, 1945
New Yorker 21:57, Apr. 21, 1945
Time 45:92+, Feb. 26, 1945

Having Wonderful Time (1938)
Canadian Magazine 90:28, Jul., 1938
Life 4:56-7, Jun. 27, 1938
New York Times XI, p. 5, Nov. 21, 1937; XII, p. 9,
Dec. 5, 1937; X, p. 3, Jun. 12, 1938; p. 11, Jul. 8,
1938; IX, p. 3, Jul. 10, 1938
Newsweek 11:23, Jun. 27, 1938
Time 31:26, Jun. 27, 1938

Hawaii Calls (1938)
New York Times XII, p. 8, Dec. 5, 1937; p. 17, Apr.
29, 1938
Time 31:53, Mar. 14, 1938

Hawaiian Nights (1939)
New York Times IX, p. 3, Jul. 16, 1939; p. 19, Sep. 29,
1939
Photoplay 53:65, Nov., 1939

Hazard (1948)
New York Times p. 29, Jun. 3, 1948
Newsweek 31:95, Jun. 14, 1948

He (1933)
New York Times p. 23, Dec. 27, 1933

He Hired the Boss (1943)
New York Times p. 17, Jun. 4, 1943

He Knew Women (1930)
New York Times p. 33, Apr. 22, 1930

He Laughed Last (1956)
National Parent-Teacher 51:38, Oct., 1956

He Married His Wife (1940)
New York Times p. 11, Jan. 20, 1940

He Ran All the Way (1951)
Christian Century 68:1087, Sep. 19, 1951
Commonweal 54:310, Jul. 6, 1951
Library Journal 76:1141, Jul., 1951
Life 30:129-30+, Jun. 4, 1951
Nation 173:38, Jul. 14, 1951
New Republic 125:23, Jul. 16, 1951
New York Times p. 24, Jun. 21, 1951
New Yorker 27:74, Jun. 30, 1951
Newsweek 37:88, Jun. 25, 1951
Saturday Review 34:34, Jun. 23, 1951
Time 57:90+, Jun. 25, 1951

He Stayed for Breakfast (1940)
Commonweal 32:410, Sep. 6, 1940
New York Times p. 16, Aug. 31, 1940
Newsweek 16:50, Aug. 26, 1940

He Walked by Night (1948)
Collier's 123:32, Mar. 5, 1949
New York Times p. 15, Feb. 7, 1949
Newsweek 33:78, Feb. 14, 1949
Rotarian 74:38, Mar., 1949

He Was Her Man (1934)
New York Times p. 28, May 17, 1934; X, p. 3, May 27, 1934

He Who Must Die (1958)
America 100:480-2, Jan. 17, 1959
Christian Century 76:327-8, Mar. 18, 1959
Commonweal 69:363, Jan. 2, 1959
Library Journal 84:184, Jan. 15, 1959
Nation 188:60, Jan. 17, 1959
New Republic 139:21-2, Nov. 24, 1959
New York Times VI, p. 24, Nov. 30, 1958; p. 21, Dec. 29, 1958; II, p. 1, Jan. 11, 1959; II, p. 8, Mar. 29, 1959
New Yorker 34:110, Jan. 10, 1959
Saturday Review 41:14, Dec. 20, 1958
Time 72:50, Dec. 29, 1958

Head (1960)
New York Times p. 29, Jun. 20, 1963

Head of a Tyrant (1960)
New York Times p. 31, Jun. 7, 1962

Head Over Heels in Love (1937)
Canadian Magazine 87:25, Mar., 1937
New York Times p. 9, Feb. 13, 1937
Time 29:25, Feb. 22, 1937

Headin' East (1937)
New York Times p. 19, Jan. 15, 1938

Headless Ghost (1959)
New York Times p. 37, Apr. 30, 1959

Headline Shooters (1933)
New York Times p. 18, Oct. 23, 1933

Heads Up (1930)
New York Times p. 31, Oct. 13, 1930

Heart of a Nation (1943)
Commonweal 38:12, Apr. 23, 1943
New York Times II, p. 3, Mar. 21, 1943; p. 27, Apr. 8, 1943; II, p. 3, Apr. 11, 1943
New Yorker 19:55, Apr. 10, 1943
Newsweek 21:86-7, Apr. 12, 1943

Heart of Arizona (1938)
New York Times p. 17, Apr. 16, 1938

Heart of New York (1932)
New York Times p. 15, Mar. 2, 1932; VIII, p. 4, Mar. 6, 1932

Heart of Paris (1939)
Nation 148:102, Jan. 21, 1939
New Republic 98:17, Feb. 8, 1939
New York Times p. 17, Jan. 13, 1939
North American Review 247 no. 1:177-8, [Mar.] 1939

Heart of the Golden West (1942)
New York Times VIII, p. 3, Jul. 19, 1942; VIII, p. 3, Sep. 20, 1942

Heart of the Matter (1954)
America 92:284, Dec. 4, 1954
Catholic World 180:303, Jan., 1955
Commonweal 61:254, Dec. 3, 1954
Nation 179:470, Nov. 27, 1954
National Parent-Teacher 49:39, Feb., 1955
New York Times p. 20, Nov. 19, 1954; II, p. 1, Nov. 28, 1954
New Yorker 30:188, Nov. 27, 1954
Newsweek 44:92, Nov. 29, 1954
Reporter 11:45-6, Dec. 30, 1954
Saturday Review 37:31, Nov. 20, 1954
Time 64:96+, Dec. 13, 1954

Heart of the North (1938)
New York Times p. 29, Dec. 21, 1938
Photoplay 53:49, Feb., 1939
Time 32:21, Dec. 19, 1938

Heart Song (1934)
New York Times p. 24, Jun. 6, 1933

Heartbeat (1939)
Commonweal 30:481, Sep. 15, 1939

Heartbeat (1939) (Continued)
New York Times p. 21, Sep. 5, 1939

Heartbeat (1946)
Commonweal 44:168, May 31, 1946
New York Times p. 22, May 11, 1946; II, p. 3, May 12,
1946
New Yorker 22:92, May 18, 1946
Newsweek 27:98, May 20, 1946
Time 47:97, May 27, 1946

*Heartbreak Ridge
Nation 180:450, May 21, 1955
National Parent-Teacher 49:39, Mar., 1955
New York Times p. 41, May 5, 1955
New Yorker 31:146, May 14, 1955
Newsweek 45:118+, May 23, 1955
Saturday Review 38:28, Apr. 30, 1955
Time 65:106+, May 9, 1955

Heart's Desire (1937)
New York Times p. 20, Jul. 12, 1937

Heart's Divided (1936)
Canadian Magazine 86:30-1, Jul., 1936
Commonweal 24:287, Jul. 10, 1936
Literary Digest 121:19, Jun. 20, 1936
New York Times p. 13, Jun. 13, 1936
Time 27:37, Jun. 22, 1936

Hearts in Dixie (1929)
Life (NY) 93:21, Mar. 29, 1929
New York Times IX, p. 8, Feb. 24, 1929; p. 30, Feb.
28, 1929; X, p. 7, Mar. 10, 1929

Hearts in Exile (1929)
New York Times p. 25, Nov. 29, 1929

Heat Lightning (1934)
New York Times p. 23, Mar. 8, 1934

Heat's On (1943)
Commonweal 39:207, Dec. 10, 1943
New York Times p. 29, Nov. 26, 1943
Time 42:94+, Dec. 13, 1943

Heaven Can Wait (1943)
Commonweal 38:421, Aug. 13, 1943

Heaven Can Wait (1943) (Continued)
Life 15:61-2+, Aug. 30, 1943
Nation 157:275, Sep. 4, 1943
New Republic 109:284, Aug. 30, 1943
New York Times p. 15, Aug. 12, 1943
Newsweek 22:84, Aug. 9, 1943
Photoplay 23:32, Sep., 1943
Time 42:96, Jul. 19, 1943

Heaven Knows, Mr. Allison (1957)
America 96:716, Mar. 23, 1957
Catholic World 185:145, May, 1957
Commonweal 65:661, Mar. 29, 1957
Good Housekeeping 144:17, Apr., 1957
Library Journal 82:974, Apr. 1, 1957
Life 42:99-100, Mar. 25, 1957
National Parent-Teacher 51:36, May, 1957
New York Times II, p. 8, Nov. 8, 1956; p. 22, Mar. 15,
    1957; II, p. 1, Mar. 24, 1957
New Yorker 33:103, Mar. 23, 1957
Newsweek 49:110, Mar. 25, 1957
Saturday Review 40:27, Apr. 6, 1957
Senior Scholastic 70:35, Apr. 12, 1957
Time 69:106, Mar. 25, 1957

Heaven on Earth (1931)
New York Times p. 16, Dec. 19, 1931
Outlook 160:23, Jan. 6, 1932

Heaven on Earth (1961)
New York Times p. 55, Oct. 11, 1960

Heaven Only Knows (1947)
New York Times II, p. 5, Dec. 15, 1946; II, p. 5, Jun.
    22, 1947; II, p. 5, Nov. 9, 1947; p. 29, Nov. 14,
    1947
Newsweek 30:82, Nov. 10, 1947

Heaven with a Barbed Wire Fence (1939)
Photoplay 53:65, Oct., 1939

Heavenly Body (1944)
Cosmopolitan 116:92, Feb., 1944
Musician 49:96, May, 1944
New York Times p. 17, Mar. 24, 1944
Newsweek 23:93+, Apr. 3, 1944
Time 43:94, Apr. 10, 1944

Heavenly Days (1944)
New York Times p. 15, Oct. 21, 1944
Time 44:94, Oct. 16, 1944

Heavens Above! (1962)
Catholic World 197:335, Aug., 1963
Christian Century 80:1380, Nov. 6, 1963
Commonweal 78:305, Jun. 7, 1963
Esquire 60:44, Oct., 1963
Nation 196:515-16, Jun. 15, 1963
New Republic 148:33+, Jun. 15, 1963
New York Times p. 28, May 21, 1963; II, p. 1, Jun. 2, 1963
New Yorker 39:153, May 25, 1963
Newsweek 61:103, May 27, 1963
Time 81:98, May 24, 1963

Hei Tiki (1935)
New York Times p. 10, Feb. 2, 1935; VIII, p. 5, Feb. 24, 1935

Heidi (1937)
Child Life 16:456-7, Oct., 1937
Commonweal 27:48, Nov. 5, 1937
Life 3:104-5, Oct. 25, 1937
New York Times p. 14, Nov. 6, 1937
Saint Nicholas 64:39, Aug., 1937
Scholastic 31:36, Nov. 13, 1937
Time 30:25, Oct. 25, 1937

Heidi (1955)
America 90:366, Jan. 2, 1954
Catholic World 178:461, Mar., 1954
Commonweal 59:473, Feb. 12, 1954
Farm Journal 78:94, Mar., 1954
Library Journal 79:56, Jan. 1, 1954
National Parent-Teacher 48:38, Feb., 1954
New York Times p. 27, Dec. 21, 1953
New Yorker 29:51, Jan. 2, 1954
Saturday Review 37:33, Jan. 9, 1954
Time 63:82, Jan. 11, 1954

*Heidi and Peter
Catholic World 182:305, Jan., 1956
National Parent-Teacher 50:38, Feb., 1956
New York Times p. 55, Dec. 13, 1955

Heiress (1949)
  Catholic World 170:149, Nov., 1949
  Christian Century 67:383, Mar. 22, 1950
  Commonweal 51:15, Oct. 14, 1949
  Cosmopolitan 127:13+, Nov., 1949
  Good Housekeeping 129:10-11, Oct., 1949
  Ladies Home Journal 66:33, Oct., 1949
  Life 27:113, 118, Oct. 17, 1949
  Musical Quarterly 37:161-75, Apr., 1951
  New Republic 121:22, Oct. 31, 1949
  New York Times II, p. 4, Aug. 15, 1948; p. 35, Oct. 7,
    1949; II, p. 1, Oct. 16, 1949
  New Yorker 25:89, Oct. 8, 1949
  Newsweek 34:94, Oct. 17, 1949
  Rotarian 76:41, May, 1950
  Scholastic 55:30, Sep. 21, 1949
  Theatre Arts 33:8, Nov., 1949
  Time 54:101-2, Oct. 24, 1949
  Woman's Home Companion 76:10-11, Nov., 1949

Helen Morgan Story (1957)
  America 97:688, Sep. 28, 1957
  Commonweal 67:19, Oct. 4, 1957
  National Parent-Teacher 52:34, Dec., 1957
  New York Times p. 33, Oct. 3, 1957; II, p. 1, Oct. 6,
    1957
  Newsweek 50:127, Sep. 30, 1957
  Time 70:116+, Oct. 14, 1957

Helen of Troy (1956)
  America 94:516, Feb. 4, 1956
  Catholic World 182:461-2, Mar., 1956
  Collier's 134:34-5, Sep. 17, 1954
  Commonweal 63:459, Feb. 3, 1956
  Library Journal 81:360, Feb. 1, 1956
  National Parent-Teacher 50:39, Oct., 1955
  New York Times II, p. 5, Aug. 8, 1954; VI, p. 28, Sep.
    25, 1955; p. 21, Jan. 27, 1956
  New York Times Magazine p. 22, Jan. 15, 1956
  New Yorker 31:65, Feb. 4, 1956
  Newsweek 47:98, Jan. 30, 1956
  Saturday Review 39:19, Jan. 28, 1956
  Time 67:62, Jan. 30, 1956

Helene (1938)
  New York Times p. 19, Jan. 22, 1938

Hell and High Water (1933)
New York Times p. 24, Dec. 18, 1933

Hell and High Water (1954)
America 90:546, Feb. 20, 1954
American Magazine 157:12, Feb., 1954
Commonweal 59:524, Feb. 26, 1954
National Parent-Teacher 48:39, Apr., 1954
New York Times p. 20, Feb. 2, 1954; p. 16, Feb. 5,
    1954; II, p. 1, Feb. 7, 1954
New Yorker 29:105, Feb. 13, 1954
Newsweek 43:106, Feb. 22, 1954
Time 63:102, Feb. 22, 1954

Hell Below (1933)
New Outlook 161:48, Jun., 1933
New York Times p. 13, Apr. 26, 1933
Newsweek 1:29, May 6, 1933

Hell Below Zero (1931)
New York Times p. 20, Jun. 27, 1931; VIII, p. 3, Jul.
    5, 1931

Hell Below Zero (1953)
Farm Journal 78:141, Jun., 1954
National Parent-Teacher 48:39, Jun., 1954
Natural History 63:188, Apr., 1954
New York Times p. 7, Jul. 17, 1954
Time 64:79, Jul. 26, 1954

Hell Bound (1931)
New York Times p. 15, May 9, 1931; VIII, p. 5, May
    17, 1931

Hell Cat (1934)
New York Times p. 16, Jul. 7, 1934; X, p. 3, Jul. 15,
    1934

Hell Divers (1932)
Commonweal 15:270-1, Jan. 6, 1932
New York Times p. 27, Dec. 23, 1931
Outlook 160:23, Jan. 6, 1932

Hell Gate (see Hellgate)

Hell Harbor (1930)
New York Times IX, p. 2, Sep. 22, 1929; IX, p. 8, Oct.

Hell Harbor (1930) (Continued)
13, 1929; X, p. 5, Dec. 15, 1929; p. 22, Mar. 28,
1930; IX, p. 5, Apr. 6, 1930

Hell in the Heavens (1934)
New York Times p. 28, Dec. 12, 1934

Hell Is a City (1960)
Commonweal 73:485, Feb. 3, 1961
New Republic 144:23, Jan. 2, 1961
New York Times p. 26, Jan. 19, 1961

Hell Is for Heroes (1962)
Commonweal 76:330, Jun. 22, 1962
New York Times II, p. 5, Jul. 23, 1961; p. 19, Jul. 12,
1962
Newsweek 60:79, Jul. 16, 1962

Hell on Earth (1934)
Nation 138:166-7, Feb. 7, 1934
New Republic 78:18, Feb. 14, 1934
New York Times p. 10, Jan. 29, 1934; IX, p. 5, Feb.
4, 1934

Hell on Frisco Bay (1956)
Commonweal 63:429, Jan. 27, 1956
National Parent-Teacher 50:39, Feb., 1956
New York Times p. 21, Jan. 27, 1956
Time 67:92, Feb. 6, 1956

Hell Raiders of the Deep (1954)
Catholic World 179:302, Jul., 1954
New York Times p. 9, Jul. 3, 1954

Hell to Eternity (1960)
America 103:680-1, Sep. 17, 1960
Commonweal 73:74, Oct. 14, 1960
New York Times II, p. 7, May 1, 1960; p. 41, Oct. 13,
1960
Time 76:47, Oct. 31, 1960

Hellcats of the Navy (1957)
National Parent-Teacher 51:37, Jun. 1957

Helldorado (1934)
New York Times p. 13, Jan. 7, 1935

Heller in Pink Tights (1960)
America 102:775, Mar. 26, 1960
Commonweal 71:629, Mar. 4, 1960
New York Times p. 28, Mar. 17, 1960; II, p. 1, Mar.
20, 1960
Newsweek 55:100, Mar. 14, 1960
Saturday Review 43:35, Mar. 5, 1960
Time 75:81, Apr. 4, 1960

Hellfire (1949)
New York Times p. 9, May 30, 1949

Hellgate (1952)
Catholic World 176:141, Nov., 1952
Newsweek 40:95, Sep. 29, 1952
Scholastic 61:28, Oct. 29, 1952

Hellions (1962)
New York Times p. 28, Mar. 15, 1962

Hello, Elephant (1954)
National Parent-Teacher 49:38, Nov., 1954
New York Times p. 18, Sep. 10, 1954

Hello, Everybody (1933)
New York Times p. 9, Jan. 30, 1933; IX, p. 3, Feb. 5,
1933

Hello, Frisco, Hello (1943)
Commonweal 37:644, Apr. 16, 1943
Cosmopolitan 114:68, May, 1943
New York Times p. 25, Mar. 25, 1943; II, p. 3, Mar.
28, 1943
Newsweek 21:67, Mar. 29, 1943
Time 41:39, Mar. 29, 1943

Hello, Sister (1933)
New York Times p. 11, May 6, 1933

Hell's Angels (1930)
Commonweal 12:499, Sep. 17, 1930
Life (NY) 96:16, Sep. 5, 1930
New Republic 64:180, Oct. 1, 1930
New York Times IX, p. 6, May 11, 1930; IX, p. 6, Jun.
8, 1930; p. 8, Aug. 16, 1930; VIII, p. 5, Aug. 24,
1930
Outlook 158:278-9, Jul. 1, 1931

Hell's Angels (1930) (Continued)
  Photoplay 37:30-33+, Apr., 1930
  Theatre Magazine 52:47-8, Oct., 1930

Hell's Cargo (1940)
  New York Times p. 15, Sep. 16, 1940

Hell's Five Hours (1958)
  New York Times p. 18, Jul. 24, 1958

Hell's Half Acre (1954)
  National Parent-Teacher 48:39, May, 1954
  New York Times p. 11, Feb. 27, 1954

Hell's Heroes (1929)
  New York Times p. 11, Dec. 28, 1929

Hell's Highway (1932)
  New York Times p. 18, Sep. 26, 1932
  Vanity Fair 39:64, Dec., 1932

Hell's Holiday (1933)
  New York Times p. 14, Jul. 15, 1933

Hell's Horizon (1955)
  National Parent-Teacher 50:39, Jan., 1956

Hell's House (1932)
  New York Times p. 24, Feb. 12, 1932

Hell's Island (1930)
  Life (NY) 96:19, Aug. 22, 1930
  New York Times p. 7, Jul. 19, 1930; VIII, p. 3, Jul. 27,
  1930

Hell's Island (1955)
  National Parent-Teacher 49:39, May, 1955
  New York Times p. 10, May 7, 1955

Hell's Kitchen (1939)
  New York Times p. 10, Jul. 3, 1939

Hell's Outpost (1954)
  National Parent-Teacher 49:39, Mar., 1955
  New York Times p. 13, Feb. 26, 1955

Hellzapoppin (1941)
  Commonweal 35:296, Jan. 9, 1942

Hellzapoppin (1941) (Continued)
New York Times p. 33, Dec. 25, 1941; p. 21, Dec. 26,
  1941
Stage 1:11, Nov., 1940; 1:12, Dec., 1940
Theatre Arts 24:93, Feb., 1940
Time 39:55, Feb. 2, 1942

Hemingway's Adventures of a Young Man (see Adventures of
a Young Man)

Henry Aldrich for President (1941)
New York Times p. 22, Oct. 18, 1941

Henry Aldrich Swings It (1943)
New York Times p. 16, Jul. 13, 1943

Henry the Fifth (see Henry V)

Henry V (1944)
Canadian Forum 26:161, Oct., 1946
Catholic World 163:457, Aug., 1946
Christian Science Monitor Magazine p. 7, Mar. 30, 1946
Commonweal 44:238-9, Jun. 21, 1946
Forum 106:77-9, Jul., 1946
Good Housekeeping 123:15, Jul., 1946
Hollywood Quarterly 2:82-7, Oct., 1946; 2:92-4, Oct.,
  1946
Life 20:38-42, May 20, 1946; 22:86+, Mar. 10, 1947
Nation 163:80, Jul. 20, 1946; 163:136, Aug. 3, 1946
New Republic 115:14, Jul. 8, 1946
New York Times II, p. 3, Feb. 27, 1944; II, p. 3, Jun.
  9, 1946; II, p. 3, Jun. 16, 1946; p. 20, Jun. 17,
  1946; p. 30, Jun. 18, 1946; II, p. 1, Jun. 23, 1946;
  II, p. 3, Sep. 1, 1946; II, p. 1, Nov. 17, 1946; p.
  42, Dec. 19, 1946; II, p. 5, Dec. 29, 1946
New York Times Magazine p. 22-3+, May 12, 1946
New Yorker 22:40-2, Jun. 22, 1946
Newsweek 27:102, Jun. 17, 1946
Photoplay 29:35, Nov., 1946
Saturday Review 29:26+, May 25, 1946
Scholastic 49:40, Sep. 16, 1946; 49:6T, Oct. 14, 1946;
  49:22-3, Oct. 21, 1946
Theatre Arts 29:337-40, 343, Jun., 1945; 30:217-18, Apr.,
  1946
Time 47:56-60, Apr. 8, 1946
Vogue 108:218-19, Sep. 1, 1946

Henry V (1958)
   Library Journal 83:835+, Mar. 15, 1958
   New York Times II, p. 1, Mar. 2, 1958

Henry the Rainmaker (1949)
   Rotarian 75:36, Sep., 1949

Her Bodyguard (1933)
   New Outlook 162:45, Sep., 1933
   New York Times p. 18, Aug. 7, 1933; IX, p. 3, Aug.
   13, 1933

Her Cardboard Lover (1942)
   New York Times p. 19, Jul. 17, 1942

Her First Mate (1933)
   New York Times p. 14, Sep. 2, 1933

Her Highness and the Bellboy (1945)
   Commonweal 42:624, Oct. 12, 1945
   Life 19:84-6, Oct. 1, 1945
   New York Times p. 16, Sep. 28, 1945; II, p. 1, Oct. 7,
   1945
   Newsweek 26:102, Oct. 8, 1945
   Photoplay 27:24, Oct., 1945
   Time 46:96, Oct. 1, 1945

Her Husband Lies (1937)
   New York Times p. 20, Mar. 18, 1937

Her Husband's Affairs (1947)
   Life 23:99-101, Sep. 15, 1947
   New York Times II, p. 5, Nov. 16, 1947; p. 29, Nov.
   14, 1947
   Newsweek 30:92, Nov. 24, 1947
   Time 50:80+, Dec. 22, 1947
   Woman's Home Companion 74:10, Nov., 1947

Her Husband's Secretary (1936)
   New York Times p. 23, Mar. 20, 1937

Her Jungle Love (1938)
   New York Times p. 27, Apr. 14, 1938

Her Kind of Man (1946)
   Commonweal 44:119, May 17, 1946
   Nation 162:701, Jun. 8, 1946

Her Kind of Man (1946) (Continued)
New York Times p. 10, May 4, 1946; II, p. 1, May 12, 1946
Newsweek 27:92+, May 13, 1946
Time 47:101, May 13, 1946

Her Mad Night (1932)
New York Times p. 24, Nov. 15, 1932

Her Majesty, Love (1931)
New York Times p. 37, Nov. 26, 1931

Her Man (1930)
New York Times p. 15, Oct. 4, 1930

Her Man Gilbey (1949)
New Republic 120:31, Jun. 20, 1949
New York Times p. 35, Jun. 9, 1949

Her Primitive Man (1944)
New York Times p. 26, Mar. 31, 1944

Her Private Affair (1929)
New York Times p. 21, Jan. 11, 1930

Her Sister's Secret (1946)
Newsweek 28:100, Sep. 16, 1946
Time 48:100+, Oct. 21, 1946

Her Sweetheart (see Christopher Bean)

Her Twelve Men (1954)
America 91:507, Aug. 21, 1954
Catholic World 179:383, Aug., 1954
Commonweal 60:557, Sep. 10, 1954
Library Journal 79:1393, Aug., 1954
National Parent-Teacher 48:39, Jun., 1954
New York Times p. 23, Aug. 12, 1954
New Yorker 30:67, Aug. 21, 1954
Newsweek 44:82, Aug. 16, 1954
Time 64:77, Aug. 30, 1954

Her Wedding Night (1930)
New York Times p. 19, Sep. 29, 1930

Her Wonderful Lie (1950)
Christian Century 67:1007, Aug. 23, 1950
Library Journal 75:570, Apr. 1, 1950

Her Wonderful Lie (1950) (Continued)
New York Times p. 15, Jul. 17, 1950
Rotarian 77:35, Oct., 1950

Herbst-Manoever (1939)
New York Times p. 9, Mar. 18, 1939

Hercules (1959)
America 101:559, Jul. 25, 1959
Library Journal 84:2171, Jul., 1959
New York Times p. 32, Jul. 23, 1959
Senior Scholastic 75:40, Sep. 16, 1959
Time 74:32, Jul. 27, 1959

Here Come the Co-Eds (1945)
Commonweal 41:495, Mar. 2, 1945
New York Times p. 21, Feb. 19, 1945
New Yorker 21:49, Mar. 3, 1945
Newsweek 25:101, Mar. 5, 1945

Here Come the Girls (1953)
Commonweal 59:282, Dec. 18, 1953
Farm Journal 78:83, Jan., 1954
National Parent-Teacher 48:39, Jan., 1954
New York Times p. 10, Dec. 26, 1953
Newsweek 42:90, Dec. 21, 1953
Saturday Review 36:30, Dec. 19, 1953
Time 62:57, Dec. 28, 1953

Here Come the Waves (1944)
New York Times p. 25, Dec. 28, 1944
New Yorker 20:57, Jan. 6, 1945
Newsweek 25:87, Jan. 8, 1945
Time 45:40, Jan. 1, 1945

Here Comes Carter (1936)
New York Times p. 23, Nov. 14, 1936

Here Comes Cookie (1935)
New York Times p. 12, Oct. 12, 1935

Here Comes Mr. Jordan (1941)
Commonweal 34:448, Aug. 29, 1941
Life 11:56-8, Aug. 18, 1941
New Republic 105:251, Aug. 25, 1941
New York Times p. 13, Aug. 8, 1941; IX, p. 3, Aug. 17, 1941

Here Comes Mr. Jordan (1941) (Continued)
New Yorker 17:52, Aug. 16, 1941
Newsweek 18:60, Aug. 11, 1941
Photoplay 19:6, Oct., 1941
Scholastic 39:28, Sep. 15, 1941
Scribner's Commentator 10:108, Oct., 1941
Time 38:74, Aug. 25, 1941

Here Comes the Groom (1934)
Literary Digest 117:31, Jun. 30, 1934
New York Times p. 20, Jun. 16, 1934; IX, p. 3, Jun. 24, 1934

Here Comes the Groom (1951)
Christian Century 68:1207, Oct. 17, 1951
Commonweal 55:64, Oct. 26, 1951
New Republic 125:21, Sep. 24, 1951
New York Times p. 19, Sep. 21, 1951; II, p. 1, Oct. 7, 1951
New Yorker 27:112, Sep. 29, 1951
Newsweek 38:88+, Oct. 1, 1951
Saturday Review 34:23, Aug. 25, 1951
Theatre Arts 35:87, Sep., 1951
Time 58:120+, Oct. 15, 1951

Here Comes the Navy (1934)
Literary Digest 118:26, Aug. 4, 1934
New Republic 80:23, Aug. 15, 1934
New York Times p. 14, Jul. 21, 1934; IX, p. 3, Jul. 29, 1934

Here Comes Trouble (1948)
New York Times p. 31, Apr. 15, 1948

Here I Am a Stranger (1939)
New York Times p. 11, Sep. 30, 1939; IX, p. 5, Oct. 8, 1939
Time 34:40-1, Oct. 9, 1939

Here Is Ireland (1940)
Commonweal 33:25, Oct. 25, 1940
New York Times p. 21, Oct. 7, 1940

Here Is My Heart (1934)
New York Times p. 21, Dec. 22, 1934; IX, p. 4, Dec. 30, 1934
Time 24:14, Dec. 31, 1934

Here We Go Again (1942)
New York Times p. 12, Oct. 12, 1942

Here's to Romance (1935)
Scholastic 27:28, Nov. 2, 1935
New York Times p. 29, Oct. 3, 1935
Time 26:29, Oct. 7, 1935
Vanity Fair 45:34, Dec., 1935

Heritage of the Desert (1933)
New York Times p. 18, Mar. 11, 1933

Heroes All (1931)
New York Times p. 30, Nov. 12, 1931

Heroes and Sinners (1959)
Commonweal 70:259, Jun. 5, 1959
New York Times p. 38, Mar. 12, 1959
Newsweek 53:118, May 18, 1959
Reporter 20:36, Jun. 25, 1959

Heroes Are Made (1944)
New York Times p. 10, Mar. 11, 1944

Heroes for Sale (1933)
New York Times p. 14, Jul. 22, 1933; IX, p. 3, Jul. 23,
1933

Heroes of the Alamo (1937)
New York Times p. 18, Apr. 2, 1938

Heroes of the Arctic (1935)
New York Times p. 24, May 24, 1935

Heroes of the Marne (1939)
New York Times p. 13, Apr. 24, 1939

Hero's Island (1962)
Saturday Review 45:22, Sep. 29, 1962

Hers to Hold (1943)
Commonweal 38:442, Aug. 20, 1943
New York Times p. 15, Jul. 22, 1943
Newsweek 22:76+, Aug. 2, 1943
Photoplay 23:28, Sep., 1943
Time 42:94, Aug. 23, 1943

Hertha's Awakening (1933)
  Nation 136:354, Mar. 29, 1933
  New York Times p. 19, Mar. 14, 1933; IX, p. 3, Mar.
    19, 1933

He's a Cockeyed Wonder (1950)
  New York Times p. 32, Oct. 20, 1950

He's My Guy (1943)
  New York Times p. 12, Mar. 12, 1943

Hesitancy (see Incertidumbre)

Hey Boy, Hey Girl (1959)
  New York Times p. 18, Aug. 6, 1959

Hey, Let's Twist (1962)
  New York Times p. 25, Feb. 8, 1962

Hi Diddle Diddle (1943)
  Commonweal 38:442, Aug. 20, 1943
  New York Times p. 26, Sep. 24, 1943
  Newsweek 22:104, Sep. 20, 1943
  Time 42:48, Jul. 26, 1943

Hi, Nellie! (1934)
  New York Times p. 15, Feb. 1, 1934; IX, p. 4, Feb.
    11, 1934
  Newsweek 3:33, Jan. 27, 1934

Hi 'Ya Chum (1943)
  New York Times p. 17, Feb. 26, 1943

Hiawatha (1952)
  Library Journal 78:211, Feb. 1, 1953
  National Parent-Teacher 47:26, Mar., 1953
  Natural History 62:92-3, Feb., 1953
  New York Times p. 20, Dec. 26, 1952

Hidden Fear (1957)
  National Parent-Teacher 51:37, Jun., 1957

*Hidden Fortress
  Esquire 56:116, Aug., 1961
  New Republic 146:28, Mar. 19, 1962
  New York Times p. 24, Jan. 24, 1962

Hidden Hand (1942)
New York Times p. 40, Nov. 26, 1942

*Hidden Hunger
American Journal of Public Health 32:319-20, Mar., 1942
Hygeia 20:250-1, Apr., 1942
New York Times p. 18, Feb. 17, 1942; VII, p. 23, Mar.
15, 1942
New York Times Magazine p. 23, Mar. 15, 1942
Time 39:17, Apr. 27, 1942

Hidden Power (1939)
New York Times p. 17, Jul. 26, 1939

Hidden Room (1949)
New Republic 122:30, Jan. 30, 1950
New York Times p. 19, Jan. 9, 1950
Newsweek 35:79, Jan. 23, 1950

Hide Out (1930)
New York Times p. 23, Apr. 12, 1930

Hide-Out (1934)
Literary Digest 118:35, Sep. 8, 1934
New York Times p. 16, Aug. 25, 1934; IX, p. 3, Sep. 2,
1934

Hideaway (1937)
New York Times p. 10, Sep. 25, 1937

Hideaway Girl (1936)
New York Times p. 20, Jan. 13, 1937

High and Dry (1954)
America 91:574, Sep. 11, 1954
Commonweal 60:582, Sep. 17, 1954
Farm Journal 78:137, Oct., 1954
National Parent-Teacher 49:38, Nov., 1954
New York Times p. 25, Aug. 31, 1954; II, p. 1, Sep. 5,
1954
New Yorker 30:77, Sep. 11, 1954
Newsweek 44:98+, Sep. 27, 1954
Reporter 11:41, Dec. 2, 1954
Saturday Review 37:25, Sep. 18, 1954
Time 64:6, Sep. 27, 1954; 64:106, Sep. 13, 1954

High and Low (1962)
New Republic 149:26-7+, Nov. 23, 1963

High and Low (1962)
New York Times p. 30, Nov. 27, 1963
New Yorker 39:197, Dec. 14, 1963
Newsweek 62:105B-106, Nov. 25, 1963

High and the Mighty (1954)
America 91:407, Jul. 17, 1954
Aviation Week 61:67, Jul. 26, 1954
Catholic World 179:303, Jul., 1954
Commonweal 60:365, Jul. 16, 1954
Farm Journal 78:101, Aug., 1954
Library Journal 79:1304, Jul., 1954
Look 18:70+, Jul. 27, 1954
National Parent-Teacher 49:38, Sep., 1954
New York Times p. 21, Jul. 1, 1954; II, p. 1, Jul. 18, 1954
New Yorker 30:59, Jul. 10, 1954
Saturday Review 37:33, Jul. 3, 1954
Time 64:94, Jul. 12, 1954

High Barbaree (1947)
Commonweal 46:240, Jun. 20, 1947
New York Times II, p. 5, Nov. 17, 1946; II, p. 5, Jun. 1, 1947; p. 27, Jun. 6, 1947
Newsweek 29:84, Jun. 23, 1947
Scholastic 50:36, Apr. 21, 1947
Time 49:100+, Jun. 9, 1947
Woman's Home Companion 74:11, Jun., 1947

High Cost of Loving (1958)
America 99:271, May 24, 1958
Commonweal 68:232, May 30, 1958
New York Times p. 12, May 17, 1958
Saturday Review 41:41, Mar. 8, 1958
Time 71:102, Mar. 24, 1958

High Flight (1958)
Library Journal 83:1389, May 1, 1958
New York Times II, p. 5, Jun. 9, 1957

High Fury (1948)
Photoplay 34:20, Feb., 1949
Rotarian 74:35, May, 1949
Scholastic 53:27, Dec. 15, 1948

High Gear (1933)
New York Times p. 16, Apr. 15, 1933

High Lonesome (1950)
New York Times p. 40, Dec. 8, 1950
Newsweek 36:92+, Sep. 25, 1950

High Noon (1952)
Catholic World 175:143, May, 1952
Christian Century 69:1046, Sep. 10, 1952
Commonweal 56:390, Jul. 25, 1952
Holiday 12:24+, Sep., 1952
Library Journal 77:1185, Jul., 1952
Life 33:73-4+, Aug. 25, 1952
Nation 174:410, Apr. 26, 1952
National Parent-Teacher 47:38, Sep., 1952
New York Times p. 14, Jul. 25, 1952; II, p. 1, Aug. 3,
   1952; II, p. 6, Jan. 25, 1953
New Yorker 28:55, Aug. 2, 1952
Newsweek 40:91, Jul. 14, 1952
Saturday Review 35:29, Jul. 5, 1952
Theatre Arts 36:45+, Jun., 1952
Time 60:92+, Jul. 14, 1952

High Pressure (1932)
Nation 134:268, Mar. 2, 1932
New York Times p. 22, Feb. 1, 1932; VIII, p. 4, Feb.
   7, 1932
Outlook 160:188, Mar., 1932

High School (1940)
New York Times p. 15, Jan. 5, 1940
Photoplay 54:62, Mar., 1940

High School Confidential (1958)
Commonweal 68:304, Jun. 20, 1958
New York Times p. 6, May 31, 1958
Saturday Review 41:26, Jun. 28, 1958

High School Girl (1935)
New York Times p. 19, Mar. 16, 1935

High Sierra (1941)
Commonweal 33:376, Jan. 31, 1941
New Republic 104:180, Feb. 10, 1941
New York Times p. 11, Jan. 25, 1941
Time 37:94, Feb. 17, 1941

High Society (1955)
America 95:472, Aug. 18, 1956

High Society (1955) (Continued)
Catholic World 183:303, Jul., 1956
Commonweal 64:397, Jul. 20, 1956
Good Housekeeping 143:142, Aug., 1956
Holiday 20:69+, Sep., 1956
Look 20:53-4+, Aug. 21, 1956
National Parent-Teacher 51:38, Oct., 1956
New York Times p. 9, Aug. 10, 1956; II, p. 1, Aug. 12, 1956
New Yorker 32:62, Aug. 18, 1956
Newsweek 48:88, Aug. 6, 1956
Saturday Review 39:29, Aug. 11, 1956
Scholastic 69:30, Sep. 13, 1956
Time 68:53, Aug. 6, 1956

High Society Blues (1930)
Life (NY) 95:18, May 9, 1930
New York Times p. 15, Apr. 19, 1930; IX, p. 5, Apr. 27, 1930

High Tension (1936)
New York Times p. 11, Jul. 11, 1936

High Tide (1947)
New York Times p. 11, Nov. 8, 1947

High Time (1960)
America 104:26, Oct. 1, 1960
Commonweal 73:48, Oct. 7, 1960
Life 49:37, Aug. 15, 1960
New York Times II, p. 9, Apr. 24, 1960; p. 15, Sep. 17, 1960
New Yorker 36:168, Oct. 1, 1960
Time 76:94, Sep. 26, 1960

High Treason (1930)
New York Times VIII, p. 4, Aug. 25, 1929
Outlook 154:712, Apr. 30, 1930

High Treason (1937)
New York Times p. 17, Jan. 27, 1937

High Treason (1952)
Catholic World 175:222, Jun., 1952
Commonweal 56:225, Jun. 6, 1952
New York Times II, p. 5, Oct. 28, 1951; p. 23, May 21, 1952; II, p. 1, Jun. 8, 1952

High Treason (1952) (Continued)
New Yorker 28:128, May 24, 1952
Newsweek 39:100, May 5, 1952
Saturday Review 35:27, Jun. 28, 1952
Theatre Arts 36:36, Jul., 1952
Time 59:110, May 19, 1952

High Wall (1948)
Commonweal 47:350, Jan. 16, 1948
New York Times p. 15, Oct. 23, 1947; II, p. 5, Dec.
    21, 1947; p. 22, Dec. 26, 1947
Newsweek 31:89, Jan. 26, 1948
Photoplay 32:20, Mar., 1948
Time 51:71, Jan. 5, 1948

High, Wide and Handsome (1937)
Commonweal 26:368, Aug. 6, 1937
Life 3:16-17, Sep. 27, 1937
New York Times X, p. 5, Feb. 21, 1937; X, p. 4, Jul.
    4, 1937; p. 15, Jul. 22, 1937; X, p. 3, Jul. 25, 1937
Newsweek 10:22, Jul. 31, 1937
Time 30:34, Aug. 2, 1937

Higher and Higher (1943)
Commonweal 39:305, Jan. 7, 1944
Cosmopolitan 116:92, Feb., 1944
Nation 158:23, Jan. 1, 1944
New York Times p. 8, Jan. 22, 1944
Time 43:88, Jan. 3, 1944

Highway Dragnet (1954)
New York Times p. 8, Feb. 20, 1954

Highway Patrol (1938)
New York Times p. 15, Aug. 4, 1938

Highway 301 (1951)
New York Times p. 13, Dec. 9, 1951
Newsweek 36:93, Dec. 18, 1950

Highway West (1941)
New York Times p. 13, Aug. 8, 1941

Highwayman (1951)
Christian Century 69:111, Jan. 23, 1952

Hilda Crane (1956)
America 95:211, May 19, 1956

515

Hilda Crane (1956) (Continued)
Commonweal 64:179, May 18, 1956
Library Journal 81:1437, Jun. 1, 1956
New York Times p. 35, May 3, 1956
New Yorker 32:172, May 12, 1956
Newsweek 47:117, May 21, 1956
Time 67:119, May 21, 1956

Hill 24 Doesn't Answer (1955)
National Parent-Teacher 50:39, Jan., 1956
New York Times p. 37, Nov. 3, 1955
Time 66:102, Nov. 28, 1955

Hills of Home (1948)
Good Housekeeping 127:196+, Dec., 1948
New York Times p. 32, Nov. 26, 1948; II, p. 5, Dec. 5,
    1948
Newsweek 32:96, Dec. 6, 1948
Rotarian 74:36, Feb., 1949
Time 52:105+, Dec. 13, 1948

Hippodrome (1961)
Commonweal 74:16, Mar. 31, 1961
New York Times p. 36, Mar. 12, 1962
Newsweek 57:100, Mar. 20, 1961

Hips, Hips, Horray (1934)
New York Times p. 18, Feb. 24, 1934

Hired Gun (1957)
National Parent-Teacher 52:37, Nov., 1957
Newsweek 50:114, Sep. 23, 1957

Hired Wife (1940)
Commonweal 32:470, Sep. 27, 1940
New York Times IX, p. 3, Jul. 28, 1940; p. 11, Sep.
    14, 1940
Photoplay 54:68, Nov., 1940

*Hiroshima
America 93:250, May 28, 1955
Commonweal 62:232, Jun. 3, 1955
Nation 180:449-50, May 21, 1955
New York Times p. 35, May 18, 1955
New Yorker 31:76, May 28, 1955
Newsweek 45:118, May 23, 1955
Saturday Review 38:45, May 21, 1955
Time 65:96+, May 23, 1955

Hiroshima, Mon Amour (1959)
America 103:383, Jun. 18, 1960
Commonweal 72:279, Jun. 10, 1960
Nation 190:479-80, May 28, 1960
National Review 10:121, Feb. 25, 1961
New Republic 142:29-30, Jun. 13, 1960
New York Times p. 43, May 17, 1960
New Yorker 35:78-80, Jul. 11, 1959; 36:133, May 28, 1960
Newsweek 55:119, May 23, 1960
Reporter 21:35-6, Aug. 20, 1960
Saturday Review 43:34, May 21, 1960
Time 75:88, May 16, 1960

His Brother's Wife (1936)
New York Times p. 6, Aug. 15, 1936
Time 28:48, Aug. 17, 1936

His Butler's Sister (1943)
New York Times II, p. 3, Nov. 28, 1943; p. 13, Dec. 30, 1943
New Yorker 19:53, Jan. 1, 1944
Newsweek 22:78, Nov. 29, 1943
Time 42:92+, Nov. 29, 1943

His Captive Woman (1929)
Life (NY) 93:29, May 17, 1929
New York Times p. 26, Apr. 3, 1929; X, p. 7, Apr. 7, 1929
Outlook 152:112, May 15, 1929

His Double Life (1933)
New York Times p. 12, Dec. 16, 1933; IX, p. 5, Dec. 24, 1933
Newsweek 2:30, Dec. 23, 1933

His Excellency (1956)
New York Times p. 19, Feb. 2, 1956

His Family Tree (1935)
Time 26:26+, Sep. 30, 1935

His First Command (1930)
New York Times p. 18, Dec. 23, 1929

His Girl Friday (1940)
Commonweal 31:287, Jan. 19, 1940
Nation 150:81, Jan. 20, 1940

517

His Girl Friday (1940) (Continued)
New Republic 102:116, Jan. 22, 1940
New York Times IX, p. 5, Oct. 8, 1939; p. 13, Jan. 12,
    1940; IX, p. 5, Jan. 14, 1940
Newsweek 15:33, Jan. 15, 1940
Photoplay 54:63, Feb., 1940
Time 35:76, Jan. 22, 1940

His Glorious Night (1929)
New York Times p. 22, Oct. 5, 1929

His Greatest Gamble (1934)
New York Times p. 20, Jul. 18, 1934; IX, p. 3, Jul. 22,
    1934

His Kind of Woman (1951)
Nation 174:18, Jan. 5, 1952
New York Times p. 20, Aug. 30, 1951
Newsweek 38:100, Sep. 10, 1951
Time 58:110, Sep. 17, 1951

His Majesty O'Keefe (1954)
America 90:518, Feb. 13, 1954
Library Journal 79:139, Jan. 15, 1954
National Parent-Teacher 48:39, Mar., 1954
Natural History 63:138-9, Mar., 1954
New York Times II, p. 5, Oct. 26, 1952; II, p. 5, Jan.
    18, 1953; p. 17, Feb. 6, 1954; II, p. 1, Feb. 14,
    1954
Scholastic 64:30, Feb. 17, 1954
Time 63:96+, Feb. 15, 1954

His Night Out (1935)
New York Times p. 19, Nov. 16, 1935
Scholastic 27:12, Dec. 7, 1935

His Tiger Lady (1928)
Life (NY) 91:23, Jun. 21, 1928
New York Times p. 23, May 28, 1928

His Woman (1931)
New York Times p. 21, Dec. 5, 1931

History Is Made at Night (1937)
Canadian Magazine 87:46+, Jun., 1937
Nation 144:419, Apr. 10, 1937
New York Times X, p. 5, Jan. 17, 1937; XI, p. 4, Mar.
    28, 1937; p. 14, Mar. 29, 1937; X, p. 3, Apr. 4, 1937

History Is Made at Night (1937) (Continued)
    Newsweek 9:48, Mar. 27, 1937
    Scholastic 30:29, Apr. 24, 1937
    Stage 14:60, Feb., 1937
    Time 29:51, Mar. 29, 1937

History of Mr. Polly (1949)
    New Republic 125:21, Dec. 3, 1951
    New York Times p. 36, Oct. 25, 1951
    New Yorker 27:152, Nov. 10, 1951
    Newsweek 38:102, Nov. 19, 1951

Hit and Run (1957)
    National Parent-Teacher 52:33, Sep., 1957

Hit of the Show (1928)
    New York Times p. 25, Jul. 9, 1928; VIII, p. 3, Jul.
    15, 1928

Hit Parade (1937)
    New York Times p. 11, May 31, 1937

Hit Parade of 1941 (1940)
    New York Times IX, p. 3, Aug. 18, 1940; p. 33, Dec.
    5, 1940

Hit Parade of 1943 (1943)
    Commonweal 37:643, Apr. 16, 1943
    New York Times p. 24, Apr. 16, 1943
    Newsweek 21:88, Apr. 5, 1943

Hit Parade of 1947 (1947)
    New York Times p. 32, May 5, 1947
    Time 49:98, Jun. 2, 1947

Hit the Deck (1930)
    Commonweal 11:454, Feb. 19, 1930
    New York Times p. 28, Jan. 15, 1930; VIII, p. 6, Jan.
    19, 1930
    Outlook 154:192, Jan. 29, 1930

Hit the Deck (1955)
    America 93:27, Apr. 2, 1955
    American Magazine 159:10, Mar., 1955
    Catholic World 181:61, Apr., 1955
    Commonweal 61:677, Apr. 1, 1955
    National Parent-Teacher 49:39, May, 1955

Hit the Deck (1955) (Continued)
New York Times p. 17, Mar. 4, 1955
New Yorker 31:76, Mar. 12, 1955
Newsweek 45:105, Mar. 14, 1955
Time 65:110, Mar. 14, 1955

Hit the Ice (1943)
Commonweal 38:302, Jul. 9, 1943
New York Times p. 27, Sep. 23, 1943
Newsweek 22:108, Jul. 5, 1943
Time 42:96, Jul. 5, 1943

Hit the Road (1941)
New York Times p. 15, Jul. 3, 1941; IX, p. 3, Jul. 6,
1941

Hitch-Hiker (1953)
Commonweal 58:201, May 29, 1953
Holiday 13:12+, Jun. , 1953
New York Times p. 39, Apr. 30, 1953
New Yorker 29:121, May 9, 1953
Newsweek 41:106, May 11, 1953
Saturday Review 36:29, Mar. 21, 1953
Theatre Arts 37:90, Apr. , 1953
Time 61:107, Apr. 6, 1953

Hitler (1962)
Newsweek 59:109, Apr. 9, 1962

Hitler, Dead or Alive (1942)
New York Times p. 23, Mar. 31, 1943

Hitler Gang (1944)
Commonweal 40:112, May 19, 1944
Life 16:25, Jan. 31, 1944; 16:78-80+, May 15, 1944
New Republic 110:739, May 29, 1944
New York Times II, p. 3, May 7, 1944; p. 15, May 8,
1944; II, p. 3, May 14, 1944
New Yorker 20:66, May 13, 1944
Newsweek 23:80, May 15, 1944
Photoplay 25:21, Jul. , 1944
Scholastic 44:27, May 22, 1944
Time 43:54+, May 8, 1944

Hitler's Children (1943)
Commonweal 37:398-9, Feb. 5, 1943
Life 14:37+, Feb. 1, 1943

Hitler's Children (1943) (Continued)
New York Times p. 27, Feb. 25, 1943; II, p. 3, Feb.
28, 1943
New Yorker 19:59, Mar. 6, 1943
Scholastic 42:27, Mar. 8, 1943
Time 41:43, Jan. 18, 1943

Hitler's Madmen (1943)
New York Times p. 15, Aug. 28, 1943

Hitler's Reign of Terror (1934)
Nation 138:574, May 16, 1934
New York Times p. 26, May 1, 1934
Newsweek 3:36, May 5, 1934

Hitting a New High (1937)
Commonweal 27:272, Dec. 31, 1937
New York Times X, p. 5, Dec. 26, 1937; p. 11, Dec.
27, 1937
Time 30:51, Dec. 20, 1937

*Hoaxters
Catholic World 176:385, Feb., 1953
Christian Century 70:495, Apr. 22, 1953
Collier's 131:70, Feb. 21, 1953
Commonweal 57:490, Feb. 20, 1953
National Parent-Teacher 47:27, Mar., 1953
New York Times p. 25, Jan. 29, 1953
Saturday Review 36:28, Jan. 24, 1953
Scholastic 61:28, Jan. 21, 1953

Hobson's Choice (1954)
America 91:387, Jul. 10, 1954
National Parent-Teacher 49:38, Sep., 1954
New Republic 131:21, Jul. 5, 1954
New York Times p. 37, Jun. 15, 1954; II, p. 1, Jun. 20,
1954
New Yorker 30:65, Jun. 19, 1954
Newsweek 43:86, Jun. 21, 1954
Saturday Review 37:30, Jun. 19, 1954
Time 63:102+, Jun. 21, 1954

Hold Back the Draw (1941)
Commonweal 34:613, Oct. 17, 1941
Life 11:89-92, Oct. 6, 1941
New York Times IX, p. 5, Apr. 20, 1941; IX, p. 4, Aug.
31, 1941; p. 29, Oct. 2, 1941; IX, p. 5, Oct. 5, 1941

Hold Back the Draw (1941) (Continued)
New Yorker 17:79, Oct. 4, 1941
Newsweek 18:55, Sep. 29, 1941
Scholastic 39:30, Oct. 20, 1941
Scribner's Commentator 11:107-8, Dec., 1941
Time 38:86, Sep. 29, 1941

Hold Back the Night (1956)
National Parent-Teacher 51:38, Oct., 1956

Hold Back Tomorrow (1955)
National Parent-Teacher 50:39, Dec., 1955

Hold 'Em, Jail (1932)
New York Times p. 7, Aug. 20, 1932

Hold 'Em Navy (1937)
New York Times p. 14, Nov. 6, 1937

Hold 'Em Yale (1935)
Literary Digest 119:30, May 11, 1935
New York Times p. 20, Apr. 27, 1935

Hold Everything (1930)
New York Times p. 24, Apr. 23, 1930

Hold Me Tight (1933)
New York Times p. 18, May 22, 1933

Hold That Blonde (1945)
New York Times p. 17, Nov. 9, 1945
Newsweek 26:104, Nov. 19, 1945
Time 46:98+, Nov. 12, 1945

Hold That Co-Ed (1938)
New York Times IX, p. 3, Jul. 17, 1938; p. 13, Sep. 24, 1938
Newsweek 12:22, Sep. 26, 1938
Time 32:50, Sep. 26, 1938

Hold That Ghost (1941)
Commonweal 34:426, Aug. 22, 1941
New York Times p. 13, Aug. 8, 1941
Time 38:74, Aug. 25, 1941

Hold That Girl (1934)
New York Times p. 20, Mar. 24, 1934

Hold That Kiss (1938)
New York Times p. 9, Jun. 11, 1938; IX, p. 3, Jun. 19,
1938

Hold Your Man (1929)
New York Times p. 20, Oct. 14, 1929

Hold Your Man (1933)
New York Times p. 16, Jul. 1, 1933; X, p. 3, Jul. 9,
1933

Hole in the Head (1959)
America 101:558, Jul. 25, 1959
Catholic World 189:394, Aug., 1959
Library Journal 84:2172, Jul., 1959
New York Times p. 31, Jul. 16, 1959; II, p. 1, Jul. 26,
1959
New Yorker 35:61, Aug. 1, 1959
Newsweek 54:83, Jul. 6, 1959
Saturday Review 42:27, Aug. 1, 1959
Time 74:65, Aug. 3, 1959

Hole in the Wall (1929)
New York Times p. 22, Apr. 15, 1929

Holiday (1930)
Commonweal 12:326, Jul. 23, 1930
Life (NY) 95:19, Jul. 25, 1930
Nation 131:160-1, Aug. 6, 1930
New York Times p. 25, Jul. 3, 1930; VIII, p. 3, Jul.
13, 1930; VIII, p. 6, Nov. 2, 1930
Outlook 155:431, Jul. 16, 1930
Theatre Magazine 52:47, Aug.-Sep., 1930

Holiday (1938)
Canadian Magazine 90:26, Jul., 1938
New Republic 95:188, Jun. 22, 1938
New York Times p. 15, Jun. 24, 1938; IX, p. 3, Jul.
10, 1938
Newsweek 11:21, Jun. 13, 1938
Stage 15:33, Jun., 1938
Time 31:23-4, Jun. 13, 1938

Holiday Affair (1949)
Christian Century 67:31, Jan. 4, 1950
Commonweal 51:268, Dec. 9, 1949
New York Times p. 48, Nov. 24, 1949

Holiday Affair (1949) (Continued)
Newsweek 34:77, Dec. 19, 1949
Time 54:92, Dec. 19, 1949

Holiday Camp (1948)
Commonweal 47:425, Feb. 6, 1948
New York Times p. 11, Jan. 24, 1948
New Yorker 23:52, Jan. 31, 1948
Newsweek 31:89-90, Feb. 16, 1948

Holiday for Henrietta (1955)
Farm Journal 79:103, Mar., 1955
Nation 180:166, Feb. 19, 1955
National Parent-Teacher 49:39, Apr., 1955
New York Times p. 21, Jan. 25, 1955; II, p. 1, Jan. 30,
    1955
New Yorker 30:103, Feb. 5, 1955
Newsweek 45:94, Jan. 24, 1955
Saturday Review 38:25, Feb. 12, 1955

Holiday for Lovers (1959)
America 101:619, Aug. 15, 1959
New York Times p. 10, Jul. 25, 1959
Newsweek 54:88, Jul. 27, 1959

Holiday for Sinners (1952)
New York Times p. 13, Sep. 20, 1952
Newsweek 40:124, Oct. 20, 1952

Holiday in Havana (1949)
New York Times p. 33, Oct. 14, 1949

Holiday in Mexico (1946)
Commonweal 44:598, Oct. 4, 1946
Cosmopolitan 121:66+, Sep., 1946
Life 21:87-8+, Sep. 9, 1946
New York Times II, p. 1, Sep. 23, 1945; II, p. 3, Aug.
    11, 1946; p. 19, Aug. 16, 1946
New Yorker 22:87, Aug. 17, 1946
Newsweek 28:89, Aug. 19, 1946
Photoplay 29:4, Nov., 1946
Time 48:92, Sep. 2, 1946
Woman's Home Companion 73:10, Oct., 1946

Holiday Inn (1942)
Commonweal 36:400, Aug. 14, 1942
New York Times VIII, p. 5, Feb. 15, 1942; p. 16, Aug.
    5, 1942; VIII, p. 3, Aug. 9, 1942

Holiday Inn (1942) (Continued)
Newsweek 20:58, Aug. 3, 1942
Time 40:94, Aug. 31, 1942

Holiday Island (1959)
New York Times p. 46, Sep. 22, 1959

Hollow Triumph (1948)
New Republic 119:30, Nov. 15, 1948
New York Times p. 29, Oct. 29, 1948
Time 52:104, Nov. 22, 1948

Holly and the Ivy (1954)
America 90:610, Mar. 6, 1954
Catholic World 178:462, Mar., 1954
Commonweal 59:497, Feb. 19, 1954
National Parent-Teacher 48:39, May, 1954
New York Times p. 16, Feb. 5, 1954
Saturday Review 37:29, Feb. 27, 1954
Time 63:91, Mar. 1, 1954

Hollywood Boulevard (1936)
New York Times p. 26, Sep. 21, 1936
Newsweek 8:27, Sep. 26, 1936

Hollywood Canteen (1944)
New York Times II, p. 4, Jul. 30, 1944; p. 19, Dec. 16, 1944
New Yorker 20:61, Dec. 16, 1944
Newsweek 24:81, Dec. 25, 1944
Time 45:92, Jan. 15, 1945; 45:8, Mar. 5, 1945

Hollywood Cavalcade (1939)
Life 7:63-4, Oct. 9, 1939
New York Times IX, p. 4, Oct. 8, 1939; p. 13, Oct. 14, 1939; IX, p. 5, Oct. 22, 1939
Newsweek 14:43, Oct. 16, 1939
Photoplay 53:62, Dec., 1939
Time 34:52, Oct. 23, 1939

Hollywood Cowboy (1937)
New York Times p. 12, Jul. 24, 1937; X, p. 3, Jul. 25, 1937

Hollywood Hotel (1938)
Canadian Magazine 89:29, Feb., 1938
Commonweal 27:300, Jan. 7, 1938

Hollywood Hotel (1938) (Continued)
New Republic 93:311, Jan. 19, 1938
New York Times p. 17, Jan. 13, 1938
Time 31:37-8, Jan. 24, 1938

Hollywood or Bust (1956)
National Parent-Teacher 51:38, Feb., 1957
New York Times p. 8, Dec. 24, 1956
Time 69:82, Jan. 21, 1957

Hollywood Party (1934)
New York Times p. 12, May 26, 1934
Newsweek 3:36, Jun. 2, 1934

Hollywood Revue (1929)
Life (NY) 94:26, Sep. 6, 1929
New York Times VIII, p. 4, Aug. 11, 1929; p. 20, Aug.
    15, 1929; VIII, p. 3, Aug. 18, 1929; VIII, p. 1, Sep.
    1, 1929
Outlook 153:156, Sep. 25, 1929

Hollywood Round-Up (1937)
New York Times p. 11, Mar. 5, 1938

Hollywood Speaks (1932)
New York Times p. 18, Aug. 12, 1932; IX, p. 3, Aug.
    21, 1932

Hollywood Story (1951)
Commonweal 54:261, Jun. 22, 1951
New Republic 124:21, Jun. 18, 1951
New York Times p. 40, Jun. 7, 1951
Newsweek 37:94, Jun. 18, 1951
Time 57:110+, Jun. 11, 1951

Holy Matrimony (1943)
Commonweal 38:586, Oct. 1, 1943
New Republic 109:457, Oct. 4, 1943
New York Times II, p. 3, Aug. 1, 1943; p. 25, Sep. 16,
    1943; II, p. 3, Sep. 19, 1943
New Yorker 19:55, Sep. 25, 1943
Newsweek 22:96, Sep. 6, 1943
Scholastic 43:34, Oct. 25, 1943
Time 42:93, Aug. 30, 1943

Holy Terror (1931)
New York Times p. 20, Jul. 20, 1931; VIII, p. 3, Jul.
    26, 1931

Holy Terror (1937)
  New York Times p. 21, Jan. 30, 1937

Home Before Dark (1958)
  America 100:296, Nov. 29, 1958
  Catholic World 188:239, Dec., 1958
  Commonweal 69:231, Nov. 28, 1958
  Library Journal 83:3237, Nov. 15, 1958
  New Republic 139:21-2, Nov. 10, 1958
  New York Times p. 23, Nov. 7, 1958
  New Yorker 34:147, Nov. 15, 1958
  Newsweek 52:99, Nov. 10, 1958
  Saturday Review 41:25, Nov. 29, 1958
  Time 72:102, Nov. 10, 1958

Home from the Hill (1960)
  America 102:746-7, Mar. 19, 1960
  Commonweal 71:676, Mar. 18, 1960
  Coronet 47:16, Apr., 1960
  McCalls 87:6, Apr., 1960
  New York Times p. 19, Mar. 4, 1960
  New Yorker 36:184, Mar. 12, 1960
  Newsweek 55:94, Mar. 7, 1960
  Saturday Review 43:35, Mar. 5, 1960
  Time 75:69, Apr. 11, 1960

Home in Indiana (1944)
  Commonweal 40:329, Jul. 21, 1944
  Life 17:74, Dec. 4, 1944
  Nation 159:24, Jul. 1, 1944
  New York Times p. 23, Jun. 22, 1944; II, p. 3, Jul. 2, 1944
  New Yorker 20:59, Jun. 24, 1944
  Newsweek 24:81, Jul. 3, 1944
  Photoplay 25:19, Jul., 1944

Home Is the Hero (1961)
  Commonweal 73:485, Feb. 3, 1961
  New York Times p. 32, Jan. 26, 1961
  Newsweek 57:84, Feb. 6, 1961

Home of the Brave (1949)
  Canadian Forum 29:116, Aug., 1949
  Commentary 8:181-3, Aug., 1949
  Commonweal 50:149, May 20, 1949
  Cosmopolitan 127:12+, Jul., 1949
  Good Housekeeping 129:201, Jul., 1949

Home of the Brave (1949) (Continued)
  Life 26:143-4+, May 23, 1949
  Nation 168:590-1, May 21, 1949
  New Republic 120:22, May 16, 1949
  New York Times II, p. 5, Mar. 6, 1949; II, p. 5, Mar.
    20, 1949; II, p. 5, Apr. 10, 1949; p. 29, May 13,
    1949; II, p. 1, May 22, 1949; p. 30, Nov. 25, 1949
  New York Times Magazine p. 56-7, May 1, 1949
  New Yorker 25:68, May 21, 1949
  Newsweek 33:86, May 16, 1949
  Photoplay 36:20, Jul., 1949
  Rotarian 75:50, Jul., 1949
  Saturday Review 32:26-7, Jun. 11, 1949
  Scholastic 54:27, May 18, 1949
  Theatre Arts 33:9, Jul., 1949
  Time 53:100, May 9, 1949

Home of the Range (1935)
  New York Times p. 24, Feb. 13, 1935

Home Sweet Homicide (1946)
  Commonweal 44:623, Oct. 11, 1946
  New York Times p. 5, Sep. 12, 1946
  Newsweek 28:106+, Sep. 9, 1946
  Scholastic 49:30, Oct. 7, 1946
  Time 48:106+, Sep. 16, 1946

Home Towners (1928)
  Life (NY) 92:22, Nov. 9, 1928
  New York Times p. 26, Oct. 24, 1928; IX, p. 7, Oct.
    28, 1928

Homecoming (1928)
  New York Times X, p. 7, Nov. 25, 1928; VIII, p. 4, Jul.
    28, 1929

Homecoming (1948)
  Commonweal 48:164, May 28, 1948
  New Republic 118:36, May 17, 1948
  New York Times p. 16, Aug. 11, 1947; p. 28, Apr. 30,
    1948; II, p. 5, May 23, 1948
  New Yorker 24:92, May 8, 1948
  Photoplay 33:22, Jul., 1948
  Time 51:100, May 10, 1948

Homestretch (1947)
  Commonweal 46:68, May 2, 1947

Homestretch (1947) (Continued)
Cosmopolitan 122:121, May, 1947
New York Times p. 30, Apr. 24, 1947; II, p. 5, Apr.
27, 1947
Newsweek 29:92, May 5, 1947
Time 49:102, May 5, 1947

Homicidal (1961)
New York Times p. 23, Jul. 27, 1961

Homicide Bureau (1938)
New York Times p. 17, Feb. 2, 1939

Homicide Squad (1931)
New York Times p. 28, Oct. 19, 1931

Hondo (1955)
America 90:327, Dec. 19, 1953
Catholic World 178:301, Jan., 1954
Commonweal 59:307, Dec. 25, 1953
Farm Journal 78:108, Feb., 1954
Life 35:125-6+, Dec. 14, 1953
National Parent-Teacher 48:39, Jan., 1954
New Yorker 29:97, Dec. 19, 1953
Newsweek 42:88+, Dec. 14, 1953
Saturday Review 36:53, Dec. 5, 1953
Time 62:112, Dec. 14, 1953

Honey (1930)
New York Times p. 23, Mar. 29, 1930; IX, p. 5, Apr.
6, 1930

Honeymoon (1947)
Commonweal 46:190, Jun. 6, 1947
Life 21:15, Aug. 12, 1946; 21:25, Sep. 9, 1946; 21:23,
Oct. 14, 1946; 22:59, Mar. 10, 1947
New Republic 116:37, Jun. 9, 1947
New York Times II, p. 1, May 12, 1946; II, p. 4, May
18, 1947; p. 27, May 19, 1947
New Yorker 23:82+, May 24, 1947
Newsweek 29:104, May 12, 1947
Time 49:102, May 26, 1947

Honeymoon Deferred (1940)
New York Times p. 23, Feb. 16, 1940

Honeymoon for Three (1941)
Commonweal 33:448, Feb. 21, 1941

Honeymoon for Three (1941) (Continued)
New York Times p. 19, Feb. 8, 1941
New Yorker 17:77, Feb. 15, 1941
Photoplay 54:62, Dec., 1940; 18:14, Jan., 1941

Honeymoon in Bali (1939)
Commonweal 30:539, Oct. 6, 1939
New York Times p. 21, Sep. 21, 1939; IX, p. 3, Sep. 24, 1939
Newsweek 14:35, Oct. 2, 1939
Time 34:49, Oct. 2, 1939

Honeymoon Lane (1930)
New York Times p. 16, Aug. 1, 1931

Honeymoon Machine (1961)
New Republic 145:28, Sep. 4, 1961
New York Times p. 25, Aug. 24, 1961; II, p. 1, Aug. 26, 1961
New Yorker 37:63, Sep. 2, 1961
Newsweek 58:77, Aug. 7, 1961
Saturday Review 44:31, Jul. 22, 1961
Time 78:60, Aug. 4, 1961

Honeymoon's Over (1939)
New York Times p. 33, Dec. 15, 1939

*Hong Kong
American Magazine 153:9, Jan., 1952
New York Times p. 20, Apr. 5, 1952
Newsweek 39:110, May 19, 1952

Honky Tonk (1929)
Life (NY) 93:23, Jun. 28, 1929
New York Times p. 32, Jun. 5, 1929; VIII, p. 5, Jun. 9, 1929

Honky Tonk (1941)
Commonweal 34:614, Oct. 17, 1941
Life 11:103-4+, Oct. 13, 1941
New York Times p. 27, Oct. 3, 1941
New Yorker 17:80, Oct. 4, 1941
Newsweek 18:60-1, Oct. 6, 1941
Photoplay 20:40-1+, Dec., 1941
Time 38:96, Oct. 13, 1941

Honolulu (1939)
Commonweal 29:497, Feb. 24, 1939

Honolulu (1939) (Continued)
  New York Times IX, p. 4, Feb. 19, 1939; p. 19, Feb.
    23, 1939; IX, p. 5, Feb. 26, 1939
  Scholastic 34:34, Feb. 25, 1939

Honor Among Lovers (1931)
  New York Times p. 15, Feb. 28, 1931; VIII, p. 5, Mar.
    8, 1931

Honor of the Family (1931)
  Life (NY) 98:19, Nov. 6, 1931
  New York Times p. 20, Oct. 17, 1931

Hoodlum (1951)
  New York Times p. 14, Jul. 6, 1951

Hoodlum Empire (1952)
  New York Times p. 25, Mar. 6, 1952

Hoodlum Priest (1961)
  America 104:799, Mar. 18, 1961
  Commonweal 74:15-16, Mar. 31, 1961
  New Republic 144:21, Feb. 27, 1961
  New York Times p. 28, Apr. 3, 1961
  Newsweek 57:104, Mar. 6, 1961
  Senior Scholastic 78:39, Apr. 12, 1961

Hoodlum Saint (1946)
  New York Times p. 29, Jun. 27, 1946; II, p. 3, Jun. 30,
    1946

Hook (1961)
  America 108:275, Feb. 23, 1963
  Commonweal 77:599, Mar. 1, 1963
  New York Times II, p. 7, Jun. 10, 1962; p. 5, Feb. 16,
    1963
  New Yorker 39:145-6, Mar. 9, 1963
  Newsweek 61:85, Mar. 4, 1963
  Saturday Review 46:26, Feb. 16, 1963
  Time 81:M17, Mar. 1, 1963

Hook, Line and Sinker (1930)
  New York Times p. 31, Dec. 25, 1930

Hoopla (1933) (The Barker)
  New York Times IX, p. 5, Nov. 12, 1933; p. 23, Dec. 1,
    1933

Hooray for Love (1935)
New York Times p. 16, Jul. 13, 1935; IX, p. 3, Jul. 21, 1935
Photoplay 48:62-3, Jul., 1935

Hopalong Rides Again (1937)
New York Times p. 19, Jan. 22, 1938

Horizon's West (1952)
National Parent-Teacher 47:38, Nov., 1952
New York Times p. 16, Nov. 22, 1952

Horizontal Lieutenant (1962)
Commonweal 76:86, Apr. 20, 1962
New York Times p. 15, May 12, 1962
Senior Scholastic 80:35, Apr. 11, 1962
Time 79:100, Apr. 13, 1962

Horn Blows at Midnight (1945)
Commonweal 42:72, May 4, 1945
Cosmopolitan 118:95, Apr., 1945
New York Times p. 18, Apr. 21, 1945
New Yorker 21:63, Apr. 28, 1945
Newsweek 25:98, May 7, 1945

Horror Island (1941)
New York Times p. 11, Mar. 31, 1941

Horror of Dracula (1957)
New York Times p. 24, May 29, 1958
America 99:358, Jun. 21, 1958

Horrors of the Black Museum (1959)
New York Times p. 37, Apr. 30, 1959

Horse Feathers (1932)
Living Age 343:371-2, Dec., 1932
Nation 135:198-9, Aug. 31, 1932
New York Times p. 12, Aug. 11, 1932; IX, p. 3, Aug. 21, 1932
Outlook 161:38, Oct., 1932
Stage 9:27, Sep., 1932

Horse Soldiers (1959)
America 101:497, Jul. 4, 1959
Catholic World 189:394-5, Aug., 1959
Commonweal 70:352, Jul. 3, 1959

Horse Soldiers (1959) (Continued)
    Cosmopolitan 147:12, Sep., 1959
    Library Journal 84:2172, Jul., 1959
    Life 46:55-8, Jun. 29, 1959
    New York Times p. 13, Jun. 27, 1959
    Newsweek 53:91, Jun. 29, 1959
    Saturday Review 42:28, Jun. 20, 1959
    Time 74:63, Jul. 20, 1959

*Horse's Mouth
    America 90:464, Jan. 30, 1954
    Commonweal 59:525, Feb. 26, 1954
    National Parent-Teacher 48:38, Mar., 1954
    New York Times p. 33, Jan. 20, 1954
    Saturday Review 37:29, Feb. 6, 1954

Horse's Mouth (1958)
    America 100:254, Nov. 22, 1958
    Catholic World 188:327, Jan., 1959
    Commonweal 69:258, Dec. 5, 1958
    Library Journal 83:3418, Dec. 1, 1958
    Life 45:98-9+, Nov. 10, 1958
    Mademoiselle 48:66, Jan., 1959
    New Republic 139:21-2, Dec. 15, 1958
    New York Times p. 41, Nov. 12, 1958; II, p. 1, Nov.
        16, 1958; II, p. 8, Mar. 15, 1959
    New York Times Magazine p. 66-7, Oct. 26, 1958
    New Yorker 34:137, Nov. 22, 1958
    Newsweek 52:113, Nov. 24, 1958
    Saturday Review 41:26, Nov. 15, 1958
    Time 72:94, Nov. 24, 1958

Horsie (see Queen for a Day)

Hostages (1943)
    New York Times VIII, p. 3, Oct. 25, 1942; p. 23, Oct.
        11, 1943
    New Yorker 19:44, Oct. 16, 1943
    Scholastic 43:32, Nov. 8, 1943
    Time 42:54, Nov. 1, 1943

Hot Blood (1956)
    National Parent-Teacher 50:39, Apr., 1956
    New York Times p. 14, Mar. 24, 1956

Hot Cars (1956)
    National Parent-Teacher 51:38, Oct., 1956

Hot for Paris (1929)
Life (NY) 95:31, Jan. 24, 1930
New York Times IX, p. 5, Nov. 17, 1929; p. 21, Jan. 4,
1930; VIII, p. 6, Jan. 12, 1930

Hot Heiress (1931)
New York Times p. 23, Mar. 14, 1931

Hot Money (1936)
New York Times p. 16, Jul. 25, 1936

Hot News (1928)
New York Times p. 11, Jul. 23, 1928; VII, p. 3, Jul.
29, 1928
Outlook 149:587, Aug. 8, 1928

Hot Pepper (1933)
New York Times p. 9, Jan. 23, 1933

Hot Saturday (1932)
New York Times p. 12, Nov. 5, 1932

Hot Spell (1958)
Catholic World 187:309, Jul., 1958
Commonweal 68:231, May 30, 1958
Library Journal 83:1913, Jun. 15, 1958
New York Times p. 37, Sep. 18, 1958; II, p. 1, Sep. 21,
1958
Saturday Review 41:26, Jun. 28, 1958
Time 71:90-1, Jun. 23, 1958

Hot Spot (1941) (see also I Wake Up Screaming)
Photoplay 20:15, Jan., 1942

Hot Steel (1940)
New York Times p. 25, Jun. 21, 1940

Hot Stuff (1929)
New York Times p. 27, May 13, 1929

Hot Summer Night (1957)
National Parent-Teacher 51:37, May, 1957

Hot Water (1937)
New York Times p. 19, Nov. 5, 1937

Hotel Berlin (1945)
Nation 160:314, Mar. 17, 1945

Hotel Berlin (1945) (Continued)
New York Times p. 11, Mar. 3, 1945; II, p. 1, Mar. 11,
1945
New Yorker 21:48, Mar. 10, 1945
Newsweek 25:108, Mar. 12, 1945
Scholastic 46:28, Apr. 2, 1945
Time 45:94, Mar. 26, 1945

Hotel Continental (1931)
New York Times p. 19, Mar. 21, 1932; VIII, p. 4, Mar.
27, 1932

Hotel Imperial (1939)
New York Times p. 31, May 11, 1939

*Hotel Sahara
Catholic World 174:143-4, Nov., 1951
New York Times p. 21, Jun. 1, 1952
Newsweek 39:82, Jan. 14, 1952
Time 58:107, Sep. 24, 1951

Hottentot (1929)
New York Times p. 15, Sep. 7, 1929; IX, p. 4, Sep. 15,
1929

Houdini (1953)
America 89:406, Jul. 18, 1953
Catholic World 177:304-5, Jul., 1953
Commonweal 58:348, Jul. 10, 1953
New York Times p. 10, Jul. 3, 1953
New Yorker 29:47, Jul. 25, 1953
Saturday Review 36:36, Jul. 11, 1953
Time 61:92, Jun. 29, 1953

Hound-Dog Man (1959)
Commonweal 71:289-90, Dec. 4, 1959
New Republic 142:21, Jan. 4, 1960
New York Times p. 29, Apr. 28, 1960
Saturday Review 42:37, Nov. 21, 1959

Hound of the Baskervilles (1939)
Commonweal 29:665, Apr. 7, 1939
Life 6:50, Apr. 10, 1939
New Republic 99:252, Jul. 5, 1939
New York Times p. 19, Mar. 25, 1939
Newsweek 13:32, Apr. 3, 1939
Time 33:40, Apr. 3, 1939

Hound of the Baskervilles (1959)
Library Journal 84:2054, Jun. 15, 1959
New York Times p. 9, Jul. 4, 1959
Newsweek 53:107, Jun. 8, 1959
Senior Scholastic 74:47, May 15, 1959

Hour Before the Dawn (1944)
New York Times II, p. 3, Nov. 7, 1943; p. 25, May 11, 1944
Time 43:94, Jun. 5, 1944

Hour of 13 (1952)
Christian Century 70:31, Jan. 7, 1953
National Parent-Teacher 47:38, Oct., 1952
New York Times p. 37, Oct. 28, 1952
Newsweek 40:105, Nov. 3, 1952
Time 60:120, Nov. 10, 1952

House Across the Bay (1940)
Commonweal 31:494, Mar. 29, 1940
New York Times p. 23, Mar. 22, 1940
Photoplay 54:69, Apr., 1940

House Across the Street (1949)
New York Times p. 14, Sep. 2, 1949

House by the River (1950)
Library Journal 75:787, May 1, 1950
New Republic 122:23, May 15, 1950
New York Times p. 25, May 2, 1950
Newsweek 35:90, May 15, 1950

House Divided (1932)
New York Times p. 21, Jan. 9, 1932; VIII, p. 4, Jan. 17, 1932

*House I Live In
Commonweal 42:238, Dec. 14, 1945
New York Times p. 23, Jun. 19, 1946
Scholastic 47:25, Nov. 19, 1945
Time 46:98, Nov. 12, 1945

House of a Thousand Candles (1936)
New York Times p. 29, Apr. 2, 1936
Time 27:34, Apr. 13, 1936

House of Bamboo (1955)
America 93:419, Jul. 23, 1955

536

House of Bamboo (1955) (Continued)
Commonweal 62:399, Jul. 22, 1955
National Parent-Teacher 50:39, Sep., 1955
New York Times p. 13, Jul. 2, 1955
Newsweek 46:83, Jul. 18, 1955
Saturday Review 38:23, Jul. 23, 1955
Time 66:60, Aug. 1, 1955

House of Dracula (1945)
New York Times p. 16, Dec. 22, 1945

House of Fear (1939)
New York Times X, p. 5, May 7, 1939

House of Fear (1945)
New York Times p. 17, Mar. 17, 1945

House of Frankenstein (1945)
New York Times II, p. 7, Dec. 10, 1944; p. 19, Dec.
16, 1944

House of Fright (1961)
Commonweal 74:306, Jun. 16, 1961
New York Times p. 25, Aug. 24, 1961

House of Horrors (1946)
New York Times p. 20, Feb. 23, 1946

House of Intrigue (1960)
New York Times p. 36, Mar. 10, 1960

House of Numbers (1957)
National Parent-Teacher 52:33, Sep., 1957
New York Times p. 15, Sep. 13, 1957
Time 70:98, Sep. 30, 1957

House of Ricordi (1954)
National Parent-Teacher 50:39, May, 1956
New York Times p. 32, Mar. 13, 1956
Newsweek 47:102, Mar. 26, 1956

House of Rothschild (1934)
American Review 3:157-8, May, 1934
Canadian Magazine 81:44, May, 1934
Commonweal 19:609, Mar. 30, 1934
Literary Digest 117:33, Mar. 31, 1934
Movie Classic 6:62, May, 1934

House of Rothschild (1934) (Continued)
Nation 138:398, Apr. 4, 1934
New Outlook 163:45, Apr., 1934
New Republic 78:216-7, Apr. 4, 1934
New York Times p. 27, Mar. 15, 1934; X, p. 3, Mar.
25, 1934; IX, p. 4, Apr. 22, 1934
Newsweek 3:38, Mar. 24, 1934
Review of Reviews 89:50, May, 1934
Time 23:20-1, Mar. 26, 1934
Vanity Fair 42:53, May, 1934

House of Secrets (1936)
New York Times p. 13, Feb. 22, 1937

House of Strangers (1949)
Commonweal 50:319, Jul. 8, 1949
Good Housekeeping 129:166-8, Sep., 1949
New Republic 121:22, Jul. 25, 1949
New York Times p. 8, Jul. 2, 1949
Newsweek 34:65, Aug. 1, 1949
Photoplay 36:23, Sep., 1949
Rotarian 75:39, Oct., 1949
Theatre Arts 33:6, Sep., 1949
Time 54:78, Jul. 18, 1949
Woman's Home Companion 76:10-11, Sep., 1949

House of the Seven Gables (1940)
New York Times IX, p. 5, Jan. 21, 1940; p. 21, Apr.
15, 1940
Photoplay 54:73, May, 1940
Scholastic 36:35, Apr. 8, 1940

House of the Seven Hawks (1959)
New York Times p. 51, Dec. 17, 1959
Newsweek 54:116, Nov. 16, 1959

House of Usher (1960)
New York Times p. 45, Sep. 15, 1960

House of Wax (1953)
America 89:229, May 23, 1953
Catholic World 177:223-4, Jun., 1953
Commonweal 58:99, May 1, 1953
National Parent-Teacher 47:37, Jun., 1953
New York Times p. 15, Apr. 11, 1953; II, p. 1, Apr.
19, 1953; II, p. 1, Apr. 26, 1953
New Yorker 29:133, Apr. 18, 1953

House of Wax (1953) (Continued)
Newsweek 41:108, Apr. 27, 1953
Time 61:114, Apr. 20, 1953

House of Women (1962)
New York Times p. 41, Apr. 12, 1962

House on 56th Street (1933)
Canadian Magazine 81:35, Jan., 1934
New York Times p. 9, Dec. 2, 1933; X, p. 7, Dec. 10,
1933

House on Haunted Hill (1959)
New York Times p. 27, Mar. 12, 1959
Newsweek 53:100, Jan. 26, 1959

House on 92nd Street (1945)
Commonweal 42:576, Sep. 28, 1945
Life 19:91-2+, Oct. 8, 1945
Nation 161:386, Oct. 13, 1945
New York Times p. 6, Sep. 13, 1945; p. 24, Sep. 27,
1945; II, p. 1, Sep. 30, 1945; II, p. 1, Oct. 28, 1945
New Yorker 21:56, Sep. 29, 1945
Newsweek 26:94, Sep. 24, 1945
Scholastic 47:38, Oct. 8, 1945
Time 46:96+, Oct. 8, 1945

House on Telegraph Hill (1951)
Library Journal 76:972, Jun. 1, 1951
New York Times p. 29, May 14, 1951
Newsweek 37:89, May 28, 1951
Scholastic 58:29, Mar. 14, 1951
Time 57:106, Jun. 18, 1951

House on the Waterfront (1959)
New York Times p. 25, Feb. 21, 1959

Houseboat (1958)
America 100:327, Dec. 6, 1958
Catholic World 188:64, Oct., 1958
Commonweal 69:232, Nov. 28, 1958
Life 45:56, Oct. 13, 1958
New York Times p. 24, Nov. 24, 1958
New York Times Magazine p. 20, Jul. 6, 1958
New Yorker 34:138, Nov. 22, 1958
Newsweek 52:106-7, Nov. 3, 1958
Saturday Review 41:36, Dec. 6, 1958
Time 72:82, Dec. 1, 1958

Householder (1963)
Commonweal 79:168, Nov. 1, 1963
New York Times p. 43, Oct. 22, 1963
New Yorker 39:206-7, Oct. 26, 1963
Newsweek 62:102, Nov. 4, 1963
Time 82:98, Nov. 8, 1963

Housekeeper's Daughter (1939)
Commonweal 31:79, Nov. 10, 1939
New York Times IX, p. 3, Aug. 13, 1939; p. 14, Aug.
14, 1939; p. 21, Dec. 2, 1939

Housemaster (1938)
New York Times X, p. 5, Apr. 9, 1939; p. 13, Apr. 10,
1939

Housewife (1934)
New York Times p. 21, Aug. 10, 1934

How Green Was My Valley (1942)
Commonweal 35:72, Nov. 7, 1941
Life 11:64-6+, Nov. 10, 1941
Nation 153:491, Nov. 15, 1941
New York Times IX, p. 3, Jun. 1, 1941; IX, p. 4, Sep.
7, 1941; p. 27, Oct. 29, 1941; IX, p. 5, Nov. 2, 1941;
p. 21, Feb. 27, 1942
New Yorker 17:72, Nov. 1, 1941
New Republic 105:733, Dec. 1, 1941
Newsweek 18:59-60, Nov. 3, 1941
Photoplay 20:14, Jan., 1942
Scholastic 39:28, Nov. 10, 1941
Theatre Arts 25:884+, Dec., 1941; 26:59, Jan., 1942
Time 38:100+, Nov. 24, 1941

How He Lied to Her Husband (1931)
Nation 132:135-6, Feb. 4, 1931
New York Times p. 35, Jan. 13, 1931; p. 23, Jan. 17,
1931; VIII, p. 5, Jan. 25, 1931; p. 10, Mar. 2, 1931;
p. 6, Mar. 3, 1931; p. 26, Mar. 4, 1931

How the West Was Won (1962)
America 108:448, Mar. 30, 1963
Commonweal 78:48, Apr. 5, 1963
Life 54:87-9, Mar. 29, 1963
National Review 15:72, Jul. 30, 1963
New Republic 148:29, Apr. 20, 1963
New York Times II, p. 7, May 21, 1961; II, p. 9, Jun.
18, 1961; p. 45, Oct. 4, 1962; p. 8, Mar. 28, 1963

How the West Was Won (1962) (Continued)
    II, p. 1, Apr. 14, 1963; p. 54, Apr. 1, 1963
    New Yorker 39:175-6, Apr. 6, 1963
    Newsweek 61:85, Mar. 4, 1963
    Saturday Review 46:42, Feb. 23, 1963
    Time 81:102+, Mar. 22, 1963

How to Be Very, Very Popular (1955)
    Library Journal 80:1674, Aug., 1955
    National Parent-Teacher 50:39, Oct., 1955
    New York Times p. 10, Jul. 23, 1955
    New Yorker 31:44, Jul. 30, 1955
    Saturday Review 38:24, Aug. 6, 1955
    Time 66:82, Aug. 8, 1955

How to Marry a Millionaire (1953)
    America 90:247+, Nov. 28, 1953
    Catholic World 178:302, Jan., 1954
    Commonweal 59:198, Nov. 27, 1953
    Farm Journal 78:83, Jan., 1954
    Library Journal 78:2098, Dec. 1, 1953
    Life 35:137-8, Nov. 23, 1953
    Nation 177:574, Dec. 26, 1953
    National Parent-Teacher 48:39, Jan., 1954
    New York Times p. 37, Nov. 11, 1953; II, p. 1, Nov.
        15, 1953
    New Yorker 29:133, Nov. 21, 1953
    Newsweek 42:104, Nov. 16, 1953
    Saturday Review 36:31, Nov. 28, 1953
    Time 62:114+, Nov. 23, 1953

How to Murder a Rich Uncle (1957)
    Library Journal 82:2918, Nov. 15, 1957
    National Parent-Teacher 52:38, Nov., 1957
    New York Times p. 19, Oct. 26, 1957
    New Yorker 33:167, Nov. 2, 1957

Howards of Virginia (1940)
    Child Life 20:61, Feb., 1941
    Commonweal 32:449, Sep. 20, 1940
    Good Housekeeping 111:14, Jul., 1940
    New York Times IX, p. 5, Apr. 14, 1940; IX, p. 3, May
        26, 1940; p. 27, Sep. 27, 1940
    Newsweek 16:60, Sep. 16, 1940
    Photoplay 54:68, Nov., 1940
    Scholastic 37:39, Sep. 23, 1940
    Time 36:88, Sep. 16, 1940

Huckleberry Finn (1931) (see also Adventures of Huckleberry Finn)
Commonweal 14:406, Aug. 26, 1931
Life (NY) 98:21, Sep. 4, 1931
New York Times VIII, p. 3, Aug. 2, 1931; p. 16, Aug. 8, 1931; VIII, p. 3, Aug. 16, 1931
Outlook 158:534, Aug. 26, 1931

Hucksters (1947)
Commonweal 46:386, Aug. 1, 1947
Cosmopolitan 123:58+, Sep., 1947
Life 22:51-2+, Mar. 31, 1947; 23:103-4+, Jul. 28, 1947
Nation 165:130, Aug. 2, 1947
New Republic 117:34, Aug. 11, 1947
New York Times p. 37, Jan. 1, 1947; II, p. 5, Jan. 19, 1947; II, p. 5, Mar. 9, 1947; II, p. 3, Jul. 13, 1947; p. 21, Jul. 18, 1947; II, p. 1, Jul. 20, 1947
New Yorker 23:46, Jul. 19, 1947
Newsweek 30:76+, Jul. 21, 1947
Photoplay 31:4, Sep., 1947
Time 50:91, Jul. 21, 1947
Woman's Home Companion 74:10-11, Oct., 1947

Hud (1963)
America 108:871-2, Jun. 15, 1963
Commonweal 78:328, Jun. 14, 1963
Esquire 60:50+, Sep., 1963
New Republic 148:27-8, May 25, 1963
New York Times p. 36, May 29, 1963; II, p. 1, Jun. 9, 1963
New Yorker 39:166, Jun. 8, 1963
Newsweek 61:84, Jun. 3, 1963
Saturday Review 46:40, May 25, 1963
Time 81:100, Jun. 7, 1963

Huddle (1932)
New York Times p. 24, Jun. 17, 1932

Hudson's Bay (1940)
Child Life 20:61, Feb., 1941
Commonweal 33:304, Jan. 10, 1941
New Republic 104:20, Jan. 6, 1941
New York Times IX, p. 3, Sep. 8, 1940; IX, p. 5, Oct. 27, 1940; p. 23, Jan. 10, 1941
Newsweek 17:62, Jan. 20, 1941
Photoplay 18:6, Mar., 1941
Scholastic 38:34, Jan. 27, 1941

Hudson's Bay (1940) (Continued)
Stage 1:22, Nov., 1940
Time 37:71, Feb. 3, 1941

Hue and Cry (1951)
New York Times p. 25, Jan. 9, 1951
Scholastic 58:23, Feb. 14, 1951

Huk (1956)
Library Journal 81:1782, Aug., 1956
National Parent-Teacher 51:39, Sep., 1956
New York Times p. 20, Dec. 15, 1956

Hullabaloo (1940)
New York Times p. 33, Dec. 19, 1940; IX, p. 5, Dec.
22, 1940

Human Adventure (1934)
New York Times p. 16, Oct. 30, 1935
Newsweek 3:36, Jun. 16, 1934

*Human Beast
Commonweal 31:435, Mar. 8, 1940
New Republic 102:346, Mar. 11, 1940
New York Times p. 17, Feb. 20, 1940; IX, p. 5, Feb.
25, 1940
Saturday Review 22:21, May 11, 1940
Time 35:68, Mar. 4, 1940

Human Cargo (1936)
New York Times p. 11, May 16, 1936

Human Comedy (1943)
Commonweal 37:543, Mar. 19, 1943
Cosmopolitan 114:68, May, 1943
Good Housekeeping 116:2, Apr., 1943
Library Journal 68:443, Jun. 1, 1943
Life 14:69-70, Mar. 5, 1943
Modern Music 20:283, May-Jun., 1943
Nation 156:426-7, Mar. 20, 1943
New Republic 108:346-7, Mar. 15, 1943
New York Times VIII, p. 3, Sep. 20, 1943; II, p. 3, Feb.
7, 1943; p. 19, Mar. 3, 1943; II, p. 3, Mar. 7, 1943;
II, p. 3, Mar. 21, 1943
Newsweek 21:78+, Mar. 15, 1943
Photoplay 22:22, May, 1943
Theatre Arts 27:283-5+, May, 1943
Time 41:56, Mar. 22, 1943

543

Human Comedy (1943) (Continued)
  Woman's Home Companion 70:2, Apr., 1943

Human Condition (1960)
  New York Times p. 56, Dec. 16, 1959

Human Desire (1954)
  National Parent-Teacher 49:39, Oct., 1954
  New York Times p. 7, Aug. 7, 1954

Human Jungle (1954)
  National Parent-Teacher 49:39, Dec., 1954
  New York Times p. 24, Nov. 26, 1954
  Newsweek 44:112, Oct. 11, 1954
  Saturday Review 37:29, Nov. 27, 1954
  Scholastic 65:25, Dec. 8, 1954

Human Monster (1940)
  New York Times p. 11, Mar. 25, 1940

Human Side (1934)
  New York Times p. 20, Sep. 15, 1934

Humanity (1933)
  New York Times p. 16, Apr. 22, 1933

Humoresque (1947)
  Commonweal 45:281, Dec. 27, 1946
  Cosmopolitan 121:72+, Nov., 1946
  Good Housekeeping 124:12-13, Feb., 1947
  New Republic 116:37, Jan. 20, 1947
  New York Times II, p. 5, Dec. 22, 1946
  New Yorker 22:44, Dec. 28, 1946
  Newsweek 28:93, Dec. 23, 1946
  Photoplay 30:9, Jan., 1947
  Time 49:97-8, Jan. 13, 1947

Hunchback of Notre Dame (1939)
  Commonweal 31:266, Jan. 12, 1940
  Life 8:37-9, Jan. 1, 1940
  New Republic 102:116, Jan. 22, 1940
  New York Times IX, p. 3, Jul. 23, 1939; IX, p. 5, Oct.
    14, 1939; p. 29, Jan. 1, 1940
  Newsweek 15:37, Jan. 8, 1940
  Photoplay 53:66-7, Nov., 1939
  Studio 119:179, May, 1940
  Theatre Arts 23:804, Nov., 1939

Hunchback of Notre Dame (1957)
Library Journal 82:3199, Dec. 15, 1957
National Parent-Teacher 52:39, Feb., 1958
New York Times VI, p. 22, Nov. 11, 1956; p. 35, Dec.
12, 1957
Time 71:77, Jan. 6, 1958

Hundred Hour Hunt (1953)
New York Times p. 32, Jun. 17, 1953
Newsweek 41:88+, Jun. 29, 1953

Hungarian Rhapsody (1929)
Life (NY) 94:23, Aug. 30, 1929
New York Times IX, p. 6, Dec. 16, 1928; p. 25, Aug. 5,
1929; VIII, p. 3, Aug. 11, 1929

Hungry Hill (1947)
New Republic 117:37, Oct. 27, 1947
New York Times p. 11, Oct. 11, 1947; II, p. 5, Oct. 12,
1947
New Yorker 23:113, Oct. 18, 1947
Newsweek 30:82, Nov. 10, 1947
Time 50:104, Nov. 10, 1947

Hunted Men (1938)
New York Times p. 9, May 21, 1938

Hunters (1958)
America 99:650, Sep. 20, 1958
Catholic World 188:65, Oct., 1958
Commonweal 68:593, Sep. 12, 1958
Library Journal 83:3098, Nov. 1, 1958
New York Times p. 33, Aug. 27, 1958
Newsweek 52:106, Sep. 15, 1958
Senior Scholastic 73:29, Nov. 7, 1958
Time 72:78, Aug. 25, 1958

Hurricane (1937)
Commonweal 27:132, Nov. 26, 1937
Life 3:106-7, Oct. 25, 1937; 3:44-7, Nov. 22, 1937
Literary Digest 124:34, Nov. 27, 1937
New York Times XI, p. 6, Oct. 24, 1937; XI, p. 5, Nov.
7, 1937; p. 31, Nov. 10, 1937; XI, p. 5, Nov. 14,
1937; XII, p. 8, Dec. 5, 1937; XI, p. 7, Dec. 12,
1937
Newsweek 10:34, Nov. 22, 1937
Saint Nicholas 64:37+, Oct., 1937

Hurricane (1937) (Continued)
Scholastic 31:10, Dec. 4, 1937
Stage 14:36-8, Sep., 1937; 15:99, Dec., 1937
Time 30:41, Nov. 15, 1937

Hurricane Smith (1952)
National Parent-Teacher 47:38, Nov., 1952
New York Times p. 15, Oct. 4, 1952
Time 60:14, Oct. 20, 1952

Hurry, Charlie, Hurry (1941)
New York Times p. 31, Nov. 12, 1941

Husband's Holiday (1931)
New York Times p. 29, Dec. 25, 1931

Hush Money (1931)
New York Times p. 7, Jul. 11, 1931; VIII, p. 3, Jul. 19,
1931

Hustler (1961)
America 106:57+, Oct. 14, 1961
Commonweal 75:71, Oct. 13, 1961
Life 51:52+, Nov. 24, 1961
New Republic 145:28, Oct. 9, 1961
New York Times II, p. 9, Mar. 19, 1961; p. 35, Sep. 27,
1961; II, p. 1, Oct. 8, 1961
New Yorker 37:140-1, Sep. 30, 1961
Newsweek 58:111, Sep. 25, 1961
Saturday Review 44:37, Oct. 7, 1961
Time 78:74, Oct. 6, 1961

Hypnotized (1932)
New York Times p. 13, Jan. 16, 1933

I Accuse (1958)
America 98:615, Feb. 22, 1958
Commonweal 67:593, Mar. 7, 1958
Library Journal 83:835, Mar. 15, 1958
New York Times p. 32, Mar. 6, 1957; II, p. 1, Mar. 9,
1957
New Yorker 34:93, Mar. 15, 1958
Newsweek 51:108, Mar. 10, 1958
Saturday Review 41:41, Mar. 8, 1958
Senior Scholastic 72:21, Apr. 11, 1958
Time 71:82, Mar. 3, 1958

I Aim at the Stars (1960)
America 104:158+, Oct. 29, 1960
Commonweal 73:96, Oct. 21, 1960
New York Times p. 15, Aug. 20, 1960; p. 42, Oct. 20,
1960; II, p. 1, Oct. 23, 1960
Newsweek 56:85, Oct. 3, 1960
Senior Scholastic 77:53, Sep. 28, 1960
Time 76:95, Oct. 17, 1960

I Am a Camera (1955)
Catholic World 181:462, Sep., 1955
Commonweal 62:565, Sep. 9, 1955
Life 39:57-8, Aug. 8, 1955
Nation 181:211, Sep. 3, 1955
National Parent-Teacher 50:39, Jan., 1956
New York Times II, p. 5, Jan. 23, 1955; p. 29, Aug. 9,
1955
New Yorker 31:69, Aug. 20, 1955
Saturday Review 38:24, Aug. 6, 1955
Time 66:58+, Aug. 15, 1955

I Am a Fugitive from a Chain Gang (1932)
Movie Classic 4:34, Mar., 1933
Nation 135:514, Nov. 23, 1932
New York Times p. 17, Nov. 11, 1932; IX, p. 5, Nov.
20, 1932; p. 22, Dec. 23, 1932
Photoplay 43:6, Feb., 1933
Stage 10:27, Dec., 1932; 10:35, Jul., 1933
Vanity Fair 39:46, Dec., 1932

I Am a Thief (1934)
New York Times p. 24, Jan. 1, 1935

I Am Suzanne (1933)
American Review 3:154-5, May, 1934
Literary Digest 117:39, Feb. 3, 1934

I Am the Law (1938)
New York Times p. 14, Aug. 26, 1938
Newsweek 12:23, Sep. 5, 1938
Time 32:33, Sep. 5, 1938

I Believe in You (1934)
New York Times p. 25, Apr. 11, 1934

I Believe in You (1953)
Library Journal 78:897, May 15, 1953

I Believe in You (1953) (Continued)
National Parent-Teacher 47:37, Jun., 1953
New York Times p. 34, May 5, 1953
Newsweek 41:108+, May 18, 1953
Saturday Review 36:29, Apr. 25, 1953
Theatre Arts 37:86, Jun., 1953
Time 61:117, Apr. 20, 1953

I Can Get It for You Wholesale (1951)
Christian Century 68:647, May 23, 1951
Library Journal 76:720, Apr. 15, 1951
New York Times II, p. 5, Sep. 24, 1950; p. 34, Apr. 5, 1951
New Yorker 27:127-8, Apr. 14, 1951
Newsweek 37:106, Apr. 16, 1951
Saturday Review 34:28, Apr. 21, 1951
Time 57:104+, Apr. 30, 1951

I Can't Give You Anything but Love, Baby (1940)
Commonweal 32:233, Jul. 5, 1940

I Confess (1953)
America 88:717-18, Mar. 28, 1953
American Photographer 47:16, Jul., 1953
Catholic World 177:63, Apr., 1953
Christian Century 70:463, Apr. 15, 1953
Commonweal 57:550, Mar. 6, 1953
Library Journal 78:437, Mar. 1, 1953
Look 17:110+, Apr. 21, 1953
Nation 176:314, Apr. 11, 1953
National Parent-Teacher 47:40, Apr., 1953
New York Times p. 28, Mar. 23, 1953
New Yorker 29:82, Apr. 4, 1953
Newsweek 41:90, Mar. 2, 1953
Saturday Review 36:33-4, Feb. 21, 1953
Theatre Arts 37:89, Apr., 1953
Time 61:92, Mar. 2, 1953

I Could Go on Singing (1963)
Commonweal 78:377, Jun. 28, 1963
New York Times p. 42, May 16, 1963; II, p. 1, May 26, 1963
Newsweek 61:98, Apr. 22, 1963
Time 81:112+, Apr. 19, 1963

I Cover the War (1937)
New York Times p. 10, Aug. 2, 1937

I Cover the Waterfront (1933)
Commonweal 18:133, Jun. 2, 1933
New York Times p. 17, May 18, 1933
Newsweek 1:30, May 27, 1933

I Died a Thousand Times (1955)
National Parent-Teacher 50:39, Jan., 1956
New York Times p. 45, Nov. 10, 1955
Newsweek 46:98, Dec. 5, 1955
Time 66:102+, Nov. 28, 1955

I Don't Care Girl (1953)
National Parent-Teacher 47:37, Feb., 1953

I Dood It (1943)
Commonweal 39:73, Nov. 5, 1943
Cosmopolitan 115:66, Aug., 1943
New York Times p. 29, Nov. 11, 1943
Time 42:92, Nov. 29, 1943

I Dream of Jeanie (1952)
New York Times p. 26, Jun. 26, 1952

I Dream Too Much (1935)
Commonweal 23:219, Dec. 20, 1935
New York Times p. 24, Nov. 29, 1935
Newsweek 6:41, Dec. 7, 1935
Scholastic 27:28, Jan. 18, 1936
Time 26:45, Dec. 9, 1935

I Found Stella Parish (1935)
Canadian Forum 15:15, Jan., 1936
New York Times p. 24, Nov. 4, 1935

I Give My Love (1934)
New York Times p. 24, Jul. 17, 1934

I Have Lived (1933)
New York Times p. 24, Sep. 6, 1933

I, Jane Doe (1948)
New York Times p. 8, Jul. 5, 1948

I Kiss Your Hand, Madame (1932)
Commonweal 16:492, Sep. 21, 1932
New York Times p. 9, Aug. 29, 1932

I Know Where I'm Going (1947)
  Commonweal 46:501-2, Sep. 5, 1947
  Life 24:64, Mar. 8, 1948
  Nation 165:264, Sep. 13, 1947
  New Republic 117:39, Sep. 22, 1947
  New York Times II, p. 4, Aug. 17, 1947; p. 25, Aug. 20,
    1947; II, p. 5, Sep. 14, 1947
  New Yorker 23:42, Aug. 23, 1947
  Newsweek 30:78, Sep. 1, 1947
  Scholastic 51:35, Oct. 20, 1947
  Theatre Arts 30:648, Nov., 1946
  Time 50:102+, Sep. 15, 1947

I Like It That Way (1934)
  New York Times p. 23, Apr. 18, 1934

I Like Money (1962)
  America 107:408-9, Jun. 16, 1962
  New Republic 146:28, May 28, 1962
  New York Times p. 18, May 19, 1962
  New Yorker 38:133, May 26, 1962
  Newsweek 59:101, May 28, 1962
  Time 79:89, May 25, 1962

I Like Your Nerve (1931)
  New York Times p. 15, Sep. 12, 1931

I Live for Love (1935)
  New York Times p. 21, Oct. 19, 1935

I Live My Life (1935)
  New York Times p. 12, Oct. 12, 1935
  Time 26:60, Oct. 14, 1935

I Live on Danger (1942)
  New York Times p. 16, Aug. 22, 1942

I Lived in Grosvenor Square (1945)
  New York Times II, p. 3, Jan. 28, 1945

I Love a Soldier (1944)
  Commonweal 40:569, Sep. 29, 1944
  New York Times p. 22, Nov. 2, 1944; II, p. 1, Nov. 12,
    1944
  Newsweek 24:104, Sep. 18, 1944
  Photoplay 25:21, Sep., 1944
  Time 44:88, Aug. 28, 1944

I Love Melvin (1953)
America 89:118, Apr. 25, 1953
Catholic World 176:462, Mar., 1953
Commonweal 57:650, Apr. 3, 1953
Look 17:93-6, Apr. 7, 1953
National Parent-Teacher 47:37, May, 1953
New York Times p. 18, Apr. 10, 1953
Saturday Review 36:29, Mar. 21, 1953
Scholastic 62:30, Mar. 11, 1953
Time 61:86, Mar. 30, 1953

I Love That Man (1933)
New Outlook 162:45, Aug., 1933
New York Times p. 11, Jul. 10, 1933
Vanity Fair 40:38-9, Jun., 1933

I Love You Again (1940)
Commonweal 32:411, Sep. 6, 1940
New York Times p. 11, Aug. 16, 1940; IX, p. 3, Aug.
18, 1940
New Yorker 16:44, Aug. 17, 1940
Newsweek 16:46, Aug. 19, 1940
Time 36:31, Sep. 2, 1940

I Love, You Love (1962)
New York Times p. 16, Nov. 10, 1962

I Loved a Woman (1933)
Canadian Magazine 80:36, Nov., 1933
New York Times p. 14, Sep. 22, 1933; IX, p. 3, Oct. 1,
1933
Newsweek 2:46, Sep. 30, 1933

I Loved You Wednesday (1933)
New York Times p. 20, Jun. 16, 1933; IX, p. 3, Jun.
25, 1933

I Married a Communist (1948) (also see Where Danger Lives)
Commonweal 51:294, Dec. 16, 1949
New York Times II, p. 9, Dec. 5, 1948; II, p. 5, Jun.
5, 1949
Photoplay 36:18, Dec., 1949
Time 54:102+, Oct. 17, 1949

I Married a Doctor (1937)
Commonweal 24:20, May 1, 1936
New York Times p. 17, Apr. 20, 1936
Time 27:28, May 4, 1936

I Married a Witch (1942)
  Commonweal 37:176, Dec. 4, 1942
  Life 13:74+, Nov. 2, 1942
  New Republic 107:715, Nov. 30, 1942
  New York Times p. 27, Nov. 20, 1942
  Newsweek 20:82, Nov. 16, 1942
  Time 40:94+, Nov. 9, 1942

I Married a Woman (1958)
  Catholic World 186:466, Mar., 1958
  New York Times p. 42, Nov. 5, 1958

I Married Adventure (1940)
  Commonweal 32:331, Aug. 9, 1940
  New Republic 103:189, Aug. 5, 1940
  New York Times p. 28, Sep. 12, 1940; p. 26, Sep. 24,
    1940
  Newsweek 16:37, Aug. 5, 1940

I Married an Angel (1942)
  New York Times p. 13, Jul. 10, 1942
  Newsweek 19:64, Jun. 29, 1942
  Time 40:83, Jul. 6, 1942

I Met a Murderer (1939)
  New Republic 100:301, Oct. 18, 1939
  New York Times p. 15, Oct. 2, 1939

I Met Him in Paris (1937)
  Life 2:48-60, May 31, 1937
  New Republic 91:159, Jun. 16, 1937
  New York Times p. 29, Jun. 3, 1937; IX, p. 3, Jun. 6,
    1937; X, p. 8, Sep. 18, 1938
  Time 29:34+, Jun. 7, 1937

I Met My Love Again (1938)
  New York Times p. 19, Jan. 15, 1938
  Time 31:37, Jan. 24, 1938

I Passed for White (1960)
  Commonweal 72:96, Apr. 22, 1960
  New York Times p. 19, Aug. 18, 1960

I Promise to Pay (1937)
  New York Times p. 15, Apr. 26, 1937

I Remember Mama (1948)
  Commonweal 47:596, Mar. 26, 1948

I Remember Mama (1948) (Continued)
  Cosmopolitan 124:12+, Apr., 1948
  Life 24:61-2, Apr. 12, 1948; 26:53, Mar. 14, 1949
  New Republic 118:29, Apr. 19, 1948
  New York Times p. 25, May 12, 1947; II, p. 5, Jun. 8,
    1947; II, p. 5, Oct. 26, 1947; p. 29, Mar. 12, 1948;
    II, p. 1, Mar. 21, 1948
  New York Times Magazine p. 13, Jan. 4, 1948
  New Yorker 24:46, Mar. 20, 1948
  Newsweek 31:80, Mar. 29, 1948
  Photoplay 33:20, Jun., 1948
  Scholastic 52:30, May 3, 1948
  Time 51:94+, Apr. 5, 1948
  Woman's Home Companion 75:10-11, Jun., 1948

I Sell Anything (1934)
  New York Times p. 25, Dec. 27, 1934

I Shot Jesse James (1949)
  New York Times p. 12, Apr. 2, 1949

I Spit on Your Grave (1962)
  New York Times p. 13, Jun. 29, 1963

I Stand Accused (1938)
  New York Times p. 17, Jan. 5, 1939

I Stand Condemned (1936)
  Commonweal 24:307, Jul. 17, 1936
  New York Times p. 27, Jul. 2, 1936; IX, p. 2, Jul. 5,
    1936
  Newsweek 8:27, Jul. 11, 1936
  Time 28:53, Jul. 13, 1936

I Stole a Million (1939)
  New York Times p. 11, Aug. 7, 1939

I Take This Woman (1931)
  New York Times p. 20, Jun. 13, 1931; VIII, p. 3, Jun.
    21, 1931

I Take This Woman (1939)
  Commonweal 31:413, Mar. 1, 1940
  New York Times IX, p. 5, Nov. 13, 1938; XI, p. 5, Mar.
    19, 1939; IX, p. 9, Dec. 3, 1939; IX, p. 7, Dec. 17,
    1939; p. 23, Feb. 16, 1940
  Newsweek 15:40, Feb. 12, 1940
  Time 35:69, Mar. 4, 1940

I Thank a Fool (1962)
America 107:825, Sep. 29, 1962
New York Times p. 15, Sep. 15, 1962
New Yorker 38:86-7, Sep. 22, 1962
Newsweek 60:60, Sep. 17, 1962

I, the Jury (1953)
America 89:584, Sep. 12, 1953
Commonweal 58:537, Sep. 4, 1953
Farm Journal 77:98, Oct., 1953
Holiday 14:99, Nov., 1953
Library Journal 78:1411, Sep. 1, 1953
National Parent-Teacher 48:37, Nov., 1953
New York Times p. 8, Aug. 22, 1953
New Yorker 29:50, Aug. 22, 1953
Newsweek 42:90, Aug. 17, 1953
Saturday Review 36:27, Aug. 22, 1953
Time 62:90, Aug. 17, 1953

I Wake Up Dreaming (see Secret Life of Walter Mitty)

I Wake Up Screaming (1941) (also see Hot Spot)
Commonweal 35:248, Dec. 26, 1941
Nation 154:101, Jan. 24, 1942
New York Times p. 13, Jan. 17, 1942
Time 38:102, Dec. 15, 1941

I Walk Alone (1948)
Commonweal 47:400, Jan. 30, 1948
Cosmopolitan 124:11+, Jan., 1948
Good Housekeeping 126:11, Jan., 1948
New York Times p. 36, Jan. 22, 1948; II, p. 1, Jan. 25, 1948
Newsweek 31:89, Jan. 26, 1948
Woman's Home Companion 75:8, Jan., 1948

I Walked with a Zombie (1943)
New York Times p. 31, Apr. 22, 1943

I Want a Divorce (1940)
Commonweal 32:531, Oct. 18, 1940
New York Times p. 31, Oct. 3, 1940
Photoplay 54:67, Sep., 1940; 54:70-74+, Oct., 1940

I Want to Be a Mother (1937)
New York Times p. 9, Feb. 27, 1937

I Want to Live! (1958)
America 100:297, Nov. 29, 1958
Catholic World 188:329, Jan., 1959
Commonweal 69:293, Dec. 12, 1958
Library Journal 83:3418, Dec. 1, 1958
Nation 187:504, Dec. 27, 1958
New Republic 139:21, Dec. 22, 1958
New York Times p. 45, Nov. 19, 1957; II, p. 1, Nov. 23,
   1957
New Yorker 34:108+, Nov. 29, 1958
Newsweek 52:109, Nov. 17, 1958
Saturday Review 41:25, Nov. 29, 1958
Time 72:94, Nov. 24, 1958

I Want You (1952)
Catholic World 174:385, Feb., 1952
Christian Century 69:207, Feb. 13, 1952
Commonweal 55:301, Dec. 28, 1951
Library Journal 76:2110, Dec. 15, 1951
Nation 174:66, Jan. 19, 1952
New Republic 125:22, Dec. 31, 1951
New York Times p. 9, Dec. 24, 1951
New Yorker 27:65, Jan. 5, 1952
Newsweek 39:59, Jan. 7, 1952
Saturday Review 34:34, Dec. 22, 1951
Time 59:96, Jan. 28, 1952

I Wanted Wings (1941)
Commonweal 33:622, Apr. 11, 1941
New York Times IX, p. 3, Jun. 2, 1940; IX, p. 3, Aug.
   18, 1940; IX, p. 4, Mar. 9, 1941; p. 29, Mar. 27,
   1941; IX, p. 5, Mar. 30, 1941
New Yorker 17:67, Mar. 29, 1941
Newsweek 17:66-7, Mar. 31, 1941
Photoplay 19:8, Jun., 1941
Scholastic 38:20, Apr. 14, 1941
Scribner's Commentator 10:107-8, Aug., 1941

I Was a Captive of Nazi Germany (1936)
New York Times p. 11, Aug. 3, 1936

I Was a Communist for the F. B. I. (1948) (also see Where
Danger Lives)
Christian Century 68:695, Jun. 6, 1951
Commonweal 54:143, May 18, 1951
New York Times p. 34, May 3, 1951; II, p. 1, May 6,
   1951
Newsweek 37:101, May 14, 1951

555

I Was a Communist for the F. B. I. (Continued)
  Saturday Review 34:26, May 19, 1951
  Time 57:104+, May 7, 1951

I Was a Convict (1939)
  New York Times p. 27, Mar. 23, 1939

I Was a Male War Bride (1949)
  Commonweal 50:509, Sep. 2, 1949
  Good Housekeeping 129:221, Nov., 1949
  Life 27:70+, Sep. 19, 1949
  New York Times II, p. 3, Aug. 7, 1949; p. 7, Aug. 27,
    1949
  New Yorker 25:62, Sep. 3, 1949
  Newsweek 34:67, Sep. 5, 1949
  Rotarian 75:34, Nov., 1949
  Scholastic 55:19, Oct. 12, 1949
  Time 54:98, Sep. 12, 1949
  Woman's Home Companion 76:10-11, Nov., 1949

I Was a Prisoner on Devil's Island (1941)
  New York Times p. 16, Jul. 28, 1941

I Was a Shoplifter (1950)
  Commonweal 52:127, May 12, 1950
  New York Times p. 26, Apr. 28, 1950

I Was a Spy (1934)
  Canadian Magazine 80:36-7, Dec., 1933
  New Outlook 163:49, Feb., 1934
  New Republic 78:18, Feb. 14, 1934
  New York Times p. 12, Jan. 15, 1934; X, p. 5, Jan. 21,
    1934

I Was a Teenage Frankenstein (1957)
  Time 71:95, Mar. 10, 1958

I Was a Teenage Werewolf (1957)
  New Republic 137:22, Aug. 26, 1957

I Was an Adventuress (1940)
  Commonweal 32:103, May 24, 1940
  New York Times IX, p. 4, Jan. 14, 1940; p. 13, May
    20, 1940
  Photoplay 54:60, Jul., 1940
  Time 35:102+, May 27, 1940

I Was an American Spy (1951)
    New York Times p. 13, Jul. 4, 1951

I Was Framed (1942)
    New York Times p. 16, Jun. 12, 1942

I Was Monty's Double (1958)
    America 100:560, Feb. 7, 1959
    Commonweal 69:467, Jan. 30, 1959
    Good Housekeeping 148:24, Feb., 1959
    Library Journal 84:421, Feb. 1, 1959
    New Republic 140:22, Jan. 26, 1959
    Saturday Review 42:72, Jan. 17, 1959
    Time 73:58, Feb. 2, 1959

I Wonder Who's Kissing Her Now (1947)
    Commonweal 46:429, Aug. 15, 1947
    New York Times II, p. 4, Jul. 20, 1947; p. 27, Jul. 24,
        1947
    New Yorker 23:47, Aug. 2, 1947
    Newsweek 30:90, Aug. 4, 1947
    Time 50:95+, Aug. 11, 1947

Ice Capades (1941)
    New York Times p. 29, Sep. 25, 1941; IX, p. 3, Sep.
        28, 1941
    Newsweek 18:50, Sep. 1, 1941

Ice Follies of 1939 (1939)
    New York Times p. 25, Mar. 17, 1939
    Photoplay 53:63, May, 1939

Ice Palace (1960)
    America 103:443, Jul. 9, 1960
    Commonweal 72:403, Aug. 5, 1960
    New York Times II, p. 7, Sep. 27, 1959; p. 22, Jun. 30,
        1960
    New Yorker 36:55-6, Jul. 9, 1960
    Newsweek 56:91, Jul. 11, 1960
    Saturday Review 43:31, Jul. 23, 1960
    Time 76:51, Jul. 4, 1960

Iceland (1942)
    Commonweal 36:594, Oct. 9, 1942
    New York Times p. 27, Oct. 15, 1942; VIII, p. 3, Oct.
        18, 1942
    New Yorker 18:58, Oct. 17, 1942

Iceland Fisherman (see Pecheurs D' Islande)

I'd Climb the Highest Mountain (1951)
    Christian Century 68:222, Feb. 14, 1951
    Library Journal 76:343, Feb. 15, 1951
    New York Times II, p. 5, Jun. 18, 1950; p. 38, May 10,
        1951
    Newsweek 37:89, Feb. 19, 1951
    Rotarian 78:40, Apr., 1951
    Saturday Review 34:32, Mar. 3, 1951
    Time 57:96, Mar. 5, 1951

I'd Give My Life (1936)
    New York Times p. 9, Aug. 17, 1936

Idaho (1943)
    Newsweek 21:74+, Mar. 8, 1943
    Scholastic 42:28, Mar. 29, 1943

Ideal Husband (1948)
    Commonweal 47:373, Jan. 23, 1948
    Life 24:60-1+, Feb. 16, 1948
    New Republic 118:34, Jan. 26, 1948
    Newsweek 31:72-3, Feb. 2, 1948
    Scholastic 52:36, Feb. 2, 1948
    Time 51:93, Feb. 9, 1948

Idiot (1960)
    New Republic 143:21, Sep. 19, 1960
    New York Times p. 11, Jul. 22, 1960; II, p. 1, Jul. 24,
        1960
    New Yorker 36:54, Jul. 30, 1960
    Saturday Review 43:28, Aug. 6, 1960

Idiot (1963)
    Commonweal 78:198, May 10, 1963
    New Republic 148:27, May 11, 1963
    New York Times p. 35, May 1, 1963
    Newsweek 61:94-5, May 6, 1963

Idiot's Delight (1939)
    Canadian Magazine 91:40, Mar., 1939
    Commonweal 29:470, Feb. 17, 1939
    Life 66:44+, Feb. 13, 1939
    Nation 148:213-4, Feb. 18, 1939
    New Republic 98:74, Feb. 22, 1939
    New York Times IX, p. 5, Mar. 13, 1938; IX, p. 3, Jul.

558

Idiot's Delight (1939) (Continued)
    3, 1938; IX, p. 5, Nov. 27, 1938; IX, p. 5, Jan. 22,
    1939; p. 13, Feb. 3, 1939; IX, p. 5, Feb. 5, 1939
Newsweek 13:24-5, Feb. 6, 1939
North American Review 247 no1:174-5, [Mar.] 1939
Photoplay 53:34-5, Mar., 1939
Stage 16:7, Mar. 15, 1939
Time 33:29, Feb. 13, 1939

Idle Rich (1929)
    New York Times p. 29, Jun. 17, 1929
    Outlook 152:396, Jul. 3, 1929

Idol of the Crowd (1937)
    New York Times p. 21, Dec. 4, 1937

If a Man Answers (1962)
    New York Times p. 43, Nov. 22, 1962
    Redbook 120:38, Nov., 1962
    Saturday Review 45:19, Sep. 1, 1962
    Time 80:93, Dec. 14, 1962

If All the Guys in the World (1957)
    America 97:244, May 18, 1957
    Commonweal 65:176, Nov. 16, 1956
    New York Times p. 34, Apr. 23, 1957
    New Yorker 33:162, May 4, 1957

If I Had a Million (1932)
    Nation 135:624, Dec. 21, 1932
    New York Times p. 21, Dec. 3, 1932; IX, p. 7, Dec. 11,
    1932

If I Had My Way (1940)
    New York Times p. 13, May 6, 1940; IX, p. 3, May 12,
    1940

If I Were Free (1933)
    New York Times p. 25, Jan. 5, 1934
    Newsweek 3:34, Jan. 13, 1934

If I Were King (1938)
    Commonweal 28:616, Oct. 7, 1938
    New York Times X, p. 3, Apr. 24, 1938; IX, p. 4, Jun.
    5, 1938; IX, p. 3, Jun. 26, 1938; p. 31, Sep. 29,
    1938; IX, p. 5, Oct. 2, 1938
    Newsweek 12:28-9, Oct. 10, 1938

If I Were King (1938) (Continued)
Saint Nicholas 65:39+, Oct., 1938
Stage 16:57, Nov., 1938
Time 32:36, Oct. 3, 1938

If I Were Single (1927)
New York Times p. 21, Mar. 5, 1928

If I'm Lucky (1946)
New York Times p. 41, Sep. 20, 1946

If This Be Sin (1950)
Christian Century 67:1151, Sep. 27, 1950
Library Journal 75:1201, Jul., 1950
New York Times p. 9, Jul. 1, 1950
Rotarian 77:36, Nov., 1950

If War Comes Tomorrow (1938)
New York Times p. 17, Jul. 14, 1938; IX, p. 3, Jul. 17,
1938

If Winter Comes (1948)
Commonweal 47:400, Jan. 30, 1948
New York Times p. 28, Jan. 23, 1948
New Yorker 23:52, Jan. 31, 1948
Newsweek 31:74, Feb. 9, 1948
Time 51:94+, Feb. 9, 1948

If You Could Only Cook (1935)
Canadian Magazine 85:38, Feb., 1936
Literary Digest 120:22, Dec. 21, 1935
New York Times p. 21, Dec. 26, 1935
Time 27:28, Jan. 6, 1936

If You Knew Susie (1948)
New York Times p. 19, Feb. 23, 1948
New Yorker 24:75, Mar. 6, 1948
Newsweek 31:94+, Mar. 22, 1948

Igloo (1932)
New York Times p. 15, Jul. 21, 1932; IX, p. 3, Jul. 31,
1932

Ikiru (1960)
Nation 190:284, Mar. 26, 1960
New Republic 142:28, Mar. 7, 1960
New York Times p. 13, Jan. 30, 1960

Ikiru (1960) (Continued)
New Yorker 35:125-6, Feb. 13, 1960
Time 75:85, Feb. 15, 1960; 80:90, Sep. 21, 1962

I'll Be Seeing You (1945)
Commonweal 41:566, Mar. 23, 1945
New Republic 112:557, Apr. 23, 1945
New Yorker 21:49, Apr. 14, 1945
Newsweek 25:88, Jan. 22, 1945
Photoplay 26:19, Mar., 1945
Theatre Arts 29:231, Apr., 1945
Time 45:91-2, Jan. 22, 1945

I'll Be Yours (1947)
Commonweal 45:493, Feb. 28, 1947
Holiday 2:173, May, 1947
New Republic 116:41, Mar. 24, 1947
New York Times p. 16, Feb. 22, 1947
Newsweek 29:92+, Mar. 10, 1947

I'll Cry Tomorrow (1956)
America 94:487, Jan. 28, 1956
Catholic World 182:137, Nov., 1955
Commonweal 63:403, Jan. 20, 1956
Library Journal 81:360, Feb. 1, 1956
Life 40:117-18+, Jan. 9, 1956
Look 19:104-7, Dec. 13, 1955
Nation 182:78, Jan. 28, 1956
National Parent-Teacher 50:39, Feb., 1956
New York Times p. 18, Jan. 13, 1956; II, p. 1, Jan. 15,
    1956
New Yorker 31:110, Jan. 21, 1956
Newsweek 46:117, Nov. 28, 1956
Saturday Review 39:56, Jan. 7, 1956
Time 67:92, Jan. 23, 1956
Woman's Home Companion 83:14-15, Jan., 1956

I'll Fix It (1934)
New York Times p. 17, Nov. 12, 1934

I'll Get By (1950)
New York Times p. 39, Nov. 2, 1950
Newsweek 36:102, Nov. 13, 1950
Time 56:104, Nov. 13, 1950

I'll Give a Million (1938)
New York Times p. 7, Jul. 16, 1938

I'll Love You Always (1935)
New York Times p. 11, Mar. 30, 1935

Ill Met By Moonlight (see Night Ambush)

I'll Never Forget You (1951)
American Magazine 153:9, Jan., 1952
Library Journal 77:44, Jan. 1, 1952
New York Times p. 9, Dec. 8, 1951; II, p. 3, Dec. 16, 1951
New Yorker 27:147, Dec. 15, 1951
Time 59:92, Jan. 14, 1952

I'll See You in My Dreams (1952)
American Magazine 153:8, Jan., 1952
Christian Century 69:111, Jan. 23, 1952
Commonweal 55:278, Dec. 21, 1951
New York Times p. 35, Dec. 7, 1951; II, p. 5, Dec. 9, 1951
New Yorker 27:67, Dec. 8, 1951
Newsweek 38:100, Dec. 17, 1951
Time 59:94+, Jan. 21, 1952

I'll Take Romance (1937)
New York Times p. 33, Dec. 17, 1937; X, p. 5, Dec. 26, 1937
Time 30:51, Dec. 20, 1937

I'll Tell the World (1934)
New York Times p. 12, Apr. 21, 1934

I'll Wait for You (1941)
New York Times p. 13, Jun. 2, 1941

Illegal (1955)
National Parent-Teacher 50:39, Nov., 1955
New York Times p. 12, Oct. 29, 1955
Newsweek 46:113, Sep. 12, 1955

Illegal Entry (1949)
New York Times p. 11, Jun. 11, 1949
Newsweek 33:89, Jun. 27, 1949

Illegal Traffic (1938)
New York Times p. 29, Nov. 17, 1938

Illicit (1931)
Life (NY) 97:20, Feb. 20, 1931

Illicit (1931) (Continued)
New York Times p. 25, Jan. 19, 1931; VIII, p. 5, Jan.
25, 1931
Outlook 157:192, Feb. 4, 1931

Illicit Interlude (1954)
Nation 179:430, Nov. 13, 1954
New York Times p. 32, Oct. 27, 1954
Time 64:114, Nov. 8, 1954

Illusion (1929)
New York Times p. 17, Sep. 28, 1929

I'm All Right Jack (1960)
Commonweal 72:229, May 27, 1960
McCalls 87:6, May, 1960
Nation 190:431, May 14, 1960
New Republic 142:21, May 30, 1960
New York Times p. 40, Apr. 26, 1960; II, p. 1, May 1,
1960
New Yorker 35:204-6, Nov. 21, 1959; 36:190-1, May 7,
1960
Newsweek 55:112, May 9, 1960
Saturday Review 43:24, Apr. 30, 1960
Time 75:34, May 2, 1960

I'm from Missouri (1939)
New York Times XI, p. 4, Mar. 19, 1939; p. 27, Mar.
23, 1939

I'm from the City (1938)
New York Times p. 13, Aug. 19, 1938

I'm No Angel (1933)
Nation 137:548, Nov. 8, 1933
New Outlook 162:43, Nov., 1933
New Republic 77:73-5, Nov. 29, 1933
New York Times p. 18, Oct. 14, 1933; IX, p. 3, Oct. 22,
1933
Newsweek 2:30, Oct. 21, 1933
Time 22:34, Oct. 16, 1933

I'm Still Alive (1940)
New York Times p. 25, Oct. 11, 1940

Imitation General (1958)
America 99:538, Aug. 23, 1958

Imitation General (1958) (Continued)
Catholic World 187:456, Sep., 1958
Commonweal 68:447, Aug. 1, 1958
New York Times p. 22, Aug. 21, 1958; II, p. 1, Aug. 31, 1958

Imitation of Life (1934)
Literary Digest 118:31, Dec. 8, 1934
New York Times p. 19, Nov. 24, 1934

Imitation of Life (1959)
America 101:314, May 9, 1959
Catholic World 189:154-5, May, 1959
Commonweal 70:82, Apr. 17, 1959
Library Journal 84:843, Mar. 15, 1959
New York Times p. 18, Apr. 18, 1959; II, p. 1, Apr. 19, 1959
New Yorker 35:167-8, Apr. 25, 1959
Newsweek 53:118, Apr. 13, 1959
Saturday Review 42:28, Apr. 11, 1959
Time 73:86, May 11, 1959

Immortal Sergeant (1943)
Commonweal 37:423, Feb. 12, 1943
New York Times p. 29, Feb. 4, 1943; II, p. 3, Feb. 7, 1943
New Yorker 18:52, Feb. 6, 1943
Newsweek 21:70, Feb. 15, 1943
Time 41:52, Feb. 15, 1943

Immortal Vagabond (1931)
Commonweal 16:158, Jun. 8, 1932
New York Times p. 15, Aug. 3, 1931; VIII, p. 3, Aug. 9, 1931

Impact (1949)
New York Times II, p. 5, Nov. 14, 1948; p. 19, Mar. 21, 1949
Newsweek 33:84, Mar. 28, 1949
Time 53:101, Mar. 28, 1949

Impatient Maiden (1932)
New York Times p. 17, Mar. 4, 1932

Impatient Years (1944)
Commonweal 40:569, Sep. 29, 1944
Nation 159:334, Sep. 16, 1944

Impatient Years (1944) (Continued)
New York Times p. 20, Sep. 20, 1944
New Yorker 20:53, Sep. 16, 1944
Newsweek 24:104+, Sep. 18, 1944
Theatre Arts 28:597, Oct., 1944
Woman's Home Companion 71:10, Oct., 1944

Imperfect Lady (1947)
Commonweal 46:142, May 23, 1947
New York Times p. 34, May 22, 1947
Newsweek 29:97-8, May 19, 1947
Time 49:101, May 19, 1947

Importance of Being Earnest (1953)
Catholic World 176:384-5, Feb., 1953
Commonweal 57:334, Jan. 2, 1953
Library Journal 78:50, Jan. 1, 1953
National Parent-Teacher 47:38, Jan., 1953
New York Times p. 17, Dec. 23, 1952
New Yorker 28:35, Jan. 3, 1953
Newsweek 41:60, Jan. 5, 1953
Saturday Review 36:31, Jan. 10, 1953
Theatre Arts 37:83, Feb., 1953; 37:72-4, Apr., 1953
Time 61:71, Jan. 5, 1953

Important Man (1961)
America 107:602, Aug. 11, 1962
Commonweal 76:426, Jul. 27, 1962
New York Times p. 25, Jun. 26, 1962
Newsweek 60:79, Jul. 16, 1962

Imposter (1944)
Commonweal 39:625, Apr. 7, 1944
Nation 158:346, Mar. 18, 1944
New York Times p. 17, Mar. 27, 1944
Scholastic 44:31, Mar. 13, 1944

Imposter (1955)
National Parent-Teacher 49:39, Jun., 1955
New York Times p. 27, Mar. 23, 1955
Newsweek 45:113, Apr. 11, 1955
Saturday Review 38:27, Apr. 16, 1955
Time 65:109, Apr. 25, 1955

In a Lonely Place (1950)
Commonweal 52:221, Jun. 9, 1950
Library Journal 75:992, Jun. 1, 1950

In a Lonely Place (1950) (Continued)
New York Times p. 37, May 18, 1950
New Yorker 26:63, May 27, 1950
Newsweek 35:85, Jun. 5, 1950
Time 55:91, Jun. 5, 1950

In a Monastery Garden (1935)
New York Times p. 16, Mar. 13, 1935

In Caliente (1935)
New York Times p. 16, Jun. 27, 1935
Time 25:50, Jun. 3, 1935

In Gay Madrid (1930)
Life (NY) 95:17, Jun. 27, 1930
New York Times p. 10, Jun. 7, 1930; VIII, p. 5, Jun.
15, 1930

In His Steps (1936)
Commonweal 24:560, Oct. 9, 1936
New York Times IX, p. 5, Oct. 4, 1936; p. 31, Oct. 29,
1936
Scholastic 29:23-4, Oct. 31, 1936

In Love and War (1959)
America 100:226, Nov. 15, 1958
Catholic World 188:329, Jan., 1959
Commonweal 69:208, Nov. 21, 1958
Library Journal 83:3237, Nov. 15, 1958
New York Times p. 14, Nov. 1, 1958
New Yorker 34:182, Nov. 8, 1958

In Love with Life (1934)
New York Times p. 12, May 12, 1934

In Name Only (1939)
Commonweal 30:400, Aug. 18, 1939
New York Times p. 11, Aug. 4, 1939; IX, p. 3, Aug. 13,
1939; p. 16, Aug. 18, 1939
Photoplay 53:64, Oct., 1939
Time 34:33, Aug. 14, 1939

In Old Arizona (1928)
New York Times VIII, p. 7, Jan. 20, 1929; p. 18, Jan.
21, 1929; IX, p. 7, Jan. 27, 1929
Outlook 151:225, Feb. 6, 1929

In Old California (1942)
New York Times p. 25, Jun. 18, 1942

In Old Chicago (1938)
Commonweal 27:358, Jan. 21, 1938
Life 4:46-9, Jan. 17, 1938
Literary Digest 125:22, Jan. 29, 1938
New York Times X, p. 3, Jun. 27, 1937; XI, p. 6, Dec.
  19, 1937; p. 15, Jan. 7, 1938; X, p. 5, Jan. 16, 1938;
  X, p. 4, Feb. 6, 1938
Newsweek 11:23, Jan. 17, 1938
Saint Nicholas 65:41, Nov., 1937
Scholastic 32:32, Feb. 5, 1938
Stage 15:40, Mar., 1938
Time 31:44-5, Jan. 17, 1938

In Old Kentucky (1935)
Literary Digest 120:24, Nov. 30, 1935
New York Times IX, p. 3, Sep. 8, 1935; p. 24, Nov. 29,
  1935
Time 26:46, Dec. 9, 1935

In Old Oklahoma (1943)
Commonweal 39:174+, Dec. 3, 1943
New York Times p. 21, Dec. 6, 1943
Newsweek 22:84, Dec. 20, 1943
Photoplay 24:6, Jan., 1944

In Old Sacramento (1946)
New York Times II, p. 5, Dec. 16, 1945; p. 24, Apr. 29,
  1946

In Our Time (1944)
New York Times p. 11, Feb. 12, 1944; II, p. 3, Feb.
  28, 1944
Newsweek 23:88, Feb. 21, 1944
Scholastic 44:36, Feb. 28, 1944
Time 43:58, Feb. 7, 1944

In Person (1935)
New York Times p. 31, Dec. 13, 1935
Time 26:41, Dec. 16, 1935

In Search of the Castaways (1962)
Commonweal 77:461, Jan. 25, 1963
New York Times p. 5, Dec. 22, 1962
Newsweek 61:73, Jan. 14, 1963

In the Cool of the Day (1963)
Commonweal 78:377, Jun. 28, 1963
New Republic 148:36, Jun. 15, 1963
New York Times p. 20, May 30, 1963
Saturday Review 46:45, Jun. 15, 1963
Time 81:99-100, Jun. 14, 1963

In the Far East (1937)
New York Times p. 27, Oct. 20, 1937

In the French Style (1963)
America 109:399, Oct. 5, 1963
Commonweal 79:46, Oct. 4, 1963
New York Times II, p. 9, Nov. 4, 1962; p. 23, Sep. 19, 1963
New Yorker 39:106+, Sep. 23, 1963
Newsweek 62:101-2, Sep. 23, 1963
Saturday Review 46:44, Sep. 28, 1963

In the Good Old Summertime (1949)
Commonweal 50:465, Aug. 19, 1949
New York Times p. 23, Aug. 5, 1949; II, p. 1, Aug. 14, 1949
New Yorker 25:66+, Aug. 13, 1949
Newsweek 34:70, Aug. 22, 1949
Photoplay 36:22, Sep., 1949
Rotarian 75:39, Oct., 1949
Time 54:76, Jul. 18, 1949

In the Navy (1941)
Commonweal 34:208, Jun. 20, 1941
Life 10:38-40, Jun. 23, 1941
New York Times p. 29, Jun. 12, 1941; IX, p. 3, Jun. 15, 1941
Newsweek 18:47, Aug. 4, 1941
Scribner's Commentator 10:106, Sep., 1941

In the Next Room (1930)
New York Times p. 21, Apr. 7, 1930

In the Rear of the Enemy (1942)
New York Times p. 11, Oct. 10, 1942

In the Wake of a Stranger (1960)
New York Times p. 23, Jun. 22, 1961

In This Our Life (1942)
Commonweal 36:112-13, May 22, 1942

In This Our Life (1942) (Continued)
Musician 47:76, May, 1942
New York Times p. 10, May 9, 1942
Newsweek 19:50, May 18, 1942
Time 39:88, May 11, 1942

In Which We Serve (1942)
Collier's 111:20-2, Jan. 2, 1943
Commonweal 37:301, Jan. 8, 1943
Life 12:106-9, May 25, 1942; 13:59+, Dec. 21, 1942
New Republic 107:858, Dec. 28, 1942
New York Times IX, p. 7, Dec. 14, 1941; VIII, p. 3,
    Apr. 5, 1942; VIII, p. 3, Jul. 19, 1942; VIII, p. 3,
    Oct. 25, 1942; VII, p. 23, Nov. 29, 1942; VIII, p. 3,
    Dec. 6, 1942; VIII, p. 3, Dec. 20, 1942; p. 18, Dec.
    24, 1942; p. 18, Dec. 30, 1942; VIII, p. 3, Jan. 3,
    1943
New York Times Magazine p. 22, Feb. 14, 1943
Newsweek 20:80-2, Dec. 21, 1942
Photoplay 22:64, Feb., 1943
Reader's Digest 42:94, Mar., 1943
Scholastic 41:27, Dec. 14, 1942
Theatre Arts 27:5, Jan., 1943
Time 40:84+, Dec. 28, 1942

Incendiary Blonde (1945)
Commonweal 42:431, Aug. 17, 1945
Life 19:67-8+, Aug. 27, 1945
New York Times p. 13, Jul. 26, 1945; II, p. 3, Feb. 11,
    1945
New Yorker 21:36, Aug. 4, 1945
Newsweek 26:85, Aug. 6, 1945
Photoplay 27:22, Sep., 1945
Time 46:98+, Aug. 6, 1945

Incertidumbre (Hesitancy) (1936)
New York Times p. 26, Sep. 21, 1936

Incident in an Alley (1962)
New York Times p. 31, May 17, 1962

Incredible Journey (1963)
Commonweal 79:349, Dec. 13, 1963
New York Times p. 43, Nov. 21, 1963
Newsweek 62:92, Dec. 9, 1963
Saturday Review 46:29, Nov. 16, 1963
Time 82:120, Dec. 6, 1963

Incredible Mr. Limpet (1963)
  Commonweal 80:91, Apr. 10, 1964
  Life 56:121-2, Mar. 20, 1964
  New York Times p. 40, Mar. 26, 1964
  Senior Scholastic 84:38, Apr. 3, 1964

Incredible Shrinking Man (1957)
  America 96:685, Mar. 16, 1957
  Commonweal 66:65, Apr. 19, 1957
  Library Journal 82:661, Mar. 1, 1957
  Life 42:143, May 13, 1957
  National Parent-Teacher 51:38, Apr., 1957
  New York Times p. 13, Feb. 23, 1957
  Newsweek 49:106, Mar. 11, 1957

India Speaks (1933)
  New York Times p. 10, May 8, 1933

Indian Fighter (1955)
  America 94:420, Jan. 7, 1956
  National Parent-Teacher 50:39, Feb., 1956
  New York Times p. 20, Dec. 22, 1955
  New Yorker 31:93, Jan. 14, 1956
  Newsweek 47:71, Jan. 9, 1956
  Time 67:92+, Jan. 23, 1956

Indianapolis Speedway (1939)
  Commonweal 30:340, Jul. 28, 1939
  New York Times p. 8, Jul. 15, 1939

Indiscreet (1931)
  Life (NY) 97:20, Jun. 5, 1931
  New York Times p. 21, May 7, 1931; VIII, p. 5, May 17,
    1931

Indiscreet (1958)
  America 99:399, Jul. 5, 1958
  Catholic World 187:457, Sep., 1958
  Commonweal 68:404, Jul. 18, 1958
  Library Journal 83:2036, Jul., 1958
  Life 45:69, Jul. 7, 1958
  New Republic 139:21, Jul. 21, 1958
  New York Times II, p. 5, Jan. 26, 1958; p. 18, Jun. 17,
    1958; II, p. 1, Jun. 24, 1958
  New Yorker 34:99, Jul. 12, 1958
  Newsweek 52:73, Jul. 7, 1958
  Saturday Review 41:25, Jul. 12, 1958
  Time 72:78, Jul. 21, 1958

Indiscretion of an American Wife (1954)
America 91:407, Jul. 17, 1954
Catholic World 179:143-4, May, 1954
Commonweal 60:117, May 7, 1954
Coronet 36:14, May, 1954
Farm Journal 78:92, Jul., 1954
National Parent-Teacher 48:39, Apr., 1954
New York Times p. 7, Jun. 26, 1954
Newsweek 43:104-5, Apr. 12, 1954
Saturday Review 37:25, Apr. 24, 1954
Time 63:110, Apr. 26, 1954

Indiscretions (1939)
New York Times p. 21, May 1, 1939

Infernal Machine (1933)
New York Times p. 16, Apr. 8, 1933; IX, p. 3, Apr. 16,
1933

Inferno (1953)
American 89:487, Aug. 15, 1953
Catholic World 177:462-3, Sep., 1953
Commonweal 58:536, Sep. 4, 1953
New York Times p. 22, Aug. 2, 1953
Newsweek 42:76, Aug. 24, 1953
Time 62:112+, Sep. 14, 1953

Informer (1935)
Catholic World 141:605-6, Aug., 1935
Commonweal 22:103, May 24, 1935; 23:525-6, Mar. 6,
1936; 23:637-8, Apr. 3, 1936; 23:666, Apr. 10, 1936
Literary Digest 119:26, May 25, 1935; 121:20, Mar. 21,
1936
Nation 140:610+, May 22, 1935
New Republic 83:76, May 29, 1935
New York Times IX, p. 3, May 5, 1935; p. 25, May 10,
1935; X, p. 3, May 12, 1935; X, p. 3, Jun. 30, 1935;
p. 15, Dec. 23, 1935; p. 21, Jan. 2, 1936; IX, p. 5,
Jan. 5, 1936; X, p. 4, Oct. 31, 1937
Newsweek 5:29, May 11, 1935
Theatre Arts 35:58-9+, Aug., 1951
Time 25:32, May 20, 1935
Vanity Fair 44:38, Jul., 1935

*Ingagi
Motion Picture 40:8+, Aug., 1930
Nature Magazine 16:66, Jul., 1930

*Ingagi (Continued)
New York Times p. 34, Mar. 17, 1931
Science 71:sup10, Jun. 6, 1930

Inherit the Wind (1960)
America 104:101, Oct. 15, 1960
Christian Century 78:48-9, Jan. 11, 1961
Commonweal 73:151, Nov. 4, 1960
Coronet 48:12, Jul., 1960
Life 49:77+, Sep. 26, 1960
Look 24:126, Oct. 25, 1960
New Republic 143:29, Oct. 31, 1960
New York Times II, p. 7, Nov. 1, 1959; p. 41, Oct. 13,
    1960; II, p. 1, Oct. 16, 1960
New Yorker 36:98+, Oct. 22, 1960
Newsweek 56:114, Oct. 17, 1960
Saturday Review 43:30, Oct. 8, 1960
Senior Scholastic 77:40, Sep. 14, 1960
Time 76:95, Oct. 17, 1960

Inheritance (1951)
Library Journal 76:1141, Jul., 1951
New York Times p. 19, Feb. 12, 1951
Scholastic 58:29, Mar. 14, 1951

Inn of the Sixth Happiness (1959)
America 100:380, Dec. 20, 1958
Catholic World 188:413, Feb., 1959
Commonweal 69:317, Dec. 19, 1958
Good Housekeeping 148:24, Jan., 1959
Life 46:45+, Jan. 12, 1959
New York Times p. 2, Dec. 14, 1958
New Yorker 34:124-5, Dec. 13, 1958; 34:98, Dec. 20,
    1958
Newsweek 52:114, Dec. 15, 1958
Saturday Review 41:26, Dec. 13, 1958
Senior Scholastic 74:30, Jan. 30, 1959
Time 72:72, Dec. 22, 1958

Innocent Affair (1948)
Commonweal 48:618, Oct. 8, 1948
Good Housekeeping 127:260, Nov., 1948
Newsweek 32:85, Oct. 4, 1948
Time 52:100, Oct. 4, 1948

Innocents (1961)
America 106:480, Jan. 13, 1962

Innocents (1961) (Continued)
Commonweal 75:414, Jan. 12, 1962
Life 52:45-6, Feb. 2, 1962
McCalls 89:14, Jan., 1962
New Republic 146:20, Jan. 8, 1962
New York Times p. 15, Dec. 26, 1961
New Yorker 37:72, Jan. 6, 1962
Newsweek 59:52, Jan. 1, 1962
Saturday Review 44:38, Dec. 23, 1961
Senior Scholastic 79:37, Jan. 17, 1962
Time 79:59, Jan. 5, 1962

Innocents in Paris (1955)
New York Times p. 9, Mar. 5, 1955
New Yorker 31:77, Mar. 12, 1955
Saturday Review 38:27, Mar. 12, 1955

Innocents of Paris (1929)
Literary Digest 101:25-6, May 18, 1929
New York Times IX, p. 8, Jan. 27, 1929; VIII, p. 6,
    Feb. 3, 1929; IX, p. 3, Feb. 10, 1929; IX, p. 8, Feb.
    17, 1929; p. 16, Apr. 27, 1929; IX, p. 7, May 5,
    1929; VIII, p. 5, Aug. 25, 1929; VIII, p. 4, Sep. 1,
    1929
Outlook 152:396, Jul. 3, 1929

Inside Detroit (1956)
National Parent-Teacher 50:39, Jan., 1956
New York Times p. 10, Jan. 28, 1956

Inside Fascist Spain (1943)
New York Times p. 5, Apr. 17, 1943
Time 41:96, May 10, 1943

Inside Job (1946)
New York Times p. 24, Jun. 15, 1946

Inside Straight (1951)
Christian Century 68:575, May 2, 1951
New York Times p. 34, Mar. 16, 1951; II, p. 1, Mar.
    18, 1951
New Yorker 27:95, Mar. 24, 1951
Newsweek 37:100, Mar. 26, 1951

Inside the Lines (1930)
New York Times p. 17, Jul. 5, 1930

Inside the Walls of Folsom Prison (1951)
    New York Times p. 17, May 28, 1951
    Newsweek 37:102, Jun. 11, 1951
    Saturday Review 34:34, Jun. 23, 1951

Inspector Calls (1954)
    Nation 179:517, Dec. 11, 1954
    National Parent-Teacher 49:39, Feb., 1955
    New York Times p. 24, Nov. 26, 1954
    New Yorker 30:228, Dec. 4, 1954
    Newsweek 44:98, Dec. 13, 1954

Inspector General (1937)
    New York Times p. 37, Nov. 25, 1937

Inspector General (1949)
    Christian Century 67:95, Jan. 18, 1950
    Commonweal 51:342, Dec. 30, 1949
    Good Housekeeping 130:92, Feb., 1950
    Library Journal 75:332, Feb. 15, 1950
    New Republic 122:20, Jan. 23, 1950
    New York Times p. 9, Dec. 31, 1949; II, p. 1, Jan. 15,
        1950
    New Yorker 25:75, Jan. 14, 1950
    Newsweek 35:79, Jan. 16, 1950
    Rotarian 76:36, Mar., 1950
    Time 55:75, Jan. 23, 1950

Inspector Hornleigh (1939)
    New York Times p. 27, Jun. 15, 1939

Inspector Maigret (1958)
    Library Journal 83:3237, Nov. 15, 1958
    New York Times p. 47, Oct. 9, 1958
    Newsweek 52:119, Oct. 13, 1958
    Time 72:104, Dec. 8, 1958

Inspiration (1931)
    Life (NY) 97:22, Mar. 6, 1931
    New York Times p. 25, Feb. 9, 1931; VIII, p. 5, Feb.
        15, 1931
    Outlook 157:312, Feb. 25, 1931

Intent to Kill (1959)
    Catholic World 188:241, Dec., 1958
    Library Journal 84:589, Feb. 15, 1959
    New York Times p. 43, Apr. 1, 1959

Interference (1929)
New York Times p. 23, Nov. 17, 1928; X, p. 7, Nov. 25,
1928; IX, p. 5, Jan. 27, 1929

*Interlude
New Republic 120:30, Jan. 17, 1949
New York Times p. 19, Jan. 3, 1949
New Yorker 24:58, Jan. 8, 1949
Newsweek 33:75, Jan. 17, 1949

Interlude (1957)
America 98:92, Oct. 19, 1957
Catholic World 185:385-6, Aug., 1957
Commonweal 66:638, Sep. 27, 1957
Library Journal 82:1994, Sep. 1, 1957
National Parent-Teacher 52:33, Sep., 1957
Saturday Review 40:27, Jul. 20, 1957; 40:24, Aug. 10, 1957

Intermezzo, a Love Story (1939)
Nation 149:534, Nov. 11, 1939
New York Times IX, p. 3, Jul. 16, 1939; IX, p. 4, Sep.
24, 1939; p. 31, Oct. 6, 1939; IX, p. 5, Oct. 15,
1939
Newsweek 14:34, Oct. 9, 1939
Photoplay 53:63, Dec., 1939
Time 34:101, Oct. 16, 1939

International Crime (1938)
New York Times p. 14, May 16, 1938

International House (1933)
Nation 136:708, Jun. 21, 1933
New York Times p. 11, May 27, 1933; IX, p. 3, Jun. 4,
1933
Vanity Fair 40:59, Jul., 1933

International Lady (1941)
Commonweal 35:145, Nov. 28, 1941
New York Times p. 29, Nov. 11, 1941
Scholastic 39:28, Nov. 17, 1941

International Settlement (1938)
New York Times p. 20, Feb. 12, 1938
Time 31:33, Feb. 14, 1938

International Squadron (1941)
New York Times p. 28, Nov. 14, 1941; IX, p. 5, Nov.
16, 1941

Interns (1962)
New York Times p. 17, Aug. 9, 1962
Newsweek 60:76, Jul. 30, 1962

Internes Can't Take Money (1937)
Canadian Magazine 87:51, Jun., 1937
New York Times p. 23, May 6, 1937
Time 29:66, Apr. 19, 1937

*Interrupted Journey
New Republic 124:22, Jun. 18, 1951
New York Times p. 20, May 29, 1951
New Yorker 27:29, Jun. 9, 1951
Newsweek 37:100, Jun. 11, 1951

Interrupted Melody (1955)
America 93:193, May 14, 1955
Catholic World 181:143, May, 1955
Commonweal 62:126, May 6, 1955
Cosmopolitan 138:18-19, Apr., 1955
Musical America 75:34, Jun., 1955
National Parent-Teacher 49:38, May, 1955
New York Times p. 18, May 6, 1955
New York Times Magazine p. 59, Feb. 27, 1955
New Yorker 31:145, May 14, 1955
Newsweek 45:108, Apr. 25, 1955
Saturday Review 38:27, Apr. 30, 1955
Scholastic 66:30, May 11, 1955
Time 65:109, May 9, 1955

Intimate Relations (1954)
New York Times p. 15, Feb. 22, 1954
Saturday Review 37:28, Mar. 6, 1954
Time 63:102+, Mar. 15, 1954

Intrigue (1947)
New York Times p. 11, Apr. 24, 1948
Newsweek 31:95, May 17, 1948

Intruder (1955)
America 92:631, Mar. 12, 1955
Nation 180:207, Mar. 5, 1955
National Parent-Teacher 49:39, Apr., 1955
New York Times p. 22, Jan. 26, 1955
New Yorker 30:104, Feb. 5, 1955
Newsweek 45:74, Feb. 7, 1955
Saturday Review 38:25, Feb. 5, 1955
Time 65:84+, Feb. 28, 1955

Intruder (1962)
America 107:277, May 19, 1962
Commonweal 76:210-11, May 18, 1962
Ebony 17:76-9, May, 1962
New Republic 146:27, May 28, 1962
New York Times p. 48, May 15, 1962
New Yorker 38:134, May 26, 1962
Newsweek 59:97, May 21, 1962
Saturday Review 45:34, Feb. 10, 1962

Intruder in the Dust (1949)
Christian Century 67:351, Mar. 15, 1950
Commonweal 51:240, Dec. 2, 1940
Library Journal 75:332, Feb. 15, 1950
Life 27:149-50, Dec. 12, 1949
Nation 170:45, Jan. 14, 1950
New Republic 121:30, Dec. 12, 1949
New York Times p. 19, Nov. 23, 1949; p. 30, Nov. 25,
    1949; II, p. 1, Nov. 27, 1949
New Yorker 25:84+, Nov. 26, 1949
Newsweek 34:81, Dec. 5, 1949
Rotarian 76:40, May, 1950
Time 54:98+, Dec. 12, 1949

Invaders (1942)
Commonweal 35:536, Mar. 20, 1942
Life 12:57-8+, Mar. 23, 1942
Nation 154:320, Mar. 14, 1942
New Republic 106:399, Mar. 23, 1942
New York Times p. 17, Mar. 6, 1942; VIII, p. 3, Mar.
    8, 1942; VIII, p. 4, Mar. 15, 1942
Newsweek 19:72-3, Mar. 16, 1942; 20:80, Sep. 21, 1942
Photoplay 20:24, May, 1942
Time 39:90+, Mar. 16, 1942

Invaders from Mars (1953)
National Parent-Teacher 47:37, Jun., 1953
New York Times p. 7, May 30, 1953

Invasion Quartet (1961)
New York Times p. 41, Dec. 11, 1961

Invasion U.S.A. (1952)
National Parent-Teacher 47:38, Dec., 1952
New York Times p. 39, Apr. 30, 1953
Saturday Review 36:34, Feb. 21, 1953
Time 61:106+, Feb. 16, 1953

Invisible Agent (1942)
Commonweal 36:450, Aug. 28, 1942
New York Times VIII, p. 3, May 31, 1942; p. 23, Aug. 6, 1942
Newsweek 20:71, Aug. 17, 1942

Invisible Boy (1957)
Catholic World 186:222, Dec., 1957
Commonweal 67:255, Dec. 6, 1957
Library Journal 82:2918, Nov. 15, 1957
National Parent-Teacher 52:33, Dec., 1957
Newsweek 50:112+, Nov. 4, 1957
Senior Scholastic 71:32, Dec. 13, 1957

Invisible Enemy (1938)
New York Times p. 18, Apr. 30, 1938

Invisible Ghost (1941)
New York Times p. 21, May 8, 1941

Invisible Man (1933)
Commonweal 19:246, Dec. 29, 1933
Nation 137:688, Dec. 13, 1933
New York Times p. 18, Nov. 18, 1933; IX, p. 5, Nov. 26, 1933; IX, p. 8, Dec. 3, 1933
Newsweek 2:33, Nov. 25, 1933

Invisible Man Returns (1940)
New York Times IX, p. 4, Jan. 14, 1940; p. 19, Jan. 16, 1940; IX, p. 5, Jan. 21, 1940
Newsweek 15:32, Jan. 22, 1940

Invisible Man's Revenge (1944)
New York Times p. 12, Jun. 10, 1944

Invisible Menace (1938)
New York Times p. 20, Feb. 14, 1938

Invisible Ray (1936)
New York Times p. 9, Jan. 11, 1936

Invisible Stripes (1940)
New York Times p. 11, Jan. 13, 1940; IX, p. 5, Jan. 21, 1940

Invisible Wall (1947)
New York Times p. 11, Nov. 1, 1947

Invisible Woman (1941)
New York Times IX, p. 5, Nov. 3, 1940; p. 27, Jan. 9,
1941
Time 37:79, Jan. 20, 1941

Invitation (1952)
Library Journal 77:426, Mar. 1, 1952
New York Times p. 22, Jan. 30, 1952
New Yorker 27:105, Feb. 9, 1952
Newsweek 39:88, Feb. 1, 1952
Time 59:72, Feb. 4, 1952

Invitation to Happiness (1939)
New York Times IX, p. 7, Dec. 18, 1938; p. 31, Jun.
8, 1939; IX, p. 3, Jun. 11, 1939; IX, p. 4, Jun. 11,
1939
Newsweek 13:34, Jun. 5, 1939
Photoplay 53:62, Jul., 1939
Time 33:74, Jun. 19, 1939

Invitation to the Dance (1956)
America 95:252, Jun. 2, 1956
Catholic World 183:305, Jul., 1956
Commonweal 64:226-7, Jun. 1, 1956
Dance Magazine 30:14-17+, Jun., 1956
Life 40:59-60+, Jun. 11, 1956
Look 17:88+, Mar. 24, 1953
Nation 182:497, Jun. 9, 1956
National Parent-Teacher 51:39, Sep., 1956
New York Times p. 35, May 23, 1956; II, p. 1, May 27,
1956
New Yorker 32:131, Jun. 2, 1956
Newsweek 47:118, Jun. 11, 1956
Saturday Review 39:25, May 26, 1956
Time 67:102+, Jun. 11, 1956

Irene (1940)
Commonweal 32:63, May 10, 1940
Etude 58:229, Apr., 1940
Life 8:59, Aug. 8, 1940
New York Times IX, p. 5, Dec. 24, 1939; p. 23, May
24, 1940; IX, p. 3, May 26, 1940
Photoplay 54:68, Jun., 1940
Time 35:82+, May 6, 1940

Irish and Proud of It (1938)
New York Times p. 12, Oct. 31, 1938

Irish Eyes Are Smiling (1944)
    Commonweal 41:125, Nov. 17, 1944
    Life 17:74, Dec. 4, 1944
    Musician 50:18, Jan., 1945
    New York Times p. 27, Nov. 8, 1944
    New Yorker 20:50-1, Nov. 18, 1944
    Newsweek 24:108, Nov. 27, 1944
    Photoplay 26:14, Jan., 1945

Irish in Us (1935)
    Literary Digest 120:29, Aug. 10, 1935
    New York Times X, p. 4, Jul. 28, 1935; p. 15, Aug. 1,
        1935
    Time 26:34, Aug. 12, 1935

Irma La Douce (1963)
    American 109:124, Aug. 3, 1963
    Commonweal 78:376, Jun. 28, 1963
    New Republic 149:29, Jun. 13, 1963
    New York Times II, p. 9, Oct. 21, 1962; II, p. 7, Jun.
        2, 1963; p. 39, Jun. 6, 1963
    New Yorker 39:54, Jun. 15, 1963
    Newsweek 61:90, Jun. 17, 1963
    Saturday Review 46:31, Jun. 22, 1963
    Time 81:92, Jun. 21, 1963

Iron Curtain (1948)
    Canadian Forum 28:89, Jul., 1948
    Commonweal 48:165, May 28, 1948
    Life 24:59-60+, May 17, 1948
    New Republic 118:30-1, May 24, 1948
    New York Times II, p. 5, Jan. 11, 1948; II, p. 5, Mar.
        28, 1948; p. 31, May 13, 1948; II, p. 1, May 16,
        1948; II, p. 5, May 30, 1948
    New Yorker 25:103, May 22, 1948
    Newsweek 31:26-7, Apr. 26, 1948; 31:95, May 24, 1948
    Time 51:102, May 17, 1948
    Woman's Home Companion 75:10, Aug., 1948

Iron Duke (1935)
    Literary Digest 119:32, Feb. 9, 1935
    New York Times p. 8, Dec. 1, 1934; IX, p. 4, Jan. 6,
        1935; p. 27, Jan. 25, 1935; VIII, p. 5, Feb. 3, 1935
    Newsweek 5:32, Feb. 2, 1935
    Time 25:38, Feb. 4, 1935

Iron Glove (1954)
    National Parent-Teacher 48:38, May, 1954

Iron Major (1943)
Commonweal 39:281, Dec. 31, 1943
New York Times p. 12, Nov. 1, 1943

Iron Man (1931)
Life (NY) 97:20, May 15, 1931
New York Times p. 17, Apr. 18, 1931; VIII, p. 5, Apr.
26, 1931

Iron Man (1951)
Commonweal 54:524, Sep. 7, 1951
Library Journal 76:1239, Aug., 1951
New Republic 125:22, Sep. 10, 1951
New York Times p. 14, Aug. 20, 1951
Newsweek 38:82, Aug. 27, 1951
Time 58:112, Sep. 17, 1951

Iron Mask (1929)
Life (NY) 93:25, Mar. 15, 1929
New York Times VIII, p. 8, Feb. 3, 1929; p. 18, Feb.
22, 1929; VIII, p. 7, Mar. 3, 1929; X, p. 8, Mar.
10, 1929
Outlook 151:382, Mar. 6, 1929
Theatre Magazine 49:29, Mar., 1929

Iron Master (1932)
New York Times p. 11, Feb. 4, 1933

Iron Mistress (1952)
Library Journal 77:2170, Dec. 15, 1952
Nation 175:536, Dec. 6, 1952
New York Times p. 39, Nov. 20, 1952
Newsweek 40:94, Dec. 8, 1952
Time 60:108+, Nov. 24, 1952

Iron Petticoat (1956)
Catholic World 184:466, Mar., 1957
Library Journal 82:349, Feb. 1, 1957
National Parent-Teacher 51:38, Feb., 1957
New York Times II, p. 5, Jan. 15, 1956; p. 12, Feb. 2,
1957; II, p. 1, Feb. 10, 1957
New Yorker 32:107, Feb. 9, 1957
Newsweek 48:61, Dec. 31, 1956
Saturday Review 40:25, Feb. 2, 1957
Senior Scholastic 70:58, Feb. 2, 1957
Time 69:103, Jan. 28, 1957

Iron Sheriff (1957)
   National Parent-Teacher 52:33, Sep., 1957

Iroquois Trail (1950)
   Library Journal 75:992, Jun. 1, 1950
   New York Times p. 24, Oct. 27, 1950

Is Everybody Happy? (1929)
   New York Times p. 14, Oct. 2, 1929

Is My Face Red? (1932)
   New York Times p. 9, Jun. 11, 1932; IX, p. 3, Jun. 19,
      1932

Island (1962)
   Commonweal 76:474, Aug. 24, 1962
   Esquire 58:62+, Nov., 1962
   McCalls 89:12, Sep., 1962
   Nation 195:185-6, Sep. 29, 1962
   New Republic 147:29-30, Jul. 30, 1962
   New York Times p. 27, Sep. 11, 1962; II, p. 1, Sep. 16,
      1962
   New Yorker 38:86-7, Sep. 22, 1962
   Newsweek 60:104, Sep. 10, 1962
   Redbook 120:16, Dec., 1962
   Reporter 27:49-50, Nov. 8, 1962
   Saturday Review 45:16, Jul. 7, 1962
   Time 80:103, Sep. 28, 1962

Island in the Sky (1953)
   America 89:611, Sep. 19, 1953
   Catholic World 177:464, Sep., 1953
   Farm Journal 77:161, Nov., 1953
   Holiday 14:99, Nov., 1953
   Library Journal 78:1927, Nov. 1, 1953
   McCalls 81:10, Oct., 1953
   Nation 177:259, Sep. 26, 1953
   National Parent-Teacher 48:39, Dec., 1953
   New York Times p. 22, Sep. 10, 1953
   Newsweek 42:100-1, Sep. 21, 1953
   Saturday Review 36:47, Sep. 12, 1953
   Time 62:86, Sep. 28, 1953

Island in the Sun (1957)
   Commentary 24:354-7, Oct., 1957
   Commonweal 66:351, Jul. 5, 1957
   Library Journal 82:1755, Jul., 1957

Island in the Sun (1957) (Continued)
Life 43:67-8, Jul. 22, 1957
Nation 184:574, Jun. 29, 1957
National Parent-Teacher 52:33, Sep., 1957
New Republic 137:21, Jul. 29, 1957
New York Times II, p. 5, Jan. 20, 1957; p. 37, Jun. 13,
    1957; II, p. 1, Jun. 23, 1957; p. 10, Jul. 27, 1957
New Yorker 33:75, Jun. 22, 1957
Saturday Review 40:22, Jun. 29, 1957
Time 69:84, Jun. 24, 1957

Island of Desire (1951)
Catholic World 175:223, Jun., 1952
Commonweal 56:462, Aug. 15, 1952
Time 60:74, Jul. 28, 1952

Island of Doom (1933)
New York Times p. 9, Jul. 17, 1933

Island of Doomed Men (1940)
New York Times p. 21, Jun. 10, 1940

Island of Lost Men (1939)
New York Times p. 16, Aug. 17, 1939
Photoplay 53:63, Sep., 1939

Island of Lost Souls (1932)
New York Times IX, p. 4, Jan. 8, 1933; p. 19, Jan. 13,
    1933; IX, p. 5, Jan. 22, 1933

Island Rescue (1952)
Christian Century 69:1046, Sep. 10, 1952
Commonweal 56:367, Jul. 18, 1952
Library Journal 77:1893, Nov. 1, 1952
National Parent-Teacher 47:37, Sep., 1952
New York Times p. 19, Jul. 1, 1952
New Yorker 28:77, Jul. 12, 1952
Newsweek 40:79, Jul. 7, 1952
Theatre Arts 36:88, Aug., 1952
Time 60:98, Jul. 21, 1952

Isle of Destiny (1940)
New York Times p. 15, Apr. 8, 1940

Isle of Lost Ships (1929)
New York Times p. 15, Oct. 26, 1929; IX, p. 5, Oct.
    27, 1929

Isle of Paradise (1932)
 Literary Digest 114:18, Sep. 3, 1932
 New York Times p. 15, Jul. 21, 1932

Isle of the Dead (1945)
 Nation 161:321, Sep. 29, 1945
 New York Times p. 12, Sep. 8, 1945
 Time 46:96+, Sep. 17, 1945

Isn't It Romantic? (1948)
 Commonweal 48:618, Oct. 8, 1948
 New York Times p. 35, Oct. 7, 1948
 Newsweek 32:108, Oct. 18, 1948
 Time 52:102, Oct. 11, 1948

Istanbul (1956)
 America 96:512, Feb. 2, 1957
 National Parent-Teacher 51:37, Jan., 1957
 New York Times p. 34, Jan. 24, 1957

It Ain't Hay (1943)
 Commonweal 37:568, Mar. 26, 1943
 New York Times p. 17, Mar. 11, 1943

It All Came True (1940)
 Etude 58:375, Jun., 1940
 New York Times p. 13, Apr. 6, 1940
 Photoplay 54:23-36, Mar., 1940; 54:52, Apr., 1940

It Always Rains on Sunday (1948)
 New Republic 120:30, Feb. 28, 1949
 New York Times p. 15, Feb. 14, 1949
 Newsweek 33:79, Feb. 28, 1949

It Came from Beneath the Sea (1955)
 National Parent-Teacher 49:39, Apr., 1955
 Newsweek 45:103, May 9, 1955

It Came from Outer Space (1953)
 America 89:366, Jul. 4, 1953
 National Parent-Teacher 48:37, Sep., 1953
 New York Times p. 38, Jun. 10, 1953
 Saturday Review 36:36, Jul. 11, 1953
 Time 62:86, Jul. 6, 1953

It Can't Last Forever (1937)
 New York Times p. 22, Jul. 30, 1937

It Comes Up Love (1942)
New York Times p. 25, Jan. 22, 1943

It Could Happen to You (1939)
New York Times p. 26, Jun. 9, 1939

It Grows on Trees (1952)
National Parent-Teacher 47:36, Dec., 1952
New York Times p. 11, Nov. 29, 1952

It Had to Be You (1947)
Commonweal 47:304, Jan. 2, 1948
Good Housekeeping 126:11, Jan., 1948
New York Times p. 35, Dec. 8, 1947; II, p. 3, Dec. 14,
     1947
Newsweek 30:69, Dec. 29, 1947
Time 50:105, Dec. 1, 1947
Woman's Home Companion 75:10-11, Feb., 1948

It Had to Happen (1936)
New York Times p. 18, Feb. 15, 1936
Time 27:58, Feb. 24, 1936

It Happened at the Inn (1946)
Commonweal 43:407, Feb. 1, 1946
Nation 162:205, Feb. 16, 1946
New Republic 114:836, Jun. 10, 1946
New York Times p. 16, Dec. 22, 1945; II, p. 3, Jan.
     13, 1946
New Yorker 21:61, Jan. 5, 1946
Newsweek 26:94, Dec. 31, 1945
Theatre Arts 30:101, Feb., 1946
Time 47:97, Jan. 21, 1946
Vogue 107:100, Feb. 15, 1946

It Happened at the World Fair (1963)
New York Times p. 20, May 30, 1963

It Happened in Athens (1962)
New York Times p. 46, Nov. 15, 1962

It Happened in Broad Daylight (1960)
Commonweal 73:97, Oct. 21, 1960
New York Times p. 30, Sep. 30, 1960
New Yorker 36:106, Oct. 8, 1960
Saturday Review 43:34, Oct. 15, 1960
Time 76:76, Nov. 7, 1960

585

It Happened in Brooklyn (1947)
  Commonweal 45:594, Mar. 28, 1947
  Nation 164:433, Apr. 12, 1947
  New Republic 116:39, Mar. 31, 1947
  New York Times II, p. 5, Mar. 9, 1947; p. 28, Mar.
    14, 1947
  New Yorker 23:88, Mar. 22, 1947
  Newsweek 29:94, Mar. 24, 1947
  Scholastic 50:29, Apr. 28, 1947
  Time 49:99, Apr. 7, 1947

*It Happened in Europe
  Commonweal 50:607, Sep. 30, 1949
  New Republic 121:22, Oct. 24, 1949
  New York Times p. 32, Oct. 4, 1949
  Newsweek 34:95, Oct. 17, 1949
  Theatre Arts 33:43, Nov., 1949
  Vogue 114:86, Oct. 15, 1949

It Happened in Flatbush (1942)
  New York Times p. 12, Jul. 3, 1942
  Newsweek 19:68, Jun. 22, 1942
  Time 40:81, Jul. 6, 1942

It Happened in Gibralter (1943)
  New York Times p. 27, Nov. 16, 1943

It Happened in Hollywood (1937)
  New York Times p. 18, Oct. 2, 1937; XI, p. 5, Oct. 10,
    1937

It Happened in New York (1935)
  New York Times p. 10, Apr. 6, 1935

It Happened in the Park (1957)
  New York Times p. 23, Aug. 13, 1957
  New Yorker 33:73, Aug. 24, 1957

It Happened on Fifth Avenue (1947)
  Commonweal 46:241, Jun. 20, 1947
  New Republic 116:35, Jun. 30, 1947
  New York Times II, p. 1, Sep. 8, 1946; II, p. 5, Jun 8,
    1954; p. 33, Jun. 11, 1947
  Newsweek 29:94, Jun. 9, 1947
  Time 49:64, Jun. 16, 1947
  Woman's Home Companion 74:10, May, 1947

It Happened One Night (1934)
Literary Digest 117:38, Mar. 10, 1934
Nation 138:314, Mar. 14, 1934; 140:426, Apr. 10, 1935
New Republic 78:364, May 9, 1934
New York Times p. 23, Feb. 23, 1934; IX, p. 5, Mar.
4, 1934; X, p. 3, May 29, 1938
Vanity Fair 42:50, Apr., 1934

It Happened Out West (1937)
New York Times p. 22, Jun. 7, 1937

It Happened to Jane (1959)
Commonweal 70:278, Jun. 12, 1959
New York Times p. 18, Aug. 6, 1959
Senior Scholastic 74:47, May 15, 1959
Time 73:72, May 25, 1959

It Happened to One Man (1941)
New York Times p. 11, Feb. 24, 1941

It Happened Tomorrow (1944)
Commonweal 39:564, Mar. 24, 1944
Nation 158:577, May 13, 1944
New Republic 110:788, Jun. 12, 1944
New York Times p. 18, May 29, 1944; II, p. 3, Jun. 4,
1944
Newsweek 23:92, Mar. 20, 1944
Theatre Arts 28:375-9+, Jun., 1944
Time 43:96, Apr. 24, 1944

It Happens Every Spring (1949)
Christian Century 66:879, Jul. 20, 1949
Commonweal 50:272, Jun. 24, 1949
Good Housekeeping 129:10, Apr., 1949
New Republic 120:22, Jun. 27, 1949
New York Times p. 11, Jun. 11, 1949; II, p. 1, Jun. 19,
1949
New Yorker 25:52, Jun. 18, 1949
Newsweek 33:82+, Jun. 13, 1949
Photoplay 36:25, Aug., 1949
Rotarian 75:36-7, Sep., 1949
Time 53:97+, Jun. 6, 1949

It Happens Every Thursday (1953)
Catholic World 177:224, Jun., 1953
National Parent-Teacher 47:36, Jun., 1953

It Pays to Advertise (1931)
Life (NY) 97:21, Mar. 13, 1931
New York Times p. 15, Feb. 21, 1931; VIII, p. 5, Mar. 1, 1931
Theatre Magazine 53:47, Apr., 1931

It Should Happen to You (1954)
America 90:426, Jan. 23, 1954
Catholic World 178:463, Mar., 1954
Commonweal 59:473, Feb. 12, 1954
Farm Journal 78:165, Apr., 1954
Life 36:37-8+, Feb. 1, 1954
National Parent-Teacher 48:39, Mar., 1954
New York Times p. 10, Jan. 16, 1954
New Yorker 29:81, Jan. 23, 1954
Saturday Review 37:28, Feb. 6, 1954
Scholastic 64:38, Apr. 7, 1954
Time 63:108, Jan. 25, 1964

It Shouldn't Happen to a Dog (1946)
New York Times p. 11, Sep. 7, 1946

It Started in Naples (1960)
Commonweal 72:425, Aug. 19, 1960
McCalls 88:6, Oct., 1960
New Republic 143:19-20, Oct. 3, 1960
New York Times II, p. 7, Aug. 28, 1960; p. 7, Sep. 3, 1960; II, p. 1, Oct. 16, 1960
New Yorker 36:169, Sep. 17, 1960
Newsweek 56:85, Aug. 29, 1960
Time 76:62, Aug. 15, 1960

*It Started in Paradise
Commonweal 58:610, Sep. 25, 1953
National Parent-Teacher 49:39, Feb., 1955
New York Times p. 8, Jul. 25, 1953
New Yorker 29:44, Aug. 1, 1953

It Started with a Kiss (1959)
America 101:679, Sep. 5, 1959
Commonweal 70:472, Sep. 4, 1959
Life 47:131-3, Sep. 14, 1959
New York Times p. 14, Aug. 20, 1959
New Yorker 35:68, Aug. 29, 1959
Newsweek 54:80, Sep. 7, 1959
Saturday Review 42:31, Sep. 5, 1959
Time 74:46, Aug. 31, 1959

It Started with Eve (1941)
  Commonweal 35:16, Oct. 24, 1941
  Etude 59:663, Oct., 1941
  Life 11:53-4+, Oct. 20, 1941
  New Republic 105:763, Dec. 8, 1941
  New York Times p. 27, Oct. 3, 1941; IX, p. 5, Oct. 12,
    1941
  Newsweek 18:67+, Oct. 13, 1941
  Scholastic 39:32, Oct. 13, 1941
  Scribner's Commentator 11:107, Dec., 1941
  Time 38:94+, Oct. 13, 1941

It Takes a Thief (1962)
  New York Times p. 24, Aug. 15, 1963

It's a Big Country (1952)
  Catholic World 174:305, Jan., 1952
  Christian Century 69:415, Apr. 2, 1952
  Commonweal 55:400, Jan. 25, 1952
  New Republic 126:22, Jan. 28, 1952
  New York Times p. 25, Jan. 9, 1952
  Newsweek 39:90, Jan. 21, 1952
  Saturday Review 35:26, Jan. 5, 1952
  Scholastic 59:26, Jan. 9, 1952
  Theatre Arts 36:32, Feb., 1952
  Time 59:96+, Jan. 28, 1952

It's a Boy (1933)
  New York Times IX, p. 2, Jul. 23, 1933; p. 18, Jun. 8,
    1934

It's a Date (1940)
  Commonweal 31:514, Apr. 5, 1940
  Etude 58:375, Jun., 1940
  New York Times p. 16, Mar. 23, 1940; IX, p. 5, Mar.
    24, 1940
  Photoplay 54:51, Apr., 1940
  Scholastic 36:37, Apr. 1, 1940
  Time 35:82, Apr. 8, 1940

It's a Dog's Life (1955)
  New York Times p. 14, Dec. 23, 1955
  New Yorker 31:92, Jan. 14, 1956
  Time 67:96, Jan. 16, 1956

It's a Gift (1934)
  Literary Digest 119:30, Jan. 19, 1935

It's a Gift (1934) (Continued)
New York Times p. 20, Jan. 5, 1935; IX, p. 5, Jan. 13,
1935

It's a Great Feeling (1949)
New York Times p. 6, Aug. 13, 1949
New Yorker 25:38, Aug. 27, 1949
Newsweek 34:72, Aug. 29, 1949
Rotarian 75:38, Dec., 1949
Time 54:102, Sep. 12, 1949

It's a Pleasure (1945)
New York Times II, p. 3, Jul. 23, 1944; p. 23, May 4,
1945; II, p. 1, May 6, 1945
Photoplay 26:18, May, 1945

It's a Small World (1935)
Time 25:61, Apr., 1935

It's a Small World (1950)
Saturday Review 34:47, Dec. 8, 1951

It's a Wise Child (1931)
New York Times p. 13, May 16, 1931; VIII, p. 5, May
24, 1931

It's a Wonderful Life (1947)
Commonweal 45:305, Jan. 3, 1947
Cosmopolitan 122:66+, Jan., 1947
Life 21:68-73, Dec. 30, 1946; 22:87, Mar. 10, 1947
Nation 164:193, Feb. 15, 1947
New Republic 116:44, Jan. 6, 1947
New York Times II, p. 3, Jun. 30, 1946; II, p. 5, Dec.
15, 1946; p. 19, Dec. 23, 1946; II, p. 5, Jan. 5,
1947; II, p. 1, Jan. 12, 1947
New Yorker 22:87, Dec. 21, 1946
Newsweek 28:72-3, Dec. 30, 1946
Photoplay 30:4, Mar., 1947; 30:48-9, Apr., 1947; 32:40,
Mar., 1948
Scholastic 50:36, Feb. 3, 1947
Theatre Arts 31:36-7, Feb., 1947
Time 48:54, Dec. 23, 1946
Woman's Home Companion 74:10, Mar., 1947

It's a Wonderful World (1939)
New Republic 99:102, May 31, 1939
New York Times p. 27, May 19, 1939

It's a Wonderful World (1939) (Continued)
Photoplay 53:63, Jul., 1939
Time 33:56, May 22, 1939

It's All Yours (1937)
New York Times p. 15, Jan. 7, 1938

It's Always Fair Weather (1955)
America 93:575, Sep. 10, 1955
Catholic World 181:59, Oct., 1955
Commonweal 62:541, Sep. 2, 1955
Dance Magazine 29:15, Oct., 1955
Life 39:75, Oct. 3, 1955
Nation 181:291, Oct. 1, 1955
National Parent-Teacher 50:39, Nov., 1955
New York Times p. 19, Sep. 16, 1955
New Yorker 31:113, Sep. 24, 1955
Saturday Review 38:20, Sep. 3, 1955
Time 66:80, Sep. 5, 1955

It's Great to Be Alive (1933)
New York Times p. 14, Jul. 8, 1933; IX, p. 3, Jul. 16,
    1933
Newsweek 1:31, Jul. 15, 1933

It's Great to Be Young (1956)
New York Times p. 23, Dec. 26, 1957

It's in the Air (1935)
New York Times p. 18, Nov. 8, 1935
Time 26:53, Oct. 28, 1935

It's in the Bag (1945)
Commonweal 42:72, May 4, 1945
Nation 160:469, Apr. 21, 1945
New York Times p. 12, Jun. 11, 1945
New Yorker 21:40, Jun. 16, 1945
Newsweek 25:100+, May 21, 1945
Photoplay 26:18, May, 1945
Scholastic 46:24, Mar. 12, 1945
Time 45:94+, Apr. 23, 1945

It's Love Again (1936)
Canadian Magazine 86:32, Jul., 1936
Literary Digest 121:20, May 23, 1936
New York Times p. 12, May 23, 1936
Newsweek 7:27, May 23, 1936
Time 27:22, Jun. 1, 1936

It's Love I'm After (1937)
Life 3:100-101, Nov. 15, 1937
New York Times X, p. 3, Jul. 11, 1937; XI, p. 6, Nov.
7, 1937; p. 31, Nov. 11, 1937; XI, p. 5, Nov. 14,
1937
Scholastic 31:35, Oct. 30, 1937
Stage 14:45, Sep., 1937
Time 30:52, Nov. 22, 1937

It's Only Money (1962)
New York Times p. 43, Nov. 22, 1962
Time 80:93, Dec. 14, 1962

It's Tough to Be Famous (1932)
New York Times p. 18, Apr. 9, 1932

Itto (1936)
New York Times X, p. 4, May 12, 1935; p. 15, Jan. 28,
1936; IX, p. 5, Feb. 2, 1936

Ivan Pavlov (1950)
New York Times p. 15, Feb. 13, 1950

Ivan the Terrible (1947)
Canadian Forum 27:40-1, May, 1947
Hollywood Quarterly 1:26-30, Oct., 1945
Life 18:90-5, Mar. 12, 1945
Nation 164:495-7, Apr. 26, 1947
New Republic 116:41-2, Mar. 24, 1947
New York Times p. 30, Oct. 22, 1946; II, p. 4, Mar. 9,
1947; p. 25, Mar. 10, 1947; II, p. 1, Mar. 16, 1947;
p. 24, Mar. 25, 1947
New Yorker 23:64, Mar. 15, 1947
Newsweek 29:94, Mar. 24, 1947
Theatre Arts 29:281-2, May, 1945; 30:533, Sep., 1946;
31:51, May, 1947
Time 47:93, Apr. 1, 1946; 49:102+, Apr. 14, 1947

Ivan the Terrible, Part II (1959)
Commonweal 71:351, Dec. 18, 1959
Nation 190:20, Jan. 2, 1960
New Republic 141:26-7, Dec. 28, 1959
New York Times p. 33, Jul. 29, 1959; p. 22, Nov. 25,
1959
Newsweek 54:113-4, Dec. 7, 1959
Saturday Review 42:30, Nov. 28, 1959
Time 75:69, Jan. 4, 1960

Ivanhoe (1952)
  Catholic World 175:381, Aug., 1952
  Christian Century 69:1271, Oct. 29, 1952
  Commonweal 56:485-6, Aug. 22, 1952
  Harper 205:92, Sep., 1952
  Library Journal 77:1299, Aug., 1952
  Life 33:53-4+, Aug. 11, 1952
  Nation 175:283, Sep. 27, 1952
  National Parent-Teacher 47:37, Sep., 1952
  New York Times II, p. 5, Aug. 26, 1951; p. 8, Aug. 1,
    1952; II, p. 1, Aug. 10, 1952
  New Yorker 28:55, Aug. 9, 1952
  Newsweek 40:85, Aug. 4, 1952
  Saturday Review 35:28, Aug. 2, 1952
  Scholastic 61:37, Sep. 17, 1952
  Time 60:76, Aug. 4, 1952

I've Always Loved You (1946)
  Cosmopolitan 121:193, Oct., 1946
  New York Times p. 11, Sep. 7, 1946; II, p. 3, Sep. 8,
    1946
  New Yorker 22:105, Sep. 14, 1946
  Photoplay 30:4, Dec., 1946
  Time 48:106, Sep. 16, 1946
  Woman's Home Companion 73:11, Feb., 1946

I've Got Your Number (1934)
  Canadian Magazine 81:44, May, 1934
  New York Times p. 9, Feb. 3, 1934

I've Lived Before (1956)
  National Parent-Teacher 51:38, Oct., 1956
  New York Times p. 13, Aug. 4, 1956

Ivory Hunter (1952)
  Catholic World 175:223, Jun., 1952
  Christian Century 69:935, Aug. 13, 1952
  Commonweal 56:268, Jun. 20, 1952
  National Parent-Teacher 47:36, Sep., 1952
  Natural History 61:286, Jun., 1952
  Nature Magazine 45:343, Aug., 1952
  New York Times p. 19, Aug. 19, 1952; II, p. 1, Aug.
    24, 1952; II, p. 1, Jan. 23, 1955
  New Yorker 28:53, Aug. 30, 1952
  Newsweek 39:108, Jun. 16, 1952
  Saturday Review 35:28, Jun. 7, 1952
  Scholastic 61:20, Oct. 1, 1952

Ivory Hunter (1952) (Continued)
Theatre Arts 36:89, Jul., 1952
Time 60:74, Aug. 25, 1952

Ivy (1947)
Commonweal 46:287, Jul. 4, 1947
Cosmopolitan 123:54+, Aug., 1947
Life 23:83-4+, Jul. 14, 1947
Nation 165:172, Aug. 16, 1947
New Republic 117:31, Jul. 28, 1947
New York Times II, p. 5, Jun. 22, 1947; p. 19, Jun. 26, 1947
Newsweek 29:77, Jun. 30, 1947
Time 50:66, Jul. 7, 1947
Woman's Home Companion 74:10, Sep., 1947

Jacare (1942)
New York Times p. 23, Dec. 28, 1942

Jack Ahoy (1935)
New York Times p. 11, Feb. 9, 1935; VIII, p. 5, Feb. 17, 1935

Jack and the Beanstalk (1952)
Christian Century 69:599, May 14, 1952
New York Times II, p. 6, Mar. 2, 1952; p. 35, Apr. 8, 1952

Jack London (1943)
Commonweal 39:281, Dec. 31, 1943
Cosmopolitan 116:134, Jan., 1944
New York Times p. 19, Mar. 3, 1944
New Yorker 20:42+, Feb. 26, 1944
Photoplay 24:22, Feb., 1944

Jack Slade (1953)
National Parent-Teacher 48:39, Jan., 1954
New York Times p. 42, Oct. 29, 1953

Jack the Giant Killer (1962)
New York Times p. 17, Jul. 26, 1962
Newsweek 60:77, Aug. 6, 1962

Jack the Ripper (1960)
New York Times p. 37, Feb. 18, 1960
Newsweek 55:103, Feb. 22, 1960

Jackass Mail (1942)
New York Times p. 25, Jul. 2, 1942

Jackie Robinson Story (1950)
Christian Century 67:775, Jun. 21, 1950
Commonweal 52:198, Jun. 2, 1950
New Republic 122:23, Jun. 12, 1950
New York Times II, p. 6, Apr. 30, 1950; p. 36, May 17,
    1950; II, p. 1, May 21, 1950
Newsweek 35:84, May 29, 1950
Rotarian 77:44, Aug., 1950
Time 55:86+, Jun. 5, 1950

Jackpot (1950)
Christian Century 67:1503, Dec. 13, 1950
Commonweal 53:198, Dec. 1, 1950
Holiday 9:85, Jan., 1951
Library Journal 75:1915, Nov. 1, 1950
Life 29:109-10+, Dec. 4, 1950
New Republic 123:28, Dec. 11, 1950
New York Times p. 55, Nov. 23, 1950; II, p. 1, Dec. 3,
    1950
New Yorker 26:115, Dec. 2, 1950
Newsweek 36:100-2, Nov. 13, 1950
Rotarian 78:38, Jan., 1951
Scholastic 57:19, Nov. 29, 1950
Time 56:100+, Nov. 27, 1950

Jade Casket (1929)
New York Times p. 27, Jun. 24, 1929

Jail Buster (1955)
National Parent-Teacher 50:39, Mar., 1956

Jail House Blues (1941)
New York Times p. 23, Feb. 6, 1942

Jailbreak (1936)
New York Times p. 22, Aug. 6, 1936

Jailbreakers (1960)
New York Times p. 27, Jan. 7, 1961

Jailhouse Rock (1957)
Catholic World 186:221, Dec., 1957
New York Times p. 41, Nov. 14, 1957
Time 70:111, Nov. 4, 1957

Jalna (1936)
New York Times p. 8, Sep. 14, 1935
Stage 12:3, Sep., 1935
Time 26:28, Aug. 19, 1935

Jam Session (1944)
New York Times p. 25, May 3, 1944

Jamaica Inn (1939)
New York Times IX, p. 4, Jan. 22, 1939; IX, p. 3, Jun.
11, 1939; p. 33, Oct. 12, 1939; IX, p. 5, Oct. 15,
1939
Theatre Arts 33:39, May, 1949
Time 34:49, Oct. 30, 1939

Jamaica Run (1953)
National Parent-Teacher 47:37, Jun., 1953

James Dean Story (1957)
National Parent-Teacher 52:33, Oct., 1957
New York Times p. 16, Oct. 19, 1957
Newsweek 50:111, Sep. 9, 1957
Saturday Review 40:20, Aug. 3, 1957
Senior Scholastic 71:37, Sep. 20, 1957
Time 70:112+, Sep. 9, 1957

*Jamming the Blues
Life 18:6-8, Jan. 22, 1945
Nation 159:753, Dec. 16, 1944
Theatre Arts 28:725, Dec., 1944
Time 44:50, Dec. 25, 1944

Jane Eyre (1944)
Commonweal 39:36-7, Oct. 29, 1943
Nation 158:197, Feb. 12, 1944
New Republic 110:346, Mar. 13, 1944
New York Times p. 12, Feb. 4, 1944; II, p. 3, Feb. 13,
1944
Newsweek 23:88, Feb. 14, 1944
Photoplay 23:40-41+, Aug., 1943; 24:22, Dec., 1943
Saturday Review 27:14, Feb. 19, 1944
Scholastic 43:27, Dec. 13, 1943; 43:37, Dec. 13, 1943
Time 43:96, Feb. 21, 1944

Janie (1944)
Commonweal 40:494, Sep. 8, 1944
Cosmopolitan 117:90, Sep., 1944

Janie (1944) (Continued)
Life 17:61-2, Aug. 21, 1944
New York Times p. 16, Aug. 5, 1944
Newsweek 24:83, Jul. 31, 1944
Photoplay 25:21, Oct., 1944
Time 44:94+, Aug. 14, 1944

Janie Gets Married (1946)
New York Times II, p. 3, Jun. 9, 1946; p. 24, Jun. 15, 1946

Japanese War Bride (1952)
New York Times p. 22, Jan. 30, 1952
Newsweek 39:90, Feb. 11, 1952
Time 59:74, Feb. 4, 1952

Jason (1962)
America 109:143, Aug. 10, 1963
New York Times p. 19, Aug. 8, 1963
New Yorker 39:65, Aug. 24, 1963
Newsweek 62:78B+, Jul. 8, 1963
Time 82:78, Jul. 19, 1963

Jason and the Golden Fleece (1961)
New York Times II, p. 7, Nov. 12, 1961

Jassy (1948)
Commonweal 47:567, Mar. 19, 1948
New York Times p. 19, Feb. 20, 1948
Newsweek 31:83, Mar. 8, 1948

Java Head (1935)
Commonweal 22:387, Aug. 16, 1935
New York Times p. 21, Jul. 31, 1935

Jaws of Hell (1931)
New York Times p. 21, Jan. 5, 1931

Jazz Age (1929)
New York Times p. 36, Jan. 7, 1929

Jazz Heaven (1929)
New York Times p. 29, Oct. 30, 1929; IX, p. 6, Nov. 3, 1929

Jazz on a Summer's Day (1960)
Commonweal 72:40-1, Apr. 8, 1960

Jazz on a Summer's Day (1960) (Continued)
Nation 190:392, Apr. 30, 1960
New York Times p. 46, Mar. 29, 1960; II, p. 1, Apr.
10, 1960
Newsweek 55:112, Apr. 4, 1960
Reporter 22:40-1, Mar. 31, 1960
Saturday Review 43:70, Mar. 12, 1960
Time 75:69, May 23, 1960

Jazz Singer (1927)
Cosmopolitan 121:51, Aug., 1946
Life (NY) Vol. 90, Oct. 27, 1927
Motion Picture Magazine 34:55, Jan., 1928
New York Times VII, p. 4, Aug. 28, 1927; p. 24, Oct.
7, 1927; IX, p. 7, Oct. 16, 1928; p. 8, Sep. 28, 1928;
IX, p. 5, Mar. 8, 1936

Jazz Singer (1953)
Christian Century 70:399, Apr. 1, 1953
Commonweal 57:451, Feb. 6, 1953
McCalls 80:12, Mar., 1953
National Parent-Teacher 47:26, Mar., 1953
New York Times p. 24, Jan. 14, 1953
Newsweek 41:98+, Jan. 26, 1953
Saturday Review 36:27, Feb. 7, 1953
Scholastic 62:29, Feb. 11, 1953
Time 61:96, Jan. 19, 1953

Jealousy (1929)
New York Times X, p. 8, Mar. 24, 1929; VIII, p. 3,
Jul. 28, 1929; p. 17, Sep. 14, 1929

Jealousy (1945)
Time 46:94+, Aug. 13, 1945

Jeanne Eagles (1957)
America 97:688, Sep. 28, 1957
Catholic World 185:383-4, Aug., 1957
Commonweal 67:19, Oct. 4, 1957
Coronet 42:13, Sep., 1957
National Parent-Teacher 52:33, Sep., 1957
New York Times p. 19, Aug. 31, 1957
New Yorker 33:74, Sep. 7, 1957
Newsweek 50:93, Aug. 12, 1957
Saturday Review 40:25, Aug. 17, 1957

Jeannie (1943)
Nation 157:536, Nov. 6, 1943

Jeannie (1943) (Continued)
New York Times p. 14, Sep. 13, 1943
Time 42:54+, Nov. 8, 1943

Jedda, the Uncivilized (1956)
National Parent-Teacher 51:38, Oct., 1956

Jennifer (1953)
National Parent-Teacher 48:39, Jan., 1954

Jennie Gerhardt (1933)
New Outlook 162:42, Jul., 1933
New York Times p. 20, Jun. 9, 1933
Newsweek 1:30, Jun. 17, 1933
Time 21:32, Jun. 19, 1933

*Jenny Lamour
Commonweal 47:566, Mar. 19, 1948
New Republic 118:33, Feb. 16, 1948
New York Times p. 17, Mar. 8, 1948; II, p. 1, Mar.
    14, 1948
New Yorker 24:81, Mar. 13, 1948
Newsweek 31:85, Apr. 5, 1948
Theatre Arts 32:50, Spring, 1948

Jeopardy (1953)
America 89:88, Apr. 18, 1953
Commonweal 58:99, May 1, 1953
Nation 176:274, Mar. 28, 1953
National Parent-Teacher 47:40, Apr., 1953
New York Times p. 36, Mar. 31, 1953
Newsweek 41:90, Apr. 6, 1953
Saturday Review 36:40, Feb. 28, 1953
Time 61:104, Mar. 9, 1953

Jericho (1937)
New York Times X, p. 3, Apr. 25, 1937; XI, p. 4, Sep.
    26, 1937

Jericho (1946)
New York Times p. 31, Dec. 16, 1946
New Yorker 22:45, Dec. 28, 1946
Newsweek 29:69, Jan. 6, 1947
Theatre Arts 31:34-5, Feb., 1947

Jesse James (1939)
Collier's 102:14+, Nov. 26, 1938

599

Jesse James (1939) (Continued)
Commonweal 29:386, Jan. 27, 1939
Life 6:40-43, Jan. 30, 1939
New York Times X, p. 4, Sep. 4, 1938; IX, p. 4, Jan.
8, 1939; p. 13, Jan. 14, 1939; IX, p. 5, Jan. 22, 1939
Newsweek 13:25, Jan. 23, 1939
Scholastic 33:30-1, Jan. 21, 1939
Stage 16:7, Mar. 15, 1939
Time 33:26, Jan. 23, 1939

Jesse James' Women (1954)
National Parent-Teacher 49:40, Dec., 1954
New York Times p. 23, Sep. 29, 1954

Jessica (1962)
Commonweal 76:153, May 4, 1962
New York Times p. 20, Apr. 20, 1962
New Yorker 38:182, May 19, 1962
Time 79:97-8, Apr. 20, 1962

Jet Over the Atlantic (1960)
New York Times p. 27, Jan. 7, 1960

Jet Pilot (1957)
Commonweal 67:49, Oct. 11, 1957
National Parent-Teacher 52:33, Oct., 1957
New York Times p. 8, Oct. 5, 1957
Newsweek 50:115, Sep. 23, 1957
Saturday Review 40:31, Oct. 12, 1957

Jew at War (1931)
New York Times p. 11, Jul. 25, 1931; VIII, p. 3, Aug.
2, 1931

Jewel Robbery (1932)
New York Times p. 6, Jul. 23, 1932; IX, p. 3, Jul. 31,
1932

Jezebel (1938)
Life 4:44-6+, Mar. 28, 1938
Nation 146:365, Mar. 26, 1938
New York Times p. 15, Mar. 11, 1938; IX, p. 4, Mar.
13, 1938; XI, p. 5, Mar. 20, 1938
Newsweek 11:25, Mar. 21, 1938
Time 31:33, Mar. 28, 1938

Jigsaw (1949)
New York Times p. 9, May 30, 1949

Jim Thorpe, All-American (1951)
Christian Century 68:1239, Oct. 24, 1951
Commonweal 54:550, Sep. 14, 1951
New York Times p. 7, Aug. 25, 1951
Newsweek 38:73, Sep. 3, 1951
Scholastic 59:30, Oct. 3, 1951
Time 58:108, Sep. 24, 1951

Jimmy and Sally (1933)
New York Times p. 12, Dec. 16, 1933

Jimmy the Gent (1934)
New York Times p. 22, Mar. 26, 1934; X, p. 3, Apr.
1, 1934

Jitterbugs (1943)
New York Times p. 12, Jun. 5, 1943

Jivaro (1954)
National Parent-Teacher 48:39, Mar., 1954
New York Times p. 11, Feb. 13, 1954
Newsweek 43:107, Feb. 22, 1954

*Joan at the Stake
New York Times Magazine p. 34-5, Apr. 11, 1954
Theatre Arts 39:30-1+, May, 1955

Joan of Arc (1948)
Catholic World 168:321, Jan., 1949
Collier's 121:24-5, Jun. 26, 1948
Commonweal 49:143, Nov. 19, 1948
Cosmopolitan 125:13+, Nov., 1948
Good Housekeeping 127:10, Oct., 1948
Harper's 198:110-11, Jan., 1949
Ladies Home Journal 65:33, Dec., 1948
Life 25:78-87, Nov. 15, 1948; 26:46, Mar. 14, 1949
Nation 167:585, Nov. 20, 1948
New Republic 119:27, Nov. 22, 1948
New York Times II, p. 6, Dec. 21, 1947; VI, p. 66, Nov.
7, 1947; p. 30, Nov. 12, 1948; II, p. 1, Nov. 21,
1948
New York Times Magazine p. 12-13, Feb. 29, 1948
New Yorker 24:130, Nov. 13, 1948
Newsweek 32:91, Nov. 22, 1948
Photoplay 34:17, Jan., 1949
Rotarian 74:38, Mar., 1949
Saturday Review 31:22-4, Dec. 18, 1948

Joan of Arc (1948) (Continued)
Scholastic 53:30-1, Nov. 10, 1948
Time 52:102, Nov. 15, 1948

Joan of Paris (1942)
Commonweal 35:419, Feb. 13, 1942
Nation 154:239, Feb. 21, 1942
New Republic 106:462, Apr. 6, 1942
New York Times IX, p. 5, Oct. 5, 1941; p. 18, Jan. 26, 1942
Newsweek 19:60, Feb. 2, 1942
Time 39:85, Feb. 23, 1942

Joan of the Angels (1962)
Commonweal 76:305, Jun. 15, 1962
Nation 194:483, May 26, 1962
New Republic 146:26+, May 21, 1962
New York Times p. 43, May 8, 1962
New Yorker 38:181, May 19, 1962
Newsweek 59:96, May 21, 1962
Saturday Review 45:23-4, May 26, 1962
Time 79:93-4, May 18, 1962

Joe and Ethel Turp Call on the President (1939)
New York Times p. 19, Jan. 4, 1940; IX, p. 5, Jan. 14, 1940
Time 35:78, Jan. 22, 1940

Joe Butterfly (1957)
America 97:292, Jun. 1, 1957
Commonweal 66:257, Jun. 7, 1957
National Parent-Teacher 51:36, May, 1957
New York Times p. 23, May 30, 1957

Joe Dakota (1957)
Commonweal 66:495, Aug. 16, 1957
National Parent-Teacher 52:38, Nov., 1957

Joe Louis Story (1953)
America 90:185, Nov. 14, 1953
Catholic World 178:141, Nov., 1953
Commonweal 59:142, Nov. 13, 1953
Nation 177:434, Nov. 21, 1953
National Parent-Teacher 48:35, Nov., 1953
New York Times VI, p. 78, Oct. 4, 1953; p. 29, Nov. 4, 1953
Newsweek 42:86, Oct. 5, 1953

Joe Louis Story (1953) (Continued)
Saturday Review 36:38, Oct. 17, 1953
Time 62:108+, Nov. 16, 1953

Joe Macbeth (1956)
America 94:264, Dec. 3, 1955
Library Journal 81:523, Feb. 15, 1956
National Parent-Teacher 50:39, Mar., 1956
New York Times p. 13, Apr. 7, 1956

Joe Palooka, Champ (1946)
New York Times p. 10, Apr. 6, 1946
Time 47:96+, Apr. 29, 1946

Joe Smith, American (1942)
Commonweal 35:536, Mar. 20, 1942
Musician 47:75, May, 1942
New York Times p. 27, Apr. 2, 1942
Newsweek 19:72, Feb. 16, 1942
Scholastic 40:34, Feb. 9, 1942
Time 39:86, Feb. 16, 1942

John and Julie (1957)
Catholic World 183:384, Aug., 1956
National Parent-Teacher 51:38, Sep., 1956
New York Times p. 40, May 7, 1957; II, p. 1, May 16, 1957
New Yorker 33:147, May 18, 1957

John Loves Mary (1949)
Commonweal 49:521, Mar. 4, 1949
Good Housekeeping 128:211, Mar., 1949
New York Times p. 11, Feb. 5, 1949
Newsweek 33:85, Feb. 7, 1949
Rotarian 74:35, May, 1949
Time 53:87, Feb. 7, 1949

John Meade's Woman (1937)
Canadian Magazine 87:25, Mar., 1937
Literary Digest 123:22, Feb. 27, 1937
New York Times p. 19, Feb. 18, 1937
Time 29:25-6, Feb. 22, 1937

John Paul Jones (1959)
America 101:559, Jul. 25, 1959
Catholic World 189:395, Aug., 1959
Commonweal 70:307, Jun. 19, 1959

John Paul Jones (1959) (Continued)
    Library Journal 84:2054, Jun. 15, 1959
    New York Times p. 39, Jun. 17, 1959
    Saturday Review 42:28, Jun. 20, 1959
    Time 73:62+, Jun. 29, 1959

*John Wesley
    Life 36:79-80+, Jun. 7, 1954
    National Parent-Teacher 49:38, Oct., 1954
    New York Times p. 26, Apr. 30, 1954
    Newsweek 43:81, May 3, 1954
    Time 63:58, May 3, 1954

Johnny Allegro (1949)
    New Republic 120:31, Jun. 20, 1949
    New York Times p. 19, May 31, 1949
    Newsweek 33:88, Jun. 20, 1949
    Rotarian 75:36, Sep., 1949
    Time 53:88, Jun. 20, 1949

Johnny Angel (1945)
    New York Times p. 12, Dec. 18, 1945
    Newsweek 26:87, Sep. 3, 1945

Johnny Apollo (1940)
    Commonweal 32:20, Apr. 26, 1940
    New York Times p. 21, Apr. 13, 1940

Johnny Belinda (1948)
    Collier's 122:74, Oct. 2, 1948
    Commonweal 49:41, Oct. 22, 1948
    Good Housekeeping 127:258, Nov., 1948
    Life 25:153-5, Oct. 25, 1948
    Nation 167:705, Dec. 18, 1948
    New York Times II, p. 5, May 30, 1948; p. 11, Oct. 2,
        1948; II, p. 1, Oct. 10, 1948; II, p. 4, Oct. 10, 1948
    New Yorker 24:111, Oct. 9, 1948
    Newsweek 32:85, Oct. 4, 1948
    Photoplay 33:22, Sep., 1948; 36:32, Oct., 1949
    Rotarian 74:52, Jan., 1949
    Theatre Arts 32:53, Oct., 1948
    Time 52:102+, Oct. 25, 1948
    Woman's Home Companion 75:10-11, Nov., 1948

Johnny Come Lately (1943)
    Commonweal 38:586, Oct. 1, 1943
    Cosmopolitan 115:128, Sep., 1943

Johnny Come Lately (1943) (Continued)
 Nation 157:536, Nov. 6, 1943
 New York Times II, p. 3, Jun. 6, 1943; p. 26, Sep. 24,
  1943
 New Yorker 19:55, Sep. 25, 1943
 Newsweek 22:105-6, Sep. 13, 1943
 Scholastic 43:34, Oct. 25, 1943
 Theatre Arts 27:733, Dec., 1943
 Time 42:92+, Sep. 27, 1943

Johnny Concho (1956)
 Catholic World 184:66, Oct., 1956
 Commonweal 64:561, Sep. 7, 1956
 National Parent-Teacher 51:38, Oct., 1956
 New York Times II, p. 5, Jan. 1, 1956; p. 30, Aug. 16,
  1956
 Newsweek 48:88, Aug. 20, 1956
 Time 68:76, Sep. 3, 1956

Johnny Cool (1963)
 New York Times p. 31, Oct. 3, 1963
 Newsweek 62:115, Oct. 14, 1963

Johnny Dark (1954)
 Farm Journal 78:101, Aug., 1954
 New York Times p. 7, Jun. 26, 1954
 Time 64:78, Jul. 26, 1954

Johnny Doughboy (1942)
 New York Times p. 25, May 6, 1943

Johnny Eager (1941)
 Commonweal 35:463, Feb. 27, 1942
 Nation 154:321, Mar. 14, 1942
 New York Times XI, p. 6, Oct. 12, 1941; p. 21, Feb.
  20, 1942; VIII, p. 3, Mar. 1, 1941
 Newsweek 19:66, Jan. 26, 1942
 Photoplay 20:6, Mar., 1942
 Time 39:86, Feb. 23, 1942

Johnny Frenchman (1947)
 Commonweal 45:117, Nov. 15, 1946
 New York Times II, p. 5, Oct. 20, 1946; p. 27, Oct. 27,
  1946; II, p. 1, Nov. 17, 1946
 New Yorker 22:109, Oct. 26, 1946
 Newsweek 28:94, Oct. 28, 1946
 Theatre Arts 30:716, Dec., 1946
 Time 48:106, Nov. 4, 1946

Johnny Guitar (1954)
America 91:287, Jun. 5, 1954
Catholic World 179:221, Jun., 1954
Commonweal 60:170, Jun. 18, 1954
Farm Journal 78:101, Aug., 1954
Library Journal 79:1048, Jun. 1, 1954
New York Times p. 19, May 28, 1954
New Yorker 30:63, Jun. 5, 1954
Newsweek 43:104, Jun. 14, 1954
Time 63:106+, Jun. 14, 1954

Johnny Holiday (1950)
Christian Century 67:879, Jul. 19, 1950
Commonweal 52:198, Jun. 2, 1950
New York Times II, p. 5, Oct. 2, 1949; p. 36, May 17,
1950; II, p. 1, May 28, 1950
Rotarian 77:38, Sep., 1950

Johnny in the Clouds (1946)
Commonweal 43:264, Dec. 21, 1945
New York Times p. 16, Nov. 16, 1945; II, p. 1, Nov.
18, 1945
New Yorker 21:67, Nov. 24, 1945
Newsweek 26:109, Nov. 26, 1945
Theatre Arts 30:47-8, Jan., 1946

Johnny O'Clock (1947)
Commonweal 46:16, Apr. 18, 1947
New Republic 116:40, Apr. 14, 1947
New York Times p. 39, Mar. 27, 1947
New Yorker 23:83, Apr. 5, 1947
Newsweek 29:87, Apr. 7, 1947
Theatre Arts 31:52, May, 1947
Time 49:100+, Apr. 14, 1947

Johnny One-Eye (1950)
Library Journal 75:787, May 1, 1950
New York Times p. 31, Nov. 17, 1950

Johnny Stool Pigeon (1949)
New York Times p. 28, Sep. 23, 1949
Newsweek 34:79, Aug. 15, 1949
Rotarian 75:38, Dec., 1949

Johnny Tremain (1957)
America 97:472, Aug. 3, 1957
Commonweal 66:449, Aug. 2, 1957

Johnny Tremain (1957) (Continued)
National Parent-Teacher 51:36, Jun., 1957
New York Times p. 21, Jul. 11, 1957
Newsweek 50:84, Jul. 22, 1957
Senior Scholastic 70:30, May 17, 1957

Johnny Trouble (1957)
National Parent-Teacher 52:38, Nov., 1957

Join the Marines (1937)
Time 29:46, Feb. 1, 1937

Joker (1961)
Commonweal 74:519, Sep. 22, 1961
Esquire 56:63, Dec., 1961
Nation 193:214, Sep. 30, 1961
New Republic 145:28, Sep. 4, 1961
New York Times p. 32, Aug. 8, 1961
New Yorker 37:68+, Aug. 12, 1961
Newsweek 58:69, Aug. 14, 1961
Saturday Review 44:27, Sep. 2, 1961
Time 78:60, Aug. 18, 1961

Joker Is Wild (1957)
America 97:688, Sep. 28, 1957
Commonweal 67:20, Oct. 4, 1957
Cosmopolitan 143:10, Oct., 1957
National Parent-Teacher 52:38, Nov., 1957
New York Times p. 16, Sep. 27, 1957
New Yorker 33:146, Oct. 5, 1957
Newsweek 50:126, Sep. 30, 1957
Time 70:98, Sep. 30, 1957

Jolson Sings Again (1949)
Commonweal 50:490, Aug. 26, 1949
Life 27:93-4+, Sep. 12, 1949
New York Times p. 16, Aug. 18, 1949; II, p. 1, Aug.
21, 1949
New Yorker 25:37, Aug. 27, 1949
Newsweek 34:73, Aug. 29, 1949
Photoplay 36:22, Oct., 1949
Rotarian 75:34, Nov., 1949
Theatre Arts 33:2+, Nov., 1949
Time 54:62, Sep. 5, 1949
Woman's Home Companion 76:10, Oct., 1949

Jolson Story (1946)
Commonweal 45:46, Oct. 25, 1946

Jolson Story (1946) (Continued)
    Cosmopolitan 121:73+, Oct., 1946
    Life 22:94, Mar. 10, 1947
    Nation 163:537, Nov. 9, 1946
    New York Times II, p. 3, Dec. 23, 1945; p. 28, Oct.
        11, 1946; II, p. 3, Oct. 13, 1946; VI, p. 31, Oct. 13,
        1946; II, p. 1, Oct. 20, 1946
    New Yorker 22:112+, Oct. 19, 1946
    Newsweek 28:112, Oct. 14, 1946
    Photoplay 29:4, Nov., 1946
    Theatre Arts 30:669-70, Nov., 1946
    Time 48:101, Oct. 7, 1946

Jonas (1959)
    New York Times p. 37, Apr. 30, 1959

Josette (1938)
    Commonweal 28:245, Jun. 24, 1938
    New York Times p. 9, Jun. 11, 1938; IX, p. 3, Jun. 19,
        1938
    Time 31:24, Jun. 13, 1938

*Jour De Fete
    New York Times p. 26, Feb. 20, 1952; II, p. 1, Mar.
        2, 1952
    New Yorker 28:77, Mar. 1, 1952
    Saturday Review 39:50, May 19, 1956
    Time 59:102, Mar. 31, 1952

Journal of a Crime (1934)
    New York Times p. 11, Apr. 28, 1934
    Newsweek 3:33, Mar. 10, 1934

Journey (1959)
    America 100:696+, Mar. 14, 1959
    Catholic World 188:413-14, Feb., 1959
    Commonweal 69:520, Feb. 13, 1959
    Nation 188:284, Mar. 28, 1959
    New Republic 140:20, Jan. 19, 1959
    New York Times p. 19, Feb. 20, 1959; II, p. 1, Mar. 1,
        1959
    New Yorker 35:106, Feb. 28, 1959
    Newsweek 53:101, Feb. 23, 1959
    Reporter 20:41-2, Mar. 19, 1959
    Saturday Review 42:73, Jan. 17, 1959
    Time 73:86, Feb. 9, 1959

Journey for Margaret (1942)
Commonweal 37:256, Dec. 25, 1942
Nation 156:140, Jan. 23, 1943
New Republic 108:22, Jan. 4, 1943
New York Times p. 36, Dec. 18, 1942
Scholastic 41:37, Jan. 11, 1943
Time 41:89, Jan. 11, 1943
Woman's Home Companion 69:2, Nov., 1942

Journey into Fear (1942)
Commonweal 37:43, Oct. 30, 1942; 37:520, Mar. 12, 1943
Nation 157:84, Jul. 17, 1943
New York Times IX, p. 5, Jan. 25, 1942; VIII, p. 3,
  Nov. 15, 1942; II, p. 4, Mar. 14, 1943; p. 15, Mar.
  19, 1943
Scholastic 42:32, Apr. 5, 1943
Time 41:50+, Feb. 15, 1943

Journey into Light (1951)
Christian Century 68:1423, Dec. 5, 1951
New York Times p. 24, Oct. 5, 1951
New Yorker 27:118, Oct. 13, 1951
Newsweek 38:94+, Oct. 15, 1951

Journey to the Center of the Earth (1960)
America 102:429-30, Jan. 9, 1960
Commonweal 71:374, Dec. 25, 1959
Good Housekeeping 150:30, Jan., 1960
Life 47:59, Dec. 21, 1959
New York Times p. 51, Dec. 17, 1959
Newsweek 54:65, Dec. 28, 1959
Senior Scholastic 76:59, Feb. 10, 1960
Time 75:85, Feb. 15, 1960

Journey to the Lost City (1960)
New York Times p. 43, Dec. 8, 1960

Journey to the Seventh Planet (1962)
New York Times p. 28, May 25, 1962
Senior Scholastic 80:43, Apr. 4, 1962

Journey Together (1946)
New York Times II, p. 3, Aug. 13, 1944; II, p. 3, Mar.
  3, 1946; p. 16, Mar. 4, 1946
Theatre Arts 30:219, Apr., 1946

Journey's End (1929)
Commonweal 11:715, Apr. 23, 1930

Journey's End (1929) (Continued)
    Life (NY) 95:20, May 2, 1930
    Literary Digest 105:18-19, May 3, 1930
    Nation 130:524-5, Apr. 30, 1930
    New York Times IX, p. 6, Mar. 2, 1930; p. 30, Mar.
       21, 1930; VIII, p. 6, Mar. 30, 1930; p. 25, Apr. 9,
       1930; X, p. 4, Apr. 13, 1930; p. 28, Apr. 15, 1930
    Outlook 154:670, Apr. 23, 1930
    Theatre Magazine 51:31, Apr., 1930; 52:44, Jul., 1930

Joy of Living (1938)
    New York Times p. 27, May 6, 1938
    Newsweek 11:24, Apr. 4, 1938
    Stage 15:29, Mar., 1938; 15:26, May, 1938

Juarez (1939)
    Commonweal 30:77, May 12, 1939
    Good Housekeeping 108:197-8, Jun., 1939
    Life 6:74-5, May 8, 1939
    Nation 148:539-40, May 6, 1939
    New Republic 99:20, May 10, 1939
    New York Times IX, p. 5, Feb. 5, 1939; XI, p. 5, Mar.
       12, 1939; X, p. 4, Apr. 23, 1939; p. 27, Apr. 26,
       1939; XI, p. 5, Apr. 30, 1939; IX, p. 4, Jul. 2, 1939
    Newsweek 13:22-3, May 8, 1939
    North American Review 247 no. 2:379-81, Jun., 1939
    Photoplay 53:22-3+, May, 1939; 53:62, Jul., 1939
    Saint Nicholas 66:41, Jun., 1939
    Scholastic 34:33, May 13, 1939
    Stage 16:38-41+, May 1, 1939; 16:26-7, May 15, 1939
    Time 33:66, May 8, 1939
    World Horizons 3:34-5, May, 1939

Jubal (1956)
    American 95:184, May 12, 1956
    Catholic World 183:60-1, Apr., 1956
    Commonweal 64:49, Apr. 13, 1956
    Library Journal 81:1146, May 1, 1956
    National Parent-Teacher 50:39, Apr., 1956
    New York Times p. 39, Apr. 25, 1956
    New Yorker 32:147, May 5, 1956
    Newsweek 47:104, Apr. 30, 1956
    Saturday Review 39:23, Apr. 28, 1956
    Time 67:108, May 7, 1956

Jubilee Trail (1954)
    Catholic World 178:461, Mar., 1954

Jubilee Trail (1954) (Continued)
Library Journal 79:314, Feb. 15, 1954
National Parent-Teacher 48:39, Mar., 1954
New York Times p. 13, May 1, 1954

Judge Hardy and Son (1939)
New York Times p. 27, Jan. 18, 1940
Photoplay 54:59, Jan., 1940

Judge Hardy's Children (1938)
New York Times p. 17, Apr. 8, 1938

Judge Priest (1934)
Canadian Magazine 82:41, Dec., 1934
Literary Digest 118:34, Oct. 27, 1934
Motion Picture 48:56-7, Nov., 1934
New York Times p. 33, Oct. 12, 1934
Vanity Fair 43:54, Nov., 1934

Judge Steps Out (1949)
Life 25:7, Aug. 9, 1948
New York Times p. 21, Jun. 3, 1949
Newsweek 33:84, May 23, 1949
Time 53:84, Jun. 20, 1949

Judgment at Nuremberg (1961)
America 106:542-3+, Jan. 20, 1962
Catholic World 195:63-4, Apr., 1962
Christian Century 79:332-3, Mar. 14, 1962
Commentary 33:56-63, Jan., 1962
Commonweal 75:318-19, Dec. 15, 1961
Esquire 57:26+, Jan., 1962
Life 51:121-3, Dec. 15, 1961
Nation 194:19-20, Jan. 6, 1962
National Review 12:254+, Apr. 10, 1962
New Republic 145:26+, Dec. 11, 1961
New York Times II, p. 9, Apr. 30, 1961; p. 49, Dec.
    15, 1961; p. 36, Dec. 20, 1961; II, p. 3, Dec. 24,
    1961; X, p. 3, Dec. 24, 1961
New Yorker 37:68, Dec. 23, 1961
Newsweek 58:72, Dec. 25, 1961
Saturday Review 44:43-5, Dec. 2, 1961
Senior Scholastic 79:25, Dec. 6, 1961
Time 78:85, Dec. 15, 1961

Juggernaut (1937)
New York Times p. 16, Jul. 15, 1937

Juggler (1953)
America 89:175, May 9, 1953
Catholic World 177:225, Jun., 1953
Commentary 15:615-17, Jun., 1953; 16:175, Aug., 1953
Commonweal 58:201, May 29, 1953
Library Journal 78:806, May 1, 1953
National Parent-Teacher 47:38, May, 1953
New York Times II, p. 5, Nov. 23, 1952; p. 39, May 6, 1953
New Yorker 29:131, May 16, 1953
Newsweek 41:110+, May 18, 1953
Saturday Review 36:28-9, May 9, 1953
Theatre Arts 37:88, Jul., 1953
Time 61:102, May 4, 1953

Juke Box Jennie (1942)
New York Times p. 21, Apr. 17, 1942

Juke Girl (1942)
Commonweal 36:256, Jul. 3, 1942
New Republic 107:22-3, Jul. 6, 1942
New York Times p. 9, Jun. 20, 1942
Newsweek 19:64, Jun. 15, 1942
Time 39:48+, May 25, 1942

Jules and Jim (1962)
Commonweal 76:153, May 4, 1962
Esquire 58:46+, Sep., 1962
Nation 194:427-8, May 12, 1962
New Republic 146:28-30, May 7, 1962
New York Times p. 32, Apr. 24, 1962
New Yorker 38:184-5, May 5, 1962
Newsweek 59:90, May 7, 1962
Saturday Review 45:50, May 12, 1962
Time 79:65, May 4, 1962

Jules Verne's Mysterious Island (see Mysterious Island)

Julia Misbehaves (1948)
Commonweal 49:41, Oct. 22, 1948
Good Housekeeping 127:258, Nov., 1948
New York Times II, p. 5, Feb. 1, 1948; p. 30, Oct. 8, 1948; II, p. 1, Oct. 17, 1948
Newsweek 32:85, Oct. 4, 1948
Time 52:102+, Oct. 11, 1948
Woman's Home Companion 75:10-11, Nov., 1948

Julie (1956)
    Catholic World 184:300, Jan., 1957
    Life 41:113-14, Nov. 19, 1956
    National Parent-Teacher 51:39, Dec., 1956
    New York Times p. 51, Nov. 22, 1956
    New Yorker 32:130, Dec. 1, 1956
    Newsweek 48:108+, Nov. 26, 1956
    Saturday Review 39:29, Nov. 17, 1956
    Time 68:110, Nov. 19, 1956

Julietta (1957)
    Commonweal 66:352, Jul. 5, 1957
    New York Times p. 38, Jun. 18, 1957

Julius Caesar (1953)
    America 89:306, Jun. 13, 1953
    Catholic World 177:303, Jul., 1953; 177:469-70, Sep.,
        1953
    Commonweal 58:273-4, Jun. 19, 1953
    Good Housekeeping 136:19+, Apr., 1953
    Library Journal 78:1102, Jun. 15, 1953
    Life 34:135-9, Apr. 20, 1953
    Look 17:17-19, Mar. 10, 1953
    McCalls 80:10-11, Jun., 1953
    National Parent-Teacher 47:38, Jan., 1953; 47:38, May,
        1953
    New Republic 129:20-1, Aug. 3, 1953
    New York Times p. 33, Nov. 25, 1952; p. 12, May 9,
        1953; p. 19, Jun. 5, 1953; II, p. 5, Jun. 7, 1953;
        II, p. 1, Jun. 14, 1953; II, p. 5, Sep. 20, 1953
    New Yorker 29:65, Jun. 13, 1953
    Newsweek 41:101, Jun. 8, 1953
    Reporter 9:35-6, Jul. 21, 1953
    Saturday Review 36:6, May 30, 1953; 36:26-8, Jun. 6,
        1953
    Scholastic 60:13T, Apr. 2, 1952; 63:37, Sep. 16, 1953
    Theatre Arts 37:84+, Jun., 1953
    Time 60:87, Oct. 27, 1952; 61:94+, Jun. 1, 1953

July 14th (see Fourteenth of July)

Jumbo (1962)
    Commonweal 77:342, Dec. 21, 1962
    Good Housekeeping 156:22, Jan., 1963
    New York Times II, p. 7, Mar. 18, 1962; p. 49, Dec.
        7, 1962
    New Yorker 38:135, Dec. 15, 1962

613

Jumbo (1962) (Continued)
  Newsweek 60:95, Dec. 17, 1962
  Saturday Review 45:50, Dec. 8, 1962
  Time 80:77, Dec. 21, 1962

Jump into Hell (1955)
  National Parent-Teacher 49:39, Jun., 1955

Jumping Jacks (1952)
  Commonweal 56:368, Jul. 18, 1952
  National Parent-Teacher 47:37, Sep., 1952
  New York Times p. 30, Jul. 24, 1952
  Newsweek 39:102, Jun. 30, 1952
  Saturday Review 35:36, Aug. 9, 1952
  Time 60:76+, Aug. 4, 1952

June Bride (1948)
  Commonweal 49:176, Nov. 26, 1948
  Cosmopolitan 125:13+, Dec., 1948
  Good Housekeeping 127:10, Dec., 1948
  New Republic 119:28, Nov. 22, 1948
  New York Times p. 10, Oct. 30, 1948
  New Yorker 24:115, Nov. 6, 1948
  Newsweek 32:91, Nov. 8, 1948
  Photoplay 34:22, Dec., 1948
  Rotarian 74:52, Jan., 1949
  Time 52:102+, Nov. 15, 1948
  Woman's Home Companion 75:10-11, Dec., 1948

June Moon (1931)
  Life (NY) 97:21, Apr. 3, 1931
  New York Times p. 23, Mar. 14, 1931; VIII, p. 5, Mar.
    22, 1931

Jungle (1952)
  New York Times p. 32, Oct. 2, 1952

Jungle Book (1942)
  Commonweal 35:649, Apr. 17, 1942
  Life 12:76-8, Mar. 16, 1942
  Nation 154:553, May 9, 1942
  New York Times IX, p. 4, Jul. 27, 1941; IX, p. 3, Aug.
    3, 1941; VII, p. 14-15, Mar. 8, 1942; p. 19, Apr. 6,
    1942; VIII, p. 3, Apr. 12, 1942
  Newsweek 19:64, Apr. 6, 1942
  Photoplay 21:6, Jun., 1942
  Scholastic 39:17-19+, Jan. 5, 1942
  Time 39:92, Apr. 13, 1942

Jungle Bride (1933)
New York Times p. 16, May 13, 1933

Jungle Captive (1945)
New York Times p. 7, Jul. 7, 1945

Jungle Cat (1960)
America 103:603, Sep. 3, 1960
Commonweal 73:17, Sep. 30, 1960
New York Times p. 21, Jun. 27, 1960; p. 19, Aug. 18, 1960
New Yorker 36:56, Aug. 27, 1960
Newsweek 56:85, Aug. 29, 1960
Senior Scholastic 77:29, Oct. 5, 1960
Time 76:53, Aug. 22, 1960

Jungle Fighters (1962) (see also Long and the Short and the Tall)
New York Times p. 28, Mar. 15, 1962

Jungle Headhunters (1951)
New York Times p. 42, Dec. 6, 1951

Jungle Heat (1957)
National Parent-Teacher 52:38, Nov., 1957

Jungle Jim (1948)
New York Times p. 9, Jan. 1, 1949

Jungle Killer (1932)
New York Times p. 11, Nov. 26, 1932

Jungle Man-Eaters (1954)
National Parent-Teacher 48:39, May, 1954

Jungle Princess (1936)
New York Times p. 21, Dec. 24, 1936

Jungle Siren (1942)
New York Times p. 11, Oct. 10, 1942

Jungle Woman (1944)
New York Times p. 19, Jul. 15, 1944

Junior Miss (1945)
Commonweal 42:263, Jun. 29, 1945
Harper's Bazaar 75:66, Dec., 1941

Junior Miss (1945) (Continued)
Life 19:51, Jul. 23, 1945
Nation 153:548, Nov. 29, 1941
New Republic 113:161, Aug. 6, 1945
New York Times p. 15, Jun. 18, 1945
New Yorker 21:40, Jun. 23, 1945
Newsweek 25:99, Jun. 25, 1945
Photoplay 27:22, Sep., 1945
Theatre Arts 26:9+, Jan., 1942

Juno and the Paycock (1930)
New York Times p. 22, Jun. 30, 1930; VIII, p. 3, Jul.
6, 1930

Jupiter's Darling (1955)
American Magazine 159:10, Jan., 1955
Farm Journal 79:103, Mar., 1955
Library Journal 80:436, Feb. 15, 1955
Look 19:70+, Feb. 22, 1955
New York Times II, p. 5, Nov. 14, 1954; p. 18, Feb.
18, 1955; II, p. 1, Feb. 27, 1955
Newsweek 45:94, Feb. 21, 1955
Saturday Review 38:27, Mar. 5, 1955
Time 65:104+, Mar. 7, 1955
Woman's Home Companion 82:24-5, Feb., 1955

Jury's Secret (1938)
New York Times p. 17, Feb. 4, 1938

Just a Gigolo (1931)
New York Times p. 20, Jun. 13, 1931; VIII, p. 3, Jun.
21, 1931

Just Across the Street (1952)
New York Times p. 12, Jun. 28, 1952
Time 60:77, Jul. 7, 1952

Just Around the Corner (1938)
New York Times p. 11, Dec. 3, 1938
Photoplay 53:44, Jan., 1939

Just for You (1952)
Catholic World 175:464, Sep., 1952
Christian Century 69:1271, Oct. 29, 1952
Library Journal 77:1801, Oct. 15, 1952
McCalls 80:18-19, Oct., 1952
National Parent-Teacher 47:36, Oct., 1952

Just for You (1952) (Continued)
New York Times p. 40, Oct. 9, 1952; II, p. 11, Nov. 9,
1952
Newsweek 40:114-15, Sep. 22, 1952
Saturday Review 35:27, Sep. 27, 1952
Scholastic 61:47, Oct. 22, 1952
Theatre Arts 36:73, Oct. , 1952
Time 60:72, Aug. 25, 1952

Just Imagine (1930)
Life (NY) 96:20, Dec. 12, 1930
New York Times VIII, p. 6, Nov. 16, 1930; p. 21, Nov.
22, 1930; IX, p. 5, Nov. 30, 1930

Just Off Broadway (1942)
New York Times p. 18, Aug. 29, 1942

Just Smith (1933)
New York Times p. 20, Apr. 23, 1934

Just This Once (1952)
Catholic World 174:387, Feb. , 1952
Library Journal 77:785, May 1, 1952
New York Times p. 22, Mar. 18, 1952
Newsweek 39:87, Mar. 31, 1952
Theatre Arts 36:73, Mar. , 1952

Justice and Caryl Chessman (1960)
Newsweek 55:100, Mar. 14, 1960

Justice Is Done (1953)
Commonweal 57:522, Feb. 27, 1953
Life 34:129-30+, Mar. 30, 1953
National Parent-Teacher 47:37, Jun. , 1953
New York Times VI, p. 52, Feb. 15, 1953; p. 23, Mar.
3, 1953; II, p. 1, Mar. 8, 1953
New York Times Magazine p. 52-3, Feb. 15, 1953
New Yorker 29:64, Mar. 7, 1953
Newsweek 41:108, Mar. 23, 1953
Saturday Review 36:39, Feb. 28, 1953; 39:51, May 19,
1956
Theatre Arts 37:89, Apr. , 1953
Time 61:112, Mar. 16, 1953

Juvenile Court (1938)
New York Times p. 13, Sep. 12, 1938

WITHDRAWAL